Subjects/Strategies

A Writer's Reader

TENTH EDITION

Subjects/Strategies

A Writer's Reader

Paul Eschholz
Alfred Rosa

University of Vermont

BEDFORD/ST. MARTIN'S
Boston • New York

For Bedford/St. Martin's

Developmental Editor: Gregory S. Johnson
Production Editor: Bernard Onken
Senior Production Supervisor: Dennis J. Conroy
Senior Marketing Manager: Rachel Falk
Art Director: Lucy Krikorian
Text Design: Books By Design, Inc.
Copy Editor: Eric Raetz
Indexer: Riofrancos & Co. Indexes
Photo Research: Alice Lundoff
Cover Design: Lucy Krikorian
Cover Photo: "Boardwalk Over Sea" © Saki Sakakibara/Photonica
Composition: Macmillan-India
Printing and Binding: Haddon Craftsmen, an R. R. Donnelley & Sons Company

President: Joan E. Feinberg
Editorial Director: Denise B. Wydra
Editor in Chief: Nancy Perry
Director of Marketing: Karen Melton Soeltz
Director of Editing, Design, and Production: Marcia Cohen
Managing Editor: Erica T. Appel

Library of Congress Control Number: 2004108136

Manufactured in the United States of America.

0   9   8   7   6   5
f   e   d   c   b   a

For information, write: Bedford/St. Martin's, 75 Arlington Street, Boston, MA 02116   (617-399-4000)

ISBN: 0-312-41309-2

EAN: 978-0-312-41309-5

Acknowledgments

Acknowledgments and copyrights are continued at the back of the book on pages 728–732, which constitute an extension of the copyright page.

Preface

Subjects/Strategies is a reader for college writers. The selections in this book will entertain, inform, and contribute to students' self-awareness and understanding of the world around them. But above all, the seventy-eight reading selections and twenty-two visual texts in this edition were chosen to help students become better observers and better writers, and especially to help them grasp and master nine widely used and versatile writing strategies.

Subjects/Strategies, as its title suggests, places equal emphasis on the content and form of an essay — that is, on what an essay has to say and on the techniques used to say it. All readers pay attention to content, to the substance of what writers are saying. Far fewer readers, however, notice the strategies that writers use to organize their writing and to make it understandable and effective. Because these strategies are such an essential element of the writer's craft, students need first to become more aware of them — most of which they intuitively use already — and then to practice using them in order to write well. The most important purpose of *Subjects/Strategies* is to help students understand how a given strategy, alone or in combination, can be used most effectively to communicate a subject to an audience.

FAVORITE FEATURES OF *SUBJECTS/STRATEGIES*

We continue to include the key features — developed and refined over nine previous editions — that have made *Subjects/Strategies* a classic.

Timely, Teachable, and Diverse Readings

Seventy-eight readings — including twelve student essays, sixty-one professional essays, and five short stories by some of the best classic and contemporary writers — offer a broad spectrum of subjects, styles, and cultural points of view. These engaging selections, by well-known writers including Thomas L. Friedman, Deborah Tannen, Alice Walker, Edward Abbey, Malcolm X, Annie Dillard, Mark Twain, Martin Luther King Jr., Sandra Cisneros, Shirley Jackson, Linda Chavez, and Jonathan Rauch, demonstrate for students the versatility and strengths of the different rhetorical strategies.

Detailed Introductions to Each Rhetorical Strategy

The introduction to each rhetorical chapter opens with a definition of the rhetorical strategy under discussion and then examines examples of the strategy put into practice. Next, after discussing the various purposes for which writers use each strategy, a complete, annotated student essay employing the strategy is presented. Finally, sound and practical advice is offered on how to write an essay using that strategy, including guidelines on selecting topics, developing thesis statements, considering audiences, gathering evidence, choosing organizational patterns, and using other rhetorical strategies in support of the dominant strategy.

Annotated Student Essays

An annotated student essay appears in each chapter introduction, offering students realistic examples of how they can successfully incorporate rhetorical strategies into their own writing. Discussion questions follow each student essay, encouraging students to analyze and evaluate the overall effectiveness of the rhetorical strategies employed in the example.

Visual Writing Prompts

In addition to each rhetorical chapter's "Seeing/Reading" pair, one professional essay per chapter features a writing suggestion incorporating a cartoon as a visual writing prompt. These cartoons demonstrate themes or strategies similar to those in the essay and offer students another way of thinking about how those themes and strategies work in visual and written formats.

Extensive Rhetorical Apparatus

The abundant study materials accompanying each essay in the book teach students how to use each strategy to make their writing more effective by linking their reading to their writing.

- *Journal writing activities* are provided before and after each professional selection. *Preparing to Read* prereading journal prompts ask students to write about their own experiences with the issues discussed in the selection. *Responding to the Text* postreading journal prompts ask students to analyze, elaborate on, or take issue with a key aspect of the selection. From time to time, discussion questions and writing assignments ask students to return to these journal writings to reflect on their early thinking before moving ahead with more formal writing tasks.

- *Engaging the Writer's Subject* questions focus students' attention on the content of each selection as well as on the author's purpose. These questions help students check their comprehension of the selection, and they provide a basis for classroom discussion.

- *Analyzing the Writer's Craft* questions direct students to the various rhetorical strategies and writing techniques the writer has used. These questions encourage students to put themselves in the writer's place and to consider how they might employ the strategies in their own writing. In addition, questions in this section ask students to identify and analyze places where the author has used one or more rhetorical strategies to enhance or develop the essay's dominant strategy.

- *Understanding the Writer's Language* questions emphasize the importance of diction, word choice, and verbal context. Each set of questions ends with a vocabulary-building exercise in which students are asked to use a dictionary to determine the meanings of certain words as they are used in the selection.

- *Writing Suggestions* following each professional essay are of three types. The first type focuses on the particular rhetorical strategy under discussion. The second type asks students to explore the topic of the essay or a related topic using a different strategy. The third type asks students to do some research, including research on the Internet. Each research-writing assignment features a cross-reference to the *Subjects/Strategies* TopLinks Web site, where students will find assignment-specific and thematically arranged annotated links to the most current and reliable research sites available on the Web.

End-of-Chapter Writing Suggestions

As in previous editions, there are a number of writing suggestions at the end of Chapters 3 through 12. These writing suggestions provide additional topics suitable to the strategy covered by the chapters. In preparing the suggestions, we made an effort to tie them to particular selections or pairs of selections in the chapter. Instructors can use these writing suggestions as complements to or substitutes for the more focused writing topics that accompany individual selections.

Advice for Writing Documented Essays

Chapter 14, "Writing Documented Essays," includes guidelines for conducting print and online research, with screen shots of sample Internet searches; evaluating the reliability and timeliness of print and online sources; taking notes and integrating quotations into an essay; and avoiding plagiarism. In addition, the chapter features model MLA citations for the most widely used sources, including electronic databases, and a sample documented student essay.

Thematic Table of Contents

Immediately after the main table of contents, a second table of contents classifies the reading selections into general thematic categories. This thematic table of contents is designed to make it easier for instructors to identify groups of essays that have common subject matter, thus providing further opportunities for discussion and writing based on the content of individual selections and on various rhetorical approaches to common themes.

Glossary of Rhetorical Terms

The glossary at the end of *Subjects/Strategies* provides concise definitions of terms useful in working with the rhetorical strategies presented in the text. Wherever we thought that information in the glossary might assist students in answering a study question in the text, we placed a cross-reference to the appropriate glossary entry next to the question.

NEW TO THIS EDITION OF *SUBJECTS/STRATEGIES*

Substantially updated for its tenth edition, *Subjects/Strategies* combines the currency of a brand new text with the effectiveness of a thoroughly class-tested one and continues to answer the needs of a wide range of students and instructors. Guided by comments and advice from instructors and students across the country who have used the previous editions, we have made some dramatic changes designed primarily to expand and strengthen the writing instruction offered in the text.

Engaging New Readings, Compelling Perspectives

Half of the selections in *Subjects/Strategies* are new to this edition and represent a wide array of writers, topics, viewpoints, and rhetorical approaches. Among the thirty-eight new professional essays are fresh pieces by contemporary writers on topics of interest to today's students — for example, Iris Chang's "Fear of SARS, Fear of Strangers," G. Anthony Gorry's "Steal This MP3 File: What Is Theft?," Dalton Conley's "Tip Jars and the New Economy," Aisha K. Finch's "If Hip-Hop Ruled the World," and Andrew Blake's "Harry Potter and the New Consumer."

Innovative "Seeing/Reading" Pairings of Images and Texts

Each rhetorical chapter and argument cluster features a "Seeing/ Reading" pair — a stimulating new photo matched with a new essay on a contemporary topic. Students can use these photos as a bridge to the essays' themes, and the accompanying "Connecting Image and Text" activities ask students to further explore the thematic connections in discussion or writing.

Expanded Coverage of Reading

Chapter 1, "Reading for Understanding and Meaning," now contains expanded coverage of close, critical reading, with specific instruction on how to read visuals and how to get the most out of selections' headnotes, journal prompts, and apparatus. Also new to Chapter 1 is a sample annotated essay, Rita Dove's "Loose Ends."

New Sentence-Level Editing Tips

The tenth edition's rhetorical chapter introductions now feature Editing Tips that address the most common sentence-level writing concerns students encounter in each strategy — for example, run-ons, comma splices, and sentence fragments in Narration; pronoun references in Process Analysis; and sentence variety in Argumentation.

Provocative New Argument Clusters

In response to current events and students' changing interests, the Argumentation chapter now features two four-reading clusters: on women in combat and on genetically modified food. These new clusters enable students to explore each issue from a number of angles, not just pro and con. Each cluster is paired with a thought-provoking photo and is followed by suggestions for exploring that cluster's topic further in discussion or writing.

New and Helpful "Writers on Writing" Chapter

In response to reviewers' requests, the tenth edition now includes a chapter offering essays about writing. Reading pieces by Linda Flower, William Zinsser, Audre Lorde, and others, students will find humor, inspiration, and advice to validate their experiences in the writing classroom and enrich their own writing processes.

ACKNOWLEDGMENTS

We are gratified by the reception and use of the nine previous editions of *Subjects/Strategies*. Composition teachers in hundreds of community colleges, liberal arts colleges, and universities have used the book. Many teachers responded to our detailed review questionnaire, thus helping tremendously in conceptualizing the improvements to this edition. We thank Carmen Acevedo Butcher, Shorter College; Elizabeth Culverson, Northwood University; Deborah A. Dusek, North Dakota State College of Science; Nathan P. Gordon, Kishwaukee College; River Karner, Ball State University; Dolores Kiesler, Brescia University; Wade King, North Dakota State College of Science; Monique Kluczykowski, Gainesville College; Joshua Lukin, SUNY Buffalo; Andrew McAlister, Gainesville College; Terrie McCoy, Drew University; Helen Molanphy, Adams State College; Angela A. Rapkin, Manatee Community College; Dina Rhoden, Shorter College; Candace Rowe, Bridgewater State College; Daniel J. Sullivan, Catonsville Community College; and Jane J. Turnbull, The Community College of Baltimore County.

At Bedford/St. Martin's, we thank our longtime friend and editor, Nancy Perry, and our talented and enthusiastic developmental editor, Gregory S. Johnson, for their commitment to *Subjects/Strategies*. Together we have charted some new territories for this enduring text, and the process has been truly exciting. Thanks go also to the rest of the Bedford/St. Martin's team: Joan Feinberg, Denise Wydra, Karen Melton Soeltz, Rachel Falk, Marcia Cohen, Erica Appel, Bernard

Onken, Donna Dennison, Lucy Krikorian, Sandy Schechter, and Nathan Odell. Special thanks go to Sarah Federman for preparing the *Instructor's Manual* and to Alice Lundoff for researching the photographs and cartoons in this book. We are also happy to recognize those students whose work appears in *Subjects/Strategies* for their willingness to contribute their time and effort in writing and rewriting their essays: Keith Eldred, Shannon Long, James Blake Wilson, Andrew Kauser, William Peterson, Barbara Bowman, Gerald Cleary, Howard Solomon Jr., Kevin Cunningham, Tara E. Ketch, and Krista Gonnerman. We are grateful to our own writing students at the University of Vermont for their enthusiasm for writing and for their invaluable responses to materials included in this book. And we also thank our families for sharing in our commitment to quality teaching and textbook writing.

Finally, we thank each other. Beginning in 1971 we have collaborated on many textbooks on language and writing, all of which have gone into multiple editions. With this tenth edition of *Subjects/Strategies,* we enter the thirty-fourth year of working together. Ours must be one of the longest-running and most mutually satisfying writing partnerships in college textbook publishing. The journey has been invigorating and challenging as we have come to understand the complexities and joys of good writing and have sought new ways to help students become better writers.

Paul Eschholz

Alfred Rosa

Contents

Preface   v

Thematic Contents   xxx

1 Reading for Understanding and Meaning   1

Getting the Most out of Your Reading   2

Prereading: Preparing Yourself to Read   3

Reading: Getting an Overview of the Selection   5

Rereading: Coming to an Understanding of the Selection   5

Responding: Annotating the Text   5

▶ *What to Annotate in a Text*   6

An Example: Annotating Rita Dove's "Loose Ends"   6

Analyzing: Asking Yourself Questions as You Read   8

▶ *Questions to Ask Yourself as You Read*   8

Practice: Reading and Annotating Thomas L. Friedman's "My Favorite Teacher"   8

About the Photographs and Visual Texts in This Book   13

Using Your Reading in the Writing Process   16

Reading as a Writer   16

2 Writing Essays   19

The Writing Process   20

Prewriting   20
  ▶ *Questions about Audience*   23

Generating Ideas and Collecting Information   23
  ▶ *Will Your Thesis Hold Water?*   27

Writing Your First Draft   31
  ▶ *Checklist for Your First Draft*   32

Peer Critiquing   32
  ▶ *A Brief Guide to Peer Critiquing*   32

Revising   33
  ▶ *Questions for Revising the Large Elements of Your Essay*   34
  ▶ *Questions for Revising Sentences*   35
  ▶ *Notes on Beginnings and Endings*   36

Editing and Proofreading   36
  ▶ *Questions to Ask during Editing and Proofreading*   37

Writing an Expository Essay: A Student Essay in Progress   37
  KEITH ELDRED, *Secular Mantras*   41

3 Exemplification   45

What Is Exemplification?   45

Why Do Writers Use Exemplification?   47

An Annotated Student Essay Using Exemplification   48
  SHANNON LONG, *Wheelchair Hell: A Look at Campus Accessibility*   49
  Analyzing Shannon Long's Essay of Exemplification: Questions for Discussion   52

Suggestions for Writing an Essay of Exemplification   52
  Gather More Examples Than You Can Use   53
  Choose Relevant Examples   54
  Be Sure Your Examples Are Representative   55
  Organize Your Examples   55
  Use Transitions   56
  Share Your Work with Others   56
  Editing Tip: Strong Topic Sentences and Unified Paragraphs   56
  ▶ *Questions for Revising and Editing: Exemplification*   58

NATALIE GOLDBERG, *Be Specific*   59

"Don't say 'fruit.' Tell what kind of fruit — 'It is a pomegranate.' Give things the dignity of their names."

CARTOON: Charles Schulz, *Dear Sweetheart . . .*   **62**

SEEING/READING

CLARO CORTES IV, *Chinese Commuter in Shanghai* (PHOTO)   63

IRIS CHANG, *Fear of SARS, Fear of Strangers*   64

". . . without the mitigating influence of sound thinking, excessive fear of this new disease can lead to discrimination against Asians, something that is not without precedent in this country."

DEBORAH TANNEN, *How to Give Orders Like a Man*   70

"I challenge the assumption that talking in an indirect way necessarily reveals powerlessness, lack of self-confidence or anything else about the character of the speaker. Indirectness is a fundamental element in human communication."

ISAAC ASIMOV, *Those Crazy Ideas*   80

"How does one go about creating or inventing or dreaming up or stumbling over a new and revolutionary scientific principle?"

ALICE WALKER, *In Search of Our Mothers' Gardens*   92

"How was the creativity of the black woman kept alive, year after year and century after century, when for most of the years black people have been in America, it was a punishable crime for a black person to read or write?"

Writing Suggestions for Exemplification   103

4 Description   105

What Is Description?   105

Why Do Writers Use Description?   107

An Annotated Student Essay Using Description   108

JAMES BLAKE WILSON, *The "Shaw"*   108

Analyzing James Blake Wilson's Essay of Description: Questions for Discussion   111

Suggestions for Writing a Descriptive Essay   111

Determine a Purpose   111

Focus the Subject of Your Description   111

Use Description in the Service of an Idea   112

Collect Sensory Details about Your Subject   112

Select Descriptive Details with Your Purpose in Mind   113

Identify Your Audience   113

Create a Dominant Impression   113

Organize Your Details to Create a Vivid Picture   114

Show, Don't Tell: Use Specific Strong Nouns and Verbs   115

Editing Tip: Figurative Language   115

▶ *Questions for Revising and Editing: Description*   118

CHEROKEE PAUL MCDONALD, *A View from the Bridge*   119
"I was coming up on the little bridge in the Rio Visto neighborhood of Fort Lauderdale, deepening my stride and my breathing to negotiate the slight incline without altering my pace. And then, as I neared the crest, I saw the kid."
CARTON: Bill Watterson, *Gone Fishing*   **123**

EDWARD ABBEY, *Aravaipa Canyon*   124
"We will never get to the end of it, never plumb the bottom of it, never know the whole of even so small and trivial and useless and precious a place as Aravaipa. Therein lies our redemption."

STEVE MARTIN, *The Death of My Father*   130
"During my teenage years, we hardly spoke except in one-way arguments — from him to me. I am sure that the number of words that passed between us could be counted."

SEEING/READING

iPodLounge.com, *Shane Holding His iPod* (PHOTO)   137

Rob Walker, *The Guts of a New Machine*   138
"So you can say that the iPod is innovative, but it's harder to nail down whether the key is what's inside, the external appearance or even the way these work together. One approach is to peel your way through the thing, layer by layer."

SANDRA CISNEROS, *The House on Mango Street* (FICTION)   151
"The house on Mango Street is ours, and we don't have to pay rent to anybody, or share the yard with the people downstairs, or be careful not to make too much noise, and there isn't a landlord banging on the ceiling with a broom."

Writing Suggestions for Description   155

5 Narration   157

What Is Narration?   157

Why Do Writers Use Narration?   159

An Annotated Student Essay Using Narration   160
ANDREW KAUSER, *Challenging My Fears*   160
Analyzing Andrew Kauser's Essay of Narration: Questions for Discussion   164

Suggestions for Writing a Narrative Essay   165
Select a Topic That Has Meaning for You   165
Determine Your Point and Purpose   165
Establish a Context   166
Choose the Most Appropriate Point of View   166
Select Details that "Show, Don't Tell"   167
Organize Your Narrative   167
Keep Your Verb Tense Consistent   168
Use Narrative Time for Emphasis   169
Use Transitional Words to Clarify Narrative Sequence   169
Use Dialogue to Bring Your Narrative to Life   169
Editing Tip: Run-on Sentences, Comma Splices, and Sentence Fragments   170
▶ *Questions for Revising and Editing: Narration*   172

MALCOLM X, *Coming to an Awareness of Language*   174
"I saw that the best thing I could do was get hold of a dictionary — to study, to learn some words."

ANNIE DILLARD, *Getting Caught*   179
"A black Buick was moving toward us down the street. We all spread out, banged together some regular snowballs, took aim, and, when the Buick drew nigh, fired."
CARTOON: Barbara Smaller, *An Appropriate Punishment*   184

BARRY WINSTON, *Stranger Than True*   186
"Some kid is in trouble and would I be interested in helping him out? He's charged with manslaughter, a felony, and driving under the influence. I tell him sure, have the kid call me."

SEEING/READING

BOB DAEMMRICH, *Nobody Knows I'm Gay* (PHOTO)   192

DAVID P. BARDEEN, *Not Close Enough for Comfort* 193
"I had wanted to tell Will I was gay since I was 12. As twins, we
shared everything back then: clothes, gadgets, thoughts, secrets.
Everything except this."

EUDORA WELTY, *A Worn Path* (FICTION)   198
"Far out in the country there was an old Negro woman with her head
tied up in a red rag, coming along a path through the pinewoods. Her
name was Phoenix Jackson."

Writing Suggestions for Narration   207

6 Process Analysis   209

What Is Process Analysis?   209

Why Do Writers Use Process Analysis?   210
Directional Process Analysis   211
Informational Process Analysis   211
Evaluative Process Analysis   212

An Annotated Student Essay Using Process Analysis   213
WILLIAM PETERSON, *I Bet You Can*   213
*Analyzing William Peterson's Essay of Process Analysis: Questions
for Discussion*   217

Suggestions for Writing a Process Analysis Essay   218
Know the Process You Are Writing About   218
Have a Clear Purpose   218
Organize the Process into Steps   218
Use Transitions to Link the Steps   219
Energize Your Writing: Use the Active Voice and Strong
Action Verbs   219
Use Consistent Verb Tense   220
Consider Your Audience, and Choose Appropriate Diction   221
Test the Effectiveness of Your Process Analysis   222
Editing Tip: Clear Pronoun References   223
▶ *Questions for Revising and Editing: Process Analysis*   225

MORTIMER ADLER, *How to Mark a Book* 226
"Full ownership [of a book] comes only when you have made it a part of yourself, and the best way to make yourself a part of it is by writing in it."

PAUL ROBERTS, *How to Say Nothing in 500 Words* 233
"You still have four hundred and sixty-eight [words] to go, and you've pretty well exhausted the subject. It comes to you that you do your best thinking in the morning, so you put away the typewriter and go to the movies."

SEEING/READING

JOEL GORDON, *World Trade Center Disaster, September 11, 2001* (PHOTO) 247

CHRISTOPHER CALLAHAN, *Anatomy of an Urban Legend* 248
"The proliferation of rumors, gossip and urban legends in the Internet age is well documented. But how do such stories spread so quickly with such flimsy factual basis?"

DIANE ACKERMAN, *Why Leaves Turn Color in the Fall* 256
". . . first there will be weeks of gushing color so bright, so pastel, so confettilike, that people will travel up and down the East Coast just to stare it — a whole season of leaves."

MATT HAUGHEY, *Building an Online Community: Just Add Water* 262
"I watched several big communities grow from nothing and prosper and I took my lead from them, but a good lot of what I know now was gained from trial and error."
CARTOON: Harry Bliss, *Click Here to Enter Amazon.com Espresso Bar* 269

Writing Suggestions for Process Analysis 270

7 Comparison and Contrast 272

What Are Comparison and Contrast? 272
    Point-by-Point and Block Comparison 273
    Analogy: A Special Form of Comparison and Contrast 274
Why Do Writers Use Comparison and Contrast? 276
An Annotated Student Essay Using Comparison and Contrast 277
    BARBARA BOWMAN, *Guns and Cameras* 277
    Analyzing Barbara Bowman's Essay of Comparison and Contrast: Questions for Discussion 280

Suggestions for Writing a Comparison and Contrast Essay   281

Compare Subjects from the Same Class   281

Determine Your Purpose, and Focus on It   282

Formulate a Thesis Statement   282

Choose the Points of Comparison   282

Organize the Points of Comparison   283

Draw a Conclusion from the Comparison   284

Editing Tip: Parallel Constructions   285

▶ *Questions for Revising and Editing: Comparison and Contrast*   287

MARK TWAIN, *Two Ways of Seeing a River*   288
"... a day came when I began to cease from noting the glories and the charms which the moon and the sun and twilight wrought upon the river's face; another day came when I ceased altogether to note them."

CARTOON: Charles Adams, *By George!*   291

SUZANNE BRITT, *Neat People vs. Sloppy People*   293
"I've finally figured out the difference between neat people and sloppy people. The distinction is, as always, moral."

SEEING/READING

**MICROSOFT, *Macs and PCs Have Never Been So Compatible*
(PHOTO)   298**

DEL MILLER, *Mac or PC: There Is Simply No Comparison!*   299
"Consumers don't care about bus topology or whether their RAM is double data rate or not ... What they do want is for their computer to serve their needs and not break."

STEPHEN E. AMBROSE, *Crazy Horse and Custer as Young Warriors*   306
"They fought for honors and because their societies expected them to fight ... But the overriding reason they fought is that they enjoyed it. As a result, they both became heroes."

DEBORAH TANNEN, *Sex, Lies, and Conversation*   312
"The communication problems that endanger marriage can't be fixed by mechanical engineering. They require a conceptual framework about the role of talk in human relationships."

Writing Suggestions for Comparison and Contrast   319

8 Division and Classification 321

What Are Division and Classification? 321

Why Do Writers Use Division and Classification? 325

An Annotated Student Essay Using Division and Classification 325
GERALD CLEARY, *How Loud? How Good? How Much?*
How Pretty? 326
Analyzing Gerald Cleary's Essay of Division and Classification:
Questions for Discussion 328

Suggestions for Writing a Division and Classification Essay 329
Determine Your Purpose, and Focus on It 329
Formulate a Thesis Statement 330
Establish Appropriate Characteristics 331
Organize the Points of Your Essay 332
State Your Conclusion 333
Use Other Rhetorical Strategies 333
Editing Tip: Headings and Subheadings for Clarification 334
▶ *Questions for Revising and Editing: Division and Classification* 336

SEEING/READING

STEFANIE FELIX, *Girls on a Stoop* (PHOTO) 337

ROSALIND WISEMAN, *The Queen Bee and Her Court* 338
"Our best politicians and diplomats couldn't do better than a teen
girl does in understanding the social intrigue and political landscape
that lead to power."

JUDITH VIORST, *The Truth about Lying* 352
"I am willing to lie. But just as a last resort — the truth's always better."
CARTOON: Scott Adams, *Translating Marketing Talk* 358

MARTIN LUTHER KING JR., *The Ways of Meeting Oppression* 360
"The problem is not purely a racial one, with Negroes set against
whites. In the end, it's not a struggle between people at all, but a tension between justice and injustice."

JUDITH ORTIZ COFER, *The Myth of the Latin Woman* 365
"There are thousands of Latinas without the privilege of an education
or the entrees into society that I have. For them life is a constant
struggle against the misconceptions perpetuated by the myth of the
Latina."

INSTITUTE FOR PROPAGANDA ANALYSIS, *How to Detect Propaganda*   372

"If American citizens are to have clear understanding of present-day conditions and what to do about them, they must be able to recognize propaganda, to analyze it, and to appraise it."

Writing Suggestions for Division and Classification   380

9 Definition   382

What Is Definition?   382

Why Do Writers Use Definition?   385

An Annotated Student Essay Using Definition   387

HOWARD SOLOMON JR., *Best Friends*   387

Analyzing Howard Solomon Jr.'s Essay of Definition: Questions for Discussion   391

Suggestions for Writing a Definition Essay   391

Determine Your Purpose   391

Formulate a Thesis Statement   392

Consider Your Audience   393

Choose a Technique of Definition   393

Develop Your Organizational Plan   394

Use Other Rhetorical Strategies   395

Editing Tip: Precise Language   396

▶ *Questions for Revising and Editing: Definition*   398

JO GOODWIN PARKER, *What Is Poverty?*   399

"Poverty is getting up every morning from a dirt- and illness-stained mattress. The sheets have long since been used for diapers. Poverty is living in a smell that never leaves."

ETHAN WATTERS, *In My Tribe*   405

"The bond is clearest in times of trouble. After earthquakes (or the recent terrorist attacks), my instinct to huddle with and protect my group is no different from what I'd feel for my own family."

CARTOON: Marisa Acocella, *He Didn't Want to End It*   **409**

SEEING/READING

TIME MAGAZINE, *What's Next for Napster* (PHOTO)   410

G. ANTHONY GORRY, *Steal This MP3 File: What Is Theft?*   411
"But in the case of digital music, where the material is disconnected from the physical moorings of conventional stores and copying is so easy, my students see matters differently."

SOJOURNER TRUTH, *Ain't I a Woman?*   417
"That man over there says women need to be helped into carriages, and lifted over ditches, and to have the best place everywhere. Nobody ever helps me into carriages, or over mud-puddles, or gives me any best place!"

ANTON CHEKHOV, *A Nincompoop* (FICTION)   420
"She murmured her little '*merci*' several times and went out. I looked after her and thought: 'How easy it is to crush the weak in this world!'"

Writing Suggestions for Definition   424

10   Cause and Effect Analysis   426

What Is Cause and Effect Analysis?   426

Why Do Writers Use Cause and Effect Analysis?   430

An Annotated Student Essay Using Cause and Effect Analysis   430
KEVIN CUNNINGHAM, *Gentrification*   431
Analyzing Kevin Cunningham's Essay of Cause and Effect Analysis: Questions for Discussion   434

Suggestions for Writing a Cause and Effect Analysis   434
Establish Your Focus   436
Determine Your Purpose   437
Formulate a Thesis Statement   437
Avoid Oversimplification and Errors of Logic   438
Select Words That Strike a Balanced Tone   439
Use Other Rhetorical Strategies   439
Editing Tip: Cause and Effect Signal Words   440
▶ *Questions for Revising and Editing: Cause and Effect Analysis*   442
Special Usage Notes for Cause and Effect   443

JON KATZ, *How Boys Become Men* 444

"Men remember receiving little mercy as boys; maybe that's why it's sometimes difficult for them to show any."

CARTOON: Ed Fisher, *It Isn't That I Don't Love You . . .* **448**

SEEING/READING

JOEL GORDON, *Tipping Is Not a City in China* (PHOTO) 449

DALTON CONLEY, *Tip Jars and the New Economy* 450

"Today you cannot order a coffee, buy a bagel, or pay for a photocopy without being asked to leave your change behind for 'better service' or, alternatively, 'good karma.'"

KENNEDY P. MAIZE, *The Great Kern County Mouse War* 456

"If one pair of adult mice produces offspring, who in turn produce offspring, who in turn produce offspring, and so on for one year, the result will be over one million mice — unless there are predators."

CARL M. CANNON, *The Real Computer Virus* 463

"One of the things that makes the Internet so appealing is that anyone can pull anything off of it. The other side of the coin is that anyone can put anything on it."

SHIRLEY JACKSON, *The Lottery* (FICTION) 472

"Although the villagers had forgotten the ritual and lost the original black box, they still remembered to use stones."

Writing Suggestions for Cause and Effect Analysis 482

11 **Argumentation** **483**

What Is Argument? 483

Informational, or Exploratory, Argument 485

Focused Argument 485

Action-Oriented Argument 485

Quiet, or Subtle, Argument 486

Reconciliation Argument 486

Why Do Writers Use Argument? 486

An Annotated Student Essay Using Argument   491

MARK JACKSON, *The Liberal Arts: A Practical View*   492

Analyzing Mark Jackson's Essay of Argumentation: Questions for Discussion   497

Suggestions for Writing an Argumentation Essay   497

Determine Your Thesis or Proposition   498

Consider Your Audience   499

Gather Supporting Evidence   499

Choose an Organizational Pattern   499

Consider Refutations to Your Argument   500

Avoid Faulty Reasoning   500

Conclude Forcefully   501

Use Other Rhetorical Strategies   501

Editing Tip: Sentence Variety   502

  ▶ *Questions for Revising and Editing: Argumentation*   506

SEEING/READING

ED BAILEY, *Rap the Vote* (PHOTO)   507

AISHA K. FINCH, *If Hip-Hop Ruled the World*   508
"The fact is, from Senegal to South Africa, from England to Japan, the export of hip-hop around the globe is more than just a pop phenomenon."

RICHARD LEDERER, *The Case for Short Words*   513
"A lot of small words, more than you might think, can meet your needs with a strength, grace, and charm that large words do not have."
CARTOON: Harry Bliss, *Your Daughter Is a Pain in the Ass*   **518**

THOMAS JEFFERSON, *The Declaration of Independence*   519
"We hold these truths to be self-evident, that all men are created equal, that they are endowed by their Creator with certain unalienable rights, that among these are Life, Liberty, and the Pursuit of Happiness."

MARTIN LUTHER KING JR., *I Have a Dream*   525
"I have a dream that my four little grandchildren will one day live in a nation where they will not be judged by the color of their skin but by the content of their character."

JULIA ALVAREZ, *Snow* (FICTION)   531
"At home, Mami and my sisters and I said a rosary for world peace. I heard a new vocabulary: *nuclear bomb, radioactive fallout, bomb shelter.*"

ARGUMENT CLUSTER: WOMEN IN COMBAT   535

SEEING/READING

MICHAEL PROBST, *Ex-POW Army Spc. Shoshana Johnson* (PHOTO)   537

ANNA QUINDLEN, *Uncle Sam and Aunt Samantha*   538
"More than 40,000 [women] managed to serve in the Persian Gulf without destroying unit cohesion or failing because of upper-body strength."

LINDA CHAVEZ, *Women in Combat Will Take a Toll on Our Culture*   542
"What remains to be seen is whether it is in our national interest — and civilization's — to send young women and mothers into battle in the first place."

ANNE APPLEBAUM, *When Women Go to War*   545
"After the long struggle for acceptance, higher-ranking women in particular loathe the idea of treating mothers and fathers differently."

JOEL BECK, *Rough Draft*   548
"Even though women are allowed to participate in more than 90 percent of military activities, Uncle Sam still doesn't want them to register for the draft."

Making Connections: Writing and Discussion Suggestions for "Women in Combat"   554

ARGUMENT CLUSTER: GENETICALLY MODIFIED FOOD   556

SEEING/READING

GEORGE OLSON, *Spraying Potato Seedlings* (PHOTO)   558

JONATHAN RAUCH, *Will Frankenfood Save the Planet?*   559
"Biotechnology will transform agriculture, and in doing so will transform American environmentalism."

DAVID EHRENFELD, *A Techno-Pox Upon the Land*   568
"With very few exceptions, the whole point of genetic engineering is to increase the sales of chemicals and bio-engineered products to dependent farmers."

JANE E. BRODY, *Gene-Altered Foods: A Case against Panic*   574
"To render a rational opinion on the subject and make reasoned choices in the marketplace, it is essential to understand what genetic engineering of foods and crops involves and its potential benefits and risks."

JIM SCHARPLAZ, *Weeding Out the Skilled Farmer* 579

"New agricultural technologies must be judged: Is their purpose the industrialization and homogenization of farming, or the benefit of humanity?"

Making Connections: Writing and Discussion Suggestions for "Genetically Modified Food" 582

Writing Suggestions for Argumentation 584

12   Combining Strategies   586

What Does It Mean to Combine Strategies? 587

Why Do Writers Combine Strategies? 587

An Annotated Student Essay Using a Combination of Strategies 589

TARA E. KETCH, *Kids, You Can't Read That Book!* 589

Analyzing Tara E. Ketch's Essay of Combining Strategies: Questions for Discussion 596

Suggestions for Writing a Combining Strategies Essay 596

Determine Your Purpose 597

Formulate a Thesis Statement 597

Determine Your Dominant Developmental Strategy 597

Determine Your Supporting Strategies 598

Editing Tip: Wordiness 599

▶ *Questions for Revising and Editing: Combining Strategies* 601

ROBERT RAMÍREZ, *The Barrio* 602

"Members of the barrio describe their entire area as their home. It is a home, but it is more than this. The barrio is a refuge from the harshness and coldness of the Anglo world."

SEEING/READING

SERGEI ILNITSKY, *Harry Potter on Sale in Moscow* (PHOTO) 608

ANDREW BLAKE, *Harry Potter and the New Consumer* 609

"Even when, wizard-cloaked and wand in hand, he is defeating monsters, Harry Potter is a contemporary boy. He therefore shops."

NANCY MAIRS, *On Being a Cripple* 622

"First, the matter of semantics. I am a cripple. I choose this word to name me. I choose from among several possibilities, the most common of which are 'handicapped and 'disabled.'"

GEORGE ORWELL, *Shooting an Elephant* 635

"When I pulled the trigger I did not hear the bang or feel the kick — one never does when a shot goes home — but I heard the devilish roar of glee that went up from the crowd."

LARS EIGHNER, *On Dumpster Diving* 644

"I like the frankness of the word scavenging. I live from the refuse of others. I am a scavenger."

CARTOON: Peter Steiner, *We've Certainly Become a Throwaway Society* **648**

Writing Suggestions for Combining Strategies 649

13 Writers on Writing 650

JACK RAWLINS, *Five Principles for Getting Good Ideas* 651

"Essays rarely begin with the subject matter alone. Why would a person say out of the blue, 'I think I'll write about linoleum, or the national debt'?"

ANNE LAMOTT, *Shitty First Drafts* 657

"All writers write them. This is how they end up with good second and terrific third drafts."

LINDA FLOWER, *Writing for an Audience* 662

"A good piece of writing closes the gap between you and the reader."

WILLIAM ZINSSER, *Simplicity* 666

"Clutter is the disease of American writing. We are society strangling in unnecessary words, circular constructions, pompous frills, and meaningless jargon."

DONALD M. MURRAY, *The Maker's Eye: Revising Your Own Manuscripts* 670

"A piece of writing is never finished. It is delivered to a deadline, torn out of the typewriter on demand, sent off with a sense of accomplishment and shame and pride and frustration."

AUDRE LORDE, *The Transformation of Silence Into Language and Action* 676

"I have come to believe over and over again that what is most important to me must be spoken, made verbal and shared, even at the risk of having it bruised or misunderstood."

14   Writing Documented Essays   681

Print Sources   681
Previewing Print Sources   682
Developing a Working Bibliography   682
Evaluating Print Sources   683

Internet Sources   684
Previewing Internet Sources   684
Developing a Working Bibliography   685
Evaluating Internet Sources   685
Internet Research: Subject Directories and Keyword Searches   687
▶ *Refining Keyword Searches on the Web*   690

Note Taking   691
Summary   693
Paraphrase   694
Direct Quotation   695
Taking Notes on Internet Sources   697

Integrating Quotations into Your Text   698

Documenting Sources   699
In-Text Citations   700
List of Works Cited   701

A Note on Plagiarism   708
Using Quotation Marks for Language Borrowed Directly   708
Using Your Own Words and Word Order When Summarizing and
Paraphrasing   709
▶ *Preventing Plagiarism*   710

A Documented Student Essay   711
KRISTA GONNERMAN, *Pharmaceutical Advertising*   712

Glossary of Rhetorical Terms   717
Student Essay Submission Form   726
Index   733

Thematic Contents

Contemporary Social Issues

RITA DOVE, *Loose Ends*   7

IRIS CHANG, *Fear of SARS, Fear of Strangers*   64

ROB WALKER, *The Guts of a New Machine*   138

DAVID P. BARDEEN, *Not Close Enough for Comfort*   193

CHRISTOPHER CALLAHAN, *Anatomy of an Urban Legend*   248

MATT HAUGHEY, *Building an Online Community: Just Add Water*   262

DEL MILLER, *Mac or PC: There Is Simply No Comparison!*   299

ROSALIND WISEMAN, *The Queen Bee and Her Court*   338

ETHAN WATTERS, *In My Tribe*   405

G. ANTHONY GORRY, *Steal This MP3 File: What Is Theft?*   411

KEVIN CUNNINGHAM, *Gentrification*   431

DALTON CONLEY, *Tip Jars and the New Economy*   450

CARL M. CANNON, *The Real Computer Virus*   463

AISHA K. FINCH, *If Hip-Hop Ruled the World*   508

ANDREW BLAKE, *Harry Potter and the New Consumer*   609

KRISTA GONNERMAN, *Pharmaceutical Advertising*   714

Education

THOMAS L. FRIEDMAN, *My Favorite Teacher*   8

ISAAC ASIMOV, *Those Crazy Ideas*   80

ALICE WALKER, *In Search of Our Mothers' Gar dens*   92

CHEROKEE PAUL MCDONALD, *A View from the Bridge*   119

STEVE MARTIN, *The Death of My Father*   130

MALCOLM X, *Coming to an Awareness of Language*   **174**
ANNIE DILLARD, *Getting Caught*   **179**
MORTIMER ADLER, *How to Mark a Book*   **226**
PAUL ROBERTS, *How to Say Nothing in 500 Words*   **233**
MARK JACKSON, *The Liberal Arts: A Practical View*   **492**
TARA E. KETCH, *Kids, You Can't Read That Book!*   **589**

Historical Perspectives

ISAAC ASIMOV, *Those Crazy Ideas*   **80**
STEPHEN E. AMBROSE, *Crazy Horse and Custer as Young Warriors*   **306**
MARTIN LUTHER KING JR., *The Ways of Meeting Oppression*   **360**
INSTITUTE FOR PROPGANDA ANALYSIS, *How to Detect Propaganda*   **372**
SOJOURNER TRUTH, *Ain't I a Woman*   **417**
THOMAS JEFFERSON, *The Declaration of Independence*   **519**
MARTIN LUTHER KING JR., *I Have a Dream*   **525**
JULIA ALVAREZ, *Snow* (FICTION)   **531**
GEORGE ORWELL, *Shooting an Elephant*   **635**

Language, Reading, and Writing

NATALIE GOLDBERG, *Be Specific*   **59**
DEBORAH TANNEN, *How to Give Orders Like a Man*   **70**
MALCOLM X, *Coming to an Awareness of Language*   **174**
MORTIMER ADLER, *How to Mark a Book*   **226**
PAUL ROBERTS, *How to Say Nothing in 500 Words*   **233**
DEBORAH TANNEN, *Sex, Lies, and Conversation*   **312**
JUDITH VIORST, *The Truth about Lying*   **352**
INSTITUTE FOR PROPAGANDA ANALYSIS, *How to Detect Propaganda*   **372**
RICHARD LEDERER, *The Case for Short Words*   **513**
JULIA ALVAREZ, *Snow* (FICTION)   **531**
JACK RAWLINS, *Five Principles for Getting Good Ideas*   **651**
ANNE LAMOTT, *Shitty First Drafts*   **657**
LINDA FLOWER, *Writing for an Audience*   **662**
WILLIAM ZINSSER, *Simplicity*   **666**
DONALD MURRAY, *The Maker's Eye: Revising Your Own Manuscripts*   **670**
AUDRE LORDE, *The Transformation of Silence into Language and Action*   **676**

The Natural World

EDWARD ABBEY, *Aravaipa Canyon*   **124**
DIANE ACKERMAN, *Why Leaves Turn Color in the Fall*   **256**

BARBARA BOWMAN, *Guns and Cameras* 277

MARK TWAIN, *Two Ways of Seeing a River* 288

KENNEDY P. MAIZE, *The Kern County Mouse War* 456

JONATHAN RAUCH, *Will Frankenfood Save the Planet?* 559

DAVID EHRENFELD, *A Techno-Pox upon the Land* 568

JANE E. BRODY, *Gene-Altered Foods: A Case against Panic* 574

JIM SCHARPLAZ, *Weeding Out the Skilled Farmer* 579

The Minority Experience

SHANNON LONG, *Wheelchair Hell: A Look at Campus Accessibility* 49

IRIS CHANG, *Fear of SARS, Fear of Strangers* 64

ALICE WALKER, *In Search of Our Mothers' Gardens* 92

SANDRA CISNEROS, *The House on Mango Street* (FICTION) 151

MALCOLM X, *Coming to an Awareness of Language* 174

DAVID P. BARDEEN, *Not Close Enough for Comfort* 193

EUDORA WELTY, *A Worn Path* (FICTION) 198

MARTIN LUTHER KING JR., *The Ways of Meeting Oppression* 360

JUDITH ORTIZ COFER, *The Myth of the Latin Woman* 365

SOJOURNER TRUTH, *Ain't I a Woman?* 417

AISHA K. FINCH, *If Hip-Hop Ruled the World* 508

MARTIN LUTHER KING JR., *I Have a Dream* 525

JULIA ALVAREZ, *Snow* (FICTION) 531

ROBERT RAMIREZ, *The Barrio* 602

NANCY MAIRS, *On Being a Cripple* 622

GEORGE ORWELL, *Shooting an Elephant* 635

AUDRE LORDE, *The Transformation of Silence into Language and Action* 676

Science, Technology, and the Internet

ISAAC ASIMOV, *Those Crazy Ideas* 80

ROB WALKER, *The Guts of a New Machine* 138

CHRISTOPHER CALLAHAN, *Anatomy of an Urban Legend* 248

MATT HAUGHEY, *Building an Online Community: Just Add Water* 262

DEL MILLER, *Mac or PC: There Is Simply No Comparison!* 299

G. ANTHONY GORRY, *Steal This MP3 File: What Is Theft?* 411

CARL M. CANNON, *The Real Computer Virus* 463

JONATHAN RAUCH, *Will Frankenfood Save the Planet?* 559

DAVID EHRENFELD, *A Techno-Pox upon the Land* 568

JANE E. BRODY, *Gene-Altered Foods: A Case against Panic* 574

JIM SCHARPLAZ, *Weeding Out the Skilled Farmer* 579

A Sense of Place

JAMES BLAKE WILSON, *The "Shaw"*   108

EDWARD ABBEY, *Aravaipa Canyon*   124

SANDRA CISNEROS, *The House on Mango Street* (FICTION)   151

EUDORA WELTY, *A Worn Path* (FICTION)   198

MARK TWAIN, *Two Ways of Seeing a River*   288

KEVIN CUNNINGHAM, *Gentrification*   431

SHIRLEY JACKSON, *The Lottery* (FICTION)   472

ROBERT RAMIREZ, *The Barrio*   602

A Sense of Self

KEITH ELDRED, *Secular Mantras*   41

STEVE MARTIN, *The Death of My Father*   130

SANDRA CISNEROS, *The House on Mango Street* (FICTION)   151

ANDREW KAUSER, *Challenging My Fears*   160

MALCOLM X, *Coming to an Awareness of Language*   174

ANNIE DILLARD, *Getting Caught*   179

DAVID P. BARDEEN, *Not Close Enough for Comfort*   193

WILLIAM PETERSON, *I Bet You Can*   213

ROSALIND WISEMAN, *The Queen Bee and Her Court*   338

JUDITH VIORST, *The Truth about Lying*   352

ETHAN WATTERS, *In My Tribe*   405

NANCY MAIRS, *On Being a Cripple*   622

LARS EIGHNER, *On Dumpster Diving*   644

AUDRE LORDE, *The Transformation of Silence into Language and Action*   676

Visual Texts

CLARO CORTES IV, *Chinese Commuter in Shanghai*   63

iPODLOUNGE.COM, *Shane Holding His iPod*   137

BOB DAEMMRICH, *Nobody Knows I'm Gay*   192

JOEL GORDON, *World Trade Center Disaster, September 11, 2001*   247

MICROSOFT, *Macs and PCs Have Never Been So Compatible*   293

STEFANIE FELIX, *Girls on a Stoop*   337

TIME MAGAZINE, *What's Next for Napster*   410

JOEL GORDON, *Tipping Is Not a City in China*   449

ED BAILEY, *Rap the Vote*   507

MICHAEL PROBST, *Ex-POW Army Spc. Shoshana Johnson*   537

GEORGE OLSON, *Spraying Potato Seedlings*   558

SERGEI ILNITSKY, *Harry Potter on Sale in Moscow*   608

Women and Men

DEBORAH TANNEN, *How to Give Orders Like a Man*   70
DEBORAH TANNEN, *Sex, Lies, and Conversation*   312
ROSALIND WISEMAN, *The Queen Bee and Her Court*   338
JUDITH ORTIZ COFER, *The Myth of the Latin Woman*   365
SOJOURNER TRUTH, *Ain't I a Woman*   417
JON KATZ, *How Boys Become Men*   444
ANNA QUINDLEN, *Uncle Sam and Aunt Samantha*   538
LINDA CHAVEZ, *Women in Combat Will Take a Toll on Our Culture*   542
ANNE APPLEBAUM, *When Women Go to War*   545
JOEL BECK, *Rough Draft*   548

Subjects/Strategies

A Writer's Reader

Reading for Understanding and Meaning

Subjects/Strategies is a reader for writers. The selections in this book will entertain you, inform you, and even contribute to your self-awareness and understanding of the world around you. In addition, they will help you grasp and master nine versatile and widely used writing strategies — exemplification, description, narration, process analysis, comparison and contrast, division and classification, definition, cause and effect analysis, and argumentation — as well as how to combine these strategies. *Subjects/Strategies* devotes one chapter to each of these strategies. In each chapter, an introduction defines the strategy, illustrates it with examples, presents an annotated student essay using the strategy, and offers suggestions for using the strategy in your own writing. Each chapter then offers selections from professional writers, chosen because they serve as excellent models of the strategy in question.

Subjects/Strategies places equal emphasis on the content and form of a selection — that is, on what an essay has to say and on the strategy used to say it. All readers pay attention to content, to the substance of what an author is saying. Far fewer, however, notice the strategies authors use to organize their writing, to make it clear, logical, and effective. Yet using these strategies is an essential element of the writer's craft, one that writers must master to write well. Because these strategies are such a vital component of the writer's craft, you will need first to become more aware of them in your reading and then to master your use of them to become a better writer.

As the readings in this text demonstrate, content and form are unified in all good writing. Indeed, the two actually help determine one another. A writer who wants to relate the details of an event, to "tell what happened," for example, will naturally choose narration; at the same time, the requirements of the narrative form will influence the content of the written story. On the other hand, if the writer wants to examine why something happened, storytelling alone will not do the job. It will be necessary to use the strategy of cause and effect analysis, and this strategy will determine the ultimate content. As you write, you will often tentatively plan your strategy before you start, consciously deciding which strategy or which combination of strategies best fits what you have to say and what you want to accomplish with your writing. Sooner or later, you will have to look back at what you have written, making sure that your choice of strategy serves the purpose of your writing and that it expresses your content accurately and effectively.

One good way for you to become a stronger writer is to become a stronger, more active reader. By becoming more familiar with different types of writing, you will sharpen your critical thinking skills and learn how good writers make decisions in their writing. After reading an article or essay, most people feel more confident talking about the content of the piece than about the style. Content is more tangible than style, which always seems so elusive. In large part, this discrepancy results from our schooling. Most of us have been taught to read for ideas. Not many of us, however, have been trained to read with a writer's eye, to ask why we like one piece of writing and not another. Likewise, most of us do not ask ourselves why one piece of writing is more believable or convincing than another. When you learn to read with a writer's eye, you begin to answer these important questions, and in the process you come to appreciate the craftsmanship involved in writing — how a writer selects descriptive details, uses an unobtrusive organizational strategy, opts for fresh and lively language, chooses representative and persuasive examples, and emphasizes important points with sentence variety.

We have designed this text to help you improve your reading and writing skills. The two processes go hand in hand and should be studied that way because writing, after all, is the making of reading. The more sensitive you become to the content and style decisions made by the writers in this text, the more skilled you will be at making similar decisions in your own writing.

GETTING THE MOST OUT OF YOUR READING

Active, analytical reading requires, first of all, that you commit time and effort. Second, try to take a positive interest in what you are reading, even if the subject matter is not immediately appealing. Remember, you are not reading for content alone but also to understand a writer's craft — to see firsthand the kinds of subjects and strategies he or she chooses.

To help you get the most out of your reading, here are some guidelines for 1) prereading, 2) reading, 3) rereading, 4) annotating, and 5) analyzing a text.

Prereading: Preparing Yourself to Read

Instead of diving right into any given selection in *Subjects/Strategies*, there are things you can do beforehand to get the most out of what you will be reading. It's helpful, for example, to get a context for what you'll be reading. What's the essay about? What do you know about the writer's background and reputation? Where was the essay first published? Who was the intended audience? And, finally, how much do you already know about the subject of the reading?

We encourage you to consider carefully the materials that precede each selection in this book: the *title, headnote,* and *journal prompt.* From the *title* you often discover the writer's position on an issue or attitude toward the topic. The title can also give clues about the intended audience and the writer's purpose in writing the piece. The *headnote* contains three essential elements. The *biographical note* provides information about the writer's life and work, as well as his or her reputation and authority to write on the chosen subject. The *publication information* tells you when the essay was published, where it appeared, and what other works the writer has published. This information can also give you insight about the intended audience. The *content and rhetorical highlights* preview the topic and outline key aspects of how the selection was written. Finally, the *journal prompt* encourages you to collect and record your thoughts and opinions about the topic before you commence reading.

Carefully review the following context-building materials that accompany Rita Dove's essay "Loose Ends" to see how they can help you preview the reading. The essay itself appears on pp. 6–7.

Title

LOOSE ENDS

Rita Dove

Headnote

Biographical note

> Pulitzer Prize–winning poet Rita Dove was born in Akron, Ohio, in 1952 and received her bachelor's degree from Miami University of Ohio in 1973. After two semesters as a Fulbright scholar at Universitat Tubingen in Germany, Dove enrolled in the

University of Iowa's Writers' Workshop, where she earned her master's in 1977. She has published seven poetry collections in-cluding The Yellow House on the Corner *(1980),* Museum *(1983),* Thomas and Beulah *(1986),* Mother Love *(1995), and* On the Bus with Rosa Parks *(1999); a book of short sto-ries,* Fifth Sunday *(1985); a novel,* Through the Ivory Gate *(1992); and a collection of essays,* The Poet's World *(1995). Dove served as poet laureate of the United States from 1993 to 1995. From 1981 to 1989, she taught at Arizona State Univer-sity; currently, she is Commonwealth Professor of English at the University of Virginia.*

Publication information

"Loose Ends" was first published in The Poet's World. *Starting with a simple anecdote about her daughter's behavior, Dove prepares readers for what she has to say about Americans, reality, and television. Notice how she uses comparison and contrast to highlight what she sees as our culture's seeming preference for television over reality.*

Content and rhetorical highlights

PREPARING TO READ

Journal prompt

What are your thoughts about the new "reality" tele-vision programs? In what ways, if at all, do these programs reflect "real" life? How do these shows differ from regular television fare?

From reading these preliminary materials, what expectations do you have for the selection? How does this knowledge equip you to engage the selection? While Dove's *title* does not give any specific in-dication of her topic, it does suggest that she will be writing about something that is chaotic or unfinished and not neatly organized or prepackaged. The *biographical note* reveals that Dove is an acclaimed poet and teacher. As a university professor and poet laureate, she has traveled widely in the United States and has closely observed popular culture. The *publication information* includes the titles of her various books, which suggest her African American heritage and her interest in the minority experience. This information suggests that the subject of the essay is likely to be reflective and explorative, perhaps intended to enlighten or provoke thought. This assumption is strengthened when you learn that the essay first appeared in *The Poet's World*, a collection of essays published during Dove's last year as poet laureate. The *content and rhetorical highlights* advise you to look at Dove's use of comparison and contrast to spotlight differences between real life and life depicted on television. Finally, the *journal prompt* asks for your thoughts and opinions about "reality" televison. After reading Dove's essay, you can compare your thoughts about "reality" television and real life with her reflections.

Reading: Getting an Overview of the Selection

Always read the selection at least twice, no matter how long it is. The first reading lets you get acquainted with the essay and form general impressions of it. You will want to get an overall sense of what the writer is saying, keeping in mind the essay's title and what you know about the writer. The essay will present information, ideas, and arguments — some you may expect, some you may not. As you read, you may find yourself modifying your sense of the writer's message and purpose. Circle words you do not recognize so that you can look them up in a dictionary. Put a question mark alongside any passages that are not immediately clear. However, you will probably want to delay most of your annotating until a second reading so that your first reading can be fast, enabling you to concentrate on the larger issues of message and purpose.

Rereading: Coming to an Understanding of the Selection

Your second reading should be quite different from your first. You will know what the essay is about, where it is going, and how it gets there; now you can relate the individual parts of the essay more accurately to the whole. Use your second reading to test your first impressions, developing and deepening your sense of how (and how well) the essay is written. Because you now have a general understanding of the essay, you can pay special attention to the author's purpose and means of achieving it. You can look for features of organization and style and adapt them to your own work.

Responding: Annotating the Text

When you annotate a text you should do more than simply underline what you think are important points. It is easy to underline so much that the notations become almost meaningless because you forget why you underlined passages in the first place. Instead, as you read, write down your thoughts in the margins or on a separate piece of paper. Mark the selection's main point when you find it stated directly. Look for the strategy or strategies the author uses to explore and support that point, and jot the information down. If you disagree with a statement or conclusion, object in the margin: "No!" If you feel skeptical, indicate that response: "Why?" or "Explain." If you are impressed by an argument or turn of phrase, compliment the writer: "Good point!" Place vertical lines or a star in the margin to indicate important points.

Jot down whatever marginal notes come naturally to you. Most readers combine brief written responses with underlining, circling, highlighting, stars, or question marks.

▶ *What to Annotate in a Text*

Here are some examples of what you may want to mark in the text as you read:

- Memorable statements of important points
- Key terms or concepts
- Central issues or themes
- Examples that support a main point
- Unfamiliar words
- Questions you have about a point or passage
- Your responses to a specific point or passage

Remember that there are no hard-and-fast rules for annotating elements. Choose a method of annotation that will make sense to you when you go back to recollect your thoughts and responses to the essay. Don't let annotating become burdensome. A word or phrase is usually as good as a sentence. One helpful way to focus your annotations is to ask yourself questions while reading the selection a second time.

An Example: Annotating Rita Dove's "Loose Ends"

Notice how one of our students recorded her responses to Dove's text with marginal annotations.

Central con-
trast of essay
revealed in
opening an-
ecdote in
first seven
paragraphs.

For years the following scene would play daily at our house: Home from school, my daughter would heave her backpack off her shoulder and let it thud to the hall floor, and then dump her jacket on top of the pile. My husband would tell her to pick it up — as he did every day — and hang it in the closet. Begrudgingly with a snort and a hrrumph, she would comply. The ritual interrogation began:

"Hi, Aviva. How was school?"

"Fine."

"What did you do today?"

"Nothing."

aughter,
viva, bored
y what
appens in
chool.

And so it went, every day. We cajoled, we pleaded, we threatened with rationed ice-cream sandwiches and new healthy vegetable casseroles, we attempted subterfuges such as: "What was Ms. Boyers wearing today?" or: "Any new pets in science class?" but her answer remained the same: I dunno.

ut she's en-
aged with
hat's on TV.

Asked, however, about that week's episodes of "MathNet," her favorite series on Public Television's *Square One,* or asked for a quick gloss of a segment of *Lois and Clark* that we happened to miss, and she'd spew out the details of a complicated story, complete with character development, gestures, every twist and back-flip of the plot.

uestions
esigned to
ngage me.

Is TV greater than reality? Are we to take as damning evidence the soap opera stars attacked in public by viewers who obstinately believe in the on-screen villainy of Erica or Jeannie's evil twin? Is an estrangement from real life the catalyst behind the escalating violence in our schools, where children imitate the gun-'em-down pyrotechnics of cop-and-robber shows? Such a conclusion is too easy. Yes, the influence of public media on our perceptions is enor-

ove intro-
uces thesis.

mous, but the relationship of projected reality — i.e., TV — to imagined reality — i.e., an existential moment — is much more complex. It is not that we confuse TV with reality, but that we prefer it to reality — the manageable struggle resolved in twenty-six minutes, the witty repartee within the family circle instead of the

eries of
oint-by-point
ontrasts
etween
TV and real
ife.

grunts and silence common to most real families; the sharpened conflict and defined despair instead of vague anxiety and invisible enemies. "Life, my friends, is boring. We must not say so," wrote John Berryman, and many years and "Dream Songs" later he leapt from a bridge in Minneapolis. But there is a devastating corollary to that statement: Life, friends, is ragged. Loose ends are the rule.

omment
a loose,
agged
ature of
fe echoes
itle...

What happens when my daughter tells the television's story better than her own is simply this: the TV offers an easier tale to tell. The salient points are there for the plucking — indeed, they're the only points presented — and all she has to do is to recall them. Instant Nostalgia! Life, on the other hand, slithers about and runs down blind alleys and sometimes just fizzles at the climax. "The

ove re-
ects on
hat our
reference
or TV
means.

world is ugly, / And the people are sad," sings the country bumpkin in Wallace Stevens's "Gubinnal." Who isn't tempted to ignore the inexorable fact of our insignificance on a dying planet? We all yearn for our own private patch of blue.

Now that you have learned about the essentials of the reading process — what you should do to prepare yourself to read a selection, what you should look for during a first reading, and what you should annotate — it is time to move on to the next step: analyzing a text by asking yourself questions as you reread it.

Analyzing: Asking Yourself Questions as You Read

As you read the essay a second time, probing for a deeper understanding of and appreciation for what the writer has done, focus your attention by asking yourself basic questions about its content and its form. Here are some questions you may find useful:

▶ *Questions to Ask Yourself as You Read*

1. What does the writer want to say? What is the writer's main point or thesis?
2. Why does the writer want to make this point? What is the writer's purpose?
3. What strategy or strategies does the writer use? Where are the strategies used?
4. How does the writer's strategy suit his or her subject and purpose?
5. What, if anything, is noteworthy about the writer's use of the strategy?
6. How effective is the essay? Does the writer make his or her points clear?

Each essay in *Subjects/Strategies* is followed by study questions similar to these but specific to the essay. The subject questions help you analyze the content of an essay while the craft questions analyze the writer's strategies. In addition, there are questions about the writer's language, which encourage you to explore unfamiliar vocabulary, as well as the writer's diction. As you read the essay a second time, look for details related to these questions, and then answer the questions as fully as you can.

Practice: Reading and Annotating Thomas L. Friedman's "My Favorite Teacher"

Before you read the following essay, think about its title, the biographical and rhetorical information in the headnote, and the journal prompt. Make some marginal notes of your expectations, and write a response to the journal prompt. Then, as you read the essay for the first time, try not to stop; take it all in as if in one breath. The second time, however, pause to annotate the text using the following six questions.

1. What does Friedman want to say? What is his main point or thesis?
2. Why does he want to make this point? What is his purpose?
3. What strategy or strategies does Friedman use?
4. How does Friedman's strategy or strategies suit his subject and purpose?
5. What is noteworthy about Friedman's use of this strategy?
6. How effective is Friedman's essay? Why?

MY FAVORITE TEACHER

Thomas L. Friedman

New York Times *foreign affairs columnist Thomas L. Friedman was born in Minneapolis, Minnesota, in 1953. He graduated from Brandeis University in 1975 and received a Marshall Scholarship to study Modern Middle East Studies at St. Anthony's College, Oxford University, where he earned a master's degree. He has worked for the* New York Times *since 1981 — first in Lebanon, then in Israel, and since 1989 in Washington, D.C. He was awarded the Pulitzer Prize for Reporting in 1983 and again in 1988, and recently his column won him his third Pulitzer Prize. Friedman's 1989 best-seller,* From Beirut to Jerusalem, *received the National Book Award for nonfiction. His most recent books are* The Lexus and the Olive Tree: Understanding Globalization *(2000) and* Longitudes and Attitudes: Exploring the World after September 11 *(2002).*

In the following essay, which first appeared in the New York Times *on January 9, 2001, Friedman pays tribute to his tenth-grade journalism teacher. As you read Friedman's profile of Hattie M. Steinberg, note the descriptive detail he selects to create the dominant impression of "a woman of clarity in an age of uncertainty."*

PREPARING TO READ

If you had to name your three favorite teachers to date, who would they be? Why do you consider each one a favorite? Which one, if any, are you likely to remember twenty-five years from now? Why?

L ast Sunday's *New York Times Magazine* published its annual review of people who died last year who left a particular mark on the world. I am sure all readers have their own such list. I certainly do. Indeed, someone who made the most important difference in my life died last year — my high school journalism teacher, Hattie M. Steinberg.

I grew up in a small suburb of Minneapolis, and Hattie was the   2
legendary journalism teacher at St. Louis Park High School, Room 313.
I took her intro to journalism course in 10th grade, back in 1969, and
have never needed, or taken, another course in journalism since. She
was that good.

Hattie was a woman who believed that the secret for success in   3
life was getting the fundamentals right. And boy, she pounded the
fundamentals of journalism into her students — not simply how to
write a lead or accurately transcribe a quote, but, more important,
how to comport yourself in a professional way and to always do
quality work. To this day, when I forget to wear a tie on assignment,
I think of Hattie scolding me. I once interviewed an ad exec for our
high school paper who used a four-letter word. We debated whether
to run it. Hattie ruled yes. That ad man almost lost his job when it
appeared. She wanted to teach us about consequences.

Hattie was the toughest teacher I ever had. After you took her   4
journalism course in 10th grade, you tried out for the paper, *The
Echo*, which she supervised. Competition was fierce. In 11th grade, I
didn't quite come up to her writing standards, so she made me business manager, selling ads to the local pizza parlors. That year,
though, she let me write one story. It was about an Israeli general
who had been a hero in the Six-Day War, who was giving a lecture
at the University of Minnesota. I covered his lecture and interviewed him briefly. His name was Ariel Sharon. First story I ever got
published.

Those of us on the paper, and the yearbook that she also super-   5
vised, lived in Hattie's classroom. We hung out there before and after
school. Now, you have to understand, Hattie was a single woman,
nearing 60 at the time, and this was the 1960's. She was the polar opposite of "cool," but we hung around her classroom like it was a malt
shop and she was Wolfman Jack. None of us could have articulated it
then, but it was because we enjoyed being harangued by her, disciplined by her and taught by her. She was a woman of clarity in an age
of uncertainty.

We remained friends for 30 years, and she followed, bragged   6
about and critiqued every twist in my career. After she died, her
friends sent me a pile of my stories that she had saved over the years.
Indeed, her students were her family — only closer. Judy Harrington,
one of Hattie's former students, remarked about other friends who
were on Hattie's newspapers and yearbooks: "We all graduated
41 years ago; and yet nearly each day in our lives something comes
up — some mental image, some admonition that makes us think of
Hattie."

Judy also told the story of one of Hattie's last birthday parties,   7
when one man said he had to leave early to take his daughter

somewhere. "Sit down," said Hattie. "You're not leaving yet. She can just be a little late."

That was my teacher! I sit up straight just thinkin' about her.   8

Among the fundamentals Hattie introduced me to was *The New York Times*. Every morning it was delivered to Room 313. I had never seen it before then. Real journalists, she taught us, start their day by reading *The Times* and columnists like Anthony Lewis and James Reston.   9

I have been thinking about Hattie a lot this year, not just because she died on July 31, but because the lessons she imparted seem so relevant now. We've just gone through this huge dot-com-Internet-globalization bubble — during which a lot of smart people got carried away and forgot the fundamentals of how you build a profitable company, a lasting portfolio, a nation state or a thriving student. It turns out that the real secret of success in the information age is what it always was: fundamentals — reading, writing and arithmetic, church, synagogue and mosque, the rule of law and good governance.   10

The Internet can make you smarter, but it can't make you smart. It can extend your reach, but it will never tell you what to say at a P.T.A. meeting. These fundamentals cannot be downloaded. You can only upload them, the old-fashioned way, one by one, in places like Room 313 at St. Louis Park High. I only regret that I didn't write this column when the woman who taught me all that was still alive.   11

Once you have read and reread Friedman's essay, write your own answers to the six basic questions listed earlier. Then compare your answers with those that follow.

1. *What does Friedman want to say?*

Friedman wants to tell his readers about his high school journalism teacher, Hattie M. Steinberg, because she was "someone who made the most important difference in my life" (paragraph 1). His main point seems to be that "Hattie was a woman who believed that the secret for success in life was getting the fundamentals right" (3). Friedman himself believes that "the real secret of success in the information age is what it always was: fundamentals" (10).

2. *Why does he want to make this point?*

Friedman's purpose is to recognize Hattie Steinberg, his former journalism teacher, and to explain the importance of the fundamentals that she taught him more than thirty years ago. He wants his readers to appreciate the examples of fundamentals offered by his journalism teacher and to realize that there are no shortcuts or quick fixes on the road to success. Without the fundamentals, success often eludes people.

3. What strategy or strategies does Friedman use?

Overall, Friedman uses the strategy of exemplification. Hattie M. Steinberg is offered up as a well-developed example of Friedman's favorite teacher. Friedman fleshes out his example of Steinberg with specific examples of the fundamentals she instilled in her students (paragraphs 3 and 9). Friedman uses description and narration as well to develop his profile of Steinberg. We learn that she was Friedman's "toughest teacher" (4), that she was "a single woman, nearing 60 at the time," that she was "the polar opposite of 'cool,'" and that she was "a woman of clarity in an age of uncertainty" (5). Finally, Friedman's brief narratives about his interview of an advertising executive, his interview of Ariel Sharon, hanging out in Steinberg's classroom, and one of the teacher's last birthday parties give readers insight into her personality by showing us what she was like instead of simply telling us.

4. How does Friedman's strategy or strategies suit his subject and purpose?

Friedman selects exemplification as a strategy because his purpose is to explain why — out of all the teachers that he has had — Hattie M. Steinberg is his favorite, the one who has had the greatest impact on his life. Friedman knew that he was not telling Steinberg's story, a narration, so much as he was showing what a great teacher she was. Friedman's examples of Steinberg in action in her classroom and of the fundamentals she insisted her students learn make her come alive for readers and illustrate the life-shaping impact she had on her students.

5. What is noteworthy about Friedman's use of the strategy?

In developing his portrait of Hattie M. Steinberg, Friedman relies on the fundamentals of good journalism. He selects brief examples that give us insight into Steinberg's character and personality. When taken collectively, these examples create a poignant picture of this unforgettable teacher. One would have to think that Steinberg herself would have been proud to see how her former student demonstrates his journalistic skills in paying tribute to the woman who taught him his craft so long ago.

6. *How effective is the essay? Why?*

Friedman's essay is effective because it serves his purpose extremely well. He helps his readers visualize Hattie M. Steinberg and understand the gifts that she gave to each of her journalism students. In his concluding two paragraphs, Friedman shows us that Steinberg's message is as relevant today as it was more than thirty years ago in St. Louis Park High School, Room 313.

ABOUT THE PHOTOGRAPHS AND VISUAL TEXTS IN THIS BOOK

We have introduced one essay in each chapter with a photograph that depicts one or more of the themes in the essay. Occasionally, the photographs also demonstrate the rhetorical mode of the chapter. Think of these photographs, then, as another type of Preparing to Read journal exercise. The questions that follow the photographs, entitled "Connecting Image and Text," are designed to encourage close observation and critical thinking. It is our hope that, by adding a new, visual medium to the mix of written essays and text-based analytical activities and assignments, we can demonstrate not only another approach to themes and strategies but also how a different medium portrays these themes and strategies.

There's nothing unnatural or wrong about looking at a photograph and naming its subject or giving it a label. For example, summarizing the content of the photograph on page 14 by Sean Sprague of a village scene in Gujarat, India, is easy enough. We'd simply say, *"Here's a photograph of a woman in native dress."*

The problem comes when we mistake *looking* for *seeing*. If we think we are seeing and truly perceiving but are only looking, we miss a lot. Our visual sense can become uncritical and nonchalant, perhaps even numbed to what's going on in a photograph.

To reap the larger rewards, we need to move in more closely on an image. If we take a closer look, we will see all kinds of important details that we missed the first time around.

If we dig a little deeper and apply our critical faculties, we can see photographs as dynamic, visual works that play with some important concepts. We see some elements in a photograph as parts of something larger. We see elements in harmony as well as conflict. We see comparisons and contrasts. We see storytelling. We see process and change. We see highlights and shadows, foreground and background, light and dark, and a myriad of shades in between. There is movement — even in still photographs. There is tension and energy,

© Sean Sprague/Stock Boston

peace and harmony, and line and texture. We see all this because we are seeing and not merely looking.

For example, we can examine the photograph of the woman again and quickly generate numerous observations that go beneath the surface and help exercise our critical reasoning faculties about what's going on in the photo.

1. The woman is holding a child. It looks as if the child is wearing a necklace but is otherwise naked. The woman is barefoot, but she's also wearing jewelry — a necklace and a bracelet. She is not necessarily poor. She is in some kind of native dress — the skirt goes down to her ankles, and there is some kind of scarf that goes over the back of her hair.

2. The woman is focusing on something to the photographer's right (her left). She is looking into the sun, which is low on the horizon. We know this because there is a large shadow behind her.

3. The second primary subject in the photograph is the satellite dish on the roof of the building the woman is standing beside. It is neither a huge dish indicating early technology nor a relatively small one indicating recent digital satellite technology. On the peak of the roof of the building is a cross.

4. There is non-Western writing on the wall of the building. Some of the writing is smudged. The writing doesn't appear to be graffiti because it is very neatly rendered.

5. At what looks like the entrance to the building are two large sacks of what may be grain, still tied at their tops.

6. There's no paving or concrete apparent, simply dirt and stone. There is some tension in the fact that the woman is standing barefoot on this surface.

7. There are trees poking out from behind the building. They are not palm trees, and it is difficult to determine exactly what kind they are.

8. The most tension in the photograph lies in the juxtaposition of the high-tech satellite dish in what appears to be a third world setting.

In short, there is more in the photograph than we suspected. Based upon these detailed observations, we can begin to identify a number of themes at work in the photo: cultural diversity, cultural contradictions, culture clashes (Eastern world versus Western world), technology, and imperialism. Likewise, we can see that several rhetorical strategies are at work: comparison and contrast predominantly, with the juxtaposition of Old- and New-World images, but also description and exemplification. A similar close analysis of the other photographs in this book will enhance your understanding of how themes and strategies work in these visual texts.

This exercise in visual analysis will, in turn, add to your understanding of how the same types of themes and strategies work in the reading selections. When it comes to reading, we need to train ourselves to pay close attention to catch all nuances and implications and to be attuned to what is not said as well as what is made clear. By sharpening our observational skills, we penetrate to another level of meaning in our reading — a level not apparent to a casual reader — and we enable ourselves to interact with essential facts and truths. For writers, the world does not exist so much in abstractions as it does in specifics — not trees but this particular tree, not leaves but this one I am holding in my hand. We need to see first, clearly and in detail, before we attempt as writers to find the proper words to make others see.

For all these reasons, then, there is value in analyzing photographs and other visual texts, just as there is value in analyzing life, as a way of understanding the processes of reading and writing.

USING YOUR READING IN THE WRITING PROCESS

Reading and writing are two sides of the same coin. Many people view writing as the making of reading, but the connection does not end there. Active reading is one of the best ways to learn to write and to improve writing skills. By reading we can see how others have communicated their experiences, ideas, thoughts, and feelings in their writing. We can study how they have effectively used the various elements of the essay — thesis, organization, beginnings and endings, paragraphs, transitions, effective sentences, word choice, tone, and figurative language — to say what they wanted to say. By studying the style, technique, and rhetorical strategies of other writers we learn how we might effectively do the same. The more we read and write, the more we begin to read as writers and, in turn, to write knowing what readers expect.

Reading as a Writer

What does it mean to read as a writer? Most of us have not been taught to read with a writer's eye, to ask why we like one piece of writing and not another. Likewise, most of us do not ask ourselves why one piece of writing is more believable or convincing than another. When you learn to read with a writer's eye, you begin to answer these important questions and, in the process, come to appreciate what is involved in selecting a subject. Also, you begin to understand the craftsmanship involved in writing — how a writer selects descriptive details, uses an unobtrusive organizational pattern, opts for fresh and lively language, chooses representative and persuasive examples, and emphasizes important points with sentence variety.

At one level, reading stimulates your imagination by providing you with subjects. After reading Malcolm X's "Coming to an Awareness of Language," David P. Bardeen's "Not Close Enough for Comfort," or Annie Dillard's "Getting Caught," you might decide to write about a "turning point" in your life or how you once succumbed to pressure in a tight situation. Or, by reading Steve Martin's "The Death of My Father," Edward Abbey's "Aravaipa Canyon," or Robert Ramirez's "The Barrio," you would see how each writer creates a dominant impression of an important person or place in his life, and you could write about a person or place of similar personal significance.

On a second level, reading provides you with information, ideas, and perspectives for developing your own essay. For example, after reading Rosalind Wiseman's "The Queen Bee and Her Court," you might want to elaborate on what she has written, agreeing with her examples or generating better ones; qualify her argument or take issue with it; or use a variation of her classification scheme to discuss male relationships (i.e., "The King and His Court"). Similarly, if you wanted to write about the "Frankenfood" (genetically modified food) debate, you will find the essays by Jonathan Rauch, David Ehrenfeld, Jane Brody, and Jim Scharplaz on contemporary farming practices in the Argument chapter an invaluable resource.

On a third level, reading can increase your awareness of how others' writing affects you, making you more sensitive to how your writing will affect readers. For example, if you have been impressed by an author who uses convincing evidence to support her claims, you might be more likely to back up your own claims carefully. If you have been impressed by an apt turn of phrase, you may be less inclined to feed your readers dull phrases. More to the point, however, the active, analytical reading that you will be encouraged to do in *Subjects/Strategies* will help you recognize and analyze the essay's essential elements. When you see, for example, how Deborah Tannen uses a strong thesis statement about the value of directness and indirectness in human communication to control the parts of her essay, you can better appreciate the importance of having a clear thesis statement in your writing. When you see the way Judith Ortiz Cofer uses transitions to link key phrases and important ideas so that readers can recognize how the parts of her essay are meant to flow together, you have a better idea of how to achieve such coherence in your writing. And when you see how Suzanne Britt uses a point-by-point organizational pattern to show the differences between neat and sloppy people, you see a powerful way in which you can organize an essay using the strategy of comparison and contrast.

Finally, another important reason to master the skill of reading like a writer is that, for everything you write, you will be your own first reader. How well you scrutinize your own drafts will affect how well you revise them, and revising well is crucial to writing well. So reading others' writing with a critical eye is useful and important practice; the more you read, the more practice you will have in sharpening your skills.

Remember, writing is the making of reading. The more sensitive you become to the content and style decisions made by the writers in *Subjects/Strategies,* the more skilled you will become at making similar decisions in your writing.

CHAPTER 2

Writing Essays

There is nothing mysterious or difficult about the nine rhetorical strategies discussed in this book. You're probably familiar with some of them already. When you want to tell a story, for example, you naturally use the strategy of narration. When you want to make a choice, you naturally compare and contrast the things you must choose between. When you want to explain how to make a pizza, you fall automatically into the strategy of process analysis. These and other strategies are ways we think about the world and our experiences in it. What might make these strategies seem unfamiliar, especially in writing, is that most people use them more or less intuitively, with little awareness of their use. Sophisticated thinking and writing do not come from simply using these structures — everyone does that — but from using them consciously and purposefully.

Writing strategies, however, are not like blueprints or plaster molds that determine in advance exactly how the final product will be shaped. Good essays usually employ components of more than one strategy, and the options for how to use them effectively are numerous. Rather, these strategies are flexible and versatile, with only a few fundamental rules or directions to define their shape — like the rules for basketball, chess, or other strategic games. Such directions leave plenty of room for all the imagination and variety you can put into your writing and for all the things you may want to write about. In addition, because these strategies are fundamental ways of thinking, they will help you in all stages of the writing process — from prewriting and writing a first draft through revising and editing your piece.

THE WRITING PROCESS

Prewriting

Writers rarely rely on inspiration to produce an effective piece of writing. Good writers plan or prewrite, write, revise and edit, and proofread. It is worth remembering, however, that the writing process is rarely as simple and straightforward as this. Often the process is recursive, moving back and forth among the four stages. Moreover, writing is personal — no two people go about it exactly the same way. Still, it is possible to describe the steps in the writing process and thereby have a reassuring and reliable method for undertaking a writing task.

Your reading can give you ideas and information, of course. But reading also helps expand your knowledge of available writing strategies, and consequently it can help direct your prewriting activities. In *prewriting*, you select your subject and topic, gather ideas and information, and determine the thesis, strategy, and organization you will use. Once you've worked through the prewriting process, you will be ready to start on your first draft. Let's explore how this works.

Understand Your Assignment. When you first receive an assignment, read it over several times to be sure you understand what you are being asked to do. For example, consider each of the following assignments:

- Tell about an experience that led you to a new understanding of relationships.
- Discuss the concept of supply and demand in the marketplace.
- Leading environmentalists agree that effective recycling efforts must be both economically and environmentally sustainable. Write an essay in which you analyze the prospects for recycling Styrofoam products.

The first assignment asks you to identify and narrate an experience that gave you some insight into human relationships. You might choose simply to narrate the experience, or you might choose to analyze it; in either case, you would have to explain to your reader what new understanding you gained. In the second assignment, you would need to define or explain exactly what is meant by supply and demand and then give several examples of how this concept applies to the marketplace. Finally, the third assignment asks you to do a number of things. First, you would need to define the concepts of economic and environmental sustainability. Second, you would probably research and explore the pros and cons of recycling Styrofoam products. Third, based on your understanding of sustainability as well as the issues involved with recycling Styrofoam, you would need to spec-ulate on the chances for setting up successful Styrofoam recycling pro-grams.

If, after rereading the assignment several times, you are still unsure about what is being asked of you or of any additional requirements (such as length or format), be sure to consult with your instructor. He or she should be willing to clear up any confusion before you start writing.

Determine Your Purpose. All effective writing is written with a purpose. Good writing seeks to accomplish any one of three purposes:

- To express thoughts and feelings about life experiences
- To inform readers by explaining something about the world around them
- To persuade readers to adopt some belief or take some action

Your purpose will often determine which strategy you choose to em-ploy in your writing. For example, if you wish to express thoughts and feelings, a personal narrative is appropriate. If, on the other hand, you wish to persuade your readers to adopt a certain belief, you will proba-bly choose to write an argument.

In *expressive writing,* or writing from experience, you put your thoughts and feelings before all other concerns. When Annie Dillard reacts to being caught throwing a snowball at a car (Chapter 5), when Malcolm X shows his frustration at not having appropriate language to express himself (Chapter 5), and when Edward Abbey describes a hike in Aravaipa Canyon with two friends (Chapter 4), each one is writing from experience. In each case, the writer has clarified an important life experience and has conveyed what he or she learned from it.

Informative writing focuses on telling the reader something about the outside world. In informative writing, you report, explain, analyze, define, classify, compare, describe a process, or examine causes and effects. When Kennedy P. Maize explains what happens when the res-idents of Kern County declare war on the mouse population (Chapter 10) and when Deborah Tannen discusses examples of orders given and received in the workplace (Chapter 3), each one is writing to in-form.

Argumentative writing seeks to influence readers' thinking and atti-tudes toward a subject and, in some cases, to move them to a particular course of action. Such persuasive writing uses logical reasoning, au-thoritative evidence, and testimony and sometimes includes emotion-ally charged language and examples. In selections reprinted in this book, Richard Lederer uses numerous examples to show us the power of short words (Chapter 11), and Jonathan Rauch uses evidence to argue that genetically modified foods could feed the hungry and help the environment (Chapter 11).

Find a Subject Area and Topic. Although you will usually be given specific assignments in your writing course, you may sometimes be given the freedom to choose your subject matter and topic. In either case, when selecting your specific topic you should determine whether you know something about it and whether it interests you.

When your instructor leaves you free to choose your own topic, begin by determining a broad subject that you like to think about and might enjoy writing about — a general subject like the Internet, biomedical ethics, amateur sports, or foreign travel. Something you've recently read — one of the essays in *Subjects/Strategies*, for example — may help bring particular subjects to mind. You might consider a subject related to your career ambitions — perhaps business, journalism, law, medicine, architecture, or computer programming. Another option is to list some subjects you enjoy discussing with friends: food, motorcycles, television programs, or politics. Select several likely subjects, and let your mind explore their potential for interesting topics. Your goal is to arrive at an appropriately limited topic.

Suppose, for example, you select as possible subject areas journalism, foreign travel, and television programs. You could develop the following focused topics:

General Subject Area	Limited Topic	More Limited Topic
Journalism ⟶	Investigative reporting ⟶	Protecting sources
Foreign travel ⟶	Study-abroad programs ⟶	Learning language by immersion
Television programs ⟶	Sitcoms ⟶	Comic devices on *The Simpsons*

Know Your Audience. The best writers always keep their audience in mind. Once they have decided upon a purpose and a topic, writers present their material in a way that empathizes with their readers, addresses their difficulties and concerns, and appeals to their rational and emotional faculties. Based on knowledge of their audience, writers make conscious decisions on content, sentence structure, and word choice.

An audience might be an individual (a parent), a group (the students in your class), a specialized group (heart surgeons), or a general readership (readers of your local newspaper). To help identify your audience, ask yourself the following questions:

▶ *Questions about Audience*

- Who are my readers?
- Are they a specialized or a general group?
- What do I know about my audience's age, gender, education, religious affiliation, economic status, and political attitudes?
- What does my audience know about my subject? Are they experts or novices?
- What does my audience need to know that I can tell them?
- Will my audience be interested, open-minded, resistant, or hostile to what I have to say?
- Do I need to explain any specialized language so that my audience can understand my subject? Is there any language that I should avoid?
- What do I want my audience to do as a result of reading my essay?

Generating Ideas and Collecting Information

Keep a Journal. Many writers keep a journal in which they record thoughts and observations that might be mined for future writing projects. They've learned not to rely on their memories to retain ideas, facts, and statistics they have heard or read about. Writers also keep all kinds of lists in journals: lists of questions they would like answers to, lists of issues that concern them, and lists of topics that they would like to write about someday.

Journals are also a great place to do *freewriting* — to run with an idea and to see where it leads. Writers often use these freewriting sessions — five to ten minutes of uninterrupted writing — to discover new materials, new strategies, and, perhaps most important, new topics. By writing about a topic before you have done any reading or research, not only will you discover what you already know about the topic, but you will find out what you think and how you feel about it. For each professional selection in *Subjects/Strategies*, we have provided a Preparing to Read question that offers you an opportunity to do some journal writing before you read the selection. After you have read a selection, it is a good practice to reflect in writing on what the author has said; to this end we provide a Responding to the Text question immediately after each professional selection.

Brainstorm for New Material. Another good way to generate ideas and information about your topic is to *brainstorm*. Simply list everything you know about your topic, freely associating one idea with another. At this point, order is not important. Try to capture everything that comes to mind because you never know what might prove valuable later. Write quickly, but if you get stalled, reread what you have written; doing so will jog your mind in new directions. Keep your list handy so that you can add to it over the course of several days. Here, for example, is a student's brainstorming list on why Martin Luther King Jr.'s "I Have a Dream" speech (page 525) is enduring:

WHY "I HAVE A DREAM" IS MEMORABLE

- Civil rights demonstration in Washington, D.C.
- Delivered on the steps of Lincoln Memorial
- Repetition of "I have a dream"
- Allusions to the Bible, spirituals
- "Bad check" metaphor
- Other memorable figures of speech
- Crowd of more than 200,000 people
- Echoes other great American writings — Declaration of Independence and Gettysburg Address
- Refers to various parts of the country
- Embraces all races and religions
- Sermon format
- Displays energy and passion

Generate Ideas Using Rhetorical Strategies. Even the most experienced writers need to generate ideas and find information for their writing. Use the rhetorical strategies to get your mind working, to make associations, and to discover meaningful things to say about your topic. Remember that writing strategies are more than techniques for composition; they are basic ways of thinking.

Suppose that you like to watch television news programs and you think you would like to write about some aspect of television news. First, you might use the strategy of division to identify the most common genres, or types, of news programs.

Network evening news shows
Network morning news shows
Headline news shows
Newsmagazines

News talk shows
News interview shows
Tabloid news shows

To get to the next level of specificity about your subject, you might want to use the strategy of *classification* and supply examples for each of your established categories.

Network evening news shows: *CBS Evening News, NBC Nightly News, ABC World News Tonight*

Network morning news shows: *Early Show, Today, Good Morning America*

Headline news shows: *CNN Headline News*

Newsmagazines: *20/20, 60 Minutes, 48 Hours, Nightline*

News talk shows: *NewsHour with Jim Lehrer, Crossfire, Hardball with Chris Matthews*

News interview shows: *Meet the Press, Larry King Live*

Tabloid news shows: *Entertainment Tonight, Inside Edition, Access Hollywood*

With these examples clearly in mind, the next step would be to describe a typical program for each of your categories, trying to capture specific representative details of each category.

CBS Evening News: Major network news program anchored by a well-known and respected reporter. Relies on a broad range of reports from around the world on news items and subjects of interest to the general public. Is broadcast once a day and is supported by commercials.

Today: Latest overnight news roundup, weather, sports, interviews with major newsmakers, and human interest features. Is interrupted periodically by local updates.

CNN Headline News: Capsule summaries of international, national, financial, sports, and entertainment news delivered at preset intervals each half hour — twenty-four hours a day, every day.

60 Minutes: Presents three in-depth stories based on investigative reporting. Usually includes a ten-minute commentary by Andy Rooney.

NewsHour with Jim Lehrer: Focused and in-depth news analysis with a reserved and quiet tone. Not commercially supported.

Larry King Live: Interview program with major personalities and newsmakers. Noted for being a great interviewer, King also tends to be somewhat sensational and controversial.

Entertainment Tonight: Developing and breaking news stories in the entertainment world, very often characterized by up-to-the-minute reports. Borders on the gossipy.

Other strategies you might choose include *comparison* and *contrast*, showing the relative amounts of hard and soft news on each type of program; *definition*, defining the niche, vision, and purpose of each type of show; and *cause and effect*, analyzing the effects of various types of program formats on viewing audiences.

Of course, when you write your essay, you probably won't use all the material you gather, and you won't necessarily organize your writing using the same strategies that helped you find your ideas. At this stage, your goal should be to search your memory for material. After choosing a subject and topic and generating ideas and information, you are ready to make connections within the material and to organize your thoughts.

Formulate a Thesis Statement. You should now be ready to commit to a controlling idea, a *thesis*. The thesis of an essay is its main idea, the point the writer is trying to make. The thesis is often expressed in one or two sentences called a *thesis statement*. Here's an example.

> The so-called serious news programs are becoming too much like tabloid news shows in both their content and their presentation.

The thesis statement should not be confused with your purpose for writing. While a thesis statement makes an assertion about your topic and actually appears in your essay as such, your purpose is what you are trying to do in the essay — to express, to explain, or to argue — and should not be stated explicitly. For example, the purpose behind the preceding thesis statement might be expressed as follows.

> By comparing the transcripts of news shows like the *CBS Evening News* and tabloid shows like *Entertainment Tonight*, I will show alarming parallels in what the two genres of programs find "newsworthy."

Again, this type of purpose statement should not appear in your essay.

A thesis statement should be

- The most important point you make about your topic
- More general than the ideas and facts used to support it
- Focused enough to be covered in the space allotted for the essay

A thesis statement should not be a question but an assertion. If you find yourself writing a question for a thesis statement, answer the question first — this answer will be your thesis statement.

An effective strategy for developing a thesis statement is to begin by writing, "What I want to say is that . . . ."

> *What I want to say is that* unless language barriers between patients and health care providers are bridged, many patients' lives in our most culturally diverse cities will be endangered.

Later you can delete the formulaic opening, and you will be left with a thesis statement.

> Unless language barriers between patients and health care providers are bridged, many patients' lives in our most culturally diverse cities will be endangered.

A good way to determine whether your thesis is too general or too specific is to think hard about how easy it will be to present information and examples to support it. If you stray too far in either direction, your task will become much more difficult. A thesis statement that is too general will leave you overwhelmed by the number of issues you must address. For example, the statement "Malls have ruined the fabric of American life" would lead to the question "How?" To answer it, you would probably have to include information about traffic patterns, urban decay, environmental damage, economic studies, and so on. You would obviously have to take shortcuts, and your paper would be ineffective. On the other hand, too specific a thesis statement will leave you with too little information to present. "The Big City Mall should not have been built because it reduced retail sales at existing Big City stores by 21.4 percent" does not leave you with any opportunity to develop an argument.

▶ *Will Your Thesis Hold Water?*

Once you have a possible thesis statement in mind for an essay, ask yourself the following questions:

- Does my thesis statement take a clear stance on an issue? If so, what is that stance?
- Is my thesis too general?
- Is my thesis too specific?
- Does my thesis apply to a larger audience than myself? If so, what is the audience, and how does the thesis apply?

The thesis statement is usually set forth near the beginning of the essay, although writers sometimes first offer a few sentences that establish a context for the piece. One common strategy is to position the thesis statement as the final sentence of the first paragraph. In the opening paragraph of an essay on the harmful effects of quick weight-loss diets, student Marcie Turple builds a context for her thesis statement, which she presents in her last sentence:

> Americans are obsessed with thinness — even at the risk of dying. In the 1930s, people took dinitrophenol, an industrial poison, to lose weight. It boosted metabolism but caused blindness and some deaths. Since then dieters have used thyroid hormone injections, amphetamines, liquid protein diets, and, most recently, the controversial fen-phen. What most dieters need to realize is that there is no magic way to lose weight — no pill, no crash diet plan. The only way to permanent weight loss is through sensible eating and exercise.

Determine Your Strategy. Once you decide what you want to write about and come up with ideas about what you might like to say, your next task is to jot down the main ideas for your essay in an order that seems both natural and logical. In other words, make a scratch outline. In constructing this outline, you might discover that one of the rhetorical strategies will help you approach your topic. If a particular strategy was especially helpful to you in generating ideas, you might consider using that as your overall organizing principle.

If you're still undecided about what strategy to use for your essay, try the following steps:

1. Summarize the point you want to make in a single phrase or sentence.
2. Restate the point as a question — in effect, the question your essay will answer.
3. Look closely at both the summary and the question for key words or concepts that go with a particular strategy.
4. Consider other strategies that would support your primary strategy.

Here are some examples:

SUMMARY: NASCAR is becoming the most popular sport in the United States.

QUESTION: Why is NASCAR becoming the most popular sport in the United States?

STRATEGY: Cause and effect analysis. Whenever a question asks *why*, answering it will require discovering a *cause* or a series of causes for a particular *effect*.

SUPPORTING STRATEGIES: Exemplification and description. Evidence includes statistics, examples, and descriptions of NASCAR's varied fan base.

SUMMARY: How to build a Web site.

QUESTION: How do you build a Web site?

STRATEGY: Process analysis. The word *how*, especially in the phrase "how to," implies a procedure that can be explained in steps or stages.

SUPPORTING STRATEGIES: Description and exemplification. It is necessary to describe the work-in-progress Web site at some points in the process, as well as explain why certain design elements — background colors, font and icon size — would or would not be good choices for the site.

SUMMARY: The threat of terrorism has changed the way people think about air travel.

QUESTION: What effects does terrorism have on air travel?

STRATEGY: Cause and effect. The word *what* asks for a listing of the effects.

SUPPORTING STRATEGY: Exemplification. The best presentation of effects is through vivid examples.

SUMMARY: The state government should fund high-speed Internet access for every elementary school.

QUESTION: What should be done to provide the state's elementary schools with high-speed Internet access?

STRATEGIES: Argument or persuasion. The word *should* signals an argument, calling for evidence and reasoning in support of the conclusion.

SUPPORTING STRATEGIES: Comparison and contrast as well as cause and effect analysis. Evidence comes from a comparison of school districts that have high-speed Internet access with those that don't, as well as from a discussion of the effects of computer and Internet use on children.

These are just a few examples of how to decide on a writing strategy and supporting strategies that are suitable for your topic. In every case, your reading can guide you in recognizing the best plan to follow. In Chapter 12, you will learn more about combining strategies.

Organize Your Paper. Before you start a draft, it's a good idea to organize your material according to the strategy you will use — that is, to create a working plan. Different strategies, of course, will suggest different kinds of working plans. A process analysis essay, in which you provide directions for someone to follow, might be mapped out in this way:

Step 1: _____

Step 2: _____

Step 3: _____

Step 4: _____

A working plan for an essay using comparison and contrast, however, would look quite different — perhaps like this:

Object A	**Object B**
Point 1: _____	Point 1: _____
Point 2: _____	Point 2: _____
Point 3: _____	Point 3: _____
Point 4: _____	Point 4: _____

A working plan for an argumentative essay might look like this:

Point to be proved: _____

Supporting arguments:

1. _____

2. _____

3. _____

Opposing argument(s): _____

Rebuttal: _____

Final argument: _____

A working plan is similar to a scratch outline; it is determined, however, much more specifically by the requirements of a particular writing strategy. You have a great deal of flexibility in determining your working plan's format; the models provided here are only suggestions. Your reading will help you understand the kinds of modifications acceptable for a given strategy.

Writing Your First Draft

First drafts are exploratory and sometimes unpredictable. While writing your first draft, you may find yourself getting away from your original plan. What started as a definition essay may develop into a process analysis or an effort at argumentation. For example, a definition of "school spirit" could turn into a process analysis of how a pep rally is organized or an argument about why school spirit is important (or detrimental). A definition of "manners" could become an instructive process analysis on how to be a good host, or it could turn into an argument that respect is based on the ways people treat one another. A definition of "democracy" could evolve into a process analysis of how democracy works in the United States or into an argument for democratic forms of government. If your draft is leaning toward another strategy, don't force yourself to revert to your original plan. Allow your inspiration to take you where it will. When you finish your draft, you can see whether the new strategy works better than the old one or whether it would be best to go back to your initial strategy. Use your first draft to explore your ideas; you will always have a chance to revise later.

It may also happen that while writing your first draft, you run into a difficulty that prevents you from moving forward. For example, suppose you want to tell about something that happened to you, but you aren't certain whether you should be using the pronoun *I* so often. If you turn to the essays in Chapter 5 to see how authors of narrative essays handle this problem, you will find that it isn't necessarily a problem at all. For an account of a personal experience, it's perfectly acceptable to write *I* as often as you need to. Or suppose that after writing several pages describing someone you think is quite a character, you find that your draft seems flat and doesn't express how lively and funny the person really is. If you read the introduction to Chapter 4, you will learn that descriptions need lots of factual, concrete detail, and the chapter selections give further proof of this. You suddenly realize that just such detail is what's missing from your draft. Reading, then, is helpful because it enables you to see how other writers successfully dealt with problems similar to yours.

If you do run into difficulties writing your first draft, don't worry or get upset. Even experienced writers run into problems at the beginning. Just try to keep going and take pressure off yourself. Think about your topic, and consider your details and what you want to say. You might even want to go back and look over the information you've gathered.

> ### ▶ Checklist for Your First Draft

- Triple-space your draft so that you can make changes more easily.
- Make revisions on a hard copy of your paper.
- Read your paper aloud, listening for parts that do not make sense.
- Have a fellow student read your essay and critique it.

Peer Critiquing

When you critique work with other students — yours or theirs — it is important to maximize the effectiveness and efficiency of the exercise. The tips outlined in the following box will help you get the most out of peer critiques.

> ### ▶ A Brief Guide to Peer Critiquing

When critiquing someone else's work:

- Read the essay carefully. Read it to yourself first and, if possible, have the writer read it to you at the beginning of the session. Some flaws become obvious when read aloud.
- Ask the writer to state his or her purpose for writing and to identify the thesis statement within the paper itself.
- Be positive, but be honest. Never denigrate the paper's content or the writer's effort, but do your best to identify how the writer can improve the paper through revision.
- Try to address the most important issues first. Think about the thesis and the organization of the paper before moving on to more specific topics like word choice.
- Do not be dismissive, and do not dictate changes. Ask questions that encourage the writer to reconsider parts of the paper that you find confusing or ineffective.

When someone critiques your work:

- Give your reviewer a copy of your essay before your meeting.
- Listen carefully to your reviewer, and try not to discuss or argue each issue. Record comments, and evaluate them later.

(continued on next page)

(*continued from previous page*)

- Do not get defensive or explain what you wanted to say if the reviewer misunderstands what you meant. Try to understand the reviewer's point of view, and learn what you need to revise to clear up the misunderstanding.
- Consider every suggestion, but only use the ones that make sense to you in your revision.
- Be sure to thank your reviewer for his or her effort on your behalf.

Revising

Once you have completed your first draft and at least one critiquing session, you are ready to revise it.

Revise the Large Elements of Your Essay. During the revision stage of the writing process, you will focus on the large issues of thesis, purpose, content, organization, and paragraph structure to make sure that your writing says what you want it to say. But first, it is crucial that you set your draft aside and give yourself a rest. Then you can come back to it with some freshness and objectivity. When you do, resist the temptation to plunge immediately into a second draft. Scattered changes will not necessarily improve the piece. Try to look at your writing as a whole and to tackle your writing problems systematically.

One way to begin the revision process is to make an informal outline of your first draft — not as you planned it, but as it actually came out. What does your outline tell you about the strategy you used? Does this strategy suit your purpose? Perhaps you meant to compare your two grandmothers, but you have not clearly shown their similarities and differences. Consequently, your draft is not one unified comparison and contrast essay but two descriptive essays spliced together. Or perhaps your outline will show you that you set out to write about your grandmothers, but you never had a definite purpose in mind. Outlining your first draft helps you see that, despite some differences in looks and habits, both grandmothers are essentially alike in all the ways that matter. This gives you both a point to make and a strategy for making it: comparison and contrast.

Even if you are satisfied with the overall strategy of your draft, an outline can still help you make improvements. Perhaps your directions for preparing a pizza leave out an important step in the process — adding oregano to the tomato sauce, for example. Or perhaps your classification essay on types of college students is confusing because you create overlapping categories: computer science majors, athletes, and foreign students (a computer science major could, of course, be an athlete, a foreign student, or both). You may uncover a flaw in your organization, such as a lack of logic in an argument or a parallelism in a comparison and contrast. Now is the time to discover these problems and to fix them.

Another method you can use in revising is to start with large-scale issues, such as your overall structure, and then concentrate on finer and finer points. As you examine your essay, ask yourself questions about what you have written. The following list of questions addresses the large elements of your essay: thesis, purpose, organization, paragraphs, and evidence.

▶ *Questions for Revising the Large Elements of Your Essay*

- Have I focused my topic?
- Does my thesis statement clearly identify my topic and make an assertion about it?
- Is my organizational pattern the best one for my purpose?
- Are my paragraphs adequately developed, and does each support my thesis?
- Have I supplied enough details and examples to support my thesis?
- Have I accomplished my purpose?
- Is my beginning effective in capturing my reader's interest and introducing my topic?
- Is my conclusion effective? Does it grow naturally from what I've said in the rest of my essay?

Having addressed these questions, you might consider constructing a formal outline of your essay that reflects the changes you want to make and the anticipated organization of the piece. At the beginning of this outline include your title, a brief statement of your purpose, and your thesis statement. As a general rule, it is advisable to write in complete sentences unless your meaning is immediately clear from a phrase. If you wish to divide any of your main categories into subcategories, make sure that you have at least two subcategories; if not, a division is not necessary. Finally, you should observe the conventions of formal outlining. Notice how each new level of specificity in the pattern below is given a new letter or number designation.

Title: _____

Purpose: _____

Thesis: _____

    I. _____

      A. _____

      B. _____

        1. _____

        2. _____

      C. _____

   II. _____

      A. _____

        1. _____

          a. _____

          b. _____

        2. _____

      B. _____

  III. _____

Revising the Small Elements of Your Essay. Once you have addressed the major problems in your essay by writing a second draft, you should turn your attention to the finer elements of sentence structure, word choice, and usage. The following questions focus on these concerns.

▶ *Questions for Revising Sentences*

- Do my sentences convey my thoughts clearly, and do they emphasize the most important parts of my thinking?
- Are all my sentences complete sentences?
- Are my sentences stylistically varied? Do I alter their pattern and rhythm for emphasis? Do I use some short sentences for dramatic effect?
- Are all my sentences written in the active voice?
- Do I use strong action verbs and concrete nouns?
- Is my diction fresh and forceful, or is my writing verbose?
- Have I committed any errors in usage?

Finally, if you find yourself dissatisfied with specific elements of your draft, look at several essays in *Subjects/Strategies* to see how other writers have dealt with similar situations. For example, if you don't like the way the essay starts, find some beginnings you think are particularly effective. If your paragraphs don't seem to flow into one another, examine how various writers use transitions. If an example seems unconvincing, examine the way other writers include details, anecdotes, facts, and statistics to strengthen their illustrations. Remember that the readings in this text are a resource for you as you write, as are the strategy chapter introductions, which outline the basic features and sentence-level concerns unique to each strategy. In addition, the six readings in Chapter 13, "Writers on Writing," will provide you with inspiration and advice to help you through the writing process.

▶ *Notes on Beginnings and Endings*

Beginnings and endings are very important to the effectiveness of an essay, but they can be daunting to write. Inexperienced writers often feel they must write their essays sequentially when, in fact, it is usually better to write both the beginning and the ending after you have completed most or all of the rest of your essay. Once you see how your essay develops, you will know better how to catch your reader's attention and introduce the rest of the essay. Particular attention should be paid to both parts during the revision process. Ask yourself:

- Does my introduction grab the reader's attention?
- Is my introduction confusing in any way? How well does it relate to the rest of the essay?
- If I state my thesis in the introduction, how effectively is it presented?
- Does my essay come to a logical conclusion or does it seem to just stop?
- How well does the conclusion relate to the rest of the essay? Am I careful not to introduce new topics or issues that I did not address in the essay?
- Does my conclusion help to underscore or illuminate important aspects of the body of the essay or is it redundant, a mechanical rehashing of what I wrote earlier?

Editing and Proofreading

Now that you have made your essay "right," it is time to think about making it "correct." During the *editing* stage of the writing process, you check your writing for errors in grammar, punctuation, capitalization, spelling, and manuscript format. The questions in the following box will guide you in the editing of your essay. Both your dictionary

---

▶ *Questions to Ask during Editing and Proofreading*

- Do my verbs agree in number with their antecedents?
- Do my pronouns have clear antecedents — that is, do they clearly refer to specific earlier nouns?
- Do I have any sentence fragments, comma splices, or run-on sentences?
- Have I made any unnecessary shifts in person, tense, or number?
- Have I used the comma properly in all instances?
- Have I checked for misspellings, mistakes in capitalization, and typos?
- Have I inadvertently confused words like *their, they're*, and *there* or *it's* and *its*?
- Have I followed the prescribed guidelines for formatting my manuscript?

---

and your grammar handbook will help you in answering specific editing questions about your essay.

Having revised and edited your essay, you are ready to print your final copy. Always proofread your work before turning it in. Even though you may have used your computer's spell-checker you might find that you have typed *worm* instead of *word* or *form* instead of *from*. Check also to be sure that your essay is properly line-spaced and that the text is legible.

WRITING AN EXPOSITORY ESSAY: A STUDENT ESSAY IN PROGRESS

When he was a first-year student at the University of Vermont, Keith Eldred was asked to write an essay using the strategy of definition; he was able to choose whatever topic he wished. Eldred began by reading the chapter on definition in an earlier edition of this text. He had recently been introduced to the Hindu concept of the mantra and decided that he would like to explore this concept as it pertained to the secular world. Having made this decision, he began to generate notes that would help him get started. These notes provided him with several examples of what he intended to call "secular mantras"; a dictionary definition of the word *mantra*; and the idea that a good starting point for his rough draft might be the story of "The Little Engine That Could." Here are the notes he jotted down.

Mantra: "a mystical formula of invocation or incantation" (Webster's)

Counting to ten when angry

"Little Engine That Could" (possible beginning)

"Let's Go Bulls" → action because crowd wants players to say it to themselves

Swearing (not always a mantra)

Tennis star — "Get serious!"

"Come on, come on" (at traffic light)

"Geronimo" "Ouch!"

Hindu mythology

After mulling over his list, Eldred began to organize his ideas with the following scratch outline:

1. Begin with story of "Little Engine That Could"
2. Talk about the magic of secular mantras
3. Dictionary definition and Hindu connections
4. Examples of individuals using mantras
5. Crowd chants as mantras — Bulls
6. Conclusion — talk about how you can't get through the day without using mantras

Based on this outline as well as what he had learned in reading about definition as a writing strategy, Eldred came up with the following rough draft.

Secular Mantras: Magic Words

Keith Eldred

Remember "The Little Engine That Could"? That's the   1
story about the tiny locomotive that pulled the train
over the mountain when the big locomotives wouldn't. Remember how the Little Engine strained and chugged, "I
think I can — I think I can — I think I can" until she
reached the top of the mountain? That's a perfect example
of a secular mantra in action.

A secular mantra (pronounced man-truh) is any word   2
or group of words that helps a person use his or her energy. The key word here is "helps" — repeating a secular
mantra doesn't <u>create</u> energy; it just makes it easier to
channel a given amount. The Little Engine, for instance,

obviously had the strength to pull the train up the mountain; apparently, she could have done it without saying a
word. But we all know she wouldn't have been able to, any
more than any one of us would be able to sky-dive the
first time without yelling "Geronimo" or not exclaim
"Ouch" if we touched a hot stove. Some words and phrases
simply have a certain magic that makes a job easier or
that makes us feel better when we repeat them. These are
secular mantras.

It is because of their magical quality that these   3
expressions are called "secular mantras" in the first
place. A mantra (Sanskrit for "sacred counsel") is "a
mystical formula of invocation or incantation" used in
Hinduism (<u>Webster's</u>). According to Hindu mythology,
Manu, lawgiver and progenitor of humankind, created the
first language by teaching people the thought-forms of
objects and substances. "VAM," for example, is the
thought-form of what we call "water." Mantras, groups of
these ancient words, can summon any object or deity if
they are miraculously revealed to a seer and properly
repeated silently or vocally. Hindus use divine mantras
to communicate with gods, acquire superhuman powers,
cure diseases, and for many other purposes. Hence,
everyday words that people concentrate on to help themselves accomplish tasks or cope with stress act as secular mantras.

All sorts of people use all sorts of secular mantras   4
for all sorts of reasons. A father counts to 10 before
saying anything when his son brings the car home dented.
A tennis player faults and chides himself, "Get serious!"
A frustrated mother pacing with her wailing baby mutters,
"You'll have your own kids someday." A college student
writhing before an exam instructs himself not to panic. A
freshly spanked child glares at his mother's back and repeatedly promises never to speak to her again. Secular
mantras are everywhere.

Usually, we use secular mantras to make ourselves   5
walk faster or keep silent or do some other act. But we
can also use them to influence the actions of other persons. Say, for instance, the Chicago Bulls are behind in
the final minutes of a game. Ten thousand fans who want

them to win scream, "Let's go, Bulls!" The Bulls are
roused and win by 20 points. Chalk up the victory to the
fans' secular mantra, which transferred their energy to
the players on the court.

If you're not convinced of the power of secular   6
mantras, try to complete a day without using any. Don't
mutter anything to force yourself out of bed. Don't
utter a sound when the water in the shower is cold.
Don't grumble when the traffic lights are long. Don't
speak to the computer when it's slow to boot up. And
don't be surprised if you have an unusually long,
painful, frustrating day.

Eldred read his paper aloud in class, and other students had an opportunity to ask him questions about secular mantras. As a result of this experience, Eldred had a good idea of what he needed to do in subsequent drafts, and he made the following notes so that he wouldn't forget.

- Get more examples, especially from everyday experiences
- Class thought Bulls example didn't work — expand or cut
- Be more specific in my definition of secular mantra — maybe tell what secular mantras are <u>not</u>
- Make use of "The Little Engine That Could" example in the body of the paper
- Get new conclusion — present conclusion doesn't follow from paper
- Explain how mantras might work and why they are important
- Don't eliminate background information about mantras

In subsequent drafts, Eldred worked on each of the areas he had listed. While revising, he found it helpful to reread portions of the selections in the definition chapter. His reading led him to new insights about how to strengthen his essay. As he revised further, he found that he needed to make yet other unanticipated changes. For example, once he made his definition more specific, he found that he then needed to do some reorganization (for example, moving the background information on mantras to a position later in the paper) and to develop a new paragraph. By the deadline, Eldred had completed the following final draft. Marginal annotations point to the revisions and comment on the paper's overall structure.

Secular Mantras
Keith Eldred

<table>
<tr><td>Introductory
example (from
first draft)</td><td>Remember "The Little Engine That Could"? That's the story about the tiny locomotive that hauled the train over the mountain when the big, rugged locomotives wouldn't. Remember how the Little Engine strained and heaved and chugged, "I think I can — I think I can — I think I can" until she reached the top of the mountain? That's a perfect example of a secular mantra in action.</td><td>1</td></tr>
<tr><td>Thesis: formal
definition (revised)

Transitional/
organizational
sentence (new)</td><td>You probably have used a secular mantra — pronounce it "mantruh" — already today. It's any word or group of words that helps you use your energy when you consciously repeat it to yourself. You must understand two things about secular mantras to be able to recognize one.</td><td>2</td></tr>
<tr><td>Qualifier no. 1
(new)</td><td>First of all, a secular mantra is not simply any word or phrase you say to yourself. It must help you use your energy. Thus, "I wish I were home" is not a secular mantra if you just think the words. But the sentence is a secular mantra if, walking home on a cold day, you repeat it each time you take a step, willing your feet to move in a fast rhythm. By the same token, every swear word you mutter to bear down on a job is a secular mantra, while every one you unthinkingly repeat is simple profanity.</td><td>3</td></tr>
<tr><td>Qualifier no. 2
(revised)</td><td>Secondly, secular mantras only help you use your energy. They don't create energy. The Little Engine, for instance, obviously had enough power to pull the train up the mountainside — she could have done it without a peep. But we all know that puffing "I think I can" somehow made her job easier, just like, say, chanting "left-right-left" makes it easier for us to march in step. Any</td><td>4</td></tr>
</table>

such word or phrase that magically seems to help you perform an action when you purposefully utter it is a secular mantra.

In fact, it is to highlight this apparent magic that I dubbed these expressions with so odd a title as "secular mantras." 5

Historical definition of mantra (revised)

"Mantra" means "sacred counsel" in Sanskrit. The term refers to a "mystical formula of invocation or incantation" used in Hinduism (<u>Webster's</u>). According to Hindu mythology, the god Manu created the first language by teaching humans the thought-form of every object and substance. "VAM," for example, was what he told them to call the stuff we call "water." But people altered or forgot most of Manu's thought-forms. Followers of Hinduism believe mantras, groups of these ancient words revealed anew by gods to seers, can summon specific objects or deities if they are properly repeated, silently or vocally. Hindus repeat mantras to gain superhuman powers, cure diseases, and for many other purposes. Sideshow fakirs chant "AUM" ("I agree" or "I accept") to become immune to pain when lying on beds of nails. 6

Definition of secular (expanded)

Our "mantras" are "secular" because, unlike Hindus, we do not attribute them to gods. Instead, we borrow them from tradition or invent them to fit a situation, as the Little Engine did. They work not by divine power but because they help us, in a way, to govern transmissions along our central nervous systems. 7

Explanation (new)

Secular mantras give our brains a sort of dual signal-boosting and signal-damping capacity. The act of repeating them pushes messages, or impulses, with extra force along our nerves or interferes with incoming messages we would rather ignore. We can then perform actions more easily or cope with 8 stress that might keep us from functioning the way we want to. We may even accomplish both tasks at once. A sky-diver might yell "Geronimo," for example, both to amplify the signals telling his legs to jump and to drown out the ones warning him he's dizzy or scared.

*Example
(elaborated)*

More examples

Any one of us can use any words in this way to help himself or herself to any task. A father might count to ten to keep from bellowing when junior brings the car home dented. A tennis player who faults may chide himself "Get serious!" as he swings, to concentrate harder on directing the ball. A sleepy mother pacing with her wailing baby can make her chore less painful by muttering, "You'll have kids someday." Chanting "Grease cartridge" always cools my temper because doing that once kept me from exploding at my father when we were working on a cantankerous Buick.

*Personal example
(new)*

9

*Revised conclusion
(more positive)*

You probably have favorite secular mantras already. Think about it. How about those phrases you mumble to force yourself from your warm bed on chilly mornings? And those words you chant to ease your impatience when the traffic lights are endless? And the reminders you mutter so you'll remember to buy bread at the store? You know what I'm talking about. And you must see how much less painful and frustrating your life is because of those magic words and phrases.

10

"Secular Mantras" is a fine essay of definition. Eldred provides a clear explanation of the concept, offers numerous examples to illustrate it, and suggests how mantras work and how we use them. More importantly, Eldred's notes and the two drafts of his paper show how writing is accomplished. By reading analytically — both his own writing and that of more experienced writers — Eldred discovered and understood the requirements of the strategy of definition.

An honest and thorough appraisal of his rough draft led to thought-ful revisions, resulting in a stronger and more effective piece of writing. Finally, note how Eldred's essay combines the strategies of exemplification and definition to become more interesting and convincing.

CHAPTER 3

Exemplification

WHAT IS EXEMPLIFICATION?

Exemplification is the use of examples — facts, opinions, samples, and anecdotes or stories — to make a generalization more vivid, understandable, and persuasive. Saying that "Kris did a wonderful job of managing her roommate's campaign for Student Government Association president" is not nearly as effective as providing concrete reasons that support this statement. For example, consider the following rewrite: "Kris did a wonderful job of managing her roommate's campaign for Student Government Association president because she kept her roommate up to date on students' concerns about parking and a proposed increase in student fees. In addition, Kris made posters to advertise her roommate's candidacy, set up dormitory meetings so that students could meet her, and on election day went through the dorms reminding students to vote for her." Examples serve to illustrate the truth or validity of the generalization you make.

In the following paragraph from "Wandering through Winter," notice how naturalist Edwin Way Teale uses examples to support his generalization that "country people" have many superstitions about how harsh the coming winter will be.

Topic sentence about weather superstitions frames the entire paragraph.   In the folklore of the country, numerous superstitions relate to winter weather. Back-country farmers examine their husks — the thicker the husk, the colder the winter. They watch the acorn crop — the more acorns, the more

Series of examples amplify and elucidate the topic sentence.

severe the season. They observe where white-faced hornets place their paper nests — the higher they are, the deeper will be the snow. They examine the size and shape and color of the spleens of butchered hogs for clues to the severity of the season. They keep track of the blooming of the dogwood in the spring — the more abundant the blooms, the more bitter the cold in January. When chipmunks carry their tails high and squirrels have heavier fur, the superstitious gird themselves for a long, hard winter. Without any specific basis, a wider-than-usual black band on a woolly-bear caterpillar is accepted as a sign that winter will arrive early and stay late. Even the way a cat sits beside the stove carries its message to the credulous. According to the belief once widely held in the Ozarks, a cat sitting with its tail to the fire indicates very cold weather is on the way.

— EDWIN WAY TEALE

Teale uses nine separate examples to illustrate and explain his topic sentence about weather-related superstitions. These examples both demonstrate his knowledge of folk traditions and entertain us. As readers, we come away from Teale's paragraph thinking that he is an authority on his subject.

Teale's examples are a series of related but varied illustrations of his main point. Not only are there many examples, but the examples are representative because they illustrate the main generalization and are typical or characteristic of the topic. Sometimes just one sustained example is more effective if the example is representative and the writer develops it well. Here is one such example by basketball legend Bill Russell from his autobiographical *Second Wind*:

Topic sentence focuses on athletes slipping into an unknown gear.

Extended example of Bob Beamon's record-shattering day exemplifies Russell's topic sentence.

Every champion athlete has a moment when everything goes so perfectly for him he slips into a gear that he didn't know was there. It's easy to spot that perfect moment in a sport like track. I remember watching the 1968 Olympics in Mexico City, where the world record in the long jump was just under 27 feet. Then Bob Beamon flew down the chute and leaped out over the pit in a majestic jump that I have seen replayed many times. There was an awed silence when the announcer said that Beamon's jump measured 29 feet 2¼ inches. Generally world records are broken by fractions of inches, but Beamon had exceeded the existing record by more than two feet. On learning what he had done, Beamon slumped down on the ground and cried. Most viewers' image of Beamon ends

Example illustrates that even Beamon did not anticipate his own performance. with the picture of him weeping on the ground, but in fact he got up and took some more jumps that day. I like to think that he did so because he had jumped for so long at his best that *even then* he didn't know what might come out of him. At the end of the day he wanted to be absolutely sure that he'd had his perfect day.

Few readers have experienced that "extra gear" that Russell describes, so he illustrates what he means with a single, extended example — in this case, an anecdote that gives substance to the idea he wants his readers to understand. Russell's example of Bob Beamon's record-breaking jump is not only concrete and specific; it is memorable because it so aptly captures the essence of his topic sentence about athletic perfection. Without this extended example, Russell's claim that every great athlete "slips into a gear that he didn't know was there" would simply be a hollow statement.

WHY DO WRITERS USE EXEMPLIFICATION?

Exemplifying a point with examples is a basic strategy of human communication, and it serves several purposes for writers. First, examples make writing more vivid and interesting. Writing that consists of loosely strung together generalizations is lifeless and difficult to read, regardless of the believability of the generalizations or our willingness to accept them. Good writers try to provide just the right kind and number of examples to make their ideas clear and convincing. For example, an essay about television bloopers will be dull and pointless without some examples of on-screen blunders — accidents, pratfalls, and "tips of the slongue," as one writer calls them. Likewise, a more serious essay on the dangers of drunk driving will have more impact if it is illustrated with descriptions of the victims' suffering and the grief and outrage of their family and friends.

Writers also use exemplification to explain or clarify their ideas. All readers want specific information and feel that it is the writer's responsibility to provide it. Even if readers can provide examples themselves, they want to see what kind of evidence the writer can present. In an essay on political leadership, for instance, the assertion "Successful leaders are often a product of their times" will certainly require further explanation. Such explanation could be provided effectively through examples: Franklin D. Roosevelt, Winston Churchill, Charles de Gaulle, Corazon Aquino, and Nelson Mandela all rose to power because their people were looking for leadership in a time of national crisis. Keep in mind, however, that the use of these specific examples paints a different picture of the term "successful leaders" than a different set of examples would; unlike leaders like Joseph Stalin, Adolf Hitler, and Benito Mussolini, who rose to power under similar circumstances, the first group of leaders exercised their power in the interest of the people. The importance of carefully selected examples cannot be overemphasized. Good examples always clearly illustrate the writer's point or idea.

All of the selections in this chapter use exemplification to heighten interest in and add substance to the work. The chapter's opening essay is Natalie Goldberg's "Be Specific," which uses a number of specific examples to illustrate a writer's need to be specific. She asserts, "Be specific. Don't say 'fruit.' Tell what kind of fruit — 'It is a pomegranate.' " In "Fear of SARS, Fear of Strangers," Iris Chang uses examples from history to show what can and does happen when people overreact to an event like the SARS outbreak. She knows that "a blanket ban on Asians isn't protection against the virus — it is simply discrimination under a different name." In her essay "How to Give Orders Like a Man," language expert Deborah Tannen uses different types of examples of the ways orders are given and received — gender-related, cross-cultural, and situational — to challenge the idea that indirectness in one's interpersonal communications necessarily conveys an undesirable powerlessness and a self-deprecating attitude. Isaac Asimov, in his essay "Those Crazy Ideas," uses the example of naturalist Charles Darwin and his theories of evolution and natural selection to explain his ideas about the nature of creativity and the creative person. Alice Walker, in the essay "In Search of Our Mothers' Gardens," gives us poignant examples of the artistic expressions of the oppressed black women who went before her. These women carried the spark of creativity that is now Walker's cherished legacy.

Exemplification is so useful and versatile a strategy that it is found in many different kinds of writing such as reports, cover letters, editorials, applications, proposals, law briefs, and reviews. In fact, there is hardly an essay in this book that does not use exemplification in one way or another.

AN ANNOTATED STUDENT ESSAY
USING EXEMPLIFICATION

Shannon Long wrote the following essay while she was a student at the University of Kentucky in Lexington. Confined to a wheelchair, Long knows firsthand the problems of accessibility on her campus. She uses this personal experience to show her readers that the physical improvements made at her university simply do not go far enough in solving the problems of wheelchair accessibility. Her examples of particular problems in specific buildings are intended to persuade readers that additional improvements are necessary.

Wheelchair Hell: A Look at
Campus Accessibility
Shannon Long

Opening example is a personal one and gives an excellent illustration of the problem of inaccessibility.

It was my first week of college, and I was going to the library to meet someone on the third floor and study. After entering the library, I went to the elevator and hit the button calling it. A few seconds later the doors opened, I rolled inside, and the doors closed behind me. Expecting the buttons to be down in front, I suddenly noticed that they were behind me — and too high to reach. There I was stuck in the elevator with no way to get help. Finally, somebody got on at the fourth floor. I'd been waiting fifteen minutes.

1

Author shows that the problem of campus accessibility is a widespread issue.

I'm not the only one who has been a victim of inaccessibility. According to Jake Karnes, the Assistant Dean of Students and the Director of Handicapped Student Services, the University of Kentucky currently has eleven buildings that are inaccessible to students in wheelchairs. Many other buildings, like the library, are accessible, but have elevators that are inoperable by handicapped students. Yet, Section 504 of the Rehabilitation Act of 1973 states,

2

Author explains the federal law regarding accessibility and financial assistance to the university.

> No qualified handicapped person shall, because a recipient's facilities are inaccessible to or unusable by handicapped persons, be denied the benefits of, be excluded from participation in, or otherwise be subjected to discrimination under any program or activity receiving Federal financial assistance (Federal 22681).

When this law went into effect in 1977, the University of Kentucky started a renovation process in which close to a million

3

Author provides examples of buildings that are still inaccessible.

dollars was spent on handicap modifications (Karnes). But even though that much money has been spent, there are still many more modifications needed. Buildings still inaccessible to wheelchair students are the Administration Building, Alumni House, Barker Hall, Bowman Hall, Bradley Hall, Engineering Quadrangle, Gillis Building, Kinkead Hall, Miller Hall, Safety and Security Building, and Scovell Hall ("Transition Plan").

Author provides examples of problems created by inaccessibility.

So many inaccessible buildings create many unnecessary problems. For example, if a handicapped student wants to meet an administrator, he or she must make an appointment to meet somewhere more accessible than the Administration Building. Making appointments is usually not a problem, but there is still the fact that able-bodied students have no problem entering the Administration Building while handicapped students cannot. Though handicapped students can enter the Gillis Building, they cannot go above the ground floor and even have to push a button to get someone to come downstairs to help them. Finally, for handicapped students to get counseling from the Career Planning Center, they must set up an appointment to meet with someone at another place. In this case, some students might not use the Center's services because of the extra effort involved (Croucher). 4

Author provides examples of problems for the handicapped even in buildings that are accessible.

Even many of the accessible buildings have elevators, water fountains, and door handles that are inoperable by handicapped students (Karnes). Elevators in the Library and Whitehall Classroom Building, for instance, have buttons too high for wheelchair students, forcing them to ask somebody else to hit the button. If there is nobody around to ask, the handicapped person simply has to wait. In the Chemistry and Physics Building, 5 a key is needed to operate the elevator, forcing wheelchair students to ride up and down the hall to find somebody to help. Many water fountains are inaccessible to people in wheelchairs. Some buildings have only <u>one</u> accessible water fountain. Finally, hardly any buildings have doorknobs that students with hand and arm impairments can operate.

Author provides examples of inaccessibility in residence halls.

Many residence halls, such as Boyd Hall, Donovan Hall, Patterson Hall, and Keenland Hall, are also completely inaccessible. If a handicapped student wanted to drop by and see a friend or attend a party in one of these dorms, he or she would have to be carried up steps. Kirivan and Blanding Towers have bathrooms that are inaccessible. Also, in Kirivan Tower the elevator is so small that someone has to lift the back of the chair into the elevator. The complex lowrises — Shawneetown, Commonwealth Village, and Cooperstown Apartments — are also inaccessible. Cooperstown has some first-floor apartments that are accessible, but a handicapped student couldn't very well live there because the bathrooms are inaccessible. All eleven sororities are inaccessible, and only five of the sixteen fraternities are accessible. Since the land sororities and fraternities are on is owned by UK, Section 504 does require that houses be accessible ("Transition Plan" 14, 15). Clearly, many UK places are still inaccessible.

Author argues that the university should make more changes to improve accessibility.

June 1980 was the deadline for meeting the requirements of Section 504 (Robinson 28). While the University of Kentucky has made significant changes to make campus buildings more accessible, many more changes are needed. Handicapped students often work to overachieve to prove their abilities. All

6

7

they ask for is a chance, and that chance
should not be blocked by high buttons, heavy
doors, or steps.

Works Cited

Croucher, Lisa. "Accessibility at U.K. for Handicapped
    Still Can Be Better." <u>Kentucky Kernal</u>. Date unknown.
<u>Federal Register</u>. Volume 42 (4 May 1977): 22681.
Karnes, Jake. Personal interview. 17 Oct. 1989.
Robinson, Rita. "For the Handicapped: Renovation Report
    Card." <u>American School & University</u> (Apr. 1980): 28.
"University of Kentucky — Transition Plan" [report]. Date
    unknown.

Analyzing Shannon Long's Essay of Exemplification: Questions for Discussion

1. What different types of examples does Long use in her essay?
2. What points do her examples serve to illustrate or support?
3. Which examples did you find most and least effective? Why?

SUGGESTIONS FOR WRITING AN ESSAY OF EXEMPLIFICATION

Begin by thinking of ideas and generalizations about your topic that you can make clearer and more persuasive by illustrating them with facts, anecdotes, or specific details. You should focus primarily on your main point, the central generalization that you will develop in your essay. But also be alert for other statements or references that may benefit from exemplification. You will find that examples add clarity, color, and weight to what you say.

Consider the following generalization:

Americans are a pain-conscious people who would rather get
rid of pain than seek and cure its root causes.

This assertion is broad and general; it raises the following questions: How so? What does this mean exactly? Why does the writer think so? The statement could be the topic sentence of a paragraph or perhaps even the thesis of an essay or an entire book. As a writer, you could make it stronger and more meaningful through exemplification. You might support this statement by pointing to the sheer number of painkillers available and the different types of pain they address or by citing specific situations or cases in which Americans have gone to the drugstore instead of a doctor. In addition, you might compare sales figures of painkillers in the United States and in other countries.

Gather More Examples than You Can Use

Before you begin to write, bring together as many examples as you can that are related to your subject — more than you can possibly use. An example may be anything from a fact or a statistic to an anecdote or a story; it may be stated in a few words — "India's population is now approaching 900 million people" — or it may go on for several pages of elaborate description or explanation.

The kinds of examples you look for and where you look for them will depend, of course, on your subject and the point you want to make about it. If you plan to write about all the quirky, fascinating people who make up your family, you can gather your examples without leaving your room: descriptions of their habits and clothing, stories about their strange adventures, facts about their backgrounds, quotations from their conversations. If, however, you are writing an essay on book censorship in American public schools, you will need to do research in the library or on the Internet and read many sources to supply yourself with examples. Your essay might well include accounts drawn from newspapers; statistics published by librarians' or teachers' professional organizations; court transcripts and judicial opinions on censorship; and interviews with school board members, parents, book publishers, and even the authors whose work has been pulled off library shelves or kept out of the classroom.

The range of sources and the variety of examples are limited only by your imagination and the time you can spend on research. One student who was trying to answer the question "Do diets really work?" remembers her research in the library very clearly: "It's really not that difficult if you stay organized. I started with *The Readers' Guide to Periodical Literature*. I also thought it was wise to use a variety of magazines, starting with popular newsmagazines such as *Time* and *U.S. News & World Report*. After this, I consulted scholarly journals in order to get a better understanding of the short- and long-term effects of diets." As she puts it, "I collected all kinds of examples because I did not know at that point which ones would be most useful when I got to actually writing my paper, and I wanted to make sure that I had more than enough to choose from."

Shannon Long, in gathering examples for her "Wheelchair Hell" essay, relied on her own experiences on the University of Kentucky campus. She had been a "victim of inaccessibility," and she had inter-viewed the director of Handicapped Student Services to help her iden-tify the buildings where problems existed and the exact nature of the problems for those in wheelchairs (problems such as inoperable door handles, locked elevators or elevators with hard-to-reach buttons, and inaccessible water fountains and bathrooms). In addition to her inter-view with the director, Long also consulted several public documents that addressed her problems — documents she includes in her Works Cited list.

Collecting an abundance of examples will allow you to choose the strongest and most representative ones for your essay, not merely the first ones that come to mind. Having enough material will also make it less likely that you will have to stop in mid-draft and hunt for further examples, losing the rhythm of your work or the thread of your ideas. Moreover, the more examples you gather, the more you will learn about your subject and the easier it will be to write about it with authority.

Choose Relevant Examples

You must make sure that your examples are relevant. Do they clarify and support the points you want to make? Suppose the main point of your planned essay is that censorship runs rampant in American pub-lic education. A newspaper story about the banning of *Catcher in the Rye* and *The Merchant of Venice* from the local high school's English curriculum would clearly be relevant because it concerns book censor-ship at a public school. The fact that James Joyce's novel *Ulysses* was first banned as obscene and then vindicated in a famous trial, al-though a landmark case of censorship in American history, has noth-ing to do with books in public schools. While the case of *Ulysses* might be a useful example for other discussions of censorship, it would not be relevant to your essay.

Sometimes more than one of your examples will be relevant. In such cases, choose the examples that are most closely related to your main idea or generalization. If you were working on the pain essay mentioned earlier, a statistic indicating the sales of a particular drug in a given year might be interesting; however, a statistic showing that over the past ten years painkiller sales in America have in-creased more rapidly than the population would be relevant to the idea that Americans are a pain-conscious people, and so this statistic could be used to support your assertion. In other words, examples may be interesting in and of themselves, but they only come alive when they illustrate and link important ideas that the writer is trying to promote.

Be Sure Your Examples Are Representative

Besides being relevant, to be most effective an example should also be representative. The story it tells or the fact it presents should be typical of the main point or concept, an example indicative of a larger pattern rather than an uncommon or isolated occurrence. Figures showing how many people use aspirin, and for what purposes, would be representative because aspirin is the most widely used painkiller in America. Statistics about a newly developed barbiturate (a highly specialized kind of painkiller) might show a tremendous increase in its use compared with other barbiturates, but the example would not be very representative because not many people use barbiturates compared with other kinds of painkillers. In fact, giving the barbiturate example might even cause readers to wonder why aspirin, which is better known, was not used as an example.

If, while working on the censorship paper, you found reports on a dozen quiet administrative hearings and orderly court cases, but only one report of a sensational incident in which books were actually burned in a school parking lot, the latter incident, however dramatic, is clearly not a representative example. You might want to mention the book burning in your essay as an extremist viewpoint, but you should not present it as typical of how censorship is handled.

What if your examples do not support your point? Perhaps you have missed some important information and need to look further. It may be, though, that the problem is with the point itself. For example, suppose you intend your censorship paper to illustrate the following thesis: "Book censorship has seriously impacted American public education." However, you have not found very many examples in which specific books were actually censored or banned outright. While many attempts at censorship have been made, most were ultimately prevented or overturned in the courts. You might then have to revise your original thesis: "Although there have been many well-publicized attempts to censor books in public schools, actual censorship is relatively rare."

Organize Your Examples

It is important to arrange your examples in an order that serves your purpose, is easy for readers to follow, and will have maximum effect. Some possible patterns of organization include chronological order and spatial order. Others include moving from the least to the most controversial, as in Martin Luther King Jr.'s "The Ways of Meeting Oppression" (page 360); or from the least to the most important, as in Jo Goodwin Parker's "What Is Poverty?" (page 399). Or you may hit upon an order that "feels right" to you, as Edwin Way Teale did in his paragraph about winter superstitions. How many examples you include depends, of course, on the length and nature of the assignment. Before starting the first draft, it may be helpful to work out your organization in a rough outline, using only enough words so that you can tell which example each entry refers to.

Use Transitions

While it is important to give the presentation of your examples an inherent logic, it is also important to link your examples to the topic sentences in your paragraphs and, indeed, to the thesis of your entire essay by using transitional words and expressions such as *for example, for instance, therefore, afterward, in other words, next,* and *finally.* Such structural devices will signal your use of examples and will make the sequencing of the examples easy to follow.

Share Your Work with Others

Students often find it particularly helpful to share the drafts of their essays with other students in their writing class. One of our students commented, "In total, I probably wrote five or six different versions of this essay. I shared them with members of the class, and their comments were extremely insightful. I remember one student's question in particular because she really got me to focus on the problems with fad diets. The students also helped me to see where I needed examples to explain what I was talking about. The very first draft that I wrote is completely different from the one I submitted in class."

Editing Tip: Strong Topic Sentences and Unified Paragraphs

Be sure to follow the guidelines and advice for editing an essay given in Chapter 2: "Writing Essays." The guidelines highlight those sentence-level concerns — grammar, mechanics, and punctuation — that are especially important in editing any piece of writing. While editing your essay of exemplification, identify the topic sentence in each paragraph and look for opportunities to focus or clarify any topic sentence that is not explicitly connected to the supporting examples in that paragraph.

Within an essay, the paragraph is the most important unit of thought. A paragraph has its own main idea, often stated directly in a topic sentence. It is also called the *controlling idea* because it limits the subject of the paragraph. And a topic sentence helps unify a paragraph; in providing direction, it helps you avoid digressions. Usually, the topic sentence appears at or near the beginning of the paragraph; this way, you let your reader know the idea that you plan to illustrate. For example, consider the following topic sentence from Thomas L. Friedman's "My Favorite Teacher":

> Hattie was a woman who believed that the secret for success in life was getting the fundamentals right.

This topic sentence limits the subject of the paragraph to "fundamentals" and leads readers to expect that Friedman will provide examples of the fundamentals that his teacher Hattie M. Steinberg stressed. Friedman fulfills these expectations.

> *Hattie was a woman who believed that the secret for success in life was getting the fundamentals right.* And boy, she pounded the fundamentals of journalism into her students — not simply how to write a lead or accurately transcribe a quote, but, more important, how to comport yourself in a professional way and to always do quality work. To this day, when I forget to wear a tie on assignment, I think of Hattie scolding me. I once interviewed an ad exec for our high school paper who used a four-letter word. We debated whether to run it. Hattie ruled yes. That ad man almost lost his job when it appeared. She wanted to teach us about consequences.

Consider another paragraph, this one the opening paragraph in Natalie Goldberg's "Be Specific." Notice how the three examples (i.e., fruit, girl, flower) are all connected to the italicized topic sentence.

> Be specific. Don't say "fruit." Tell what kind of fruit — "It is a pomegranate." *Give things the dignity of their names.* Just as with human beings, it is rude to say, "Hey, girl, get in line." That "girl" has a name. (As a matter of fact, if she's at least twenty years old, she's a woman, not a "girl" at all.) Things, too, have names. It is much better to say "the geranium in the window" than "the flower in the window." "Geranium" — that one word gives us a much more specific picture. It penetrates more deeply into the beingness of that flower. It immediately gives us the scene by the window — red petals, green circular leaves, all straining toward sunlight.

In paragraphs like Goldberg's or Friedman's, every sentence belongs, and together the sentences make a unified whole. This, however, may not be the case with all the paragraphs in your essays.

To check for paragraph unity while editing your essay, boldface or underline the topic sentence in each of your paragraphs. By calling special attention to each topic sentence, you see how the other sentences in the paragraph relate to the topic sentence and to each other. In paragraphs where you find no topic sentence, you need to decide whether to add a topic sentence or whether your controlling idea is clearly implied in the examples themselves. In other paragraphs where you do have a topic sentence, ask yourself if this sentence adequately captures the essence of your examples. If it doesn't, rewrite the topic sentence until it articulates your controlling idea.

Next, ask yourself whether you need all of your examples and whether any of your examples upon closer scrutiny is inappropriate. If you discover you have too many examples, simply drop the weakest. If you think that an example may be inappropriate, you should supply another, more fitting example.

▶ *Questions for Revising and Editing: Exemplification*

1. Is my topic well focused?
2. Does my thesis statement clearly identify my topic and make an assertion about it?
3. Are my examples well chosen to support my thesis? Are there other examples that might work better?
4. Are my examples representative? That is, are they typical of the main point or concept, rather than bizarre or atypical?
5. Do I have enough examples to be convincing, or do I have too many examples?
6. Have I developed my examples in enough detail so as to be clear to readers?
7. Have I organized my examples in some logical pattern, and is that pattern clear to readers?
8. Does the essay accomplish my purpose?
9. Are my topic sentences strong? Are my paragraphs unified?

Be Specific

Natalie Goldberg

Author Natalie Goldberg has made a specialty of writing about writing. Her first and best-known work, Writing Down the Bones: Freeing the Writer Within, *was published in 1986. Goldberg's advice to would-be writers is, on the one hand, practical and pithy; on the other, it is almost mystical in its call to know and appreciate the world. "Be Specific," the excerpt that appears below, is representative of the book as a whole. Amid widespread acclaim for the book, one critic commented, "Goldberg teaches us not only how to write better, but how to live better."* Writing Down the Bones *was followed by three more successful books about writing:* Wild Mind: Living the Writer's Life *(1990),* Living Color: A Writer Paints Her World *(1996), and* Thunder and Lightning: Cracking Open the Writer's Craft *(2000). Altogether, more than three-quarters of a million copies of these books are now in print. Goldberg has also written fiction; her first novel,* Banana Rose, *was published in 1994. Her most recent book,* Top of My Lungs *(2002), is a collection of poetry and paintings.*

Notice the way in which Goldberg demonstrates her advice to be specific in the following selection.

PREPARING TO READ

Suppose someone says to you, "I walked in the woods." What do you envision? Write down what you see in your mind's eye. Now suppose someone says, "I walked in the redwood forest." Again, write what you see. What's different about your two descriptions, and why?

B e specific. Don't say "fruit." Tell what kind of fruit — "It is a pomegranate." Give things the dignity of their names. Just as with human beings, it is rude to say, "Hey, girl, get in line." That "girl" has a name. (As a matter of fact, if she's at least twenty years old, she's a woman, not a "girl" at all.) Things, too, have names. It is much better to say "the geranium in the window" than "the flower in the window." "Geranium" — that one word gives us a much more specific picture. It penetrates more deeply into the beingness of that flower. It immediately gives us the scene by the window — red petals, green circular leaves, all straining toward sunlight.

About ten years ago I decided I had to learn the names of plants and flowers in my environment. I bought a book on them and walked down the tree-lined streets of Boulder, examining leaf, bark, and seed, trying to match them up with their descriptions and names in the book. Maple, elm, oak, locust. I usually tried to cheat by asking people working in their yards the names of the flowers and trees growing there. I was amazed how few people had any idea of the names of the live beings inhabiting their little plot of land.

When we know the name of something, it brings us closer to the ground. It takes the blur out of our mind; it connects us to the earth. If I walk down the street and see "dogwood," "forsythia," I feel more friendly toward the environment. I am noticing what is around me and can name it. It makes me more awake. 3

If you read the poems of William Carlos Williams, you will see how specific he is about plants, trees, flowers — chicory, daisy, locust, poplar, quince, primrose, black-eyed Susan, lilacs — each has its own integrity. Williams says, "Write what's in front of your nose." It's good for us to know what is in front of our noses. Not just "daisy," but how the flower is in the season we are looking at it — "The dayseye hugging the earth / in August . . . brownedged, / green and pointed scales / armor his yellow."[1] Continue to hone your awareness: to the name, to the month, to the day, and finally to the moment. 4

Williams also says: "No idea, but in things." Study what is "in front of your nose." By saying "geranium" instead of "flower," you are penetrating more deeply into the present and being there. The closer we can get to what's in front of our nose, the more it can teach us everything. "To see the World in a Grain of Sand, and a heaven in a Wild Flower . . ."[2] 5

In writing groups and classes too, it is good to quickly learn the names of all the other group members. It helps to ground you in the group and make you more attentive to each other's work. 6

Learn the names of everything: birds, cheese, tractors, cars, buildings. A writer is all at once everything — an architect, French cook, farmer — and at the same time, a writer is none of these things. 7

RESPONDING TO THE TEXT

Natalie Goldberg found that she wasn't the only one in her neighborhood who didn't know the names of local trees and flowers. Are you unable to name individual members of some categories of things that you encounter often? What are these categories? What are some that would be pleasing or useful for you to learn? How might you go about learning them? (Consider why Goldberg says it was "cheating" to ask people the names of their flowers and trees.) What would you gain by knowing them?

---

[1] William Carlos Williams, "Daisy," in *The Collected Earlier Poems* (New York: New Directions, 1938).

[2] William Blake, "The Auguries of Innocence."

ENGAGING THE WRITER'S SUBJECT

1. In paragraphs 3, 5, and 6, Goldberg cites a number of advantages to be gained by knowing the names of things. Review these advantages. What are they? Do they ring true?

2. Throughout the essay, Goldberg instructs readers to be specific and to be aware of the world around them. Of what besides names are the readers advised to be aware? Why?

ANALYZING THE WRITER'S CRAFT

1. How does Goldberg "specifically" follow the advice she gives writers in this essay?

2. Goldberg makes several lists of the names of things. What purpose do these lists serve? How does she use these specifics to exemplify her point?

3. What specific audience is Goldberg addressing in this essay? (Glossary: *Audience*) How do you know?

4. The strategies of definition and exemplification are closely intertwined in this essay; to name a thing precisely, after all, is to take the first step in defining it. (Glossary: *Definition*) What central concept is defined by Goldberg's many illustrations of naming? How might a writer use exemplification to make definitions richer and more meaningful?

UNDERSTANDING THE WRITER'S LANGUAGE

1. Goldberg says that to name an object gives it dignity (1) and integrity (4). What does she mean in each case?

2. In paragraph 1, Goldberg writes, "It [the word *geranium*] penetrates more deeply into the beingness of that flower." The word *beingness* does not appear in the dictionary. Where does it come from? Why does Goldberg use it, and what does she mean by her statement?

3. In his poem "Daisy," quoted in paragraph 4, William Carlos Williams calls the flower "dayseye." How does this spelling reinforce the central idea of the paragraph? Of the essay as a whole?

4. Refer to your desk dictionary to determine the meanings of the following words as Goldberg uses them in this selection: *pomegranate* (1), *integrity* (4).

WRITING SUGGESTIONS

1. Write a brief essay advising your readers of something they should do. Title your essay, as Goldberg does, with a directive ("Be Specific"). Tell your readers how they can improve their lives by taking your advice, and give strong examples of the behavior you are recommending.

2. Consider the following comic strip by Charles Schulz. What point about "being specific" does Schulz make? How do you think Goldberg would respond to this comic strip? Is it possible to be too specific? Explain. What do you think of Snoopy's response to Lucy's request? How appropriate is Snoopy's response given the context? How else could Snoopy have been more specific? Using Goldberg's essay, Schulz's comic strip, and your own experiences and observations as examples, write an essay on what it means to be specific and how being specific can and should depend on the situation.

3. In the final paragraph, the three occupations that Goldberg names are probably familiar to you, but many of the tools and products connected to them may not be familiar at all. With several classmates, brainstorm an expanded list of such occupations. Choose one that interests you and learn about the activities and functions of a person in that profession. Use the Internet to help you brainstorm and research. Write a report to share what you have learned.

- To begin your research online, go to **bedfordstmartins.com /subjectsstrategies** and click on "Exemplification" or browse the thematic directory of annotated links.

Chinese Commuter in Shanghai

Claro Cortes IV

Claro Cortes IV/Reuters/CORBIS

CONNECTING IMAGE AND TEXT

When SARS (Severe Acute Respiratory Syndrome) first broke out in the spring of 2003, it was largely confined to Southeast Asia. In time, cases were diagnosed elsewhere, including South Africa and Canada. When this photograph appeared in newspapers in May 2003, it was captioned: "A Chinese commuter wearing a skull and crossbones protective mask waits for a ride at a Shanghai subway late May 20, 2003. As of May 20, Shanghai has had no new SARS cases for the past 11 consecutive days. Nationwide, China has reported 5,248 SARS infections, including 294 deaths." How do you "read" this photograph? What do you see in the woman's face, particularly her eyes? How do you react to the skull and crossbones on her mask? What statement does she make with this mask? Your observations will help guide you to the key themes and strategies in the essay that follows.

Fear of SARS, Fear of Strangers

Iris Chang

A freelance journalist and lecturer, Iris Chang was born in Princeton, New Jersey, in 1968, the daughter of two university professors. She gradu- ated from the University of Illinois in 1989 with a degree in journalism and worked briefly for the Associated Press and Chicago Tribune *before accepting a fellowship at Johns Hopkins University, where she earned her master's in 1991. Interest in her family's history led her to research and write* The Rape of Nanking: The Forgotten Holocaust of World War II *(1997), the first full-length narrative of the Japanese slaughter, rape, and torture of more than three hundred thousand Chinese civilians dur- ing World War II. Chang is the author of two other books on the Chinese experience:* Thread of the Silkworm *(1995) and* The Chinese in Amer- ica: A Narrative History *(2003).*

In the following article, first published in the New York Times *on May 2, 2003, Chang uses historical examples to give readers another per- spective on what can and does happen when people overreact to an event like the SARS virus outbreak.*

PREPARING TO READ

What kinds of events make you fearful? How do you explain and deal with your fear? Have you ever been surprised or relieved to find that your fear is unfounded?

Earlier this month, the University of California at Berkeley banned from its summer programs all students from mainland China, Hong Kong, Taiwan and Singapore, out of fear that some might be in- fected by the SARS (Severe Acute Respiratory Syndrome) virus. The university's response to the epidemic illustrates how easily the fear of SARS can degenerate into a generalized antipathy toward Asians, even on college campuses.

After facing sharp criticism for its decision, Berkeley modified its policy, announcing that it would permit some students from the banned countries to enroll, though not nearly as many as it had originally expected. It also said it would reserve special rooms on campus to isolate or quarantine people if any should fall ill, and that the Asian students would be closely monitored by campus health authorities.

There is no question that precautions should be taken to protect 3 people from SARS: after all, scientists have not yet found a cure for the disease or a vaccination to prevent it. But without the mitigating influence of sound thinking, excessive fear of this new disease can lead to discrimination against Asians, something that is not without precedent in this country.

In the late 19th century, anti-Chinese sentiment arose, fueled by a 4 bad economy and workers threatened by an influx of cheap Chinese labor. Anti-Chinese propaganda tended to focus on issues of health and disease. In 1875, the American Medical Association sponsored a study to investigate assertions that Chinese women were spreading a unique, "Chinese" strain of syphilis. Though the study found no evidence to support the claim, one medical publication, *The Medico-Literary Journal,* nevertheless accused the Chinese of "infusing a poison in the Anglo-Saxon blood."

Elements of the American press helped fan the flames, portraying 5 the Chinese as an unsanitary and dangerous race. An editorial in *The Santa Cruz Sentinel* in 1879, for example, described the Chinese as "half-human, half-devil, rat-eating, rag-wearing, law-ignoring, Christian-civilization-hating, opium-smoking, labor-degrading, entrail-sucking Celestials."

Another California newspaper, *The Dutch Flat Forum,* struck a simi- 6 lar chord at the time. "Women of California," it asked, "why do you persist in having your dirty linen fouled by unclean hands, under the pretense of having it cleansed? Do you not know that (in these exciting times when the Chinese are losing employment, and naturally mad at the white race) you are taking desperate chances of having disease introduced among us that will render desolate our firesides? And in fact we don't know but that the diseases among our children during the past year, which have baffled the skill of our most eminent physicians, and depopulated many households, have emanated from the Chinese."

Sensational news accounts of Chinese men luring innocent young 7 white women into opium dens were complemented by advertising. For instance, ads for "Rough on Rats," a pest control product, featured a picture of a pigtailed Chinese man with his head tilted back, devouring a live rodent. The image was accompanied, not so subtly, by the anti-Chinese slogan of the era: "They must go."

Some Chinese-Americans found profit in perpetuating these stereo- 8 types. Up through the 1930's, white and Chinese tour guides alike invented stories about a mysterious, labyrinthine world under Chinatown streets, filled with narcotics and brothels. In San Francisco, they ushered white tourists into fake leper colonies and fake opium dens and staged elaborate fights in which residents posing as opium-crazed gangsters dueled with knives in the streets.

Anti-Chinese sentiment was met with sympathy in Washington, where Democrats and Republicans adopted discriminatory platforms in order to win votes in California. Under pressure from the Working-men's Party in California, Congress in 1882 passed the Chinese Exclusion Act, which specifically barred laborers and permitted only certain classes of Chinese, like scholars, diplomats and merchants, to enter. 9

Consequently, Chinese immigrants endured much greater scrutiny than their European counterparts. To make sure no Chinese were using false identification papers to gain entrance under one of the permitted categories, immigration officers detained all new arrivals from China and interrogated them intensely about their identity, sometimes for months. 10

In 1910, the government set up a new immigration center at Angel Island in San Francisco Bay, formerly the site of a quarantine station that fumigated foreign ships and inspected passengers for signs of contagious diseases. Officials claimed that the physical isolation would stop the epidemics that they had been led to believe were "prevalent among aliens from Oriental countries." 11

Although Angel Island was meant to contain disease, it produced the opposite effect by cramming healthy and sick Chinese immigrants together into close quarters. Hospitals in San Francisco refused to admit patients from Angel Island — even though there were no medical facilities on the island to treat the critically ill. When one detainee came down with cerebral spinal meningitis, immigration officials moved him into a tent, where he was kept until he died. 12

Perhaps the most severe example of medical panic transforming itself into racial prejudice took place in 1899, when bubonic plague broke out in Hawaii. Though the disease hit whites as well as Chinese, the local board of health focused its efforts on the Chinese alone, placing them under quarantine, preventing them from sailing to the continental United States and burning down parts of Honolulu's Chinatown. 13

In 1900, officials in San Francisco followed Hawaii's example, closing Chinatown businesses, forcing Chinese residents to submit to inoculation and cordoning off the neighborhood with a nine-foot-tall fence — a quarantine that a federal court later ruled unconstitutional. San Francisco authorities also tried to raze and burn down Chinese neighborhoods; it took the combined efforts of the ethnic San Francisco Chinese community, their lawyers and China's ambassador to the United States to save the community from complete destruction. 14

Suspicion of Chinese-Americans has waxed and waned over the 20th century, but it has never completely gone away. It is no wonder, then, that given this not-so-distant history Chinese-Americans are uneasy about the way in which people have responded to the threat of SARS. While we are right to expect the government to take all necessary steps to slow the spread of the disease, we are also right to demand more careful reasoning from American institutions. 15

Though Berkeley's desire to protect its campus from SARS is understandable, its willingness to bar Asian students admitted to summer school was unfortunate. (According to the school's Web site, hundreds of other students from Asian countries — those who had hoped to take English as a Second Language classes — will not be able to come this summer.) 16

The university's actions have had particular force for many Asians, in large measure because California has historically been home to the oldest and most virulent strains of anti-Chinese sentiment. As long as the university maintains criteria for exclusion based on nationality, not sound medical diagnosis, it will continue to face charges of anti-Asian prejudice. After all, SARS is a global disease. A blanket ban on Asians isn't protection against the virus — it is simply discrimination under a different name. 17

RESPONDING TO THE TEXT

How did you react when you read how Berkeley handled Asian students in its summer programs after the outbreak of SARS? How does your reaction compare to Chang's? Do you think Chang makes a sound point about excessive fear leading to discrimination or is she being alarmist? Explain.

ENGAGING THE WRITER'S SUBJECT

1. How did the University of California–Berkeley respond to the SARS outbreak in Southeast Asia in the spring of 2003? What does Chang find objectionable about this response?

2. In the past, newspapers stirred up anti-Chinese sentiments in California. What kinds of stereotypes of the Chinese were created?

3. In paragraph 8, Chang reveals that some Chinese Americans benefited economically by perpetuating negative stereotypes of the Chinese. Why do you suppose she chose to include this piece of history? In what ways, if any, do your feelings about the author and her argument change as a result of knowing this? (Glossary: *Argument*)

4. According to Chang, why should Berkeley's actions be considered discriminatory?

ANALYZING THE WRITER'S CRAFT

1. What is Chang's thesis, and where is it stated? (Glossary: *Thesis*) What expectations does this thesis raise?

2. What is the meaning of Chang's title? How does it relate to her thesis?

3. How has Chang organized her examples in paragraphs 4 through 14? (Glossary: *Organization*) Why do you suppose she saved the example of the bubonic plague outbreak in Hawaii for last?

4. Chang uses examples to argue for a link between "excessive fear" and "discrimination against Asians." (Glossary: *Argument*) Which examples work best for you? What about these examples makes her argument particularly effective? In the end, does she convince you of the link between fear and prejudice?

UNDERSTANDING THE WRITER'S LANGUAGE

1. How would you describe Chang's diction in this essay — angry, reasoned, confrontational, tempered, or something else? (Glossary: *Diction*) How does her diction differ from that of the quoted passages in her examples? Be specific in explaining the differences you see as well as how these differences affect the reader's response to the subject matter and the author herself.

2. Refer to your desk dictionary to determine the meanings of the following words as Chang uses them in this selection: *epidemic* (paragraph 1), *quarantine* (2), *propaganda* (4), *sensational* (7), *platforms* (9), *raze* (14), *blanket* (17).

WRITING SUGGESTIONS

1. Using examples from your own experience, observation, or reading, write an essay in which you explore the links between fear and prejudice or discrimination. How have diseases like AIDS, science issues like cloning, sexual orientation issues like gay marriage, medical issues like stem cell research, gender issues like women in the military, or social issues like abortion affected the ways we behave toward one another? You may want to review your response to Preparing to Read for this selection before you start to write.

2. Chang provides historical examples of what can happen when disease is linked with the label *Chinese*, characterizing the reaction to SARS as "medical panic transforming itself into racial prejudice" (paragraph 13). Drawing on examples from Chang's essay or your own observations, experiences, or research, write an essay comparing and contrasting media reactions to the initial outbreaks of two diseases such as AIDS, SARS, or hantavirus. (Glossary: *Comparison and Contrast*) How is media coverage of the outbreaks similar or different? Is one group the focus of attention? If so, do you find this focus unfair? Explain. Does coverage vary from one media source to another? If so, how? Before you write, you

might find it helpful to refer to your Connecting Image and Text response for this selection.

3. Since Chang wrote this article in May 2003, what advances have been made against SARS? What lessons did we learn from the initial outbreak? How is SARS treated? What precautions have been taken to prevent the global spread of the disease? What negative effects, if any, have these measures had? (Glossary: *Cause and Effect Analysis*) Research SARS in your college library and on the Internet; then present your findings in a report to your class.

- To begin your research online, go to **bedfordstmartins.com /subjectsstrategies** and click on "Exemplification" or browse the thematic directory of annotated links.

How to Give Orders Like a Man

Deborah Tannen

Deborah Tannen, professor of linguistics at Georgetown University, was born in 1945 in Brooklyn, New York. Tannen received her B.A. in English from the State University of New York at Binghamton in 1966 and taught English in Greece until 1968. She then earned an M.A. in English literature from Wayne State University in 1970. While pursuing her Ph.D. in linguistics at the University of California–Berkeley, she received several prizes for her poetry and short fiction. Her work has appeared in New York, Vogue, *and the* New York Times Magazine. *In addition, she has authored three best-selling books on how people communicate:* You Just Don't Understand *(1990),* That's Not What I Meant *(1991), and* Talking from Nine to Five *(1994). The success of these books attests to the public's interest in language, especially when it pertains to gender differences. Tannen's most recent books include* The Argument Culture: Stopping America's War of Words *(1998) and* I Only Say This Because I Love You: Talking to Your Parents, Partners, Sibs, and Kids When You're All Adults *(2002).*

In this essay, first published in the New York Times Magazine *in August 1994, Tannen looks at the variety of ways in which orders are given and received. Interestingly, she concludes that, contrary to popular belief, directness is not necessarily logical or effective and indirectness is not necessarily manipulative or insecure.*

PREPARING TO READ

Write about a time in your life when you were ordered to do something. Who gave you the order — a friend, a parent, maybe a teacher? Did the person's relationship to you affect how you carried out the order? Did it make a difference to you whether the order giver was male or female? Why?

A university president was expecting a visit from a member of the board of trustees. When her secretary buzzed to tell her that the board member had arrived, she left her office and entered the reception area to greet him. Before ushering him into her office, she handed her secretary a sheet of paper and said: "I've just finished drafting this letter. Do you think you could type it right away? I'd like to get it out before lunch. And would you please do me a favor and hold all calls while I'm meeting with Mr. Smith?"

When they sat down behind the closed door of her office, Mr. Smith began by telling her that he thought she had spoken inappropriately to her secretary. "Don't forget," he said. "*You're* the president!"

Putting aside the question of the appropriateness of his admonish- 3
ing the president on her way of speaking, it is revealing — and representative of many Americans' assumptions — that the indirect way in
which the university president told her secretary what to do struck
him as self-deprecating. He took it as evidence that she didn't think
she had the right to make demands of her secretary. He probably
thought he was giving her a needed pep talk, bolstering her self-
confidence.

I challenge the assumption that talking in an indirect way nec- 4
essarily reveals powerlessness, lack of self-confidence or anything
else about the character of the speaker. Indirectness is a fundamental element in human communication. It is also one of the elements
that varies most from one culture to another, and one that can
cause confusion and misunderstanding when speakers have different habits with regard to using it. I also want to dispel the assumption that American women tend to be more indirect than American
men. Women and men are both indirect, but in addition to differences associated with their backgrounds — regional, ethnic and
class — they tend to be indirect in different situations and in different ways.

At work, we need to get others to do things, and we all have differ- 5
ent ways of accomplishing this. Any individual's ways will vary depending on who is being addressed — a boss, a peer or a subordinate.
At one extreme are bald commands. At the other are requests so indirect that they don't sound like requests at all, but are just a statement
of need or a description of a situation. People with direct styles of asking others to do things perceive indirect requests — if they perceive
them as requests at all — as manipulative. But this is often just a way
of blaming others for our discomfort with their styles.

The indirect style is no more manipulative than making a tele- 6
phone call, asking "Is Rachel there?" and expecting whoever answers
the phone to put Rachel on. Only a child is likely to answer "Yes" and
continue holding the phone — not out of orneriness but because of
inexperience with the conventional meaning of the question. (A mis-
chievous adult might do it to tease.) Those who feel that indirect orders are illogical or manipulative do not recognize the conventional
nature of indirect requests.

Issuing orders indirectly can be the prerogative of those in power. 7
Imagine, for example, a master who says "It's cold in here" and expects a servant to make a move to close a window, while a servant
who says the same thing is not likely to see his employer rise to correct
the situation and make him more comfortable. Indeed, a Frenchman
raised in Brittany tells me that his family never gave bald commands to
their servants but always communicated orders in indirect and highly

polite ways. This pattern renders less surprising the finding of David Bellinger and Jean Berko Gleason that fathers' speech to their young children had a higher incidence than mothers' of both direct imperatives like "Turn the bolt with the wrench" *and* indirect orders like "The wheel is going to fall off."

The use of indirectness can hardly be understood without the 8 cross-cultural perspective. Many Americans find it self-evident that directness is logical and aligned with power while indirectness is akin to dishonesty and reflects subservience. But for speakers raised in most of the world's cultures, varieties of indirectness are the norm in communication. This is the pattern found by a Japanese sociolinguist, Kunihiko Harada, in his analysis of a conversation he recorded between a Japanese boss and a subordinate.

The markers of superior status were clear. One speaker was a 9 Japanese man in his late 40's who managed the local branch of a Japanese private school in the United States. His conversational partner was a Japanese-American woman in her early 20's who worked at the school. By virtue of his job, his age and his native fluency in the language being taught, the man was in the superior position. Yet when he addressed the woman, he frequently used polite language and almost always used indirectness. For example, he had tried and failed to find a photography store that would make a black-and-white print from a color negative for a brochure they were producing. He let her know that he wanted her to take over the task by stating the situation and allowed her to volunteer to do it: (This is a translation of the Japanese conversation.)

> On this matter, that, that, on the leaflet? This photo, I'm thinking of changing it to black-and-white and making it clearer. . . . I went to a photo shop and asked them. They said they didn't do black-and-white. I asked if they knew any place that did. They said they didn't know. They weren't very helpful, but anyway, a place must be found, the negative brought to it, the picture developed.

Harada observes, "Given the fact that there are some duties to be 10 performed and that there are two parties present, the subordinate is supposed to assume that those are his or her obligation." It was precisely because of his higher status that the boss was free to choose whether to speak formally or informally, to assert his power or to play it down and build rapport — an option not available to the subordinate, who would have seemed cheeky if she had chosen a style that enhanced friendliness and closeness.

The same pattern was found by a Chinese sociolinguist, Yuling 11 Pan, in a meeting of officials involved in a neighborhood youth program. All spoke in ways that reflected their place in the hierarchy. A subordinate addressing a superior always spoke in a deferential way, but a superior addressing a subordinate could either be authoritarian, demonstrating his power, or friendly, establishing rapport. The ones in power had the option of choosing which style to use. In this spirit, I have been told by people who prefer their bosses to give orders indirectly that those who issue bald commands must be pretty insecure; otherwise why would they have to bolster their egos by throwing their weight around?

I am not inclined to accept that those who give orders directly are   12
really insecure and powerless, any more than I want to accept that judgment of those who give indirect orders. The conclusion to be drawn is that ways of talking should not be taken as obvious evidence of inner psychological states like insecurity or lack of confidence. Considering the many influences on conversational style, individuals have a wide range of ways of getting things done and expressing their emotional states. Personality characteristics like insecurity cannot be linked to ways of speaking in an automatic, self-evident way.

Those who expect orders to be given indirectly are offended when   13
they come unadorned. One woman said that when her boss gives her instructions, she feels she should click her heels, salute, and say "Yes, boss!" His directions strike her as so imperious as to border on the militaristic. Yet I received a letter from a man telling me that indirect orders were a fundamental part of his military training. He wrote:

> Many years ago, when I was in the Navy, I was training to be a radio technician. One class I was in was taught by a chief radioman, a regular Navy man who had been to sea, and who was then in his third hitch. The students, about 20 of us, were fresh out of boot camp, with no sea duty and little knowledge of real Navy life. One day in class the chief said it was hot in the room. The students didn't react, except perhaps to nod in agreement. The chief repeated himself: "It's hot in this room." Again there was no reaction from the students.
>
> Then the chief explained. He wasn't looking for agreement or discussion from us. When he said that the room was hot, he expected us to do something about it — like opening the window. He tried it one more time, and this time all of us left our workbenches and headed for the windows. We had learned. And we had many opportunities to apply what we had learned.

This letter especially intrigued me because "It's cold in here" is the   14
standard sentence used by linguists to illustrate an indirect way of getting someone to do something — as I used it earlier. In this example, it is the very obviousness and rigidity of the military hierarchy that makes the statement of a problem sufficient to trigger corrective action on the part of subordinates.

A man who had worked at the Pentagon reinforced the view that   15
the burden of interpretation is on subordinates in the military — and
he noticed the difference when he moved to a position in the private
sector. He was frustrated when he'd say to his new secretary, for example, "Do we have a list of invitees?" and be told, "I don't know; we
probably do" rather than "I'll get it for you." Indeed, he explained, at
the Pentagon, such a question would likely be heard as a reproach that
the list was not already on his desk.

The suggestion that indirectness is associated with the military   16
must come as a surprise to many. But everyone is indirect, meaning
more than is put into words and deriving meaning from words that
are never actually said. It's a matter of where, when and how we each
tend to be indirect and look for hidden meanings. But indirectness has
a built-in liability. There is a risk that the other will either miss or
choose to ignore your meaning.

On January 13, 1982, a freezing cold, snowy day in Washington,   17
Air Florida Flight 90 took off from National Airport, but could not
get the lift it needed to keep climbing. It crashed into a bridge
linking Washington to the state of Virginia and plunged into the Po-
tomac. Of the 79 people on board, all but 5 perished, many floundering and drowning in the icy water while horror-stricken bystanders
watched helplessly from the river's edge and millions more watched,
aghast, on their television screens. Experts later concluded that the
plane had waited too long after deicing to take off. Fresh buildup of
ice on the wings and engine brought the plane down. How could
the pilot and co-pilot have made such a blunder? Didn't at least
one of them realize it was dangerous to take off under these
conditions?

Charlotte Linde, a linguist at the Institute for Research on Learn-   18
ing in Palo Alto, Calif., has studied the "black box" recordings of cockpit conversations that preceded crashes as well as tape recordings of
conversations that took place among crews during flight simulations
in which problems were presented. Among the black box conversations she studied was the one between the pilot and co-pilot just before the Air Florida crash. The pilot, it turned out, had little experience
flying in icy weather. The co-pilot had a bit more, and it became
heartbreakingly clear on analysis that he had tried to warn the pilot,
but he did so indirectly.

The co-pilot repeatedly called attention to the bad weather and to   19
ice building up on other planes:

> Co-pilot: Look how the ice is just hanging on his, ah, back,
> back there, see that?
> . . .

> Co-pilot: See all those icicles on the back there and everything?
> Captain: Yeah.

He expressed concern early on about the long waiting time be- 20
tween deicing:

> Co-pilot: Boy, this is a, this is a losing battle here on trying to
> de-ice those things, it [gives] you a false feeling of security, that's all
> that does.

Shortly after they were given clearance to take off, he again ex- 21
pressed concern:

> Co-pilot: Let's check these tops again since we been setting
> here awhile.
> Captain: I think we get to go here in a minute.

When they were about to take off, the co-pilot called attention to 22
the engine instrument readings, which were not normal:

> Co-pilot: That don't seem right, does it? [three-second pause]
> Ah, that's not right. . . .
> Captain: Yes, it is, there's 80.
> Co-pilot: Naw, I don't think that's right. [seven-second pause]
> Ah, maybe it is.
> Captain: Hundred and twenty.
> Co-pilot: I don't know.

The takeoff proceeded, and 37 seconds later the pilot and co-pilot 23
exchanged their last words.

The co-pilot had repeatedly called the pilot's attention to danger- 24
ous conditions but did not directly suggest they abort the takeoff. In
Linde's judgment, he was expressing his concern indirectly, and the
captain didn't pick up on it — with tragic results.

That the co-pilot was trying to warn the captain indirectly is sup- 25
ported by evidence from another airline accident — a relatively minor
one — investigated by Linde that also involved the unsuccessful use of
indirectness.

On July 9, 1978, Allegheny Airlines Flight 453 was landing at 26
Monroe County Airport in Rochester, when it overran the runway by
728 feet. Everyone survived. This meant that the captain and co-pilot
could be interviewed. It turned out that the plane had been flying too
fast for a safe landing. The captain should have realized this and
flown around a second time, decreasing his speed before trying to
land. The captain said he simply had not been aware that he was
going too fast. But the co-pilot told interviewers that he "tried to

warn the captain in subtle ways, like mentioning the possibility of a tail wind and the slowness of flap extension." His exact words were recorded in the black box. The crosshatches indicate words deleted by the National Transportation Safety Board and were probably expletives:

> Co-pilot: Yeah, it looks like you got a tail wind here.
> Captain: Yeah.
> [?]: Yeah [it] moves awfully # slow.
> Co-pilot: Yeah the # flaps are slower than a #.
> Captain: We'll make it, gonna have to add power.
> Co-pilot: I know.

The co-pilot thought the captain would understand that if there 27 was a tail wind, it would result in the plane going too fast, and if the flaps were slow, they would be inadequate to break the speed sufficiently for a safe landing. He thought the captain would then correct for the error by not trying to land. But the captain said he didn't interpret the co-pilot's remarks to mean they were going too fast.

Linde believes it is not a coincidence that the people being indirect 28 in these conversations were the co-pilots. In her analyses of flight-crew conversations she found it was typical for the speech of subordinates to be more mitigated — polite, tentative or indirect. She also found that topics broached in a mitigated way were more likely to fail, and that captains were more likely to ignore hints from their crew members than the other way around. These findings are evidence that not only can indirectness and other forms of mitigation be misunderstood, but they are also easier to ignore.

In the Air Florida case, it is doubtful that the captain did not real- 29 ize what the co-pilot was suggesting when he said, "Let's check these tops again since we been setting here awhile" (though it seems safe to assume he did not realize the gravity of the co-pilot's concern). But the indirectness of the co-pilot's phrasing certainly made it easier for the pilot to ignore it. In this sense, the captain's response, "I think we get to go here in a minute," was an indirect way of saying, "I'd rather not." In view of these patterns, the flight crews of some airlines are now given training to express their concerns, even to superiors, in more direct ways.

The conclusion that people should learn to express themselves 30 more directly has a ring of truth to it — especially for Americans. But direct communication is not necessarily always preferable. If more direct expression is better communication, then the most direct-speaking crews should be the best ones. Linde was surprised to find in her research that crews that used the most mitigated speech were often judged the best crews. As part of the study of talk among cockpit crews in flight simulations, the trainers observed and rated the performances of the simulation crews. The crews they rated top in performance had a higher rate of mitigation than crews they judged to be poor.

This finding seems at odds with the role played by indirectness in   31
the examples of crashes that we just saw. Linde concluded that since every utterance functions on two levels — the referential (what it says) and the relational (what it implies about the speaker's relationships), crews that attend to the relational level will be better crews. A similar explanation was suggested by Kunihiko Harada. He believes that the secret of successful communication lies not in teaching subordinates to be more direct, but in teaching higher-ups to be more sensitive to indirect meaning. In other words, the crashes resulted not only because the co-pilots tried to alert the captains to danger indirectly but also because the captains were not attuned to the co-pilots' hints. What made for successful performance among the best crews might have been the ability — or willingness — of listeners to pick up on hints, just as members of families or longstanding couples come to understand each other's meaning without anyone being particularly explicit.

It is not surprising that a Japanese sociolinguist came up with this   32
explanation; what he described is the Japanese system, by which good communication is believed to take place when meaning is gleaned without being stated directly — or at all.

While Americans believe that "the squeaky wheel gets the grease"   33
(so it's best to speak up), the Japanese say, "The nail that sticks out gets hammered back in" (so it's best to remain silent if you don't want to be hit on the head). Many Japanese scholars writing in English have tried to explain to bewildered Americans the ethics of a culture in which silence is often given greater value than speech, and ideas are believed to be best communicated without being explicitly stated. Key concepts in Japanese give a flavor of the attitudes toward language that they reveal — and set in relief the strategies that Americans encounter at work when talking to other Americans.

Takie Sugiyama Lebra, a Japanese-born anthropologist, explains   34
that one of the most basic values in Japanese culture is *omoiyari*, which she translates as "empathy." Because of *omoiyari*, it should not be necessary to state one's meaning explicitly; people should be able to sense each other's meaning intuitively. Lebra explains that it is typical for a Japanese speaker to let sentences trail off rather than complete them because expressing ideas before knowing how they will be received seems intrusive. "Only an insensitive, uncouth person needs a direct, verbal, complete message," Lebra says.

Sasshi, the anticipation of another's message through insightful guesswork, is considered an indication of maturity. 35

Considering the value placed on direct communication by Americans in general, and especially by American business people, it is easy to imagine that many American readers may scoff at such conversational habits. But the success of Japanese businesses makes it impossible to continue to maintain that there is anything inherently inefficient about such conversational conventions. With indirectness, as with all aspects of conversational style, our own habitual style seems to make sense — seems polite, right and good. The light cast by the habits and assumptions of another culture can help us see our way to the flexibility and respect for other styles that is the only best way of speaking. 36

RESPONDING TO THE TEXT

In her essay, Tannen states that "indirectness is a fundamental element in human communication" (paragraph 4). Do you agree with Tannen on this point? What does she mean when she says that it is just as important to notice what we do not say as what we actually say?

ENGAGING THE WRITER'S SUBJECT

1. How does Tannen define indirect speech? What does she see as the built-in liability of indirect speech? Do you see comparable liability inherent in direct speech?

2. Tannen doesn't contest a finding that fathers had a higher incidence of both direct imperatives and indirect orders than mothers. How does she interpret these results?

3. Why do you think Tannen doesn't tell her audience how to deal with an insecure boss?

4. Why is it typical for Japanese speakers to let their sentences trail off?

ANALYZING THE WRITER'S CRAFT

1. What is Tannen's thesis, and where does she present it? (Glossary: *Thesis*)

2. Tannen mostly uses examples in which men give direct orders. In what ways do these examples support her thesis?

3. For what audience has Tannen written this essay? Does this help to explain why she focuses primarily on indirect communication? Why or why not? (Glossary: *Audience*)

4. Tannen gives two examples of flight accidents that resulted from indirect speech, and yet she then explains that top-performing flight teams used indirect speech more often than poorly performing teams. How do these seemingly contradictory examples support the author's argument?

5. Explain how Tannen uses comparison and contrast to document the assertion that "indirectness is a fundamental element in human communication. It is also one of the elements that varies most from one culture to another, and one that can cause confusion and misunderstanding when speakers have different habits with regard to using it" (4). (Glossary: *Comparison and Contrast*) How does this strategy enhance or support the dominant strategy of exemplification in the essay?

UNDERSTANDING THE WRITER'S LANGUAGE

1. In paragraph 13, what irony does Tannen point out in the popular understanding of the word *militaristic*? (Glossary: *Irony*)

2. How would you describe Tannen's diction in this essay? (Glossary: *Diction*) Does she ever get too scientific for the general reader? If so, where do you think her language gets too technical? Why do you think she uses such language?

3. Refer to your desk dictionary to determine the meanings of the following words as Tannen uses them in this selection: *admonishing* (paragraph 3), *self-deprecating* (3), *manipulative* (5), *prerogative* (7), *subservience* (8), *cheeky* (10), *deferential* (11), *imperious* (13), *liability* (16), *mitigated* (28), *broached* (28), *gleaned* (32), *relief* (33), *empathy* (34).

WRITING SUGGESTIONS

1. Tannen concludes that "the light cast by the habits and assumptions of another culture can help us see our way to the flexibility and respect for other styles that is the only best way of speaking" (paragraph 36). Write an essay in which you use concrete examples from your own experience, observation, or readings to agree or disagree with her conclusion.

2. Write an essay comparing the command styles of two people — either people you know or fictional characters. You might consider your parents, professors, coaches, television characters, or characters from movies or novels. What conclusions can you draw from your analysis? (Glossary: *Comparison and Contrast*)

3. Tannen often refers to the communication practices of other cultures and the options these practices open for us. Do some research in the sociology and anthropology sections of your library and possibly on the Internet. Using your research, write an essay in which you illustrate the importance of understanding and learning from other cultures' communication habits, in terms of both speech and body language.

• To begin your research online, go to **bedfordstmartins.com /subjectsstrategies** and click on "Exemplification" or browse the thematic directory of annotated links.

Those Crazy Ideas

Isaac Asimov

Born in Russia in 1920, Isaac Asimov immigrated to the United States three years later. His death in 1992 ended a long career as a science-fiction and nonfiction writer. Asimov was uniquely talented at making topics from Shakespeare to physics not only comprehensible but entertaining to the average reader. He grew up in Brooklyn, New York, and went to Columbia University, earning his doctorate in 1948. At the time of his death, he had published more than five hundred books. It's Been a Good Life, *published in 2002, was compiled from selections from Asimov's three previous autobiographical volumes and contains "A Way of Thinking," Asimov's four-hundredth essay for the* Magazine of Fantasy and Science Fiction. *His science fiction includes the novels* The Gods Themselves *(1972) and* Foundation's Edge *(1982), and two of his short stories — "Nightfall" and "Bicentennial Man" — are sci-fi classics.*

When a Boston consulting firm contacted Asimov to learn where his futuristic ideas came from, Asimov's response was the essay "Those Crazy Ideas," which was subsequently published in the Magazine of Fantasy and Science Fiction *in January 1960. The example of Darwin's principles of evolution and natural selection spell out Asimov's theory of creativity.*

PREPARING TO READ

For you, what are the characteristics of a creative person? Do you consider yourself creative? Why or why not? What is it that separates a creative idea from an ordinary one? Explain.

Time and time again I have been asked (and I'm sure others who have, in their time, written science fiction have been asked too): "Where do you get your crazy ideas?"

Over the years, my answers have sunk from flattered confusion to a shrug and a feeble smile. Actually, I don't really know, and the lack of knowledge doesn't really worry me, either, as long as the ideas keep coming.

But then some time ago, a consultant firm in Boston, engaged in a sophisticated space-age project for the government, got in touch with me.

What they needed, it seemed, to bring their project to a successful conclusion were novel suggestions, startling new principles, conceptual breakthroughs. To put it into the nutshell of a well-turned phrase, they needed "crazy ideas."

Unfortunately, they didn't know how to go about getting crazy ₅
ideas, but some among them had read my science fiction, so they
looked me up in the phone book and called me to ask (in essence),
"Dr. Asimov, where do you get your crazy ideas?"

Alas, I still didn't know, but as speculation is my profession, I am ₆
perfectly willing to think about the matter and share my thoughts
with you.

The question before the house, then, is: How does one go about ₇
creating or inventing or dreaming up or stumbling over a new and
revolutionary scientific principle?

For instance — to take a deliberately chosen example — how did ₈
Darwin come to think of evolution?

To begin with, in 1831, when Charles Darwin was twenty-two, he ₉
joined the crew of a ship called the *Beagle*. This ship was making a
five-year voyage about the world to explore various coast lines and to
increase man's geographical knowledge. Darwin went along as ship's
naturalist, to study the forms of life in far-off places.

This he did extensively and well, and upon the return of the *Bea-* ₁₀
gle Darwin wrote a book about his experiences (published in 1840)
which made him famous. In the course of this voyage, numerous
observations led him to the conclusion that species of living creatures
changed and developed slowly with time; that new species descended
from old. This, in itself, was not a new idea. Ancient Greeks had had
glimmerings of evolutionary notions. Many scientists before Darwin,
including Darwin's own grandfather, had theories of evolution.

The trouble, however, was that no scientist could evolve an expla- ₁₁
nation for the *why* of evolution. A French naturalist, Jean-Baptiste de
Lamarck, had suggested in the early 1800s that it came about by a
kind of conscious effort or inner drive. A tree-grazing animal, attempting to reach leaves, stretched its neck over the years and transmitted a
longer neck to its descendants. The process was repeated with each
generation until a giraffe in full glory was formed.

The only trouble was that acquired characteristics are not inher- ₁₂
ited and this was easily proved. The Lamarckian explanation did not
carry conviction.

Charles Darwin, however, had nothing better to suggest after sev- ₁₃
eral years of thinking about the problem.

But in 1798, eleven years before Darwin's birth, an English clergy- ₁₄
man named Thomas Robert Malthus had written a book entitled *An
Essay on the Principle of Population*. In this book Malthus suggested that
the human population always increased faster than the food supply
and that the population had to be cut down by either starvation, disease, or war; that these evils were therefore unavoidable.

In 1838 Darwin, still puzzling over the problem of the develop- ₁₅
ment of species, read Malthus's book. It is hackneyed to say "in a

flash" but that, apparently, is how it happened. In a flash, it was clear to Darwin. Not only human beings increased faster than the food supply; all species of living things did. In every case, the surplus population had to be cut down by starvation, by predators, or by disease. Now no two members of any species are exactly alike; each has slight individual variations from the norm. Accepting this fact, which part of the population was cut down?

Why — and this was Darwin's breakthrough — those members of 16 the species who were less efficient in the race for food, less adept at fighting off or escaping from predators, less equipped to resist disease, went down.

The survivors, generation after generation, were better adapted, on 17 the average, to their environment. The slow changes toward a better fit with the environment accumulated until a new (and more adapted) species had replaced the old. Darwin thus postulated the reason for evolution as being the action of *natural selection*. In fact, the full title of his book is *On the Origin of Species by Means of Natural Selection, or the Preservation of Favored Races in the Struggle for Life*. We just call it *The Origin of Species* and miss the full flavor of what it was he did.

It was in 1838 that Darwin received this flash and in 1844 that he 18 began writing his book, but he worked on for fourteen years gathering evidence to back up his thesis. He was a methodical perfectionist and no amount of evidence seemed to satisfy him. He always wanted more. His friends read his preliminary manuscripts and urged him to publish. In particular, Charles Lyell (whose book *Principles of Geology*, published in 1830–1833, first convinced scientists of the great age of the earth and thus first showed there was *time* for the slow progress of evolution to take place) warned Darwin that someone would beat him to the punch.

While Darwin was working, another and younger English natural- 19 ist, Alfred Russel Wallace, was traveling in distant lands. He too found copious evidence to show that evolution took place and he too wanted to find a reason. He did not know that Darwin had already solved the problem.

He spent three years puzzling, and then in 1858, he too came 20 across Malthus's book and read it. I am embarrassed to have to become hackneyed again, but in a flash he saw the answer. Unlike Darwin, however, he did not settle down to fourteen years of gathering and arranging evidence.

Instead, he grabbed pen and paper and at once wrote up his the- 21 ory. He finished this in two days.

Naturally, he didn't want to rush into print without having his 22 notions checked by competent colleagues, so he decided to send it to some well-known naturalist. To whom? Why, to Charles Darwin. To whom else?

I have often tried to picture Darwin's feeling as he read Wallace's essay which, he afterward stated, expressed matters in almost his own words. He wrote to Lyell that he had been forestalled "with a vengeance."

Darwin might easily have retained full credit. He was well-known and there were many witnesses to the fact that he had been working on his project for a decade and a half. Darwin, however, was a man of the highest integrity. He made no attempt to suppress Wallace. On the contrary, he passed on the essay to others and arranged to have it published along with a similar essay of his own. The year after, Darwin published his book.

Now the reason I chose this case was that here we have two men making one of the greatest discoveries in the history of science independently and simultaneously and under precisely the same stimulus. Does that mean *anyone* could have worked out the theory of natural selection if they had but made a sea voyage and combined that with reading Malthus?

Well, let's see. Here's where the speculation starts.

To begin with, both Darwin and Wallace were thoroughly grounded in natural history. Each had accumulated a vast collection of facts in the field in which they were to make their breakthrough. Surely this is significant.

Now every man in his lifetime collects facts, individual pieces of data, items of information. Let's call these "bits" (as they do, I think, in information theory). The "bits" can be of all varieties: personal memories, girls' phone numbers, baseball players' batting averages, yesterday's weather, the atomic weights of the chemical elements.

Naturally, different men gather different numbers of different varieties of "bits." A person who has collected a larger number than usual of those varieties that are held to be particularly difficult to obtain — say, those involving the sciences and the liberal arts — is considered "educated."

There are two broad ways in which the "bits" can be accumulated. The more common way, nowadays, is to find people who already possess many "bits" and have them transfer those "bits" to your mind in good order and in predigested fashion. Our schools specialize in this transfer of "bits" and those of us who take advantage of them receive a "formal education."

The less common way is to collect "bits" with a minimum amount of live help. They can be obtained from books or out of personal experience. In that case you are "self-educated." (It often happens that "self-educated" is confused with "uneducated." This is an error to be avoided.)

In actual practice, scientific breakthroughs have been initiated by those who were formally educated, as for instance by Nicolaus

Copernicus, and by those who were self-educated, as for instance by Michael Faraday.

To be sure, the structure of science has grown more complex over   33
the years and the absorption of the necessary number of "bits" has become more and more difficult without the guidance of someone who has already absorbed them. The self-educated genius is therefore becoming rarer, though he has still not vanished.

However, without drawing any distinction according to the man-   34
ner in which "bits" have been accumulated, let's set up the first criterion for scientific creativity:

1) The creative person must possess as many "bits" of information   35
as possible; i.e., he must be educated.

Of course, the accumulation of "bits" is not enough in itself. We   36
have probably all met people who are intensely educated, but who manage to be abysmally stupid, nevertheless. They have the "bits," but the "bits" just lie there.

But what is there one can do with "bits"?   37

Well, one can combine them into groups of two or more. Every-   38
one does that; it is the principle of the string on the finger. You tell yourself to remember a (to buy bread) when you observe b (the string). You enforce a combination that will not let you forget a because b is so noticeable.

That, of course, is a conscious and artificial combination of "bits."   39
It is my feeling that every mind is, more or less unconsciously, continually making all sorts of combinations and permutations of "bits," probably at random.

Some minds do this with greater facility than others; some minds   40
have greater capacity for dredging the combinations out of the unconscious and becoming consciously aware of them. This results in "new ideas," in "novel outlooks."

The ability to combine "bits" with facility and to grow consciously   41
aware of the new combinations is, I would like to suggest, the measure of what we call "intelligence." In this view, it is quite possible to be educated and yet not intelligent.

Obviously, the creative scientist must not only have his "bits" on   42
hand but he must be able to combine them readily and more or less consciously. Darwin not only observed data, he also made deductions — clever and far-reaching deductions — from what he observed. That is, he combined the "bits" in interesting ways and drew important conclusions.

So the second criterion of creativity is: 43

2) The creative person must be able to combine "bits" with facil-   44
ity and recognize the combinations he has formed; i.e., he must be intelligent.

Even forming and recognizing new combinations is insufficient in itself. Some combinations are important and some are trivial. How do you tell which are which? There is no question but that a person who cannot tell them apart must labor under a terrible disadvantage. As he plods after each possible new idea, he loses time and his life passes uselessly.

There is also no question but that there are people who somehow have the gift of seeing the consequences "in a flash" as Darwin and Wallace did; of feeling what the end must be without consciously going through every step of the reasoning. This, I suggest, is the measure of what we call "intuition."

Intuition plays more of a role in some branches of scientific knowledge than others. Mathematics, for instance, is a deductive science in which, once certain basic principles are learned, a large number of items of information become "obvious" as merely consequences of those principles. Most of us, to be sure, lack the intuitive powers to see the "obvious."

To the truly intuitive mind, however, the combination of the few necessary "bits" is at once extraordinarily rich in consequences. Without too much trouble they see them all, including some that have not been seen by their predecessors.

It is perhaps for this reason that mathematics and mathematical physics has seen repeated cases of first-rank breakthroughs by youngsters. Evariste Galois evolved group theory at twenty-one. Isaac Newton worked out calculus at twenty-three. Albert Einstein presented the theory of relativity at twenty-six, and so on.

In those branches of science which are more inductive and require larger numbers of "bits" to begin with, the average age of the scientists at the time of the breakthrough is greater. Darwin was twenty-nine at the time of his flash, Wallace was thirty-five.

But in any science, however inductive, intuition is necessary for creativity. So:

3) The creative person must be able to see, with as little delay as possible, the consequences of the new combinations of "bits" which he has formed; i.e., he must be intuitive.

But now let's look at this business of combining "bits" in a little more detail. "Bits" are at varying distances from each other. The more closely related two "bits" are, the more apt one is to be reminded of one by the other and to make the combination. Consequently, a new idea that arises from such a combination is made quickly. It is a "natural consequence" of an older idea, a "corollary." It "obviously follows."

The combination of less related "bits" results in a more startling idea; if for no other reason than that it takes longer for such a combination to be made, so that the new idea is therefore less "obvious." For a scientific breakthrough of the first rank, there must be a combination of "bits" so widely spaced that the random chance of the combination being made is small indeed. (Otherwise, it will be made quickly and be considered but a corollary of some previous idea which will then be considered the "breakthrough.")

But then, it can easily happen that two "bits" sufficiently widely spaced to make a breakthrough by their combination are not present in the same mind. Neither Darwin nor Wallace, for all their education, intelligence, and intuition, possessed the key "bits" necessary to work out the theory of evolution by natural selection. Those "bits" were lying in Malthus's book, and both Darwin and Wallace had to find them there.

To do this, however, they had to read, understand, and appreciate the book. In short, they had to be ready to incorporate other people's "bits" and treat them with all the ease with which they treated their own.

It would hamper creativity, in other words, to emphasize intensity of education at the expense of broadness. It is bad enough to limit the nature of the "bits" to the point where the necessary two would not be in the same mind. It would be fatal to mold a mind to the point where it was incapable of accepting "foreign bits."

I think we ought to revise the first criterion of creativity, then, to read:

1) The creative person must possess as many "bits" as possible, falling into as wide a variety of types as possible; i.e., he must be broadly educated.

As the total amount of "bits" to be accumulated increases with the advance of science, it is becoming more and more difficult to gather enough "bits" in a wide enough area. Therefore, the practice of "brain-busting" is coming into popularity; the notion of collecting thinkers into groups and hoping that they will cross-fertilize one another into startling new breakthroughs.

Under what circumstances could this conceivably work? (After all, anything that will stimulate creativity is of first importance to humanity.)

Well, to begin with, a group of people will have more "bits" on hand than any member of the group singly since each man is likely to have some "bits" the others do not possess.

However, the increase in "bits" is not in direct proportion to the number of men, because there is bound to be considerable overlapping. As the group increases, the smaller and smaller addition of completely new "bits" introduced by each additional member is quickly outweighed by the added tensions involved in greater numbers; the longer wait to speak, the greater likelihood of being interrupted, and so on. It is my (intuitive) guess that five is as large a number as one can stand in such a conference.

Now of the three criteria mentioned so far, I feel (intuitively) that intuition is the least common. It is more likely that none of the group will be intuitive than that none will be intelligent or none educated. If no individual in the group is intuitive, the group as a whole will not be intuitive. You cannot add non-intuition and form intuition.

If one of the group is intuitive, he is almost certain to be intelligent and educated as well, or he would not have been asked to join the group in the first place. In short, for a brain-busting group to be creative, it must be quite small and it must possess at least one creative individual. But in that case, does that one individual need the group? Well, I'll get back to that later.

Why did Darwin work fourteen years gathering evidence for a theory he himself must have been convinced was correct from the beginning? Why did Wallace send his manuscript to Darwin first instead of offering it for publication at once?

To me it seems that they must have realized that any new idea is met by resistance from the general population who, after all, are not creative. The more radical the new idea, the greater the dislike and distrust it arouses. The dislike and distrust aroused by a first-class breakthrough are so great that the author must be prepared for unpleasant consequences (sometimes for expulsion from the respect of the scientific community; sometimes, in some societies, for death).

Darwin was trying to gather enough evidence to protect himself by convincing others through a sheer flood of reasoning. Wallace wanted to have Darwin on his side before proceeding.

It takes courage to announce the results of your creativity. The greater the creativity, the greater the necessary courage in much more than direct proportion. After all, consider that the more profound the breakthrough, the more solidified the previous opinions; the more "against reason" the new discovery seems, the more against cherished authority.

Usually a man who possesses enough courage to be a scientific genius seems odd. After all, a man who has sufficient courage or irreverence to fly in the face of reason or authority must be odd, if you define "odd" as "being not like most people." And if he is courageous and irreverent in such a colossally big thing, he will certainly be courageous and irreverent in many small things so that being odd in one way, he is apt to be odd in others. In short, he will seem to the non-creative, conforming people about him to be a "crackpot."

So we have the fourth criterion:

4) The creative person must possess courage (and to the general 72
public may, in consequence, seem a crackpot).

As it happens, it is the crackpottery that is most often most notice- 73
able about the creative individual. The eccentric and absentminded
professor is a stock character in fiction; and the phrase "mad scientist"
is almost a cliché.

(And be it noted that I am never asked where I get my interesting 74
or effective or clever or fascinating ideas. I am invariably asked where I
get my *crazy* ideas.)

Of course, it does not follow that because the creative individual is 75
usually a crackpot, that any crackpot is automatically an unrecognized
genius. The chances are low indeed, and failure to recognize that the
proposition cannot be so reversed is the cause of a great deal of trouble.

Then, since I believe that combinations of "bits" take place quite 76
at random in the unconscious mind, it follows that it is quite possible
that a person may possess all four of the criteria I have mentioned in
superabundance and yet may never happen to make the necessary
combination. After all, suppose Darwin had never read Malthus.
Would he ever have thought of natural selection? What made him
pick up the copy? What if someone had come in at the crucial time
and interrupted him?

So there is a fifth criterion which I am at a loss to phrase in any 77
other way than this:

5) A creative person must be lucky. 78

To summarize: 79

A creative person must be 1) broadly educated, 2) intelligent, 80
3) intuitive, 4) courageous, and 5) lucky.

How, then, does one go about encouraging scientific creativity? 81
For now, more than ever before in man's history, we must; and the
need will grow constantly in the future.

Only, it seems to me, by increasing the incidence of the various 82
criteria among the general population.

Of the five criteria, number 5 (luck) is out of our hands. We can 83
only hope; although we must also remember Louis Pasteur's famous
statement that "Luck favors the prepared mind." Presumably, if we
have enough of the four other criteria, we shall find enough of number five as well.

Criterion 1 (broad education) is in the hands of our school system. 84
Many educators are working hard to find ways of increasing the quality of education among the public. They should be encouraged to continue doing so.

Criteria 2 (intelligence) and 3 (intuition) are inborn and their inci- 85
dence cannot be increased in the ordinary way. However, they can be
more efficiently recognized and utilized. I would like to see methods devised for spotting the intelligent and intuitive (particularly the latter)

early in life and treating them with special care. This, too, educators are concerned with.

To me, though, it seems that it is criterion 4 (courage) that re- 86 ceives the least concern, and it is just the one we may most easily be able to handle. Perhaps it is difficult to make a person more courageous than he is, but that is not necessary. It would be equally effective to make it sufficient to be less courageous; to adopt an attitude that creativity is a permissible activity.

Does this mean changing society or changing human nature? I 87 don't think so. I think there are ways of achieving the end that do not involve massive change of anything, and it is here that brain-busting has its greatest chance of significance.

Suppose we have a group of five that includes one creative indi- 88 vidual. Let's ask again what that individual can receive from the non-creative four.

The answer to me, seems to be just this: Permission! 89

They must permit him to create. They must tell him to go ahead 90 and be a crackpot.[1]

How is this permission to be granted? Can four essentially non- 91 creative people find it within themselves to grant such permission? Can the one creative person find it within himself to accept it?

I don't know. Here, it seems to me, is where we need experimenta- 92 tion and perhaps a kind of creative breakthrough about creativity. Once we learn enough about the whole matter, who knows — I may even find out where I get those crazy ideas.

RESPONDING TO THE TEXT

Asimov notes, "I am never asked where I get my interesting or effective or clever or fascinating ideas. I am invariably asked where I get my *crazy* ideas" (paragraph 74). Why do you suppose people react to Asimov this way? What does this tell you about society's willingness to accept potentially innovative or breakthrough thinking?

ENGAGING THE WRITER'S SUBJECT

1. For Asimov, what are the five criteria for a creative person? Which criteria separate intelligent from creative people?

2. Asimov uses the example of Charles Darwin and Alfred Russel Wallace to illustrate the discovery of a "new and revolutionary scientific principle"

---

[1]Always with the provision, of course, that the crackpot creation that results survives the test of hard inspection. Though many of the products of genius seem crackpot at first, very few of the creations that seem crackpot turn out, after all, to be products of genius.

(paragraph 7). What principle did these men discover, and how did each make his discovery?

3. How did Darwin react when he read Wallace's manuscript, which articulated the same theory Darwin himself had first discovered fourteen years earlier?

4. Asimov believes that an educated person is one who has accumulated many pieces of information, which he calls "bits." According to Asimov, what are the two ways people accumulate "bits"?

5. What advice does Asimov offer concerning the practice of "brainbusting"? What does Asimov think are the essential ingredients of an effective group?

ANALYZING THE WRITER'S CRAFT

1. What is Asimov's purpose in writing this essay? (Glossary: *Purpose*)

2. Asimov takes care to tell us that the example of Charles Darwin was "deliberately chosen" (paragraph 8). How effective did you find this example? How does it illustrate each of the points that Asimov makes about creativity?

3. Asimov informs us that a creative person must be educated, intelligent, and intuitive — and then, after some discussion, he decides to "revise the first criterion for creativity" (paragraph 58). What does Asimov gain by adding the stipulation that the education should be "broad" at this point in his essay? Why do you think he organized his essay this way? (Glossary: *Organization*)

4. Asimov carefully compares how Darwin and Wallace made "one of the greatest discoveries in the history of science independently and simultaneously" (paragraph 25). What about these two scientists' careers does he compare? What insights into the creative person does this yield? (Glossary: *Comparison and Contrast*)

5. Asimov tells us that in "mathematics and mathematical physics" there have been a number of "first-rank breakthroughs by youngsters" (paragraph 49). What examples does he provide to document his case? Are they convincing? Explain.

6. How effective did you find Asimov's beginning and ending? How are the two linked? Explain.

UNDERSTANDING THE WRITER'S LANGUAGE

1. In talking about creativity's fourth criterion, courage, Asimov uses the words *crackpot* and *crackpottery*. Why do you suppose he chose these particular words? What alternatives might he have used? When noncreative, conforming people use the label *crackpot* to describe genius, what does Asimov imply they are saying about themselves?

2. Refer to your desk dictionary to determine the meanings of the following words as Asimov uses them in this selection: *evolution* (paragraph 8), *hackneyed* (15), *postulated* (17), *copious* (19), *stimulus* (25), *permutations* (39), *intuition* (47), *inductive* (50).

WRITING SUGGESTIONS

1. Asimov writes, "A creative person must be lucky" (paragraph 78). Is there more to creativity than just "dumb luck"? Is luck ever "dumb"? Is creativity something that happens passively or something one works at actively? Write an essay based on examples from your own experience, observation, and reading to agree or disagree with Asimov's assertion.

2. As Asimov reminds us, "it does not follow that because the creative individual is usually a crackpot, that any crackpot is automatically an unrecognized genius" (paragraph 75). What for you constitutes real genius? Using examples from your own experience and reading, write an essay in which you compare and contrast your thinking about creativity and genius with Asimov's. (Glossary: *Comparison and Contrast*) Before you start to write, you may find it helpful to refer to your Preparing to Read response for this selection.

3. Asimov writes, "The more radical the new idea, the greater the dislike and distrust it arouses. The dislike and distrust aroused by a first-class breakthrough are so great that the author [or inventor or scientist or artist] must be prepared for unpleasant consequences . . ." (paragraph 67). Using your college library and the Internet, research a figure from history — for example, Galileo, Albert Einstein, Pablo Picasso, Elizabeth Cady Stanton, or Rosa Parks — whose revolutionary ideas challenged the status quo. Write an essay in which you explore the general reaction to this figure's ideas. Why were the ideas so controversial? What values, beliefs, or institutions did these ideas challenge? What consequences did the figure bear? How long did it take for the public to embrace the figure's ideas, if at all? Why?

• To begin your research online, go to **bedfordstmartins.com /subjectsstrategies** and click on "Exemplification" or browse the thematic directory of annotated links.

In Search of Our Mothers' Gardens

Alice Walker

Best known for her Pulitzer Prize–winning novel The Color Purple, *Alice Walker is a prolific writer of poetry, essays, and fiction. Walker was born in Georgia in 1944, the youngest of eight children in a sharecropping family. She took advantage of educational opportunities to escape a life of poverty and servitude, attending Spelman College in Georgia and then graduating from the prestigious Sarah Lawrence College in New York. An African American activist and feminist, Walker often deals with controversial subjects in her writing;* The Color Purple *(1982), the novel* Possessing the Secret of Joy *(1992), and the nonfiction* Warrior Marks *(1993) are known for this characteristic. Other widely acclaimed works by Walker include her collected poems,* Her Blue Body Everything We Know: Earthling Poems, 1965–1990 *(1991); a memoir entitled* The Same River Twice: Honoring the Difficult *(1996); a collection of essays,* Anything We Love Can Be Saved: A Writer's Activism *(1997); and a collection of stories,* The Way Forward Is with a Broken Heart *(2000). Walker's most recent work includes* Sent by Earth: A Message from the Grandmother Spirit after the Bombing of the World Trade Center and the Pentagon *(2001) and* Absolute Trust in the Goodness of the Earth: New Poems *(2003). Although much of her writing deals with pain and life's hardships, her work is not pessimistic; in the words of one reviewer, Walker's writing represents a "quest for peace and joy in a difficult world."*

In the following essay, the title piece from a collection of essays published in 1983, she explores what it has meant in the past — and, by implication, what it means today — to be a black woman in America.

PREPARING TO READ

Is everyone born with creative impulses, with the urge to indulge artistic expression of some kind, or is creativity a special gift granted only to a few? Are there ways to satisfy creativity other than with art? What happens to a person whose artistic drive is discouraged? Explain.

I described her own nature and temperament. Told how they needed a larger life for their expression.... I pointed out that in lieu of proper channels, her emotions had overflowed into paths that dissipated them. I talked, beautifully I thought, about an art that would be born, an art that would open the way for women the likes of her. I asked her to hope, and build up an inner life against the coming of that day.... I sang, with a strange quiver in my voice, a promise song.

— JEAN TOOMER,
"Avey," Cane

The poet speaking to a prostitute who falls asleep while he's talking— 1

When the poet Jean Toomer walked through the South in the early 2
twenties, he discovered a curious thing: black women whose spirituality was so intense, so deep, so *unconscious*, that they were themselves
unaware of the richness they held. They stumbled blindly through
their lives: creatures so abused and mutilated in body, so dimmed and
confused by pain, that they considered themselves unworthy even of
hope. In the selfless abstractions their bodies became to the men who
used them, they became more than "sexual objects," even more than
mere women: they became "Saints." Instead of being perceived as
whole persons, their bodies became shrines, what was thought to be
their minds became temples suitable for worship. These crazy Saints
stared out at the world, wildly, like lunatics — or quietly, like suicides;
and the "God" that was in their gaze was as mute as a great stone.

Who were these Saints? These crazy, loony, pitiful women? 3

Some of them, without a doubt, were our mothers and grand- 4
mothers.

In the still heat of the post-Reconstruction South, this is how they 5
seemed to Jean Toomer: exquisite butterflies trapped in an evil honey,
toiling away their lives in an era, a century, that did not acknowledge
them, except as "the *mule* of the world." They dreamed dreams that
no one knew — not even themselves, in any coherent fashion — and
saw visions no one could understand. They wandered or sat about the
countryside crooning lullabies to ghosts, and drawing the mother of
Christ in charcoal on courthouse walls.

They forced their minds to desert their bodies and their striving 6
spirits sought to rise, like frail whirlwinds from the hard red clay. And
when those frail whirlwinds fell, in scattered particles, upon the ground,
no one mourned. Instead, men lit candles to celebrate the emptiness
that remained, as people do who enter a beautiful but vacant space to
resurrect a God.

Our mothers and grandmothers, some of them: moving to music 7
not yet written. And they waited.

They waited for a day when the unknown thing that was in them 8
would be made known; but guessed, somehow in their darkness, that
on the day of their revelation they would be long dead. Therefore to
Toomer they walked, and even ran, in slow motion. For they were
going nowhere immediate, and the future was not yet within their
grasp. And men took our mothers and grandmothers, "but got no
pleasure from it." So complex was their passion and their calm.

To Toomer, they lay vacant and fallow as autumn fields, with har- 9
vest time never in sight: and he saw them enter loveless marriages,
without joy; and become prostitutes, without resistance, and become
mothers of children, without fulfillment.

For these grandmothers and mothers of ours were not Saints, 10
but Artists; driven to a numb and bleeding madness by the springs
of creativity in them for which there was no release. They were Creators, who lived lives of spiritual waste, because they were so rich in
spirituality — which is the basis of Art — that the strain of enduring
their unused and unwanted talent drove them insane. Throwing away
this spirituality was their pathetic attempt to lighten the soul to a
weight their work-worn, sexually abused bodies could bear.

What did it mean for a black woman to be an artist in our grand- 11
mothers' time? In our great-grandmothers' day? It is a question with
an answer cruel enough to stop the blood.

Did you have a genius of a great-great-grandmother who died 12
under some ignorant and depraved white overseer's lash? Or was she
required to bake biscuits for a lazy backwater tramp, when she cried
out in her soul to paint watercolors of sunsets, or the rain falling on
the green and peaceful pasturelands? Or was her body broken and
forced to bear children (who were more often than not sold away from
her) — eight, ten, fifteen, twenty children — when her one joy was
the thought of modeling heroic figures of rebellion, in stone or clay?

How was the creativity of the black woman kept alive, year after 13
year and century after century, when for most of the years black people have been in America, it was a punishable crime for a black person
to read or write? And the freedom to paint, to sculpt, to expand the
mind with an action did not exist. Consider, if you can bear to imagine it, what might have been the result if singing, too, had been forbidden by law. Listen to the voices of Bessie Smith, Billie Holiday,
Nina Simone, Roberta Flack, and Aretha Franklin, among others, and
imagine those voices muzzled for life. Then you may begin to compre-
hend the lives of our "crazy," "Sainted" mothers and grandmothers.
The agony of the lives of women who might have been Poets, Novel-
ists, Essayists, and Short-Story Writers (over a period of centuries),
who died with their real gifts stifled within them.

And, if this were the end of the story, we would have cause to cry 14
out in my paraphrase of Okot p'Bitek's great poem:

O, my clanswomen
Let us all cry together!
Come,
Let us mourn the death of our mother,
The death of a Queen
The ash that was produced
By a great fire!
O, this homestead is utterly dead
Close the gates
With *lacari* thorns,
For our mother

The creator of the Stool is lost!
And all the young women
Have perished in the wilderness!

But this is not the end of the story, for all the young women —
our mothers and grandmothers, *ourselves* — have not perished in the
wilderness. And if we ask ourselves why, and search for and find the
answer, we will know beyond all efforts to erase it from our minds,
just exactly who, and of what, we black American women are. [15]

One example, perhaps the most pathetic, most misunderstood
one, can provide a backdrop for our mothers' work: Phillis Wheatley,[1]
a slave in the 1700s. [16]

Virginia Woolf,[2] in her book *A Room of One's Own*, wrote that in
order for a woman to write fiction she must have two things, certainly: a room of her own (the key and lock) and enough money to
support herself. [17]

What then are we to make of Phillis Wheatley, a slave, who owned
not even herself? This sickly, frail black girl who required a servant of
her own at times — her health was so precarious — and who, had she
been white, would have been easily considered the intellectual superior
of all women and most of the men in the society of her day. [18]

Virginia Woolf wrote further, speaking of course not of our Phillis,
that "any woman born with a great gift in the sixteenth century [in-
sert "eighteenth century," insert "black woman," insert "born or made
a slave"] would certainly have gone crazed, shot herself, or ended her
days in some lonely cottage outside the village, half witch, half wizard
[insert "Saint"], feared and mocked at. For it needs little skill and psychology to be sure that a highly gifted girl who had tried to use her
gift for poetry would have been so thwarted and hindered by contrary
instincts [add "chains, guns, the lash, the ownership of one's body by
someone else, submission to an alien religion"], that she must have
lost her health and sanity to a certainty." [19]

The key words, as they relate to Phillis, are "contrary instincts."
For when we read the poetry of Phillis Wheatley — and when we read
the novels of Nella Larsen or the oddly false-sounding autobiography
of that freest of all black women writers, Zora Hurston[3] — evidence of
"contrary instincts" is everywhere. Her loyalties were completely divided, as was, without question, her mind. [20]

---

[1]Wheatley (1753?–1784) published several volumes of poetry and is considered the first important African American writer in the United States.

[2]Woolf (1882–1941) was an acclaimed English essayist and novelist.

[3]Larsen (1891–1964) wrote realistic novels about the relationships between
different races; Hurston (1903–1960) is known for her folklore research, novels, and stories that convey the nuances of southern black speech.

But how could this be otherwise? Captured at seven, a slave of 21
wealthy, doting whites who instilled in her the "savagery" of the
Africa they "rescued" her from . . . one wonders if she was even able to
remember her homeland as she had known it, or as it really was.

Yet, because she did not try to use her gift for poetry in a world that 22
made her a slave, she was "so thwarted and hindered by . . . contrary
instincts, that she . . . lost her health. . . ." In the last years of her brief
life, burdened not only with the need to express her gift but also with a
penniless, friendless "freedom" and several small children for whom
she was forced to do strenuous work to feed, she lost her health, certainly. Suffering from malnutrition and neglect and who knows what
mental agonies, Phillis Wheatley died.

So torn by "contrary instincts" was black, kidnapped, enslaved 23
Phillis that her description of "the Goddess" — as she poetically called
the Liberty she did not have — is ironically, cruelly humorous. And, in
fact, has held Phillis up to ridicule for more than a century. It is usually
read prior to hanging Phillis's memory as that of a fool. She wrote:

> The Goddess comes, she moves divinely fair,
> Olive and laurel binds her *golden* hair.
> Wherever shines this native of the skies,
> Unnumber'd charms and recent graces rise. [My italics]

It is obvious that Phillis, the slave, combed the "Goddess's" hair 24
every morning; prior, perhaps, to bringing in the milk, or fixing her
mistress's lunch. She took her imagery from the one thing she saw ele-
vated above all others.

With the benefit of hindsight we ask, "How could she?" 25

But at last, Phillis, we understand. No more snickering when your 26
stiff, struggling, ambivalent lines are forced on us. We know now that
you were not an idiot or a traitor; only a sickly little black girl,
snatched from your home and country and made a slave; a woman
who still struggled to sing the song that was your gift, although in a
land of barbarians who praised you for your bewildered tongue. It is
not so much what you sang, as that you kept alive, in so many of our
ancestors, *the notion of song.*

Black women are called, in the folklore that so aptly identifies one's 27
status in society, "the *mule* of the world," because we have been handed
the burdens that everyone else — *everyone* else — refused to carry. We
have also been called "Matriarchs," "Superwomen," and "Mean and Evil
Bitches." Not to mention "Castrators" and "Sapphire's Mama." When
we have pleaded for understanding, our character has been distorted;
when we have asked for simple caring, we have been handed empty in-
spirational appellations, then stuck in the farthest corner. When we
have asked for love, we have been given children. In short, even our

plainer gifts, our labors of fidelity and love, have been knocked down our throats. To be an artist and a black woman, even today, lowers our status in many respects, rather than raises it: and yet, artists we will be.

Therefore we must fearlessly pull out of ourselves and look at and identify with our lives the living creativity some of our great-grandmothers were not allowed to know. I stress *some* of them because it is well known that the majority of our great-grandmothers knew, even without "knowing" it, the reality of their spirituality, even if they didn't recognize it beyond what happened in the singing at church — and they never had any intention of giving it up. 28

How they did it — those millions of black women who were not Phillis Wheatley, or Lucy Terry or Frances Harper or Zora Hurston or Nella Larsen or Bessie Smith; or Elizabeth Catlett, or Katherine Dunham,[4] either — brings me to the title of this essay, "In Search of Our Mothers' Gardens," which is a personal account that is yet shared, in its theme and its meaning, by all of us. I found, while thinking about the far-reaching world of the creative black woman, that often the truest answer to a question that really matters can be found very close. 29

In the late 1920s my mother ran away from home to marry my father. Marriage, if not running away, was expected of seventeen-year-old girls. By the time she was twenty, she had two children and was pregnant with a third. Five children later, I was born. And this is how I came to know my mother: she seemed a large, soft, loving-eyed woman who was rarely impatient in our home. Her quick, violent temper was on view only a few times a year when she battled with the white landlord who had the misfortune to suggest to her that her children did not need to go to school. 30

She made all the clothes we wore, even my brothers' overalls. She made all the towels and sheets we used. She spent the summers canning vegetables and fruits. She spent the winter evenings making quilts enough to cover all our beds. 31

During the "working" day, she labored beside — not behind — my father in the fields. Her day began before sunup, and did not end until late at night. There was never a moment for her to sit down, undisturbed, to unravel her own private thoughts; never a time free from interruption — by work or the noisy inquiries of her many children. And yet, it is to my mother — and all our mothers who were not famous — that I went in search of the secret of what has fed that muzzled 32

---

[4]Accomplished African American female artists; the first five were writers, Smith was a singer and songwriter, Catlett a sculptor, and Dunham a choreographer and dancer.

and often mutilated, but vibrant, creative spirit that the black woman has inherited, and that pops out in wild and unlikely places to this day.

But when, you will ask, did my overworked mother have time to know or care about feeding the creative spirit? 33

The answer is so simple that many of us have spent years discovering it. We have constantly looked high, when we should have looked high — and low. 34

For example: in the Smithsonian Institution in Washington, D.C., there hangs a quilt unlike any other in the world. In fanciful, inspired, and yet simple and identifiable figures, it portrays the story of the Crucifixion. It is considered rare, beyond price. Though it follows no known pattern of quilt-making, and though it is made of bits and pieces of worthless rags, it is obviously the work of a person of powerful imagination and deep spiritual feeling. Below this quilt I saw a note that says it was made by "an anonymous Black woman in Alabama, a hundred years ago." 35

If we could locate this "anonymous" black woman from Alabama, she would turn out to be one of our grandmothers — an artist who left her mark in the only materials she could afford, and in the only medium her position in society allowed her to use. 36

As Virginia Woolf wrote further, in *A Room of One's Own:* 37

> Yet genius of a sort must have existed among women as it must have existed among the working class. [Change this to "slaves" and "the wives and the daughters of sharecroppers."] Now and again an Emily Brontë or a Robert Burns [change this to "a Zora Hurston or a Richard Wright"] blazes out and proves its presence. But certainly it never got itself on to paper. When, however, one reads of a witch being ducked, of a woman possessed by devils [or "Sainthood"], of a wise woman selling herbs [our root workers], or even a very remarkable man who had a mother, then I think we are on the track of a lost novelist, a suppressed poet, of some mute and inglorious Jane Austen. . . . Indeed, I would venture to guess that Anon, who wrote so many poems without signing them, was often a woman. . . .

And so our mothers and grandmothers have, more often than not anonymously, handed on the creative spark, the seed of the flower they themselves never hoped to see: or like a sealed letter they could not plainly read. 38

And so it is, certainly, with my own mother. Unlike "Ma" Rainey's[5] songs, which retained their creator's name even while blasting forth from Bessie Smith's mouth, no song or poem will bear my mother's name. Yet so many of the stories that I write, that we all write, are my 39

---

[5]Rainey (1886–1939) was a famous blues singer and songwriter.

mother's stories. Only recently did I fully realize this: that through years of listening to my mother's stories of her life, I have absorbed not only the stories themselves, but something of the manner in which she spoke, something of the urgency that involves the knowledge that her stories — like her life — must be recorded. It is probably for this reason that so much of what I have written is about characters whose counterparts in real life are so much older than I am.

But the telling of these stories, which came from my mother's lips   40
as naturally as breathing, was not the only way my mother showed herself as an artist. For stories, too, were subject to being distracted, to dying without conclusion. Dinners must be started, and cotton must be gathered before the big rains. The artist that was and is my mother showed itself to me only after many years. This is what I finally noticed:

Like Mem, a character in *The Third Life of Grange Copeland*, my   41
mother adorned with flowers whatever shabby house we were forced to live in. And not just your typical straggly country stand of zinnias, either. She planted ambitious gardens — and still does — with over fifty different varieties of plants that bloom profusely from early March until late November. Before she left home for the fields, she watered her flowers, chopped up the grass, and laid out new beds. When she returned from the fields she might divide clumps of bulbs, dig a cold pit, uproot and replant rose, or prune branches from her taller bushes or trees — until night came and it was too dark to see.

Whatever she planted grew as if by magic, and her fame as a   42
grower of flowers spread over three counties. Because of her creativity with her flowers, even my memories of poverty are seen through a screen of blooms — sunflowers, petunias, roses, dahlias, forsythia, spirea, delphiniums, verbena . . . and on and on.

And I remember people coming to my mother's yard to be given   43
cuttings from her flowers; I hear again the praise showered on her because whatever rocky soil she landed on, she turned into a garden. A garden so brilliant with colors, so original in its design, so magnificent with life and creativity, that to this day people drive by our house in Georgia — perfect strangers and imperfect strangers — and ask to stand or walk in my mother's art.

I notice that it is not only when my mother is working in her flow-   44
ers that she is radiant, almost to the point of being invisible — except as Creator: hand and eye. She is involved in work her soul must have. Ordering the universe in the image of her personal conception of Beauty.

Her face, as she prepares the Art that is her gift, is a legacy of respect   45
she leaves to me, for all that illuminates and cherishes life. She has handed down respect for the possibilities — and the will to grasp them.

For her, so hindered and intruded upon in so many ways, being an   46
artist has still been a daily part of her life. This ability to hold on, even in very simple ways, is work black women have done for a very long time.

This poem is not enough, but it is something, for the woman who   47
literally covered the holes in our walls with sunflowers:

> They were women then
> My mama's generation
> Husky of voice — Stout of
> Step
> With fists as well as
> Hands
> How they battered down
> Doors
> And ironed
> Starched white
> Shirts
> How they led
> Armies
> Headragged Generals
> Across mined
> Fields
> Booby-trapped
> Kitchens
> To discovery books
> Desks
> A place for us
> How they knew what we
> *Must* know
> Without knowing a page
> Of it
> Themselves.

Guided by my heritage of a love of beauty and a respect for   48
strength — in search of my mother's garden, I found my own.

And perhaps in Africa over two hundred years ago, there was just   49
such a mother; perhaps she painted vivid and daring decorations in
oranges and yellows and greens on the walls of her hut; perhaps she
sang — in a voice like Roberta Flack's — *sweetly* over the compounds
of her village; perhaps she wove the most stunning mats or told the
most ingenious stories of all the village storytellers. Perhaps she was
herself a poet — though only her daughter's name is signed to the
poems that we know.

Perhaps Phillis Wheatley's mother was also an artist.   50

Perhaps in more than Phillis Wheatley's biological life is her   51
mother's signature made clear.

RESPONDING TO THE TEXT

Walker finds art in a quilt and a garden. Where have you encountered examples of artistic expression in unusual forms or in everyday places? Describe one or two. What do they suggest to you about the nature and motivation of their creators?

ENGAGING THE WRITER'S SUBJECT

1. Why does Walker open her essay with a quote from Jean Toomer? What surprising discovery did he make many years ago about black women in America? Where did his understanding of them fall short?

2. Who was Phillis Wheatley? Why might modern blacks consider her a "traitor"? What is Walker's opinion of her? What does she exemplify?

3. Walker gives two examples of her mother's artistry. What are these examples? What is the impact of each upon Walker herself?

ANALYZING THE WRITER'S CRAFT

1. Near the end of the essay, Walker includes a poem of her own, written in tribute to her mother and other black women of her mother's generation. Why is it appropriate here? What central idea does it support and exemplify? How does mixing two forms, prose and poetry, emphasize her main point?

2. Paragraph 11 uses a rhetorical question to introduce a turning point in the essay: "What did it mean for a black woman to be an artist in our grandmothers' time?" (Glossary: *Rhetorical Question*) What shift of emphasis does this question bring about? Although Walker says the answer is "cruel enough to stop the blood," she does not state it directly. In your own words, what is the answer?

3. Examples and illustrations have a purpose; usually they support an argument. (Glossary: *Argument*) Walker uses different types of examples throughout this essay. Find and identify several different kinds of examples. What idea or argument does each support?

4. Walker tells of her mother's natural gift for narrative. (Glossary: *Narration*) The only brief examples of narrative in this essay occur when Walker tells about her mother. Find these examples, and explain why they are effective in their context.

5. Walker quotes Virginia Woolf, a white author, to support her vision of the suppressed female artist, but she also draws a contrast between Woolf's ancestors and her own. (Glossary: *Comparison and Contrast*) How does she make the contrast explicit? Why does Walker use Woolf as an example?

UNDERSTANDING THE WRITER'S LANGUAGE

1. In paragraph 44, what does Walker imply when she describes her mother as "radiant, almost to the point of being invisible"? What is the metaphor in this paragraph, and how does it relate to the earlier description of black women as "Saints"? Through these metaphors, what is Walker trying to express about the process of art? (Glossary: *Figures of Speech*)

2. What does Walker mean, in paragraph 34, when she says that "we should have looked high — and low" to find examples of the creative spirit? What kinds of places does she mean?

3. Walker, a poet, chooses words precisely. Be sure you know the meanings of these words as she uses them: *abstractions* (paragraph 2), *post-Reconstruction* (5), *revelation* (8), *depraved* (12), *precarious* (18), *doting* (21), *ambivalent* (26), *matriarchs* (27), *appellations* (27), *vibrant* (32).

WRITING SUGGESTIONS

1. Walker equates creative artistry with spirituality. Do you agree with the connection she makes? What does she mean by these two terms? How would you define them? What do you believe to be the wellspring of art? Write an essay in which you use numerous illustrations to define and exemplify the creative spirit. You might find it helpful to refer to your Preparing to Read and Responding to the Text entries.

2. Why are there so few women among the best-known writers in Western culture? Walker cites the work of Virginia Woolf and Zora Hurston, one white woman and one black, who wrote their landmark works early in the twentieth century. Read either *A Room of One's Own* by Woolf or *Dust Tracks on a Road* by Hurston. Write an essay to discuss how the work you chose exemplifies the limits society laid on its author and the ways in which she overcame or sought to overcome those limits.

3. Interview a female artist (author, painter, singer, quilt maker, etc.) within your community. Before you conduct your interview, you might want to check your library, local newspapers, or the Internet to find out what some female artists have to say about their lives. What were the advantages and limitations the artist experienced as an artist because of her gender? What does she believe to be the wellspring of the creative spirit? What role, if any, did her mother, grandmother, or other female relative play in her choice and pursuit of art? Write an essay profiling this artist.

- To begin your research online, go to **bedfordstmartins.com /subjectsstrategies** and click on "Exemplification" or browse the thematic directory of annotated links.

WRITING SUGGESTIONS FOR EXEMPLIFICATION

1. Write an essay on one of the following statements, using examples to illustrate your ideas. You should be able to draw some of your examples from personal experience and firsthand observations.

   a. Fads never go out of style.
   b. Television has produced a number of "classic" programs.
   c. Every college campus has its own unique slang terms.
   d. Making excuses sometimes seems like a national pastime.
   e. A liberal arts education can have many practical applications.
   f. All good teachers (*or* doctors, secretaries, auto mechanics, sales representatives) have certain traits in common.
   g. Television talk shows are an accurate (*or* inaccurate) reflection of our society.
   h. Good literature always teaches us something about our humanity.
   i. Grades are not always a good indication of what has been learned.
   j. Recycling starts with the individual.

2. Write an essay on one of the following statements, using examples to illustrate your ideas. Draw your examples from a variety of sources: your library's print and Internet resources, interviews, and information gathered from lectures and the media. As you plan your essay, consider whether you will want to use a series of short examples or one or more extended examples.

   a. Much has been (*or* should still be) done to eliminate barriers for the physically handicapped.
   b. Nature's oddities are numerous.
   c. Throughout history, dire predictions have been made about the end of the world.
   d. Boxing should be outlawed.
   e. The past predictions of science fiction are today's realities.
   f. The world has not seen an absence of warfare since World War II.
   g. Young executives have developed many innovative management strategies.
   h. A great work of art may come out of an artist's most difficult period.
   i. The misjudgments of our presidents can be useful lessons in leadership.
   j. Genius is 10 percent talent and 90 percent hard work.
   k. Drugs have taken an economic toll on American business.
   l. Democracy has attracted renewed interest in countries outside of the United States.

3. College students are not often given credit for the community volunteer work they do. Write a letter to the editor of your local newspaper in which you demonstrate, with several extended examples, the beneficial impact that you and your fellow students have had on the community.

4. How do advertisers portray older people in their advertisements? Based on your analysis of some real ads, how fair are advertisers to senior citizens? What tactics do advertisers use to sell their products to senior citizens? Write an essay in which you use actual ads to illustrate two or three such tactics.

5. Most students would agree that in order to be happy and "well ad-justed," people need to learn how to relieve stress and to relax. What strategies do you and your friends use to relax? What have been the benefits of these relaxation techniques for you? Write an article for the school newspaper in which you give examples of several of these tech-niques and encourage your fellow students to try them.

6. The Internet has profoundly altered the way people around the world communicate and share information. One area in which significant change is especially evident is education. While having so much infor-mation at your fingertips can be exciting, such technology is not with-out its problems. What are the advantages and disadvantages of the Internet for teachers and students? Write an essay in which you analyze the Internet's educational value. Document your assessment with spe-cific examples.

7. Some people think it's important to look their best and, therefore, give careful attention to the clothing they wear. Others do not seem to care. How much stock do you put in the old saying, "Clothes make the per-son"? Use examples of the people on your own campus or in your com-munity to argue your position.

CHAPTER 4

Description

WHAT IS DESCRIPTION?

Description is conveying, through words, the perceptions of our five senses. We see, hear, smell, taste, and feel; and through description we try to re-create those sensations to share them with others. Some sensations are so basic that they almost precede thought: the color and dazzle of fireworks, the crunch of snow underfoot, the savory aroma of fried onion rings, the tartness of lemonade, the soothing coolness of aloe vera on sunburned skin, the pleasant tiredness of leg muscles after a brisk run. Other perceptions appeal more directly to the mind, like the intricate architecture of a spider web or the multilayered sounds of a symphony. All are the province of description.

It is often said that to describe is to paint a verbal picture — of a thing, a place, a person — and the analogy is a helpful one. Both description and painting seek to transform fleeting perceptions into lasting images through the use of a foreign medium: words in the case of description, oils or watercolors in the case of a painting. Although the original perception may have taken place in a flash, both description and painting are created bit by bit, word by word, or brushstroke by brushstroke. Yet while we can view a painting in a single glance (though appreciation may take longer), we take in a description only piece by piece, or word by word, just as the writer created it. And of course, a picture is purely visual and textural, while a description may draw on all of our sense perceptions, evoking not just sight, but also sound, texture, taste, and smell.

Consider, for example, the following description by Bernd Heinrich from his book *One Man's Owl* (1987). In this selection, Heinrich describes trekking through the woods in search of owls. First, allow the words of his description to build up a concrete mental image. Try to experience in your mind what Heinrich experienced firsthand; try to see, hear, smell, and feel what his words suggest. Form the jigsaw puzzle of words and details into a complete experience. Once you've built this mental image, define the dominant impression Heinrich creates.

Writer sets the scene with description of the landscape.

By mid-March in Vermont, the snow from the winter storms has already become crusty as the first midday thaws refreeze during the cold nights. A solid white cap compacts the snow, and you can walk on it without breaking through to your waist. The maple sap is starting to run on warm days, and one's blood quickens.

Writer describes the sights and sounds of the birds in early spring.

Spring is just around the corner, and the birds act as if they know. The hairy and downy woodpeckers drum on dry branches and on the loose flakes of maple bark, and purple finches sing merrily from the spruces. This year the reedy voices of the pine siskins can be heard everywhere on the ridge where the hemlocks grow, as can the chickadees' two-note, plaintive song. Down in the bog, the first red-winged blackbirds have just returned, and they can be heard yodeling from the tops of dry cattails. Flocks of rusty blackbirds fly over in long skeins, heading north.

Writer reveals his position and relies on auditory details as night approaches.

From where I stand at the edge of the woods overlooking Shelburne Bog, I feel a slight breeze and hear a moaning gust sweeping through the forest behind me. It is getting dark. There are eery creaking and scraping noises. Inside the pine forest it is becoming black, pitch black. The songbirds are silent. Only the sound of the wind can be heard above the distant honks of Canada geese flying below the now starry skies. Suddenly I hear a booming hollow "hoo-hoo-*hoo*-hoo—." The deep resonating hoot can send a chill down any spine, as indeed it has done to peoples of many cultures. But I know what the sound is, and it gives me great pleasure.

Heinrich could have described the scene with far fewer words, but that description would likely not have conveyed his dominant impression — one of comfort with the natural surroundings. Heinrich reads the landscape with subtle insight; he knows all the different birds and understands their springtime habits. The reader can imagine the smile on Heinrich's face when he hears the call of the owl.

WHY DO WRITERS USE DESCRIPTION?

Writers often use description to inform — to provide readers with specific data. You may need to describe the results of a chemical reaction for a lab report; the style of a Renaissance painting for an art history term paper; the physical capabilities and limitations of a stroke patient for a case study; or the acting of Halle Berry in a movie you want your friends to see. Such descriptions will sometimes be scientifically objective, sometimes intensely impressionistic. The approach you use will depend on the subject itself, the information you want to communicate about it, and the format in which the description appears.

Another important use of description is to create a mood or atmosphere or even to convey your own views — to develop a *dominant impression*. Edward Abbey captures the beauty and mystery of the twelve-mile-long Aravaipa Canyon in Arizona. Here is Abbey's description of part of the canyon:

> The walls bristle with spiky rock gardens of formidable desert vegetation. Most prominent is the giant saguaro cactus, growing five to fifty feet tall out of crevices in the stone you might think could barely lodge a flower. The barrel cactus, with its pink fishhook thorns, thrives here on the sunny side; and clusters of hedgehog cactus, and prickly pear with names like clockface and cows-tongue, have wedged roots into the rock. Since most of the wall is vertical, parallel to gravity, these plants grow first outward then upward, forming right-angled bends near the base. It looks difficult but they do it. They like it here.

Each of the descriptions in this chapter, whether informative, entertaining, or both is distinguished by the strong dominant impression the writer creates.

There are essentially two types of description: objective and subjective. *Objective description* is as factual as possible, emphasizing the actual qualities of the subject being described while subordinating the writer's personal responses. For example, a holdup witness would try to give authorities a precise, objective description of the assailant, unaffected by emotional responses, so that positive identification could be made and an innocent person would not be arrested by mistake. In the excerpt from his book, Bernd Heinrich objectively describes what he sees: "The hairy and downy woodpeckers drum on dry branches and on the loose flakes of maple bark, and purple finches sing merrily from the spruces." *Subjective* or *impressionistic description*, on the other hand, conveys the writer's personal opinion or impression of the object, often in language rich in modifiers and figures of speech. A food critic describing a memorable meal would inevitably write about it impressionistically, using colorful or highly subjective language; in fact, relatively few words in English can describe the subtleties of smell and taste in neutral terms. In "Aravaipa Canyon," Edward Abbey uses subjective description to capture the subtle beauty that he witnesses when walking through a desert canyon in America's Southwest. Notice that with objective description, it is usually the person, place, or thing being described that stands out, whereas with subjective description the response of the person doing the describing is the most prominent feature. Most subjects, however, lend themselves to both objective and subjective description, depending on the writer's purpose. You could write, for example, that you had "exactly four weeks" to finish a history term paper (objective) or that you had "all the time in the world" or "an outrageously short amount of time" (subjective). Each type of description can be accurate and useful in its own way.

Although descriptive writing can stand alone, and often does, it is also used with other types of writing. In a narrative, for example, descriptions provide the context for the story — and make the characters, settings, and events come alive. Description may also help to define an unusual object or thing, such as a giraffe, or to clarify the steps of a process, such as diagnosing an illness. Wherever it is used, good description creates vivid and specific pictures that clarify, create a mood, build a dominant impression, inform, and entertain.

AN ANNOTATED STUDENT ESSAY USING DESCRIPTION

James Blake Wilson wrote the following essay while he was a student at the University of California–Riverside. Drawing details from his teenage memories of Crenshaw Boulevard in South Central Los Angeles, where he grew up, Wilson gives an insightful view of an infamous place — a place that has gotten much media attention, mostly negative and sensational. His observations offer readers a picture of the region that they won't see on the eleven o'clock news or on the front page of the *Los Angeles Times*.

The "Shaw"

James Blake Wilson

Ah yes, my home. It feels good to be   1

*Writer sets context —
Sunday afternoon walk down Crenshaw Boulevard in South Central Los Angeles.*

back. It's just another Sunday afternoon in the beautiful city of Los Angeles. As I walk down the street I see all the little things that make me remember all of the good times I have had out here on this street, and all the bad things that I wish I could put in the back of my memory. I'm standing on the corner of Slauson Avenue and Crenshaw Boulevard, the center of liveliness here on the "Shaw." As I stand here and close my eyes, I can hear many different noises and sounds that would convince anyone that they were in the big city. I hear the diesel exhaust of the "108" metro bus line throttle up to take its passengers up and down Crenshaw every twenty minutes. I hear the mingling of car horns honking from impatient drivers trying to get from point A to point B in a matter of minutes, squeaking wheels of a homeless man's shopping cart that he uses to collect cans. These cans, which to me conveniently hold soda, are a source of income for him. It's amazing to see that what one man takes for granted, another man may cherish.

I open my eyes and see street vendors of all shapes and sizes. I see little children trying to sell ten dollar cutlery sets to every motorist that stops at a street light, and grown adults selling the latest in scandal fashion. With clothes bearing slogans such as "Let the Juice Loose" or "Free O.J.," you can't help but think that people will try to make money off of anything these days. Alongside the street vendors, you can see members of The Nation of Islam, dressed in their single breasted suits with afrocentric bowties, selling bean pies for five dollars and copies of the <u>Final Call</u> for fifty cents. I walk up the street and see Willie on the corner of Crenshaw and 54th Street. It is here that Willie waits for his bus with a Walkman and his hyperactive body which dances, slides, and gyrates to the music that he hears in his own world. People watch and laugh at the zany actions of a man we call crazy. But who are we to call someone crazy?

Writer focuses on details of sound.

Writer selects details to highlight both sights and sounds.

Writer's description portrays a sense of movement.

2

Well-selected details of the "Wall of Fame"

Writer uses description to depict emotion.

I look up the block and see the paint 3
on the Crenshaw "Wall of Fame" fading from
the sun. This wall symbolizes those in the
Black community who have struggled, fought,
and sometimes died for the Black race in
America. With portraits of Martin Luther
King Jr., Malcolm X, Louis Farrakhan, Frederick Douglass, and many others, this wall
is highly respected and remains untouched by
graffiti and vandalism all year round. Of
course with every pro, there's a con. It
only takes a glimpse down the street to see
gang colors on the white walls of a neighborhood liquor store. It's heartbreaking to
know that hundreds of kids, male and female,
mark up, fight and die over territory that
isn't even theirs. I wonder what these kids
could accomplish if their efforts were taken
away from gang violence and put into something more productive. Maybe their efforts
could go towards cleaning up the infamous
Leimert Park, a home to many homeless people. The park is a truly diverse landmark,
where one day you might see an organized
marketplace of vendors selling clothing and
food, and the next day the sirens and lights
of police cars at the scene of a drug deal
gone bad.

As the sun goes down, and the moon il- 4
luminates the dark gray, almost black, asphalt of the street, Crenshaw Boulevard
turns into the "Shaw." It all starts with
the first sonic thumps of bass extending
from the oversized speakers of a car stereo.

"The name of the game is . . . Boom- 5
Boom."

I hear the two thundering thumps muffle 6
out the lyrics and hit me in my chest. Ten-,
twelve-, or fifteen-inch diameter speakers
can be commonly found in the trunks of these
attention hungry motorists. Out here there's

no telling what kind of car you'll see: anything from a new Lexus to a fully restored
1964 Chevrolet Impala with hydraulic lifts
on every wheel and axle. I've seen a lot of
things on this street, some good, some bad.
But no matter how hard I try, I can never
repress my inner feeling that this is my
home.

Analyzing James Blake Wilson's Essay of Description: Questions for Discussion

1. What senses does Wilson call on to describe the "Shaw"?
2. Why is it significant that no graffiti mar the "Wall of Fame"? What does much of the graffiti elsewhere symbolize to Wilson?
3. Why is the "Shaw" a paradoxical place for Wilson? How does his description serve to strengthen his conflicted emotions about the place?

SUGGESTIONS FOR WRITING A DESCRIPTIVE ESSAY

Determine a Purpose

Begin by determining your purpose: Are you trying to inform, express your emotions, or persuade? While it is not necessary, or even desirable, to state your purpose explicitly, it is necessary that you have one that your readers recognize. If your readers do not see a purpose in your writing they may be tempted to respond by asking, "So what?" Making your reason for writing clear in the first place will help you avoid this pitfall.

Focus the Subject of Your Description

Next, fix the subject of your description firmly in your mind. If it's an inanimate object, get it and keep it handy as you work on your essay; if it's a place, go there and spend some time taking in the sights, sounds, and smells; if it's a person, dig out old photographs and let-ters, or go visit. Observe, observe, observe, and make notes of your sensory impressions: not just what you can see, but also what you hear, smell, taste, touch, and feel. If you must work from memory — if, for example, you are describing your great-grandmother — try to "observe" with your mind's eye, to conjure up the half-forgotten face, the quirky way of talking, the special walk. If you must rely on others' writing (to describe Pompeii before the eruption of Mount Vesuvius, for example), try to imagine a picture of your own from the pieces you find in your sources. Without vivid perceptions of your own to work from, you can hardly create a detailed, accurate description. The way you develop your perceptions will depend, first, on your purpose for writing the description.

Use Description in the Service of an Idea

Your readers will appreciate your description of an object, event, person, or experience, but what they really want to know is why you chose to describe what you did. You would not describe a person, a horse, or a canoe trip and let it go at that because you write description with a thesis in mind, an idea you want to convey to your readers. For example, you would describe the canoe trip as one of both serenity and exhilarating danger, which you came to realize symbolizes the contrasting aspects of nature. When Steve Martin describes his father he wants us to get to know him so that we can figure out along with Martin why his father was the way he was and learn of the jealousy and envy, and yet pride, he had for his son's accomplishments. Without such a description it would be hard to show the difficulties Martin had communicating with his father and how meaningful Martin's efforts at reaching out were before his father's death. It is his use of description in the service of an idea that makes his description so effective and rewarding for us as readers.

Collect Sensory Details about Your Subject

Writing a description requires that you gather a great many details about your subject — more, in fact, than you are likely to use. Like a reporter at the scene of an accident, you will take notes about what you see and hear directly, but you may also need to list details that you remember or that you have learned from other sources.

When collecting descriptive details, it's easy to forget to use *all* your senses. Sight is so important that we tend to pay attention only to what we can see, and inexperienced writers often rely almost completely on visual detail. While observing an emergency room, for example, you would by all means take notes about the medical equipment, the blank white walls, the unnaturally brilliant lighting, and the efficient movements of the medical staff. But don't stop there. Keep your ears open for the hiss of trolley tires on linoleum and the odd, mechanical noises that interrupt the emergency room hush; sniff the hospital smells; touch the starched sheets on the stretchers and the cold stainless steel that seems to be everywhere. Your observations, and the notes you make about them, will give you the details you need when you write your description.

Select Descriptive Details with Your Purpose in Mind

Why you are writing will influence the kinds of descriptive details you use and the way you use them. In describing the emergency room, if your purpose is mainly to entertain, then you might want to create an atmosphere of intricate technology, as in a mad scientist's laboratory, or of controlled chaos, as in the operating room on *ER*. If your chief purpose is to inform your readers, however, you will use a more objective approach, relying on factual descriptions of individual staff members and pieces of emergency equipment, as well as explaining the functions of each.

Identify Your Audience

Whom do you expect to read your essay? What do they know already, and what do they want to learn from you? If you are describing the hospital emergency room for an audience of medical professionals, you will only need to mention a nuclear magnetic resonance scanner for them to know what it looks like and what it does. A less specialized audience, however, will appreciate a more detailed description. In addition, the general audience will be more receptive to impressionistic description and to details like the color of the staff's uniforms and the strong antiseptic smell; professional readers will consider such things obvious or irrelevant.

Create a Dominant Impression

From the catalog of details that you have collected, select those that will be most helpful in developing a dominant impression. Suppose that you wish to depict the hospital emergency room as a place of great tension. You will then naturally choose details to reinforce that sense of tension: the worried looks on the faces of a couple sitting in the corner, the quick movements of the medical staff as they tend a patient on a wheeled stretcher, the urgent whisperings of two interns out in the hallway, the incessant paging of Dr. Thomas. If the dominant impression you want to create is of the emergency room's sterility, however, you will choose different details: the smell of disinfectant, the spotless white uniforms of the staff members, the stainless steel tables and chairs, the gleaming instruments the nurse hands to the physician. Building a convincing dominant impression depends on the selection of such details.

Of course, it is equally important to omit any details that conflict with the dominant impression. Perhaps there was an orderly lounging in a corner, chewing gum and reading a magazine, who did not feel the tension of the emergency room; perhaps the room's sterility was marred by several used Styrofoam coffee cups left on a corner table. Deciding which details to include and which to exclude is up to you.

Organize Your Details to Create a Vivid Picture

A photographer can capture a large, complicated scene with the press of a button. The writer has to put descriptive details down on paper one at a time. It's not enough to decide which details to include and which to leave out; you also need to arrange your chosen details in a particular order, one that serves your purpose and is easy for the reader to follow.

Imagine what the reader would experience first. A description of an emergency room could begin at the entrance, move through the waiting area, pass the registration desk, and proceed into the treatment cubicles. A description of a restaurant kitchen might conjure up the smells and sounds that escape through the swinging doors even before moving on to the first glimpse inside the kitchen.

Other patterns of organization include moving from general to specific, from smallest to largest, from least to most important, or from the usual to the unusual. Keep in mind that the last details you present will probably stay in the reader's mind the longest and that the first details will also have special force. Those in the middle of your description, though they will have their effect, may not have the same impact as those before and after them.

Before you begin your first draft, you may find it useful to sketch out an outline of your description. Here's a sample outline for Bernd Heinrich's description earlier in this introduction:

Description of Shelburne Bog

Dominant impression: Comfort with the natural surroundings

Paragraph 1: Snow-crusted landscape in mid-March

Paragraph 2: Activity and sounds of the birds (e.g., woodpeckers, finches, chickadees, and red-winged blackbirds) described from the edge of the woods

Paragraph 3: Activity and sounds inside the pine forest behind the speaker, culminating with the call of the familiar owl

Such an outline can remind you of the dominant impression you want to create and can suggest which specific details may be most useful to you.

Show, Don't Tell: Use Specific Strong Nouns and Verbs

Inexperienced writers often believe that adjectives and adverbs are the basis for effective descriptions. They're right in one sense, but not wholly so. Although strong adjectives and adverbs are crucial, description also depends on well-chosen nouns and verbs. *Vehicle* is not nearly as descriptive as something more specific — *Jeep, snowmobile,* or *Honda Civic.* Why write *see* when what you mean is *glance, stare, spy, gaze, peek, examine,* or *witness*? The more specific and strong you make your nouns and verbs, the more lively and interesting your descriptions will be.

When you have difficulty thinking of strong, specific nouns and verbs to use, reach for a thesaurus — but only if you are sure you can discern the best word for your purpose. Inexpensive paperback editions are available at any bookstore, and most word-processing programs have a thesaurus utility. A thesaurus will help you keep your descriptions from getting repetitive and will be invaluable when you need to find a specific word with just the right meaning.

Editing Tip: Figurative Language

Be sure to follow the guidelines and advice for editing an essay given in Chapter 2: "Writing Essays." The guidelines highlight those sentence-level concerns of style — grammar, mechanics, and punctuation — that are especially important in editing any piece of writing. While editing your essay of description, look for opportunities to both enliven and clarify your description through the use of figurative language — similes, metaphors, and personification.

With figurative language we speak and write imaginatively rather than in a literal or strict sense. Often we associate figurative language with poetry, but it can be just as effective in prose. Figurative language enriches our writing. It allows us to create images out of our thoughts and emotions and to share them with our readers so that they, too, can experience our excitement.

A *simile* is an explicit comparison between two essentially different ideas or objects using *like* or *as* to link them. After the speaker in

Cherokee Paul McDonald's "A View from the Bridge" retrieves the fish that the young boy catches, the boy says, "Hey, mister, tell me what he looks like." The speaker goes on to describe the fish. Instead of saying, "He has all these big scales all over his body," he says, "He has all these big *scales, like armor* all over his body." Here's another example:

PLAIN   The water in this pool has a dark clarity, transparent but obscure.

DESCRIPTIVE   "The water in this pool has a dark clarity, *like smoked glass,* transparent but obscure."

—EDWARD ABBEY
"Aravaipa Canyon," Page 126

A *metaphor,* on the other hand, makes an implicit comparison between dissimilar ideas or things without using *like* or *as.*

PLAIN   Feeling the tree for better understanding, I hear a clatter of loose stones, look up, and see six, seven, eight bighorn sheep perched on the rimrock a hundred feet above us. Three rams, five ewes. They are eating brittlebush, desert holly, bursage, and jojoba — aware of us but not alarmed.

DESCRIPTIVE   "Feeling the tree for better understanding, I hear a clatter of loose stones, look up, and see six, seven, eight bighorn sheep perched on the rimrock a hundred feet above us. Three rams, five ewes. They are *browsing at the local salad bar* — brittlebush, desert holly, bursage, and jojoba — aware of us but not alarmed."

—EDWARD ABBEY
"Aravaipa Canyon," Page 127

The addition of the metaphor, while seemingly a small change, makes a big difference in Abbey's description. It is clear that Abbey has an image in mind that he wants to get across, the image of the sheep acting like people at a salad bar, excited about the array of tasty choices available to them and satisfying their desires.

In order to take full advantage of the richness of a particular comparison, writers sometimes use several sentences or even a whole paragraph to develop a metaphor. Such a comparison is called an *extended metaphor.*

The point is that you have to strip down your writing before you can build it back up. You must know what the essential tools are and what job they were designed to do. If I may belabor the metaphor on carpentry, it is first necessary to saw wood neatly and drive nails. Later you can bevel the edges or add elegant finials, if that is your taste. But you can never forget that you are practicing a craft that is based on certain principles. If the nails are weak, your house will collapse. If your verbs are weak and your syntax is rickety, your sentences will fall apart.

—WILLIAM ZINSSER
On Writing Well

A word of caution about using extended metaphors is necessary because they can easily become overdone and tedious. Zinsser himself hints at this potential problem in his begging our indulgence as he extends his metaphor a bit further than his first two sentences. So for the most part, keep your metaphors simple unless the added clarity is worth going the extra distance.

Mixed metaphors are figures of speech that contain two metaphors that do not go together logically. Be sure that all metaphors, simple or extended, are consistent.

MIXED   We were sailing along smoothly until we hit a roadblock.

CONSISTENT   We were *sailing* along smoothly until we hit *rough seas*.

In *personification* the writer attributes human qualities to animals, inanimate objects, or ideas.

Blond October comes striding over the hills wearing a crimson shirt and faded green trousers.

—HAL BORLAND

"Back now beyond the tracks, *the train creeks and groans, the cars jostle each other down the tracks, and the light begins its pulsing, the barrio, with all its meanings, greets a new dawn with yawns and restless stretchings.*"

—ROBERT RAMÍREZ
"The Barrio"

In each of the preceding examples, the writer more vividly communicates an idea or the presence of an object by comparing it to something familiar and concrete. In all cases, too, the figurative language grows out of the writer's thinking, reflecting the way he or she sees the material.

▶ *Questions for Revising and Editing: Description*

1. Do I have a clear purpose for my description? Have I answered the "so what" question?
2. Is the subject of my description interesting and relevant to my audience?
3. What senses have I chosen to use to describe it? For example, what does it look like, sound like, or smell like? Does it have a texture or taste that is important to mention?
4. Which details must I include in my essay? Which are irrelevant or distracting to my purpose and should be discarded?
5. Have I achieved the dominant impression I wish to leave with my audience?
6. Does the organization I have chosen for my essay make it easy for the reader to follow my description?
7. How carefully have I chosen my descriptive words? Are my nouns and verbs strong and specific?
8. Have I used figurative language, if appropriate, to further strengthen my description?

A View from the Bridge

Cherokee Paul McDonald

A fiction writer and journalist, Cherokee Paul McDonald was raised and schooled in Fort Lauderdale, Florida. In 1970, he returned home from a tour of duty in Vietnam and joined the Fort Lauderdale Police Department, where he remained until 1980, resigning with the rank of sergeant. During this time, McDonald received a degree in criminal science from Broward Community College. He left the police department to become a writer and worked a number of odd jobs before publishing his first book, The Patch, *in 1986. McDonald has said that almost all of his writing comes from his police work, and his common themes of justice, balance, and fairness reflect his life as part of the "thin blue line" (the police department). In 1991, he published* Blue Truth, *a memoir. His first novel,* Summer's Reason, *was released in 1994. His most recent book is a memoir of his three years as an artillery forward observer in Vietnam,* Into the Green: A Reconaissance by Fire *(2001).*

"A View from the Bridge" was originally published in Sunshine *magazine in 1990. The essay shows McDonald's usual expert handling of fish and fishermen, both in and out of water, and reminds us that things are not always as they seem.*

PREPARING TO READ

There's an old saying that "familiarity breeds contempt." We've all had the experience of becoming numb to sights or experiences that once struck us with wonderment; but sometimes, with luck, something happens to renew our appreciation. Think of an example from your own experience. What are some ways we can retain or recover our appreciation of the remarkable things we have come to take for granted?

I was coming up on the little bridge in the Rio Vista neighborhood of Fort Lauderdale, deepening my stride and my breathing to negotiate the slight incline without altering my pace. And then, as I neared the crest, I saw the kid.

He was a lumpy little guy with baggy shorts, a faded T-shirt and heavy sweat socks falling down over old sneakers.

Partially covering his shaggy blond hair was one of those blue baseball caps with gold braid on the bill and a sailfish patch sewn onto the peak. Covering his eyes and part of his face was a pair of those stupid-looking '50s-style wrap-around sunglasses.

He was fumbling with a beat-up rod and reel, and he had a little bait bucket by his feet. I puffed on by, glancing down into the empty bucket as I passed.

"Hey, mister! Would you help me, please?"   5

The shrill voice penetrated my jogger's concentration, and I was   6
determined to ignore it. But for some reason, I stopped.

With my hands on my hips and the sweat dripping from my nose   7
I asked, "What do you want, kid?"

"Would you please help me find my shrimp? It's my last one and   8
I've been getting bites and I know I can catch a fish if I can just find
that shrimp. He jumped outta my hand as I was getting him from the
bucket."

Exasperated, I walked slowly back to the kid, and pointed.   9

"There's the damn shrimp by your left foot. You stopped me for   10
that?"

As I said it, the kid reached down and trapped the shrimp.   11

"Thanks a lot, mister," he said.   12

I watched as the kid dropped the baited hook down into the   13
canal. Then I turned to start back down the bridge.

That's when the kid let out a "Hey! Hey!" and the prettiest tarpon   14
I'd ever seen came almost six feet out of the water, twisting and turning as he fell through the air.

"I got one!" the kid yelled as the fish hit the water with a loud   15
splash and took off down the canal.

I watched the line being burned off the reel at an alarming rate.   16
The kid's left hand held the crank while the extended fingers felt for
the drag setting.

"No, kid!" I shouted. "Leave the drag alone . . . just keep that   17
damn rod tip up!"

Then I glanced at the reel and saw there were just a few loops of   18
line left on the spool.

"Why don't you get yourself some decent equipment?" I said, but   19
before the kid could answer I saw the line go slack.

"Ohhh, I lost him," the kid said. I saw the flash of silver as the fish   20
turned.

"Crank, kid, crank! You didn't lose him. He's coming back toward   21
you. Bring in the slack!"

The kid cranked like mad, and a beautiful grin spread across his face.   22

"He's heading in for the pilings," I said. "Keep him out of those   23
pilings!"

The kid played it perfectly. When the fish made its play for the   24
pilings, he kept just enough pressure on to force the fish out. When
the water exploded and the silver missile hurled into the air, the kid
kept the rod tip up and the line tight.

As the fish came to the surface and began a slow circle in the mid-   25
dle of the canal, I said, "Whooee, is that a nice fish or what?"

The kid didn't say anything, so I said, "Okay, move to the edge of   26
the bridge and I'll climb down to the seawall and pull him out."

When I reached the seawall I pulled in the leader, leaving the fish 27
lying on its side in the water.

"How's that?" I said. 28

"Hey, mister, tell me what it looks like." 29

"Look down here and check him out," I said, "He's beautiful." 30

But then I looked up into those stupid-looking sunglasses and it 31
hit me. The kid was blind.

"Could you tell me what he looks like, mister?" he said again. 32

"Well, he's just under three, uh, he's about as long as one of 33
your arms," I said. "I'd guess he goes about 15, 20 pounds. He's
mostly silver, but the silver is somehow made up of *all* the colors, if
you know what I mean." I stopped. "Do you know what I mean by
colors?"

The kid nodded. 34

"Okay. He has all these big scales, like armor all over his body. 35
They're silver too, and when he moves they sparkle. He has a
strong body and a large powerful tail. He has big round eyes, bigger
than a quarter, and a lower jaw that sticks out past the upper one
and is very tough. His belly is almost white and his back is a
gunmetal gray. When he jumped he came out of the water about
six feet, and his scales caught the sun and flashed it all over the
place."

By now the fish had righted itself, and I could see the bright-red 36
gills as the gill plates opened and closed. I explained this to the kid,
and then said, more to myself, "He's a beauty."

"Can you get him off the hook?" the kid asked. "I don't want to 37
kill him."

I watched as the tarpon began to slowly swim away, tired but still 38
alive.

By the time I got back up to the top of the bridge the kid had his 39
line secured and his bait bucket in one hand.

He grinned and said, "Just in time. My mom drops me off here, 40
and she'll be back to pick me up any minute."

He used the back of one hand to wipe his nose. 41

"Thanks for helping me catch that tarpon," he said, "and for help- 42
ing me to see it."

I looked at him, shook my head, and said, "No, my friend, thank 43
you for letting *me* see that fish."

I took off, but before I got far the kid yelled again. 44

"Hey, mister!" 45

I stopped. 46

"Someday I'm gonna catch a sailfish and a blue marlin and a giant 47
tuna and *all* those big sportfish!"

As I looked into those sunglasses I knew he probably would. I 48
wished I could be there when it happened.

RESPONDING TO THE TEXT

The jogger and the kid are very different from each other, but they share a passionate interest in fishing. What role does the tarpon play in this story? What can a shared interest do for a relationship between two people?

ENGAGING THE WRITER'S SUBJECT

1. What clues lead up to the revelation that the kid is blind? Why does it take the narrator so long to realize it?

2. "Why don't you get yourself some decent equipment?" the narrator asks the kid (paragraph 19). Why does McDonald include this question? Speculate about the answer.

3. Near the end of the story, why does the narrator say to the kid, "No, my friend, thank you for letting *me* see that fish" (paragraph 43)?

ANALYZING THE WRITER'S CRAFT

1. Notice the way the narrator chooses and actually adjusts some of the words he uses to describe the fish to the kid. Why does he do this? What is McDonald's desired effect?

2. By the end of the essay, we know much more about the kid than the fact that he is blind, but, after the initial description, McDonald characterizes him only indirectly. As the essay unfolds, what do we learn about the kid, and by what techniques does the author convey this knowledge?

3. Reread the description of the kid (paragraphs 2 and 3). Which details gain significance as events unfold over the course of the essay?

4. This essay, descriptive in theme and intent, is structured as a narrative. (Glossary: *Narration*) What makes the combination of story and description effective? Suppose McDonald had started his essay with a statement like this: "If you really want to see something clearly, try describing it to a blind child." How would such an opening change the impact of the piece? Which other rhetorical strategies might McDonald have used along with the new opening?

UNDERSTANDING THE WRITER'S LANGUAGE

1. What is the metaphor in paragraph 24? Why is it apt? How does this metaphor enhance McDonald's description? (Glossary: *Figures of Speech*)

2. What is the connotation of the word *view* in the title? Of the word *bridge?* (Glossary: *Connotation/Denotation*)

3. You may be unfamiliar with some of the fishing-related vocabulary in this essay. What sort of fish is a tarpon? In the context of fishing, define *drag* (paragraph 16), *pilings* (23), *seawall* (26), *leader* (27).

WRITING SUGGESTIONS

1. Divide the class into groups of three or four. In your group, take turns describing some specific beautiful or remarkable thing to the others as if they were blind. You may actually want to bring an object to observe while your classmates cover their eyes. Help each other find the best words to create a vivid verbal picture. Write your description in a couple of brief paragraphs, retaining the informal style of your speaking voice.

2. McDonald's "A View from the Bridge" and the *Calvin and Hobbes* cartoon reprinted below are just two "fish stories" in the long and rich tradition of that genre. In their own ways, both the essay and the cartoon play upon the ironic notion that fishing is a quiet sport but one in which participants come to expect the unexpected. For the narrator in McDonald's story, there is a lesson in not merely looking but truly seeing. For Calvin, there is the story of "latchin' on to the big one." It is interesting that a sport in which "nothing happens" can be the source of so much storytelling. Write an essay in which you tell a "fish story" of your own, making sure that it reveals a larger, significant truth or life lesson. Try to incorporate the element of surprise.

3. There are many services available to visually impaired people. Working with a classmate, have one partner learn about the accommodations and services for visually impaired students at your college or university, while the other partner searches the community and the Internet to learn about resources and adaptive technology for the blind in your area. Share your findings, and write a report to present them.

• To being your research online, go to **bedfordstmartins.com /subjectsstrategies** and click on "Description" or browse the thematic directory of anotated links.

Aravaipa Canyon

Edward Abbey

Edward Abbey (1927–1989) wrote numerous novels, including two that were adapted for film: The Brave Cowboy *(1958), which was released as a film in 1962 under the title* Lonely Are the Brave, *and* Fire on the Mountain *(1962). He is best known, however, for his many volumes of nature writings. Variously called an ecologist, a naturalist, and an environmental activist, Abbey described himself simply as "one who loves the unfenced country." He had a particular love for the American Southwest, where he worked for many years as a ranger in the National Park Service. In his collections of nonfiction essays, including* Desert Solitaire *(1968),* The Journey Home *(1977), and* Abbey's Road *(1979), Abbey celebrated the Southwest and made a passionate case for the preservation of its natural wonders.*

"Aravaipa Canyon," first published in Down River *(1982), is a strong example of the rich descriptive prose in which he expressed his belief in the sacred power of the landscape.*

PREPARING TO READ

Recall a natural setting that you found particularly beautiful, impressive, or awe-inspiring. Describe this setting using rich and evocative details.

Southeast of Phoenix and northeast of Tucson, in the Pinal Mountains, is a short deep gorge called Aravaipa Canyon. It is among the few places in Arizona with a permanent stream of water and in popular estimation one of the most beautiful. I am giving away no secrets here: Aravaipa Canyon has long been well known to hikers, campers, horsemen, and hunters from the nearby cities. The federal Bureau of Land Management (BLM), charged with administration of the canyon, recently decreed it an official Primitive Area, thus guaranteeing its fame. Demand for enjoyment of the canyon is so great that the BLM has been obliged to institute a rationing program: no one camps here without a permit and only a limited number of such permits are issued. 1

Two friends and I took a walk into Aravaipa Canyon a few days ago. We walked because there is no road. There is hardly even a foot trail. Twelve miles long from end to end, the canyon is mostly occupied by the little river which gives it its name, and by stream banks piled with slabs of fallen rock from the cliffs above, the whole overgrown with cactus, trees, and riparian desert shrubbery. 2

Aravaipa is an Apache name (some say Pima, some say Papago) and the commonly accepted meaning is "laughing waters." The name 3 fits. The stream is brisk, clear, about a foot deep at normal flow levels, churning its way around boulders, rippling over gravelbars, plunging into pools with bright and noisy vivacity. Schools of loach minnow, roundtail chub, spike dace, and Gila mudsuckers — rare and endemic species — slip and slither past your ankles as you wade into the current. The water is too warm to support trout or other varieties of what are called game fish; the fish here live out their lives undisturbed by anything more than horses' hooves and the sneaker-shod feet of hikers. (PLEASE DO NOT MOLEST THE FISH.)

The Apaches who gave the name to this water and this canyon are   4
not around anymore. Most of that particular band — unarmed old men, women, children — huddled in a cave near the mouth of Aravaipa Canyon, were exterminated in the 1880s by a death squad of American pioneers, aided by Mexicans and Papagos, from the nearby city of Tucson. The reason for this vigilante action is obscure (suspicion of murder and cattle stealing) but the results were clear. No more Apaches in Aravaipa Canyon. During pauses in the gunfire, as the pioneers reloaded their rifles, the surviving Indians could have heard the sound of laughing waters. One hundred and twenty-five were killed, the remainder relocated in the White Mountain Reservation to the northeast. Since then those people have given us no back talk at all.

Trudging upstream and over rocky little beaches, we are no more   5
troubled by ancient history than are the mudsuckers in the pools. We prefer to enjoy the scenery. The stone walls stand up on both sides, twelve hundred feet high in the heart of the canyon. The rock is of volcanic origin, rosy-colored andesites and buff, golden, consolidated tuff. Cleavages and fractures across the face of the walls form perfect stairways and sometimes sloping ramps, slick as sidewalks. On the beaches lie obsidian boulders streaked with veins of quartzite and pegmatite.

The walls bristle with spiky rock gardens of formidable desert   6
vegetation. Most prominent is the giant saguaro cactus, growing five to fifty feet tall out of crevices in the stone you might think could barely lodge a flower. The barrel cactus, with its pink fishhook thorns, thrives here on the sunny side; and clusters of hedgehog cactus, and prickly pear with names like clockface and cows-tongue, have wedged roots into the rock. Since most of the wall is vertical, parallel to gravity, these plants grow first outward then upward, forming right-angled bends near the base. It looks difficult but they do it. They like it here.

Also present are tangles of buckhorn, staghorn, chainfruit, and   7
teddybear cholla; the teddybear cholla is a cactus so thick with spines it glistens under the sun as if covered with fur. From more comfortable niches in the rock grow plants like the sotol, a thing with sawtooth leaves and a flower stalk ten feet tall. The agave, a type of lily, is even bigger, and its leaves are long, rigid, pointed like bayonets. Near the

summit of the cliffs, where the moisture is insufficient to support cactus, we see gray-green streaks of lichen clinging to the stone like a mold.

The prospect at streamside is conventionally sylvan, restful to 8 desert-weary eyes. Great cottonwoods and sycamores shade the creek's stony shores; when we're not wading in water we're wading through a crashing autumn debris of green-gold cottonwood and dusty-red sycamore leaves. Other trees flourish here — willow, salt cedar, alder, desert hackberry, and a kind of wild walnut. Cracked with stones, the nuts yield a sweet but frugal meat. At the water's edge is a nearly continuous growth of peppery-flavored watercress. The stagnant pools are full of algae; and small pale frogs, treefrogs, and leopard frogs leap from the bank at our approach and dive into the water; they swim for the deeps with kicking legs, quick breaststrokes.

We pass shadowy, intriguing side canyons with names like 9 Painted Cave (ancient pictographs), Iceberg (where the sun seldom shines), and Virgus (named in honor of himself by an early settler in the area). At midday we enter a further side canyon, one called Horse-camp, and linger here for a lunch of bread, cheese, and water. We contemplate what appears to be a bottomless pool.

The water in this pool has a dark clarity, like smoked glass, trans- 10 parent but obscure. We see a waterlogged branch six feet down resting on a ledge but cannot see to the bottom. The water feels intensely cold to hand and foot; a few tadpoles have attached themselves to the stony rim of the pool just beneath the surface of the water. They are sluggish, barely animate. One waterbug, the kind called boatman, propels itself with limp oars down toward darkness when I extend my hand toward it.

Above the pool is a thirty-foot bluff of sheer, vesiculated, fine- 11 grained, monolithic gray rock with a glossy chute carved down its face. Flash floods, pouring down that chute with driving force, must have drilled this basin in the rock below. The process would require a generous allowance of time — ten thousand, twenty thousand years — give or take a few thousand. Only a trickle of water from a ring of seeps enters the pool now, on this hot still blazing day in December. Feels like 80°F; a month from now it may be freezing; in June 110°. In the silence I hear the rasping chant of locusts — that universal lament for mortality and time — here in this canyon where winter seldom comes.

The black and bottomless pool gleams in the shining rock — a sin- 12 ister paradox, to a fanciful mind. To any man of natural piety this pool, this place, this silence, would suggest reverence, even fear. But I'm an apostate Presbyterian from a long-ago Pennsylvania: I shuck my clothes, jump in, and touch bottom only ten feet down. Bedrock bottom, as I'd expected, and if any Grendels dwell in this inky pool they're not inclined to reveal themselves today.

We return to the Aravaipa. Halfway back to camp and the canyon 13
entrance we pause to inspect a sycamore that seems to be embracing a
boulder. The trunk of the tree has grown around the rock. Feeling the
tree for better understanding, I hear a clatter of loose stones, look up,
and see six, seven, eight bighorn sheep perched on the rimrock a hundred feet above us. Three rams, five ewes. They are browsing at the
local salad bar — brittlebush, desert holly, bursage, and jojoba —
aware of us but not alarmed. We watch them for a long time as they
move casually along the rim and up a talus slope beyond, eating as
they go, halting now and then to stare back at the humans staring up
at them.

Once, years before, I had glimpsed a mountain lion in this 14
canyon, following me through the twilight. It was the only mountain
lion I had ever seen, so far, in the wild. I stopped, the big cat stopped,
we peered at each other through the gloom. Mutual curiosity: I felt
more wonder than fear. After a minute, or perhaps it was five minutes,
I made a move to turn. The lion leaped up into the rocks and melted
away.

We see no mountain lions this evening. Nor any of the local 15
deer, either Sonoran whitetail or the desert mule deer, although the
little heart-shaped tracks of the former are apparent in the sand.
Javelina, or peccary, too, reside in this area; piglike animals with
tusks, oversized heads, and tapering bodies, they roam the slopes
and gulches in family bands (like the Apaches), living on roots, tu-
bers, and innards of barrel cactus, on grubs, insects, and carrion.
Omnivorous, like us, and equally playful, if not so dangerous. Any
desert canyon with permanent water, like Aravaipa, will be as full of
life as it is beautiful.

We stumble homeward over the stones and through the anklebone- 16
chilling water. The winter day seems alarmingly short; it is.

We reach the mouth of the canyon and the old trail uphill to the 17
roadhead in time to see the first stars come out. Barely in time. Nightfall is quick in this arid climate and the air feels already cold. But we
have earned enough memories, stored enough mental-emotional images in our heads, from one brief day in Aravaipa Canyon, to enrich
the urban days to come. As Thoreau found a universe in the woods
around Concord, any person whose senses are alive can make a world
of any natural place, however limited it might seem, on this subtle
planet of ours.

"The world is big but it is comprehensible," says R. Buckminster 18
Fuller. But it seems to me that the world is not nearly big enough and
that any portion of its surface, left unpaved and alive, is infinitely rich
in details and relationships, in wonder, beauty, mystery, comprehensible
only in part. The very existence of existence is itself suggestive of the
unknown — not a problem but a mystery.

We will never get to the end of it, never plumb the bottom of it,   19
never know the whole of even so small and trivial and useless and precious a place as Aravaipa. Therein lies our redemption.

RESPONDING TO THE TEXT

Aravaipa Canyon is under the protection of the Bureau of Land Management. For what reasons should the government restrict land use in a nation
with a relatively unrestricted economy? Given Abbey's commentary in this
essay, how might he answer that question? What are some aspects of the
question that he doesn't address?

ENGAGING THE WRITER'S SUBJECT

1. Abbey writes that he and his companions "are no more troubled by ancient history than are the mudsuckers in the pools" (paragraph 5). Why
   not? What does he mean by this statement? If his assertion is true, why
   does he include a long paragraph about the canyon's ancient history?
   Why is his tone in paragraph 4 ironic? (Glossary: *Irony*)

2. Why, in your opinion, does Abbey dive into the pool? (Before answering, consider the final sentence of paragraph 18.)

3. What does the last paragraph mean, particularly in regard to the word
   redemption? How does this paragraph contradict the Buckminster Fuller
   quotation in paragraph 18?

ANALYZING THE WRITER'S CRAFT

1. Abbey gives a chronological account of his explorations of Aravaipa
   Canyon; that is, he recounts the events of the day in the order in which
   they happened. How does he organize his descriptions of what he experienced?

2. Abbey pays close attention to the sounds of words, using techniques
   such as the alliteration found in this sentence in paragraph 5: "Cleavages and fractures across the face of the walls form perfect stairways and
   sometimes sloping ramps, slick as sidewalks." How does the repeated
   sound of *s* add to the effectiveness of his description? Find other instances where the author uses repetition of sound to good effect.

3. Much of this essay is composed of objective, factual description, but
   Abbey also shares with the reader some subjective thoughts inspired by
   his exploration of Aravaipa Canyon. (Glossary: *Objective/Subjective*) Note
   the places where he expresses his own opinions. As a writer, what effect
   does he achieve through the contrast between objective and subjective
   detail?

4. This primarily descriptive essay makes clear the author's opinion about
   the relationship of humans to nature. What is his argument? Does it
   take the form of a thesis statement? Explain. Why does Abbey place the

direct argument at the end of the piece rather than at the beginning, where arguments are usually stated?

UNDERSTANDING THE WRITER'S LANGUAGE

1. Paragraph 3 ends with an unexpected warning: "(PLEASE DO NOT MOLEST THE FISH.)" Why is it written in capitals and parenthesized? What is the effect on the reader?

2. The words *obscure* (paragraph 10) and *comprehensible* (18) bring strong connotations to the passages in which they are used. What multiple meanings are implied?

3. What similarities does Abbey perceive between the peccary and the human? Why does he choose to highlight these similarities? (Glossary: *Comparison and Contrast*)

4. Abbey uses a great deal of precise terminology in naming what he sees. The following descriptive words, all equally important to the essay, are not restricted to the land and wildlife of Aravaipa Canyon. Be sure you know their meanings to appreciate the description fully: *riparian* (paragraph 2), *vivacity* (3), *endemic* (3), *vigilante* (4), *formidable* (6), *sylvan* (8), *vesiculated* (11), *apostate* (12), *Grendel* (12).

WRITING SUGGESTIONS

1. Write about a trip you have taken into a natural setting. Using "Aravaipa Canyon" as a model, tell about the trip in chronological order, describing in detail what you saw and experienced. In your writing, make sure you convey the impact the natural setting had on you.

2. Refer to your Responding to the Text answer. Land-use restrictions are a matter of considerable controversy in America today. Which is more important, the development of natural resources or the preservation of wilderness? To reach a decision about any particular piece of land, what issues should be taken into consideration? Who should have the right to decide? Write an essay in support of your own stance toward land use.

3. We learn in this essay that the federal Bureau of Land Management decreed Aravaipa Canyon an official Primitive Area. What are the criteria by which a piece of land is named a Primitive Area? How does this designation differ from Wilderness Area or National Park? Which human activities are permitted in a Primitive Area, and which are not? What are some other Primitive Areas in the United States? Use government publications and other relevant sources to answer these questions and others that may occur to you on the subject; write a report to present your findings. You might also consider writing a research essay that explores the various designations that government agencies assign to protect natural resources in the United States.

• To begin your research online, go to **bedfordstmartins.com /subjectsstrategies** and click on "Description" or browse the thematic directory of annotated links.

The Death of My Father

Steve Martin

Born in Waco, Texas, in 1945, Steve Martin is a comedian, actor, screen-writer, producer, dancer, magician, recording star, and author. While still in his twenties, Martin wrote for the leading television comedies of his day, including The Smothers Brothers Comedy Hour, *for which he won an Emmy in 1969. He also won Grammys for his recordings* Let's Get Small *(1977) and* A Wild and Crazy Guy *(1978). Martin has made dozens of movies, among them* Father of the Bride *(1991) and a sequel, both of which earned him People's Choice and Golden Globe nomina-tions;* Bringing Down the House *(2003); and* The Pink Panther *(2005). His published works include* Picasso at the Lapin Agile and Other Plays *(1996);* Pure Drivel *(1998), a collection of short comic pieces;* Shopgirl, a novel *(2001); and* The Pleasure of My Company: A Novel *(2003).*

In the following essay, which appeared in the New Yorker *on June 17, 2002, Martin paints a portrait of his father and tells how his death brought the family together.*

PREPARING TO READ

How might you describe your mother, father, or legal guardian? What would be the best approach for your description? Would you describe the person physically or in terms of personality, character, occupation, tenacity, appreciation for life, and an ability to grow old gracefully? What dominant impression would you try to create?

In his death, my father, Glenn Vernon Martin, did something he could not do in life. He brought our family together.

After he died, at the age of eighty-three, many of his friends told me how much they loved him — how generous he was, how outgoing, how funny, how caring. I was surprised at these descriptions. I re-member him as angry. There was little said to me, that I recall, that was not criticism. During my teenage years, we hardly spoke except in one-way arguments — from him to me. I am sure that the number of words that passed between us could be counted. At some point in my preteens, I decided to officially "hate" him. When he came into a room, I would wait five minutes, then leave.

But now, when I think of him, five years after his death, I recall events that seem to contradict my memory of him. When I was six-teen, he handed down to me the family's 1957 Chevy. Neither one of us knew at the time that it was the coolest car anyone my age could have. When I was seven or eight, I discovered on Christmas morning a brand-new three-speed bike illuminated by the red, green, and blue of the tree lights in the predawn blackness of Christmas Day. When I was in the third grade, he proudly accompanied me to the school tumbling contest, where I won first prize. One day, while I was in the single digits, he suggested we play catch in the front yard. The offer to spend time together was so anomalous that I didn't quite understand what I was supposed to do.

When I graduated from high school, my father offered to buy me a tuxedo. I refused; he had raised me to reject all aid and assistance, and he detested extravagance. Because my father always shunned gifts, I felt that, in my refusal, I was somehow, in a convoluted, perverse way, being a good son. I wish now that I had let him buy me a tuxedo.

My father sold real estate, but he wanted to be in show business. I must have been five years old when I saw him in a bit part at the Call Board Theatre, on Melrose Place in Hollywood. He came on in the second act and served a drink. Somewhere in our memorabilia is a publicity photo of him staged with the entire family: he is a criminal being taken away by the police, and his five-year-old son, me, surrounded by my mother and sister, is tugging at his shirtsleeve, pleading with him to stay. There was no way to explain to a five-year-old that this was not actually happening. During the war, he was in a U.S.O. performance of *Our Town* in England with Raymond Massey. Later, when I was probably nineteen, he wrote Raymond Massey a letter, reminding Mr. Massey who he was and promoting his son who wanted to be in show business. He never heard back.

Generally, however, my father was critical of my show-business accomplishments. Even after I won an Emmy at twenty-three as a writer for *The Smothers Brothers Comedy Hour*, he advised me to finish college so that I'd have something to fall back on. Years later, my friends and I took him to the premiere of my first movie, *The Jerk*, and afterward we went to dinner. For a long time, he said nothing. My friends noted his silence and were horrified. Finally, one friend said, "What did you think of Steve in the movie?" And my father said, "Well, he's no Charlie Chaplin."

My father did not believe that he was hurting me. He was just being honest. After my first appearance on *Saturday Night Live*, in 1976, he wrote a bad review of me in the newsletter of the Newport Board of Realtors, of which he was the president. Later, he related this news to me slightly shamefacedly, and said that after it appeared his best friend came into his office holding the paper, placed it on his desk, and shook his head sternly, indicating a wordless "No." My father did not understand what I was doing in my work and was slightly embarrassed by it. Perhaps he believed that his friends would be embarrassed by it, too, and the review was his way of refusing to sanction this new comedy.

In the early eighties, a close friend of mine, whose own father was killed crossing a street, and whose mother committed suicide on

Mother's Day, told me that if I had anything to work out with my parents I should do it now, because one day they wouldn't be there anymore. I had no idea that there was anything to work out. But after the remark had stewed in my brain for years, I decided to try to get to know my parents. I took them to lunch every Sunday that I could, and goaded them into talking. My father was cantankerous, and usually, when my mother said anything, he would contradict her; then she would contradict him; and soon the conversation would disintegrate into silence, with my mother afraid to speak and my father angry. This went on for years, until finally I struck upon the idea of taking them out separately. This resulted in the telling of wonderful histories, of interest only to me and my sister Melinda. My mother's recollections could finally be aired without fear of an explosion from my father, and my father could remain calm in the telling of his stories without the presence of my mother, who seemed mostly to annoy him.

Around this time, my sister told me she wanted to make a deter- 9 mined effort to "get to know my brother." I accepted this casually, but found, as we began swapping stories, that we were united by our view of a peculiar family portrait. Until then, we had seldom seen each other. My sister was four years older, which meant that we had always been in separate schools when we were children and never saw each other during the day. In the early eighties, my father began having heart attacks (three) and strokes (many), and my sister and I began to see more and more of each other. It took me thirty-five years to understand that all siblings separated by four years are not necessarily uncommunicative.

My father then had a quadruple-bypass operation. I remember the 10 two of us together, during one of my Sunday lunches at a restaurant, as he held the menu in one hand and his newly prescribed list of dietary restrictions in the other. He glanced back and forth between the standard restaurant fare on his left and the healthy suggestions on his right, looked up at the waiter, and said resignedly, "Oh, I'll just have the fettuccine Alfredo."

It was our routine that after our lunches my mother and father, now 11 in their eighties, would walk me to the car. I would kiss my mother on the cheek, and my father and I would wave or awkwardly say goodbye. But one time we hugged each other and he whispered, "I love you," with a voice that was barely audible. This was the first time these words were ever spoken between us. I returned the phrase with the same awkward, broken delivery. Several days later, I wrote him a letter that began, "I heard what you said. . . ."

But as my father ailed he grew even more irritable. He made un- 12 reasonable demands, such as waking his twenty-four-hour nurse at three in the morning and insisting that she take him for a drive. He also became heartrendingly emotional. He might be in the middle of a story and begin to laugh, which then provoked sudden tears, and he would be unable to continue. These poignant moments became more frequent. Sometimes his eyes filled for no reason at all, and he would look down to hide his face.

We convinced him that he should visit a shrink, even though therapy did not fit his definition of manhood — fashioned in Texas, during the Depression. The therapist was a callow young man, a recent graduate. My father and I went together on one visit and talked out a few things in an emotionally charged hour, and I still regret how much we said in front of this stranger. My mother, also Texas born, and raised by a strict Baptist mother — no dancing, no card playing — was enlisted to visit the shrink, too, in the hope of shedding some light on their relationship. I waited outside, and when she came out I said, "How was it?" She said, "Well, I didn't say anything bad."

In my youth, my father stubbornly resisted and criticized anything new, from rock and roll to flower power (how right he was!), but as he aged I sensed in him a willingness to try new things, even though he indignantly rejected egg-white omelets and green salads to the very end. Once, a male nurse produced a bag of pot, and I, having heard of its analgesic qualities for cancer patients, suggested that my father try some — which he did, willingly. He took several hits. Eventually, his eyes glazed over and his leg stopped shaking. He looked around the room with dilated pupils and said, "I don't feel anything."

There must be an instinct about when the end is near, and one day in May, 1997, we all found ourselves gathered at my parents' home, in Orange County, California. I walked into the house they had lived in for thirty-five years, and my weeping sister said, "He's saying goodbye to everyone." A hospice nurse said to me, "This is when it all happens." I didn't know what she meant, but I soon would.

I walked into the bedroom where he lay, his mind alert but his body failing. He said, almost buoyantly, "I'm ready now." I understood that his intensifying rage of the last few years had been against death, and now his resistance was abating. I stood at the end of the bed, and we looked into each other's eyes for a long, unbroken time. At last he said, "You did everything I wanted to do."

I said, "I did it because of you." It was the truth. Looking back, I'm sure that we both had different interpretations of what I meant.

I sat on the edge of the bed. Another silence fell over us. Then he said, "I wish I could cry, I wish I could cry."

At first, I took this as a comment on his plight but am forever thankful that I pushed on. "What do you want to cry about?" I finally said.

"For all the love I received and couldn't return."

He had kept this secret, his desire to love his family, from me and 21 from my mother his whole life. It was as though an early misstep had kept us forever out of stride. Now, two days from his death, our pace was aligning, and we were able to speak.

I sometimes think of our relationship graphically, as a bell curve. 22 In my infancy, we were perfectly close. Then the gap widened to accommodate our differences and indifference. In the final days of his life, we again became perfectly close.

My father's death has a thousand endings. I continue to absorb 23 its messages and meanings. He stripped death of its spooky morbidity and made it tangible and passionate. He prepared me in some way for my own death. He showed me the responsibility of the living to the dying. But the most enduring thought was expressed by my sister. Afterward, she told me she had learned something from all this. I asked her what it was. She said, "Nobody should have to die alone."

RESPONDING TO THE TEXT

Martin writes that he sometimes thought of his relationship with his father as being represented by a bell curve: "In my infancy, we were perfectly close. Then the gap widened to accommodate our differences and indifference. In the final days of his life, we again became perfectly close" (22). Reflect on the relationship you have with your parents or another relative. Would you say that the bell-curve relationship is typical? If so, what might be some reasons for the widening and narrowing of the "gap"? Is another analogy more apt for your relationships? (Glossary: *Analogy*) Explain.

ENGAGING THE WRITER'S SUBJECT

1. Explain the irony of Martin's statement that his father did something in death that he could not do in life. (Glossary: *Irony*)

2. What causes the conflict between Martin and his father?

3. What significance is there in Martin's remembrance of his father five years after his death? What perspective has the passing of time lent to Martin's impression of his father?

4. What effect did the Depression have on Martin's father and a strict Baptist upbringing have on his mother, in your opinion? What effect might their backgrounds have had on their children?

5. In paragraph 17, Martin tells his father that he did everything "because of [him]." Martin goes on to write: "Looking back, I'm sure that we both had different interpretations of what I meant." What could those differing interpretations be?

6. What does Martin mean when he writes, "My father's death has a thousand endings" (paragraph 23)?

ANALYZING THE WRITER'S CRAFT

1. What picture do you have of Martin's father from the description of him? What do we learn about his physical being and personality? Is there a dominant impression in Martin's description of his father? (Glossary: *Dominant Impression*) Explain.

2. Martin organizes the examples in paragraph 3 in reverse chronological order. What would be gained or lost if he presented them in the order in which they happened? (Glossary: *Organization*)

3. What about Martin's audience for this essay? (Glossary: *Audience*) The readers of the *New Yorker* are thought to be fairly sophisticated and sensitive readers. Why might this essay be a good choice for them?

4. What might Martin's purpose be in writing this essay? (Glossary: *Purpose*) Do you think he is trying to "sort things out" for himself? Teach us some kind of lesson? Warn us in some way? Encourage us in some direction? Explain.

5. Martin describes his father by using examples to illustrate his father's character and behavior. For example, he uses exemplification to support his claim that "as my father ailed he grew even more irritable. He made unreasonable demands, such as waking his twenty-four-hour nurse at three in the morning and insisting that she take him for a drive" (paragraph 12). Find several other examples of exemplification. How do these enhance Martin's description of his father? (Glossary: *Exemplification*)

UNDERSTANDING THE WRITER'S LANGUAGE

1. What is Martin's tone in this essay? (Glossary: *Tone*) Is he angry, resentful, loving, tender, sad, or regretful? How do you know?

2. Refer to your desk dictionary to determine the meanings of the following words as Martin uses them in this selection: *shamefacedly* (paragraph 7), *goaded* (8), *ailed* (12), *callow* (13), *glazed* (14), *dilated* (14), *hospice* (15), *abating* (16), *bell curve* (22).

WRITING SUGGESTIONS

1. Using Martin's essay as a model, write a description of one of your parents or a person who has acted as a parent for you. Keep in mind that effective description requires examples drawn from sense perceptions, telling details, thoughtful organization, showing and not telling, and the use of concrete nouns and strong action verbs, as well as figurative language. Above all, think about the dominant impression you wish to create and your larger purpose in describing this person.

2. In paragraphs 12 through 14 Martin cites several examples of how he fulfilled his obligation of caring for his ailing father. What family obligations do you have — or do others have toward you? How do you feel about these obligations? Write an essay in which you explore these

obligations and your thoughts and feelings about them. Which obligations would you classify as chores? Which would you classify as willing acts of love? Are there obligations that you could classify as both? (Glossary: *Classification; Division*) Explain.

3. Just like Martin, many adults find themselves responsible for caring for elderly parents or relatives. In some cases this means providing financial support for home–health care or a nursing home; in other cases the elderly relative moves in with the adult child. This trend is so widespread that a new term, "sandwich generation," has been coined to describe adults caught between responsibilities for both children and an elderly relative. Drawing on your own observations, experiences, and library and Internet research, write an essay on the emergence of the sandwich generation. What are the causes of this trend? What are the effects? (Glossary: *Cause and Effect Analysis*) What options or services are available to those in this predicament? Has this situation arisen in your own family? If so, how was it handled?

- To begin your research online, go to **bedfordstmartins.com /subjectsstrategies** and click on "Description" or browse the thematic directory of annotated links.

SEEING/READING

Shane Holding His iPod
iPodLounge.com

CONNECTING IMAGE AND TEXT

This is a candid shot of an iPod user mimicking an iPod advertisement at Penn Station in Philadelphia, Pennsylvania. This photograph was submitted anonymously and posted in the North American Gallery at iPodLounge.com, an online community for iPod enthusiasts. How do you "read" this photograph? What statement does Shane make by striking this pose? What parallels do you see between Shane and the silhouette? How do you react to the "double ad" in this image? Your observations about this photograph will help guide you to the key themes and strategies in the essay that follows.

The Guts of a New Machine

Rob Walker

Rob Walker was born in Houston, Texas, in 1968 and graduated from the University of Texas–Austin with a degree in radio, television, and film. Walker has worked as a writer and editor and has had articles published in the American Lawyer, Money, GQ, *the* New Republic, *and the* Wall Street Journal. *He often writes about marketing, most notably in columns called "Ad Report Card" for Slate.com and "Consumed" for the* New York Times Magazine. *Walker's first book, a collection of essays entitled* Letters from New Orleans, *was published in 2005.*

In "The Guts of a New Machine," first published in the New York Times Magazine *on November 30, 2003, Walker describes the Apple iPod from a variety of angles.*

PREPARING TO READ

Do you sometimes wonder how devices such as CD players, personal digital assistants, cell phones, and wireless devices actually work? Or do you prefer just to use such products and leave the design and mechanics to the experts? Does it matter if we know how things work? Is how something looks more important than how it works?

Two years ago this month, Apple Computer released a small, sleek-looking device it called the iPod. A digital music player, it weighed just 6.5 ounces and held about 1,000 songs. There were small MP3 players around at the time, and there were players that could hold a lot of music. But if the crucial equation is "largest number of songs" divided by "smallest physical space," the iPod seemed untouchable. And yet the initial reaction was mixed: the thing cost $400, so much more than existing digital players that it prompted one online skeptic to suggest that the name might be an acronym for "Idiots Price Our Devices." This line of complaint called to mind the Newton, Apple's pen-based personal organizer that was ahead of its time but carried a bloated price tag to its doom.

Since then, however, about 1.4 million iPods have been sold. (It has been updated twice and now comes in three versions, all of which improved on the original's songs-per-space ratio, and are priced at $300, $400 and $500, the most expensive holding 10,000 songs.) For the months of July and August, the iPod claimed the No. 1 spot in the MP3 player market both in terms of unit share (31 percent) and revenue share (56 percent), by Apple's reckoning. It is now Apple's highest-volume product. "It's something that's as big a brand to Apple as the Mac," is how Philip Schiller, Apple's senior vice president of worldwide product marketing, puts it. "And that's a pretty big deal."

Of course, as anyone who knows the basic outline of Apple's history is aware, there is no guarantee that today's innovation leader will not be copycatted and undersold into tomorrow's niche player. Apple's recent and highly publicized move to make the iPod and its related software, iTunes, available to users of Windows-based computers is widely seen as a sign that the company is trying to avoid that fate this time around. But it may happen anyway. The history of innovation is the history of innovation being imitated, iterated, and often overtaken. 3

Whether the iPod achieves truly mass scale — like, say, the cassette-tape Walkman, which sold an astonishing 186 million units in its first 20 years of existence — it certainly qualifies as a hit and as a genuine breakthrough. It has popped up on *Saturday Night Live*, in a 50 Cent video, on Oprah Winfrey's list of her "favorite things," and in recurring "what's on your iPod" gimmicks in several magazines. It is, in short, an icon. A handful of familiar clichés have made the rounds to explain this — it's about ease of use, it's about Apple's great sense of design. But what does that really mean? "Most people make the mistake of thinking design is what it looks like," says Steve Jobs, Apple's C.E.O. "People think it's this veneer — that the designers are handed this box and told, 'Make it look good!' That's not what we think design is. It's not just what it looks like and feels like. Design is how it works." 4

So you can say that the iPod is innovative, but it's harder to nail down whether the key is what's inside it, the external appearance or even the way these work together. One approach is to peel your way through the thing, layer by layer. 5

The Aura

If you want to understand why a product has become an icon, you of course want to talk to the people who dreamed it up and made it. And you want to talk to the design experts and the technology pros and the professors and the gurus. But what you really want to do is talk to Andrew Andrew. Andrew Andrew is a "highly diversified company" made of two personable young men, each named Andrew. They dress identically and seem to agree on everything; they say, among other things, that they have traveled from the future "to set things on the right course for tomorrow." They require interviewers to sign a form agreeing not to reveal any differences between Andrew and Andrew, because to do so might undermine the Andrew Andrew brand — and since this request is more interesting than whatever those differences might be, interviewers sign it. 6

Among other things, they do some fashion design and they are ⁊
DJs who "spin" on iPods, setting up participatory events called iPar-
ties. Thus they've probably seen more people interact with the player
than anyone who doesn't work for Apple. More important, they put
an incredible amount of thought into what they buy, and why: In a
world where, for better or worse, aesthetics is a business, they are not
just consumers but consumption artists. So Andrew remembers exactly where he was when he first encountered the iPod: 14th Street
near Ninth Avenue in New York City. He was with Andrew, of course.
A friend showed it to them. Andrew held the device in his hand. The
main control on the iPod is a scroll wheel: you spin it with your
thumb to navigate the long list of songs (or artists or genres), touch a
button to pick a track and use the wheel again to adjust the volume.
The other Andrew also tried it out. "When you do the volume for the
first time, that's the key moment," says Andrew. "We knew: We had
to have one." (Well, two.)

Before you even get to the surface of the iPod, you encounter 8
what could be called its aura. The commercial version of an aura is a
brand, and while Apple may be a niche player in the computer market, the fanatical brand loyalty of its customers is legendary. A journalist, Leander Kahney, has even written a book about it, *The Cult of Mac*,
to be published in the spring. As he points out, that base has supported the company with a faith in its will to innovate — even during
stretches when it hasn't. Apple is also a giant in the world of industrial
design. The candy-colored look of the iMac has been so widely copied
that it's now a visual cliché.

But the iPod is making an even bigger impression. Bruce Claxton, 9
who is the current president of the Industrial Designers Society of
America and a senior designer at Motorola, calls the device emblematic of a shift toward products that are "an antidote to the hyper
lifestyle," which might be symbolized by hand-held devices that bristle with buttons and controls that seem to promise a million functions
if you only had time to figure them all out. "People are seeking out
products that are not just simple to use but a joy to use." Moby, the
recording artist, has been a high-profile iPod booster since the product's debut. "The kind of insidious revolutionary quality of the iPod,"
he says, "is that it's so elegant and logical, it becomes part of your life
so quickly that you can't remember what it was like beforehand."

Tuesday nights, Andrew Andrew's iParty happens at a club called 10
APT on the spooky, far western end of 13th Street. They show up at
about 10 in matching sweat jackets and sneakers, matching eyeglasses,
matching haircuts. They connect their matching iPods to a modest
Gemini mixer that they've fitted with a white front panel to make it
look more iPodish. The iPods sit on either side of the mixer, on their
backs, so they look like tiny turntables. Andrew Andrew change into

matching lab coats and ties. They hand out long song lists to patrons, who take a number and, when called, are invited up to program a seven-minute set. At around midnight, the actor Elijah Wood (Frodo from the *Lord of the Rings* trilogy) has turned up and is permitted to plug his own iPod into Andrew Andrew's system. His set includes a Squarepusher song.

Between songs at APT, each Andrew analyzed the iPod. In talking about how hard it was, at first, to believe that so much music could be stuffed into such a tiny object, they came back to the scroll wheel as the key to the product's initial seductiveness. "It really bridged the gap," Andrew observed, "between fantasy and reality." 11

The idea of innovation, particularly technological innovation, has a kind of aura around it, too. Imagine the lone genius, sheltered from the storm of short-term commercial demands in a research lab somewhere, whose tinkering produces a sudden and momentous breakthrough. Or maybe we think innovation begins with an epiphany, a sudden vision of the future. Either way, we think of that one thing, the lightning bolt that jolted all the other pieces into place. The Walkman came about because a Sony executive wanted a high-quality but small stereo tape player to listen to on long flights. A small recorder was modified, with the recording pieces removed and stereo circuitry added. That was February 1979, and within six months the product was on the market. 12

The iPod's history is comparatively free of lightning-bolt moments. Apple was not ahead of the curve in recognizing the power of music in digital form. It was practically the last computer maker to equip its machines with CD burners. It trailed others in creating jukebox software for storing and organizing music collections on computers. And various portable digital music players were already on the market before the iPod was even an idea. Back when Napster was inspiring a million self-styled visionaries to predict the end of music as we know it, Apple was focused on the relationship between computers and video. The company had, back in the 1990's, invented a technology called FireWire, which is basically a tool for moving data between digital devices — in large quantities, very quickly. Apple licensed this technology to various Japanese consumer electronics companies (which used it in digital camcorders and players) and eventually started adding FireWire ports to iMacs and creating video editing software. This led to programs called iMovie, then iPhoto and then a conceptual view of the home computer as a "digital hub" that would complement a range of devices. Finally, in January 2001, iTunes was added to the mix. 13

And although the next step sounds prosaic — we make software that lets you organize the music on your computer, so maybe we should make one of those things that lets you take it with you — it 14 was also something new. There were companies that made jukebox software, and companies that made portable players, but nobody made both. What this meant is not that the iPod could do more, but that it would do less. This is what led to what Jonathan Ive, Apple's vice president of industrial design, calls the iPod's "overt simplicity." And this, perversely, is the most exciting thing about it.

The Surface

Ive introduces himself as Jony, but really he seems like more of a Jonathan: Friendly and soft-spoken, almost sheepish at times, but also, with his shaved head and English accent and carefully chosen words, an extremely precise man. We spoke in a generic conference room in Apple's Cupertino, California, headquarters, decorated mostly with the company's products.   15

Before I really had a chance to ask a question, Ive spent about 10 minutes talking about the iPod's packaging — the way the box opens, how the foam is cut. He talked about the unusually thin and flexible FireWire cable, about the "taut, crisp" cradle that the iPod rests in, about the white headphones. "I remember there was a discussion: 'Headphones can't be white; headphones are black, or dark gray.'" But uniform whiteness seemed too important to the product to break the pattern, and indeed the white headphones have become a kind of secondary, unplanned icon — as Apple's current ads featuring white-headphoned silhouettes now underscore. It's those details, he said, that make the iPod special: "We are surrounded by so many things that are flippant and trivial. This could have been just another self-important plastic thing."   16

When it came to pinning Ive down on questions of how specific aspects of the product came to be, he stressed not epiphanies but process. Asked about the scroll wheel, he did not mention the Bang & Olufsen BeoCom phones that use a similar radial dial; rather, he talked about the way that his design group collaborates constantly with engineers and manufacturers. "It's not serial," he insisted. "It's not one person passing something on to the next." I'd push for a lightning-bolt moment, and he'd trail off. Finally, at one point, he interrupted himself and said, with sudden energy, "It's almost easier to talk about it as what it's not."   17

The surface of the iPod, white on front and stainless steel behind, is perfectly seamless. It's close to impenetrable. You hook it up to a computer with iTunes, and whatever music you have collected there flows (incredibly fast, thanks to that FireWire cable) into the iPod — again, seamless. Once it's in there, the surface of the iPod is not likely to cause problems for the user, because there's almost nothing on it.   18

Just that wheel, one button in the center, and four beneath the device's LCD screen. (The look, with the big circle at the bottom, is reminiscent of a tiny stereo speaker.)

"Steve" — that would be Steve Jobs — "made some very interesting observations very early on about how this was about navigating content," Ive says. "It was about being very focused and not trying to do too much with the device — which would have been its complication and, therefore, its demise. The enabling features aren't obvious and evident, because the key was getting rid of stuff." [19]

Later he said: "What's interesting is that out of that simplicity, and almost that unashamed sense of simplicity, and expressing it, came a very different product. But difference wasn't the goal. It's actually very easy to create a different thing. What was exciting is starting to realize that its difference was really a consequence of this quest to make it a very simple thing." [20]

Before Ive came to Apple, he worked independently, often on projects that never got out of the prototype phase; one working model would be made, and then it would sit on a shelf in his office. You can think of innovation as a continuum, and this phase is one end of it. The dreams and experiments that happen outside of — and in a state of indifference toward — the marketplace. At the other end of the continuum are the fast followers, those who are very attuned to the marketplace, but are not particularly innovative. They let someone else do the risky business of wild leaps, then swoop in behind with an offering that funnels some aspect of the innovation into a more marketable (cheaper? watered down? easier to obtain?) package — and dominates. Fairly or not, the shorthand version of this in the technology world would have at one end of the continuum Xerox PARC, the famous R&D lab where all manner of bleeding-edge innovations (including some of the "look and feel" of the Mac) were researched but never developed into marketable products. And at the other end you'd have companies like Microsoft and Dell. [21]

Apple presents itself as a company whose place on this continuum is unique. Its headquarters in Cupertino is a series of connected buildings arranged in a circle. Behind this surface is a kind of enclosed park. It looks like public space, but of course it isn't: You can't get to it unless you're an Apple employee or are accompanied by one. Along one side of this hermetic oasis are a bunch of tables, set just outside the company cafeteria, and a sign that says Cafe Macs. Here I sat with my P.R. minder and watched Steve Jobs approach in long, energetic strides. It was a perfect day, and he wore shorts with his black turtleneck, and sneakers. [22]

He was very much on message, and the message was that only Apple could have developed the iPod. Like the device itself, Apple appears seamless: it has the hardware engineers, the software engineers, [23] the industrial designers, all under one roof and working together. "As technology becomes more complex, Apple's core strength of knowing how to make very sophisticated technology comprehensible to mere mortals is in even greater demand." This is why, he said, the barrage of devices made by everyone from Philips to Samsung to Dell that are imitating and will imitate the iPod do not make him nervous. "The Dells of the world don't spend money" on design innovation, he said. "They don't think about these things."

As he described it, the iPod did not begin with a specific techno-   24
logical breakthrough, but with a sense, in early 2001, that Apple could give this market something better than any rival could. So the starting point wasn't a chip or a design; the starting point was the question, What's the user experience? "Correct," Jobs said. "And the pieces come together. If you start to work on something, and the time is right, pieces come in from the periphery. It just comes together."

The Guts

What, then, are the pieces? What are the technical innards of the seam-   25
less iPod? What's underneath the surface? "Esoterica," says Schiller, an Apple V.P., waving away any and all questions about the iPod's innards. Consumers, he said, don't care about technical specs; they care about how many songs it holds, how quickly they can transfer them, how good the sound quality is.

Perhaps. But some people are interested in esoterica, and a lot of   26
people were interested in knowing what was inside the iPod when it made its debut. One of them was David Carey, who for the past three years has run a business in Austin, Texas, called Portelligent, which tears apart electronic devices and does what might be called guts checks. He tore up his first iPod in early 2002.

Inside was a neat stack of core components. First, the power   27
source: a slim, squarish rechargeable battery made by Sony. Atop that was the hard disk — the thing that holds all the music files. At the time, small hard disks were mostly used in laptops, or as removable data-storage cards for laptops. So-called 2.5-inch hard disks, which are protected by a casing that actually measures about $2^{3}/_{4}$ inches by 4 inches, were fairly commonplace, but Toshiba had come up with an even smaller one. With a protective cover measuring just over 2 inches by 3 inches, 0.2 inches thick and weighing less than two ounces, its 1.8-inch disk could hold five gigabytes of data — or, in practical terms, about a thousand songs. This is what Apple used.

On top of this hard disk was the circuit board. This included com-   28
ponents to turn a digitally encoded music file into a conventional audio file, the chip that enables the device to use FireWire both as a

pipe for digital data and battery charging and the central processing unit that acts as the sort of taskmaster for the various components. Also here was the ball-bearing construction underlying the scroll wheel. (The newer iPod models got slimmer by replacing that wheel with a solid-state version and by using a smaller battery.) It is, as Carey notes, an admirable arrangement.

Exactly how all the pieces came together — there were parts from at least a half-dozen companies in the original iPod — is not something Apple talks about. But one clue can be found in the device itself. Under the Settings menu is a selection called Legal, and there you find not just Apple's copyright but also a note that "portions" of the device are copyrighted by something called PortalPlayer Inc. That taskmaster central processing unit is a PortalPlayer chip. The Silicon Valley company, which describes itself as a "supplier of digital media infrastructure solutions for the consumer marketplace," has never publicly discussed its role in the iPod. Its vice president for sales and marketing, Michael Maia, would talk to me only in general terms. 29

PortalPlayer was founded a little more than four years ago with an eye toward creating basic designs for digital computer peripherals, music players in particular. Specifically, the company wanted to build an architecture around tiny hard disks. Most early MP3 players did not use hard disks because they were physically too large. Rather, they used another type of storage technology (referred to as a "flash" chip) that took up little space but held less data — that is, fewer songs. PortalPlayer's setup includes both a hard disk and a smaller memory chip, which is actually the thing that's active when you're listening to music; songs are cleverly parceled into this from the hard disk in small groups, a scheme that keeps the energy-hog hard disk from wearing down the battery. More recently, PortalPlayer's work has formed the guts of new players released by Samsung and Philips. A trade journal called *Electronics Design Chain* described PortalPlayer as having developed a "base platform" that Apple at least used as a starting point and indicated that PortalPlayer picked other members of the iPod "design chain" and helped manage the process. 30

Interestingly, the legal section in the first version of the iPod used to include another copyright notice on behalf of a company called Pixo, which is reported to have created the original operating system for the iPod. Pixo has since been bought by Sun Microsystems, and the credit has disappeared from both newer iPods and even more recent software upgrades for the original model. 31

Apple won't comment on any of this, and the nondisclosure agreements it has in place with its suppliers and collaborators are described as unusually restrictive. Presumably this is because the company prefers the image of a product that sprang forth whole from the corporate godhead — which was certainly the impression the iPod created 32 when it seemed to appear out of nowhere two years ago. But the point here is not to undercut Apple's role: the iPod came together in somewhere between six and nine months, from concept to market, and its coherence as a product given the time frame and the number of variables is astonishing. Jobs and company are still correct when they point to that coherence as key to the iPod's appeal; and the reality of technical innovation today is that assembling the right specialists is critical to speed, and speed is critical to success.

Still, in the world of technology products, guts have traditionally mattered quite a bit; the PC boom viewed from one angle was nothing but an endless series of announcements about bits and megahertz and RAM. That 1.8-inch hard disk, and the amount of data storage it offered in such a small space, isn't the only key to the iPod, but it's a big deal. Apple apparently cornered the market for the Toshiba disks for a while. But now there is, inevitably, an alternative. Hitachi now makes a disk that size, and it has at least one major buyer: Dell.

The System

My visit to Cupertino happened to coincide with the publication of a pessimistic installment of *The Wall Street Journal*'s "Heard on the Street" column pointing out that Apple's famous online music store generates little profit. The more interesting point, noted in the back half of the column, is that Apple doesn't expect it to generate much profit — it's a "Trojan horse" whose real function is to help sell more iPods. Given that the store was widely seen as a pivotal moment in the tortuous process of creating a legitimate digital music source that at least some paying consumers are willing to use, this is an amazing notion: Apple, in a sense, was willing to try and reinvent the entire music business in order to move iPods.

The column also noted that some on Wall Street were waiting to see what would happen to the iPod once Dell came out with its combination of music store and music player. (The Dell DJ is slightly bigger than the iPod but claims a longer battery life, which the company says is what its consumer research indicated people wanted; it costs $250 for a 15-gigabyte version, $300 for 20 gigabytes, or nearly 5,000 songs.) Napster's name has been bought by another company that has launched a pay service with a hardware partner, Samsung. But it was Dell that one investor quoted in the *Journal* article held out as the rival with the greatest chance of success: "No one markets as well as Dell does." This was causing some eye-rolling in Cupertino; Dell is not a marketer at all. Dell has no aura; there is no Cult of Dell. Dell is a merchandiser, a shiller of gigs-per-dollar. A follower. Dell had not released its product when I met Jobs, but he still dismissed it as "not any good."

About a week later Jobs played host to one of the "launch" events for which the company is notorious, announcing the availability of iTunes and access to the company's music store for Windows users. (In what seemed an odd crack in Apple's usually seamless aura maintenance, he did his demo on what was clearly a Dell computer.) The announcement included a deal with AOL and a huge promotion with Pepsi. The message was obvious: Apple is aiming squarely at the mainstream.

This sounded like a sea change. But while you can run iTunes on Windows and hook it up to an iPod, that iPod does not play songs in the formats used by any other seller of digital music, like Napster or Rhapsody. Nor will music bought through Apple's store play on any rival device. (The iPod does, of course, work easily with the MP3 format that's common on free file-swapping services, like KaZaA, that the music industry wants to shut down but that are still much more popular than anything requiring money.) This means Apple is, again, competing against a huge number of players across multiple business segments, who by and large will support one another's products and services. In light of this, says one of those competitors, Rob Glaser, founder and C.E.O. of RealNetworks, "It's absolutely clear now why five years from now, Apple will have 3 to 5 percent of the player market."

Glaser says he admires Apple and likes Jobs, but contends that this is simply the latest instance of the company's tendency, once again, to sacrifice commercial logic in the name of "ideology." Not that Apple can't maintain a business by catering to the high end and operating in a closed world. But maintaining market leadership, while easy when the field of competitors is small, will become impossible as rivals flood the market with their own innovations and an agnostic attitude about what works with what. "The history of the world," he says, "is that hybridization yields better results." With Dell and others aiming a big push at the Christmas season, it's even possible that Apple's market share has peaked.

Jobs, of course, has heard the predictions and has no patience for any of it. Various contenders have come at the iPod for two years, and none have measured up. Nothing has come close to Apple's interface. Even the look-alike products are frauds. "They're all putting their dumb controls in the shape of a circle, to fool the consumer into thinking it's a wheel like ours," he says. "We've sort of set the vernacular. They're trying to copy the vernacular without understanding it." (The one company that did plan a wheel-driven product, Samsung, changed course after Apple reportedly threatened to sue.)

"We don't underestimate people," Jobs said later in the interview. "We really did believe that people would want something this good, that they'd see the value in it. And that rather than making a far inferior product for a hundred dollars less, giving people the product that they want and that will serve them for years, even though it's a little pricier. People are smart; they figure these things out."

The point that companies — like Dell — that have no great repu- 41
tation as innovators but a track record of winning by playing a price-driven, low-margin volume game was dismissed. The iPod has already been improved several times, Jobs said, and will keep improving in ways that keep it ahead of the pack. (He wouldn't get specific.) "For whatever reason," he said with finality, "the superior product has the largest share. Sometimes the best product does win. This may be one of those times."

The Core

Actually, Jobs seemed a little annoyed. Looking back at my notes, I 42
found it remarkable how many of his answers begin with some variation of "No," as if my questions were out of sync with what he wanted to say. (Before I could finish a question about the significance of Apple's pitching a product to Windows users, for instance, he corrected me: "We're not pitching the Windows user. We're pitching the music lover.") After half an hour of this, my inquiries really did start to fall apart, so I didn't expect much when I resorted to asking, in so many words, whether he thinks consciously about innovation.

"No," he said, peevishly. "We consciously think about making 43
great products. We don't think, 'Let's be innovative!'" He waved his hands for effect. " 'Let's take a class! Here are the five rules of innovation, let's put them up all over the company!'"

Well, I said defensively, there are people who do just that. 44

"Of course they do." I felt his annoyance shift elsewhere. "And it's 45
like . . . somebody who's not cool trying to be cool. It's painful to watch. You know what I mean?" He looked at me for a while, and I started to think he was trying to tell me something. Then he said, "It's like . . . watching Michael Dell try to dance." The P.R. minder guffawed. "Painful," Jobs summarized.

What I had been hoping to do was catch a glimpse of what's there 46
when you pull back all those layers — when you penetrate the aura, strip off the surface, clear away the guts. What's under there is innovation, but where does it come from? I had given up on getting an answer to this question when I made a jokey observation that before long somebody would probably start making white headphones so that people carrying knockoffs and tape players could fool the world into thinking they had trendy iPods.

Jobs shook his head. "But then you meet the girl, and she says, 47
'Let me see what's on your iPod.' You pull out a tape player, and she walks away." This was an unanticipated, and surprisingly persuasive,

response. That's thinking long-term, I said. "No," said Steve Jobs. "That's being an optimist."

RESPONDING TO THE TEXT

Walker's description of the Apple iPod is complicated and interesting because it describes an invention that he contends has become a cultural icon. As such the description can't really be divorced from its aura and the people and the corporation that produced it. Yet, for all that, the iPod is a machine that Apple's vice president Jonathan Ive says is characterized by "overt simplicity" (paragraph 14). He says, "It's almost easier to talk about it as what it's not" (17). How would you describe what it's not?

ENGAGING THE WRITER'S SUBJECT

1. What does Andrew of Andrew Andrew mean when he says of the iPod, "It really bridged the gap between fantasy and reality" (11)?
2. Why do Ive and Jobs think that only Apple could have developed the iPod?
3. What does Jobs say is key to innovation?
4. What are the arguments for and against Apple's losing its market share?
5. What does Walker mean by the last category of his description: The Core?

ANALYZING THE WRITER'S CRAFT

1. For what audience do you think Walker is writing? (Glossary: *Audience*) Explain.
2. Into what categories does Walker divide his description of the iPod? (Glossary: *Classification; Division*) How would you describe those categories in your own words? What for you is the most interesting of the categories? Why?
3. How does Walker organize those categories? (Glossary: *Organization*) What does he mean when he says that "One approach is to peel your way through the thing, layer by layer" (paragraph 5)?
4. Does Walker describe each category objectively, subjectively, or with some combination of the two? (Glossary: *Objective/Subjective*) Take a category or two and explain the method of description used.
5. Walker describes the iPod, but why does he also describe the company that developed it? Are the two somehow inseparable? Explain.
6. Walker uses several strategies in his description of the iPod. For example, he uses narrative details to describe his visit to Apple's corporate campus and to add insight into his interactions with his interview subjects. (Glossary: *Narration*) Walker also incorporates the strategies of cause and effect analysis, comparison and contrast, classification, and division into his essay. (Glossary: *Cause and Effect Analysis, Classification; Comparison and Contrast; Division*) Find examples of Walker's use of

these strategies. How does each enrich Walker's description? How effective or interesting would Walker's description be if he didn't incorporate other strategies into his writing?

UNDERSTANDING THE WRITER'S LANGUAGE

1. Refer to your desk dictionary to determine the meanings of the following words as Walker uses them in this selection: *iterated* (paragraph 3), *icon* (4), *gurus* (6), *aesthetics* (7), *epiphany* (12), *prosaic* (14), *flippant* (16), *esoterica* (25), *godhead* (32), *shiller* (35), *agnostic* (38), *hybridization* (38), *vernacular* (39).

WRITING SUGGESTIONS

1. Write an essay in which you describe an inanimate object that you value such as your prom dress, first car, or a special gift. First, describe the object in objective terms: its size, color, weight, distinguishing characteristics, and so on. Then describe the object in subjective terms, explaining how you obtained it and why it is important to you. (Glossary: *Objective/Subjective*) Create a dominant impression of the object, and use concrete nouns and strong action verbs to make your description come alive. (Glossary: *Dominant Impression*)

2. In paragraph 46, Walker writes, "I made a jokey observation that before long somebody would probably start making white headphones so that people carrying knockoffs and tape players could fool the world into thinking they had trendy iPods." Have you ever fallen prey to a passing fad or trend? Have you ever gotten a particular haircut, dressed a certain way, bought a certain product, or listened to a particular type of music to fit in or feel like part of a group? Drawing on your own observations and experiences, as well as your Connecting Image and Text response for this selection, write a narrative essay about a time when you tried — either successfully or unsuccessfully — to fit in. (Glossary: *Narration*) Be sure to use specific details when describing your transformation.

3. Walker states that the iPod is, "in short, an icon" (paragraph 4). Every so often, an object surpasses fad status and becomes emblematic — an icon — of a time, place, or state of mind, instantly connecting the viewer of the object to what the object-icon symbolizes. For example, Volkswagen Beetles are tied to the 1960s, platform shoes to the 1970s, and Rubik's Cubes to the 1980s. Using the library or the Internet to do your research, write an essay in which you describe the process by which objects become iconographic. (Glossary: *Process Analysis*) Based on your research, do you agree with Walker that the iPod is an icon? If so, what do you think the iPod symbolizes? Are there other or more recent examples that better deserve the label *icon*? If so, what are they?

- To begin your research online, go to **bedfordstmartins.com /subjectsstrategies** and click on "Description" or browse the thematic directory of annotated links.

The House on Mango Street (FICTION)

Sandra Cisneros

Sandra Cisneros was born in Chicago in 1954. She received her B.A. from Loyola University in Chicago in 1976 and her M.F.A. from the University of Iowa in 1978. Cisneros has had numerous occupations in education and the arts and has been a visiting writer at various universities, including the University of California–Berkeley and the University of Michigan. Although she has written two well-received books of poetry, My Wicked, Wicked Ways *(1987) and* Loose Woman *(1994), she is better known for the autobiographical fiction of* The House on Mango Street *(1984) and for* Woman Hollering Creek and Other Stories *(1991), for which she won the PEN West Award for Fiction in 1991. In 1995 she was awarded a grant from the prestigious MacArthur Foundation. Her latest novel,* Caramelo, *was published in 2003.*

The following selection is an excerpt from The House on Mango Street.

PREPARING TO READ

Reflect on the place you call home or the various places you may have lived during your lifetime. How have the places where you have lived helped define you, for better or worse? How important is your home as a reflection of who you are?

We didn't always live on Mango Street. Before that we lived on 1 Loomis on the third floor, and before that we lived on Keeler. Before Keeler it was Paulina, and before that I can't remember. But what I remember most is moving a lot. Each time it seemed there'd be one more of us. By the time we got to Mango Street we were six — Mama, Papa, Carlos, Kiki, my sister Nenny and me.

The house on Mango Street is ours, and we don't have to pay rent 2 to anybody, or share the yard with the people downstairs, or be careful not to make too much noise, and there isn't a landlord banging on the ceiling with a broom. But even so, it's not the house we'd thought we'd get.

We had to leave the flat on Loomis quick. The water pipes broke 3 and the landlord wouldn't fix them because the house was too old. We had to leave fast. We were using the washroom next door and carrying water over in empty milk gallons. That's why Mama and Papa looked for a house, and that's why we moved into the house on Mango Street, far away, on the other side of town.

They always told us that one day we would move into a house, a   4
real house that would be ours for always so we wouldn't have to
move each year. And our house would have running water and pipes
that worked. And inside it would have real stairs, not hallway stairs,
but stairs inside like the houses on T.V. And we'd have a basement
and at least three washrooms so when we took a bath we wouldn't
have to tell everybody. Our house would be white with trees around
it, a great big yard and grass growing without a fence. This was the
house Papa talked about when he held a lottery ticket and this was
the house Mama dreamed up in the stories she told us before we
went to bed.

But the house on Mango Street is not the way they told it at all.   5
It's small and red with tight steps in front and windows so small you'd
think they were holding their breath. Bricks are crumbling in places,
and the front door is so swollen you have to push hard to get in. There
is no front yard, only four little elms the city planted by the curb. Our
back is a small garage for the car we don't own yet and a small yard
that looks smaller between the two buildings on either side. There are
stairs in our house, but they're ordinary hallway stairs, and the house
has only one washroom. Everybody has to share a bedroom — Mama
and Papa, Carlos and Kiki, me and Nenny.

Once when we were living on Loomis, a nun from my school   6
passed by and saw me playing out front. The laundromat downstairs
had been boarded up because it had been robbed two days before and
the owner had painted on the wood YES WE'RE OPEN so as not to lose
business.

Where do you live? she asked.   7

There, I said pointing up to the third floor.   8

You live *there?*   9

There. I had to look to where she pointed — the third floor, the   10
paint peeling, wooden bars Papa had nailed on the windows so we
wouldn't fall out. You live *there?* The way she said it made me feel
like nothing. *There.* I lived *there.* I nodded.

I knew then I had to have a house. A real house. One I could   11
point to. But this isn't it. The house on Mango Street isn't it. For the
time being, Mama says. Temporary, says Papa. But I know how those
things go.

RESPONDING TO THE TEXT

In paragraph 9, the nun says to the narrator, "You live *there?*" The narrator
then says, "The way she said it made me feel like nothing." Do you think
the nun meant to insult the narrator, or was she simply expressing shock at
the narrator's living conditions? Could the nun have anticipated she would
make the narrator feel bad?

ENGAGING THE WRITER'S SUBJECT

1. Who is the narrator? What do you know about her?

2. What role does the nun play in the narrator's desire for a house?

3. What does the narrator learn about the relationship between where she lives and her sense of self-worth?

ANALYZING THE WRITER'S CRAFT

1. How does the narrator describe the house on Mango Street? How does it differ from previous houses? What is her purpose in describing the house on Mango Street? (Glossary: *Purpose*)

2. How does the narrator describe her dream house? Is the description objective or subjective? How do you know?

3. How does the house on Mango Street both meet and fail to meet the narrator's expectations?

4. Cisneros describes the house in paragraphs 2 and 5. What information separates those paragraphs? Why do you suppose she organized her description as she did? (Glossary: *Organization*)

5. What dominant impression of housing in general does the narrator create? What details does she use to develop that dominant impression? (Glossary: *Dominant Impression*)

6. How does Cisneros use comparison and contrast to support her description of the house on Mango Street? (Glossary: *Comparison and Contrast*) What are the similarities and differences between the house that Cisneros moves into, the house that she lived in previously, and the house that she dreams about?

UNDERSTANDING THE WRITER'S LANGUAGE

1. Cinsneros's style is a good example of informal colloquial writing, meaning it is written as one might describe something orally. What examples can you find within Cisneros's writing of this style? (Glossary: *Style*) Why do you think she chose this style?

2. Cisneros uses the italicized word *there* five times near the end of the selection. What is her purpose in using italics? How effective are they in your judgment? (Glossary: *Emphasis*)

WRITING SUGGESTIONS

1. Have you ever dreamed about possessing or doing something only to be disappointed by following through on that dream? For example, have you ever fantasized taking a trip someplace only to be disappointed in actually seeing it? Using Cisneros's description as a model, write a descriptive essay in which you contrast what you anticipated with reality. (Glossary: *Comparison and Contrast*) How were your anticipated ideal

and reality similar or different? Do you think your expectations were too high? If so, why? What did you learn from the experience? Be sure to use specific strong nouns and verbs as well as figurative language to make your descriptions lively and engaging.

2. Write an essay in which you compare and contrast your dream house and your current home. (Glossary: *Comparison and Contrast*). What features, if any, of your current home would you like in your dream house? What features — for example, a pool, media room, mountain view, or large kitchen — would you like in your dream house? Why? Before you write, you might want to refer to your Preparing to Read response.

3. Research what housing options are available to low-income families in your area. What social services do the local government and private charities provide? Drawing on your research, write an essay in which you evaluate the resources available to people in need in your area. How do the services provided compare to those provided in wealthier or poorer areas? (Glossary: *Comparison and Contrast*) What suggestions, if any, do you have for improving the housing "safety net" in your area?

- To begin your research online, go to **bedfordstmartins.com /subjectsstrategies** and click on "Description" or browse the thematic directory of annotated links.

WRITING SUGGESTIONS FOR DESCRIPTION

1. Most description is predominantly visual; that is, it appeals to our sense of sight. Good description, however, often goes beyond the visual; it appeals as well to one or more of the other senses — hearing, smell, taste, and touch. One way to heighten your awareness of these other senses is to purposefully deemphasize the visual impressions you receive. For example, while standing on a busy street corner, sitting in a classroom, or shopping in a supermarket, carefully note what you hear, smell, taste, or feel. (It may help if you close your eyes to eliminate visual distractions as you carry out this experiment.) Use these sense impressions to write a brief description of the street corner, the classroom, the supermarket, or another spot of your choosing.

2. Select one of the following topics, and write an objective description of it. Remember that your task in writing an objective description is to inform the reader about the object, not to convey to the reader the mood or feeling that the object evokes in you.

   a. a pine tree
   b. a personal computer
   c. a café
   d. a dictionary
   e. a fast-food restaurant
   f. a basketball
   g. the layout of your campus
   h. a stereo system
   i. a houseplant
   j. your room

3. Writers of description often rely on factual information to make their writing more substantial and interesting. Using facts, statistics, or other information found in standard reference works in your college library (encyclopedias, dictionaries, almanacs, atlases, biographical dictionaries, or yearbooks), write an essay of several paragraphs describing one of the people, places, or things in the following list. Be sure that you focus your description, that you have a purpose for your description, and that you present your facts in an interesting manner.

   a. the Statue of Liberty
   b. the telephone
   c. Gloria Steinem
   d. the Grand Canyon
   e. the Great Wall of China
   f. Colin Powell
   g. Aretha Franklin
   h. the Tower of London
   i. the sun
   j. Disney World

k. the Hubble Space Telescope
l. Toni Morrison
m. Rosie O'Donnell
n. a local landmark

4. Select one of the following places, and write a multiparagraph description that captures your subjective sense impressions of that particular place.

a. a busy intersection
b. a bakery
c. a dorm room
d. a factory
e. a service station
f. a zoo
g. a cafeteria
h. a farmers' market
i. a concert hall
j. a locker room
k. a bank
l. a library

5. At college you have the opportunity to meet many new people, students as well as teachers; perhaps you would like to share your impressions of these people with a friend or family member. In a letter to someone back home, describe one of your new acquaintances. Try to capture the essence of the person you choose and to explain why this person stands out from all the other people you have met at school.

6. As a way of getting to know your campus, select a building, statue, sculpture, or other familiar landmark and research it. What's its significance or meaning to your college or university? Are there any ceremonies or rituals associated with the object? What are its distinctive or unusual features? When was it erected? Who sponsored it? Is it currently being used as originally intended? Once you have completed your informal research, write a description of your subject in which you create a dominant impression of your landmark's importance to the campus community.

You and your classmates may wish to turn this particular assignment into a collaborative class project: the compilation of a booklet of essays that introduces readers to the unique physical and historic features of your campus. To avoid duplication, the class should make a list of campus landmarks, and students should sign up for the one that they would like to write about.

CHAPTER 5

Narration

WHAT IS NARRATION?

We all love a good story. We want to find out what happens. The tremendous popularity of current fiction and biography reflects our avid interest in stories. Knowing of our interest in stories, many writers and speakers use them to their advantage. A science writer, for example, wishing to assert that many important scientific discoveries have been made by accident, could tell the story of how Sir Alexander Fleming discovered penicillin: Fleming noticed that a bit of mold had fallen into a culture plate in his laboratory and had destroyed bacteria around it. Or a religious leader writing a sermon about charity could illustrate the point that charity should not always be measured in monetary terms by telling the story of an old woman who spends hours every week visiting hospital patients. Or a politician giving a speech could engage the audience by starting off with a humorous anecdote.

Whenever you recount an event or tell a story or anecdote to illustrate an idea, you are using narration. In its broadest sense, narration includes all writing that gives an account of an event or a series of events in a logical sequence. Although you are already very familiar with narratives, you probably associate narration with novels, short fiction, poetry, and even movies. But narration is effective and useful in most nonfiction writing, such as biography, autobiography, history, and news reporting. A good narrative essay provides a meaningful account of some significant event — anything from an account of the U.S. involvement with Iraq to a personal experience that gave you new insight about yourself or others.

Consider, for example, the following narrative by E. J. Kahn Jr. about the invention of Coca-Cola as both a medicine and a soft drink, from his book *The Big Drink: The Story of Coca-Cola.*

Writer establishes context for his narrative about Pemberton and Coca-Cola.

Writer uses third-person point of view.

Writer organizes the narrative chronologically, using time markers.

Writer focuses on the discovery that led to Coca-Cola's becoming a popular soft drink.

The man who invented Coca-Cola was not a native Atlantan, but on the day of his funeral every drugstore in town testimonially shut up shop. He was John Styth Pemberton, born in 1833 in Knoxville, Georgia, eighty miles away. Sometimes known as Doctor, Pemberton was a pharmacist who, during the Civil War, led a cavalry troop under General Joe Wheeler. He settled in Atlanta in 1869, and soon began brewing such patent medicines as Triplex Liver Pills and Globe of Flower Cough Syrup. In 1885, he registered a trademark for something called French Wine Coca — Ideal Nerve and Tonic Stimulant; a few months later he formed the Pemberton Chemical Company, and recruited the services of a bookkeeper named Frank M. Robinson, who not only had a good head for figures but, attached to it, so exceptional a nose that he could audit the composition of a batch of syrup merely by sniffing it. In 1886 — a year in which, as contemporary Coca-Cola officials like to point out, Conan Doyle unveiled Sherlock Holmes and France unveiled the Statue of Liberty — Pemberton unveiled a syrup that he called Coca-Cola. He had taken out the wine and added a pinch of caffeine, and, when the end product tasted awful, had thrown in some extract of cola (or kola) nut and a few other oils, blending the mixture in a three-legged iron pot in his back yard and swishing it around with an oar. He distributed it to soda fountains in used beer bottles, and Robinson, with his flowing bookkeeper's script, presently devised a label on which "Coca-Cola" was written in the fashion that is still employed. Pemberton looked upon his concoction less as a refreshment than as a headache cure, especially for people whose throbbing temples could be traced to overindulgence. On a morning late in 1886, one such victim of the night before dragged himself into an Atlanta drugstore and asked for a dollop of Coca-Cola. Druggists customarily stirred a teaspoonful of syrup into a glass of water, but in this instance the factotum on duty was too lazy to walk to the fresh-water tap, a couple of feet off. Instead, he mixed the syrup with some charged water, which was closer at hand. The suffering customer perked up almost at once, and word quickly spread that the best Coca-Cola was a fizzy one.

A good narrative essay, like the paragraph above, has four essential features. The first is *context*: The writer makes clear when the action happened, where it happened, and to whom. The second is *point of view*: The writer establishes and maintains a consistent relationship to the action, either as a participant or as a reporter looking on. The third is *selection of detail*: The writer carefully chooses what to include, focusing on those actions and details that are most important to the story while playing down or even eliminating others. The fourth is *organization*: The writer arranges the events of the narrative in an appropriate sequence, often a strict chronology with a clear beginning, middle, and end.

As you read the selections in this chapter, watch for these features and for how each writer uses them to tell his or her story. Think about how each writer's choices affect the way you reacted to the selections.

WHY DO WRITERS USE NARRATION?

Good stories are compelling; we're hungry for them. We read novels and short stories, and we watch dramatized stories on television, at the movies, and in the theater because we're curious about others' lives. We want to know what happened to other people to gain insights into our own lives. The most basic and most important purpose of narration is to instruct, to share a meaningful experience with readers.

Another important purpose of narration is to report — to give the facts, to tell what happened. Journalists and historians, in reporting events of the near and more distant past, provide us with information that we can use to form opinions about a current issue or to better understand the world around us. A biographer gives us another person's life as a document of an individual's past but also, perhaps, as a portrait of more general human potential. Scientists recount studies and experiments so that we may judge for ourselves whether their conclusions are to be believed. We expect writers to make these narratives as objective as possible and to distinguish between facts and opinions.

Narration is often used in combination with one or more of the other rhetorical strategies. In an essay that is written primarily to explain a process — reading a book, for example — a writer might find it useful to tell a brief story or anecdote demonstrating an instance when the process worked especially well (Mortimer Adler, "How to Mark a Book," Chapter 6). In the same way, a writer attempting to define the term *poverty* might tell several stories to illustrate clearly the many facets of poverty (Jo Goodwin Parker, "What Is Poverty?" Chapter 9). Finally, a writer could use narrative examples to persuade — for example, to argue that growing genetically altered crops is a step backward for agriculture (Jim Scharplaz, "Weeding Out the Skilled Farmer," Chapter 11) or to demonstrate for readers the power and clarity of monosyllabic words (Richard Lederer, "The Case for Short Words,"

Chapter 11). Essays that use process analysis, definition, and argumentation as their dominant strategies are addressed in detail in Chapters 6, 9, and 11, respectively.

A narrative may present a straightforward moral, or it may make a more subtle point about ourselves and the world we live in. In each of the narratives in this chapter, we witness a slice of the ongoing human drama. In "Coming to an Awareness of Language," Malcolm X tells of his discovery of the power of the written and spoken word. Annie Dillard reveals the surprising lesson learned from a childhood prank in "Getting Caught." In "Stranger Than True," attorney Barry Winston tells a story to explain why he defends guilty clients. In David P. Bardeen's essay "Not Close Enough for Comfort," he takes us inside his relationship with his twin brother and shows us what happens when David finally reveals a long-kept secret. And in "A Worn Path," Eudora Welty shows us the character of former slave Phoenix Jackson as she encounters and overcomes obstacles on her journey to Natchez, Mississippi.

AN ANNOTATED STUDENT ESSAY USING NARRATION

Andrew Kauser, a student at the University of Vermont, was born in Montreal, Canada, where he grew up and still makes his home. As a youngster, he often went on weekend-long flying trips with his father, who is a pilot; these experiences instilled in him a passion for flying and a desire to get his own pilot's license. In the following essay, Kauser writes how he felt as he took that most important step in becoming a licensed pilot, the first solo flight.

Challenging My Fears

Andrew Kauser

Context is set — writer driving to airport on chilly autumn morning for first solo flight.

Cedars Airport, just off the western tip of Montreal, is about a half-hour drive from my house. Today's drive is boring as usual except for the chill which runs up the back of my legs because of the cold breeze entering through the rusted floorboards. I peer through the dew-covered windshield to see the leaves changing color. Winter is on its way.

Writer tells story in present tense and uses first-person point of view.

Finally, I arrive at the airport; while my instructor waits, I do my aircraft check. I curse as I touch the steely cold parts of the aircraft. Even though the discomfort is

1

2

great, I do my check slowly. Hurrying could
make me miss a potential problem. It is better to find a problem on the ground instead
of in the air. The check takes about fifteen
minutes, and by this time my fingertips are
white. Everything appears to be in order so
now it is time to start up.

*Writer presents
events in
chronological
order.*

My instructor and I climb into the   3
cockpit of the airplane and strap ourselves
in. The plane has been out all night, and it
is just as cold inside as it is outside. My
back shivers as I sit in the seat, and the
controls are painfully cold to touch. The
plane starts without a hint of trouble, and
in one continuous motion I taxi onto the
runway. At full throttle we begin to increase our speed down the runway. In a matter of seconds we leave the ground. The
winds are calm and the visibility is endless. It's a beautiful day to fly.

The object of today's lesson is to prac-   4
tice taking off and landing. The first "touch
and go" is so smooth that I surprise both myself and my instructor. Unfortunately, my
next two attempts are more like "smash and
goes." I land once more; this time it is not

*Writer introduces
central idea — solo
flight.*

as jarring as my last two, and my instructor
gives me the O.K. to do a circuit alone. We
taxi to the hangar, and he gets out.

Confined in the small cockpit with my   5
seatbelt strapped around me as tightly as it
will go, I look out the window and watch my
human security blanket walking back toward
the hangars. The calm feeling with which I

*Writer uses
figurative language
to describe his
feelings.*

began the day quickly disappears. I feel like
a soldier being sent to the front lines. I
begin to feel smothered by the enclosed cockpit. My stomach tightens around the breakfast
I ate and squeezes out my last breath. I gulp
for air, and my breathing becomes irregular.
My mind still functions, though, and I begin
to taxi toward the runway.

Key word taxi *is repeated to make a transition.*

It is a long taxi, and I have ample time to think about what I am about to do. I remember the time when my father had to land on a football field when his engine quit. My eyes scan the instruments quickly in hope of finding something comforting in all the dials. My hands are still feeling quite cool. I reach out and pull the lever

Writer's selection of detail reveals his state of mind.

for cabin heat. A rush of warm air saturated with the smell of the engine fills the cockpit. This allows me some comfort as my mind begins to wander. The radio crackles and breaks my train of thought. A student pilot in the air with his instructor announces that he is on final approach for landing. While still taxiing, I look through the Plexiglas windscreen to watch him land. The plane hits hard and bounces right back into the air. It comes down again, and as though on springs, leaps back into the air. Once again it comes down and this time stays.

At the parking area off the runway, I close the throttle and bring the plane to a stop. I check the instruments and request clearance for take-off from the tower. While I wait, I try to calm down.

Now hold your breath and count to ten. Look, the chances of dying in a car accident are twenty times greater, I think to myself. Somehow that isn't very comforting. The radio crackles, and I exhale quickly. Permission is granted.

Dramatic short sentence announces the start of the solo.

I taxi onto the runway and come to a stop. I mentally list my options, but they are very few. One is to get up the courage to challenge my fears; the other, to turn the plane around and shamefully go back to the

Writer makes connection to title.

hangar. Well, the choices are limited, but the ultimate decision seems fairly obvious. I reach out and push the throttle into the

6

7

8

9

full open position. The engine roars to life. The decision to go has been made. The plane screams down the runway, and at fifty-five knots I pull back on the controls. In one clean movement, the plane and I leave the ground.

The noise of the engine is the only   10
thing I can hear as the air pressure begins to clog my ears. My mind still racing, I check my instruments. The winds are still calm, and the plane cuts through the air without a hint of trouble. Warm gas-laden air streams through the vents as the sun streaks into the cockpit through the passenger window, and I begin to feel quite hot. At seven hundred feet above the ground, I turn left, check for any traffic, and continue climbing. At twelve hundred feet, I turn left onto the downward portion of the circuit which is parallel to the runway.

This is a longer stretch, and I take a   11
moment to gaze down at the ground below. The view is simply amazing. The trees are all rich bright colors, and I can see for miles. Then it hits me. I'm flying alone. It's great, almost tranquil, no instructor yelling

Writer's choice of details shows his growing calm once airborne.

things into my ear, just the machine and myself. A relaxed feeling comes over me, and I start to enjoy the flight. I check my instruments again and start to descend as I turn left.

Turning on the final approach, I an-   12
nounce my intentions on the radio. The nice feeling of calm leaves me just as quickly as it came. What is there to worry about, Andrew? All you have to do is land the airplane, preferably on the runway. My heart starts to pound quickly, almost to the beat of the motor. Where is my instructor? Why am I alone?

Writer addresses himself directly as he once again challenges his fears.

Short sentences enhance tension and drama of landing.

13   Lower the nose, Andrew. Don't lose speed. Give it some more power, maintain your glidepath. That's it. Bank a little to the left. Now you're doing it, just a little further. My ears begin to pop as the pressure on them decreases, and the motor gets quieter as I start to decrease power. The plane passes over the threshold of the runway. I begin to raise the nose. The wheels utter a squeal as they touch down, but the impact quickly sends the plane back into the air. The wheels hit again; this time they stay down, and I roll to a stop.

Writer comments on the meaning of his first solo flight.

14   Back at the hangar, I climb out of the plane and shudder as the cool air hits me again. A smile comes across my face, and it persists. I told myself that I would just be cool about it and not try to show any emotion, but it isn't going to work. I can't stop smiling as my instructor congratulates me. I smile because I know that I was successful in challenging and overcoming my fears.

Analyzing Andrew Kauser's Essay of Narration: Questions for Discussion

1. What context does Kauser provide for his narrative? What else, if anything, would you have liked to have known about the situation?

2. Kauser tells his story in the first person. How would the narrative have changed had he used a third-person point of view?

3. What details in Kauser's narrative did you find most effective? Are there places where you think he could have used more detail? Explain.

4. Kauser uses a straightforward chronological organization in his narrative. How might he have used flashbacks in his narrative? What would have been the effect?

5. What meaning or importance do you think this experience holds for Kauser?

SUGGESTIONS FOR WRITING A NARRATIVE ESSAY

Keep in mind the basic features of narration, and use them when plaɪ ning, writing, and revising your narrative essay. How you use those features will depend on the story you have to tell and your purpose for telling it.

Select a Topic That Has Meaning for You

In your writing course, you may have the freedom to choose the story you want to narrate, or your instructor may give you a list of topics from which to choose. Instead of jumping at the first topic that looks good, brainstorm a list of events that have had an impact on your life and that you could write about. For example, such a list might include your first blind date, catching frogs as a child, making a team or a club, the death of a loved one, a graduation celebration, a trip to the Grand Canyon, the loss of a pet, learning to drive a car, or even the breakup of a relationship. As you narrow down your options, look for an event or an incident that is particularly memorable for you. Memorable experiences are memorable for a reason; they offer us important insights into our lives. Such experiences are worth narrating because people want to read about them. Before you begin writing, ask yourself why the experience you have chosen is meaningful to you. What did you learn from it? How are you different as a result of the experience? What has changed?

Determine Your Point and Purpose

Right from the beginning, ask yourself what the significance is of the event you are narrating and why you are telling your story. Your narrative point (the meaning of your narrative) and purpose in writing will influence which events and details you include and which you leave out. Suppose, for example, you choose to write about how you learned to ride a bicycle. In some neighborhoods, learning to ride a bike is a real rite of passage. If, however, you mean mainly to entertain, you will probably include a number of unusual and amazing incidents unique to your experience. If your purpose is mainly to report or inform, it will make more sense to concentrate on the kinds of details that are common to most people's experience. However, if your purpose is to tell your readers step-by-step how to ride a bicycle, you should use process analysis, a strategy used by writers whose purpose is to give directions for how something is done or to explain how something works (see Chapter 6).

The most successful narrative essays, however, do more than entertain or inform. While narratives do not have a formal thesis statement, readers will more than likely expect your story to make a statement or to arrive at some meaningful conclusion — implied or explicit — about your experience. The student essay by Andrew Kauser, for example, shows how important it was for him to challenge his fears. In overcoming his fears of flying solo, he gains a measure of control over his life. Certainly, you will not be happy if your story is dismissed as essentially "pointless." So as you prepare to write, look for the significance in the story you want to tell — some broader, more instructive points it could make about the ways of the world. Learning to ride a bicycle may not suggest such points to you, and it may therefore not be a very good subject for your narrative essay. However, the subject does have possibilities. Here's one: Learning to master a difficult, even dangerous, but definitely useful skill like riding a bicycle is an important experience to have in life. Here's another: Learning to ride a bicycle is an opportunity for you to acquire and use some basic physics, such as the laws of gravity and the behavior of a gyroscope. Perhaps you can think of others. If, however, you do not know why you are telling the story and it seems pointless even to you, your readers will pick up on the ambivalence in your writing, and you should probably find another, more meaningful story to tell.

Establish a Context

Early in your essay, perhaps in the opening paragraphs, establish the context, or setting, of your story — the world within which the action took place:

> *When it happened* — morning; afternoon; 11:37 on the dot; 1997; winter
>
> *Where it happened* — in the street; at Wendy's; in Pocatello, Idaho
>
> *To whom it happened* — to me; to my father; to the assistant; to Teri Hopper

Without a clear context, your readers can easily get confused or even completely lost. And remember, readers respond well to specific contextual information because such details make them feel like they are present, ready to witness the narrative.

Choose the Most Appropriate Point of View

Consider what point of view to take in your narrative. Did you take part in the action? If so, it will seem most natural for you to use the first-person (*I, we*) point of view. On the other hand, if you weren't there at all and must rely on other sources for your information, you will probably choose the third-person (*he, she, it, they*) point of view, as did the author writing about the invention of Coca-Cola earlier in this chapter. However, if you were a witness to part or all of what happened but not a participant, then you will need to choose between the more immediate and subjective quality of the first person and the more distanced, objective effect of the third person. Whichever you choose, you should maintain the same point of view throughout your narrative.

Select Details That "Show, Don't Tell"

When writing your essay, you should include enough detail about the action, the people involved, and the context to let your readers understand what is going on. Start collecting details by asking yourself the traditional reporter's questions:

- Who was involved?
- What happened?
- Where did it happen?
- When did it happen?
- Why did it happen?
- How did it happen?

Generate as many details as you can because you never know which ones will prove valuable in developing your narrative point so that your essay *shows* and doesn't *tell* too much. For example, instead of telling readers that he is scared, Andrew Kauser shows us his irregular breathing and tightening stomach and lets us draw our own conclusion about his state of mind. As you write, you will want to select and emphasize details that support your point, serve your purpose, and show the reader what is happening. Above all, you should not get so carried away with details that your readers become confused or bored by excess information. In good storytelling, deciding what to leave out can be as important as deciding what to include. In his narrative about the discovery of Coca-Cola, E. J. Kahn Jr. gives us just enough information about inventor John Styth Pemberton to make him interesting but not so much as to distract readers from the story.

Organize Your Narrative

Storytellers tend to follow an old rule: Begin at the beginning, and go on till you come to the end; then stop. Chronological organization is natural in narration because it is a retelling of the original order of events; it is also easiest for the writer to manage and the reader to understand.

Some narratives, however, are organized using a technique common in movies and theater called *flashback*: The writer may begin midway through the story, or even at the end, with an important or exciting event, then use flashbacks to fill in what happened earlier to lead up to that event. Some authors begin in the present and then use flashbacks to shift to the past to tell the story. Whatever organizational pattern you choose, words and phrases like *for a month, afterward,* and *three days earlier* are examples of devices that will help you and your reader keep the sequence of events straight.

It may help you in organizing to jot down a quick outline before tackling the first draft of your narrative. Here's the outline that Andrew Kauser used to order the events in his narrative chronologically.

> Narration about My First Solo Airplane Flight
>
> Point: You don't get anywhere by just sitting around being afraid.
>
> Context: Cedars Airport outside Montreal, early morning, autumn.
>
> 1. Drive to airport sets scene.
> 2. Perform my aircraft safety check.
> 3. Practice takeoffs and landings with instructor.
> 4. Wait for clearance to take off on solo.
> 5. Decide to solo in spite of my fears.
> 6. Take off on my first solo.
> 7. Thrill at the reality of flying alone.
> 8. Fears return as I think about landing alone.
> 9. Celebrate my victory over my fears.

Such an outline can remind you of your point, your organization, and the emphasis you want when you write your first draft.

Keep Your Verb Tense Consistent

Most narratives are in the past tense, and this is logical: They recount events that have already happened, even if very recently. But writers sometimes use the present tense to create an effect of intense immediacy, as if the events were happening as you read about them. The essay by Andrew Kauser is an example of a narrative using the present tense. The important thing to remember is to be consistent. If you are recounting an event that has already occurred, use the past tense throughout. For an event in the present, use the present tense consistently. If you find yourself jumping from a present event to a past event, as in the case of a flashback, you will need to switch verb tenses to signal the change in time.

Use Narrative Time for Emphasis

The number of words or pages you devote to an event does not usually correspond to the number of minutes or hours the event took to happen. You may require several pages to recount an important or complex quarter of an hour, but then pass over several hours or days in a sentence or two. Length has less to do with chronological time than with the amount of detail you include, and that's a function of the amount of emphasis you want to give to a particular incident.

Use Transitional Words to Clarify Narrative Sequence

Transitional words like *after, next, then, earlier, immediately,* and *finally* are useful, as they help your readers smoothly connect and understand the sequence of events that makes up your narrative. Likewise, a specific time mark like *on April 20, two weeks earlier,* and *in 2004* can indicate time shifts and can signal to readers how much time has elapsed between events. But inexperienced writers sometimes overuse these words; this makes their writing style wordy and tiresome. Use these conventional transitions when you really need them, but when you don't — when your readers can follow your story without them — leave them out.

Use Dialogue to Bring Your Narrative to Life

Having people in a narrative speak is a very effective way of showing rather than telling or summarizing what happened. Snippets of actual dialogue make a story come alive and feel immediate to the reader.

Consider the following passages from a student narrative, an early draft without dialogue:

> I hated having to call a garage, but I knew I couldn't do the work myself and I knew they'd rip me off. Besides, I had to get the car off the street before the police had it towed. I felt trapped without any choices.

Now compare this early draft, in which the writer summarizes and tells us what happened in very general terms, with the revised draft below, in which the situation is revealed through dialogue.

> "University Gulf, Glen speaking. What can I do for ya?"
>
> "Yeah, my car broke down. I think it's the timing belt, and I was wondering if you could give me an estimate."
>
> "What kind of car is it?" asked Glen.
>
> "A Nissan Sentra."
>
> "What year?"
>
> "1995," I said, emphasizing the 95.
>
> "Oh, those are a bitch to work on. Can ya hold on for a second?"
>
> I knew what was coming before Glen came back on the line.

With dialogue, readers can hear the direct exchange between the car owner and the mechanic. You can use dialogue in your own writing to deliver a sense of immediacy to the reader.

Editing Tip: Run-on sentences, comma splices, and sentence fragments

Be sure to follow the guidelines and advice for editing an essay given in Chapter 2, "Writing Essays." The guidelines highlight those sentence-level concerns — grammar, mechanics, and punctuation — that are especially important in editing any piece of writing. When writing personal narratives and other types of stories, writers can become so absorbed in capturing the flow of events that occasionally they run sentences together without proper punctuation or create incomplete or fragmentary sentences. While editing your narrative essay, look for instances of three common sentence faults: run-on sentences, comma splices, and sentence fragments.

A *run-on sentence*, or *fused sentence*, occurs when a writer joins two sentences with no punctuation and no coordinating conjunction.

TWO CORRECT SENTENCES	A black Buick was moving toward us down the street. We all spread out, banged together some regular snowballs, took aim, and, when the Buick drew nigh, fired.

— ANNIE DILLARD,
"Getting Caught," page 180

RUN-ON SENTENCE   A black Buick was moving toward us down the street we all spread out, banged together some regular snowballs, took aim, and, when the Buick drew nigh, fired.

A *comma splice* occurs when a writer uses only a comma to join two sentences.

COMMA SPLICE   A black Buick was moving toward us down the street, we all spread out, banged together some regular snowballs, took aim, and, when the Buick drew nigh, fired.

There are five ways to fix run-on sentences and comma splices.

1. Create two separate sentences with a period.

A black Buick was moving toward us down the street. We all spread out, banged together some regular snowballs, took aim, and, when the Buick drew nigh, fired.

2. Use a comma and a coordinating conjunction (and, or, nor, for, so, but, yet) to join the two sentences.

A black Buick was moving toward us down the street, *so* we all spread out, banged together some regular snowballs, took aim, and, when the Buick drew nigh, fired.

3. Use a semicolon to separate the two sentences.

A black Buick was moving toward us down the street; we all spread out, banged together some regular snowballs, took aim, and, when the Buick drew nigh, fired.

4. Use a semicolon followed by a transitional word or expression and a comma to join the two sentences.

A black Buick was moving toward us down the street; *therefore*, we all spread out, banged together some regular snowballs, took aim, and, when the Buick drew nigh, fired.

5. Subordinate one sentence to the other, using a subordinate conjunction or a relative pronoun.

As a black Buick was moving toward us down the street, we all spread out, banged together some regular snowballs, took aim, and, when the Buick drew nigh, fired.

A **sentence fragment** is a part of a sentence presented as if it were a complete sentence. That is, it begins with a capital letter and ends with a period, question mark, or exclamation point, but it does not include one of the two essential elements — a subject or a verb — required of a grammatically complete sentence.

SENTENCE   Alec called and made an appointment to see me. A nice
FRAGMENT   kid, fresh out of high school.

You can correct sentence fragments in one of two ways.

1. Integrate the fragment into a nearby sentence.

> Alec — *a nice kid, fresh out of high school* — called and made an appointment to see me.

2. Develop the fragment itself into a complete sentence by adding a subject or a verb.

> Alec called and made an appointment to see me. *He's* a nice kid, fresh out of high school.

Sentence fragments are not always wrong. In fact, if not overused, a deliberate sentence fragment can add emphasis. In narratives, deliberate sentence fragments are most commonly used in dialogue and in descriptive passages that set a mood or tone. In the following passage, David P. Bardeen uses fragments to set the stage for the unsettling luncheon meeting he had with his brother Will:

> I asked him about his recent trip. He asked me about work. Short questions. One-word answers. Then an awkward pause.
>
> — DAVID P. BARDEEN
> "Not Close Enough for Comfort," page 193

▶ *Questions for Revising and Editing: Narration*

1. Is my narrative well focused, or do I try to cover too long a period of time?
2. What is my reason for telling this story? Is that reason clearly stated or implied for readers?
3. Have I established a clear context for my readers? Is it clear when the action happened, where it happened, and to whom?

(*continued on next page*)

(*continued from previous page*)

4. Have I used the most effective point of view to tell my story? How would my story be different had I used another point of view?

5. Have I selected details that help readers understand what is going on in my narrative, or have I included unnecessary details that distract readers or get in the way of what I'm trying to say? Do I give enough examples of the important events in my narrative?

6. Is the chronology of events in my narrative clear? Have I taken advantage of opportunities to add emphasis, drama, or suspense with flashbacks or other complications of the chronological organization?

7. Have I used transitional expressions or time markers to help readers follow the sequencing of events in my narrative?

8. Have I employed dialogue in my narrative to reveal a situation, or have I told about or summarized the situation too much?

9. Have I avoided run-on sentences and comma splices? Have I used sentence fragments only deliberately to convey mood or tone?

10. Is the meaning of my narrative clear? Or have I left my readers thinking, "So what?"

Coming to an Awareness of Language

Malcolm X

In the course of Malcolm X's brief life, he rose from a world of street crime to become one of the most powerful and articulate African American leaders in the United States during the 1960s. On February 21, 1965, his life was cut short at age thirty-nine; he was shot and killed as he addressed an afternoon rally in Harlem. Malcolm X told his life story in The Autobiography of Malcolm X *(1964), written with the assistance of* Roots *author Alex Haley. The book, a moving account of his life and his struggle for fulfillment, is still read by hundreds of thousands each year. In 1992, the life of this influential African American leader was reexamined in Spike Lee's film* Malcolm X.

The following selection from The Autobiography *refers to a period Malcolm X spent in federal prison. In the selection, Malcolm X explains how he was frustrated by his inability to express his ideas and how this frustration led him to a goal: acquiring the skills of reading and writing.*

PREPARING TO READ

Our educational system places a great emphasis on our having a large and varied working vocabulary. Has anyone ever stressed to you the importance of developing a good vocabulary? What did you think when you heard this advice? In what ways can words be used as powerful tools? How would you judge your own vocabulary?

I've never been one for inaction. Everything I've ever felt strongly about, I've done something about. I guess that's why, unable to do anything else, I soon began writing to people I had known in the hustling world, such as Sammy the Pimp, John Hughes, the gambling house owner, the thief Jumpsteady, and several dope peddlers. I wrote them all about Allah and Islam and Mr. Elijah Muhammad. I had no idea where most of them lived. I addressed their letters in care of the Harlem or Roxbury bars and clubs where I'd known them.

I never got a single reply. The average hustler and criminal was too uneducated to write a letter. I have known many slick, sharp-looking hustlers, who would have you think they had an interest in Wall Street; privately, they would get someone else to read a letter if they received one. Besides, neither would I have replied to anyone writing me something as wild as "the white man is the devil."

What certainly went on the Harlem and Roxbury wires was that Detroit Red was going crazy in stir, or else he was trying some hype to shake up the warden's office.

During the years that I stayed in the Norfolk Prison Colony, never did any official directly say anything to me about those letters, although, of course, they all passed through the prison censorship. I'm sure, however, they monitored what I wrote to add to the files which every state and federal prison keeps on the conversion of Negro inmates by the teachings of Mr. Elijah Muhammad.

But at that time, I felt that the real reason was that the white man knew that he was the devil.

Later on, I even wrote to the Mayor of Boston, to the Governor of Massachusetts, and to Harry S. Truman. They never answered; they probably never even saw my letters. I handscratched to them how the white man's society was responsible for the black man's condition in this wilderness of North America.

It was because of my letters that I happened to stumble upon starting to acquire some kind of a homemade education.

I became increasingly frustrated at not being able to express what I wanted to convey in letters that I wrote, especially those to Mr. Elijah Muhammad. In the street, I had been the most articulate hustler out there — I had commanded attention when I said something. But now, trying to write simple English, I not only wasn't articulate, I wasn't even functional. How would I sound writing in slang, the way I would *say* it, something such as, "Look, daddy, let me pull your coat about a cat. Elijah Muhammad —"

Many who today hear me somewhere in person, or on television, or those who read something I've said, will think I went to school far beyond the eighth grade. This impression is due entirely to my prison studies.

It had really begun back in the Charlestown Prison, when Bimbi first made me feel envy of his stock of knowledge. Bimbi had always taken charge of any conversation he was in, and I had tried to emulate him. But every book I picked up had few sentences which didn't contain anywhere from one to nearly all of the words that might as well have been in Chinese. When I just skipped those words, of course, I really ended up with little idea of what the book said. So I had come to the Norfolk Prison Colony still going through only book-reading motions. Pretty soon, I would have quit even these motions, unless I had received the motivation that I did.

I saw that the best thing I could do was get hold of a dictionary — to study, to learn some words. I was lucky enough to reason also that I should try to improve my penmanship. It was sad. I couldn't even write in a straight line. It was both ideas together that moved me to request a dictionary along with some tablets and pencils from the Norfolk Prison Colony school.

I spent two days just riffling uncertainly through the dictionary's 12 pages. I'd never realized so many words existed! I didn't know *which* words I needed to learn. Finally, just to start some kind of action, I began copying.

In my slow, painstaking, ragged handwriting, I copied into my 13 tablet everything printed on that first page, down to the punctuation marks.

I believe it took me a day. Then, aloud, I read back, to myself, 14 everything I'd written on the tablet. Over and over, aloud, to myself, I read my own handwriting.

I woke up the next morning, thinking about those words — 15 immensely proud to realize that not only had I written so much at one time, but I'd written words that I never knew were in the world. Moreover, with a little effort, I also could remember what many of these words meant. I reviewed the words whose meanings I didn't remember. Funny thing, from the dictionary first page right now, that "aardvark" springs to my mind. The dictionary had a picture of it, a long-tailed, long-eared, burrowing African mammal, which lives off termites caught by sticking out its tongue as an anteater does for ants.

I was so fascinated that I went on — I copied the dictionary's next 16 page. And the same experience came when I studied that. With every succeeding page, I also learned of people and places and events from history. Actually the dictionary is like a miniature encyclopedia. Finally the dictionary's A section had filled a whole tablet — and I went on into the B's. That was the way I started copying what eventually became the entire dictionary. It went a lot faster after so much practice helped me to pick up handwriting speed. Between what I wrote in my tablet, and writing letters, during the rest of my time in prison I would guess I wrote a million words.

I suppose it was inevitable that as my word-base broadened, I 17 could for the first time pick up a book and read and now begin to understand what the book was saying. Anyone who has read a great deal can imagine the new world that opened. Let me tell you something: from then until I left that prison, in every free moment I had, if I was not reading in the library, I was reading on my bunk. You couldn't have gotten me out of books with a wedge. Between Mr. Muhammad's teachings, my correspondence, my visitors . . . and my reading of books, months passed without my even thinking about being imprisoned. In fact, up to then, I never had been so truly free in my life.

RESPONDING TO THE TEXT

We are all to one degree or another prisoners of our own language. Sometimes we lack the ability to communicate as effectively as we would like. Why do you think this happens, and what do you think can be done to remedy it? How can improved language skills also improve a person's life?

ENGAGING THE WRITER'S SUBJECT

1. In paragraph 8, Malcolm X refers to the difference between being "articulate" and being "functional" in his speaking and writing. What is the distinction he makes? In your opinion, is it a valid one?

2. Malcolm X offers two possible reasons for the warden's keeping track of African American inmates' conversion to the teachings of Elijah Muhammad. What are those two assertions, and what is their effect on the reader?

3. What is the nature of the freedom that Malcolm X refers to in the final sentence? In what sense can language be said to be liberating?

ANALYZING THE WRITER'S CRAFT

1. Malcolm X narrates his experiences as a prisoner using the first-person *I*. Why is the first person particularly appropriate? What would be lost or gained had he narrated his story using the third-person pronoun *he?*

2. In the opening paragraph, Malcolm X refers to himself as a man of action and conviction. What details does he include to support this assertion?

3. Many people think of "vocabulary building" as learning strange, multisyllabic, difficult-to-spell words. But acquiring an effective vocabulary does not have to be so intimidating. How would you characterize Malcolm X's vocabulary in this narrative? Did you find his word choice suited to what he was trying to accomplish in this selection?

4. What is Malcolm X's narrative point in this passage? How do you know? What does he learn about himself as a result of this experience?

5. In reflecting on his years in prison, Malcolm X comes to an understanding of the events that caused him to reassess his life and take charge of his own education. Identify those events, and discuss the changes that resulted from Malcolm X's actions. How does his inclusion of these causal links enhance the overall narrative? (Glossary: *Cause and Effect Analysis*)

UNDERSTANDING THE WRITER'S LANGUAGE

1. Although Malcolm X taught himself to be articulate, we can still "hear" a street-savvy voice in his writing. Cite examples of his diction that convey a streetwise sound. (Glossary: *Diction*)

2. What do you do when you encounter new words in your reading? Do you skip those words as Malcolm X once did, do you take the time to

look them up, or do you try to figure out their meanings from the context? Explain the strategies you use to determine the meaning of a word from its context. Can you think of other strategies?

3. Refer to your desk dictionary to determine the meanings of the following words as Malcolm X uses them in this selection: *hustler* (paragraph 2), *slick* (2), *hype* (3), *frustrated* (8), *emulate* (10), *riffling* (12), *inevitable* (17).

WRITING SUGGESTIONS

1. Using Malcolm X's essay as a model, write a narrative about some goal you have set and achieved in which you were motivated by a strong inner conflict. What was the nature of your conflict? What feeling did it arouse in you, and how did the conflict help you to accomplish your goal?

2. Malcolm X solved the problems of his own near-illiteracy by carefully studying the dictionary. Would this be a practical solution to the national problem of illiteracy? In your experience, what does it mean to be literate? Write a proposal on what can be done to promote literacy in this country. You might also consider what is being done now in your community.

3. There are a tremendous number of language resources on the Internet. Explore the Internet; what language Web sites can you find? Do you think the Internet is a good medium for building a stronger vocabulary? Why or why not? Write an essay about how people can use libraries and the Internet to improve their language skills.

• To begin your research online, go to **bedfordstmartins.com /subjectsstrategies** and click on "Narration" or browse the thematic directory of annotated links.

Getting Caught

Annie Dillard

Born in Pittsburgh, Pennsylvania, in 1945, Annie Dillard has written in many genres. Her first two books were both published in 1974, before she was thirty years old; the first was a collection of poems entitled Tickets for a Prayer Wheel *and the second was* Pilgrim at Tinker Creek, *a Pulitzer Prize–winning book of essays based on her observations of and reflections about nature. She has explored the world of fiction, writing books of criticism (*Living by Fiction, *1982, and* Encounters with Chinese Writers, *1984) and a novel (*The Living, *1992). Most recently, she published a collection of essays,* For the Time Being *(2000).*

In one of her early essays, Dillard expressed a mistrust of memoirs, saying, "I don't recommend, or even approve, writing personally. It can lead to dreadful writing." By 1987, however, she had put this warning aside to publish an autobiography, An American Childhood, *from which this selection is taken. The book details Dillard's memories of her years growing up in Pittsburgh and is filled with the wonder and joy of living. "Getting Caught" (the editors' title) reflects the tone of the book as a whole.*

PREPARING TO READ

What activity are you passionate about — an activity that makes you give your all? A sport is a good example of a pursuit that demands and rewards total involvement, but you might also want to consider other types of activities. What satisfactions result from wholehearted participation in the activity of your choice?

Some boys taught me to play football. This was fine sport. You 1
thought up a new strategy for every play and whispered it to the others. You went out for a pass, fooling everyone. Best, you got to throw yourself mightily at someone's running legs. Either you brought him down or you hit the ground flat out on your chin, with your arms empty before you. It was all or nothing. If you hesitated in fear, you would miss and get hurt: you would take a hard fall while the kid got away, or you would get kicked in the face while the kid got away. But if you flung yourself wholeheartedly at the back of his knees — if you gathered and joined body and soul and pointed them diving fearlessly — then you likely wouldn't get hurt, and you'd stop the ball. Your fate, and your team's score, depended on your concentration and courage. Nothing girls did could compare with it.

Boys welcomed me at baseball, too, for I had, through enthusiastic 2
practice, what was weirdly known as a boy's arm. In winter, in the

snow, there was neither baseball nor football, so the boys and I threw
snowballs at passing cars. I got in trouble throwing snowballs, and
have seldom been happier since.

On one weekday morning after Christmas, six inches of new snow   3
had just fallen. We were standing up to our boot tops in snow on a
front yard on trafficked Reynolds Street, waiting for cars. The cars traveled Reynolds Street slowly and evenly; they were targets all but
wrapped in red ribbons, cream puffs. We couldn't miss.

I was seven; the boys were eight, nine, and ten. The oldest two   4
Fahey boys were there — Mikey and Peter — polite blond boys who
lived near me on Lloyd Street, and who already had four brothers and
sisters. My parents approved Mikey and Peter Fahey. Chickie McBride
was there, a tough kid, and Billy Paul and Mackie Kean too, from
across Reynolds, where the boys grew up dark and furious, grew up
skinny, knowing, and skilled. We had all drifted from our houses that
morning looking for action, and had found it here on Reynolds Street.

It was cloudy but cold. The cars' tires laid behind them on the   5
snowy street a complex trail of beige chunks like crenellated castle walls.
I had stepped on some earlier; they squeaked. We could have wished for
more traffic. When a car came, we all popped it one. In the intervals between cars we reverted to the natural solitude of children.

I started making an iceball — a perfect iceball, from perfectly white   6
snow, perfectly spherical, and squeezed perfectly translucent so no
snow remained all the way through. (The Fahey boys and I considered
it unfair actually to throw an iceball at somebody, but it had been
known to happen.)

I had just embarked on the iceball project when we heard tire chains   7
come clanking from afar. A black Buick was moving toward us down the
street. We all spread out, banged together some regular snowballs, took
aim, and, when the Buick drew nigh, fired.

A soft snowball hit the driver's windshield right before the driver's   8
face. It made a smashed star with a hump in the middle.

Often, of course, we hit our target, but this time, the only time in   9
all of life, the car pulled over and stopped. Its wide black door opened;
a man got out of it, running. He didn't even close the car door.

He ran after us, and we ran away from him, up the snowy Reynolds   10
sidewalk. At the corner, I looked back; incredibly, he was still after us.
He was in city clothes: a suit and tie, street shoes. Any normal adult
would have quit, having sprung us into flight and made his point. This
man was gaining on us. He was a thin man, all action. All of a sudden,
we were running for our lives.

Wordless, we split up. We were on our turf; we could lose our-   11
selves in the neighborhood backyards, everyone for himself. I paused

and considered. Everyone had vanished except Mikey Fahey, who was just rounding the corner of a yellow brick house. Poor Mikey, I trailed him. The driver of the Buick sensibly picked the two of us to follow. The man apparently had all day.

He chased Mikey and me around the yellow house and up a back- 12 yard path we knew by heart: under a low tree, up a bank, through a hedge, down some snowy steps, and across the grocery store's delivery driveway. We smashed through a gap in another hedge, entered a scruffy backyard and ran around its back porch and tight between houses to Edgerton Avenue; we ran across Edgerton to an alley and up our own sliding woodpile to the Halls' front yard; he kept coming. We ran up Lloyd Street and wound through mazy backyards toward the steep hilltop at Willard and Lang.

He chased us silently, block after block. He chased us silently over 13 picket fences, through thorny hedges, between houses, around garbage cans, and across streets. Every time I glanced back, choking for breath, I expected he would have quit. He must have been as breathless as we were. His jacket strained over his body. It was an immense discovery, pounding into my hot head with every sliding, joyous step, that this ordinary adult evidently knew what I thought only children who trained at football knew: that you have to fling yourself at what you're doing, you have to point yourself, forget yourself, aim, dive.

Mikey and I had nowhere to go, in our own neighborhood or out 14 of it, but away from this man who was chasing us. He impelled us forward; we compelled him to follow our route. The air was cold; every breath tore my throat. We kept running, block after block; we kept improvising, backyard after backyard, running a frantic course and choosing it simultaneously, failing always to find small places or hard places to slow him down, and discovering always, exhilarated, dismayed, that only bare speed could save us — for he would never give up, this man — and we were losing speed.

He chased us through the backyard labyrinths of ten blocks before 15 he caught us by our jackets. He caught us and we all stopped.

We three stood staggering, half blinded, coughing, in an obscure 16 hilltop backyard: a man in his twenties, a boy, a girl. He had released our jackets, our pursuer, our captor, our hero: he knew we weren't going anywhere. We all played by the rules. Mikey and I unzipped our jackets. I pulled off my sopping mittens. Our tracks multiplied in the backyard's new snow. We had been breaking new snow all morning. We didn't look at each other. I was cherishing my excitement. The man's lower pants legs were wet; his cuffs were full of snow, and there was a prow of snow beneath them on his shoes and socks. Some trees bordered the little flat backyard, some messy winter trees. There was no one around: a clearing in a grove, and we the only players.

It was a long time before he could speak. I had some difficulty at   17
first recalling why we were there. My lips felt swollen; I couldn't see
out of the sides of my eyes; I kept coughing.

"You stupid kids," he began perfunctorily.   18

We listened perfunctorily indeed, if we listened at all, for the   19
chewing out was redundant, a mere formality, and beside the point.
The point was that he had chased us passionately without giving up,
and so he had caught us. Now he came down to earth. I wanted the
glory to last forever.

But how could the glory have lasted forever? We could have run   20
through every backyard in North America until we got to Panama. But
when he trapped us at the lip of the Panama Canal, what precisely
could he have done to prolong the drama of the chase and cap its
glory? I brooded about this for the next few years. He could only have
fried Mikey Fahey and me in boiling oil, say, or dismembered us piece-
meal, or staked us to anthills. None of which I really wanted, and
none of which any adult was likely to do, even in the spirit of fun. He
could only chew us out there in the Panamanian jungle, after months
or years of exalting pursuit. He could only begin, "You stupid kids,"
and continue in his ordinary Pittsburgh accent with his normal righ-
teous anger and the usual common sense.

If in that snowy backyard the driver of the black Buick had cut off   21
our heads, Mikey's and mine, I would have died happy, for nothing
has required so much of me since as being chased all over Pittsburgh
in the middle of winter — running terrified, exhausted — by this
sainted, skinny, furious red-headed man who wished to have a word
with us. I don't know how he found his way back to his car.

RESPONDING TO THE TEXT

As a child, did you ever do something exhilarating, satisfying, or fun even
though you knew that it was "wrong"? Compare your experience to Dillard's. To what extent should children be held responsible for their deliberate misbehavior? What would have been an appropriate consequence for
Dillard and her companions? If you had chased them down, what would
you have done?

ENGAGING THE WRITER'S SUBJECT

1. In this essay, Dillard separates the behavior of boys from that of both
   girls and adults. What characteristics does she identify that distinguish
   the actions of boys? Why is she able to play with them?

2. What is Dillard's main point? Where does she state it explicitly?

3. Why was the driver "sensible" to choose Mikey and the author as the
   targets of his chase?

4. What made the chase so unusual and exciting? Why was the end of the chase disappointing? Was there any way it could have ended that would have been more satisfying to the author? Why or why not?

ANALYZING THE WRITER'S CRAFT

1. In an unusual rhetorical strategy, Dillard opens her essay in the first person but immediately switches to second person. (Glossary: *Point of View*) What is her purpose for using two points of view, and especially for shifting from one to the other? In what ways does Dillard's use of the second-person point of view evoke childhood?

2. This narrative essay begins with two nonnarrative introductory paragraphs whose connection to the rest of the story may not be immediately apparent. Note especially the apparently paradoxical sentence that closes the introduction: "I got in trouble throwing snowballs, and have seldom been happier since." (Glossary: *Paradox*) How do these paragraphs, and particularly this sentence, help the reader understand the story that follows?

3. The event that prompted this narrative was in itself small and seemingly insignificant, but Dillard describes it with such intensity that the reader is left in no doubt as to its tremendous significance for her. Show how she uses carefully crafted description to lift her story from the ordinary to the remarkable. (Glossary: *Description*)

UNDERSTANDING THE WRITER'S LANGUAGE

1. In paragraph 14, Dillard describes the chase using parallel word structures: "He impelled us forward; we compelled him to follow our route." In paragraph 16, find the parallel noun phrases that Dillard uses to characterize the young man who chased them. What is the impact on the reader of these parallel word structures? (Glossary: *Parallelism*) This essay contains numerous examples of parallelism; find several others that add to the impact you have identified.

2. Notice the use of strong verbs (*flung, popped, smashed*) throughout the narrative. How do strong verbs work to enhance a narrative?

3. Dillard uses a great deal of description in her narrative essay. Look up and define these words, vital to her descriptions, as she uses them: *crenellated* (paragraph 5), *reverted* (5), *turf* (11), *impelled* (14), *compelled* (14), *labyrinths* (15), *obscure* (16), *perfunctorily* (18, 19), *exalting* (20). How do these words contribute to the impact of the finished piece?

WRITING SUGGESTIONS

1. Children know what it means to plunge headlong, fearlessly and eagerly, into a challenging situation. One of the most wonderful encounters a child can have is with an adult who is still able to summon up that childlike enthusiasm — one who can put aside grown-up ideas of

respectability and caution in order to accomplish something. In this narrative, Dillard reveres a man who is willing to pursue his young tormentors until he catches them. Recall and write about an enthusiastic adult — a parent, a relative, a teacher, a chance acquaintance — who abandoned grown-up behavior to inspire you as a child. In what way did he or she do so? As Annie Dillard does, make your story lively and detailed.

2. Consider the following cartoon by Barbara Smaller. What do you think Smaller is saying here? After reading "Getting Caught," how do you think Annie Dillard would respond to Smaller's cartoon? Explain. Now review what you wrote in Responding to the Text. How accountable should children be for their misconduct or lack of performance? Using Smaller's cartoon, Dillard's essay, and your own experience, write an essay in which you look at the question of holding people responsible for their actions. Your essay could take the form of an argument in which you take a definite position or a narrative in which you tell the story of a childhood punishment that you received or witnessed. If you choose to narrate a childhood experience, be sure to be clear about your response to the punishment: Was it justified? Appropriate? Effective? Why or why not? It might be useful to trade stories with classmates and discuss the issues that arise before you start writing.

"What do I think is an appropriate punishment? I think an appropriate punishment would be to make me live with my guilt."

3. When Annie Dillard was a child, it was more unusual for girls to participate in athletic programs in schools and universities. This all changed

in 1972 with the passage of Title IX, which legislated equal funding of school athletics for males and females. Since then, the involvement of girls and women in sports has grown tremendously. What kind of impact have competitive sports had on the lives of female athletes? Interview some female athletes and their coaches about the effects of sports on the lives of girls and women. You might also consider doing research in your college library and on the Internet to find out more about women in sports. Write an essay to present your findings; be sure to include appropriate quotations and examples.

- To begin your research online, go to **bedfordstmartins.com /subjectsstrategies** and click on "Narration" or browse the thematic directory of annotated links.

Stranger Than True

Barry Winston

*Barry Winston is a practicing attorney in Chapel Hill, North Carolina.
He was born in New York City in 1934 and graduated from the University of North Carolina, from which he also received his law degree. His
specialty is criminal law.*

"Stranger Than True" was published in Harper's *magazine in December 1986. In the story, Winston recounts his experience defending a
young college graduate accused of driving while under the influence of alcohol and causing his sister's death. The story is characterized by Winston's energetic and strong voice. In commenting on his use of narrative
detail, Winston says, "I could have made it twice as long, but it wouldn't
have been as good a story."*

PREPARING TO READ

The American judicial system works on the basis of the presump-
tion of innocence. In short, you are innocent until proven guilty.
But what about a situation in which all the evidence seems to point
to a person's guilt? What's the purpose of a trial in such a case?

L et me tell you a story. A true story. The court records are all there if 1
anyone wants to check. It's three years ago. I'm sitting in my office,
staring out the window, when I get a call from a lawyer I hardly know.
Tax lawyer. Some kid is in trouble and would I be interested in helping him out? He's charged with manslaughter, a felony, and driving
under the influence. I tell him sure, have the kid call me.

So the kid calls and makes an appointment to see me. He's a nice 2
kid, fresh out of college, and he's come down here to spend some time
with his older sister, who's in med school. One day she tells him
they're invited to a cookout with some friends of hers. She's going directly from class and he's going to take her car and meet her there. It's
way out in the country, but he gets there before she does, introduces
himself around, and pops a beer. She shows up after a while and he
pops another beer. Then he eats a hamburger and drinks a third beer.
At some point his sister says, "Well, it's about time to go," and they
head for the car.

And, the kid tells me, sitting there in my office, the next thing he 3
remembers, he's waking up in a hospital room, hurting like hell, ban-
dages and casts all over him, and somebody is telling him he's charged
with manslaughter and DUI because he wrecked his sister's car, killed
her in the process, and blew fourteen on the Breathalyzer. I ask him

what the hell he means by "the next thing he remembers," and he looks me straight in the eye and says he can't remember anything from the time they leave the cookout until he wakes up in the hospital. He tells me the doctors say he has post-retrograde amnesia. I say of course I believe him, but I'm worried about finding a judge who'll believe him.

I agree to represent him and send somebody for a copy of the wreck report. It says there are four witnesses: a couple in a car going the other way who passed the kid and his sister just before their car ran off the road, the guy whose front yard they landed in, and the trooper who investigated. I call the guy whose yard they ended up in. He isn't home. I leave word. Then I call the couple. The wife agrees to come in the next day with her husband. While I'm talking to her, the first guy calls. I call him back, introduce myself, tell him I'm representing the kid and need to talk to him about the accident. He hems and haws and I figure he's one of those people who think it's against the law to talk to defense lawyers. I say the D.A. will tell him it's O.K. to talk to me, but he doesn't have to. I give him the name and number of the D.A. and he says he'll call me back.

Then I go out and hunt up the trooper. He tells me the whole story. The kid and his sister are coming into town on Smith Level Road, after it turns from fifty-five to forty-five. The Thornes — the couple — are heading out of town. They say this sports car passes them, going the other way, right after that bad turn just south of the new subdivision. They say it's going like a striped-ass ape, at least sixty-five or seventy. Mrs. Thorne turns around to look and Mr. Thorne watches in the rearview mirror. They both see the same thing: halfway into the curve, the car runs off the road on the right, whips back onto the road, spins, runs off on the left, and disappears. They turn around in the first driveway they come to and start back, both terrified of what they're going to find. By this time, Trooper Johnson says, the guy whose front yard the car has ended up in has pulled the kid and his sister out of the wreck and started CPR on the girl. Turns out he's an emergency medical technician. Holloway, that's his name. Johnson tells me that Holloway says he's sitting in his front room, watching television, when he hears a hell of a crash in his yard. He runs outside and finds the car flipped over, and so he pulls the kid out from the driver's side, the girl from the other side. She dies in his arms.

And that, says Trooper Johnson, is that. The kid's blood/alcohol content was fourteen, he was going way too fast, *and* the girl is dead. He had to charge him. It's a shame, he seems a nice kid, it was his own sister and all, but what the hell can he do, right?

The next day the Thornes come in, and they confirm everything Johnson said. By now things are looking not so hot for my client, and

I'm thinking it's about time to have a little chat with the D.A. But Holloway still hasn't called me back, so I call him. Not home. Leave word. No call. I wait a couple of days and call again. Finally I get him on the phone. He's very agitated, and won't talk to me except to say that he doesn't have to talk to me.

I know I better look for a deal, so I go to the D.A. He's very sympa-   8
thetic. But. There's only so far you can get on sympathy. A young woman is dead, promising career cut short, all because somebody has too much to drink and drives. The kid has to pay. Not, the D.A. says, with jail time. But he's got to plead guilty to two misdemeanors: death by vehicle and driving under the influence. That means probation, a big fine. Several thousand dollars. Still, it's hard for me to criticize the D.A. After all, he's probably going to have the MADD mothers all over him because of reducing the felony to a misdemeanor.

On the day of the trial, I get to court a few minutes early. There   9
are the Thornes and Trooper Johnson, and someone I assume is Holloway. Sure enough, when this guy sees me, he comes over and introduces himself and starts right in: "I just want you to know how serious all this drinking and driving really is," he says. "If those young people hadn't been drinking and driving that night, that poor young girl would be alive today." Now, I'm trying to hold my temper when I spot the D.A. I bolt across the room, grab him by the arm, and say, "We gotta talk. Why the hell have you got all those people here? That jerk Holloway. Surely to God you're not going to call him as a witness. This is a guilty plea! My client's parents are sitting out there. You don't need to put them through a dog-and-pony show."

The D.A. looks at me and says, "Man, I'm sorry, but in a case like   10
this, I gotta put on witnesses. Weird Wally is on the bench. If I try to go without witnesses, he might throw me out."

The D.A. calls his first witness. Trooper Johnson identifies himself,   11
tells about being called to the scene of the accident, and describes what he found when he got there and what everybody told him. After he finishes, the judge looks at me. "No questions," I say. Then the D.A. calls Holloway. He describes the noise, running out of the house, the upside-down car in his yard, pulling my client out of the window on the left side of the car and then going around to the other side for the girl. When he gets to this part, he really hits his stride. He describes, in minute detail, the injuries he saw and what he did to try and save her life. And then he tells, breath by breath, how she died in his arms.

The D.A. says, "No further questions, your Honor." The judge looks   12
at me. I shake my head, and he says to Holloway, "You may step down."

One of those awful silences hangs there, and nothing happens for   13
a minute. Holloway doesn't move. Then he looks at me, and at the D.A., and then at the judge. He says, "Can I say something else, your Honor?"

All my bells are ringing at once, and my gut is screaming at me, 14
Object! Object! I'm trying to decide in three quarters of a second
whether it'll be worse to listen to a lecture on the evils of drink from
this jerk Holloway or piss off the judge by objecting. But all I say
is, "No objections, your Honor." The judge smiles at me, then at
Holloway, and says, "Very well, Mr. Holloway. What did you wish to
say?"

It all comes out in a rush. "Well, you see, your Honor," Holloway 15
says, "it was just like I told Trooper Johnson. It all happened so fast. I
heard the noise, and I came running out, and it was night, and I was
excited, and the next morning, when I had a chance to think about it,
I figured out what had happened, but by then I'd already told Trooper
Johnson and I didn't know what to do, but you see, the car, it was upside down, and I did pull that boy out of the left-hand window, but
don't you see, the car was upside down, and if you turned it over on its
wheels like it's supposed to be, the left-hand side is really on the right-
hand side, and your Honor, that boy wasn't driving that car at all. It
was the girl that was driving, and when I had a chance to think about
it the next morning, I realized that I'd told Trooper Johnson wrong,
and I was scared and I didn't know what to do, and that's why" — and
now he's looking right at me — "why I wouldn't talk to you."

Naturally, the defendant is allowed to withdraw his guilty plea. 16
The charges are dismissed and the kid and his parents and I go into
one of the back rooms in the courthouse and sit there looking at one
another for a while. Finally, we recover enough to mumble some Oh
my Gods and Thank yous and You're welcomes. And that's why I can
stand to represent somebody when I know he's guilty.

RESPONDING TO THE TEXT

Much abuse is heaped on lawyers who defend clients whose guilt seems obvious. How does Winston's story help explain why lawyers need to defend
"guilty" clients?

ENGAGING THE WRITER'S SUBJECT

1. Why does the D.A. bring in witnesses for a case that has been plea-
   bargained? What is ironic about that decision? (Glossary: *Irony*)

2. Why was Holloway reluctant to be interviewed by Winston about what
   he saw and did in the aftermath of the accident? What might he have
   been afraid of?

3. Why did Holloway finally ask to speak to the court? Why do you suppose Winston chose not to object to Holloway's request?

4. What do you think is the point of Winston's narrative?

ANALYZING THE WRITER'S CRAFT

1. Winston establishes the context for his story in the first three paragraphs. What basic information does he give readers?

2. What details does Winston choose to include in the story? Why does he include them? Is there other information that you would like to have had? Why do you suppose Winston chose to omit that information?

3. Explain how Winston uses sentence variety to pace his narrative. What effect do his short sentences and sentence fragments have on you?

4. What does Winston gain as a writer by telling us that this is "a true story," one that we can check out in the court records?

5. During the courtroom scene (paragraphs 9–15), Winston relies heavily on dialogue. (Glossary: *Dialogue*) What does he gain by using dialogue? Why do you suppose he uses dialogue sparingly in the other parts of his narrative?

6. How does Winston use description to differentiate the four witnesses to the accident? (Glossary: *Description*) Why is it important for him to give his readers some idea of their differing characters?

UNDERSTANDING THE WRITER'S LANGUAGE

1. How would you characterize Winston's voice in this story? How is that voice established?

2. What, if anything, does Winston's diction tell you about Winston himself ? (Glossary: *Diction*) What effect does his diction have on the tone of his narrative? (Glossary: *Tone*)

3. Refer to your desk dictionary to determine the meanings of the following words as Winston uses them in this selection: *felony* (paragraph 1), *agitated* (7), *misdemeanor* (8), *probation* (8), *bolt* (9).

WRITING SUGGESTIONS

1. "Stranger Than True" is a first-person narrative told from the defense lawyer's point of view. Imagine that you are a newspaper reporter covering this case. What changes would you have to make in Winston's narrative to make it a news story? Make a list of the changes you would have to make, and then rewrite the story.

2. Holloway's revelation in the courtroom catches everyone by surprise. Analyze the chain of events in the accident and the assumptions that people made based on the accounts of those events. Write a cause and effect essay in which you explain some of the possible reasons why Holloway's confession is so unexpected. (Glossary: *Cause and Effect Analysis*)

3. The Sixth Amendment to the U.S. Constitution states that "In all criminal prosecutions, the accused shall enjoy the right to . . . Assistance of Counsel for his defense." However, some critics have argued that wealthy defendants who can afford to hire the best defense lawyers and

expert witnesses are essentially able to "buy" themselves an acquittal while poorer defendants — who rely on low-paid or court-appointed lawyers — are often convicted, regardless of guilt or innocence. Do you agree or disagree? Why or why not? Do you propose changing the system? How? Research this topic in your college library and on the Internet and write a paper in which you present your findings.

• To begin your research online, go to **bedfordstmartins.com /subjectsstrategies** and click on "Narration" or browse the thematic directory of annotated links.

Nobody Knows I'm Gay

Bob Daemmrich

Bob Daemmrich/The Image Works

CONNECTING IMAGE AND TEXT

This photograph of college students at a gay rights rally was taken on October 11, 2003 — National Coming Out Day — in Austin, Texas.

How do you "read" this photograph? Why do you suppose viewers' eyes are drawn to the young man's T-shirt? How do you interpret the message on his T-shirt? What significance, if any, do you attach to his being the only one wearing sunglasses? Imagine for a moment that the young man in the middle is wearing a plain white T-shirt. How would you then react to this photograph? Your observations will help guide you to the key themes and strategies in the essay that follows.

Not Close Enough for Comfort

David P. Bardeen

David P. Bardeen was born in 1974 in New Haven, Connecticut, and grew up in Seattle, Washington. He graduated cum laude from Harvard University in 1996 and then worked for J. P. Morgan & Co. as an investment banking analyst. In 2002, he received his J.D. from the New York University School of Law, where he was the managing editor of the Law Review. *After graduation, he joined the law firm of Cleary, Gottleib, Steen & Hamilton and became a member of the New York Bar. Bardeen is proficient in Spanish, and his practice focuses on international business transactions involving clients in Latin America.*

In the following article, which appeared in the New York Times Magazine *on February 29, 2004, Bardeen tells the story of a lunch meeting at which he reveals a secret to his twin brother, a secret that had derailed their relationship for almost fifteen years.*

PREPARING TO READ

Recall a time when a parent, sibling, friend, teacher, or some other person close to you kept a secret from you. How did the secret affect your relationship? How did you feel once the secret was revealed? How has the relationship fared since?

I had wanted to tell Will I was gay since I was 12. As twins, we shared everything back then: clothes, gadgets, thoughts, secrets. Everything except this. So when we met for lunch more than a year ago, I thought that finally coming out to him would close the distance that had grown between us. When we were kids, we created our own language, whispering to each other as our bewildered parents looked on. Now, at 28, we had never been further apart.

I asked him about his recent trip. He asked me about work. Short questions. One-word answers. Then an awkward pause.

Will was one of the last to know. Partly it was his fault. He is hard to pin down for brunch or a drink, and this was not the sort of conversation I wanted to have over the phone. I had actually been trying to tell him for more than a month, but he kept canceling at the last minute — a friend was in town, he'd met a girl.

But part of me was relieved. This was the talk I had feared the most. Coming out is, in an unforgiving sense, an admission of fraud. Fraud against yourself primarily, but also fraud against your family and friends. So, once I resolved to tell my secret, I confessed to my most recent "victims" first. I told my friends from law school — those

I had met just a few years earlier and deceived the least — then I worked back through college to the handful of high-school friends I still keep in touch with.

Keeping my sexuality from my parents had always seemed permissible, so our sit-down chat did not stress me out as much as it might have. We all mislead our parents. "I'm too sick for school today." "No, I wasn't drinking." "Yes, Mom, I'm fine. Don't worry about me." That deception is understood and, in some sense, expected. But twins expect complete transparency, however romantic the notion.

Although our lives unfolded along parallel tracks — we went to college together, both moved to New York and had many of the same friends — Will and I quietly drifted apart. When he moved abroad for a year, we lost touch almost entirely. Our mother and father didn't think this was strange, because like many parents of twins, they wanted us to follow divergent paths. But friends were baffled when we began to rely on third parties for updates on each other's lives. "How's Will?" someone would ask. "You tell me," I would respond. One mutual friend, sick of playing the intermediary, once sent me an e-mail message with a carbon copy to Will. "Dave, meet Will, your twin," it said. "Will, let me introduce you to Dave."

Now, here we were, at lunch, just the two of us. "There's something I've been meaning to tell you," I said. "I'm gay." I looked at him closely, at the edges of his mouth, the wrinkles around his eyes, for some hint of what he was thinking.

"O.K.," he said evenly.

"I've been meaning to tell you for a while," I said.

"Uh-huh." He asked me a few questions but seemed slightly uneasy, as if he wasn't sure he wanted to hear the answers. Do Mom and Dad know? Are you seeing anyone? How long have you known you were gay? I hesitated.

I've known since I was young, and to some degree, I thought Will had always known. How else to explain my adolescent melancholy, my withdrawal, the silence when the subject changed to girls, sex, and who was hot. As a teenager I watched, as if from a distance, as my demeanor went from outspoken to sullen. I had assumed, in the self-centered way kids often do, that everyone noticed this change — and that my brother had guessed the reason. To be fair, he asked me once in our 20's, after I had ended yet another brief relationship with a woman. "Of course I'm not gay," I told him, as if the notion were absurd.

"How long have you known?" he asked again.

"About 15 years," I said. Will looked away.

Food arrived. We ate and talked about other things. Mom, Dad, the mayor and the weather. We asked for the check and agreed to get together again soon. No big questions, no heart to heart. Just disclosure, explanation, follow-up, conclusion. But what could I expect? I had shut him out for so long that I suppose ultimately he gave up. Telling my brother I was gay hadn't made us close, as I had naively hoped it would; instead it underscored just how much we had strayed apart.

As we left the restaurant, I felt the urge to apologize, not for being gay, of course, but for the years I'd kept him in the dark, for his being among the last to know. He hailed a cab. It stopped. He stepped inside, the door still open. 15

"I'm sorry," I said. 16

He smiled. "No, I think it's great." 17

A nice gesture. Supportive. But I think he misunderstood. 18

A year later, we are still only creeping toward the intimacy everyone expects us to have. Although we live three blocks away from each other, I can't say we see each other every week or even every two weeks. But with any luck, next year, I'll be the one updating our mutual friends on Will's life. 19

RESPONDING TO THE TEXT

How do you think Will felt when David announced that he was gay? Do you think Will had any clue about David's sexual orientation? What in Will's response to David's announcement led you to this conclusion? Why has it been so difficult for them to recapture the "intimacy everyone expects [them] to have" (paragraph 19) in the year following David's coming out to Will?

ENGAGING THE WRITER'S SUBJECT

1. Why do you suppose Bardeen chose to keep his sexual orientation a secret from his brother? Why was this particular "coming-out" so difficult? Was Bardeen realistic in thinking that "Will had always known" (paragraph 11) that he was gay?

2. What does Bardeen mean when he says, "But twins expect complete transparency, however romantic the notion" (paragraph 5)?

3. Why does Bardeen feel the need to apologize to his brother as they part? Do you think his brother understood the meaning of the apology? Why or why not?

4. What do you think Bardeen had hoped would happen after he confided his secret to his brother? Was this hope unrealistic?

5. What harm had Bardeen's secret done to his relationship with his brother? What is necessary to heal the relationship?

ANALYZING THE WRITER'S CRAFT

1. Bardeen narrates his coming-out using the first-person pronoun *I*. (Glossary: *Point of View*) Why is the first person particularly appropriate for telling a story such as this one? Explain.

2. How has Bardeen organized his narrative? (Glossary: *Organization*) In paragraphs 3 through 6, Bardeen uses flashbacks to give readers a context for his relationship with his twin. What would have been lost or gained had he begun his essay with paragraphs 3 through 6?

3. During the lunch meeting part of the narrative (paragraphs 7–17), Bardeen uses dialogue. (Glossary: *Dialogue*) What does he gain by doing this? Why do you suppose he uses dialogue sparingly elsewhere?

4. Bardeen uses a number of short sentences and deliberate sentence fragments. What effect do these have on you? Why do you suppose he uses some sentence fragments instead of complete sentences?

5. Bardeen's title plays on the old saying "too close for comfort." What does his title suggest to you? (Glossary: *Title*) How effectively does it capture the essence of his relationship with his brother? Explain.

6. In paragraphs 6 and 11 Bardeen uses comparison and contrast to highlight the similarities and differences between himself and Will. (Glossary: *Comparison and Contrast*) Which did you find more interesting and revealing, the similarities or differences? Why?

UNDERSTANDING THE WRITER'S LANGUAGE

1. How would you describe Bardeen's voice in this narrative? How is that voice established? What, if anything, does Bardeen's diction tell you about him as a person? (Glossary: *Diction*) Explain.

2. Bardeen says that "coming out is, in an unforgiving sense, an admission of fraud" (paragraph 4). Why do you suppose he uses the word *fraud* to describe how he felt about his coming-out? What does he mean when he says "in an unforgiving sense"? What other words might he have used instead of *fraud*?

3. Refer to your desk dictionary to determine the meanings of the following words as Bardeen uses them in this selection: *baffled* (paragraph 6), *melancholy* (11), *demeanor* (11), *sullen* (11), *intimacy* (19).

WRITING SUGGESTIONS

1. Using your Preparing to Read response for this selection, write an essay about a secret you once had and how it affected relationships with those close to you. What exactly was your secret? Why did you decide to keep this information secret? How did you feel while you kept your secret? What happened when you revealed your secret? What insights into secrets do you have as a result of this experience?

2. In paragraph 4 Bardeen states, "So, once I resolved to tell my secret, I confessed to my most recent 'victims' first. I told my friends from law school — those I had met just a few years earlier and deceived the least — then I worked back through college to the handful of high-school friends I still keep in touch with." Write an essay in which you compare and contrast your level of honesty among your friends or a

larger community and your level of honesty among your family or people with whom you are very close. (Glossary: *Comparison and Contrast*) Are there secrets you would be more likely to share with one group than another? If so, how would you classify those secrets? (Glossary: *Classification; Division*) Do you think it is easier to be honest with people who do or do not know you very well? Why? Before you write, you might find it helpful to refer to your Connecting Image and Text response for this selection.

3. After doing some research in the library and on the Internet, write an essay about the history of the words *gay* and *queer*. What did these words originally mean? How have their meanings changed over time? How did these words become associated with the gay, lesbian, bisexual, and transgender community? What is the current status of these words? Twenty years ago could Americans have imagined watching television shows titled *Queer Eye for the Straight Guy, Queer as Folk, The L-Word,* or *Boy Meets Boy*? Why or why not?

• To begin your research online, go to **bedfordstmartins.com /subjectsstrategies** and click on "Narration" or browse the thematic directory of annotated links.

A Worn Path (FICTION)

Eudora Welty

Eudora Welty (1909–2001) was born in Jackson, Mississippi, and lived there for most of her life. She received her B.A. from the University of Wisconsin in 1929 and then studied advertising at Columbia University. Advertising jobs being scarce during the Depression, Welty returned home and began to write. Her published works include many short stories, available as her Collected Stories *(1980), five novels, and a collection of essays,* The Eye of the Story *(1978). Welty's autobiographical* One Writer's Beginnings *(1984) recounts childhood events that influenced her development as a writer.*

In "A Worn Path," we meet Phoenix Jackson, one of Welty's most memorable characters, on her way to town to perform an errand. Welty's story provides rich insights into character, daily routines, growing old, and family relationships and duties.

PREPARING TO READ

Have you ever walked from one place to another — for example, from home to a friend's house or from one class to another across campus — so many times that it seemed you could do it with your eyes closed? What was your purpose behind this routine trip? What sights, sounds, and smells do you still remember?

It was December — a bright frozen day in the early morning. Far out in the country there was an old Negro woman with her head tied in a red rag, coming along a path through the pinewoods. Her name was Phoenix Jackson. She was very old and small and she walked slowly in the dark pine shadows, moving a little from side to side in her steps, with the balanced heaviness and lightness of a pendulum in a grandfather clock. She carried a thin, small cane made from an umbrella, and with this she kept tapping the frozen earth in front of her. This made a grave and persistent noise in the still air, that seemed meditative like the chirping of a solitary little bird.

She wore a dark striped dress reaching down to her shoe tops, and an equally long apron of bleached sugar sacks, with a full pocket: all neat and tidy, but every time she took a step she might have fallen over her shoelaces, which dragged from her unlaced shoes. She looked straight ahead. Her eyes were blue with age. Her skin had a pattern all its own of numberless branching wrinkles and as though a whole little tree stood in the middle of her forehead, but a golden color ran underneath, and the two knobs of her cheeks were illumined by a yellow burning under the dark. Under the red rag her hair came down on her neck in the frailest of ringlets, still black, and with an odor like copper.

Now and then there was a quivering in the thicket. Old Phoenix said, "Out of my way, all you foxes, owls, beetles, jack rabbits, coons and wild animals! . . . Keep out from under these feet, little bob-whites. . . . Keep the big wild hogs out of my path. Don't let none of those come running my direction. I got a long way." Under her small black-freckled hand her cane, limber as a buggy whip, would switch at the brush as if to rouse up any hiding things.

On she went. The woods were deep and still. The sun made the pine needles almost too bright to look at, up where the wind rocked. The cones dropped as light as feathers. Down in the hollow was the mourning dove — it was not too late for him.

The path ran up a hill. "Seem like there is chains about my feet, time I get this far," she said, in the voice of argument old people keep to use with themselves. "Something always take a hold of me on this hill — pleads I should stay."

After she got to the top she turned and gave a full, severe look behind her where she had come. "Up through pines," she said at length. "Now down through oaks."

Her eyes opened their widest, and she started down gently. But before she got to the bottom of the hill a bush caught her dress.

Her fingers were busy and intent, but her skirts were full and long, so that before she could pull them free in one place they were caught in another. It was not possible to allow the dress to tear. "I in the thorny bush," she said. "Thorns, you doing your appointed work. Never want to let folks pass, no sir. Old eyes thought you was a pretty little *green* bush."

Finally, trembling all over, she stood free, and after a moment dared to stoop for her cane.

"Sun so high!" she cried, leaning back and looking, while the thick tears went over her eyes. "The time getting all gone here."

At the foot of this hill was a place where a log was laid across the creek.

"Now comes the trial," said Phoenix.

Putting her right foot out, she mounted the log and shut her eyes. Lifting her skirt, leveling her cane fiercely before her, like a festival figure in some parade, she began to march across. Then she opened her eyes and she was safe on the other side.

"I wasn't as old as I thought," she said.

But she sat down to rest. She spread her skirts on the bank around her and folded her hands over her knees. Up above her was a tree in a pearly cloud of mistletoe. She did not dare to close her eyes, and when a little boy brought her a plate with a slice of marble-cake on it she spoke to him. "That would be acceptable," she said. But when she went to take it there was just her own hand in the air.

So she left that tree, and had to go through a barbed-wire fence. 16 There she had to creep and crawl, spreading her knees and stretching her fingers like a baby trying to climb the steps. But she talked loudly to herself: she could not let her dress be torn now, so late in the day, and she could not pay for having her arm or her leg sawed off if she got caught fast where she was.

At last she was safe through the fence and risen up out in the 17 clearing. Big dead trees, like black men with one arm, were standing in the purple stalks of the withered cotton field. There sat a buzzard.

"Who you watching?" 18

In the furrow she made her way along. 19

"Glad this not the season for bulls," she said, looking sideways, 20 "and the good Lord made his snakes to curl up and sleep in the winter. A pleasure I don't see no two-headed snake coming around that tree, where it come once. It took a while to get by him, back in the summer."

She passed through the old cotton and went into a field of dead 21 corn. It whispered and shook and was taller than her head. "Through the maze now," she said, for there was no path.

Then there was something tall, black, and skinny there, moving 22 before her.

At first she took it for a man. It could have been a man dancing in 23 the field. But she stood still and listened, and it did not make a sound. It was as silent as a ghost.

"Ghost," she said sharply, "who be you the ghost of? For I have 24 heard of nary death close by."

But there was no answer — only the ragged dancing in the wind. 25

She shut her eyes, reached out her hand, and touched a sleeve. 26 She found a coat and inside that an emptiness, cold as ice.

"You scarecrow," she said. Her face lighted. "I ought to be shut up 27 for good," she said with laughter. "My senses is gone. I too old. I the oldest people I ever know. Dance, old scarecrow," she said, "while I dancing with you."

She kicked her foot over the furrow, and with mouth drawn down, 28 shook her head once or twice in a little strutting way. Some husks blew down and whirled in streamers about her skirts.

Then she went on, parting her way from side to side with the cane, 29 through the whispering field. At last she came to the end, to a wagon track where the silver grass blew between the red ruts. The quail were walking around like pullets, seeming all dainty and unseen.

"Walk pretty," she said. "This the easy place. This the easy going." 30

She followed the track, swaying through the quiet bare fields, 31 through the little strings of trees silver in their dead leaves, past cabins silver from weather, with the doors and windows boarded shut, all like old women under a spell siting there. "I walking in their sleep," she said, nodding her head vigorously.

In a ravine she went where a spring was silently flowing through a 32 hollow log. Old Phoenix bent and drank. "Sweetgum makes the water sweet," she said, and drank more. "Nobody know who made this well, for it was here when I was born."

The track crossed a swampy part where the moss hung as white as 33 lace from every limb. "Sleep on, alligators, and blow your bubbles." Then the track went into the road.

Deep, deep the road went down between the high green-colored 34 banks. Overhead the live-oaks met, and it was as dark as a cave.

A black dog with a lolling tongue came up out of the weeds by the 35 ditch. She was meditating, and not ready, and when he came at her she only hit him a little with her cane. Over she went in the ditch, like a little puff of milkweed.

Down there, her senses drifted away. A dream visited her, and she 36 reached her hand up, but nothing reached down and gave her a pull. So she lay there and presently went to talking. "Old woman," she said to herself, "that black dog come up out of the weeds to stall you off, and now there he sitting on his fine tail, smiling at you."

A white man finally came along and found her — a hunter, a 37 young man, with his dog on a chain.

"Well, Granny!" he laughed. "What are you doing there?" 38

"Lying on my back like a June-bug waiting to be turned over, mis- 39 ter," she said, reaching up her hand.

He lifted her up, gave her a swing in the air, and set her down. 40 "Anything broken, Granny?"

"No sir, them old dead weeds is springy enough," said Phoenix, 41 when she had got her breath. "I thank you for your trouble."

"Where do you live, Granny?" he asked, while the two dogs were 42 growling at each other.

"Away back yonder, sir, behind the ridge. You can't even see it 43 from here."

"On your way home?" 44

"No sir, I going to town." 45

"Why, that's too far! That's as far as I walked when I come out 46 myself, and I get something for my trouble." He patted the stuffed bag he carried, and there hung down a little closed claw. It was one of the bob-whites, with its beak hooked bitterly to show it was dead. "Now you go on home, Granny!"

"I bound to go to town, mister," said Phoenix. "The time come 47 around."

He gave another laugh, filling the whole landscape. "I know you old 48 colored people! Wouldn't miss going to town to see Santa Claus!"

But something held old Phoenix very still. The deep lines in her 49 face went into a fierce and different radiation. Without warning, she had seen with her own eyes a flashing nickel fall out of the man's pocket onto the ground.

"How old are you, Granny?" he was saying.   50

"There is no telling, mister," she said, "no telling."   51

Then she gave a little cry and clapped her hands and said, "Git on   52
away from here, dog! Look! Look at that dog!" she laughed as if in admiration. "He ain't scared of nobody. He a big black dog." She whispered, "Sic him!"

"Watch me get rid of that cur," said the man. "Sic him, Pete! Sic   53
him!"

Phoenix heard the dogs fighting, and heard the man running and   54
throwing sticks. She even heard a gunshot. But she was slowly bending forward by that time, further and further forward, the lids stretched
down over her eyes, as if she were doing this in her sleep. Her chin
was lowered almost to her knees. The yellow palm of her hand came
out from the fold of her apron. Her fingers slid down and along the
ground under the piece of money with the grace and care they would
have in lifting an egg from under a setting hen. Then she slowly straight-
ened up, she stood erect, and the nickel was in her apron pocket. A bird
flew by. Her lips moved. "God watching me the whole time. I come to
stealing."

The man came back, and his own dog panted about them. "Well, I   55
scared him off that time," he said, and then he laughed and lifted his
gun and pointed it at Phoenix.

She stood straight and faced him.   56

"Doesn't the gun scare you?" he said, still pointing it.   57

"No, sir, I seen plenty go off closer by, in my day, and for less than   58
what I done," she said, holding utterly still.

He smiled, and shouldered the gun. "Well, Granny," he said, "you   59
must be a hundred years old, and scared of nothing. I'd give you a
dime if I had any money with me. But you take my advice and stay
home, and nothing will happen to you."

"I bound to go on my way, mister," said Phoenix. She inclined her   60
head in the red rag. Then they went in different directions, but she
could hear the gun shooting again and again over the hill.

She walked on. The shadows hung from the oak trees to the road   61
like curtains. Then she smelled wood-smoke, and smelled the river,
and she saw a steeple and the cabins on their steep steps. Dozens of
little black children whirled around her. There ahead was Natchez
shining. Bells were ringing. She walked on.

In the paved city it was Christmas time. There were red and green   62
electric lights strung and crisscrossed everywhere, and all turned on
in the daytime. Old Phoenix would have been lost if she had not
distrusted her eyesight and depended on her feet to know where to
take her.

She paused quietly on the sidewalk where people were passing by. 63
A lady came along in the crowd, carrying an armful of red-, green-,
and silver-wrapped presents; she gave off perfume like the red roses in
hot summer, and Phoenix stopped her.

"Please, missy, will you lace up my shoe?" She held up her foot. 64

"What do you want, Grandma?" 65

"See my shoe," said Phoenix. "Do all right for out in the country, 66
but wouldn't look right to go in a big building."

"Stand still then, Grandma," said the lady. She put her packages 67
down on the sidewalk beside her and laced and tied both shoes
tightly.

"Can't lace 'em with a cane," said Phoenix. "Thank you, missy. I 68
doesn't mind asking a nice lady to tie up my shoe, when I gets out on
the street."

Moving slowly and from side to side, she went into the big build- 69
ing, and into a tower of steps, where she walked up and around and
around until her feet knew to stop.

She entered a door, and there she saw nailed up on the wall the 70
document that had been stamped with the gold seal and framed in
the gold frame, which matched the dream that was hung up in her
head.

"Here I be," she said. There was a fixed and ceremonial stiffness 71
over her body.

"A charity case, I suppose," said an attendant who sat at the desk 72
before her.

But Phoenix only looked above her head. There was sweat on her 73
face, the wrinkles in her skin shone like a bright net.

"Speak up, Grandma," the woman said. "What's your name? We 74
must have your history, you know. Have you been here before? What
seems to be the trouble with you?"

Old Phoenix only gave a twitch to her face as if a fly were bother- 75
ing her.

"Are you deaf?" cried the attendant. 76

But then the nurse came in. 77

"Oh, that's just old Aunt Phoenix," she said. "She doesn't come 78
for herself — she has a little grandson. She makes these trips just as
regular as clockwork. She lives away back off the Old Natchez Trace."
She bent down. "Well, Aunt Phoenix, why don't you just take a seat?
We won't keep you standing after your long trip." She pointed.

The old woman sat down, bolt upright in the chair. 79

"Now, how is the boy?" asked the nurse. 80

Old Phoenix did not speak. 81

"I said, how is the boy?" 82

But Phoenix only waited and stared straight ahead, her face very 83
solemn and withdrawn into rigidity.

"Is his throat any better?" asked the nurse. "Aunt Phoenix, don't 84
you hear me? Is your grandson's throat any better since the last time
you came for the medicine?"

With her hands on her knees, the old woman waited, silent, erect 85
and motionless, just as if she were in armor.

"You mustn't take up our time this way, Aunt Phoenix," the nurse 86
said. "Tell us quickly about your grandson, and get it over. He isn't
dead, is he?"

At last there came a flicker and then a flame of comprehension 87
across her face, and she spoke.

"My grandson. It was my memory had left me. There I sat and for- 88
got why I made my long trip."

"Forgot?" The nurse frowned. "After you came so far?" 89

Then Phoenix was like an old woman begging a dignified forgive- 90
ness for waking up frightened in the night. "I never did go to school, I
was too old at the Surrender," she said in a soft voice. "I'm an old
woman without an education. It was my memory fail me. My little
grandson, he is just the same, and I forgot it in the coming."

"Throat never heals, does it?" said the nurse, speaking in a loud, 91
sure voice to old Phoenix. By now she had a card with something written on it, a little list. "Yes. Swallowed lye. When was it? — January —
two-three years ago —"

Phoenix spoke unasked now. "No, missy, he not dead, he just the 92
same. Every little while his throat begin to close up again, and he not
able to swallow. He not get his breath. He not able to help himself. So the
time come around, and I go on another trip for the soothing medicine."

"All right. The doctor said as long as you came to get it, you could 93
have it," said the nurse. "But it's an obstinate case."

"My little grandson, he sit up there in the house all wrapped up, 94
waiting by himself," Phoenix went on. "We is the only two left in the
world. He suffer and it don't seem to put him back at all. He got a
sweet look. He going to last. He wear a little patch quilt and peep out
holding his mouth open like a little bird. I remembers so plain now. I
not going to forget him again, no, the whole enduring time. I could
tell him from all the others in creation."

"All right." The nurse was trying to hush her now. She brought her a 95
bottle of medicine. "Charity," she said, making a check mark in a book.

Old Phoenix held the bottle close to her eyes, and then carefully 96
put it into her pocket.

"I thank you," she said. 97

"It's Christmas time, Grandma," said the attendant. "Could I give 98
you a few pennies out of my purse?"

"Five pennies is a nickel," said Phoenix stiffly. 99

"Here's a nickel," said the attendant. 100

Phoenix rose carefully and held out her hand. She received the 101
nickel and then fished the other nickel out of her pocket and laid it

beside the new one. She stared at her palm closely, with her head on one side.

Then she gave a tap with her cane on the floor. 102

"This is what come to me to do," she said. "I going to the store and 103 buy my child a little windmill they sells, made out of paper. He going to find it hard to believe there such a thing in the world. I'll march myself back where he waiting, holding it straight up in this hand."

She lifted her free hand, gave a little nod, turned around, and 104 walked out of the doctor's office. Then her slow step began on the stairs, going down.

RESPONDING TO THE TEXT

Imagine that you encountered Phoenix Jackson on her way to Natchez. How would you react? Would you ask where she's going or whether she needs any help? What else would you ask her? How do you think she might respond?

ENGAGING THE WRITER'S SUBJECT

1. Why is Phoenix going to Natchez? Whom does she tell, and why?

2. What obstacles does Phoenix encounter? How, emotionally, does she cope with these obstacles? What does this reveal about her character?

3. How does Phoenix get the money she plans to spend at the end of the story? What will she be bringing home to her grandson? What is the significance of his gift?

4. In paragraph 90 Phoenix says, "I never did go to school, I was too old at the Surrender." What does she mean?

5. What does the title of the story mean to you? (Glossary: *Title*) Does the name Phoenix or the title have any metaphorical meaning? (Glossary: *Figures of Speech*) Explain.

6. How would the story be different if Phoenix had good eyesight? What role does sight play in this story?

7. After reading this story, many people have asked, "Is Phoenix Jackson's grandson really dead?" Did this question occur to you? Is the answer important to an understanding of the story? Explain.

ANALYZING THE WRITER'S CRAFT

1. Why do we only learn about the grandson through Phoenix and the nurse? What effect does this have on the reader?

2. Compare Phoenix's speech with that of the hunter and the nurse. When Phoenix talks to another character does she seem to understand what's going on? Does a difference in age account for the difference in speech? Explain. (Glossary: *Dialogue*) How does the diction of the characters vary according to their backgrounds? (Glossary: *Diction*) Cite examples of the differences you find.

3. How has Welty organized her story? (Glossary: *Organization*)

4. Comment on the landscape in this story. How does it change? Which characters blend into it and which stick out? Why do you suppose Welty ends her story in Natchez?

UNDERSTANDING THE WRITER'S LANGUAGE

1. Identify several passages where Welty uses descriptions to create verbal pictures of the characters, the setting, and the action. What metaphors and similes can you find in her descriptions? (Glossary: *Figures of Speech*) What do these descriptions add to her narrative? (Glossary: *Description*)

2. Refer to your desk dictionary to determine the meanings of the following words as Welty uses them in this selection: *nary* (paragraph 24), *furrow* (28), *pullets* (29), *cur* (53), *lye* (91).

WRITING SUGGESTIONS

1. Write a narrative essay about a routine trip you took that was interrupted by something unexpected such as a forced detour, a car accident, or bumping into an old friend. Where were you going? Why? What route did you take? Was anyone with you? What was the unexpected event, and how did it affect your trip? Be sure to use concrete, descriptive details so that your essay *shows* and doesn't *tell*. (Glossary: *Description*) Also use dialogue to deliver a sense of immediacy to your readers. (Glossary: *Dialogue*) Before you write, you might find it helpful to refer to your Preparing to Read response for this selection.

2. Welty uses precise details to describe Phoenix Jackson — "Her eyes were blue with age. Her skin had a pattern all its own of numberless branching wrinkles . . ." (paragraph 2). Using Welty's short story as a model, write a character sketch describing someone you know — a friend, relative, teacher, neighbor, or roommate — engaged in an activity typical for him or her such as washing dishes, watching television, reading a book, or cracking a joke. (Glossary: *Description*) What is notable about the person's appearance during this activity or how the person performs this activity? Is the person relaxed or agitated? Happy or sad? Focused or distracted? How can you tell? Be sure to use concrete, descriptive details as well as metaphors and similes to make your character sketch vivid and memorable. (Glossary: *Figures of Speech*)

3. Though brought up where racial discrimination was widespread, Eudora Welty writes of Phoenix Jackson with understanding and love. Is this typical of Welty? Read some of her other work — perhaps the story "Powerhouse" or the essay "A Pageant of Birds" — and then write an essay in which you assess the image of African Americans in her work. You may want to do some additional research on this topic in your college library or on the Internet.

- To begin your research online, go to **bedfordstmartins.com /subjectsstrategies** and click on "Narration" or browse the thematic directory of annotated links.

WRITING SUGGESTIONS FOR NARRATION

1. Using Malcolm X's or David P. Bardeen's essay as a model, narrate an experience that gave you a new awareness of yourself. Use enough telling detail in your narrative to help your reader visualize your experience and understand its significance for you. You may find the following suggestions helpful in choosing an experience to narrate in the first person:

    a. my greatest success
    b. my biggest failure
    c. my most embarrassing moment
    d. my happiest moment
    e. a truly frightening experience
    f. an experience that, in my eyes, turned a hero or idol into an ordinary person
    g. an experience that turned an ordinary person I know into one of my heroes
    h. the experience that was the most important turning point in my life

2. Each of us can tell of an experience that has been unusually significant in teaching us about our relationship to society or to life's institutions — schools, social or service organizations, religious groups, government. Think about your past, and identify one experience that has been especially important for you in this way. After you have considered this event's significance, write an essay recounting it. In preparing to write your narrative, you might enjoy reading George Orwell's account of acting against his better judgement in "Shooting an Elephant" (635–641). To bring your experience into focus and to help you decide what to include in your essay, ask yourself, Why is this experience important to me? What details are necessary for me to re-create the experience in an interesting and engaging way? How can my narrative be most effectively organized? What point of view will work best?

3. As a way of gaining experience with third-person narration, write an article intended for your school or community newspaper in which you report on what happened at one of the following:

    a. the visit of a state or national figure to your campus or community
    b. a dormitory meeting
    c. a current event of local, state, or national significance
    d. an important sports event
    e. a current research project of one of your professors
    f. a campus gathering or performance
    g. an important development at a local business or at your place of employment

4. Imagine that you are a member of a campus organization that is seeking volunteers for a community project. Your job is to write a piece for the school newspaper to solicit help for your organization. To build support

for the project, narrate one or more stories about the rewards of lending a hand to others within the community.

5. Many people love to tell stories (that is, they use narration!) to illustrate an abstract point, to bring an idea down to a personal level, or to render an idea memorable. Often, the telling of such stories can be entertaining as well as instructive. Think about a belief or position that you hold dear (e.g., every individual deserves respect, recycling matters, voluntarism creates community, people need artistic outlets, nature renews the individual), and try to capture that belief in a sentence or two. Then, narrate a story that illustrates your thesis.

6. Like Annie Dillard in "Getting Caught," we have all done something we know we should not have done. Sometimes we have gotten away with our transgressions, sometimes not. Sometimes our actions have no repercussions; sometimes they have very serious ones. Tell the story of one of your escapades, and explain why you have remembered it so well.

CHAPTER 6

Process Analysis

WHAT IS PROCESS ANALYSIS?

A process is a series of actions or stages that follow one another in a specific order and that lead to a particular end. People have invented many processes, like assembling pickup trucks or making bread; others occur naturally, like the erosion of a coastline or the development of a fetus in its mother's womb. All are processes because, if each step occurs correctly and in the right order, the results will be predictable: A completed pickup will roll off the assembly line, or a healthy baby will be born. Process analysis essays involve separating an event, an operation, or a cycle of development into distinct steps, describing each step precisely, and arranging the steps in their proper order.

Whenever you explain how something occurs or how it can (and should) be done — how plants create oxygen, how to make ice cream, or merely how to get to your house — you are using process analysis. Each year, thousands of books and magazine articles tell us how to make home repairs, how to lose weight and get physically fit, how to improve our memories, how to play better tennis, how to manage our money. They try to satisfy our curiosity about how television shows are made, how jet airplanes work, and how monkeys, bees, or whales mate. People simply want to know how things work and how to do things for themselves, so it's not surprising that process analysis is one of the most widespread and popular forms of writing today.

Process analysis resembles narration because both strategies present a series of events occurring over time. But a narration is the story of how things happened in a particular way during one particular period of time; process analysis relates how things always happen — or always should happen — in essentially the same way time after time.

Here is a process analysis written by Bernard Gladstone to explain how to light a fire in a fireplace.

The writer tells us this will be an explanation of a method for building a fire in a fireplace.

Though "experts" differ as to the best technique to follow when building a fire, one generally accepted method consists of first laying a generous amount of crumpled newspaper on the hearth between the andirons. Kindling wood is then spread generously over this layer of newspaper and one of the thickest logs is placed across the back of the andirons.

In one paragraph the writer takes us through six steps: the result is a wood-and-paper structure.

This should be as close to the back of the fireplace as possible, but not quite touching it. A second log is then placed an inch or so in front of this, and a few additional sticks of kindling are laid across these two. A third log is then placed on top to form a sort of pyramid with air space between all logs so that flames can lick freely up between them.

The next three paragraphs present three common mistakes.

A mistake frequently made is in building the fire too far forward so that the rear wall of the fireplace does not get properly heated. A heated back wall helps increase the draft and tends to suck smoke and flames rearward with less chance of sparks or smoke spurting out into the room.

Another common mistake often made by the inexperienced fire-tender is to try to build a fire with only one or two logs, instead of using at least three. A single log is difficult to ignite properly, and even two logs do not provide an efficient bed with adequate fuel burning capacity.

The writer reinforces his directions by telling us what not to do.

Use of too many logs, on the other hand, is also a common fault and can prove hazardous. Building too big a fire can create more smoke and draft than the chimney can safely handle, increasing the possibility of sparks or smoke being thrown out into the room. For best results, the homeowner should start with three medium-sized logs as described above, then add additional logs as needed if the fire is to be kept burning.

WHY DO WRITERS USE PROCESS ANALYSIS?

There are essentially two major reasons for writing a process analysis: to give directions, known as *directional process analysis*, and to inform, known as *informational process analysis*. Writers often combine one of these reasons with other rhetorical strategies to evaluate the process in question; this is known as *evaluative process analysis*. Let's take a look at each of these forms of process analysis more closely.

Directional Process Analysis

Writers use directional process analysis to provide readers with the necessary steps to achieve a desired result. The directions may be as simple as the instructions on a frozen-food package ("Heat in microwave on high for six to eight minutes. Rotate one-quarter turn halfway through cooking time, stir, and serve") or as complex as the operator's manual for a personal computer. In his student essay on juggling, William Peterson takes us through the process of learning how to juggle one step at a time. Mortimer Adler proposes a method for getting the most out of reading in his essay "How to Mark a Book." First he compares what he sees as the "two ways in which one can own a book" and classifies book lovers into three categories. Then he presents his directions for how one should make marginal comments to get the most out of a book. In his "How to Say Nothing in 500 Words," Paul Roberts lays out the steps by which a writer can turn a dull subject into a lively, interesting one. No matter their length or complexity, however, all directions have the same purpose: to guide the reader through a clear and logically ordered series of steps toward a particular goal.

Informational Process Analysis

This strategy deals not with processes that readers are able to perform for themselves, but with processes that readers are curious about or would like to understand better: how presidents are elected, how plants reproduce, how an elevator works, how the brain processes and generates language. In the following selection from his *Lives Around Us*, Alan Devoe explains what happens to an animal when it goes into hibernation.

> The woodchuck's hibernation usually starts about the middle of September. For weeks he has been foraging with increased appetite among the clover blossoms and has grown heavy and slow-moving. Now, with the coming of mid-September, apples and corn and yarrow tops have become less plentiful, and the nights are cool. The woodchuck moves with slower gait, and emerges less and less frequently for feeding trips. Layers of fat have accumulated around his chest and shoulders, and there is thick fat in the axils of his legs. He has extended his summer burrow to a length of nearly thirty feet, and has fashioned a deep nest-chamber at the end of it, far below the level of the frost. He has carried in, usually, a little hay. He is ready for the Long Sleep.
> When the temperature of the September days falls below 50 degrees or so, the woodchuck becomes too drowsy to come forth from his burrow in the chilly dusk to forage. He remains in the deep

nest-chamber, lethargic, hardly moving. Gradually, with the passing of hours or days, his coarse-furred body curls into a semicircle, like a fetus, nose-tip touching tail. The small legs are tucked in, the hand-like clawed forefeet folded. The woodchuck has become a compact ball. Presently the temperature of his body begins to fall.

In normal life the woodchuck's temperature, though fluctuant, averages about 97 degrees. Now, as he lies tight-curled in a ball with the winter sleep stealing over him, this body heat drops ten degrees, twenty degrees, thirty. Finally, by the time the snow is on the ground and the woodchuck's winter dormancy has become complete, his temperature is only 38 or 40. With the falling of the body heat there is a slowing of his heartbeat and his respiration. In normal life he breathes thirty or forty times each minute; when he is excited, as many as a hundred times. Now he breathes slower and slower: ten times a minute, five times a minute, once a minute, and at last only ten or twelve times in an hour. His heartbeat is a twentieth of normal. He has entered fully into the oblivion of hibernation.

The process Devoe describes is natural to woodchucks but not to humans, so obviously he cannot be giving instructions. Rather, he has created an informational process analysis to help us understand what happens during the remarkable process of hibernation. As Devoe's analysis reveals, hibernation is not a series of well-defined steps but a long, slow change from the activity of late summer to the immobility of a deep winter's sleep. The woodchuck does not suddenly stop feeding, nor do his temperature, pulse, and rate of respiration plummet at once. Using a transitional expression and time markers, Devoe shows us that the process lasts for weeks, even months. He connects the progress of hibernation with changes in the weather because the woodchuck's body responds to the dropping temperature as autumn sets in rather than to the passage of specific periods of time.

Evaluative Process Analysis

People often want to understand processes in order to evaluate them — to make improvements in how things are done, to better understand how events occur — and usually to improve those processes or to profit from their increased understanding. They want to improve processes by making them simpler, quicker, safer, or more efficient. They may also wish to analyze processes to understand them more deeply or accurately in order to base subsequent actions on more reliable information. An evaluative process analysis might give the reader insight into the writer's thinking about the pros and cons, the pitfalls, and the rewards of altering a widely understood and accepted process. In other words, an evaluative process analysis may offer a reconsideration of our understanding of a known process. If we look at Paul

Roberts's "How to Say Nothing in 500 Words," we see that throughout the essay he describes an ineffective writing process used by some students and then compares and contrasts it with a more effective process. Whether used to direct, inform, or evaluate, process analysis is an invaluable critical thinking skill.

AN ANNOTATED STUDENT ESSAY
USING PROCESS ANALYSIS

William Peterson grew up in New Hartford, New York. After completing a business major at the University of Vermont, he entered the music business and now works as a booking agent. He had extensive experience organizing campus concerts for his university's student association. Peterson is also an avid juggler, and he enjoys teaching others the craft. In "I Bet You Can," he shares with us, step-by-step, the basics of how to juggle. Try it.

I Bet You Can

William Peterson

Context-setting introduction invites reader to learn how to juggle.

Have you ever seen Michael Davis on television? He's a standup comic and a juggler. His antics got me interested in learning how to juggle. Several years ago after watching his act on "Saturday Night Live" I went out to my garage and started to experiment with some tennis balls. At first I felt helpless after tossing and chasing the balls for what seemed like countless hours. However, I actually did start to learn how to juggle. To my surprise I discovered that juggling is much easier than it had at first appeared. If you'd like to learn how to juggle, I recommend that you find some tennis balls or lacrosse balls and continue reading.

Transition links to next section.

First step in process is introduced: the simple toss.

Step one is the simple toss. Stand erect and hold one ball in your right hand. Carefully toss the ball up to approximately an inch above your head and to about half an arm's length in front of you. The ball should arch from your right hand across to your left. This step should now be repeated, starting with your left hand and tossing to

1

2

Recommendation is given to practice first step until it is perfected.

your right. Be sure that the ball reaches the same height and distance from you and is not simply passed from your left hand to your right. Keep tossing the ball back and forth until you have become thoroughly disgusted with this step. If you have practiced this toss enough, we can now call

Writer labels step one as "the perfect toss."

this step "the perfect toss." If it is not quite perfect, then you have not become disgusted enough with the step. We'll

Transition links to next section.

assume that you've perfected it. Now you're ready to take a little breather and move on.

Writer labels the second step in process: the toss and return.

Step two is the toss and return. Get back on your feet and this time hold a ball in each hand. Take a deep breath and make a perfect toss with the ball in your right hand. As that ball reaches its peak make another perfect toss with the ball in your left hand. The second ball should end up passing under the first one and reaching approximately the same height. When the second ball peaks, you should be grabbing — or already have grabbed, depending on timing — the first ball. The second ball should then gently drop into your awaiting right hand. If it was not that easy, then don't worry about the "gently" bit. Most people do not

Writer emphasizes the need to practice step two.

achieve perfection at first. Step two is the key factor in becoming a good juggler and should be practiced at least five times as much as step one.

Don't deceive yourself after a few successful completions. This maneuver really must be perfected before step three can be

A helpful suggestion is provided.

approached. As a way to improve dexterity, you should try several tosses and returns starting with your left hand. Let's call

Writer labels step two as "the exchange."

step two "the exchange." You're now ready for another well-deserved breather before you proceed.

3

4

Writer labels third step in process: addition of third ball.

Ready or not, here it goes. Step three 5 is merely a continuum of "the exchange" with the addition of a third ball. Don't worry if you are confused — I will explain. Get back up again, and now hold two balls in your right hand and one in your left. Make a perfect toss with one of the balls in your right hand and then an exchange with the one in your left hand. The ball coming from your left hand should now be exchanged with the, as of now, unused ball in your right hand. This process should be continued until you find yourself reaching under nearby chairs for bouncing tennis balls. It is true that many persons' backs and legs become sore when learning how to juggle because they've been picking up balls that they've inadvertently tossed around the room. Try practicing over a bed; you won't have to reach down so far. Don't get too upset if things aren't going well; you're probably keeping the same pace as everyone else at this stage. You're certainly doing better than I was because you've had me as a teacher.

Transitional paragraph links to next section.

Don't worry, this teacher is not going 6 to leave you stranded with hours of repetition of the basic steps. I am sure that you have already run into some basic problems. I will now try to relate some of my beginner's troubles and some of the best solutions you can try for them.

Writer discusses problem one and its solutions.

Problem one, you are getting nowhere 7 after the simple toss. This requires a basic improvement of hand to eye coordination. Solution one is to just go back and practice the simple toss again and again. Unfortunately, this becomes quite boring. Solution two is not as tedious and involves quite a bit of skill. Try juggling two balls in one hand. Some people show me this when I ask them if they can juggle — they're not fooling anyone. Real juggling is what you're here to learn. First try circular juggling in one hand. This involves tosses similar to "the perfect toss." They differ in that the balls go half as far towards the opposite hand, are tossed and grabbed by the same hand, and end up making their own circles (as opposed to going up and down in upside down V's like exchanges). Then try juggling the balls in the same line style. I think this is harder. You have to keep two balls traveling in their own vertical paths (the balls should go as high as they do in a "perfect toss") with only one hand. I think this is harder than the circular style because my hands normally tend to make little circles when I juggle.

Writer discusses problem two and its solution.

Problem two, you can make exchanges but you just can't accomplish step three. The best solution to this is to just continue practicing step two, but now add a twist. As soon as the first ball is caught by the left hand in our step two, throw it back up in another perfect toss for another exchange. Continue this and increase speed up to the point where two balls just don't seem like enough. You should now be ready to add the third ball and accomplish what you couldn't before — real Michael Davis kind of juggling.

8

Writer discusses problem three and its solutions.

Problem three, you have become the "runaway juggler." This means you can successfully achieve numerous exchanges but you're always chasing after balls tossed too far in front of you. The first solution is to stand in front of a wall. This causes you to end up catching a couple of balls bouncing off the wall or else you'll end up consciously keeping your tosses in closer to your body. The second solution is to put your back up against a wall. This will tend to make you toss in closer to yourself

9

because you will be restricted to keeping your back up against the wall. This solution can work, but more often than not you'll find yourself watching balls fly across the room in front of you! I've told you about the back-on-the-wall method because some people find it effective. As you can tell, I don't.

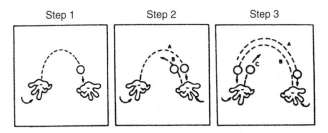

Writer concludes with visual presentation of three-step process.

Juggling is a simple three-step process. Following my routine is the easiest way to get from being a spastic ball chaser to an accomplished juggler. Patience and coordination are really not required. The only requirements are a few tennis balls, the ability to follow some basic instructions, and the time to have some fun.

10

Analyzing William Peterson's Essay of Process Analysis: Questions for Discussion

1. Peterson uses personal experience as a basis for his essay. How do his experiences learning to juggle help the reader, who is presumably playing the role of novice juggler?

2. Successful juggling depends on successfully tying together a series of basic steps, so the transitions in the above essay are extremely important. Identify what Peterson does to create smooth transitions between the steps, which are presented in a series of paragraphs.

3. Peterson presents the whole process of learning to juggle before presenting common problems. Why does he address the problems after the fact? How does this organization help his readers reach their goal?

SUGGESTIONS FOR WRITING
A PROCESS ANALYSIS ESSAY

In a process analysis, always aim for precision and clarity. Few things are more frustrating to readers of directions than an unclear, misplaced, or omitted step that prevents them from achieving the results the writer has promised. The same sort of error in an informational process analysis will cause misunderstanding and confusion. Whatever your purpose, process analysis requires a systematic, logical approach.

Know the Process You Are Writing About

There's no substitute for thorough knowledge of your subject. Be sure that you have more than a vague or general grasp of the process you are writing about. Make sure you analyze it fully, from beginning to end. You can sometimes convince yourself that you understand an entire process when, in fact, your understanding is somewhat superficial. If you were analyzing the process by which children learn language, you wouldn't want to rely on only one expert's account. Instead, it would be a good idea to read explanations by several authorities on the subject. Turning to more than one account not only reinforces your understanding of key points in the process, but also points out various ways the process is performed; you may want to consider these alternatives in your writing.

Have a Clear Purpose

Giving directions for administering cardiopulmonary resuscitation and explaining how the El Niño phenomenon unfolds are worthy purposes for writing a process analysis paper. Many process analysis papers go beyond these fundamental purposes, however. They lay out processes to evaluate them, to suggest alternative steps, to point out shortcomings in generally accepted practices, and to suggest improvements. In short, process analysis papers are frequently persuasive or argumentative; they use an understanding and discussion of process analysis to achieve another goal: to persuade readers that there is a better way of doing or understanding a given process.

Organize the Process into Steps

As much as possible, make each step a simple and well-defined action, preferably a single action. To guide yourself in doing so, write a scratch outline listing the steps. Here, for example, is an outline of Bernard Gladstone's directions for building a fire.

Process Analysis of Building a Fire in a Fireplace

1. Put down crumpled newspaper.
2. Lay kindling.
3. Place back log near rear wall but not touching.
4. Place front log an inch forward.
5. Bridge logs with kindling.
6. Place third log on top of kindling bridge.

Next, check your outline to make sure that the steps are in the right order and that none has been omitted. Then analyze your outline more carefully. Are any steps so complex that they need to be described in some detail — or perhaps divided into more steps? Will you need to explain the purpose of a certain step because the reason for it is not obvious? Especially in an informational process analysis, two steps may take place at the same time; perhaps they are performed by different people or different parts of the body. Does your outline make this clear? (One solution is to assign both steps the same number but divide them into substeps by labeling one of them "A" and the other "B.") When you feel certain that the steps of the process are complete and correct, ask yourself two more questions. Will the reader need any other information to understand the process — definitions of unusual terms, for example, or descriptions of special equipment? Should you anticipate common mistakes or misunderstandings and discuss them, as Gladstone does? If so, be sure to add an appropriate note or two to your scratch outline as a reminder.

Use Transitions to Link the Steps

Transitional words and phrases like *then, next, after doing this,* and *during the summer months* can both emphasize and clarify the sequence of steps in your process analysis. The same is true of sequence markers like *first, second, third,* and so on. Devoe uses such words to make clear which stages in the hibernation process are simultaneous and which are not; Gladstone includes an occasional *first* or *then* to alert us to shifts from one step to the next. But both writers are careful not to overuse these words, and you should exercise the same caution. Transitional words are a resource of language, but they should not be used arbitrarily.

Energize Your Writing: Use the Active Voice and Strong Action Verbs

Writers prefer the active voice because it stresses the doer of an action, is lively and emphatic, and uses strong descriptive verbs. The passive voice, on the other hand, stresses what was done rather than who did it and uses forms of the weak verb *to be*.

ACTIVE   The coaches analyzed the game film, and the fullback de-
                cided to rededicate herself to playing defense.

PASSIVE   A game film analysis was performed by the coaches, and a
                rededication to playing defense was decided upon by the
                fullback.

Sometimes, however, the doer of an action is unknown or less important than the recipient of an action. In this case, it is acceptable to use the passive voice:

The Earth's moon was formed more than 4 billion years ago.

When you revise your drafts, scan your sentences for passive constructions and weak verbs. Put your sentences into the active voice and find strong action verbs to replace weak verbs. Instead of the weak verb *run*, use *fly, gallop, hustle, jog, race, rush, scamper, scoot, scramble, tear,* or *trot,* for example. Instead of the weak verb *say,* use *declare, express, muse, mutter, pronounce, report, respond, recite, reply, snarl,* or *utter,* for example. Forms of the verb *to be* (*is, are, was, were, will be, should be*) are weak and nondescriptive and, therefore, should be avoided whenever possible. If you can't form a picture of a verb's action in your mind, it is most likely a weak verb. Here are some common weak verbs you should replace with strong action verbs in your writing:

have, had, has	get
make	involve
concern	determine
reflect	become
provide	go
do	appear
use	

Use Consistent Verb Tense

A verb's tense indicates when an action is taking place: some time in the past, right now, or in the future. Using verb tense consistently helps your readers understand time changes in your writing. Inconsistent verb tenses — or *shifts* — within a sentence confuse readers and are especially noticeable in narration and process analysis writing, which are sequence and time oriented. Generally, you should write in the past or present tense and maintain that tense throughout your sentence:

INCONSISTENT   I mixed the eggs and sugar and then add the flour.

Mixed is past tense; *add* is present tense.

CORRECTED   I mix the eggs and sugar and then add the flour.

The sentence is now consistently in the present tense. The sentence can also be revised to be consistently in the past tense:

CORRECTED   I mixed the eggs and sugar and then added the flour.

Here's another example:

INCONSISTENT   The painter studied the scene and pulls a fan brush decisively from her cup.

Studied is past tense, indicating an action that has already taken place; *pulls* is present tense, indicating an action taking place now.

CORRECTED   The painter studies the scene and pulls a fan brush decisively from her cup.

CORRECTED   The painter studied the scene and pulled a fan brush decisively from her cup.

Consider Your Audience, and Choose Appropriate Diction

The success of a process analysis essay depends heavily on how well you consider your audience. Are your readers very familiar, moderately familiar, or completely unfamiliar with the process you are trying to explain? If you are preparing a set of directions for processing film in the photo lab for a beginners' photography club, your readers will not know the meanings of technical terms and will not be able to accomplish the task without specific directions; thus you will need to include definitions and detailed explanations. If you are writing a process analysis of how tornadoes are formed for your classmates in a meteorology course, you will naturally have a fairly good sense of how much your audience already knows. Remember, in either case, that you should keep audience assessment and choice of diction — from concrete to abstract, from specific to general — in mind as you write.

Test the Effectiveness of Your Process Analysis

After finishing the first draft of your essay, have someone else read it. If you are writing a directional process analysis, ask your reader to follow the instructions and then to tell you whether he or she was able to understand each step and perform it satisfactorily. Was the desired result achieved? Did the fire burn well, the computer program run, the lasagna taste good? If not, examine your process analysis step by step, looking for errors and omissions that would explain the unsatisfactory result (no kindling wood, perhaps, or a loop in the program, or too much garlic).

In fact, William Peterson gave his essay on juggling to some friends to have them test his directions. "I gave it to people who had never tried juggling to see if there were any 'bugs' or unclear sections in my instructions. This helped me a lot as a writer because they told me where certain things were not clear or outright confusing. This enabled me to go back and revise, knowing exactly what the problem was." Peterson's readers had difficulty understanding his directions for the simple toss in his rough draft. Peterson agreed with their criticism: "I just couldn't get detailed enough in my rough draft. I had real trouble with paragraph 2, the explanation of the simple toss." Here is an early draft of that paragraph:

> Step one is the simple toss. Stand erect and hold one object (we'll call it a ball from now on) in your most adroit hand (we'll say the right). Toss the ball into the air to approximately an inch above your head and to about half an arm's length in front of you. The ball should take an arched path traveling from your right hand to your left. This step should now be repeated using your left hand first and returning it to your right hand. Repeat this until completely proficient. We'll now call this action the "perfect toss." Take a breather and then move on.

"After several drafts," Peterson says, "I finally felt satisfied with my directions." To see what changes he made, compare the paragraph above with paragraph 2 in his final essay.

With an informational process analysis, it may be a bit trickier to ensure that your reader really understands. Test your reader's comprehension by asking a few questions. If there seems to be any confusion, try rereading what you have written with an objective eye. Sometimes an especially intricate or otherwise difficult step can be made clear by rewriting it in everyday language; sometimes a recognizable comparison or analogy will help, especially if you are analyzing a scientific or otherwise unfamiliar process. For example, American readers might better understand the British game of rugby if you compare it with American football; nonspecialists might grasp the circulation of blood more easily through an analogy between the cardiovascular system and domestic plumbing. (See the introduction to Chapter 7 for discussions of *comparison and contrast* and *analogy*.) Again, try to pin down the specific cause of any misunderstanding — the step or steps that are confusing your reader. Make sure the sequence is consistently clear. Keep on revising until your reader can demonstrate a thorough understanding of the process you've tried to explain.

Editing Tip: Clear Pronoun References

Be sure to follow the guidelines and advice for editing an essay given in Chapter 2, "Writing Essays." The guidelines highlight those sentence-level concerns of style — grammar, mechanics, and punctuation — that are especially important in editing any piece of writing. In a process analysis essay, certain nouns that are key to the process the writer is explaining keep coming up. In order not to sound repetitive, writers substitute pronouns for these recurring nouns.

REPETITIVE   Children love to play in piles of *leaves*, hurling *the leaves* in the air, like confetti, leaping into soft unruly mattresses of *the leaves*.

WITH PRONOUNS   Children love to play in piles of *leaves*, hurling *them* in the air, like confetti, leaping into soft unruly mattresses of *them*.

— DIANE ACKERMAN
"Why Leaves Turn Color in the Fall," page 258

The noun to which a pronoun refers is called its *antecedent* or *referent*. Be sure to place a pronoun as close to its antecedent as possible so that the relationship between the pronoun and its antecedent is clear. The more words that intervene between the antecedent and the pronoun, the more chance there is for confusion. When the relationship between a pronoun and its antecedent is unclear, the sentence is inaccurate or ambiguous and can have two or more meanings. While editing your process analysis essay, look for and correct ambiguous, vague, or implied pronoun references.

Ambiguous Reference. Make sure all your pronouns clearly refer to specific antecedents. If a pronoun can refer to more than one antecedent, the sentence is ambiguous.

AMBIGUOUS   Adler sought to convince the reader to mark up *his* book.

In this sentence the antecedent of the pronoun *his* could be either *Adler* or *reader*. Does Adler want his particular book marked up, or does he want readers to mark up their own books? To make an ambiguous antecedent clear, either repeat the correct antecedent or rewrite the sentence.

CLEAR   Adler sought to convince the reader to mark up *Adler's* book.

CLEAR   Adler sought to convince readers to mark up *their* books.

Vague Reference. Use *this, that, which,* and *such* carefully to refer to a general idea in a preceding clause or sentence. If an idea is relatively simple, no confusion results from such a construction.

> Or, consider the word *intellectual. This* would seem to be a complimentary term, but in point of fact it is not, for it has picked up associations of impracticality and ineffectuality and general dopiness.
>
> — PAUL ROBERTS
> "How to Say Nothing in 500 Words," page 243

If the pronoun refers to a broader or more general idea, however, vagueness can result. To correct the problem, either substitute a noun for the pronoun or provide an antecedent to which the pronoun can clearly refer.

VAGUE   Some students follow Adler's advice while others do not, *which* is not surprising.

CLEAR   Some students follow Adler's advice while others do not, *an outcome that* is not surprising.

Implied References. Make every pronoun refer to a stated, not an implied, antecedent. Every time you use a pronoun in a sentence, you should be able to identify its noun equivalent. If you cannot, use a noun instead.

IMPLIED   In Christopher Callahan's "Anatomy of an Urban Legend," *he* explains how urban legends get started and travel with electronic speed around the globe.

CLEAR   In "Anatomy of an Urban Legend," *Christopher Callahan* explains how urban legends get started and travel with electronic speed around the globe.

▶ *Questions for Revising and Editing: Process Analysis*

1. Do I have a thorough knowledge of the process I chose to write about?
2. Have I clearly informed readers about how to perform the process (directional process analysis), or have I explained how a process occurs (informational process analysis)? Does my choice reflect the overall purpose of my process analysis paper?
3. Have I divided the process into clear, readily understandable steps?
4. Did I pay particular attention to transitional words to take readers from one step to the next?
5. Are all my sentences in the active voice?
6. Have I used strong action verbs, and is my tense consistent?
7. Have I succeeded in tailoring my diction to my audience's familiarity with the subject?
8. Are my pronoun antecedents clear?
9. How did my test reader respond to my essay? Did he or she find any confusing passages or any missing steps?

How to Mark a Book

Mortimer Adler

Writer, editor, and educator Mortimer Adler (1902–2001) was born in New York City. A high school dropout, Adler completed the undergraduate program at Columbia University in three years, but he did not graduate because he refused to take the mandatory swimming test. Adler is recognized for his editorial work on the Encyclopaedia Britannica *and for his leadership of the Great Books Program at the University of Chicago, where adults from all walks of life gathered twice a month to read and discuss the classics.*

In the following essay, which first appeared in the Saturday Review of Literature *in 1940, Adler offers a timeless lesson: He explains how to take full ownership of a book by marking it up, by making it "a part of yourself."*

PREPARING TO READ

When you read a book that you must understand thoroughly and remember for a class or for your own purposes, what techniques do you use to help you understand what you are reading? What helps you remember important parts of the book and improve your understanding of what the author is saying?

You know you have to read "between the lines" to get the most out of anything. I want to persuade you to do something equally important in the course of your reading. I want to persuade you to "write between the lines." Unless you do, you are not likely to do the most efficient kind of reading. 1

I contend, quite bluntly, that marking up a book is not an act of mutilation but of love. 2

You shouldn't mark up a book which isn't yours. Librarians (or your friends) who lend you books expect you to keep them clean, and you should. If you decide that I am right about the usefulness of marking books, you will have to buy them. Most of the world's great books are available today in reprint editions. 3

There are two ways in which one can own a book. The first is the property right you establish by paying for it, just as you pay for clothes and furniture. But this act of purchase is only the prelude to possession. Full ownership comes only when you have made it a part of yourself, and the best way to make yourself a part of it is by writing in it. An illustration may make the point clear. You buy a beefsteak and transfer it from the butcher's icebox to your own. But you do not 4 own the beefsteak in the most important sense until you consume it and get it into your bloodstream. I am arguing that books, too, must be absorbed in your bloodstream to do you any good.

Confusion about what it means to *own* a book leads people to a false reverence for paper, binding, and type — a respect for the physical thing — the craft of the printer rather than the genius of the author. They forget that it is possible for a man to acquire the idea, to possess the beauty, which a great book contains, without staking his claim by pasting his bookplate inside the cover. Having a fine library doesn't prove that its owner has a mind enriched by books; it proves nothing more than that he, his father, or his wife, was rich enough to buy them.

There are three kinds of book owners. The first has all the standard sets and best-sellers — unread, untouched. (This deluded individual owns woodpulp and ink, not books.) The second has a great many books — a few of them read through, most of them dipped into, but all of them as clean and shiny as the day they were bought. (This person would probably like to make books his own, but is restrained by a false respect for their physical appearance.) The third has a few books or many — every one of them dog-eared and dilapidated, shaken and loosened by continual use, marked and scribbled in from front to back. (This man owns books.)

Is it false respect, you may ask, to preserve intact and unblemished a beautifully printed book, an elegantly bound edition? Of course not. I'd no more scribble all over a first edition of *Paradise Lost* than I'd give my baby a set of crayons and an original Rembrandt! I wouldn't mark up a painting or a statue. Its soul, so to speak, is inseparable from its body. And the beauty of a rare edition or of a richly manufactured volume is like that of a painting or a statue.

But the soul of a book *can* be separated from its body. A book is more like the score of a piece of music than it is like a painting. No great musician confuses a symphony with the printed sheets of music. Arturo Toscanini reveres Brahms, but Toscanini's score of the C-minor Symphony is so thoroughly marked up that no one but the maestro himself can read it. The reason why a great conductor makes notations on his musical scores — marks them up again and again each time he returns to study them — is the reason why you should mark your books. If your respect for magnificent binding or typography gets in the way, buy yourself a cheap edition and pay your respects to the author.

Why is marking up a book indispensable to reading? First, it keeps you awake. (And I don't mean merely conscious; I mean wide awake.) In the second place, reading, if it is active, is thinking, and thinking tends to express itself in words, spoken or written. The marked book is usually the thought-through book. Finally, writing helps you remember the thoughts you had, or the thoughts the author expressed. Let me develop these three points.

If reading is to accomplish anything more than passing time, it   10
must be active. You can't let your eyes glide across the lines of a book and come up with an understanding of what you have read. Now an ordinary piece of light fiction, like say, *Gone with the Wind*, doesn't require the most active kind of reading. The books you read for pleasure can be read in a state of relaxation, and nothing is lost. But a great book, rich in ideas and beauty, a book that raises and tries to answer great fundamental questions, demands the most active reading of which you are capable. You don't absorb the ideas of John Dewey[1] the way you absorb the crooning of Mr. Vallee.[2] You have to reach for them. That you cannot do while you're asleep.

If, when you've finished reading a book, the pages are filled with   11
your notes, you know that you read actively. The most famous active reader of great books I know is President Hutchins, of the University of Chicago. He also has the hardest schedule of business activities of any man I know. He invariably reads with a pencil, and sometimes, when he picks up a book and pencil in the evening, he finds himself, instead of making intelligent notes, drawing what he calls "caviar factories" on the margins. When that happens, he puts the book down. He knows he's too tired to read, and he's just wasting time.

But, you may ask, why is writing necessary? Well, the physical act   12
of writing, with your own hand, brings words and sentences more sharply before your mind and preserves them better in your memory. To set down your reaction to important words and sentences you have read, and the questions they have raised in your mind, is to preserve those reactions and sharpen those questions.

Even if you wrote on a scratch pad, and threw the paper away   13
when you had finished writing, your grasp of the book would be surer. But you don't have to throw the paper away. The margins (top and bottom, as well as side), the end-papers, the very space between the lines, are all available. They aren't sacred. And, best of all, your marks and notes become an integral part of the book and stay there forever. You can pick up the book the following week or year, and there are all your points of agreement, disagreement, doubt, and inquiry. It's like resuming an interrupted conversation with the advantage of being able to pick up where you left off.

---

[1]John Dewey (1859–1952) was an educational philosopher who had a profound influence on learning through experimentation.

[2]Rudy Vallee (1901–1986) was a popular singer of the 1920s, famous for his crooning high notes.

And that is exactly what reading a book should be: a conversation   14
between you and the author. Presumably he knows more about the
subject than you do; naturally, you'll have the proper humility as you
approach him. But don't let anybody tell you that a reader is supposed
to be solely on the receiving end. Understanding is a two-way operation; learning doesn't consist in being an empty receptacle. The learner
has to question himself and question the teacher. He even has to argue
with the teacher, once he understands what the teacher is saying. And
marking a book is literally an expression of your differences, or agreements of opinion, with the author.

There are all kinds of devices for marking a book intelligently and   15
fruitfully. Here's the way I do it:

1. *Underlining:* of major points, of important or forceful statements.   16

2. *Vertical lines at the margin:* to emphasize a statement already un-   17
derlined.

3. *Star, asterisk, or other doo-dad at the margin:* to be used sparingly,   18
to emphasize the ten or twenty most important statements in the
book. (You may want to fold the bottom corner of each page on which
you use such marks. It won't hurt the sturdy paper on which most modern books are printed, and you will be able to take the book off the
shelf at any time and, by opening it at the folded-corner page, refresh
your recollection of the book.)

4. *Numbers in the margin:* to indicate the sequence of points the au-   19
thor makes in developing a single argument.

5. *Numbers of other pages in the margin:* to indicate where else in the   20
book the author made points relevant to the point marked; to tie up
the ideas in a book, which, though they may be separated by many
pages, belong together.

6. *Circling:* of key words or phrases.   21

7. *Writing in the margin, or at the top or bottom of the page, for the sake*   22
of: recording questions (and perhaps answers) which a passage raised in
your mind; reducing a complicated discussion to a simple statement;
recording the sequence of major points right through the book. I use
the end-papers at the back of the book to make a personal index of the
author's points in the order of their appearance.

The front end-papers are, to me, the most important. Some people   23
reserve them for a fancy bookplate. I reserve them for fancy thinking.
After I have finished reading the book and making my personal index
on the back end-papers, I turn to the front and try to outline the book,
not page by page, or point by point (I've already done that at the back),
but as an integrated structure, with a basic unity and an order of parts.
This outline is, to me, the measure of my understanding of the work.

If you're a die-hard anti-book-marker, you may object that the   24
margins, the space between the lines, and the end-papers don't give
you room enough. All right. How about using a scratch pad slightly

smaller than the page-size of the book — so that the edges of the sheets won't protrude? Make your index, outlines, and even your notes on the pad, and then insert these sheets permanently inside the front and back covers of the book.

Or, you may say that this business of marking books is going to slow up your reading. It probably will. That's one of the reasons for doing it. Most of us have been taken in by the notion that speed of reading is a measure of our intelligence. There is no such thing as the right speed for intelligent reading. Some things should be read quickly and effortlessly, and some should be read slowly and even laboriously. The sign of intelligence in reading is the ability to read different things differently according to their worth. In the case of good books, the point is not to see how many of them you can get through, but rather how many can get through you — how many you can make your own. A few friends are better than a thousand acquaintances. If this be your aim, as it should be, you will not be impatient if it takes more time and effort to read a great book than it does a newspaper. 25

You may have one final objection to marking books. You can't lend them to your friends because nobody else can read them without being distracted by your notes. Furthermore, you won't want to lend them because a marked copy is a kind of intellectual diary, and lending it is almost like giving your mind away. 26

If your friend wishes to read your *Plutarch's Lives*, *Shakespeare*, or *The Federalist Papers*, tell him gently but firmly to buy a copy. You will lend him your car or your coat — but your books are as much a part of you as your head or your heart. 27

RESPONDING TO THE TEXT

After you have read Adler's essay, compare your answer to the Preparing to Read prompt with Adler's guidelines for reading. What are the most significant differences between Adler's guidelines and your own? How can you better make the books you read part of yourself?

ENGAGING THE WRITER'S SUBJECT

1. What are the three kinds of book owners Adler identifies? What are their differences? (Glossary: *Classification; Division*)

2. According to Adler, why is marking up a book indispensable to reading? Do you agree with his three arguments? (Glossary: *Argument*) Why or why not?

3. Adler says that reading a book should be a conversation between the reader and the author. What characteristics does he say the conversation should have? How does marking a book assist in carrying on and preserving the conversation?

ANALYZING THE WRITER'S CRAFT

1. In the first paragraph, Adler writes, "I want to persuade you to do something equally important in the course of your reading. I want to persuade you to 'write between the lines.'" What assumptions does Adler make about his audience when he chooses to use the parallel structure of "I want to persuade you . . ."? (Glossary: *Audience; Parallelism*) Is stating his intention so blatantly an effective way of presenting his argument? (Glossary: *Argument*) Why or why not?

2. Adler expresses himself very clearly throughout the essay and his topic sentences are carefully crafted. (Glossary: *Topic Sentence*) Reread the topic sentences for paragraphs 3–6, and identify how each introduces the main idea for the paragraph and unifies it.

3. Throughout the essay, Adler provides the reader with a number of verbal cues ("There are two ways," "Let me develop these three points"). What do these verbal cues indicate about the organizational connections of the essay? (Glossary: *Organization*) Explain how Adler's organization creates an essay that logically follows from sentence to sentence and from paragraph to paragraph.

4. Summarize in your own words Adler's process analysis about how one should mark a book. Explain how Adler's process analysis is also an argument for the correct way to read. (Glossary: *Argument*)

5. Adler's process analysis is also a description of an event or a sequence of events (how to read). Does he claim that his recommended reading process will aid the reader's understanding, increase the reader's interest, or both? (Glossary: *Cause and Effect Analysis*)

UNDERSTANDING THE WRITER'S LANGUAGE

1. Adler makes an analogy that links reading books with the statement, "A few friends are better than a thousand acquaintances" (paragraph 25). (Glossary: *Analogy*) Explain how this analogy works. Why is this analogy important to Adler's overall argument?

2. Throughout the essay, Adler uses the personal pronoun *I* to describe his reading experience. (Glossary: *Point of View*) How does this personalized voice help or hinder the explanation of the process of reading?

3. Refer to your desk dictionary to determine the meanings of the following words as Adler uses them in this selection: *deluded* (paragraph 6), *dilapidated* (6), *typography* (8), *integral* (13), *protrude* (24).

WRITING SUGGESTIONS

1. Write a directional process analysis in which you present your techniques for getting the most enjoyment out of a common activity. For example, perhaps you have a set routine you follow for spending an evening watching television — preparing popcorn, checking the program listings, clearing off the coffee table, finding the remote control,

settling into your favorite chair, and so on. Choose from the following topics:

How to listen to music

How to eat an ice-cream cone

How to reduce stress

How to wash a dog

How to play a sport or game

2. Adler devotes a large portion of his essay to persuading his audience that marking books is a worthwhile task. (Glossary: *Persuasion*) Write an essay in which you instruct your audience about how to do something they do not necessarily wish to do or they do not think they need to do. For instance, before explaining how to buy the best MP3 player, you may need to convince readers that they *should* buy an MP3 player. Write your directional process analysis after making a convincing argument for the validity of the process you wish to present. (Glossary: *Argument*)

3. Adler provides good advice for close, active reading by explaining the process of marking books. However, how does one go about learning how to read? In your college library and on the Internet, research phonics or whole-language learning. Choose one of these methods and write an informational process analysis essay in which you explain how it works.

- To begin your research online, go to **bedfordstmartins.com /subjectsstrategies** and click on "Process Analysis" or browse the thematic directory of annotated links.

How to Say Nothing in 500 Words

Paul Roberts

Paul Roberts (1917–1967) was a linguist, a teacher, and a writer at San Jose State College from 1946 to 1960 and at Cornell University from 1962 to 1964. His books on writing, including English Syntax *(1954) and* Patterns of English *(1956), have helped generations of high school and college students become better writers.*

"How to Say Nothing in 500 Words" is taken from his best-known book, Understanding English *(1958). Although written over forty years ago, the essay is still relevant for student writers today. Good writing, Roberts tells us, is not simply a matter of filling up a page; rather, the words have to hold the reader's interest, and they must say something. In this essay, Roberts uses lively prose and a step-by-step process to guide the student from the blank page to the finished essay. His bag of writing strategies holds good advice for anyone who wants to write well.*

PREPARING TO READ

How do you feel about writing? Do you find writing difficult? What are some of your most memorable experiences with writing in school or during your free time? How have these experiences affected your current attitude toward writing? Explain.

NOTHING ABOUT SOMETHING

It's Friday afternoon, and you have almost survived another week of classes. You are just looking forward dreamily to the weekend when the English instructor says: "For Monday you will turn in a five-hundred word composition on college football." 1

Well, that puts a good big hole in the weekend. You don't have any strong views on college football one way or the other. You get rather excited during the season and go to all the home games and find it rather more fun than not. On the other hand, the class has been reading Robert Hutchins in the anthology and perhaps Shaw's "Eighty-Yard Run," and from the class discussion you have got the idea that the instructor thinks college football is for the birds. You are no fool, you. You can figure out what side to take. 2

After dinner you get out the portable typewriter that you got for high school graduation. You might as well get it over with and enjoy Saturday and Sunday. Five hundred words is about two double-spaced pages with normal margins. You put in a sheet of paper, think up a title, and you're off: 3

WHY COLLEGE FOOTBALL SHOULD
BE ABOLISHED

College football should be abolished because it's bad for the school and also bad for the players. The players are so busy practicing that they don't have any time for their studies.

This, you feel, is a mighty good start. The only trouble is that it's only thirty-two words. You still have four hundred and sixty-eight to go, and you've pretty well exhausted the subject. It comes to you that you do your best thinking in the morning, so you put away the typewriter and go to the movies. But the next morning you have to do your washing and some math problems, and in the afternoon you go to the game. The English instructor turns up too, and you wonder if you've taken the right side after all. Saturday night you have a date, and Sunday morning you have to go to church. (You shouldn't let English assignments interfere with your religion.) What with one thing and another, it's ten o'clock Sunday night before you get out the typewriter again. You make a pot of coffee and start to fill out your views on college football. Put a little meat on the bones.

WHY COLLEGE FOOTBALL SHOULD
BE ABOLISHED

In my opinion, it seems to me that college football should be abolished. The reason why I think this to be true is because I feel that football is bad for the colleges in nearly every respect. As Robert Hutchins says in his article in our anthology in which he discusses college football, it would be better if the colleges had race horses and had races with one another, because then the horses would not have to attend classes. I firmly agree with Mr. Hutchins on this point, and I am sure that many other students would agree too.

One reason why it seems to me that college football is bad is that it has become too commercial. In the olden times when people played football just for the fun of it, maybe college football was all right, but they do not play football just for the fun of it now as they used to in the old days. Nowadays college football is what you might call a big business. Maybe this is not true at all schools, and I don't think it is especially true here at State, but certainly this is the case at most colleges and universities in America nowadays, as Mr. Hutchins points out in his very interesting article. Actually the coaches and alumni go around to the high schools and offer the high school stars large salaries to come to their colleges and play football for them. There was one case where a high school star was offered a convertible if he would play football for a certain college.

Another reason for abolishing college football is that it is bad for the players. They do not have time to get a college education, because they are so busy playing football. A football player has to practice every afternoon from three to six, and then he is so tired that he can't concentrate on his studies. He just feels like dropping off to sleep after dinner, and then the next day he goes to his classes without having studied and maybe he fails the test.

(Good ripe stuff so far, but you're still a hundred and fifty-one words from home. One more push.)

Also I think college football is bad for the colleges and the universities because not very many students get to participate in it. Out of a college of ten thousand students only seventy-five or a hundred play football, if that many. Football is what you might call a spectator sport. That means that most people go to watch it but do not play it themselves.

(Four hundred and fifteen. Well, you still have the conclusion, and when you retype it, you can make the margins a little wider.)

These are the reasons why I agree with Mr. Hutchins that college football should be abolished in American colleges and universities.

5 On Monday you turn it in, moderately hopeful, and on Friday it comes back marked "weak in content" and sporting a big "D."

6 This essay is exaggerated a little, not much. The English instructor will recognize it as reasonably typical of what an assignment on college football will bring in. He knows that nearly half of the class will contrive in five hundred words to say that college football is too commercial and bad for the players. Most of the other half will inform him that college football builds character and prepares one for life and brings prestige to the school. As he reads paper after paper all saying the same thing in almost the same words, all bloodless, five hundred words dripping out of nothing, he wonders how he allowed himself to get trapped into teaching English when he might have had a happy and interesting life as an electrician or a confidence man.

7 Well, you may ask, what can you do about it? The subject is one on which you have few convictions and little information. Can you be expected to make a dull subject interesting? As a matter of fact, this is precisely what you are expected to do. This is the writer's essential task. All subjects, except sex, are dull until somebody makes them interesting. The writer's job is to find the argument, the approach, the angle, the wording that will take the reader with him. This is seldom easy, and it is particularly hard in subjects that have been much discussed: College Football, Fraternities, Popular Music, Is Chivalry Dead?, and the like. You will feel that there is nothing you can do with such subjects except repeat the old bromides. But there are some things you

can do which will make your papers, if not throbbingly alive, at least less insufferably tedious than they might otherwise be.

AVOID THE OBVIOUS CONTENT

Say the assignment is college football. Say that you've decided to be against it. Begin by putting down the arguments that come to your mind: it is too commercial, it takes the students' minds off their studies, it is hard on the players, it makes the university a kind of circus instead of an intellectual center, for most schools it is financially ruinous. Can you think of any more arguments just off hand? All right. Now when you write your paper, *make sure that you don't use any of the material on this list.* If these are the points that leap to your mind, they will leap to everyone else's too, and whether you get a "C" or a "D" may depend on whether the instructor reads your paper early when he is fresh and tolerant or late, when the sentence "In my opinion, college football has become too commercial," inexorably repeated, has brought him to the brink of lunacy. 8

Be against college football for some reason or reasons of your own. If they are keen and perceptive ones, that's splendid. But even if they are trivial or foolish or indefensible, you are still ahead so long as they are not everybody else's reasons too. Be against it because the colleges don't spend enough money on it to make it worthwhile, because it is bad for the characters of spectators, because the players are forced to attend classes, because the football stars hog all the beautiful women, because it competes with baseball and is therefore un-American and possibly Communist inspired. There are lots of more or less unused reasons for being against college football. 9

Sometimes it is a good idea to sum up and dispose of the trite and conventional points before going on to your own. This has the advantage of indicating to the reader that you are going to be neither trite nor conventional. Something like this: 10

> We are often told that college football should be abolished because it has become too commercial or because it is bad for the players. These arguments are no doubt very cogent, but they don't really go to the heart of the matter.

Then you go to the heart of the matter.

TAKE THE LESS USUAL SIDE

One rather simple way of getting interest into your paper is to take the side of the argument that most of the citizens will want to avoid. If 11 the assignment is an essay on dogs, you can, if you choose, explain that dogs are faithful and lovable companions, intelligent, useful as guardians of the house and protectors of children, indispensable in police work — in short, when all is said and done, man's best friends. Or you can suggest that those big brown eyes conceal, more often than not, a vacuity of mind and an inconstancy of purpose; that the dogs you have known most intimately have been mangy, ill-tempered brutes, incapable of instruction; and that only your nobility of mind and fear of arrest prevent you from kicking the flea-ridden animals when you pass them on the street.

Naturally, personal convictions will sometimes dictate your approach. If the assigned subject is "Is Methodism Rewarding to the Individual?" and you are a pious Methodist, you have really no choice. But few assigned subjects, if any, will fall in this category. Most of them will lie in broad areas of discussion with much to be said on both sides. They are intellectual exercises and it is legitimate to argue now one way and now another, as debaters do in similar circumstances. Always take the side that looks to you hardest, least defensible. It will almost always turn out to be easier to write interestingly on that side. 12

This general advice applies where you have a choice of subjects. If you are to choose among "The Value of Fraternities" and "My Favorite High School Teacher" and "What I Think about Beetles," by all means plump for the beetles. By the time the instructor gets to your paper, he will be up to his ears in tedious tales about the French teacher at Bloombury High and assertions about how fraternities build character and prepare one for life. Your views on beetles, whatever they are, are bound to be a refreshing change. 13

Don't worry too much about figuring out what the instructor thinks about the subject so that you can cuddle up with him. Chances are his views are no stronger than yours. If he does have convictions and you oppose them, his problem is to keep from grading you higher than you deserve in order to show he is not biased. This doesn't mean that you should always cantankerously dissent from what the instructor says; that gets tiresome too. And if the subject assigned is "My Pet Peeve," do not begin, "My pet peeve is the English instructor who assigns papers on 'my pet peeve.'" This was still funny during the War of 1812, but it has sort of lost its edge since then. It is in general good manners to avoid personalities. 14

SLIP OUT OF ABSTRACTION

If you will study the essay on college football . . . you will perceive that one reason for its appalling dullness is that it never gets down to particulars. It is just a series of not very glittering generalities: "football 15 is bad for the colleges," "it has become too commercial," "football is a big business," "it is bad for the players," and so on. Such round phrases thudding against the reader's brain are unlikely to convince him, though they may well render him unconscious.

If you want the reader to believe that college football is bad for the players, you have to do more than say so. You have to display the evil. Take your roommate, Alfred Simkins, the second-string center. Picture poor old Alfy coming home from football practice every evening, bruised and aching, agonizingly tired, scarcely able to shovel the mashed potatoes into his mouth. Let us see him staggering up to the room, getting out his econ textbook, peering desperately at it with his good eye, falling asleep and failing the test in the morning. Let us share his unbearable tension as Saturday draws near. Will he fail, be demoted, lose his monthly allowance, be forced to return to the coal mines? And if he succeeds, what will be his reward? Perhaps a slight ripple of applause when the third-string center replaces him, a moment of elation in the locker room if the team wins, of despair if it loses. What will he look back on when he graduates from college? Toil and torn ligaments. And what will be his future? He is not good enough for pro football, and he is too obscure and weak in econ to succeed in stocks and bonds. College football is tearing the heart from Alfy Simkins and, when it finishes with him, will callously toss aside the shattered hulk. 16

This is no doubt a weak enough argument for the abolition of college football, but it is a sight better than saying, in three or four variations, that college football (in your opinion) is bad for the players. 17

Look at the work of any professional writer and notice how constantly he is moving from the generality, the abstract statement, to the concrete example, the facts and figures, the illustration. If he is writing on juvenile delinquency, he does not just tell you that juveniles are (it seems to him) delinquent and that (in his opinion) something should be done about it. He shows you juveniles being delinquent, tearing up movie theatres in Buffalo, stabbing high school principals in Dallas, smoking marijuana in Palo Alto. And more than likely he is moving toward some specific remedy, not just a general wringing of the hands. 18

It is no doubt possible to be *too* concrete, too illustrative or anecdotal, but few inexperienced writers err this way. For most the soundest advice is to be seeking always for the picture, to be always turning general remarks into seeable examples. Don't say, "Sororities teach girls the social graces." Say, "Sorority life teaches a girl how to carry on a conversation while pouring tea, without sloshing the tea into the saucer." Don't say, "I like certain kinds of popular music very much." Say, "Whenever I hear Gerber Spinklittle play 'Mississippi Man' on the trombone, my socks creep up my ankles." 19

GET RID OF OBVIOUS PADDING

The student toiling away at his weekly English theme is too often tor-   20
mented by a figure: five hundred words. How, he asks himself, is he to
achieve this staggering total? Obviously by never using one word
when he can somehow work in ten.

He is therefore seldom content with a plain statement like "Fast   21
driving is dangerous." This has only four words in it. He takes thought,
and the sentence becomes:

> In my opinion, fast driving is dangerous.

Better, but he can do better still:

> In my opinion, fast driving would seem to be rather dangerous.

If he is really adept, it may come out:

> In my humble opinion, though I do not claim to be an expert
> on this complicated subject, fast driving, in most circumstances,
> would seem to be rather dangerous in many respects, or at least so
> it would seem to me.

Thus four words have been turned into forty, and not an iota of content has been added.

Now this is a way to go about reaching five hundred words, and if   22
you are content with a "D" grade, it is as good a way as any. But if you
aim higher, you must work differently. Instead of stuffing your sentences with straw, you must try steadily to get rid of the padding, to
make your sentences lean and tough. If you are really working at it,
your first draft will greatly exceed the required total, and then you will
work it down, thus:

> It is thought in some quarters that fraternities do not con-
> tribute as much as might be expected to campus life.
> Some people think that fraternities contribute little to cam-
> pus life.
> The average doctor who practices in small towns or in the
> country must toil night and day to heal the sick.
> Most country doctors work long hours.
> When I was a little girl, I suffered from shyness and embarrass-
> ment in the presence of others.
> I was a shy little girl.
> It is absolutely necessary for the person employed as a marine
> fireman to give the matter of steam pressure his undivided atten-
> tion at all times.
> The fireman has to keep his eye on the steam gauge.

You may ask how you can arrive at five hundred words at this 23 rate. Simply. You dig up more real content. Instead of taking a couple of obvious points off the surface of the topic and then circling warily around them for six paragraphs, you work in and explore, figure out the details. You illustrate. You say that fast driving is dangerous, and then you prove it. How long does it take to stop a car at forty and at eighty? How far can you see at night? What happens when a tire blows? What happens in a head-on collision at fifty miles an hour? Pretty soon your paper will be full of broken glass and blood and headless torsos, and reaching five hundred words will not really be a problem.

CALL A FOOL A FOOL

Some of the padding in freshman themes is to be blamed not on anxi- 24 ety about the word minimum but on excessive timidity. The student writes, "In my opinion, the principal of my high school acted in ways that I believe every unbiased person would have to call foolish." This isn't exactly what he means. What he means is, "My high school principal was a fool." If he was a fool, call him a fool. Hedging the thing about with "in-my-opinion's" and "it-seems-to-me's" and "as-I-see-it's" and "at-least-from-my-point-of-view's" gains you nothing. Delete these phrases whenever they creep into your paper.

The student's tendency to hedge stems from a modesty that in 25 other circumstances would be commendable. He is, he realizes, young and inexperienced, and he half suspects that he is dopey and fuzzy-minded beyond the average. Probably only too true. But it doesn't help to announce your incompetence six times in every paragraph. Decide what you want to say and say it as vigorously as possible, without apology and in plain words.

Linguistic diffidence can take various forms. One is what we call 26 *euphemism.* This is the tendency to call a spade "a certain garden implement" or women's underwear "unmentionables." It is stronger in some eras than others and in some people than others but it always operates more or less in subjects that are touchy or taboo: death, sex, madness, and so on. Thus we shrink from saying, "He died last night" but say instead, "passed away," "left us," "joined his Maker," "went to his reward." Or we try to take off the tension with a lighter cliché: "kicked the bucket," "cashed in his chips," "handed in his dinner pail." We have found all sorts of ways to avoid saying *mad:* "mentally ill," "touched," "not quite right upstairs," "feeble-minded," "innocent," "simple," "off his trolley," "not in his right mind." Even such a now plain word as *insane* began as a euphemism with the meaning "not healthy."

Modern science, particularly psychology, contributes many poly- 27
syllables in which we can wrap our thoughts and blunt their force. To
many writers there is no such thing as a bad schoolboy. Schoolboys
are maladjusted or unoriented or misunderstood or in need of guidance or lacking in continued success toward satisfactory integration of
the personality as a social unit, but they are never bad. Psychology no
doubt makes us better men or women, more sympathetic and tolerant,
but it doesn't make writing any easier. Had Shakespeare been confronted with psychology, "To be or not to be" might have come out,
"To continue as a social unit or not to do so. That is the personality
problem. Whether 'tis a better sign of integration at the conscious
level to display a psychic tolerance toward the maladjustments and re-
pressions induced by one's lack of orientation in one's environment
or —" But Hamlet would never have finished the soliloquy.

Writing in the modern world, you cannot altogether avoid mod- 28
ern jargon. Nor, in an effort to get away from euphemism, should you
salt your paper with four-letter words. But you can do much if you will
mount guard against those roundabout phrases, those echoing polysyllables that tend to slip into your writing to rob it of its crispness
and force.

BEWARE OF THE PAT EXPRESSION

Other things being equal, avoid phrases like "other things being equal." 29
Those sentences that come to you whole, or in two or three doughy
lumps, are sure to be bad sentences. They are no creation of yours but
pieces of common thought floating in the community soup.

Pat expressions are hard, often impossible, to avoid, because they 30
come too easily to be noticed and seem too necessary to be dispensed
with. No writer avoids them altogether, but good writers avoid them
more often than poor writers.

By "pat expressions" we mean such tags as "to all practical intents 31
and purposes," "the pure and simple truth," "from where I sit," "the
time of his life," "to the ends of the earth," "in the twinkling of an
eye," "as sure as you're born," "over my dead body," "under cover of
darkness," "took the easy way out," "when all is said and done," "told
him time and time again," "parted the best of friends," "stand up and
be counted," "gave him the best years of her life," "worked her fingers
to the bone." Like other clichés, these expressions were once forceful.
Now we should use them only when we can't possibly think of anything else.

Some pat expressions stand like a wall between the writer and 32
thought. Such a one is "the American way of life." Many student writers feel that when they have said that something accords with the

American way of life or does not they have exhausted the subject. Actually, they have stopped at the highest level of abstraction. The American way of life is the complicated set of bonds between a hundred and eighty million ways. All of us know this when we think about it, but the tag phrase too often keeps us from thinking about it.

So with many another phrase dear to the politician: "this great land of ours," "the man in the street," "our national heritage." These may prove our patriotism or give a clue to our political beliefs, but otherwise they add nothing to the paper except words.

COLORFUL WORDS

The writer builds with words, and no builder uses a raw material more slippery and elusive and treacherous. A writer's work is a constant struggle to get the right word in the right place, to find that particular word that will convey his meaning exactly, that will persuade the reader or soothe him or startle or amuse him. He never succeeds altogether — sometimes he feels that he scarcely succeeds at all — but such successes as he has are what make the thing worth doing.

There is no book of rules for this game. One progresses through everlasting experiment on the basis of ever-widening experience. There are few useful generalizations that one can make about words as words, but there are perhaps a few.

Some words are what we call "colorful." By this we mean that they are calculated to produce a picture or induce an emotion. They are dressy instead of plain, specific instead of general, loud instead of soft. Thus, in place of "Her heart beat," we may write "Her heart *pounded, throbbed, fluttered, danced.*" Instead of "He sat in his chair," we may say, "He *lounged, sprawled, coiled.*" Instead of "It was hot," we may say, "It was *blistering, sultry, muggy, suffocating, steamy, wilting.*"

However, it should not be supposed that the fancy word is always better. Often it is as well to write "Her heart beat" or "It was hot" if that is all it did or all it was. Ages differ in how they like their prose. The nineteenth century liked it rich and smoky. The twentieth has usually preferred it lean and cool. The twentieth-century writer, like all writers, is forever seeking the exact word, but he is wary of sounding feverish. He tends to pitch it low, to understate it, to throw it away. He knows that if he gets too colorful, the audience is likely to giggle.

See how this strikes you: "As the rich, golden glow of the sunset died away along the eternal western hills, Angela's limpid blue eyes looked softly and trustingly into Montague's flashing brown ones, and her heart pounded like a drum in time with the joyous song surging in her soul." Some people like that sort of thing, but most modern readers would say, "Good grief," and turn on the television.

COLORED WORDS

Some words we would call not so much colorful as colored — that is, 39
loaded with associations, good or bad. All words — except perhaps
structure words — have associations of some sort. We have said that
the meaning of a word is the sum of the contexts in which it occurs.
When we hear a word, we hear with it an echo of all the situations in
which we have heard it before.

In some words, these echoes are obvious and discussable. The 40
word *mother*, for example, has, for most people, agreeable associations.
When you hear *mother* you probably think of home, safety, love, food,
and various other pleasant things. If one writes, "She was like a mother
to me," he gets an effect which he would not get in "She was like an
aunt to me." The advertiser makes use of the associations of *mother* by
working it in when he talks about his product. The politician works it
in when he talks about himself.

So also with such words as *home, liberty, fireside, contentment, pa-* 41
triot, tenderness, sacrifice, childlike, manly, bluff, limpid. All of these
words are loaded with favorable associations that would be rather hard
to indicate in a straightforward definition. There is more than a literal
difference between "They sat around the fireside" and "They sat around
the stove." They might have been equally warm and happy around the
stove, but *fireside* suggests leisure, grace, quiet tradition, congenial company, and *stove* does not.

Conversely, some words have bad associations. *Mother* suggests 42
pleasant things, but *mother-in-law* does not. Many mothers-in-law are
heroically lovable and some mothers drink gin all day and beat their
children insensible, but these facts of life are beside the point. The
thing is that *mother* sounds good and *mother-in-law* does not.

Or consider the word *intellectual*. This would seem to be a compli- 43
mentary term, but in point of fact it is not, for it has picked up associations of impracticality and ineffectuality and general dopiness. So
also with such words as *liberal, reactionary, Communist, Socialist, capi-*
talist, radical, schoolteacher, truck driver, undertaker, operator, salesman,
huckster, speculator. These convey meanings on the literal level, but beyond that — sometimes, in some places — they convey contempt on
the part of the speaker.

The question of whether to use loaded words or not depends on 44
what is being written. The scientist, the scholar, try to avoid them; for
the poet, the advertising writer, the public speaker, they are standard
equipment. But every writer should take care that they do not substitute for thought. If you write, "Anyone who thinks that is nothing but
a Socialist (or Communist or capitalist)" you have said nothing except
that you don't like people who think that, and such remarks are effective only with the most naïve readers. It is always a bad mistake to think
your readers more naïve than they really are.

COLORLESS WORDS

But probably most student writers come to grief not with words that are 45
colorful or those that are colored but with those that have no color at
all. A pet example is *nice*, a word we would find it hard to dispense with
in casual conversation but which is no longer capable of adding much
to a description. Colorless words are those of such general meaning that
in a particular sentence they mean nothing. Slang adjectives, like *cool*
("That's real cool.") tend to explode all over the language. They are applied to everything, lose their original force, and quickly die.

Beware also of nouns of very general meaning, like *circumstances,* 46
cases, instances, aspects, factors, relationships, attitudes, eventualities, etc. In
most circumstances you will find that those cases of writing which contain too many instances of words like these will in this and other aspects have factors leading to unsatisfactory relationships with the reader
resulting in unfavorable attitudes on his part and perhaps other eventualities, like a grade of "D." Notice also what "etc." means. It means "I'd
like to make this list longer, but I can't think of any more examples."

RESPONDING TO THE TEXT

In this essay, Roberts points out certain features, positive and negative,
found in the work of many writers. Does your writing exhibit any of these
features? How would you rate your writing with respect to each of these features?

ENGAGING THE WRITER'S SUBJECT

1. According to Roberts, what is the job of the writer? Why, in particular,
   is it difficult for college students to do this job well? Discuss how your
   college experience leads you to agree or disagree with Roberts.

2. The author offers several "tricks" or techniques of good writing in his
   essay. What are they? Do you find them more useful than other techniques? Explain.

3. If, according to Roberts, a good writer never uses unnecessary words,
   what then are the legitimate ways a student can reach the goal of the
   five-hundred-word essay?

4. According to Roberts, how has modern psychology made it more difficult to write well?

ANALYZING THE WRITER'S CRAFT

1. Make a scratch outline of Roberts's essay. What are the similarities between his organization of material and the process analysis he outlines
   for students? (Glossary: *Organization*) Explain.

2. What kind of information does the title of Roberts's essay lead you to expect? (Glossary: *Title*) Does the author deliver what the title promises? Why do you think he chose this title?

3. What are Roberts's main points? How do his examples help him explain and clarify his main points? (Glossary: *Exemplification*)

4. Roberts's writing style is well-suited to his student audience; he includes examples that would be familiar to many students. How would you describe his writing style? What are some of the ways he uses narration and exemplification to make the process analysis easy to follow? (Glossary: *Exemplification; Narration*)

UNDERSTANDING THE WRITER'S LANGUAGE

1. Roberts wrote this essay more than forty years ago, and at some points the facts he cites indicate this; he gives the population of the United States as 180 million (paragraph 32), whereas today it is closer to 293 million. Is there anything in his diction or word choice that makes Roberts's writing seem dated, or does it sound contemporary? Choose examples from the text to support your answer. (Glossary: *Diction*)

2. What is Roberts's tone in this essay? What words does he use to create this tone? Explain how the tone affects you as a reader. (Glossary: *Tone*)

3. Refer to your desk dictionary to determine the meanings of the following words as Roberts uses them in this selection: *contrive* (paragraph 6), *bromides* (7), *cogent* (10), *cantankerously* (14), *diffidence* (26), *soliloquy* (27).

WRITING SUGGESTIONS

1. In paragraph 16, Roberts explains how a brief but good essay on college football might be written. He obeys a major rule of good writing — show, don't tell. Thus, instead of a dry lump of words, his brief "essay" uses humor, exaggeration, and concrete details to breathe life into the football player. Review Roberts's strategies for good writing. Then choose one of the dull topics he suggests or one of your own, and following the steps he lays out, write a five-hundred-word essay.

2. Roberts's essay was first published in 1958 — before personal computers and word processing programs became ubiquitous. Write an essay in which you compare and contrast the process of writing an essay on a typewriter and on a computer. (Glossary: *Comparison and Contrast*) How is the process similar? How is it different? What equipment and supplies does each require? Which do you prefer? Why?

3. Fraternities and sororities, political action groups such as the Young Republicans, social interest groups such as Amnesty International, and many other types of national student groups are represented at colleges across the country. In your college library and on the Internet, research a group not represented on your campus and read your college's policy for organizing or chartering student groups. What group would you be

interested in starting? Why? What do the national group and your college require for establishing a chapter on your campus? Using the information you gather, write an essay in which you explain how to start a group on your campus.

- To begin your research online, go to **bedfordstmartins.com /subjectsstrategies** and click on "Process Analysis" or browse the thematic directory of annotated links.

SEEING/READING

World Trade Center Disaster, September 11, 2001

Joel Gordon

Joel Gordon 2001

CONNECTING IMAGE AND TEXT

The attack on the World Trade Center on September 11, 2001, was a defining moment not only for Americans but for people around the world. Images of the hijacked airplanes and the burning twin towers have been etched into the public consciousness. How do you "read" this photograph? What response do you have to this scene? What memories or images come to mind as you reflect on the photograph? What do you imagine the people in the foreground are thinking as they stare at, or turn away from, the burning building? What would be gained or lost if the photograph did not contain images of witnesses? Your observations will help guide you to the key themes and strategies in the essay that follows.

Anatomy of an Urban Legend
Christopher Callahan

Christopher Callahan was born in Brooklyn, New York, in 1960. He received his B.S. degree from Boston University in 1982 and his master's of public administration degree from Harvard University in 1990. Callahan began his journalism career as an intern with the Boston Globe *and* New York Newsday. *He later worked as an Associated Press reporter, covering politics in New England and Washington D.C. Callahan is currently a senior editor of the* American Journalism Review *and associate dean of the Phillip Merrill College of Journalism at the University of Maryland. He is the author of* A Journalist's Guide to the Internet: The Net as a Reporting Tool *(2002).*

In the following article, first published in the American Journalism Review *in November 2001, Callahan explains the process by which a post–September 11 Internet posting took on a life of its own.*

PREPARING TO READ

An urban legend is an incredible tale, passed from one person to the next with amazing speed. Often such tales recount horrible consequences, sometimes mixed with humor. What urban legends do you know? Do your friends know similar tales? How do you think those tales got started?

The night after the September 11 attacks, a sociology graduate student from Brazil named Marcio A. V. Carvalho tapped out an e-mail and sent it to an obscure Internet mailing list. The 488-word missive, which implied that U.S. policy brought on the terrorist strike, led with a startling accusation: CNN video of Palestinians celebrating the attack was really Persian Gulf War–era file footage from a decade earlier.

1

Carvalho's note, riddled with spelling and syntax errors and peppered with exclamation points and capitalizations for emphasis, offered no proof, saying only that the grad student had heard the claim from a professor, whom he did not name.

The story, as it turns out, was untrue. The video that aired on CNN and other networks was shot by a Reuters TV crew in the hours after the attacks on the World Trade Center and the Pentagon. Yet with no further corroboration or elaboration from others, Carvalho's e-mail dispatch raced around the world at a speed only the Internet can provide. Within 24 hours, the story had spread so widely that the *St. Petersburg Times* began preparing a piece to debunk September 11 rumors such as this one.

And despite a speedy retraction from Carvalho, denials from CNN and Reuters and no offers of proof from others, the story continued to spiral outward to the point where even CNN officials believe it could go down as a classic urban legend, as immortal as it is inaccurate.

The proliferation of rumors, gossip and urban legends in the Internet age is well documented. But how do such stories spread so quickly with such flimsy factual basis? Chris Cramer, president of CNN International Networks, believes "cyberterrorism" is the culprit. "This was a concerted attempt to distort the news," Cramer says. Experts on Internet rumors, however, say how stories such as the Palestinian celebration video enter the public arena so quickly and with such force and credibility is a much subtler, more complex, and less organized process than Cramer's "cyberterrorism" label might imply.

The chain of events that rocketed the CNN rumor around the world started at 9:07 p.m. on September 12 when Carvalho hit the send button and dispatched his note to the Social Theory Network, a British-based electronic mailing list with 567 subscribers worldwide who share an interest in "the relationship between psychological and sociological explanations of the human condition."

In the message, Carvalho said one of his professors claimed to have videotapes from 1991 "with the very same images" as the tape that aired on CNN. He urged his social theory colleagues to try to find a copy of the 1991 tapes and said he would do the same. While Carvalho stated as fact "THOSE IMAGES WERE SHOT BACK IN 1991!!!," he never claimed to have the tapes or any proof of their existence.

Less than 31 hours later, an apologetic Carvalho posted a second note saying he had talked to the professor and she told him she was convinced she had seen the images 10 years earlier, but that she did not have any tapes. "I firmly believed that source, which proved to be untrustworthy," Carvalho wrote in a third e-mail to the list.

The genesis of rumors often comes from misunderstandings as 9 opposed to organized attacks by so-called cyberterrorists, folklore experts say.

"Some might start as attempts to undermine corporations, [but] 10 most begin as innocent misunderstandings that escalate, snowball literally, because people think they might be true," says Mike Coggeshall, a cultural anthropologist and folklorist at Clemson University.

And once the rumor resonates with the public and is loose on the 11 Internet, it's nearly impossible to stop.

Carvalho's initial missive got little reaction from the Social Theory 12 Network. Two members sent short responses. But within hours, the note had escaped the relative isolation of the Social Theory Network as it began to be forwarded to friends and colleagues and posted on Internet newsgroups around the world.

Within six hours, it was posted on Independent Media Center, a 13 Web site created by activists in the wake of the Seattle world trade protests. The center describes its mission as "the creation of radical, accurate and passionate tellings of the truth." That Web posting triggered an avalanche of e-mails and newsgroup postings under headings such as "Media Manipulation," "CNN Footage of Celebrating Palestinians Images a Hoax," "Media Lies About Celebrating Palestinians," and "CNN's Lies and Manipulations."

But a review of dozens of these early messages show that they 14 were little more than e-mailers adding their own opinions on top of Carvalho's forwarded message. So why did so many people believe it to be true? Scholars say the answer lies in the basic foundations for all folklore, no matter the medium.

"The reason [urban legends] spread and the reason they are semi- 15 believed is that they capture something in the mood of the people," says Clemson's Coggeshall. "They capture the hopes and concerns and fears."

David Emery, who runs the Urban Legends and Folklore Web site 16 (urbanlegends.about.com), says this was the case with the CNN video rumor. "You have to look at who most of the people who are passing it around are," he says. "And they are not people who have something against CNN. They are people who trust CNN and are suddenly gripped by the [notion] that maybe they can't."

The Internet, however, has changed the dynamics of folklore and 17 the spread of urban legends.

Emery says the medium of e-mail makes it easier for people to pass 18 along uncorroborated information. "It takes some effort and some sense of responsibility to spread a rumor by word of mouth. You actually have to call somebody or go next door," Emery says. People who would hesitate to pass along such information verbally often don't think twice about forwarding e-mail, he says.

Specialists in the world of folklore on the Internet also believe that   19
e-mail dispatches carry more weight than verbal communications.
"People are much more willing to grant credibility to anything that's
written down," says Emery. "There is just something inherently more
powerful in the written word than the spoken word."

Sreenath Sreenivasan, an associate professor of journalism at Co-   20
lumbia University who specializes in Internet communication, recalls
the child's game "telephone," in which a message gets passed from
one person to the next, often with changes that by the end make the
final iteration unrecognizable. "In e-mail, you see the exact thread in
front of you. All the facts are there. It seems like you can't misreport
it," he says. "Something I hear can be misreported."

But Sreenivasan believes the power of e-mail rumors goes beyond   21
the simple fact that they are transmitted in text form. He says e-mail
recipients often weigh the credibility of the sender, who typically is
known to the recipient, as opposed to the original, usually unknown,
author. "Your friend has sent you . . . an e-mail," Sreenivasan says. "In
a way, I'm [thinking], 'I trust this guy, and he wouldn't just send me
crap. He's serious, he's likeable.' I have a [credibility] rating in my
mind for him, and he's acceptable."

And of course, there is the speed that comes with a mass delivery   22
system such as e-mail.

"If I have a hot, juicy story, how many people can I call?" Sreeni-   23
vasan asks. "It's really a problem to spread anything [verbally]." But
with the Internet, he says, "in seconds I can tell 20 people or 100 people, and they can tell 20 people."

The CNN story reached critical mass less than 24 hours after the   24
original dispatch — lightning speed even by today's digital standards.
Reporters from around the world began calling CNN to check out the
Internet rumor the day after Carvalho's original posting, says Nigel
Pritchard, vice president for public relations at CNN International Net-
works.

"It is extremely frustrating when you are trying to do the job of a   25
busy press office" and have to spend time knocking down a rumor
"that is quite preposterous and obviously not true," Pritchard says.

Jim Romenesko says e-mails on the CNN rumor were "coming in   26
fast and furious" to him at MediaNews, the popular Web site he runs
in conjunction with the Poynter Institute (poynter.org/medianews).
Romenesko says he received so many e-mails by the following day that
he felt obliged to post one of the inquiries in the hopes of getting a response from CNN. Romenesko posted a brief inquiry from *Miami Herald*
humor columnist Dave Barry — who said he assumed "this charge is
nonsense" but was wondering if CNN had officially responded — and
provided a link to Carvalho's e-mail posted on the Independent Media
Center.

The response came swiftly from Eason Jordan, the network's chief news executive. Jordan posted an e-mail in which he explained the video was shot in East Jerusalem by a Reuters crew on September 11 "and included comments from a Palestinian praising Osama bin Laden, who was not a gulf war player."

But to try to kill a rumor once it has reached a mass audience is a near-impossible task. The proliferation of the misguided e-mail continued, as did calls to CNN.

Even Emery, whose Web site is devoted to debunking rumors and clarifying facts, says little can be done. "I have no illusions that we stop the rumor or even slow rumors down very much, but you just try to get another viewpoint out there and get some facts out there to balance it so that people who do care [receive the] truth," Emery says. "It's just a fact that a lot of people don't really care. If it's a good [rumor], or meaningful to them emotionally, they simply pass it along."

The CNN rumor took a new turn on September 18, six days after the Carvalho posting. An e-mail began circulating under the name of Russell Grossman, head of internal communications for the BBC in London. A new flurry of e-mails traversed the Internet with what was described as confirmation from an "official source" — Grossman. The Islamic News and Information Network sent to its mailing list the new e-mail, noting that the network "is very careful to ensure that [its] reports come from reliable sources."

But even a cursory glance at the alleged smoking gun shows that it was not written by Grossman, but rather was a truncated version of Carvalho's original note with a single edit: Carvalho's "A teacher of mine, here in Brazil, has videotapes recorded in 1991" was replaced with "At the BBC here, we have these footages on videotapes recorded in 1991."

"The e-mail which is circulating wasn't sent by me or BBC Internal Communication and was not issued by the BBC," Grossman wrote in an e-mail to the *American Journalism Review*. "It seems to be the work of someone seeking to make mischief." Cyberterrorists may not have started the rumor or even aided significantly in its speedy promulgation around the world, but it seems they had a hand in keeping the story afloat.

Two days later, CNN posted an official denial, along with a similar statement from Reuters and a statement from Carvalho's school, Universidad Estatala de Campinas-Brasil. The CNN statement urged readers to copy it and "send it to anyone you know who may have the false information." But Internet folklorists say such corrections of popular rumors rarely get the same dissemination as the original story.

Indeed, both CNN and Romenesko continued to get calls and e-mail queries about the rumor. News organizations such as the *Atlanta*

Journal-Constitution, Milwaukee Journal Sentinel, and *Columbus Dispatch* ran stories days after the Carvalho retraction and CNN denials to answer readers' continued inquiries about the rumor and to try to set the record straight.

In October, CNN's Pritchard told the *American Journalism Review* 35 he was receiving calls from Greek reporters saying they had received a press release allegedly confirming that the CNN video was from 1991. "I was told [there] was a press release," he says, but "nobody was able to show me."

"It spreads very quickly," a frustrated Pritchard says. "Like a wild- 36 fire."

RESPONDING TO THE TEXT

What's your opinion about urban legends? Are they acts of mischief, cases of misunderstanding, dangerous assaults on the truth that can have serious consequences, or a manifestation of society's fears and apprehensions? What do urban legends say about us and the way we live?

ENGAGING THE WRITER'S SUBJECT

1. What is cyberterrorism? Is it a good explanation for what happened in the CNN case? Why or why not? According to Callahan, is the story simply a misunderstanding or might there have been some mischief involved? Explain.

2. How has the Internet "changed the dynamics of folklore and the spread of urban legends" (paragraph 17)?

3. What can people who are concerned about urban legends do about them? Why is it difficult to correct them and get the true story to the public?

4. Why do people pass along urban legends?

ANALYZING THE WRITER'S CRAFT

1. What is Callahan's purpose in writing this piece? (Glossary: *Purpose*)

2. Explain how the CNN rumor got started and spread. Explain what Callahan means when he says in paragraph 5 that the process was "a much subtler, more complex, and less organized process than Cramer's 'cyberterrorism' label might imply."

3. How does Callahan organize this piece to explain the process that unfolded in the CNN incident? (Glossary: *Organization*)

4. Callahan's explanation of the CNN incident is an informational process analysis. Do you think it is a representative example of the process behind the origination and dissemination of urban legends? Why or why not?

5. Callahan uses a number of authorities' opinions to help him explain the process he describes. Chose several of those authorities (for example, Associate Professor Sreenath Sreenivasan or Chris Cramer, president of CNN International Networks) and explain what they add to readers' understanding of the spread of urban legends. (Glossary: *Evidence*)

6. Callahan's paragraphs are relatively short. What effect do such short paragraphs have on you as a reader? Do they make his article easier to read or do they detract from the continuity of his presentation? Explain.

UNDERSTANDING THE WRITER'S LANGUAGE

1. Callahan makes use of strong verbs to enliven his prose. For example, he says in paragraph 2 that the original note Carvalho sent was "riddled with spelling and syntax errors and peppered with exclamation points and capitalizations." Later in paragraph 6, he gives another example: "the chain of events that rocketed the CNN rumor around the world started at 9:07. . . ." What other examples of strong verbs can you find? How effective are they?

2. Refer to your desk dictionary to determine the meanings of the following words as Callahan uses them in this selection: *missive* (paragraph 1), *syntax* (2), *corroboration* (3), *elaboration* (3), *concerted* (5), *dispatched* (6), *avalanche* (13).

WRITING SUGGESTIONS

1. Have you ever been a participant — knowingly or not — in the creation or dissemination of a rumor? Have you ever been the subject of a rumor? What was the rumor? How widely did it spread? How did the process unfold? Did it spread "like a wildfire" (paragraph 36)? At what point, if at all, did you realize the spread of the rumor was beyond your control? Write a process analysis essay in which you trace the development of your chosen rumor.

2. Images of the September 11 terrorist attacks bring back memories for each of us, particularly of what we were doing when we first heard the news. Write a narrative essay about your September 11 experience. (Glossary: *Narration*) Where were you when you found out? Did you know anyone who perished? What did you do in the hours, days, and weeks afterward? How has September 11 affected you personally? Before you write, refer to your Connecting Image and Text response for this selection.

3. Mike Coggeshall, cultural anthropologist and folklorist, says, "The reason [urban legends] spread and the reason they are semi-believed is that they capture something in the mood of the people . . . They capture the hopes and concerns and fears" (paragraph 15). In your college library and on the Internet, research an urban legend with which you are familiar — for example, the female ghost hitchhiking to the prom, HIV-infected syringes in pay phone change slots, the drugged man

waking up to find that his kidney has been removed, or some other tale. What does this legend warn against? Where did it start and why? How did it spread? Using your research — and Callahan's article as a model — write an essay in which you recount the legend, explain its moral, and trace its development and dissemination.

- To begin your research online, go to **bedfordstmartins.com /subjectsstrategies** and click on "Process Analysis" or browse the thematic directory of annotated links.

Why Leaves Turn Color in the Fall

Diane Ackerman

*Diane Ackerman was born in Waukegan, Illinois, in 1948. She received
her B.A. from Pennsylvania State University and her M.F.A., M.A.,
and Ph.D. from Cornell University. Ackerman has worked as a writer-
in-residence at several major universities, has directed the Writer's
Program at Washington University in St. Louis, and has been a staff
writer at the* New Yorker. *She has written several books of poetry
and several collections of essays, among them:* The Moon by Whale
Light, and Other Adventures among Bats, Penguins, Crocodilians,
and Whales *(1991);* A Natural History of Love *(1994);* The Rarest
of the Rare: Vanishing Animals, Timeless Worlds *(1995);* The
Curious Naturalist *(1998);* and A Natural History of My Garden
(2001).

The following selection is from Ackerman's acclaimed A Natural
History of the Senses *(1990). Notice the way she shares her enthusiasm
for the natural world as she explains the process by which autumn leaves
assume their brilliant colors.*

PREPARING TO READ

What is your favorite season? What about the season makes it your
favorite — the weather, the activities and memories, the time of the
year, or a combination of these factors? Is there something about
your particular geographic region that makes this season different
from how it is manifested in other parts of the country?

The stealth of autumn catches one unaware. Was that a goldfinch   1
perching in the early September woods, or just the first turning
leaf? A red-winged blackbird or a sugar maple closing up shop for the
winter? Keen-eyed as leopards, we stand still and squint hard, looking for signs of movement. Early-morning frost sits heavily on the
grass, and turns barbed wire into a string of stars. On a distant hill, a
small square of yellow appears to be a lighted stage. At last the truth
dawns on us: Fall is staggering in, right on schedule, with its baggage
of chilly nights, macabre holidays, and spectacular, heart-stoppingly
beautiful leaves. Soon the leaves will start cringing on the trees, and
roll up in clenched fists before they actually fall off. Dry seedpods
will rattle like tiny gourds. But first there will be weeks of gushing
color so bright, so pastel, so confettilike, that people will travel up
and down the East Coast just to stare at it — a whole season of
leaves.

Where do the colors come from? Sunlight rules most living things with its golden edicts. When the days begin to shorten, soon after the summer solstice on June 21, a tree reconsiders its leaves. All summer it feeds them so they can process sunlight, but in the dog days of summer the tree begins pulling nutrients back into its trunk and roots, pares down, and gradually chokes off its leaves. A corky layer of cells forms at the leaves' slender petioles, then scars over. Undernourished, the leaves stop producing the pigment chlorophyll, and photosynthesis ceases. Animals can migrate, hibernate, or store food to prepare for winter. But where can a tree go? It survives by dropping its leaves, and by the end of autumn only a few fragile threads of fluid-carrying xylem hold leaves to their stems.

/ A turning leaf stays partly green at first, then reveals splotches of yellow and red as the chlorophyll gradually breaks down. Dark green seems to stay longest in the veins, outlining and defining them. During the summer, chlorophyll dissolves in the heat and light, but it is also being steadily replaced. In the fall, on the other hand, no new pigment is produced, and so we notice the other colors that were always there, right in the leaf, although chlorophyll's shocking green hid them from view. With their camouflage gone, we see these colors for the first time all year, and marvel, but they were always there, hidden like a vivid secret beneath the hot glowing greens of summer.

The most spectacular range of fall foliage occurs in the northeastern United States and in eastern China, where the leaves are robustly colored, thanks in part to a rich climate. European maples don't achieve the same flaming reds as their American relatives, which thrive on cold nights and sunny days. In Europe, the warm, humid weather turns the leaves brown or mildly yellow. Anthocyanin, the pigment that gives apples their red and turns leaves red or red-violet, is produced by sugars that remain in the leaf after the supply of nutrients dwindles. Unlike the carotenoids, which color carrots, squash, and corn, and turn leaves orange and yellow, anthocyanin varies from year to year, depending on the temperature and amount of sunlight. The fiercest colors occur in years when the fall sunlight is strongest and the nights are cool and dry (a state of grace scientists find vexing to forecast). This is also why leaves appear dizzyingly bright and clear on a sunny fall day: The anthocyanin flashes like a marquee.

(Not all leaves turn the same colors. Elms, weeping willows, and the ancient ginkgo all grow radiant yellow, along with hickories, aspens, bottlebrush buckeyes, cottonweeds, and tall, keening poplars. Basswood turns bronze, birches bright gold. Water-loving maples put on a symphonic display of scarlets. Sumacs turn red, too, as do flowering dogwoods, black gums, and sweet gums. Though some oaks yellow, most turn a pinkish brown. The farmlands also change color, as tepees of cornstalks and bales of shredded-wheat-textured hay stand drying in the fields. In some spots, one slope of a hill may be green and the other already in bright color, because the hillside facing south gets more sun and heat than the northern one.

An odd feature of the colors is that they don't seem to have any special purpose. We are predisposed to respond to their beauty, of course. They shimmer with the colors of sunset, spring flowers, the tawny buff of a colt's pretty rump, the shuddering pink of a blush. Animals and flowers color for a reason — adaptation to their environment — but there is no adaptive reason for leaves to color so beautifully in the fall any more than there is for the sky or ocean to be blue. It's just one of the haphazard marvels the planet bestows every year. We find the sizzling colors thrilling, and in a sense they dupe us. Colored like living things, they signal death and disintegration. In time, they will become fragile and, like the body, return to dust. They are as we hope our own fate will be when we die: Not to vanish, just to sublime from one beautiful state into another. Though leaves lose their green life, they bloom with urgent colors, as the woods grow mummified day by day, and Nature becomes more carnal, mute, and radiant.

We call the season "fall," from the Old English *feallan*, to fall, which leads back through time to the Indo-European *phol*, which also means to fall. So the word and the idea are both extremely ancient, and haven't really changed since the first of our kind needed a name for fall's leafy abundance. As we say the word, we're reminded of that other Fall, in the garden of Eden, when fig leaves never withered and scales fell from our eyes. Fall is the time when leaves fall from the trees, just as spring is when flowers spring up, summer is when we simmer, and winter is when we whine from the cold.

Children love to play in piles of leaves, hurling them into the air like confetti, leaping into soft unruly mattresses of them. For children, leaf fall is just one of the odder figments of Nature, like hailstones or snowflakes. Walk down a lane overhung with trees in the never-never land of autumn, and you will forget about time and death, lost in the sheer delicious spill of color. Adam and Eve concealed their nakedness with leaves, remember? Leaves have always hidden our awkward secrets.

But how do the colored leaves fall? As a leaf ages, the growth hormone, auxin, fades, and cells at the base of the petiole divide. Two or three rows of small cells, lying at right angles to the axis of the petiole, react with water, then come apart, leaving the petioles hanging on by only a few threads of xylem. A light breeze, and the leaves are airborne. They glide and swoop, rocking in invisible cradles. They are all wing and may flutter from yard to yard on small whirlwinds or updrafts, swiveling as they go. Firmly tethered to earth, we love to see things rise up and fly — soap bubbles, balloons, birds, fall leaves. They remind us that the end of a season is capricious, as is the end of life. We especially like the way leaves rock, careen, and swoop as they fall. Everyone knows the motion. Pilots sometimes do a maneuver called a "falling leaf," in which the plane loses altitude quickly and on purpose, by slipping first to the right, then to the left. The machine weighs a ton or more, but in one pilot's mind it is a weightless thing, a falling leaf. She has seen the motion before, in the Vermont woods where she played as a child. Below her the trees radiate gold, copper, and red. Leaves are falling, although she can't see them fall, as she falls, swooping down for a closer view.

At last the leaves leave. But first they turn color and thrill us for weeks on end. Then they crunch and crackle underfoot. They *shush*, as children drag their small feet through leaves heaped along the curb. Dark, slimy mats of leaves cling to one's heels after a rain. A damp, stuccolike mortar of semidecayed leaves protects the tender shoots with a roof until spring, and makes a rich humus. An occasional bulge or ripple in the leafy mounds signals a shrew or a field mouse tunneling out of sight. Sometimes one finds in fossil stones the imprint of a leaf, long since disintegrated, whose outlines remind us how detailed, vibrant, and alive are the things of this earth that perish.

RESPONDING TO THE TEXT

In paragraphs 2 and 6 Ackerman attributes some human qualities to Nature and to the trees. What effect does her personification have on you as a reader? Why do you think she chose to use these figures of speech in a process analysis essay? (Glossary: *Figures of Speech*)

ENGAGING THE WRITER'S SUBJECT

1. What causes leaves to change color?

2. Why do we call the season "fall"? Why do you suppose Ackerman chooses to give us this language lesson in paragraph 7?

3. What does Ackerman mean when she says, "Leaves have always hidden our awkward secrets" (paragraph 8)? Explain.

4. What, according to Ackerman, is the function of leaves underfoot? Does her assertion make sense to you? Explain.

ANALYZING THE WRITER'S CRAFT

1. Briefly summarize the steps of the process by which leaves turn color in autumn.

2. How has Ackerman organized her essay? (Glossary: *Organization*) Explain why this organization seems most appropriate for her subject.

3. Ackerman is fond of asking questions. (Glossary: *Rhetorical Question*) Locate four or five questions, and explain the different functions they serve within this essay.

4. Reread Ackerman's concluding sentence. What does she mean? Why do you suppose she has chosen to end her essay by discussing "fossil stones" and things that perish? In what ways is this a particularly appropriate ending? (Glossary: *Beginnings/Endings*)

5. When discussing the process of leaves changing colors, Ackerman adds some personal associations yet remains in the third-person point of view. (Glossary: *Point of View*) How would the essay differ if she wrote in the first person? How would this affect the scientific information in the essay?

6. Ackerman uses several strategies to support her process analysis. For example, she uses cause and effect analysis to explain why leaves are bright in certain years and dull in others, why trees change color at different rates, and why leaves finally fall to earth. (Glossary: *Cause and Effect Analysis*) She also uses description throughout her process analysis. (Glossary: *Description*) How effective would Ackerman's essay be without these supporting strategies? What do they add to your appreciation for her process analysis?

UNDERSTANDING THE WRITER'S LANGUAGE

1. Identify several similes and metaphors that Ackerman uses, and explain how each functions in this essay. (Glossary: *Figures of Speech*)

2. What is Ackerman's attitude toward her subject? (Glossary: *Attitude*) Cite examples from her essay to support your answer.

3. How would you describe the level of Ackerman's diction in this essay? (Glossary: *Diction*) Does she ever get too scientific for the average reader? If so, where?

4. Refer to your desk dictionary to determine the meanings of the following words as Ackerman uses them in this selection: *stealth* (paragraph 1), *clenched* (1), *gushing* (1), *camouflage* (3), *tawny* (6), *figments* (8), *stuccolike* (10), *vibrant* (10).

WRITING SUGGESTIONS

1. Write an essay using directional process analysis for a "simple" task that could prove disastrous if not explained precisely — for example, changing a tire, driving a standard-shift car, packing for a camping trip, or loading film into a camera. Be sure to explain why your directions are the best and what could happen if readers did not follow them exactly.

2. There are a number of famous writers such as Henry David Thoreau, Aldo Leopold, and Janisse Ray who have made careers out of writing about the processes of the natural world. Read several essays by a nature writer. How does his or her writing compare with Ackerman's?

(Glossary: *Comparison and Contrast*) Write an essay in which you compare and contrast two nature writers with respect to their style, tone, organization, or theme. (Glossary: *Organization; Style; Tone*)

3. Our world is filled with countless natural processes — for example, the cycle of the moon, the germination of a seed, the movement of the tides, the formation of a tornado, and the flowering of a tree. Use your college library and the Internet to research one process. Using Ackerman's essay as a model, write an informational process analysis about the topic you have researched.

- To begin your research online, go to **bedfordstmartins.com /subjectsstrategies** and click on "Process Analysis" or browse the thematic directory of annotated links.

Building an Online Community: Just Add Water

Matt Haughey

Matt Haughey is a Web site developer and designer. He received his B.S. and M.S. degrees in environmental science from the University of California–Riverside and went on to work as a freelance Webmaster and Web developer. His MetaFilter.com, a community weblog, or blog, has been featured in Fortune, the New Yorker, Entertainment Weekly, *and* Newsweek. *He has contributed to several books, including* We Blog: Publishing Online with Weblogs *(2002),* We've Got Blog: How Websites Are Changing Our Culture *(2002), and* Design for Community: The Art of Connecting Real People in Virtual Places *(2002).*

In this piece, first published in Digital Web Magazine *in 2001, Haughey explains what he learned from the not-so-orderly process he followed to build his blog.*

PREPARING TO READ

What is blogging? Are you a blogger? If so, how long have you been keeping a weblog? Do you read any blogs regularly? If so, what are they?

'm frequently asked how Metafilter came to be, what the secret is, and what I've learned in the process of building it. I didn't have a tidy plan or set path when I started. I watched several big communities grow from nothing and prosper, and I took my lead from them, but a good lot of what I know now was gained from trial and error. During those first few months, I picked up a lot of experience in dealing with new members, and got a chance to try out several different techniques to help growth and deal with problems. I noticed a lot of trends, I made a few mistakes, but above all I learned a lot in the process. 1

I'm here today to tell you the dos-and-don'ts of building a website community, but I can only give general guidelines. Every community is different, and every administrator of a community is different, so an aspiring community leader needs to adjust accordingly. 2

... In case you were wondering, the title is a bit of a joke, building a website into a vibrant community filled with many contributors is very difficult, and it is impossible to break down the exact steps, but I'll do my best. 3

1. Make Sure You Really Want to Do This

You know how interviewers ask someone who has lived a full life and   4
is near death, if they could relive their life again, what they would do
different. You have to ask yourself that before you lift a finger building
a community. Are you ready to be a leader? Are you ready to do all the
work necessary to create not just a normal, engaging website, but one
that many others can use? Are you ready to spend every waking moment watching it? Are you ready to stay up all night re-coding main
areas of the site after someone hacks the files? Are you ready to keep it
up, day in and day out for as long as you can stand it?

I can't overestimate how much time you will spend on a commu-   5
nity website. It will take longer to create, often months to get rolling,
with constant tweaking and twiddling of the code to keep everything
running smoothly. I was lucky when I started MetaFilter because at
that point in my life, I had plenty of free time, I was itching to learn a
new programming language, and I had a laid-back job where I could
take lots of little breaks to check in on the site. If someone asked me if
I'd do it all over again starting today with my current life, I probably
wouldn't because I don't really have the time and energy to start a
new multi-user community site from scratch.

This is the most challenging point in the list, but it's good to get   6
this one figured out before you plunge full speed into new development.

2. Have Both a Compelling Idea and Compelling Content

There are lots of possible reasons to start a community, but generally   7
it's good to focus on a specific topic. Having a specific topic means
you'll have an easier time explaining your site's purpose, and quickly
find like-minded people to contribute their thoughts and content to
your community. MetaFilter was created with the loosest of intentions,
to simply have a weblog that covered anything on the Web, and it
took about nine months of daily posting before anyone noticed it
existed. I guess having comments and allowing others to post was a
compelling enough idea that led to a busy site, but a frequent question from first time visitors was (and still is) "What's this site all about?"
If my site was a model airplane owner's group site with a well-defined
mission and idea for its purpose, I'm sure I could have found other
members a lot sooner.

Compelling content is more important than you probably think.   8
The most well-defined group purpose, with lots of motivated members,
will go nowhere unless there is something to draw everyone together

and get people contributing. This rule could go for any site really, but it's important to have the best possible writing, design, photography, etc. that you can, and update as often as possible. This is where community sites can excel over single-person operations. With a diverse enough membership, you can have expert artists, fantastic writers, great photographers, and senior programmers to build the best community site imaginable, and everyone pitching in can update the content on a frequent basis. It's not exactly easy to get big membership numbers on which to draw for ongoing content; first you have to convince people to join your site, and contribute or comment on other work, and for that you need to start with good content. It's sort of a catch-22, but once you get a group of members creating good content, it creates a strong positive feedback loop that leads to growth, popularity, and quality.

3. Seed Content Sets the Stage

In the early months of a community site, it's important that there is good content there, and that the comments or audience interaction are as close to optimal as possible, so that others reading the site can get a feel for how they are expected to act. If you're building a site that covers politics and you're dreaming of lively debate with a specific slant, make sure your first few articles, essays, or threads cover a good topic, and that some discussion follows where users (more than one) are debating things in an intelligent way. New members will see what is currently on the site, and react accordingly. If there is considerate and helpful criticism, others will usually follow. If there are "first posts!" and posts making threats on other members, other such garbage will follow that as well.

If it's a company discussion forum, set up some threads and have some friends start discussions. If it's a community of airplane enthusiasts, try and find two or three people to help start the site off the same way, by finding content and discussing it in a proper manner. You're not shooting for having hundreds of fake discussion posts with no one; you're just trying to convey a code of conduct by starting with things you can use as examples, and new members can follow.

4. Create Some Basic Guidelines and Be as Fair as Possible

When you're the administrator on a community site, it's important that you set the examples to follow. Post regularly and intelligently, and keep a high profile on the site so others know of your presence (this keeps some troublemakers away, since they know that the site owner will quickly catch wind of their mischief). Follow the Golden Rule, treat others as you would like to be treated, and watch for unsavory patterns that form. If you catch something that's happening with some regularity, and you'd like to see it stop, make it part of the rules of the site, and explain somewhere why people shouldn't do it (start by putting a pointer somewhere near the posting forms, so curious contributors can read them if they like). Keep track of these rules, and put them somewhere people can easily find them on the site. When you have to enforce them, be nice about it, and show people the rules and how they broke them. The world isn't a black-and-white place, so a lot of things will be up to your judgment, but explain as fully as you can why you chose to enforce a certain thing, and point out what the person can do to prevent it from happening again.

What users of a community don't want to see is a headstrong 12 leader who rules with an iron fist, and seems to take pleasure in enforcement. Users also don't want to see a leader who changes his or her mind from day to day, enforcing rules with some users, while letting friends or longtime members get away with murder. Users don't want to be yelled at publicly when they make their first mistake, and they want to be given second chances. Fairness and consistency are key practices when you're running an online community.

5. Have a Place to Talk about the Site, Somewhere on the Site

I've had a lot of success with a special section of MetaFilter designed to 13 talk about issues around the site, bugs and features users wish for, or any etiquette that may have been breached, and I created it because I noticed people were talking about the site on the site itself fairly regularly. Gone unchecked, I noticed it created circular discussions where people talked about other parts of the site on the site itself and it appeared to be senseless navelgazing. Having a separate section conveniently allows that to run in an organized fashion, while at the same time keeping the main site free of looking like one big game of Duck-Duck-Goose. It doesn't necessarily have to be on the site itself, or even on the web. It could be a many-to-many email list for interested parties to participate in, if that will be easier for you to implement.

6. Spread the Work Out as Much as Possible

If it's possible, have a few trusted friends act as moderators and admin- 14 istrators and allow people to contribute and streamline the code that runs the site. When the day-to-day maintenance can be spread out among several people, it's okay if someone goes on vacation, gets busy with work or gets ill, or takes some time off from the site. If lots of new features are being requested, several people can work on them, and debug them faster. This situation isn't always possible, and there are only a few projects that come to mind, such as evolt.org where a sizeable, diverse group keeps a site running.

7. Deal with Troublemakers as Quickly and Nicely as Possible

If you're running a community site of some sort, there's a good chance   15 that people are going to try and mess with it, push the envelope, and hack at it for no good reason. The important thing for you to do as the administrator is deal with problem members as soon as possible and as carefully as possible. If you act rashly or too strongly, you may incite a casual hacker into a full-blown making-your-life-a-living-hell type of hacker. You want to defuse any situation before it gets out of hand.

Start by emailing the person as soon as you can (but give yourself   16 a little time to think; don't send anything too rashly or in the heat of the moment) and asking them gently if perhaps they didn't catch the guidelines pages, or that you'd prefer if they did their thing in a different way. Be careful of your wording in these emails — you don't want to sound threatening or patronizing in any way. You might want to have a friend review the message before sending it to make sure it's neither of those things. A short email reminding a trouble-making member of the error of their ways can usually take care of 90% of problems. Even if a member is doing something obviously malicious, they'll usually stop when called on it.

If that doesn't stop the problem member, the next thing to do is   17 enforce some sort of penalty. This would usually be something like taking away posting rights or moderation rights, posing some new limit on their participation in the site. You will probably want to email them, letting them know what you've done, why you've done it, and most importantly what they can do to get the ban lifted. Hopefully, you'll never need to proceed after these first two measures because a situation can quickly escalate into a war of willpower. If you have to start banning members, doing so will prove quite difficult. You may take all rights away from their account, block their IP address or range of IP addresses, and/or remove their contributions from the site. There are trickier means of hiding a problem user's activity from the rest, but I won't go into that here. It's not a path you'll ever want to take, and no one "wins" in the end; it's just a big waste of energy for all involved.

The bottom line is to stop unsavory behavior by defusing nasty   18
situations as early as possible, in as nice of a way as possible.

8. Highlight the Good, Recognize the Work of Others

I'm still searching for the perfect way to do this, but you'll encourage   19
good contributions by recognizing and highlighting the best your
community has to offer. This is especially true when your community is larger, and you need something to point to as a casual "Hall
of Fame" that new users can take their cue from. This can take many
forms: you can use voting/moderation to let the community pick its
favorites, you can utilize some sort of Brownie Point system where
members earn credits for good contributions which are displayed
somewhere (an ego stroking stop, basically), or if you're lacking the
extra technology, just keep track of them by hand in a "Best of" setting.

Building an inviting place that attracts users and maintaining high   20
quality content on a bustling community site is far from easy, but these
key points should help get you going in the right direction.

RESPONDING TO THE TEXT

After reading Haughey's process analysis, are you encouraged or discouraged
from starting your own online community Web site? Explain. If you are encouraged, what ideas do you have for a site?

ENGAGING THE WRITER'S SUBJECT

1. What is Haughey's purpose in this essay? (Glossary: *Purpose*)

2. In his third section, "Seed Content Sets the Stage," what does Haughey
   mean by "seed content"? He then writes that "the comments or audience
   interaction" should be "as close to optimal as possible" (paragraph 9).
   What does he mean by "optimal"?

3. What problems in establishing an online community does Haughey
   warn about?

4. What problems face the single-person operator of a weblog that are less-
   ened by having a larger group working on the site?

5. Why is content so important for Haughey? What lessons are there
   about writing generally in his emphasis on content?

ANALYZING THE WRITER'S CRAFT

1. What type of process analysis has Haughey provided? Directional, informational, evaluative, or some mixture of all three? Explain.

2. Haughey does not provide steps to follow in his process analysis. Why not?

3. What parallels do you see between the writing advice in Chapter 2 of *Subjects/Strategies* and the advice Haughey gives about establishing a Web site?

4. Why is Haughey concerned about mixing general content and meta-content about the site itself? What solutions does he have for maintaining a clear focus and keeping content discreet?

5. What warning does Haughey provide at the beginning of his essay? What effect does the warning have on you? Do you appreciate his honesty, are you skeptical about how helpful his description will be, or do you take a wait-and-see attitude? (Glossary: *Beginnings/Endings*) Explain.

UNDERSTANDING THE WRITER'S LANGUAGE

1. Why does Haughey write that the title of his essay "is a bit of a joke" (paragraph 3)? (Glossary: *Title*) Do you agree with him? Explain.

2. How would you describe Haughey's tone? (Glossary: *Tone*) Is it forceful? Easygoing? Egocentric or boastful? Businesslike? What words and phrases help him establish his tone?

3. Refer to your desk dictionary to determine the meanings of the following words as Haughey uses them in this selection: *re-coding* (paragraph 4), *hacks* (4), *tweaking* (5), *weblog* (7), *threads* (10), *headstrong* (12), *navelgazing* (13), *mess* (15), *incite* (15), *patronizing* (16).

WRITING SUGGESTIONS

1. In his seventh section, "Deal with Troublemakers as Quickly and Nicely as Possible," Haughey states, "The bottom line is to stop unsavory behavior by defusing nasty situations as early as possible, in as nice of a way as possible" (paragraph 18). Do you agree with Haughey's assertion? Why or why not? If you were in a leadership role on your campus, how would you deal with discipline problems? How are situations such as underage drinking, absenteeism, plagiarism, rowdiness in dorms, vandalism, or "hate speech" handled on your campus? Identify a situation and the process by which the perpetrators are disciplined. Write an evaluative process analysis essay in which you discuss the parts of the disciplinary process that work, the parts that don't, and your suggestions for improving the process.

2. A community is traditionally defined as a group of people who live in close proximity, share the same services, make various contributions for the betterment of all, and relate to one another — face to face — as friends, relatives, and neighbors. However, chat rooms, e-mail, and blogs have changed what it means to be a member of a community. Consider the following cartoon by Harry Bliss. What does it say about the nature of community in the Internet age? Can virtual communities truly satisfy

the need for human contact that traditional communities provide? How do you think Haughey would respond to Bliss's cartoon? Write an essay in which you explore the idea of community in the Internet age. What is the process by which real and virtual communities come into being and endure? Compare and contrast the virtues and shortcomings of each type of community. (Glossary: *Comparison and Contrast*) Are the differences as great as they seem? Explain.

3. The vast majority of blogs are online journals — spaces where individuals recount their daily activities and opinions on subjects ranging from astronomy to fly-fishing — and most of them go unread by anybody other than their authors. However, there are a handful of blogs and blog-like sites such as MetaFilter.com, DrudgeReport.com, AndrewSullivan.com, and AlterNet.org that have cultivated very large followings. Some have argued that these blogs are a brand-new media source that supplements traditional print, radio, television, and Internet news reporting. In your college library and on the Internet, research the effects of blogs on traditional media. (Glossary: *Cause and Effect Analysis*) How have blogs shaped the way traditional media report the news? Are there any stories that blogs broke before traditional media sources? If so, what were the stories? How did traditional media sources follow up? In your opinion, are blogs good or bad for traditional news reporting? Explain.

• To begin your research online, go to **bedfordstmartins.com /subjectsstrategies** and click on "Process Analysis" or browse the thematic directory of annotated links.

WRITING SUGGESTIONS
FOR PROCESS ANALYSIS

1. Write a directional or evaluative process analysis on one of the following topics:
   a. how to make chocolate-chip cookies
   b. how to adjust brakes on a bicycle
   c. how to change a tire
   d. how to throw a party
   e. how to use the memory function on a calculator
   f. how to add, drop, or change a course
   g. how to play a specific card game
   h. how to wash a sweater
   i. how to develop black-and-white film
   j. how to make a pizza
   k. how to build a Web page
   l. how to select a major course of study
   m. how to winterize a car
   n. how to rent an apartment
   o. how to develop confidence
   p. how to start and operate a small business
   q. how to run for student government office
   r. how to do a magic trick

2. Write an informational or evaluative process analysis on one of the following topics:
   a. how your heart functions
   b. how a U.S. president is elected
   c. how ice cream is made
   d. how a hurricane forms
   e. how hailstones form
   f. how a volcano erupts
   g. how the human circulatory system works
   h. how a camera works
   i. how photosynthesis takes place
   j. how an atomic bomb or reactor works
   k. how fertilizer is made
   l. how a refrigerator works
   m. how water evaporates
   n. how flowers bloom
   o. how a recession occurs
   p. how an automobile is made
   q. how a bill becomes law in your state
   r. how a caterpillar becomes a butterfly

3. Think about your favorite pastime or activity. Write an essay in which you explain one or more of the processes you follow in participating in that activity. For example, if basketball is your hobby, how do you go

about making a layup? If you are a photographer, how do you develop and print a picture? If you are an actor, how do you go about learning your lines? Do you follow standard procedures, or do you personalize the process in some way?

4. Although each of us hopes never to be in an automobile accident, many of us have been or will be. Accidents are unsettling, and it is important that people know what to do if they ever find themselves in a collision. Write an essay in which you explain the steps that a person should follow to protect life and property.

5. All college students have to register for courses each term. What is the registration process like at your college? Do you find any part of the process unnecessarily frustrating or annoying? In a letter to your campus newspaper or an appropriate administrator, evaluate your school's current registration procedure, offering suggestions for making the process more efficient and pleasurable.

6. Writing to a person who is a computer novice, explain how to do a Web search using popular Web search engines like Yahoo!, AltaVista, Google, or Dogpile. Be sure to define key terms and to illustrate the steps in your process with screen shots of search directories and search results.

CHAPTER 7

Comparison and Contrast

WHAT ARE COMPARISON AND CONTRAST?

A comparison presents two or more subjects (people, ideas, or objects), considers them together, and shows in what ways they are alike; a contrast shows how they differ. These two perspectives, apparently in contradiction to each other, actually work so often in conjunction that they are commonly considered a single strategy, called comparison and contrast or simply comparison for short.

Comparison and contrast are so much a part of daily life that we are often not aware of using them. Whenever you make a choice — what to wear, where to eat, what college to attend, what career to pursue — you implicitly use comparison and contrast to evaluate your options and arrive at your decision. Consider a simple choice, like picking a shirt to wear for the day. You probably have at least a few to choose from, and all are comparable in certain ways — they fit you reasonably well, they are clean and ready to wear, and in some way each of them reflects your taste in clothes. To make a choice, you must reflect first on the situation in which the shirt will be worn: the weather, the people you will see, the work or play you will engage in, whether the occasion calls for casual or formal attire. Then you consider the shirts themselves and decide whether you want long sleeves or short; white, colored, or patterned fabric; a fastidious button-down collar, a sweatshirt, or a T-shirt with a sports logo. Even though you may not consciously realize it, you make your choice by comparing and contrasting the items in your wardrobe and the context that makes one item more suitable than the others.

The strategy of comparison and contrast is most commonly used in writing when the subjects under discussion belong to the same class or general category: four makes of car, for example, or two candidates for the Senate. (See Chapter 8, "Division and Classification," for a more complete discussion of classes.) Such subjects are said to be *comparable*, or to have a strong basis for comparison.

Point-by-Point and Block Comparison

There are two basic ways to organize an essay of comparison and contrast. In the first, *point-by-point comparison*, the author starts by comparing both subjects in terms of a particular point, then moves on to a second point and compares both subjects, then moves on to a third point, and so on. The other way to organize a comparison is called *block comparison*. In this pattern, the information about one subject is gathered into a block, which is followed by a block of comparable information about the second subject. Each pattern of comparison has advantages and disadvantages. Point-by-point comparison allows the reader to grasp fairly easily the specific points of comparison the author is making; it may be harder, though, to pull together the details and convey a distinct impression of what each subject is like. The block comparison guarantees that each subject will receive a more unified discussion; however, the points of comparison between them may be less clear.

The first of the following two annotated passages illustrates a point-by-point comparison. This selection, written before the dissolution of the Soviet Union, is from *Why They Behave Like Russians* by John Fischer.

Point-by-point comparison in second sentence (five points in one sentence)

The basis of comparison: subjects similar in class, attitude, and geographic region

The Ukrainians are the Texans of Russia. They believe they can fight, drink, ride, sing, and make love better than anybody else in the world, and if pressed will admit it. Their country, too, was a borderland — that's what "Ukraine" means — and like Texas it was originally settled by outlaws, horse thieves, land-hungry farmers, and people who hadn't made a go of it somewhere else. Some of these hard cases banded together, long ago, to raise hell and some livestock. They called themselves Cossacks, and they would have felt right at home in any Western movie. Even today the Ukrainians cherish a wistful tradition of horsemanship, although most of them would feel as uncomfortable in a saddle as any Dallas banker. They still like to wear knee-high boots and big, furry hats, made of gray or black Persian lamb, which are the local equivalent of a Stetson.

Explicit comparison between Texas and Ukraine in description of country

Implicit comparison: Ukrainians described in terms of familiar Texas mythology

Even the country looks a good deal like Texas — flat, dry prairie, shading off in the south to semidesert. Through the middle runs a strip of dark, rich soil, the Chernozom Belt, which is almost identical with the black waxy soil of central Texas. It grows the best wheat in the Soviet Union. The Ukraine is also famous for its cattle, sheep, and cotton, and — again like Texas — it has been in the throes of an industrial boom for the last twenty years. On all other people the Ukrainians look with a sort of kindly pity. They might have thought up for their own use the old Western rule of etiquette: "Never ask a man where he comes from. If he's a Texan, he'll tell you; if he's not, don't embarrass him."

In the following example from *Harper's* magazine, Otto Friedrich uses a block format to contrast a newspaper story with a newsmagazine story.

Subjects of comparison: newspaper story and magazine story. Each belongs to the same class.

There is an essential difference between a news story, as understood by a newspaperman or a wire-service writer, and a newsmagazine story. The chief purpose of the conventional news story is to tell what happened. It starts with the most important information and continues into increasingly inconsequential details, not only because the reader may not read beyond the first paragraph, but because an editor working on galley proofs a few minutes before press time likes to be able to cut freely from the end of the story.

Block comparison: each paragraph deals with one type of story.

A newsmagazine is very different. It is written to be read consecutively from beginning to end, and each of its stories is designed, following the critical theories of Edgar Allan Poe, to create one emotional effect. The news, what happened that week, may be told in the beginning, the middle, or the end; for the purpose is not to throw information at the reader but to seduce him into reading the whole story, and into accepting the dramatic (and often political) point being made.

In this selection, Friedrich has two purposes: to offer information that explains the differences between a newspaper story and a newsmagazine story, and to persuade readers that magazine stories tend to be more biased than newspaper stories.

Analogy: A Special Form of Comparison and Contrast

When the subject under discussion is unfamiliar, complex, or abstract, the resourceful writer may use a special form of comparison called *analogy* to help readers understand the difficult subject. An analogy compares two largely dissimilar subjects to look for illuminating similarities. Most comparisons analyze items within the same class. For example, an exploration of the similarities and differences between short stories and novels — two forms of fiction — would constitute a logical comparison. Short stories and novels belong to the same class, and your purpose would be to tell something about both. In contrast, analogy pairs things of different classes. In analogy, the only basis for comparison lies in the writer's imagination. In addition, while the typical comparison seeks to illuminate specific features of both subjects, the primary purpose of analogy is to clarify one subject that is complex or unfamiliar by pointing out its similarities to a more familiar or concrete subject. If, for example, your purpose were to explain the craft of fiction writing, you might note its similarities to the craft of carpentry. In this case, you would be drawing an analogy, because the two subjects clearly belong to different classes. Your imagination will suggest many ways in which the concrete work of the carpenter can be used to help readers understand the more abstract work of the novelist. You can use analogy in one or two paragraphs to clarify a particular aspect of the larger topic, or you can use it as the organizational strategy for an entire essay.

In the following example from *The Mysterious Sky* (1960), observe how Lester Del Rey explains the functions of the Earth's atmosphere (a subject that people have difficulty with because they can't "see" it) by making an analogy with an ordinary window.

> The atmosphere of Earth acts like any window in serving two very important functions. It lets light in and it permits us to look out. It also serves as a shield to keep out dangerous or uncomfortable things. A normal glazed window lets us keep our houses warm by keeping out cold air, and it prevents rain, dirt, and unwelcome insects and animals from coming in. As we have already seen, Earth's atmospheric window also helps to keep our planet at a comfortable temperature by holding back radiated heat and protecting us from dangerous levels of ultraviolet light.
>
> Lately, we have discovered that space is full of a great many very dangerous things against which our atmosphere guards us. It is not a perfect shield, and sometimes one of these dangerous objects does get through. There is even some evidence that a few of these messengers from space contain life, though this has by no means been proved yet.

You'll notice that Del Rey's analogy establishes no direct relationship between the subjects under comparison. The analogy is effective precisely because it enables the reader to visualize the atmosphere, which is unobservable, by comparing it to something quite different — a window — that is familiar and concrete.

WHY DO WRITERS USE COMPARISON AND CONTRAST?

To compare one thing or idea with another, to discover the similarities and differences between them, is one of the most basic human strategies for learning, evaluating, and making decisions. Because it serves so many fundamental purposes, comparison and contrast is a particularly useful strategy for the writer. It may be the primary mode for essay writers who seek to educate or persuade the reader; to evaluate things, people, or events; and to differentiate between apparently similar subjects or to reconcile the differences between dissimilar ones.

The essays in this chapter illustrate a number of uses of comparison and contrast. For example, an author who wishes primarily to impart information about two related subjects can bring each into clear focus by comparing and contrasting them. In "Crazy Horse and Custer as Young Warriors" (p. 306), Stephen E. Ambrose opens by dismissing romantic descriptions of Custer that appeared in the popular press in the nineteenth century. Having cleared the air, he compares Crazy Horse and Custer, two young warriors who have come to represent their respective cultures.

Sometimes, instead of giving specifics about individuals, the author seeks to emphasize the particular qualities of two types of people. Such generalization may lead to evaluation, as in Suzanne Britt's essay entitled "Neat People vs. Sloppy People" (p. 293), in which she makes an unexpected argument for the virtues of sloppiness. Generalization of types may also lead to a better understanding of the computers we've come to rely on. Del Miller, in "Mac or PC: There Is Simply No Comparison!" (p. 299), explains how some people always hear of the virtues of PCs and end up never giving Macs a chance. In addressing some of the basic reasons people give for preferring a PC over a Mac, he takes some of the fear out of purchasing an Apple product. In "Sex, Lies, and Conversation" (p. 312), a complex exploration of two types of people, Deborah Tannen compares and contrasts the ways in which men and women communicate, drawing an analogy between cross-cultural communication and communication between the sexes. Instead of arguing that one conversational style is superior, Tannen uses the strategy of comparison and contrast to educate the reader about how to reconcile the differences between the styles.

Writers may choose to compare objects or processes rather than people. Student author Barbara Bowman's primary goal (p. 277) is to persuade the reader that cameras are more desirable than guns in the hands of those who hunt animals. But Mark Twain has a more subtle purpose in "Two Ways of Seeing a River" (p. 288); Twain shows how the Mississippi River, and indeed many aspects of life, may appear different to two different observers, or to a single observer at different times in life.

Comparison and contrast may be combined readily with other writing strategies and often serves to sharpen, clarify, and add interest to essays written in a different primary mode. For example, an essay of argumentation gains credibility when the writer contrasts desirable and undesirable reasons or examples. In the Declaration of Independence (p. 519), Thomas Jefferson effectively contrasts the actual behavior of the English king with the ideals of a democratic society. In "I Have a Dream" (p. 525), Martin Luther King Jr. compares 1960s America with the promise of what ought to be to argue that the realization of the dream of freedom for all American citizens is long overdue. Likewise, Richard Lederer, in "The Case for Short Words" (p. 513), uses comparison and contrast to showcase the virtues of one-syllable words when measured against their multisyllabic counterparts. Finally, each of the writers in the "Genetically Modified Foods" Argument Cluster compare "Frankenfood" and "real" food to argue their positions.

Many descriptive essays rely heavily on comparison and contrast; one of the most effective ways to describe any person, place, or thing is to show how it is like another model of the same class and how it differs. Robert Ramírez ("The Barrio," p. 602) describes his Hispanic neighborhood against "the harshness and the coldness of the Anglo world." Definition is also clarified and enriched by the use of comparison and contrast. Virtually all the essays in Chapter 9 employ this strategy to some degree.

AN ANNOTATED STUDENT ESSAY
USING COMPARISON AND CONTRAST

A studio art major from Pittsburgh, Pennsylvania, Barbara Bowman has a special interest in photography. In her writing courses, Bowman has discovered many similarities between the writing process and the process that an artist follows. Her essay "Guns and Cameras," however, explores similarities of another kind: those between hunting with a gun and hunting with a camera.

Guns and Cameras

Barbara Bowman

Discussion of the objects of comparison

With a growing number of animals heading toward extinction, and with the idea of protecting such animals on game reserves increasing in popularity, photographic safaris are replacing hunting safaris. This may seem odd because of the obvious differences between guns and cameras. Shooting is aggressive, photography is passive; shooting eliminates, photography preserves. However, some hunters are willing to trade their guns for cameras because of similarities in the way the equipment is used, as well as in the relationship among equipment, user, and "prey."

Block One (the hunter) begins.

Point A: equipment

The hunter has a deep interest in the apparatus he uses to kill his prey. He carries various types of guns, different kinds of ammunition, and special sights and telescopes to increase his chances of success. He knows the mechanics of his guns and understands how and why they work. This fascination with the hardware of his sport is practical — it helps him achieve his goal — but it frequently becomes an end, almost a hobby in itself.

Point B: stalking

Not until the very end of the long process of stalking an animal does a game hunter use his gun. First he enters into the animal's world. He studies his prey, its habitat, its daily habits, its watering holes and feeding areas, its migration patterns, its enemies and allies, its diet and food chain. Eventually the hunter himself becomes animal-like, instinctively sensing the habits and moves of his prey. Of course, this instinct gives the hunter a better chance of killing the animal; he knows where and when he will get the best shot. But it gives him more than that. Hunting is not just pulling the trigger and killing the prey. Much of it is a multifaceted and ritualistic identification with nature.

Point C: the result

After the kill, the hunter can do a number of things with his trophy. He can sell the meat or eat it himself. He can hang the animal's head on the wall or lay its hide on the floor or even sell these objects. But any of these uses is a luxury, and its

2

3

4

cost is high. An animal has been destroyed; a life has been eliminated.

Block Two (the photographer) begins.

Like the hunter, the photographer has a great interest in the tools he uses. He carries various types of cameras, lenses, and film to help him get the picture he wants. He understands the way cameras work, the uses of telephoto and micro lenses, and

Point A: equipment

often the technical procedures of printing and developing. Of course, the time and interest a photographer invests in these mechanical aspects of his art allow him to capture and produce the image he wants. But as with the hunter, these mechanics can and often do become fascinating in themselves.

Point B: stalking

The wildlife photographer also needs to stalk his "prey" with knowledge and skill in order to get an accurate "shot." Like the hunter, he has to understand the animal's patterns, characteristics, and habitat; he must become animal-like in order to succeed. And like the hunter's, his pursuit is much more prolonged and complicated than the shot itself. The stalking processes are almost identical and give many of the same satisfactions.

Point C: the result

The successful photographer also has something tangible to show for his efforts. A still picture of an animal can be displayed in a home, a gallery, a shop; it can be printed in a publication, as a postcard, or as a poster. In fact, a single photograph can be used in all these ways at once; it can be reproduced countless times. And despite all these ways of using his "trophies," the photographer continues to preserve his prey.

Conclusion: The two activities are similar and give the same satisfaction, so why kill?

Photography is obviously the less violent and to me the more acceptable method for obtaining a trophy of a wild animal. We no longer need to hunt in order to feed or clothe ourselves, and hunting for "sport"

5

6

7

8

seems to be barbaric. Luckily, the excitement of pursuing an animal, learning its
habits and patterns, outsmarting it on its
own level, and finally "getting" it can all
be done with a camera. So why use guns?

Analyzing Barbara Bowman's Essay of Comparison and Contrast: Questions for Discussion

1. What is Bowman's thesis in this essay?
2. What are her main points of comparison between hunting with a gun and hunting with a camera?
3. How has Bowman organized her comparison? Why do you suppose she decided on this option? Explain.
4. How else could she have organized her essay? Would this alternative organization have been as effective as the one she used? Explain.
5. How does Bowman conclude her essay? In what ways is her conclusion a reflection of her thesis?

In discussing how she came to write about cameras and guns, Bowman said, "Photography is a big part of my life right now. I'm a studio art major, and this summer I'll be an intern with the local weekly newspaper, their only staff photographer. So you can see why my bias is toward cameras instead of guns." As to how she came up with the idea of comparing guns and cameras, she said, "I was reading a photography book and it mentioned a safari in Africa that used cameras instead of guns. I thought that was very interesting, so I thought I'd use it for a writing subject. I don't know that much about guns, but there's a guy in my English class who's a big hunter — he wrote a paper for the class about hunting — so I asked him about it. I could tell from what he said that he got the same gratification from it that a nature photographer would. Other people I know who hunt do it mostly for the meat and for the adventure of stalking prey. So that's how I got what I needed to know about hunting. Photography I knew lots about already, of course."

As to why she chose to use a block method of organization rather than a point-by-point method, Bowman explained, "Well, the first draft was a point-by-point comparison, and it was very bumpy, shifting back and forth between the hunter and the photographer, and I thought it was probably confusing. As I kept developing the paper, it just made more sense to switch to the block comparison. Unfortunately, this meant that I had to throw out some paragraphs in the first draft that

I liked. That's hard for me — throw out some writing that seems different and new — but it wasn't fitting right, so I had to make the cuts."

Asked if she made any other large-scale changes as she revised,
Bowman responded, "Nothing in particular, but each time I revised I
threw things out that I didn't need, and now the essay is only half as
long as it used to be. For example, here's a sentence from the next-to-
last draft: 'Guns kill, cameras don't; guns use ammunition, cameras use
film; shooting eliminates, photography preserves.' Everybody knows
this, and the first and last parts say the same thing. I liked the last
part, the way the words go together, so I kept that, but I cut out the
rest. I did a lot of that."

Finally, in reflecting on the purpose of her writing, Bowman turned
to her dislike of killing. "I don't like the idea of killing things for sport. I
can see the hunter's argument that you've got to keep the animals'
numbers under control, but I still would rather they weren't shot to
death. That was the point of the comparison right from the first draft."

SUGGESTIONS FOR WRITING A
COMPARISON AND CONTRAST ESSAY

Many assignments in college ask you to use the strategy of comparison and contrast. As you read an assignment, look for one or more of
the words that suggest the use of this strategy. When you are asked to
compare and *contrast* one item with another or to identify the *similarities* and *differences* between two items, you should use comparison and
contrast. Other assignments might ask you to determine which of two
options is *better* or to select the *best* solution to a particular problem.
Again, the strategy of comparison and contrast will help you make
this evaluation and arrive at a sound, logical conclusion. As you start
planning and writing an essay of comparison and contrast, keep in
mind the basic requirements of this writing strategy.

Compare Subjects from the Same Class

Remember that the subjects of your comparison should be in the same
class or general category, so that you can establish a clear basis for comparison. (There are any number of possible classes, such as particular
types of persons, places, and things, as well as occupations, activities,
philosophies, points in history, and even concepts and ideas.) If your
subject is difficult, complex, or unobservable, you may find that analogy, a special form of comparison, is the most effective strategy to
explain that subject. Remember, also, that if the similarities and differences between the subjects are obvious, your reader is certain to lose
interest quickly.

Determine Your Purpose, and Focus on It

Suppose you choose to compare and contrast solar energy with wind energy. It is clear that both are members of the same class — energy — so there is a basis for comparing them; there also seem to be enough interesting differences to make a comparison and contrast possible. But before going any further, you must ask yourself why you want to compare and contrast these particular subjects. What audience do you seek to address? Do you want to inform, to emphasize, to explain, to evaluate, to persuade? Do you have more than one purpose? Whatever your purpose, it will influence the content and organization of your comparison.

In comparing and contrasting solar and wind energy, you will certainly provide factual information; yet you will probably also want to evaluate the two energy sources to determine whether either is a practical means of producing energy. You may also want to persuade your readers that one technology is superior to the other.

Formulate a Thesis Statement

Once you have your purpose clearly in mind, formulate a preliminary thesis statement. At this early stage in the writing process, the thesis statement is not cast in stone; you may well want to modify it later on, as a result of research and further consideration of your subject. A preliminary thesis statement has two functions: First, it fixes your direction so that you will be less tempted to stray into byways while doing research and writing drafts; second, establishing the central point of the essay makes it easier for you to gather supporting material and to organize your essay.

Suppose, for example, that you live in the Champlain Valley of Vermont, one of the cloudiest areas of the country, where the wind whistles along the corridor between the Green Mountains and the Adirondacks. If you were exploring possible alternative energy sources for the area, your purpose might be to persuade readers of a local environmental journal that wind is preferable to sun as a source of energy for this region. The thesis statement for this essay will certainly differ from that of a writer for a national newsmagazine whose goal is to offer general information about alternative energy sources to a broad readership.

Choose the Points of Comparison

Points of comparison are the qualities and features of your subjects on which you base your comparison. For some comparisons, you will find the information you need in your own head; for others, you will have to search for that information in the library or on the Internet. At this stage, if you know only a little about the subjects of your comparison, you may have only a few hazy ideas for points of comparison. Perhaps wind energy means no more to you than an image of giant windmills lined up on a California ridge, and solar energy brings to mind only the reflective, glassy roof on a Colorado ski lodge. Even so, it is possible to list points of comparison that will be relevant to your subjects and your purpose. Here, for example, are important points of comparison in considering energy sources:

> Cost
> Efficiency
> Convenience
> Environmental impact

As you learn more about your subjects and think about what you are learning, you may want to change some of these points or add new ones. Meanwhile, a tentative list will help you by suggesting the kind of information you need to gather for your comparison and contrast. Let your tentative points of comparison be your guide, but remain alert for others you may not have thought of. For example, as you conduct research, you may find that maintenance requirements are another important factor in considering energy systems, and thus you might add that point to your list.

Organize the Points of Comparison

Once you have gathered the necessary information, you should decide which organizational pattern, block or point-by-point, will best serve your purpose. In deciding which pattern to use, you may find it helpful to jot down a scratch outline before beginning your draft.

Block organization works best when the two objects of comparison are relatively straightforward and when the points of comparison are rather general, few in number, and can be stated succinctly. As a scratch outline illustrates, block organization makes for a unified discussion of each object, which can help your readers understand the information you have to give them.

Block Organization Outline
BLOCK ONE **Solar Energy**
> Point 1. Cost
> Point 2. Efficiency
> Point 3. Convenience
> Point 4. Maintenance requirements
> Point 5. Environmental impact

BLOCK TWO **Wind Energy**
Point 1. Cost
Point 2. Efficiency
Point 3. Convenience
Point 4. Maintenance requirements
Point 5. Environmental impact

If your essay will be more than two or three pages long, however, block organization may be a poor choice. By the time your readers come to your discussion of the costs of wind energy, they may well have forgotten what you had to say about solar energy costs several pages earlier and may have to flip back and forth to grasp the comparison. If such difficulties are a possibility, you would do better to use point-by-point organization, in which comparisons are made immediately as each point is raised.

Point-by-Point Outline

POINT ONE **Cost**
Subject 1. Solar energy
Subject 2. Wind energy

POINT TWO **Efficiency**
Subject 1. Solar energy
Subject 2. Wind energy

POINT THREE **Convenience**
Subject 1. Solar energy
Subject 2. Wind energy

POINT FOUR **Maintenance Requirements**
Subject 1. Solar energy
Subject 2. Wind energy

POINT FIVE **Environmental Impact**
Subject 1. Solar energy
Subject 2. Wind energy

Draw a Conclusion from the Comparison

Only after you have gathered your information and made your comparisons will you be ready to decide on a conclusion. When drawing the conclusion to your essay, remember your purpose in writing, the claim made in your thesis statement, and your audience and emphasis. Perhaps, having presented information about both technologies, your comparison shows that solar and wind energy are both feasible, with solar energy having a slight edge on most points. If your purpose has been evaluation for a general audience, you might conclude, "Both solar and wind energy are practical alternatives to conventional energy sources." If you asserted in your thesis statement that one of the technologies is superior to the other, your comparison will support a more persuasive conclusion. For the general audience, you might say, "While both solar and wind energy are practical technologies, solar energy now seems the better investment." However, for a readership made up of residents of the cloudy Champlain Valley, you might conclude, "While both solar and wind energy are practical technologies, wind energy makes more economic sense for investors in northwest Vermont."

Editing Tip: Parallel Constructions

Be sure to follow the guidelines and advice for editing an essay given in Chapter 2, "Writing Essays." The guidelines highlight those sentence-level concerns — grammar, mechanics, and punctuation — that are especially important in editing any piece of writing. While editing your essay of comparison and contrast, use parallel grammatical structures to emphasize the similarities and differences between the items being compared.

Parallelism is the repetition of word order or grammatical form either within a single sentence or in several sentences that develop the same central idea. As a rhetorical device, parallel structure can aid coherence and add emphasis. Franklin Roosevelt's famous Depression-era statement "I see one-third of a nation *ill-housed*, *ill-clad*, and *ill-nourished*" illustrates effective parallelism. Look for opportunities to use parallel constructions with 1) paired items or items in a series, 2) correlative conjunctions, and 3) the words *as* or *than*.

1. **Use parallel constructions to balance a word with a word, a phrase with a phrase, or a clause with a clause whenever you use paired items or items in a series, as in the Roosevelt example above.**

   Consider the following examples taken from Barbara Bowman's essay "Guns and Cameras" (p. 277), in which she compares and contrasts the experiences of hunters and photographers in pursuit of their quarry.

BALANCE A WORD WITH A WORD

> Like the hunter, he [the photographer] has to understand the animal's *patterns, characteristics,* and *habitat.*

> A still picture of an animal can be displayed in a *home,* a *gallery,* a *shop*; it can be printed in a *publication,* as a *postcard,* or as a *poster.*

BALANCE A PHRASE WITH A PHRASE

> He carries *various types of guns, different kinds of ammunition,* and *special sights and telescopes* to increase his chances of success.

> Luckily, the excitement of *pursuing an animal, learning its habits and patterns, outsmarting it on its own level,* and finally *"getting"* it can all be done with a camera.

BALANCE A CLAUSE WITH A CLAUSE

> *Shooting is aggressive, photography is passive; shooting eliminates, photography preserves.*

2. **Use parallel constructions when linking paired items with a correlative conjunction (*either/or, neither/nor, not only/but also, both/and, whether/or*) in a sentence.**

> Both men lived in societies in which drugs, especially alcohol, were widely used, but *neither* Custer *nor* Crazy Horse drank.
>
> — STEPHEN E. AMBROSE
> "Crazy Horse and Custer," page 307

> A patriarchy is a patriarchy, *whether* civilized *or* primitive, and patriarchs think alike about women.
>
> — STEPHEN E. AMBROSE
> "Crazy Horse and Custer," page 308

3. **Use parallel constructions in comparisons with *than* or *as*.**

> Neat people are lazier and meaner *than* sloppy people.
>
> — SUZANNE BRITT
> "Neat People vs. Sloppy People," page 293

> It is more accurate to say that Apple machines are more competitive in some price ranges and in some configurations *than* in others.
>
> — DEL MILLER
> "Mac or PC: There Is Simply No Comparison!" page 302

As a hunter Crazy Horse killed for a living; *as* a soldier, so did Custer.

— Stephen E. Ambrose
"Crazy Horse and Custer," page 309

Women's conversational habits are *as* frustrating to men *as* men's are to women.

— Deborah Tannen
"Sex, Lies, and Conversation," page 315

► **Questions for Revising and Editing: Comparison and Contrast**

1. Are the subjects of my comparison comparable; that is, do they belong to the same class of items (for example, two cars, two advertisements, two landscape paintings) so that there is a clear basis for comparison?

2. Are there any complex or abstract concepts that might be clarified by using an analogy, in which I convey what the concept has in common with a more familiar or concrete subject?

3. Is the purpose of my comparison clearly stated?

4. Have I presented a clear thesis statement?

5. Have I chosen my points of comparison well? Have I avoided obvious points of comparison, concentrating instead on similarities between obviously different items or differences between essentially similar items?

6. Have I developed my points of comparison in sufficient detail so that my readers can appreciate my thinking?

7. Have I chosen the best pattern — block or point-by-point — to organize my information?

8. Have I drawn a conclusion that is in line with my thesis and purpose?

9. Have I used parallel constructions correctly in my sentences?

Two Ways of Seeing a River

Mark Twain

Mark Twain, the pen name of Samuel L. Clemens (1835–1910), was born in Florida, Missouri, and raised in Hannibal, Missouri. He created Tom Sawyer *(1876),* The Prince and the Pauper *(1882),* Huckleberry Finn *(1884), and* A Connecticut Yankee in King Arthur's Court *(1889), among other classics. One of America's most popular writers, Twain is generally regarded as the most important practitioner of the realistic school of writing, a style that emphasizes observable details.*

The following passage is taken from Life on the Mississippi *(1883), Twain's study of the great river and his account of his early experiences learning to be a river steamboat pilot. As you read the passage, notice how Twain uses figurative language in describing two quite different ways of seeing the Mississippi River.*

PREPARING TO READ

Our way of seeing an event or a place in our life often changes over time. Recall an important event or a place you visited in the past. Tell a story based on your memories. Has your view of this event or place changed over time? How?

Now when I had mastered the language of this water and had come to know every trifling feature that bordered the great river as familiarly as I knew the letters of the alphabet, I had made a valuable acquisition. But I had lost something, too. I had lost something which could never be restored to me while I lived. All the grace, the beauty, the poetry, had gone out of the majestic river! I still kept in mind a certain wonderful sunset which I witnessed when steamboating was new to me. A broad expanse of the river was turned to blood; in the middle distance the red hue brightened into gold, through which a solitary log came floating, black and conspicuous; in one place a long, slanting mark lay sparkling upon the water; in another the surface was broken by boiling, tumbling rings that were as many-tinted as an opal; where the ruddy flush was faintest was a smooth spot that was covered with graceful circles and radiating lines, ever so delicately traced; the shore on our left was densely wooded, and the somber shadow that fell from this forest was broken in one place by a long, ruffled trail that shone like silver; and high above the forest wall a clean-stemmed dead tree waved a single leafy bough that glowed like a flame in the unobstructed splendor that was flowing from the sun. There were graceful curves, reflected images, woody heights, soft distances, and over the whole scene, far and near, the dissolving lights drifted steadily, enriching it every passing moment with new marvels of coloring.

I stood like one bewitched. I drank it in, in a speechless rapture. The world was new to me and I had never seen anything like this at home. But as I have said, a day came when I began to cease from noting the glories and the charms which the moon and the sun and the twilight wrought upon the river's face; another day came when I ceased altogether to note them. Then, if that sunset scene had been repeated, I should have looked upon it without rapture and should have commented upon it inwardly after this fashion: "This sun means that we are going to have wind tomorrow; that floating log means that the river is rising, small thanks to it; that slanting mark on the water refers to a bluff reef which is going to kill somebody's steamboat one of these nights, if it keeps on stretching out like that; those tumbling 'boils' show a dissolving bar and a changing channel there; the lines and circles in the slick water over yonder are a warning that that troublesome place is shoaling up dangerously; that silver streak in the shadow of the forest is the 'break' from a new snag and he has located himself in the very best place he could have found to fish for steamboats; that tall dead tree, with a single living branch, is not going to last long, and then how is a body ever going to get through this blind place at night without the friendly old landmark?"

No, the romance and beauty were all gone from the river. All the value any feature of it had for me now was the amount of usefulness it could furnish toward compassing the safe piloting of a steamboat. Since those days, I have pitied doctors from my heart. What does the lovely flush in a beauty's cheek mean to a doctor but a "break" that ripples above some deadly disease? Are not all her visible charms sown thick with what are to him the signs and symbols of hidden decay? Does he ever see her beauty at all, or doesn't he simply view her professionally and comment upon her unwholesome condition all to himself? And doesn't he sometimes wonder whether he has gained most or lost most by learning his trade?

RESPONDING TO THE TEXT

In the essay, Twain points to a change of attitude he underwent as a result of seeing the river from a new perspective, that of a steamboat pilot. Why and how do you think perspectives change? How would you characterize Twain's change of perspective?

ENGAGING THE WRITER'S SUBJECT

1. What points of contrast does Twain refer to between his two ways of seeing the river?

2. What point does Twain make regarding the difference between appearance and reality, between romance and practicality? What role does knowledge play in Twain's inability to see the river as he once did?

3. Now that he has learned the trade of steamboating, does Twain feel he has "gained most or lost most" (paragraph 3)? What has he gained, and what has he lost?

ANALYZING THE WRITER'S CRAFT

1. What method of organization does Twain use in this selection? (Glossary: *Organization*) What alternative methods might he have used? What would have been gained or lost?

2. Explain the analogy that Twain uses in paragraph 3. (Glossary: *Analogy*) What is his purpose in using this analogy?

3. Reread Twain's conclusion. (Glossary: *Beginnings/Endings*) How effective do you find it? Why does he switch the focus to a doctor's perspective?

4. In reflecting on his two ways of seeing the river, Twain relies on a combination of subjective and objective descriptions. (Glossary: *Description*) Identify places in the essay where Twain uses description. How does the inclusion of these descriptions enhance his overall comparison and contrast?

UNDERSTANDING THE WRITER'S LANGUAGE

1. Twain uses a number of similes and metaphors in this selection. (Glossary: *Figures of Speech*) Identify three of each, and explain what is being compared in each case. What do these figures add to Twain's writing?

2. What effect do the italicized words have in each of the following quotations from this selection? What do these words contribute to Twain's description?
   a. "ever so *delicately* traced" (paragraph 1)
   b. "shadow that *fell* from this forest" (1)
   c. "*wrought* upon the river's face" (2)
   d. "show a *dissolving* bar" (2)
   e. "get through this *blind* place at night" (2)
   f. "lovely *flush* in a beauty's cheek" (3)

3. Refer to your desk dictionary to determine the meanings of the following words as Twain uses them in this selection: *acquisition* (paragraph 1), *hue* (1), *opal* (1), *rapture* (2), *romance* (3).

WRITING SUGGESTIONS

1. Consider the following cartoon from the *New Yorker*. What perspective does the cartoon give you on Twain's point about his different views of the Mississippi River? How does Twain's essay help you understand the cartoon? Is it possible for a person to have two different views of a single

scene, event, or issue at the same time? How might experience or perspective change how we view something? Write an essay modeled on Twain's in which you offer two different views of a scene, an event, or an issue. You might consider a reporter's view compared with a victim's view, a teacher's view compared with a student's view, or a customer's view compared with a salesclerk's view.

"*By George, your'e right! I thought there was something familiar about it.*"

2. Write an essay in which you use comparison and contrast to help you describe one of the following places or another place of your choice. (Glossary: *Description*)

   a. a place of worship
   b. a fast-food restaurant
   c. your dormitory
   d. your college library

   e. your favorite place
   f. your college student center
   g. your hometown

3. Think of a public event from the past, such as the death of Princess Diana, the impeachment of Bill Clinton, the disputed election of

George W. Bush, the events of September 11, or the war in Iraq. Go to the library and find commentary on the event that addresses the event at the time it happened. You might look in the newspaper or in newsmagazines like *U.S. News & World Report, Time,* or *Newsweek.* You might also check the Internet sites of major newsmagazines or newspapers or other electronic sources for news, such as Lexis/Nexis. Write an essay in which you compare and contrast the view that you read about from the past with your own view of the event today.

- To begin your research online, go to **bedfordstmartins.com /subjectsstrategies** and click on "Comparison and Contrast" or browse the thematic directory of annotated links.

Neat People vs. Sloppy People

Suzanne Britt

Born in Winston-Salem, North Carolina, Suzanne Britt now makes her home in Raleigh. She graduated from Salem College and Washington University, where she received her M.A. in English. A freelance writer, Britt has a regular column in North Carolina Gardens and Homes. *Her work has appeared in the* New York Times, Newsweek, *and the* Boston Globe. *Her essays have been collected in two books,* Skinny People Are Dull and Crunchy Like Carrots *and* Show and Tell. *Currently, she teaches English at Meredith College in North Carolina and continues to write.*

In the following essay taken from Show and Tell, *Britt takes a humorous look at the differences between neat and sloppy people by giving us some insights about several important personality traits.*

PREPARING TO READ

Many people in our society are fond of comparing people, places, and things. Often, these comparisons are premature and even damaging. Consider the ways people judge others based on clothes, appearance, or hearsay. Write about a time in your life when you made such a comparison about someone or something. Did your initial judgment hold up? If not, why did it change?

I've finally figured out the difference between neat people and sloppy people. The distinction is, as always, moral. Neat people are lazier and meaner than sloppy people. 1

Sloppy people, you see, are not really sloppy. Their sloppiness is merely the unfortunate consequence of their extreme moral rectitude. Sloppy people carry in their mind's eye a heavenly vision, a precise plan, that is so stupendous, so perfect, it can't be achieved in this world or the next. 2

Sloppy people live in Never-Never Land. Someday is their métier. Someday they are planning to alphabetize all their books and set up home catalogs. Someday they will go through their wardrobes and mark certain items for tentative mending and certain items for passing on to relatives of similar shape and size. Someday sloppy people will make family scrapbooks into which they will put newspaper clippings, postcards, locks of hair, and the dried corsage from their senior prom. Someday they will file everything on the surface of their desks, including the cash receipts from coffee purchases at the snack shop. Someday they will sit down and read all the back issues of *The New Yorker*. 3

For all these noble reasons and more, sloppy people never get   4
neat. They aim too high and wide. They save everything, planning
someday to file, order, and straighten out the world. But while these
ambitious plans take clearer and clearer shape in their heads, the books
spill from the shelves onto the floor, the clothes pile up in the hamper
and closet, the family mementos accumulate in every drawer, the surface of the desk is buried under mounds of paper and the unread magazines threaten to reach the ceiling.

Sloppy people can't bear to part with anything. They give loving   5
attention to every detail. When sloppy people say they're going to
tackle the surface of the desk, they really mean it. Not a paper will go
unturned; not a rubber band will go unboxed. Four hours or two weeks
into the excavation, the desk looks exactly the same, primarily because the sloppy person is meticulously creating new piles of papers
with new headings and scrupulously stopping to read all of the old
book catalogs before he throws them away. A neat person would just
bulldoze the desk.

Neat people are bums and clods at heart. They have cavalier atti-   6
tudes toward possessions, including family heirlooms. Everything is just
another dust-catcher to them. If anything collects dust, it's got to go
and that's that. Neat people will toy with the idea of throwing the
children out of the house just to cut down on the clutter.

Neat people don't care about process. They like results. What they   7
want to do is get the whole thing over with so they can sit down and
watch the rasslin' on TV. Neat people operate on two unvarying principles: never handle any item twice, and throw everything away.

The only thing messy in a neat person's house is the trash can.   8
The minute something comes to a neat person's hand, he will look at
it, try to decide if it has immediate use and, finding none, throw it in
the trash.

Neat people are especially vicious with mail. They never go through   9
their mail unless they are standing directly over a trash can. If the trash
can is beside the mailbox, even better. All ads, catalogs, pleas for chari-
table contributions, church bulletins and money-saving coupons go
straight into the trash can without being opened. All letters from home,
postcards from Europe, bills and paychecks are opened, immediately
responded to, then dropped in the trash can. Neat people keep their
receipts only for tax purposes. That's it. No sentimental salvaging of
birthday cards or the last letter a dying relative ever wrote. Into the
trash it goes.

Neat people place neatness above everything, even economics. They   10
are incredibly wasteful. Neat people throw away several toys every time
they walk through the den. I knew a neat person once who threw away
a perfectly good dish drainer because it had mold on it. The drainer
was too much trouble to wash. And neat people sell their furniture

when they move. They will sell a La-Z-Boy recliner while you are re-
clining in it.

Neat people are no good to borrow from. Neat people buy every-   11
thing in expensive little single portions. They get their flour and sugar
in two-pound bags. They wouldn't consider clipping a coupon, saving
a leftover, reusing plastic nondairy whipped cream containers or rins-
ing off tin foil and draping it over the unmoldy dish drainer. You can
never borrow a neat person's newspaper to see what's playing at the
movies. Neat people have the paper all wadded up and in the trash by
7:05 A.M.

Neat people cut a clean swath through the organic as well as the   12
inorganic world. People, animals, and things are all one to them. They
are so insensitive. After they've finished with the pantry, the medicine
cabinet, and the attic, they will throw out the red geranium (too many
leaves), sell the dog (too many fleas), and send the children off to
boarding school (too many scuffmarks on the hardwood floors).

RESPONDING TO THE TEXT

Suzanne Britt reduces people to two types: sloppy and neat. What does she
see as the defining characteristics of each type? Do you consider yourself
a sloppy or a neat person? Perhaps you are neither. If this is the case, make up
your own category, and explain why Britt's categories are not broad enough.

ENGAGING THE WRITER'S SUBJECT

1. Why do you suppose Britt characterizes the distinction between sloppy
   and neat people as a "moral" one (paragraph 1)? What is she really poking fun at with this reference? (Glossary: *Irony*)

2. In your own words, what is the "heavenly vision," the "precise plan,"
   Britt refers to in paragraph 2? How does Britt use this idea to explain
   why sloppy people can never be neat?

3. Exaggeration, as Britt uses it, is only effective if it departs from some
   shared idea of the truth. What commonly understood ideas about
   sloppy and neat people does Britt rely on? Do you agree with her? Why
   or why not?

ANALYZING THE WRITER'S CRAFT

1. Note Britt's use of transitions as she moves from trait to trait. (Glossary:
   Transitions) How well does she use transitions to achieve unity in her
   essay? Explain.

2. One of the ways Britt achieves a sense of the ridiculous in her essay is to
   switch the commonly accepted attributes of sloppy and neat people.
   Cite examples of this technique, and discuss the ways in which it adds

to her essay. What does it reveal to the reader about her purpose in writing the essay? (Glossary: *Purpose*)

3. Britt uses block comparison to point out the differences between sloppy and neat people. Make a side-by-side list of the traits of sloppy and neat people. After reviewing your list, determine any ways in which sloppy and neat people may be similar. Why do you suppose Britt does not include any of the ways in which they are the same?

4. Why do you think Britt has chosen to use a block comparison? What would have been gained or lost had she used a point-by-point system of contrast?

5. Throughout the essay, Britt uses numerous examples to show the differences between sloppy and neat people. (Glossary: *Exemplification*) Cite five examples that Britt uses to exemplify these points. How effective do you find Britt's use of examples? What do they add to her essay of comparison and contrast?

UNDERSTANDING THE WRITER'S LANGUAGE

1. Cite examples of Britt's diction that indicate her change of tone when she is talking about either sloppy or neat people. (Glossary: *Diction; Tone*)

2. How would you characterize Britt's vocabulary in the essay — easy or difficult? What does her choice of vocabulary say about her intended audience? In which places does Britt use precise word choice to particularly good effect?

3. Refer to your desk dictionary to determine the meanings of the following words as Britt uses them in this selection: *rectitude* (paragraph 2), *tentative* (3), *meticulously* (5), *heirlooms* (6), *salvaging* (9), *swath* (12).

WRITING SUGGESTIONS

1. Write an essay in which you describe yourself as either sloppy or neat. In what ways does your behavior compare or contrast with the traits Britt offers? You may follow Britt's definition of sloppy and neat, or you may come up with your own.

2. Take some time to reflect on a relationship in your life — perhaps one with a friend, a family member, or a teacher. Write an essay in which you discuss what it is about you and that other person that makes the relationship work. You may find it helpful to think of a relationship that doesn't work to better understand why the relationship you're writing about does work. What discoveries about yourself did you make while working on this essay? Explain. (Glossary: *Description*)

3. Despite what Britt claims, neat people are often considered to be well mannered, while sloppy people are considered to be rude or to have poor manners. In your college library and on the Internet, research the history or function of manners (manners are also known as *etiquette*).

Write an essay on the topic of etiquette; you might want to argue that etiquette is important or that it is not as important as some people think. (Glossary: *Argument*) You might also consider writing an essay on the etiquette of cyberspace (often referred to as *netiquette*).

- To begin your research online, go to **bedfordstmartins.com /subjectsstrategies** and click on "Comparison and Contrast" or browse the thematic directory of annotated links.

SEEING/READING

Macs and PCs Have Never Been So Compatible

Microsoft

CONNECTING IMAGE AND TEXT

One of the raps against Macs has been the nagging question of compatibility — "Will my PC software and files work on a Mac?" The validity of this bad rap continues to be debated by PC- and Mac-lovers alike. How do you "read" this Microsoft Office advertisement, which appeared in *Wired* magazine in November 2003? How does the ad address the concept of compatibility? What statement, if any, does the ad make about "Mac people" and "PC people"? About identity and life in the twenty-first century? What are some of the "telling" details in this photograph, and how do they work to support the print message? Your observations will help guide you to the key themes and strategies in the essay that follows.

Mac or PC: There Is Simply No Comparison!

Del Miller

Del Miller was born in 1945 in Waynesville, Missouri. He earned his B.S. in mechanical engineering from the University of Missouri in 1977 and has spent the past twenty-five years in a variety of engineering, sales and marketing, and management positions. He lives in Southern California, and in his spare time designs sensing equipment for materials-testing applications. Miller's experiences with computers led to his writing articles about Apple's Macintosh, the computer platform he favors. Since 1998 Miller's pieces have appeared regularly in the "Difference Engine" column at MacOpinion.com and the "Abacus" column at AppleLinks.com.

In "Mac or PC: There Is Simply No Comparison!," first published by MacOpinion.com on July 25, 2003, Miller uses comparison and contrast to address the question "Why don't more people buy Macintosh?" His answer might surprise you.

PREPARING TO READ
The Mac vs. PC debate has raged for decades, with each side claiming superiority. Do you consider yourself a "Mac person" or a "PC person": that is, have you been using your computer system long enough to establish what might be called a "relationship" with your machine? Or do you not have a preference or use whichever system is available to you? Would you ever consider using another computer system or one system over the other? Why or why not?

Why don't more people buy Macintosh? Mac fans ask this question all the time it seems, in spite of the fact that each asking prompts a cornucopia of helpful and often not so helpful answers. Perhaps the old saying applies: "When you have lots of different answers, it means none of them are very good."

Sure, there's probably some validity to everyone's take on the matter. If somebody says Macs are too expensive then that represents at least one data point on the chart. If another claims there is no software for the Macintosh, you can assume that at least someone couldn't find a specific program on the shelf. Others mention lack of upgradeability, the cost of replacing PC software, compatibility or some other reason — and these all likely have some basis in reality.

But for those of us who have been using the Macintosh for lo these many years, these reasons don't ring quite true. We inhabit the same planet as the critics, yet we have happily and productively used Apple computers and find that, whatever anyone else says, these drawbacks either don't seem to exist or else are insignificant in light of all the advantages the Macintosh returns.

When I look around at what the bulk of the computing public actually uses their computer for, I see absolutely no reason why a significant portion of them couldn't switch to the Macintosh tomorrow and be perfectly pleased with the results.

Now I'm not talking about the Slashdotters and the Ars-onists and Tom's Hardwarriors and the denizens of other, technical computer forums spread across the internet. Many of these folks might actually have requirements, or at least some unrequited desire, for computing specifications that disfavor the Mac. These guys and gals (OK, mostly guys) might be programmers or engineers, or at least power users grown up in a system that really doesn't lend itself to an Apple solution. For some of them the economics of web serving or system administration might cause them to conclude that the Macintosh doesn't meet their needs. Debatable points for sure.

But if you take all of these technically oriented people and add up their numbers, they wouldn't amount to a significant fraction of the consumer market for computers. Apple could easily grow its customer base tenfold without needing a single computer enthusiast to change his stripes. No, the enormous consumer market is composed of ordinary folks for whom a Macintosh would be a perfectly fine home computer, and many of them would actually be happier with a Mac.

Consumers don't care about bus topology or whether the RAM is double data rate or not. They don't know what a SPEC benchmark is, and I doubt most could tell you the clock rate of their CPU. What they do want is for their computer to serve their needs and not break. They want it to be a good value. For this, Macintoshes positively shine.

SO WHY DON'T MORE CONSUMERS BUY MACINTOSH?

The consumers that make up the pig-in-the-python part of the bell curve primarily use a web browser and an email client and they aren't terribly picky about either one. Good grief, millions use the AOL browser, so how demanding could they be? These people don't wait up for the nightly Mozilla builds to make sure they are operating with the latest browser technology, or fuss at length about some obscure email feature so that Aunt Edna knows how the kids are doing.

What else does the average Joe need for his computing pleasure? A word processor, of course, but Microsoft Word works just fine on a Macintosh, and even that is such extravagant overkill for most people as to be comical. The typical person doesn't need, use, or is even aware of annotations, style sheets, or ninety percent of the bells and whistles that Word offers. The functionality needed by all but a few people is available for free with Appleworks, which can open and save Word documents anyway.

Excel? Please. Excel is a wonderful program and I'm a bona fide power user. But the percentage of people that make use of even a fraction of Excel's features disappears into the demographic haze. Appleworks' spreadsheet would do practically everyone just fine.

Tax programs? The Macs got 'em. Drawing programs? The same. You can go down the list for days and the answer is nearly always identical — the Macintosh can easily do what the majority of computer users need it to do, and can do it as well as any PC and ofttimes better.

But wait, what about the cost of replacing all those Windows programs with Macintosh equivalents? Apple bundles all kinds of nifty software with each iMac, software of just the sort that a consumer needs. For most people additional software expense is not necessary because the really necessary stuff comes with the computer — for free. Specialty software is most often available for a cross-platform upgrade fee and generally speaking, if you need to upgrade your computer it's probably time to upgrade your most treasured software. Besides, the average consumer doesn't use Photoshop or AutoCad or really pricy programs anyway. There just isn't that much they need to upgrade.

GAMES

But then there's games, and we all know that the hot new games come out first and sometimes only for PCs. This is seen by many as the reason why Macintoshes can't break out of their niche. But this doesn't really make a lot of sense either.

Now I know that many of you might find this astoundingly difficult to believe, but there are a huge number of people who do *not* play computer games — really, it's true. These sad cases do other things with their lives besides run mazes and shoot demons. 'Tis a pity, I know, but for these people the vast arsenal of PC games holds no attraction.

Of the households who do play computer games close to half of 15
them have a console for the purpose. If you have a Playstation in the
house, you might as well have a Macintosh as your computer. Besides,
it's not like there isn't a very large assortment of games for the Macintosh as well.

In other words, over half the households in the United States, and 16
a significantly higher percentage worldwide, don't need a rip-snorting
PC to play games. If even a tiny fraction of these people chose a Macintosh it could triple Apple's market share.

MONEY

And we all know that Macintoshes are more expensive than PCs. Well 17
not exactly: It is more accurate to say that Apple machines are more
competitive in some price ranges and in some configurations than in
others. But for an all-purpose computer with the features and qualities
that many households would find both useful and attractive, the iMac
or an eMac is hard to beat.

Now, anyone can look up some vendor's pricelists and construct a 18
comparison that shows whatever one wants to show. This game is constantly played on bulletin board battlegrounds all over the web, and
I'll not try to settle this issue here.

Did your next-door neighbors buy the cheapest car on the lot? 19
Did they buy their clothes at a thrift store? Probably not. In fact, if
you look around you'll see that people will consistently pay more for a
better experience — it is the rule not the exception. There's no reason
to believe that consumers would avoid the Mac because of price, if
they thought it would serve them better.

Suffice it to say that there are a vast number of consumers that 20
have no particular need to choose a PC over a Macintosh. Going a bit
further let's say there is a significant fraction that would actually be
happier with a Mac if they would only give it a try. So what keeps
them from choosing Apple?

SO WHY DON'T MORE PEOPLE
BUY MACINTOSH?

The answer is simply this: People don't even look at the Macintosh as 21
an option.

When the typical consumer decides to buy a new computer, the 22
Macintosh is seldom even considered — *there is simply no comparison*
performed.

I've seen it dozens of times: A friend or relative mentions buying a   23
computer and describes a range of uses that almost define a Macintosh. So I ask, "Have you considered looking at a Mac?"

The reply is . . . well, there isn't a reply, generally. What I nor-   24
mally get is a slight frown and a glazed eyeball, wary expression of
something like incomprehension; as if I had suggested that they smear
butter all over their bodies.

There is seldom a defineable objection and certainly not a rea-   25
soned and knowledgeable discussion of the technical merits of the
Windows operating system. The decision to buy the PC has nothing
to do with a purchasing matrix, and even if Macintoshes were cheaper
than PCs, had higher clock rates, included every piece of software the
buyer would ever need, and vacuumed the rug every Saturday, the decision would still be the same.

No, for most people, the Macintosh is just not a consideration. In   26
the eyes of the masses, a computer is perceived as something like what
sits on their desk at work, or what their brother-in-law Elroy has. A
computer has a **Start** button.

SIMPLY NO COMPARISON

I laugh when I hear people suggest that Apple should change its adver-   27
tising to focus on features and specifications. Sure, four percent of the
population would really care about such things, while the rest would
slip into a mild coma. For the biggest chunk of the consumer market,
there is simply no comparison performed of any kind and a technical description as long as your arm isn't going to sell computers if no one
bothers to compare the data.

So how does Apple convince a non-technical, risk-averse, late-   28
adopting, reluctant-to-compare public to seriously consider switching
to a Macintosh?

Apple Computer's "Switch" campaign was designed to get the   29
public's attention and to simply open their minds to the possibility of
buying a Macintosh. The message is, "Buy a Mac and you'll be happy."
In the final analysis, that's what people really want.

Those Apple retail stores weren't located in the fancy-shmancy   30
shopping malls by accident either. Those are the venues where people
shop for the finer things, and Apple is trying to make that association
crystal clear.

"The Digital Hub" is pushed as a lifestyle enhancer, something for   31
which people generally have a soft spot in their wallet. This, like the
rest of Apple's marketing scheme, is not about competing feature for
feature against PCs, it's a flank attack on the psychology of a buying
public that is reluctant to compare.

But will it work? The latest market-share numbers seem to say no, 32
but it's still early in the game. If the public begins to embrace Apple's
suggestion that they will be happier with a Macintosh, the numbers
should start to turn around within the next year.

If so, then Apple's marketing campaign will be taught in business 33
schools for the next fifty years.

RESPONDING TO THE TEXT

What is your opinion of Apple's "Switch" advertising campaign? What is the
thrust of this campaign? Would you be more likely to buy a computer
whose advertising focused on the user's experience or on technical features
and specifications? Explain.

ENGAGING THE WRITER'S SUBJECT

1. What are some reasons people give for not buying a Mac? How do Mac
users dismiss these drawbacks?

2. What group of computer users does Miller target as potential Mac buyers?
What makes him think the Mac is a good computer for these people?

3. According to Miller, what are the basic needs of the average computer
user? How does Miller support his claim that "the Macintosh can easily
do what the majority of computer users need it to do, and can do it as
well as any PC and ofttimes better" (paragraph 11)?

4. According to Miller, how does the American public buy computers?
What does he say is the real answer to the question "Why don't more
people buy Macintosh?"

5. What were your expectations when you read Miller's title? (Glossary:
Title) What does the title mean to you after reading his article? Explain.

ANALYZING THE WRITER'S CRAFT

1. What is Miller's purpose in writing this essay? (Glossary: *Purpose*) Do
you think he accomplishes what he sets out to? Explain.

2. Who is Miller's audience? (Glossary: *Audience*) What is his attitude toward his subject? (Glossary: *Attitude*) What in his essay led you to these
conclusions?

3. Miller does not provide readers with a long list of comparable features
and specifications for Macs and PCs. On what points does Miller compare Macs and PCs? How does he organize his comparison? (Glossary:
Organization)

UNDERSTANDING THE WRITER'S LANGUAGE

1. Explain Miller's "pig-in-the-python" metaphor in paragraph 8. (Glossary: *Figures of Speech*)

2. How would you describe Miller's diction in this essay? (Glossary: *Diction*) Did you find his language overly technical? If so, point out examples of his use of computer jargon. (Glossary: *Technical Language*)

3. Refer to your desk dictionary to determine the meanings of the following words as Miller uses them in this selection: *cornucopia* (paragraph 1), *unrequited* (5), *topology* (7), *bell curve* (8), *functionality* (9), *ofttimes* (11), *market share* (16), *seldom* (22).

WRITING SUGGESTIONS

1. What role do computers play in your day-to-day life as a student? Do you take class notes on a computer? Do you e-mail professors and classmates? Do you use the Internet to do research? Using examples from your own experiences and observations, write an essay in which you compare and contrast what your life as a student would be like with and without a computer. What school tasks require a computer? What school tasks would you be able to complete just as easily without a computer? Are computers indispensable tools for today's students? Why or why not?

2. Many educators question whether computers, the Internet, and dot-com-based learning services actually result in a better education than students received a hundred years ago. As Thomas L. Friedman writes in "My Favorite Teacher" (p. 9), "The real secret of success in the information age is what it always was: fundamentals — reading, writing and arithmetic, church, synagogue and mosque, the rule of law and good governance" (paragraph 10). Do you agree? Why or why not? Does technology provide quick and easy access to useful information or blur our vision with "information smog"? Is always being "plugged in" a good or bad thing? Why? In your opinion, is technology a tool or a crutch? Why? Drawing on your own experiences and observations, write an essay in which you argue for or against technology-based education. (Glossary: *Argument*) Before you write, you might find it helpful to refer to your Connecting Image and Text response for this selection.

3. Bill Gates, Steve Jobs, and Stephen Wozniak are three major figures in the world of computers. What do you know about these three men? In preparation for writing an essay about the contributions one of them has made to the computer and technology industries, conduct some research in your college library and on the Internet. How did the person you chose first get into the computer business? What enabled him to climb to the top of the industry? What is he most likely to be remembered for?

• To begin your research online, go to **bedfordstmartins.com/subjectsstrategies** and click on "Comparison and Contrast" or browse the thematic directory of annotated links.

Crazy Horse and Custer as Young Warriors

Stephen E. Ambrose

A prolific and highly regarded writer of American history, Stephen E. Ambrose (1936–2002) was born in Decatur, Illinois, and grew up in Whitewater, Wisconsin. His lifelong interest in history took root during his undergraduate years at the University of Wisconsin, where he earned his B.A. in 1957 and Ph.D. in 1963. Ambrose wrote extensively about the American Civil War, presidents Dwight D. Eisenhower and Richard Nixon, World War II, and Lewis and Clark's expedition to the American West. The author of more than twenty-five books, his best-sellers include Eisenhower: Soldier, General of the Army, President-Elect, 1890–1952 *(1983);* D-Day: June 6, 1944: The Climactic Battle of World War II *(1994);* Undaunted Courage: Meriwether Lewis, Thomas Jefferson, and the Owning of the American West *(1996);* Citizen Soldiers: The U.S. Army from the Normandy Beaches to the Bulge to the Surrender of Germany, June 7, 1944–May 7, 1945 *(1997); and* Lewis and Clark: Voyage of Discovery *(1998).*

The following essay first appeared as a chapter in Ambrose's book Crazy Horse and Custer: The Parallel Lives of Two American Warriors *(1975). Here Ambrose uses comparison and contrast to bring into focus the similarities between these two different young men as well as the cultures they represent.*

PREPARING TO READ

Every culture and every generation has its own heroes. Who are your heroes, and why do you hold these people in such high esteem? Explain.

C uster did not look like a Sioux chieftain, no matter what the news- papers said, nor did he think or act like one. To describe him as such, even though he rather liked the description and saved the clipping, only revealed how little the Americans understood Indians. The phrase also indicated the gap between reality and romance in Custer's Civil War. It was pure romance to describe him as anything other than what he was, a young soldier who had led a series of charges, most of them successful and all of them bloody, against an outgunned and outnumbered opponent. By one Sioux test — bravery — Custer had covered himself with honors, but by another Sioux test — bringing home the loot with minimal losses — he was a miserable failure. For the Sioux, reality was life, not fame and power. For Custer, the reverse was true — fame and power were real, while life was cheap. "To promotion — or death!" always continued to be his watchword.

Crazy Horse, judged by white standards, was also a failure. His bravery was there for all to see and earned him his promotion to shirt-wearer. But he could not hold his fighting men together, could not make them act as a unit, could not inspire them to carry out a sustained campaign, could not obey orders himself.

It was bravery, above and beyond all other qualities, that Custer and Crazy Horse had in common. Each man was an outstanding warrior in war-mad societies. Thousands upon thousands of Custer's fellow whites had as much opportunity as he did to demonstrate their courage, just as all of Crazy Horse's associates had countless opportunities to show that they equaled him in bravery. But no white warrior, save his younger brother, Tom, could outdo Custer, just as no Indian warrior, save his younger brother, Little Hawk, could outdo Crazy Horse. And for both white and red societies, no masculine virtue was more admired than bravery. To survive, both societies felt they had to have men willing to put their lives on the line. For men who were willing to do so, no reward was too great, even though there were vast differences in the way each society honored its heroes.

Beyond their bravery, Custer and Crazy Horse were individualists, each standing out from the crowd in his separate way. Custer wore outlandish uniforms, let his hair fall in long, flowing golden locks across his shoulders, surrounded himself with pet animals and admirers, and in general did all he could to draw attention to himself. Crazy Horse's individualism pushed him in an opposite direction — he wore a single feather in his hair when going into battle, rather than a war bonnet. Custer's vast energy set him apart from most of his fellows; the Sioux distinguished Crazy Horse from other warriors because of Crazy Horse's quietness and introspection. Both men lived in societies in which drugs, especially alcohol, were widely used, but neither Custer nor Crazy Horse drank. Most of all, of course, each man stood out in battle as a great risk taker.

Custer's men went into battle in uniform, perhaps partly so that they could not be told apart. Any single soldier, it was hoped, would act just as would any other soldier in the same situation. Crazy Horse's men went into battle in the most extreme, individualistic manner possible, painting weird figures all over their bodies and their horses, so that they would stand out as individuals; an observer, they hoped, would be able to pick them out from among a hundred other warriors. Both Custer and Crazy Horse led by example, but Custer knew that his men would follow because they were disciplined, while Crazy Horse could only hope that his example would suffice to get the warriors to follow him.

But if Custer's society gave him invaluable aid in his leadership role   6
by making certain that his men would do what he told them to do, it
also thrust upon him an enormous responsibility. At age twenty-four,
he was in command of a body of troops that outnumbered the warrior
population of the entire Sioux tribe. He was responsible for their well-
being, their organization, their battle tactics, their behavior, and much
else. Crazy Horse had no comparable experience; as a young warrior
promoted to shirt-wearer he assumed certain duties and made stringent vows, but he was not responsible for his warriors to any degree as
Custer was for his soldiers.

Which was one reason Custer got more rewards than Crazy Horse.   7
Both men fought for prestige, although in Crazy Horse's case it was
prestige for its own sake, while in Custer's case the prestige led to additional power. Until the very end Crazy Horse never had real power
over other men. Nor did his great prestige lead to additional material
comforts; indeed, in accord with his sworn oath, Crazy Horse had less
of those than did the majority of his tribesmen. Custer's camp life was
much more comfortable than that of his soldiers, but his real goals were
power and fame. He wanted power for its own sake, not to use to
bring about some reform or revolution, as Custer was in perfect agreement with the prevailing structure and ideology of his society and had
no intention of changing it in any way.

Least of all did Custer want any change in the status of women.   8
Like Crazy Horse, he regarded women as inferior, mentally as well as
physically, and treated them almost as a species of property. Custer
expected Libbie to devote her life, her time, her talents, and her energy to him, just as Crazy Horse would have expected the same from
Black Buffalo Woman had things worked out between them. This attitude, of course, was precisely that held by both red and white societies and by the women themselves. Both societies were sufficiently
flexible and realistic to allow such young men as Custer and Crazy
Horse, each from a modest background, to assume leadership roles, but
made absolutely no provision for any woman of any age or ability to
assume any institutionalized leadership position. A patriarchy is a patriarchy, whether civilized or primitive, and patriarchs think alike about
women.

But not about other things. Custer embraced ambition; Crazy   9
Horse hardly knew ambition at all. Custer worked hard, driving himself to get ahead. He never really relaxed — even his entertainment
had to have a purpose beyond the immediate moment. Thus, in his
social life, he chose his friends on the basis of what they could do for
him, not how well he got along with them, much less liked them.
Crazy Horse hardly worked at all — as Claude Lévi-Strauss points out,
the notion that savages have to struggle for their existence is not

altogether correct. Certainly Crazy Horse and his friends did not have to struggle — two or three successful buffalo hunts a year, plus some occasional sporadic hunting for other game, was sufficient to feed and shelter the tribe. Three or four war parties per year might set out from Crazy Horse's village, although by no means would he go on every expedition. The rest of the time Crazy Horse, like other Sioux men, enjoyed himself, courting girls, talking, sleeping, telling stories.

There were obvious vast differences between the two men, but at bottom they shared a fundamental trait. Both were aggressive. As a hunter Crazy Horse killed for a living; as a soldier, so did Custer. Both found the rush of hot, fresh blood exciting. Both would take great personal risks to make the blood flow. Crazy Horse was most completely himself when he rode pell-mell into a herd of buffalo, shooting his arrows clear through the beasts, or when he charged the enemy alone and unaided, or when during a winter hunt he drove a herd of elk out of a valley and into the deep drifts, then, on snow-shoes, caught them and moved quickly from one elk to the next, cutting their throats as he proceeded, the bright red blood spurting out to cover him and the snow. Custer was most completely himself when on a hunt, or when he led his troops with a whoop and a shout on a charge into the heart of the enemy lines, cutting and thrusting with his saber, his horse falling beneath him, the band playing, and the newspaper correspondents watching. Neither man hated his enemy, nor did either man fight for a cause. They fought for honors and because their societies expected them to fight, and in Custer's case for personal power and fame. But the overriding reason they fought was that they enjoyed it. As a result, they both became heroes.

RESPONDING TO THE TEXT

What was the most interesting aspect of Ambrose's comparison between Crazy Horse and Custer? Did anything about these two figures surprise you? Did you learn something new?

ENGAGING THE WRITER'S SUBJECT

1. When judged by the standards of each other's culture, how were Crazy Horse and Custer both failures?

2. What does Ambrose see as the essential similarities between Crazy Horse and Custer? Between their respective cultures?

3. What conclusions does Ambrose draw about Crazy Horse and Custer as a result of his comparison?

ANALYZING THE WRITER'S CRAFT

1. How does the sentence "Each man was an outstanding warrior in war-mad societies" (paragraph 3) serve to control and direct the content of Ambrose's essay? (Glossary: *Thesis*)

2. How has Ambrose organized his essay? (Glossary: *Organization*) Does he use a block or point-by-point organization, or some combination of the two? You might find it helpful to create a scratch outline in answering this question.

3. What transitional devices does Ambrose use to move smoothly between paragraphs? (Glossary: *Transitions*) Identify a representative example of each device.

4. In paragraph 9 Ambrose enumerates a number of key differences between Crazy Horse and Custer. Why do you suppose he doesn't devote more than this paragraph to the "vast differences between the two men" (paragraph 10)?

5. Identify the physical details about Crazy Horse and Custer that Ambrose includes in his essay. (Glossary: *Description*) How do these details strengthen his comparison and contrast?

UNDERSTANDING THE WRITER'S LANGUAGE

1. Ambrose's focus in this essay is on Crazy Horse and Custer as "young warriors." What words does he use to enhance his description of each man as a warrior? What connotations do these words have for you? (Glossary: *Connotation/Denotation*) Why do you suppose he chose the word *warrior* and not *leader*? Explain.

2. Ambrose was a writer of history that appeals to a wide audience. He was also a scholar. How would you describe Ambrose's tone in this essay? (Glossary: *Tone*) Is it academic, conversational, or a balance of the two? What in his diction leads you to this conclusion? (Glossary: *Diction*)

3. Refer to your desk dictionary to determine the meanings of the following words as Ambrose uses them in this selection: *romance* (paragraph 1), *miserable* (1), *outlandish* (4), *stringent* (6), *prestige* (7), *patriarchy* (8), *sporadic* (9), *pell-mell* (10).

WRITING SUGGESTIONS

1. Crazy Horse and Custer were leaders in their respective societies, but as Ambrose tells us, their leadership styles differed. What different styles of leadership have you observed in political, business, religious, or educational leaders? What impressed or failed to impress you about the different styles these people used? Write an essay in which you compare and contrast two or more leadership styles with the purpose of highlighting the strengths of each.

2. Ideas of what makes a hero are as numerous as there are people. Write an essay in which you define what a hero is to you. (Glossary: *Definition*)

In your mind, must a hero be someone famous? Rich? Brave? Must a hero be a man or woman? A child or an adult? A person or an animal? An individual or a group? Must a hero be someone who saves lives? Shows extraordinary physical strength? Has great mental ability? Before you write, you might find it helpful to refer to your Preparing to Read response for this selection.

3. Using Ambrose's essay as a model, write an essay in which you compare and contrast two world leaders, sports figures, or celebrities who — like Crazy Horse and Custer — were alive and active at the same time or whose careers crossed in a dramatic or decisive way. Consider, for example, John F. Kennedy and Richard Nixon, Serena Williams and Lindsay Davenport, Sir Thomas Moore and Henry VIII, Bill Clinton and Ken Starr, Biggie Smalls and Tupac Shakur, George W. Bush and Saddam Hussein, Bette Davis and Joan Crawford, or two people of your own choosing. Research your two famous people in your college library and on the Internet.

• To begin your research online, go to **bedfordstmartins.com /subjectsstrategies** and click on "Comparison and Contrast" or browse the thematic directory of annotated links.

Sex, Lies, and Conversation

Deborah Tannen

Deborah Tannen, professor of linguistics at Georgetown University, was born in 1945 in Brooklyn, New York. Tannen received her B.A. in English from the State University of New York at Binghamton in 1966 and taught English in Greece until 1968. She then earned an M.A. in English literature from Wayne State University in 1970. While pursuing her Ph.D. in linguistics at the University of California–Berkeley, she received several prizes for her poetry and short fiction. Her work has appeared in New York *magazine,* Vogue, *and the* New York Times Magazine. *In addition, she has authored three best-selling language books:* You Just Don't Understand *(1990),* That's Not What I Meant *(1991), and* Talking from Nine to Five *(1994). The success of these books attests to the public's interest in language, especially when it pertains to gender differences. Tannen's most recent books include* The Argument Culture: Stopping America's War of Words *(1998) and* I Only Say This Because I Love You: Talking to Your Parents, Partners, Sibs, and Kids When You're All Adults *(2000).*

In this essay, which first appeared in the Washington Post *in 1990, Tannen examines the differences between men's and women's public and private speech. Interestingly, she concludes that cross-gender conversation, when seen as cross-cultural communication, "allows us to understand the problem and forge solutions without blaming either party."*

PREPARING TO READ

How important is it for people to be aware of gender and cultural differences when interacting with others? What are some of the potential benefits of such awareness?

I was addressing a small gathering in a suburban Virginia living room — a women's group that had invited men to join them. Throughout the evening, one man had been particularly talkative, frequently offering ideas and anecdotes, while his wife sat silently beside him on the couch. Toward the end of the evening, I commented that women frequently complain that their husbands don't talk to them. This man quickly concurred. He gestured toward his wife and said, "She's the talker in our family." The room burst into laughter; the man looked puzzled and hurt. "It's true," he explained. "When I come home from work I have nothing to say. If she didn't keep the conversation going, we'd spend the whole evening in silence." 1

This episode crystallizes the irony that although American men tend to talk more than women in public situations, they often talk less at home. And this pattern is wreaking havoc with marriage. 2

The pattern was observed by political scientist Andrew Hacker in 3
the late '70s. Sociologist Catherine Kohler Riessman reports in her new
book *Divorce Talk* that most of the women she interviewed — but only
a few of the men — gave lack of communication as the reason for
their divorces. Given the current divorce rate of nearly 50 percent,
that amounts to millions of cases in the United States every year — a
virtual epidemic of failed conversation.

In my own research, complaints from women about their hus- 4
bands most often focused not on tangible inequities such as having
given up the chance for a career to accompany a husband to his, or
doing far more than their share of daily life-support work like cleaning, cooking, social arrangements, and errands. Instead, they focused
on communication: "He doesn't listen to me," "He doesn't talk to
me." I found, as Hacker observed years before, that most wives want
their husbands to be, first and foremost, conversational partners, but
few husbands share this expectation of their wives.

In short, the image that best represents the current crisis is the ste- 5
reotypical cartoon scene of a man sitting at the breakfast table with a
newspaper held up in front of his face, while a woman glares at the
back of it, wanting to talk.

LINGUISTIC BATTLE OF THE SEXES

How can women and men have such different impressions of commu- 6
nication in marriage? Why the widespread imbalance in their interests
and expectations?

In the April issue of *American Psychologist*, Stanford University's 7
Eleanor Maccoby reports the results of her own and others' research
showing that children's development is most influenced by the social
structure of peer interactions. Boys and girls tend to play with children of their own gender, and their sex-separate groups have different
organizational structures and interactive norms.

I believe these systematic differences in childhood socialization 8
make talk between women and men like cross-cultural communication, heir to all the attraction and pitfalls of that enticing but difficult
enterprise. My research on men's and women's conversations uncov-
ered patterns similar to those described for children's groups.

For women, as for girls, intimacy is the fabric of relationships, 9
and talk is the thread from which it is woven. Little girls create and
maintain friendships by exchanging secrets; similarly, women regard
conversation as the cornerstone of friendship. So a woman expects her
husband to be a new and improved version of a best friend. What is
important is not the individual subjects that are discussed but the

sense of closeness, of a life shared, that emerges when people tell their thoughts, feelings, and impressions.

Bonds between boys can be as intense as girls', but they are based less on talking, more on doing things together. Since they don't assume talk is the cement that binds a relationship, men don't know what kind of talk women want, and they don't miss it when it isn't there. 10

Boys' groups are larger, more inclusive, and more hierarchical, so boys must struggle to avoid the subordinate position in the group. This may play a role in women's complaints that men don't listen to them. Some men really don't like to listen, because being the listener makes them feel one-down, like a child listening to adults or an employee to a boss. 11

But often when women tell men, "You aren't listening," and the men protest, "I am," the men are right. The impression of not listening results from misalignments in the mechanics of conversation. The misalignment begins as soon as a man and a woman take physical positions. This became clear when I studied videotapes made by psychologist Bruce Dorval of children and adults talking to their same-sex best friends. I found that at every age, the girls and women faced each other directly, their eyes anchored on each other's faces. At every age, the boys and men sat at angles to each other and looked elsewhere in the room, periodically glancing at each other. They were obviously attuned to each other, often mirroring each other's movements. But the tendency of men to face away can give women the impression they aren't listening even when they are. A young woman in college was frustrated: Whenever she told her boyfriend she wanted to talk to him, he would lie down on the floor, close his eyes, and put his arm over his face. This signaled to her, "He's taking a nap." But he insisted he was listening extra hard. Normally, he looks around the room, so he is easily distracted. Lying down and covering his eyes helped him concentrate on what she was saying. 12

Analogous to the physical alignment that women and men take in conversation is their topical alignment. The girls in my study tended to talk at length about one topic, but the boys tended to jump from topic to topic. The second-grade girls exchanged stories about people they knew. The second-grade boys teased, told jokes, noticed things in the room, and talked about finding games to play. The sixth-grade girls talked about problems with a mutual friend. The sixth-grade boys talked about 55 different topics, none of which extended over more than a few turns. 13

LISTENING TO BODY LANGUAGE

Switching topics is another habit that gives women the impression men aren't listening, especially if they switch to a topic about themselves. 14

But the evidence of the 10th-grade boys in my study indicates otherwise. The 10th-grade boys sprawled across their chairs with bodies parallel and eyes straight ahead, rarely looking at each other. They looked as if they were riding in a car, staring out the windshield. But they were talking about their feelings. One boy was upset because a girl had told him he had a drinking problem, and the other was feeling alienated from all his friends.

Now, when a girl told a friend about a problem, the friend responded by asking probing questions and expressing agreement and understanding. But the boys dismissed each other's problems. Todd assured Richard that his drinking was "no big problem" because "sometimes you're funny when you're off your butt." And when Todd said he felt left out, Richard responded, "Why should you? You know more people than me."

Women perceive such responses as belittling and unsupportive. But the boys seemed satisfied with them. Whereas women reassure each other by implying, "You shouldn't feel bad because I've had similar experiences," men do so by implying, "You shouldn't feel bad because your problems aren't so bad."

There are even simpler reasons for women's impression that men don't listen. Linguist Lynette Hirschman found that women make more listener-noise, such as "mhm," "uhuh," and "yeah," to show "I'm with you." Men, she found, more often give silent attention. Women who expect a stream of listener-noise interpret silent attention as no attention at all.

Women's conversational habits are as frustrating to men as men's are to women. Men who expect silent attention interpret a stream of listener-noise as overreaction or impatience. Also, when women talk to each other in a close, comfortable setting, they often overlap, finish each other's sentences, and anticipate what the other is about to say. This practice, which I call "participatory listenership," is often perceived by men as interruption, intrusion, and lack of attention.

A parallel difference caused a man to complain about his wife, "She just wants to talk about her own point of view. If I show her another view, she gets mad at me." When most women talk to each other, they assume a conversationalist's job is to express agreement and support. But many men see their conversational duty as pointing out the other side of an argument. This is heard as disloyalty by women, and refusal to offer the requisite support. It is not that women don't want to see other points of view, but that they prefer them phrased as suggestions and inquiries rather than as direct challenges.

In his book *Fighting for Life*, Walter Ong points out that men use "agonistic" or warlike, oppositional formats to do almost anything; thus discussion becomes debate, and conversation a competitive sport. In contrast, women see conversation as a ritual means of establishing rapport. If Jane tells a problem and June says she has a similar one, they walk away feeling closer to each other. But this attempt at establishing rapport can backfire when used with men. Men take too literally women's ritual "troubles talk," just as women mistake men's ritual challenges for real attack.

THE SOUNDS OF SILENCE

These differences begin to clarify why women and men have such different expectations about communication in marriage. For women, talk creates intimacy. Marriage is an orgy of closeness: you can tell your feelings and thoughts, and still be loved. Their greatest fear is being pushed away. But men live in a hierarchical world, where talk maintains independence and status. They are on guard to protect themselves from being put down and pushed around. [21]

This explains the paradox of the talkative man who said of his silent wife, "She's the talker." In the public setting of a guest lecture, he felt challenged to show his intelligence and display his understanding of the lecture. But at home, where he has nothing to prove and no one to defend against, he is free to remain silent. For his wife, being home means she is free from the worry that something she says might offend someone, or spark disagreement, or appear to be showing off; at home she is free to talk. [22]

The communication problems that endanger marriage can't be fixed by mechanical engineering. They require a new conceptual framework about the role of talk in human relationships. Many of the psychological explanations that have become second nature may not be helpful, because they tend to blame either women (for not being assertive enough) or men (for not being in touch with their feelings). A sociolinguistic approach by which male–female conversation is seen as cross-cultural communication allows us to understand the problem and forge solutions without blaming either party. [23]

Once the problem is understood, improvement comes naturally, as it did to the young woman and her boyfriend who seemed to go to sleep when she wanted to talk. Previously, she had accused him of not listening, and he had refused to change his behavior, since that would be admitting fault. But then she learned about and explained to him the differences in women's and men's habitual ways of aligning themselves in conversation. The next time she told him she wanted to talk, he began, as usual, by lying down and covering his eyes. When the familiar negative reaction bubbled up, she reassured herself that he really was listening. But then he sat up and looked at her. Thrilled, she asked why. He said, "You like me to look at you when we talk, so I'll try to do it." Once he saw their differences as cross-cultural rather than right and wrong, he independently altered his behavior. [24]

Women who feel abandoned and deprived when their husbands   25
won't listen to or report daily news may be happy to discover their
husbands trying to adapt once they understand the place of small talk
in women's relationships. But if their husbands don't adapt, the women
may still be comforted that for men, this is not a failure of intimacy.
Accepting the difference, the wives may look to their friends or family
for that kind of talk. And husbands who can't provide it shouldn't feel
their wives have made unreasonable demands. Some couples will still
decide to divorce, but at least their decisions will be based on realistic
expectations.

In these times of resurgent ethnic conflicts, the world desperately   26
needs cross-cultural understanding. Like charity, successful cross-cultural
communication should begin at home.

RESPONDING TO THE TEXT

Consider the times in your life when you have experienced problems in conversation. Do you think that these problems might have occurred as a result
of gender or cultural differences, as Tannen explains?

ENGAGING THE WRITER'S SUBJECT

1. In paragraph 8, Tannen compares conversational problems between
   men and women to the problems of "cross-cultural communication."
   What does she mean by this comparison?

2. In paragraph 7, Tannen reports on a study that shows boys' and girls'
   conversational development follows different patterns. How does she
   think these patterns carry over into adult conversational patterns?

3. Throughout the essay, Tannen makes a conscious effort to treat both
   her male and female readers fairly. In what ways has she sought to encourage understanding rather than attach blame?

ANALYZING THE WRITER'S CRAFT

1. How does Tannen organize her essay — point-by-point or block organization? (Glossary: *Organization*) Why do you think she makes this
   choice, and is it effective?

2. In hopes of explaining conversational differences between men and
   women, Tannen employs the analogy of cross-cultural communication.
   (Glossary: *Analogy*) How well does the analogy work? Did it help you
   gain a better understanding of her topic? Explain.

3. In keeping with her role as a popularizer of linguistic research, Tannen
   assumes an informal, almost conversational tone in the essay. (Glossary:
   Tone) Why do you think she chose to keep her own experiences out of
   the essay? What could she have gained or lost by including personal experience?

4. In discussing speech differences, Tannen attempts to explain the causes of our different approaches to conversation. How does a knowledge of these causes help us better understand their effects on cross-gender conversations? Explain how Tannen's use of cause and effect strengthens her overall argument. (Glossary: *Cause and Effect Analysis*)

UNDERSTANDING THE WRITER'S LANGUAGE

1. Tannen's essay appeals to a wide audience because of her informal, conversational diction. (Glossary: *Audience; Diction*) Is there anything in her choice of words that reveals her academic background?

2. In paragraph 18, Tannen introduces her term "participatory listenership." What does she mean by it? (Glossary: *Definition*) How does Tannen's use of this term point to the larger problem of gender miscommunication?

3. Refer to your desk dictionary to determine the meanings of the following words as Tannen uses them in this selection: *fabric* (paragraph 9), *hierarchical* (11), *mechanics* (12), *rapport* (20), *paradox* (22), *framework* (23).

WRITING SUGGESTIONS

1. Write an essay modeled on Tannen's in which you analyze the characteristics of conversation she has labeled as particularly "masculine" or "feminine," using examples from your own experience. How does your own experience of what men and women do when they converse compare with Tannen's explanation?

2. Imagine that your college is considering the adoption of a course entitled "Language, Gender, and Communication." As a concerned student, position yourself to argue for or against such a course. (Glossary: *Argument*) Present your argument as an essay or as a letter to the editor of your school newspaper.

3. There are many ethnic newspapers and magazines that offer multicultural perspectives on contemporary issues. Research some of these publications; search in the library with *Ethnic Information Sources of the United States,* or look for periodicals on the Internet. Spend some time reading several of the periodicals that you find. What does the continuing popularity of these periodicals suggest about the status of cultural relations in society today? Do you think such periodicals create greater understanding or more divisions within society? Write an essay in which you explain your analysis of one or more of these periodicals.

- To begin your research online, go to **bedfordstmartins.com /subjectsstrategies** and click on "Comparison and Contrast" or browse the thematic directory of annotated links.

WRITING SUGGESTIONS FOR COMPARISON AND CONTRAST

1. Write an essay in which you compare and contrast two objects, people, or events to show at least one of the following.

   a. their important differences
   b. their significant similarities
   c. their relative value
   d. their distinctive qualities

2. Select a topic from the list that follows. Write an essay using comparison and contrast as your primary means of development. Be sure that your essay has a definite purpose and a clear direction.

   a. two methods of dieting
   b. two television situation comedies
   c. two types of summer employment
   d. two people who display different attitudes toward responsibility
   e. two restaurants
   f. two courses in the same subject area
   g. two friends who exemplify different lifestyles
   h. two network television or local news programs
   i. two professional quarterbacks
   j. two ways of studying for an exam
   k. two rooms in which you have classes
   l. two of your favorite magazines
   m. two attitudes toward death
   n. two ways to heat a home

3. Use one of the following "before and after" situations as the basis for an essay of comparison and contrast.

   a. before and after an examination
   b. before and after seeing a movie
   c. before and after reading an important book
   d. before and after dieting
   e. before and after a long trip

4. Most of us have seen something important in our lives — a person, place, or thing — undergo a significant change, either in the subject itself or in our own perception of it. Write an essay comparing and contrasting the person, place, or thing before and after the change. First, reread Mark Twain's "Two Ways of Seeing a River" in this chapter (p. 288) and Malcolm X's "Coming to an Awareness of Language" in Chapter 5 (p. 174), and then consider your topic. There are many possibilities to consider. Perhaps a bucolic vista of open fields has become a shopping mall; perhaps a favorite athletic team has gone from glory to shame; perhaps a loved one has been altered by decisions, events, or illness.

5. Interview a professor who has taught for many years at your college or university. Ask the professor to compare and contrast the college as it

was when he or she first taught there with the way it is now; encourage reminiscence and evaluation. Combine strategies of description, comparison and contrast, and possibly definition as you write your essay. (Glossary: *Definition; Description*)

6. Six of the essays in this book deal, more or less directly, with issues related to the definition, achievement, or nature of manhood in America. The essays are "How to Give Orders Like a Man" (p. 70) and "Sex, Lies, and Conversation" (p. 312), both by Deborah Tannen; "The Death of My Father" by Steve Martin (p. 130); "Crazy Horse and Custer as Young Warriors" by Steven E. Ambrose (p. 306); "How Boys Become Men" by Jon Katz (p. 444); and "Shooting an Elephant" by George Orwell (p. 635). Read these essays, and discuss with classmates the broad issues they raise. Choose one topic of particular interest to you, and study the three or four essays that seem to bear most directly on this topic. Write an essay in which you compare, contrast, and evaluate the assertions in these essays.

CHAPTER 8

Division and Classification

WHAT ARE DIVISION AND CLASSIFICATION?

Like comparison and contrast, division and classification are separate yet closely related operations. Division involves breaking down a single large unit into smaller subunits or separating a group of items into discrete categories. For example, a state government can be divided into its three main branches and even further into departments or agencies within those branches; the whole pool of registered voters in the United States can be divided among political affiliations: Democrat, Republican, independent, and so forth. Classification, on the other hand, entails placing individual items into established categories: a boxer is classified with other boxers according to weight, a movie is placed in a rating category according to content, a library book is shelved according to an elaborate system of subject codes, and a voter can be categorized according to his or her political party. Division, then, takes apart, whereas classification groups together. But even though the two processes can operate separately, writers tend to use them together.

Division can be the most effective method for making sense of one large, complex, or multifaceted entity. Consider, for example, the following passage from E. B. White's *Here Is New York*, in which he discusses New Yorkers and their city.

Division into categories occurs in the opening sentence.   There are roughly three New Yorks. There is, first, the New York of the man or woman who was born here, who takes the city for granted and accepts its size and its turbulence as natural and inevitable. Second, there is the New York of the commuter — the city that is devoured by locusts each day and spat out each night. Third, there is the New York of the person who was born somewhere else and came to New York in quest of something. Of these three trembling cities the greatest is the last — the city of final destination, the city that is a goal. It is this third city that accounts for New York's highstrung disposition, its poetical deportment, its dedication to the arts, and its incomparable achievements. Commuters give the city its tidal restlessness; natives give it solidarity and continuity; but the settlers give it passion. And whether it is a farmer arriving from Italy to set up a small grocery store in a slum, or a young girl arriving from a small town in Mississippi to escape the indignity of being observed by her neighbors, or a boy arriving from the Corn Belt with a manuscript in his suitcase and a pain in his heart, it makes no difference: each embraces New York with the intense excitement of first love, each absorbs New York with the fresh eyes of an adventurer, each generates heat and light to dwarf the Consolidated Edison Company.

Author explains the nature of people in each category.

In his opening sentences, White suggests a principle for dividing the population of New York, establishing his three categories on the basis of a person's relationship to the city. There is the New York of the native, the New York of the commuter, and the New York of the immigrant. Although White gives specific examples for only his third grouping, it is easy to see where any individual would be classified. The purpose and result of White's divisions are clear and effective. They help him make a point about the character of New York City, depicting its restlessness, its solidarity, and its passion.

In contrast to breaking a large idea into parts, classification can be used to draw connections between disparate elements based on a common category — price, for example. Often, classification is used in conjunction with another rhetorical strategy, such as comparison and contrast. Consider, for example, how in the following passage from Toni Cade Bambara's "The Lesson" she classifies a toy in F.A.O. Schwarz and other items in the $35 category to compare the relative value of things in the life of two girls, Sylvia and Sugar.

Same thing in the store. We all walkin on tiptoe and hardly touchin the games and puzzles and things. And I watched Miss Moore who is steady watchin us like she waitin for a sign. Like Mama Drewery watches the sky and sniffs the air and takes note of just how much slant is in the bird formation. Then me and Sugar bump smack into each other, so busy gazing at the toys, 'specially the sailboat. But

First mention of price

we don't laugh and go into our fat-lady bump-stomach routine. We just stare at that price tag. Then Sugar run a finger over the whole boat. And I'm jealous and want to hit her. Maybe not her, but I sure want to punch somebody in the mouth.

"Whatcha bring us here for, Miss Moore?"

"You sound angry, Sylvia. Are you mad about something?" Givin me one of them grins like she tellin a grown-up joke that never turns out to be funny. And she's lookin very closely at me like maybe she plannin to do my portrait from memory. I'm mad, but I won't give her that satisfaction. So I slouch around the store being very bored and say, "Let's go."

Me and Sugar at the back of the train watchin the tracks whizzin by large then small then getting gobbled up in the dark. I'm thinkin about this tricky toy I saw in the store. A clown that somersaults on a bar then does chin-ups just cause you yank lightly at his leg. Cost $35. I could see me askin my mother for a $35 birthday clown. "You wanna who that costs what?" she'd say, cocking her head to the side to get a better view of the hole in my head.

Classification used along with comparison and contrast

Thirty-five dollars could buy new bunk beds for Junior and Gretchen's boy. Thirty-five dollars and the whole household could go visit Grand-daddy Nelson in the country. Thirty-five dollars would pay for the rent and the piano bill too. Who are these people that spend that much for performing clowns and $1000 for toy sailboats? What kinda work they do and how they live and how come we ain't in on it?

Another example may help clarify how division and classification work hand in hand. Suppose a sociologist wants to determine whether the socioeconomic status of the people in a particular neighborhood has any influence on their voting behavior. Having decided on her purpose, the sociologist chooses as her subject the fifteen families living on Maple Street. Her goal then becomes to group these families in a way that will be relevant to her purpose. She immediately knows that she wants to divide the neighborhood in two ways: (1) according to socioeconomic status (low-income earners, middle-income earners, and high-income earners) and (2) according to voting behavior (voters and nonvoters). However, her process of division won't be complete until she can classify individual families into her various groupings.

In confidential interviews with each family, the sociologist learns first its income and then whether any member of the household has voted in a state or federal election during the last four years. Based on this information, she begins to classify each family according to her established categories and at the same time to divide the neighborhood into the subclasses crucial to her study. Her work leads her to construct the following diagram of her divisions/classifications. This diagram allows the sociologist to visualize her division and classification system and its essential components: subject, basis or principle of division, subclasses or categories, and conclusion. It is clear that her ultimate conclusion depends on her ability to work back and forth between the potential divisions or subclasses and the actual families to be classified.

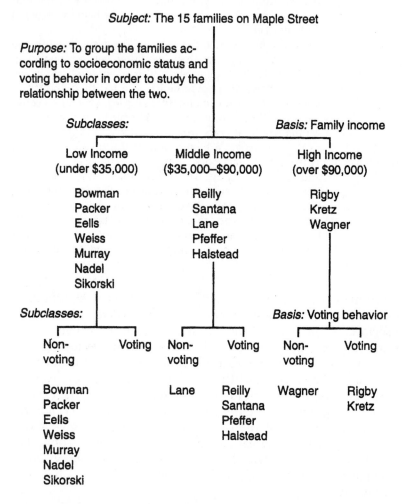

Subject: The 15 families on Maple Street

Purpose: To group the families according to socioeconomic status and voting behavior in order to study the relationship between the two.

Subclasses: *Basis:* Family income

Low Income (under $35,000)	Middle Income ($35,000–$90,000)	High Income (over $90,000)
Bowman	Reilly	Rigby
Packer	Santana	Kretz
Eells	Lane	Wagner
Weiss	Pfeffer	
Murray	Halstead	
Nadel		
Sikorski		

Subclasses: *Basis:* Voting behavior

Non-voting	Voting	Non-voting	Voting	Non-voting	Voting
Bowman		Lane	Reilly	Wagner	Rigby
Packer			Santana		Kretz
Eells			Pfeffer		
Weiss			Halstead		
Murray					
Nadel					
Sikorski					

Conclusion: On Maple Street there seems to be a relationship between socioeconomic status and voting behavior: The low-income families are nonvoters.

WHY DO WRITERS USE DIVISION AND CLASSIFICATION?

As the work of the Maple Street sociologist shows, division and classification are used primarily to demonstrate a particular point about the subject under discussion. In a paper about the emphasis a television network places on reaching various audiences, you could begin by dividing prime-time programming into suitable subclasses: shows primarily for adults, shows for families, shows for children, and so forth. You could then classify each of that network's individual programs into one of these categories. Ultimately, you would want to analyze how the programs are divided among the various categories; in this way you could make a point about which audiences the network tries hardest to reach.

Classification and division can also help to explain a broadly complicated subject by reducing it to its more manageable parts. In "How to Detect Propaganda" later in this chapter, for example, the writer identifies and classifies the many different propaganda techniques that are used to shape our opinions.

Another purpose of division and classification is to help writers and readers make choices. A voter may classify politicians on the basis of their attitudes toward nuclear energy or abortion; *Consumer Reports* classifies laptop computers on the basis of available memory, screen size, processor speed, repair record, and warranty; high school seniors classify colleges and universities on the basis of selectivity, geographic location, programs available, and tuition fees. In such cases, division and classification have an absolutely practical end: making a decision about whom to vote for, which laptop to buy, and where to apply for admission to college.

Finally, writers use division and classification as a basic organizational strategy, one that brings a sense of order to a large amorphous whole. As you'll see later in this chapter, for example, Rosalind Wiseman's system of classification in "The Queen Bee and Her Court" establishes seven categories of roles played by young girls in school cliques to help us better understand how those cliques function.

AN ANNOTATED STUDENT ESSAY USING DIVISION AND CLASSIFICATION

Gerald Cleary studied mathematics as an undergraduate and later attended law school at Cornell University. He spent his last two years of high school in West Germany as a military dependent. During that time, Cleary sold stereo equipment at a large post exchange. In this essay, Cleary has fun dividing and classifying the different types of customers he dealt with in his job.

How Loud? How Good? How Much?
How Pretty?
Gerald Cleary

As stereo equipment gets better and prices go down, stereo systems are becoming household necessities rather than luxuries. People are buying stereos by the thousands. During my year as a stereo salesman, I witnessed this boom firsthand. I dealt with hundreds of customers, and it didn't take long for me to learn that people buy stereos for different reasons. Eventually, though, I was able to divide all the stereo buyers into four basic categories: the looks buyer, the wattage buyer, the price buyer, and the quality buyer.

Introduction: Division of stereo buyers into four categories. Labels make for ease of reference.

The looks buyer cannot be bothered with the question of how her stereo will sound. Her only concern is how the stereo looks, making her the buyer least respected by the stereo salesperson. The looks buyer has an irresistible attraction to flashing lights, knobs, switches, and frivolous features. Even the loudspeakers are chosen on the basis of appearance — the looks buyer always removes the grille to make sure a couple of knobs are present. Enjoyment for her is watching the output meters flash on her amplifier, or playing with her cassette deck's remote control. No matter what component she is shopping for, the looks buyer always decides on the flashiest, exclaiming, "Wait 'til my friends see this!"

Organization: Least appealing buyer to salesperson is discussed.

Typical statement used as example

Slightly more respected is the wattage buyer, who is most easily identified by his trademark question: "How many watts does it put out?" He will not settle for less than

Organization: Second, more appealing, buyer is discussed.

1

2

3

100 watts from his amp, and his speakers must be able to handle all this power. He is interested only in the volume level his stereo can produce, for the wattage buyer always turns it up loud — so loud that most would find it painful. The wattage buyer genuinely enjoys his music — either soul or heavy metal — at this volume. He is actually proud of his stereo's ability to put out deafening noise. As a result, the wattage buyer becomes as well-known to his neighbors as he is to the salesperson. His competitive nature makes him especially obvious as he pays for his new system, telling his friend, "Man, this is gonna blow Jones's stereo away!"

Typical statement used as example

In this money-conscious world, the price buyer has the understanding, if not the respect, of the salesperson. Often, she is ashamed of her budget limitations and will try to disguise herself as one of the other types of buyers, asking, "What's the loudest receiver I can buy for $200?" Or, "What's the best turntable for under $150?" It is always obvious that price is this buyer's greatest worry — she doesn't really want the "loudest" or the "best." The price buyer can be spotted looking over the sale items or staring open-mouthed at the price tag of an expensive unit. After asking the salesperson where the best deal in the store can be found, she cringes at the standard reply: "You usually get what you pay for." But the price buyer still picks the cheapest model, telling her friends, "You won't believe the deal I got on this!"

Organization: Third, still more appealing, buyer is discussed.

Dialogue

Only one category remains: the quality buyer. He is the buyer most respected by the salesperson, although he is often not even in the store to buy — he may simply want to

Organization: Fourth, and most appealing, buyer is discussed.

4

5

listen to the new compact-disc player tested in his latest issue of <u>High Fidelity</u>. The quality buyer never buys on impulse; he has already read about and listened to any piece of equipment he finally buys. But along with high quality comes high price. The quality buyer can often be seen fingering the price tag of that noise-reduction unit he just has to own but can't yet afford. He never considers a cheaper model, preferring to wait until he can afford the high standard of quality he demands. The quality buyer shuns salespeople, believing that he knows more than they do anyway. Asking him "May I help you?" is the greatest insult of all.

Conclusion: How classifying buyers helped the author do his job

Recognizing the kind of buyer I was dealing with helped me steer her to the right corner of the store. I took looks buyers to the visually dazzling working displays, and wattage buyers into the soundproof speaker rooms. I directed price buyers to the sale items and left quality buyers alone. By the end of the year, I was able to identify the type of buyer almost instantly. My expertise paid off, making me the most successful salesperson in the store.

6

Analyzing Gerald Cleary's Essay of Division and Classification: Questions for Discussion

1. What categories does Cleary use to classify his subject? Brainstorm about other categories of stereo shoppers that might exist. Could these alternate categories be used to make a similar point?

2. How did Cleary organize the categories in his essay? Is his organization effective, or could he have chosen a better way?

3. What other strategies might Cleary have used to strengthen his essay? Be specific about the benefits of each strategy.

SUGGESTIONS FOR WRITING A DIVISION AND CLASSIFICATION ESSAY

Begin by making certain that your subject represents a single, coherent entity. To do so, you will have to set definite limits for yourself and then stick to them. For example, the sociologist whose purpose was to survey relationships between family income and voting patterns limited her study to residents of Maple Street. Including a family from Oak Street would introduce new variables: a different neighborhood, possibly different socioeconomic conditions, and so on. Not abiding by a strict set of limits upsets the established system and, consequently, suggests the need to set new limits. Similarly, if you take as your subject for classification the student body at your school, you obviously cannot include students who are visiting from somewhere else unless you first redefine your subject.

As you define your classification essay, pay particular attention to your purpose, the divisions of your subject, your organization, and your conclusion. The later processes of planning and writing will depend on your purpose and on how that purpose leads you to divide your subject.

Determine Your Purpose, and Focus on It

The principle you use to divide your subject into categories depends on your larger purpose. It is crucial, then, that you determine a clear purpose for your division and classification before you begin to examine your subject in detail. For example, in studying the student body at your school, you might have any number of purposes: to discover how much time your classmates spend in the library during the week, to explain how financial aid is distributed, to discuss the most popular movies or music on campus, to describe styles of dorm-room decor. The categories into which you divide the student body will vary according to your chosen purpose.

Let's say, for example, that you are in charge of writing an editorial for your school newspaper that will make people aware of how they might reduce the amount of trash going to the landfill. How might you approach such a task using division and classification? Having established your purpose, your next task might be to identify the different ways objects can be handled to avoid sending them to the landfill. For instance, you might decide that there are four basic ways to prevent things from ending up in the trash. Then you could establish a sequence or order of importance in which they should be addressed. Your first draft might start something like the following.

```
    Over the course of the last semester, more trash was
removed from our campus than in any semester in history.
But was it all trash that had to go to the landfill? For
example, many of us love to wear fleece vests, but did
you know that they are made from recycled plastic bot-
tles? Much of what is considered trash need not go to the
landfill at all. There are four ways we can prevent trash
from being sent to the landfill. I call them the four
R's. First, we can all either reduce the amount of indi-
vidually packaged goods that we send to the landfill by
buying frequently used items in family-size or bulk con-
tainers. Next, we can reuse those containers, as well as
other items, either for their original purpose or for an-
other. Be creative. After a while, though, things will
wear out after repeated use. Then it's a good time to try
to restore them. If that, too, can no longer be done,
then they should be recycled. Only after these options
have failed should items be considered "real" trash and
be removed to the landfill. Using the four R's — Reduce,
Reuse, Restore, Recycle — we can reduce the amount of
trash our campus sends to the landfill every semester.
```

This introduction should make the purpose of the editorial clear. In the editorial the author attempts to change readers' behavior and to reduce the amount of trash they throw out. Once items have been divided or classified, the classification can be used to persuade readers toward or away from certain types of actions. As we will see in the essay "The Ways of Meeting Oppression" later in this chapter, Martin Luther King Jr., by identifying three categories of protest, is able to cite historical precedents to argue against violent forms of protest and in favor of nonviolent ones. Argumentation, especially in conjunction with other strategies, can be one of the most powerful rhetorical modes and will be explained in detail in Chapter 11.

Formulate a Thesis Statement

When writing a division and classification essay, be sure that your thesis statement presents clearly both the type and the number of categories that you will be using to make your point. Here are a few examples from this chapter.

- "There are roughly three New Yorks." E. B. White's thesis statement asserts that there are three different ways of interpreting New York City.

- "Eventually, though, I was able to divide all the stereo buyers into four basic categories: the looks buyer, the wattage buyer, the price buyer, and the quality buyer." This thesis statement, from the annotated student essay by Gerald Cleary, presents the subject — stereo buyers — and the four different categories into which they fall. This statement makes it clear to the reader what the essay will be about and the points that the author will make.

- "Because girls' social hierarchies are complicated and overwhelming in their detail, I'm going to take you through a general breakdown of the different positions in the clique." This thesis statement is from Rosalind Wiseman's "The Queen Bee and Her Court" later in the chapter. From this opening statement, the reader knows exactly what Wiseman intends to discuss and how.

When you begin to formulate your thesis statement, keep these examples in mind. You could also look for other examples of thesis statements in the essays throughout this book. As you begin to develop your thesis statement, ask yourself, "What is my point?" Next ask yourself, "What categories will be most useful in making my point?" If you can't answer these questions, write some ideas down, and try to determine your main point from these ideas.

Once you have settled on an idea, go back to the two questions above, and write down your answers to them. Then combine the answers into a single thesis statement like the examples above. Your thesis statement does not necessarily have to be one sentence; making it one sentence, though, can be an effective way of focusing both your point and your categories.

By answering these two questions you should be well on your way to writing a clear and effective thesis statement. Use this thesis statement to guide readers through your essay and to help them understand your point and purpose.

Establish Appropriate Characteristics

Once you have decided on a subject and determined a purpose, your principle of division will usually be obvious. The sociologist studying voting patterns on Maple Street immediately divided her topic into three socioeconomic classes and into voters and nonvoters. Her important task was then to classify families according to these categories. In a study of how much time students spend in the library, you might just as readily divide your subject into categories: for example, those who spend less than five hours a week, those who spend between five and twenty hours, and those who spend more than twenty hours. You would then use these categories as your basis for classifying various individuals.

When establishing categories, make sure that they meet three criteria:

- *The categories must be appropriate to your purpose.* In determining the factors affecting financial aid distribution, you might consider family income, academic major, and athletic participation, but obviously you would not consider style of dress or preferred brand of toothpaste.
- *The categories must be consistent and mutually exclusive.* For example, dividing the student body into the classes of men, women, and athletes would be illogical because athletes can be either male or female. Instead, you could divide the student body into male athletes, female athletes, male nonathletes, and female nonathletes.
- *The categories must be complete, and they must account for all the members or aspects of your subject.* In dividing the student body according to place of birth, it would be inaccurate to consider only states in the United States; such a division would not account for foreign students or citizens born outside the country.

You may often find that a diagram (such as the one of families on Maple Street), a chart, or a table can help you visualize your organization and help you make sure that your categories meet the three criteria. It can help you determine whether your classes are appropriate, mutually exclusive, and complete.

For some subjects and purposes, appropriate divisions will not be immediately apparent. In fact, your most challenging task will often be the creation of interesting and accurate classes based on careful observation. Dividing dorm rooms according to style of decor, for example, will require some canvassing before a system of classification becomes clear. Once you have developed a system, though, you can easily classify individual rooms: homey, bare, youthful, contemporary, cluttered, and so on. The effect of many informal essays depends on the writer's ability to establish clever yet useful divisions and classifications that the reader might not otherwise notice.

Organize the Points of Your Essay

Essays of division and classification, when sensibly planned, can generally be organized with little trouble; the essay's chief divisions will reflect the classes into which the subject itself has been divided. A scratch outline can help you see those divisions and plan your order of presentation. For example, here is an outline of student Gerald Cleary's essay "How Loud? How Good? How Much? How Pretty?"

Four Types of Stereo Shoppers

1. The Looks Buyer
   a. Least respected by salespeople
   b. Appearance of stereo paramount
2. The Wattage Buyer
   a. More respected
   b. Volume level capability paramount
3. The Price Buyer
   a. Not respected but understood
   b. Cost concerns paramount
4. The Quality Buyer
   a. Most respected
   b. Quality and sound reproduction paramount

Such an outline clearly reveals the essay's overall structure.

State Your Conclusion

Your essay's purpose will determine the kinds of conclusions you reach. For example, a study of the student body of your college might show that 35 percent of all male athletes receive scholarships, compared with 20 percent of all female athletes, 15 percent of all male nonathletes, and 10 percent of all female nonathletes. These facts could provide a conclusion in themselves, or they might be the basis for a more controversial assertion about your school's athletic program. A study of dorm-room decor might conclude with the observation that juniors and seniors tend to have more elaborate rooms than first-year students. Your conclusion will depend on the way you work back and forth between the various classes you establish and the individual items available for you to classify.

Use Other Rhetorical Strategies

Although division and classification can be used effectively as a separate writing strategy, writers more commonly use it in combination with other strategies. For an essay about waste disposal, for example, it would be logical to add excerpts from interviews or dialogue between people discussing the subject. By combining narration (see Chapter 5) with division and classification, you could make your categories clearer and more powerful. Additionally, you could incorporate argumentation (see Chapter 11) to try to persuade the reader to act in a certain manner or to take a specific position on the issue of waste disposal.

When you are writing a division and classification essay, ask yourself how you might use other strategies. Consider, for example, Gerald Cleary's essay on stereo buyers. How might adding narration have changed or strengthened Cleary's essay? What other strategies might he have used? Comparison and contrast? Description? Exemplification? By using multiple strategies, you will make your writing more effective and evocative.

Editing Tip: Headings and Subheadings for Clarification

Be sure to follow the guidelines and advice for editing an essay given in Chapter 2, "Writing Essays." The guidelines highlight those sentence-level concerns of style — grammar, mechanics, and punctuation — that are especially important in editing any piece of writing. With long or complex essays it is sometimes very helpful to have some signposts to orient both you and your reader. Headings and subheadings break an extended piece of writing into sections; they quickly reveal an essay's organization, allow the reader to enter into your train of thought, and make it clear what's to come in a piece of writing. In short, headings and subheadings are an excellent road map for the reader.

Maintaining consistency in the style of your headings and subheadings is highly recommended. First you must be consistent in the way that you phrase heads. Most headings are a single word, usually a noun (Proteins, Carbohydrates, Fats) or a phrase such as Judith Viorst uses in her essay "The Truth About Lying" (Social Lies, Peace-keeping Lies, Protective Lies). Often headings are gerund phrases (Increasing Protein Consumption, Cutting Back on Carbohydrates, Maintaining a Balanced Diet). Using the same parts of speech sets your reader at ease by making the headings immediately recognizable as such and indicates that the headings are of the same organizational value. Whichever heading format you start with, however, you should continue using that same format throughout your essay. If you are using both headings and subheadings, you can make all your headings the same type (say, single-word nouns) and your subheadings another type (perhaps gerund phrases). While consistency in grammar should be a sought-after goal, it is worth noting that it is not always a practice followed by writers, even those included in *Subjects/Strategies*. If you examine the essay "How to Say Nothing in 500 Words" by Paul Roberts (p. 233), for example, you will see that he uses headings that are of mixed grammatical construction. Some are labels that are noun phrases ("Nothing about Something" and "Colorful Words," "Colored Words," and "Colorless Words") and some are directions that are complete imperative sentences (without periods), for example, "Avoid the Obvious Content," "Take the Less Usual Side," and "Slip Out of Abstraction," and so forth. While it should always be a goal to create consistent headings, be flexible rather than create an awkward heading.

It is necessary to be consistent in the type and style and size of your headings. Suppose your text is 10-point Times New Roman. All your headings should also be in Times New Roman, but you might put your main headings in 14-point and your subheadings in 12-point type. You also have some options in how you present your headings and subheadings: boldface (heavier type), underlining, italics or bold italics, all capitals, and capitals and lowercase. Notice the style used by Rosalind Wiseman in "The Queen Bee and her Court." She begins with a main heading: The Queen Bee.

The Queen Bee [noun phrase label in bold Roman type]

Under this main heading, she uses the following subheadings, which she has set in italics so as to differentiate them from the main heading:

Your Daughter Is a Queen Bee If . . . [lead-in clause in bold italic type]
What Does She Gain by Being a Queen Bee? [question in bold italic type]
What Does She Lose by Being a Queen Bee? [question in bold italic type]

With the discussion of each type of girl, Wiseman repeats the style of the headings.

The placement of the headings and subheadings should be consistent throughout your essay. Wiseman, for example, places all of the headings at the left-hand margin and relies on different type styles to differentiate main headings and subheadings. Other writers may center main headings and place subheadings are at the left margin. Wiseman could have used this style:

The Banker
Your Daughter Is a Banker If . . .
What Does She Gain by Being a Banker?
What Does She Lose by Being a Banker?

Main headings and subheadings can improve the readability of a piece of writing, especially one using division and classification as an organizing principle and where there may be a number of equally weighted parts that the reader will have difficulty keeping in mind.

Notice, for example, the way the various sections of the first two chapters of *Subjects/Strategies* and the chapter introductions have made use of headings and subheadings to organize the discussions and to make their comprehension easier for the reader. Finally, you will do well not to use too many headings and subheadings because they can be annoying unless used for major categories, not minor points.

▶ **Questions for Revising and Editing: Division and Classification**

1. Is my subject a coherent entity that readily lends itself to analysis by division and classification?
2. Does the manner in which I divide my subject into categories help me achieve my purpose in writing the essay?
3. Does my thesis statement clearly identify the number and type of categories I will be using in my essay?
4. Do I stay focused on my subject and stay within the limits of my categories throughout my essay?
5. Do my categories meet the following three criteria: Are they appropriate to my purpose, consistent and mutually exclusive, and complete?
6. Have I organized my essay in a way that makes it easy for the reader to understand my categories and how they relate to my purpose?
7. Are there other rhetorical strategies that I can use to help me achieve my purpose?
8. Is my use of headings and subheadings consistent? Could I use headings and subheadings to clarify the organization of my essay?

SEEING/READING

Girls on a Stoop

Stefanie Felix

Stefanie Felix — Susie Fitzhugh Photography

CONNECTING IMAGE AND TEXT

This photograph depicts a common scene of a group of girls sitting, talking, and passing the time together. How do you "read" this photograph? What might the girls' facial expressions, body language, hairstyles, and dress tell you about them as individuals? As members of the group? What does their configuration on the steps tell you about the girls as a group? About their roles in the group? How would your reading differ if a group of boys were depicted? Your observations will help guide you to the key themes and strategies in the essay that follows.

The Queen Bee and Her Court

Rosalind Wiseman

Rosalind Wiseman was born in 1969 in Philadelphia, Pennsylvania. She received her B.A. in political science from Occidental College in Los Angeles, California, in 1988. Wiseman is the cofounder and president of the Empower Program, a nonprofit organization whose "mission is to work with youth to end the culture of violence" and is certified through the Program for Young Negotiators at Harvard University. Her articles have appeared in Principal Leadership Magazine, Educational Digest, *and* New York Newsday, *and she has spoken extensively in the media about young people and violence. Wiseman's books include* Defending Ourselves: A Guide to Prevention, Self-Defense, and Recovery from Rape *(1995) and* Queen Bees and Wannabees: Helping Your Daughter Survive Cliques, Gossip, Boyfriends, and Other Realities of Adolescence *(2002), on which the film* Mean Girls *(2004) is based. She is currently at work on a book about the social pecking orders of parents.*

In "The Queen Bee and Her Court," an excerpt from Queen Bees and Wannabees, *Wiseman divides and classifies young schoolgirls into various hierarchical social classes dominated by the "Queen Bee."*

PREPARING TO READ

How did the various cliques work in your elementary and high schools? What roles did you play within those cliques? Did the existence of cliques bother you, or did you regard them as merely a reflection of society as a whole?

We need to give girls credit for the sophistication of their social structures. Our best politicians and diplomats couldn't do better than a teen girl does in understanding the social intrigue and political landscape that lead to power. Cliques are sophisticated, complex, and multilayered, and every girl has a role within them. However, positions in cliques aren't static. Especially from the sixth to eighth grade, a girl can lose her position to another girl, and she can move up and down the social totem pole. Also, your daughter doesn't have to be in the "popular" group to have these roles within her group of friends. Because girls' social hierarchies are complicated and overwhelming in their detail, I'm going to take you through a general breakdown of the different positions in the clique. However, when you talk to your daughter about cliques, encourage her to come up with her own names and create roles she thinks I've missed. If you can answer yes to the majority of items for each role, you've identified your daughter. So, here are the different roles that your daughter and her friends might play:

Queen Bee
Sidekick
Banker
Floater
Torn Bystander
Pleaser/Wannabe/Messenger
Target

The Queen Bee

For the girl whose popularity is based on fear and control, think of a combination of the Queen of Hearts in *Alice in Wonderland* and Barbie. I call her the Queen Bee. Through a combination of charisma, force, money, looks, will, and manipulation, this girl reigns supreme over the other girls and weakens their friendships with others, thereby strengthening her own power and influence. Indeed, she appears omnipotent. Never underestimate her power over other girls (and boys as well). She can and will silence her peers with a look. If your daughter's the Queen Bee and you could spy on her, you would (or should) be mortified by how she treats other girls.

Your Daughter Is a Queen Bee If . . .

- Her friends do what she wants to do.
- She isn't intimidated by any other girl in her class.
- Her complaints about other girls are limited to the lame things they did or said.
- When she's young, you have to convince her to invite everyone to her birthday party. When she does invite everyone you want, she ignores and excludes some of her guests. (When she's older, you lose your privilege to tell her who she can invite.)

- She can persuade her peers to do just about anything she wants.
- She can argue anyone down, including friends, peers, teachers, and parents.
- She's charming to adults, a female Eddie Haskell.
- She can make another girl feel "anointed" by declaring her a special friend.
- She's affectionate, but often that affection is deployed to demonstrate her rejection of another girl. For example, she sees two girls in her group, one she's pleased with and one she isn't. When she sees them, she'll throw her arms around one and insist that they sit together and barely say anything to the other.
- She won't (or is very reluctant to) take responsibility when she hurts someone's feelings.
- If she thinks she's been wronged she feels she has the right to seek revenge. She has an eye-for-an-eye worldview.

> *She thinks she's better than everyone else. She's in control, intimidating, smart, caring, and has the power to make others feel good or bad. She'll make stuff up about people and everyone will believe her.*
>
> — ANNE, 15

4

Who was the Queen Bee in your junior and/or high school? (If you were the Queen Bee, it's okay to admit it.) Remember how much power she had? Keep in mind that Queen Bees are good at slipping under adults' radar (including parents, teachers, and myself). Some of the nicest girls in my classes, who speak the most eloquently about how terrible they feel when girls are mean to each other, turn out to be the most cruel.

5

> *We're like an army.*
>
> — AMANDA, 13

6

Most Queen Bees aren't willing to recognize the cruelty of their actions. They believe their behavior is justified because of something done to them first. Justifications usually begin with, "For no reason, this girl got really upset about not being in the group. I mean we told her nicely and she just wasn't getting the hint. We tried to be nice but she just wasn't listening." When a Queen Bee does this, she's completely bypassing what she did and defining right and wrong by whether the individual was loyal (i.e., not challenging her authority).

7

If that sinking feeling in your stomach is because you just realized your daughter is a Queen Bee, congratulate yourself. Honesty is the first step to parenting an adolescent successfully.

8

What Does She Gain by Being a Queen Bee?

She feels power and control over her environment. She's the center of [9] attention and people pay homage to her.

What Does She Lose by Being a Queen Bee?

A real sense of self. She's so busy maintaining her image that she loses [10] herself in the process. She can be incredibly cynical about her friendships with both boys and girls ("They're only sucking up to me because I'm popular; they don't really like me."). She's vulnerable to having intimate relationships where she believes her image is dependent on the relationship. She may easily feel that she can't admit to anyone when she's in over her head because her reputation dictates that she always has everything and everyone in control.

The Sidekick

She's the lieutenant or second in command, the girl who's closest [11] to the Queen Bee and will back her no matter what because her power depends on the confidence she gets from the Queen Bee. All girls in a clique tend to dress similarly, but the Sidekick wears the most identical clothes and shares the mannerisms and overall style closest to the Queen Bee. Together they appear to other girls as an impenetrable force. They commonly bully and silence other girls to forward their own agenda. These girls are usually the first to focus on boys and are often attracted to older boys. This is particularly true in seventh and eighth grade (and their behavior is even worse if they're physically mature and going to high school parties). The difference between the two is if you separate the Sidekick from the Queen Bee, the Sidekick can alter her behavior for the better, while the Queen Bee would be more likely to find another Sidekick and begin again.

Your Daughter Is a Sidekick If . . .

- She has a best friend (the Queen Bee) who tells her what to do, [12] think, dress, etc.
- The best friend is your daughter's authority figure, not you.

- She feels like it's the two of them and everyone else is a Wannabe.
- You think her best friend pushes her around.

> *She notices everything about the Queen Bee. She will do everything*   13
> *the Queen Bee says and wants to be her. She lies for the Queen Bee but*
> *she isn't as pretty as the Queen Bee.*
>
> — MADELINE, 14

What Does She Gain by Being a Sidekick?

Power over other girls that she wouldn't have without the Queen Bee.   14
She also gains a close friend (whom you may not like) who makes her
feel popular and included.

What Does She Lose by Being a Sidekick?

The right to express her personal opinions. If she sticks around the   15
Queen Bee too long, she may forget she even has her own opinion.

The Banker

Information about each other is currency in Girl World. The Banker   16
creates chaos everywhere she goes by banking information about girls
in her social sphere and dispensing it at strategic intervals for her own
benefit. For instance, if a girl has said something negative about another girl, the Banker will casually mention it to someone in conversation because she knows it's going to cause a conflict and strengthen
her status as someone "in the know." She can get girls to trust her because when she pumps them for information it doesn't seem like gossip; instead, she does it in an innocent, I'm-trying-to-be-your-friend
way.

> *Her power lies in getting girls to confide in her. Once they figure out*   17
> *she can't be trusted, it's too late because she already has information on*
> *them, and in order to keep her from revealing things, girls will be nice*
> *to her.*
>
> — LEIGH, 17

The Banker is almost as powerful as the Queen Bee, but it's easy to   18
mistake her for the Messenger. She's usually quiet and withdrawn in
front of adults and can be physically immature in comparison to her
friends. This is the girl who sneaks under adult radar all the time because she seems so cute and harmless.

Your Daughter Is a Banker If . . .

- She is extremely secretive.   19
- She thinks in complex, strategic ways.
- She seems to be friends with everyone; some girls even treat her like a pet.
- She's rarely the subject of fights.
- She's rarely excluded from the group.

What Does She Gain by Being a Banker?

Power and security. The Banker is very confusing to other girls because   20
she seems harmless and yet everyone is afraid of her.

What Does She Lose by Being a Banker?

Once other girls figure out what she's doing, they don't trust her.   21
With her utilitarian mind-set, she can forget to look to other girls as a
trusted resource.

> *The girls can't oust the Banker from the clique because she has in-*   22
> *formation on everyone and could make or break reputations based on the*
> *information she knows.*
>
> — CHARLOTTE, 15

The Floater

You can usually spot this girl because she doesn't associate with only   23
one clique. She has friends in different groups and can move freely
among them. She usually has protective characteristics that shield her
from other girls' cruelty — for example, she's beautiful but not too
beautiful, nice, not terribly sophisticated, and avoids conflicts. She's
more likely to have higher self-esteem because she doesn't base her
self-worth on how well she's accepted by one group. Because she has
influence over other girls but doesn't use it to make them feel bad, I
call her the Floater. Girls want to be the Floater because she has confidence, people genuinely like her, and she's nice to everyone. She has
the respect of other girls because she doesn't rule by meanness. When
backed into a corner, the Floater is one of the few girls who will actually stand up to the Queen Bee. While Floaters have some power, they
don't have the same influence and impact as Queen Bees. Why? Because Floaters don't gain anything by sowing seeds of discontent and
insecurity among the other girls; Queen Bees do.

I have always felt that many potential Floaters are either swallowed 24
up by the popular crowd or choose not to identify with popular people at
all and instead create their own groups. In every girl there is a Floater
who wants to get out.

— JOANNA, 17

I don't think there are real *Floaters. Maybe I'm just bitter, but most* 25
of the time they are too good to be true.

— LIZA, 17

Your Daughter Is a Floater If . . .

- She doesn't want to exclude people; you aren't always having fights 26
  with her about spending time with people she considers "losers."
- Her friends are comfortable around her and don't seem intimidated; she's not "winning" all the conversations.
- She's not exclusively tied to one group of friends; she may have a
  jock group she hangs with, then the kids in the band, then her
  friends in the neighborhood.
- She can bring another person into a group on her own with some
  success.

What Does She Gain by Being a Floater?

Her peers like her for who she is as a person. She'll be less likely to 27
sacrifice herself to gain and keep social status.

What Does She Lose by Being a Floater?

Nothing! Count yourself truly blessed that she's your daughter. 28

If you're thinking this is your daughter, wait. It isn't that I don't be- 29
lieve you, but please read all the roles before making your final decision.
We all want to believe the best about the people we love, but sometimes
our love blinds us to reality. I've met countless parents who truly believe
their daughters are Floaters, and they're not. It should go without saying
that just because your daughter isn't a Floater doesn't mean she won't
become an amazing young woman and/or that you haven't done a
good job raising her. But if you insist on seeing her in a way that she
isn't, you won't be able to be as good a parent as she needs you to be.

The Torn Bystander

She's constantly conflicted between doing the right thing and her alle- 30
giance to the clique. As a result, she's the one most likely to be caught

in the middle of a conflict between two girls or two groups of girls. She'll often rationalize or apologize for the Queen Bee and Sidekick's behavior, but she knows it's wrong. She often feels more uncomfortable around boys, but can be very easily influenced by the clique to do what it wants (for example, getting together with a boy they decide is right for her). The status she gets from the group is very important, and the thought of standing up to the more powerful girls in the clique is terrifying. She's honest enough with herself (and maybe with you as well) to know that she doesn't like what the Queen Bee does but feels powerless to stop it.

Your Daughter Is a Torn Bystander If . . .

- She's always finding herself in situations where she has to choose   31
  between friends.
- She tries to accommodate everyone.
- She's not good at saying no to her friends.
- She wants everyone "to get along."
- She can't imagine standing up to anyone she has a conflict with; she goes along to get along.

> *She's confused and insecure because her reputation is over if she*   32
> *doesn't stick with the Queen Bee, but she can be really cool when she's*
> *alone.*
>
> — ANNE, 13

What Does She Gain by Being a Torn Bystander?

By associating herself with more powerful girls, she has access to popu-   33
larity, high social status, and boys.

What Does She Lose by Being a Torn Bystander?

She has to sacrifice a great deal. She may not try new things or she   34
may stop doing things she's interested in (plays, band, "geeky" clubs, etc.) because her friends make fun of her. She may dumb herself down to get along with others. This doesn't mean her grades will suffer, although they could. Lots of girls hide their academic accomplishments from their peers for this reason. ("I know I totally failed that test.") It more likely means that she presents herself as less intelligent than she is. This is merely irritating when she's a teen, but literally stupid when she's an adult in a job interview.

The Pleaser/Wannabe/Messenger

Almost all girls are pleasers and wannabes; some are just more obvious   35
than others. This is one of the more fascinating roles. She can be in
the clique or on the perimeter trying to get in. She will do anything to
be in the good graces of the Queen Bee and the Sidekick. She'll enthu-
siastically back them up no matter what. She'll mimic their clothes,
style, and anything else she thinks will increase her position in the
group. She's a careful observer, especially of the girls in power. She's
motivated above all else to please the person who's standing above her
on the social totem pole. She can easily get herself into messy conflicts
with other people because she'll change her mind depending on who
she's interacting with.

As a Pleaser/Wannabe/Messenger her security in the clique is   36
precarious and depends on her doing the Queen Bee's "dirty work,"
such as spreading gossip about a Target. While the Banker gathers information to further her own causes, the Pleaser/Wannabe/Messenger
does it to service the Queen Bee and get in her good graces and feel
important. But she can easily be dropped and ridiculed if she's seen
as trying too hard to fit in. (One of the worst accusations you can
make of a teen is to say she's trying too hard. In Girl World, all actions must appear effortless.) The Queen Bee and Sidekick enjoy the
convenience of making her their servant, but they love talking
behind her back. ("Can you believe what a suck-up she is? That's so
pathetic.")

When there's a fight between two girls or two groups of girls, she   37
often serves as a go-between. Her status immediately rises when she's
in active duty as a Messenger. It's also the most powerful position she
can attain, which means she has a self-interest in creating and maintaining conflicts between girls so she doesn't get laid off.

Your Daughter Is a Pleaser/Wannabe/ Messenger If . . .

- Other girls' opinions and wants are more important than her   38
own.
- Her opinions on dress, style, friends, and "in" celebrities constantly
change.
- She can't tell the difference between what she wants and what the
group wants.
- She's desperate to have the "right" look (clothes, hair, etc.).
- She'll stop doing things she likes because she fears the clique's dis-
approval.
- She's always in the middle of a conflict.

- She feels better about herself when the other girls are coming to her for help, advice, or when she's doing their dirty work.
- She loves to gossip — the phone and e-mail are her lifeline.

What Does She Gain by Being a Pleaser?

The feeling that she belongs; she's in the middle of the action and has power over girls. 39

What Does She Lose by Being a Pleaser?

Personal authenticity — she hasn't figured out who she is or what she values. She's constantly anticipating what people want from her and doesn't ask herself what she wants in return. She feels insecure about her friendships — do girls really like her, or do they only value her for the gossip she trades in? She has trouble developing personal boundaries and the ability to communicate them to others. 40

> *She's insecure and you can't trust her.* 41
>
> — Carrie, 14

The Target

She's the victim, set up by the other girls to be humiliated, made fun of, excluded. Targets are assumed to be out of the clique, one of the class "losers." While this is sometimes true, it's not always the case. Just because a girl is in the clique doesn't mean she can't be targeted by the other members. Often the social hierarchy of the clique is maintained precisely by having someone clearly at the bottom of the group's totem pole. Girls outside the clique tend to become Targets because they've challenged the clique or because their style of dress, behavior, and such are outside the norms acceptable to the clique. Girls inside the clique tend to become Targets if they've challenged someone higher on the social totem pole (i.e., the Queen Bee, Sidekick, or Banker) and need to be taken down a peg. 42

Your Daughter Is a Target If . . .

- She feels helpless to stop the girls' behavior. 43
- She feels she has no allies. No one will back her up.
- She feels isolated.
- She can mask her hurt by rejecting people first, saying she doesn't like anyone.

This role can be harder to figure out than you would think, and your daughter may be too embarrassed to tell you. She might admit she feels excluded, or she might just withdraw from you and "not want to talk about it."

44

> *Targets don't want to tell their parents because they don't want their parents to think they're a loser or a nobody.*
>
> — JENNIFER, 16

45

What Does She Gain by Being a Target?

This may seem like an odd question, but being a Target can have some hidden benefits. There's nothing like being targeted to teach your daughter about empathy and understanding for people who are bullied and/or discriminated against. Being a Target can also give her objectivity. She can see the costs of fitting in and decide she's better off outside the clique because at least she can be true to herself and/or find good friends who like her for who she is, not for her social standing.

46

What Does She Lose by Being a Target?

She feels totally helpless in the face of other girls' cruelty. She feels ashamed of being rejected by the others girls because of who she is. She'll be tempted to change herself in order to fit in. She feels vulnerable and unable to affect the outcome of her situation. She could become so anxious that she can't concentrate on schoolwork.

47

> *I didn't understand why I was so unhappy in sixth grade. I couldn't have told my parents that girls were being mean to me.*
>
> — ERIN, 17

48

> *Girls will almost always withdraw instead of telling a parent.*
>
> — CLAIRE, 14

49

> *If a girl's stuck in a degrading clique, it's the same as when she's later in a bad relationship. She doesn't expect to be treated any better.*
>
> — ELLEN, 15

50

OK, now you know the different roles girls play in cliques. The next questions are: How were these roles created in the first place? Who and what determine these positions and power plays? Why are girls able to get away with treating each other so badly?

51

It isn't really that big a secret. As girls become teens, the world be-   52
comes a much bigger, scarier place. Many girls go from a small elementary school to a much larger, more impersonal institutional school.

In elementary school, students are usually based in one room,   53
with one teacher. The principal sees them on a daily basis and parents
are often active in the school's activities, going on field trips, bringing
food for bake sales, and volunteering in after-school programs. By the
end of fifth or sixth grade, girls are beginning to prepare to leave this
safe, comfy haven of elementary school. They alternatively look forward to and dread moving on to middle school or junior high.

Then comes the first day at the middle school or junior high —   54
and everything changes. Adults, in our profound wisdom, place them
in a setting where they're overwhelmed by the number of students,
and they become nameless faces with ID security cards. If you ever
want to remember what it feels like, go to your daughter's school and
hang out in the hall when the bell rings right before a lunch period
(you probably have lots of times to choose from since most schools
have so many students that they need multiple lunch periods, which
means some students eat their midday meal at ten A.M.). When the
bell rings, walk from one end of the hall to the other. It's hard enough
simply navigating through this noisy throng. Now imagine navigating
the same hallway and caring what each person thinks of you as you
walk by.

We put our girls in this strange new environment at exactly the   55
same time that they're obsessively microanalyzing social cues, rules,
and regulations and therefore are at their most insecure. Don't underestimate how difficult and frightening this is for girls, and give your
daughter credit for getting out of bed in the morning.

RESPONDING TO THE TEXT

How real for you is the social classification system that Wiseman establishes in this piece? As a young woman, where would you place yourself
in the hierarchy? Were you a Queen Bee, a Banker, a Floater? If you are a
young man, do Wiseman's classifications of girls strike you as accurate?
Explain.

ENGAGING THE WRITER'S SUBJECT

1. What characteristics does the Queen Bee possess, according to Wiseman? Would you agree or disagree with her assessment of the girl at the
   top of the social totem pole? Would you add or subtract any characteristics? Explain.

2. Throughout her essay, Wiseman includes quoted passages in which
   young girls offer their own accounts of the characters. How effective do

you find these passages? What do they add, if anything, to Wiseman's classification system?

3. For every character type Wiseman includes a formulaic set of questions: "What does she gain by being an X?" and "What does she lose by being an X?" Why do you suppose she uses that formula? (Glossary: *Cause and Effect Analysis*)

4. Wiseman states that each character in the hierarchy gains from her position — even the Target. Do you agree? Explain.

5. What explanation does Wiseman give for the development of cliques? (Glossary: *Cause and Effect Analysis*)

ANALYZING THE WRITER'S CRAFT

1. What does Wiseman mean when she writes that "cliques are sophisticated, complex, and multilayered, and every girl has a role within them" (paragraph 1)? Is that statement her thesis? (Glossary: *Thesis*)

2. What does Wiseman hope to gain when she advises that, "when you talk to your daughter about cliques, encourage her to come up with her own names and create roles she thinks I've missed" (paragraph 1)? Why is her advice a useful strategy, given her subject and audience? (Glossary: *Audience; Subject*)

3. Into what classes does Wiseman divide all young girls in her classification system?

4. Explain how Wiseman has organized her essay. (Glossary: *Organization*) Is that organizational pattern effective? Explain.

5. Wiseman's division and classification is supported by her use of definition, exemplification, and comparison and contrast. (Glossary: *Comparison and Contrast; Definition; Exemplification*) How do these supporting strategies strengthen Wiseman's essay?

UNDERSTANDING THE WRITER'S LANGUAGE

1. How effective is Wiseman's title? (Glossary: *Title*) How effective are the names she gives each class in her classification? Would you change any of those names? If so, why?

2. What is Wiseman's attitude toward cliques? (Glossary: *Attitude*) What in her diction indicates that attitude? (Glossary: *Diction*)

3. Refer to your desk dictionary to determine the meanings of the following words as Wiseman uses them in this selection: *clique* (paragraph 1), *omnipotent* (2), *mortified* (2), *anointed* (3), *cynical* (10), *agenda* (11), *utilitarian* (21), *oust* (22), *rationalize* (30), *perimeter* (35), *precarious* (36).

WRITING SUGGESTIONS

1. Rosalind Wiseman offers her classification system for the roles that young girls play in cliques. Her system is based on interviews with

young girls, their friends, their teachers, and their mothers. But girls are not the only ones who belong to cliques. What about boys' cliques? Write a classification essay in which you divide and classify schoolboys on the basis of their behavioral characteristics and the roles they play within cliques. Review Wiseman's organization. Model your organization on hers, modify her design, or create an entirely new approach. Before you write, you might find it helpful to refer to your Connecting Image and Text response for this selection.

2. What about parents? Can we classify them into some recognizable and meaningful classes and subclasses? Jim Faye of the Love and Logic Institute in Boulder, Colorado, thinks so. He classifies parents into three groups: the Consultant who "provides guidance," the Helicopter "who hovers over children and rescues them from the hostile world in which they live," and the Drill Sargeant "who commands and directs the lives of children." Think about your parents and talk to your friends, the students in your dormitory, and others to gather opinions about the various parenting approaches that people demonstrate. Use the information to write an essay in which you classify parents. Be sure to define each class clearly and provide examples of their members' behavior. (Glossary: *Definition; Exemplification*)

3. Wiseman says that everyone in school belongs to a clique, even though that person may only be a "Target." Wiseman says of the Target, "She's the victim, set up by the other girls to be humiliated, made fun of, excluded. Targets are assumed to be out of the clique, one of the class 'losers' " (paragraph 42). Wiseman indicates that becoming a Target can render a person anxiety-ridden and ineffectual. She also suggests that we make a mistake by putting our girls in the middle of a junior high setting "where they're overwhelmed by the number of students, and they become nameless faces with ID security cards . . . at exactly the same time that they're obsessively microanalyzing social cues, rules, and regulations and therefore are at their most insecure" (54–55). We know that some students can't endure the pressure of being Targets and take violent action in retaliation for bullying, taunting, and other abuse. After researching in your college library and on the Internet the believed causes of recent outbreaks of violence in schools, write an essay on the relationship between cliques and retaliation by Targets, not only against others in school who oppress them but also against themselves for their inability to cope with social stress. (Glossary: *Cause and Effect Analysis*)

- To begin your research online, go to **bedfordstmartins.com /subjectsstrategies** and click on "Division and Classification" or browse the thematic directory of annotated links.

The Truth about Lying

Judith Viorst

Judith Viorst, poet, journalist, author of children's books, and novelist, was born in 1931. She has chronicled her life in such books as It's Hard to Be Hip Over Thirty and Other Tragedies of Married Life *(1968),* How Did I Get to Be Forty and Other Atrocities *(1976), and* When Did I Stop Being Twenty and Other Injustices: Selected Prose from Single to Mid-Life *(1987). In 1981, she went back to school, taking courses at the Washington Psychoanalytic Institute. This study, along with her personal experience of psychoanalysis, helped to inspire* Neces-sary Losses *(1986), a popular and critical success. Combining theory, poetry, interviews, and anecdotes, Viorst approaches personal growth as a shedding of illusions. Her recent work includes* Imperfect Control: Our Lifelong Struggles with Power and Surrender *(1998) and* Suddenly Sixty: And Other Shocks of Later Life *(2000).*

In this essay, first published in the March 1981 issue of Redbook, *the author approaches lying with delicacy and candor as she carefully classifies the different types of lies we all encounter.*

PREPARING TO READ

Lying happens every day in our society, whether it is a politician hiding behind a subtly worded statement or a guest fibbing to a host about the quality of a meal. What, for you, constitutes lying? Are all lies the same? In other words, are there different degrees or types of lying?

I've been wanting to write on a subject that intrigues and challenges me: the subject of lying. I've found it very difficult to do. Everyone I've talked to has a quite intense and personal but often rather intoler-ant point of view about what we can — and can never *never* — tell lies about. I've finally reached the conclusion that I can't present any ulti-mate conclusions, for too many people would promptly disagree. In-stead, I'd like to present a series of moral puzzles, all concerned with lying. I'll tell you what I think about them. Do you agree?

SOCIAL LIES

Most of the people I've talked with say that they find social lying ac-ceptable and necessary. They think it's the civilized way for folks to behave. Without these little white lies, they say, our relationships would be short and brutish and nasty. It's arrogant, they say, to insist on being so incorruptible and so brave that you cause other people unnecessary embarrassment or pain by compulsively assailing them with your honesty. I basically agree. What about you?

Will you say to people, when it simply isn't true, "I like your new hairdo," "You're looking much better," "It's so nice to see you," "I had a wonderful time"? 3

Will you praise hideous presents and homely kids? 4

Will you decline invitations with "We're busy that night — so sorry we can't come," when the truth is you'd rather stay home than dine with the So-and-sos? 5

And even though, as I do, you may prefer the polite evasion of "You really cooked up a storm" instead of "The soup" — which tastes like warmed-over coffee — "is wonderful," will you, if you must, proclaim it wonderful? 6

There's one man I know who absolutely refuses to tell social lies. "I can't play that game," he says; "I'm simply not made that way." And his answer to the argument that saying nice things to someone doesn't cost anything is, "Yes, it does — it destroys your credibility." Now, he won't, unsolicited, offer his views on the painting you just bought, but you don't ask his frank opinion unless you want *frank*, and his silence at those moments when the rest of us liars are muttering, "Isn't it lovely?" is, for the most part, eloquent enough. My friend does not indulge in what he calls "flattery, false praise and mellifluous comments." When others tell fibs he will not go along. He says that social lying is lying, that little white lies are still lies. And he feels that telling lies is morally wrong. What about you? 7

PEACE-KEEPING LIES

Many people tell peace-keeping lies; lies designed to avoid irritation or argument; lies designed to shelter the liar from possible blame or pain; lies (or so it is rationalized) designed to keep trouble at bay without hurting anyone. 8

I tell these lies at times, and yet I always feel they're wrong. I understand why we tell them, but still they feel wrong. And whenever I lie so that someone won't disapprove of me or think less of me or holler at me, I feel I'm a bit of a coward, I feel I'm dodging responsibility, I feel . . . guilty. What about you? 9

Do you, when you're late for a date because you overslept, say that you're late because you got caught in a traffic jam? 10

Do you, when you forget to call a friend, say that you called several times but the line was busy? 11

Do you, when you didn't remember that it was your father's birth- 12
day, say that his present must be delayed in the mail?

And when you're planning a weekend in New York City and 13
you're not in the mood to visit your mother, who lives there, do you
conceal — with a lie, if you must — the fact that you'll be in New
York? Or do you have the courage — or is it the cruelty? — to say, "I'll
be in New York, but sorry — I don't plan on seeing you"?

(Dave and his wife Elaine have two quite different points of view 14
on this very subject. He calls her a coward. She says she's being wise.
He says she must assert her right to visit New York sometimes and not
see her mother. To which she always patiently replies: "Why should
we have useless fights? My mother's too old to change. We get along
much better when I lie to her.")

Finally, do you keep the peace by telling your husband lies on the 15
subject of money? Do you reduce what you really paid for your shoes?
And in general do you find yourself ready, willing and able to lie to
him when you make absurd mistakes or lose or break things?

"I used to have a romantic idea that part of intimacy was confess- 16
ing every dumb thing that you did to your husband. But after a couple
of years of that," says Laura, "have I changed my mind!"

And having changed her mind, she finds herself telling peace- 17
keeping lies. And yes, I tell them too. What about you?

PROTECTIVE LIES

Protective lies are lies folks tell — often quite serious lies — because 18
they're convinced that the truth would be too damaging. They lie because they feel there are certain human values that supersede the
wrong of having lied. They lie, not for personal gain, but because they
believe it's for the good of the person they're lying to. They lie to
those they love, to those who trust them most of all, on the grounds
that breaking this trust is justified.

They may lie to their children on money or marital matters. 19

They may lie to the dying about the state of their health. 20

They may lie about adultery, and not — or so they insist — to save 21
their own hide, but to save the heart and the pride of the men they
are married to.

They may lie to their closest friend because the truth about her tal- 22
ents or son or psyche would be — or so they insist — utterly devastating.

I sometimes tell such lies, but I'm aware that it's quite presumptuous 23
to claim I know what's best for others to know. That's called playing
God. That's called manipulation and control. And we never can be
sure, once we start to juggle lies, just where they'll land, exactly where
they'll roll.

And furthermore, we may find ourselves lying in order to back up 24
the lies that are backing up the lie we initially told.

And furthermore — let's be honest — if conditions were reversed, 25
we certainly wouldn't want anyone lying to us.

Yet, having said all that, I still believe that there are times when 26
protective lies must nonetheless be told. What about you?

If your Dad had a very bad heart and you had to tell him some 27
bad family news, which would you choose: to tell him the truth or lie?

If your former husband failed to send his monthly child-support 28
check and in other ways behaved like a total rat, would you allow your
children — who believed he was simply wonderful — to continue to
believe that he was wonderful?

If your dearly beloved brother selected a wife whom you deeply 29
disliked, would you reveal your feelings or would you fake it?

And if you were asked, after making love, "And how was that for 30
you?" would you reply, if it wasn't too good, "Not too good"?

Now, some would call a sex lie unimportant, little more than so- 31
cial lying, a simple act of courtesy that makes all human intercourse
run smoothly. And some would say all sex lies are bad news and unac-
ceptably protective. Because, says Ruth, "a man with an ego that fragile doesn't need your lies — he needs a psychiatrist." Still others feel
that sex lies are indeed protective lies, more serious than simple social
lying, and yet at times they tell them on the grounds that when it
comes to matters sexual, everybody's ego is somewhat fragile.

"If most of the time things go well in sex," says Sue, "I think 32
you're allowed to dissemble when they don't. I can't believe it's good
to say, 'Last night was four stars, darling, but tonight's performance
rates only a half.' "

I'm inclined to agree with Sue. What about you? 33

TRUST-KEEPING LIES

Another group of lies are trust-keeping lies, lies that involve triangula- 34
tion, with *A* (that's you) telling lies to *B* on behalf of *C* (whose trust
you'd promised to keep). Most people concede that once you've agreed
not to betray a friend's confidence, you can't betray it, even if you
must lie. But I've talked with people who don't want you telling them
anything that they might be called on to lie about.

"I don't tell lies for myself," says Fran, "and I don't want to have to 35
tell them for other people." Which means, she agrees, that if her best
friend is having an affair, she absolutely doesn't want to know about it.

"Are you saying," her best friend asks, "that if I went off with a 36
lover and I asked you to tell my husband I'd been with you, that you
wouldn't lie for me, that you'd betray me?"

Fran is very pained but very adamant. "I wouldn't want to betray   37
you, so . . . don't ask me."

Fran's best friend is shocked. What about you?   38

Do you believe you can have close friends if you're not prepared   39
to receive their deepest secrets?

Do you believe you must always lie for your friends?   40

Do you believe, if your friend tells a secret that turns out to be   41
quite immoral or illegal, that once you've promised to keep it, you
must keep it?

And what if your friend were your boss — if you were perhaps one   42
of the President's men — would you betray or lie for him over, say,
Watergate?

As you can see, these issues get terribly sticky.   43

It's my belief that once we've promised to keep a trust, we must tell   44
lies to keep it. I also believe that we can't tell Watergate lies. And if
these two statements strike you as quite contradictory, you're right —
they're quite contradictory. But for now they're the best I can do. What
about you?

Some say that truth will out and thus you might as well tell the   45
truth. Some say you can't regain the trust that lies lose. Some say that
even though the truth may never be revealed, our lies pervert and
damage our relationships. Some say . . . well, here's what some of
them have to say.

"I'm a coward," says Grace, "about telling close people important,   46
difficult truths. I find that I'm unable to carry it off. And so if something is bothering me, it keeps building up inside till I end up just not
seeing them any more."

"I lie to my husband on sexual things, but I'm furious," says Joyce,   47
"that he's too insensitive to know I'm lying."

"I suffer most from the misconception that children can't take the   48
truth," says Emily. "But I'm starting to see that what's harder and more
damaging for them is being told lies, is *not* being told the truth."

"I'm afraid," says Joan, "that we often wind up feeling a bit of   49
contempt for the people we lie to."

And then there are those who have no talent for lying.   50

"Over the years, I tried to lie," a friend of mine explained, "but I   51
always got found out and I always got punished. I guess I gave myself
away because I feel guilty about any kind of lying. It looks as if I'm
stuck with telling the truth."

For those of us, however, who are good at telling lies, for those of   52
us who lie and don't get caught, the question of whether or not to lie
can be a hard and serious moral problem. I liked the remark of a friend
of mine who said, "I'm willing to lie. But just as a last resort — the
truth's always better."

"Because," he explained, "though others may completely accept   53
the lie I'm telling, I don't."

I tend to feel that way too.   54

What about you?   55

RESPONDING TO THE TEXT

The title of the essay plays with the relationship between lies and the truth. Viorst discusses lies that help to conceal the truth, but she's quick to point out that not all lies are malicious. Look at her subsections about "protective lies" (paragraphs 18–33) and "trust-keeping lies" (34–44). Do you think that these lies are necessary? Or would it be easier to tell the truth? Explain.

ENGAGING THE WRITER'S SUBJECT

1. Why is Viorst wary of giving advice on the subject of lying?

2. Viorst admits to contradicting herself in her section on "trust-keeping lies." Where else do you see her contradicting herself?

3. In telling a "protective lie," what assumption about the person hearing the lie does Viorst make? Would you make the same assumption? Why or why not?

4. What's the difference between a "peace-keeping lie" and a "protective lie"?

ANALYZING THE WRITER'S CRAFT

1. Into what main categories does Viorst divide lying? Do you agree with her division or do some of her categories seem to overlap? Explain.

2. Viorst recognizes that many people have steadfast views on lying. What accommodations does she make for this audience? (Glossary: *Audience*) How does she challenge this audience?

3. There are at least two parties involved in a lie — the liar and the listener. How much significance does the author give to each of these parties? How does she make the distinction?

4. Viorst presents the reader with a series of examples or moral puzzles. How do these puzzles encourage further thought on the subject of lying? Are they successful? Why or why not?

5. Viorst chooses an unconventional way to conclude her essay by showing different people's opinions of lying. What do you think she's doing in this last section, beginning in paragraph 45? Does this ending intensify any of the points she has made? Explain. (Glossary: *Beginnings/ Endings*)

6. Viorst wants us to see that a lie is not a lie is not a lie is not a lie (i.e., that not all lies are the same). To clarify the various types of lies, she uses division and classification. She also uses exemplification to illustrate the

ways in which people lie. (Glossary: *Exemplification*) Using several of the examples that work best for you, discuss how Viorst's use of exemplification strengthens and enhances her classification.

UNDERSTANDING THE WRITER'S LANGUAGE

1. How would you characterize Viorst's diction in this essay? (Glossary: *Diction*) Consider the essay's subject and audience. (Glossary: *Audience; Subject*) Cite specific examples of her word choice to support your conclusions.

2. Refer to your desk dictionary to determine the meanings of the following words as Viorst uses them in this selection: *mellifluous* (paragraph 7), *supersede* (18), *dissemble* (32).

WRITING SUGGESTIONS

1. The popular comic strip *Dilbert* derives humor from workplace situations that are absurd but nevertheless come too close to the truth for many readers. Examine the following cartoon. Although the cartoon character's statement might be considered a euphemism rather than an outright lie, what it communicates is certainly not true. How do you think Viorst would classify such a statement? How would she react to it? Write an essay in which you discuss Viorst's attitude toward such statements in relation to your own. Do you find such "business-speak" amusing or infuriating? Are there any categories of lying that Viorst has failed to consider? What are they?

DILBERT reprinted by permission of United Feature Syndicate, Inc.

2. Viorst wrote this essay for *Redbook*, which is usually considered a women's magazine. If you were writing this essay for a male audience, would you change the examples? If so, how would you change them? If not, why not? Do you think men are more likely to tell lies of a certain category? Explain. Write an essay in which you discuss whether men and women share similar perspectives about lying. (Glossary: *Comparison and Contrast*)

3. It is often difficult to discern the truths in advertising or news reporting. Select a current print advertisement or news story for analysis. In your college library and on the Internet, research the ad or story and determine just how much factual material is included. Based on your research and analysis, write an essay in which you argue for more consumer education in the area of advertising or news reporting.

- To begin your research online, go to **bedfordstmartins.com /subjectsstrategies** and click on "Division and Classification" or browse the thematic directory of annotated links.

The Ways of Meeting Oppression

Martin Luther King Jr.

Martin Luther King Jr. (1929–1968) was the son of a Baptist minister. Ordained at the age of eighteen, King went on to study at Morehouse College, Crozer Theological Seminary, Boston University, and Chicago Theological Seminary. He came to prominence in 1955 in Montgomery, Alabama, when he led a successful boycott against the city's segregated bus system. A powerful orator and writer, King went on to become the leading spokesman for the civil rights movement during the 1950s and 1960s. In 1964, he was awarded the Nobel Peace Prize for his policy of nonviolent resistance to racial injustice, a policy that he explains in the following selection. King was assassinated in April 1968 after speaking at a rally in Memphis, Tennessee.

This selection is excerpted from the book Stride Toward Freedom *(1958).*

PREPARING TO READ

Summarize what you know about the civil rights movement of the late 1950s and early 1960s. What tactics did its leaders use? How successful were those tactics? What is your impression of the movement as part of American history? How did this movement change American society?

Oppressed people deal with their oppression in three characteristic ways. One way is acquiescence: the oppressed resign themselves to their doom. They tacitly adjust themselves to oppression, and thereby become conditioned to it. In every movement toward freedom some of the oppressed prefer to remain oppressed. Almost 2800 years ago Moses set out to lead the children of Israel from the slavery of Egypt to the freedom of the promised land. He soon discovered that slaves do not always welcome their deliverers. They become accustomed to being slaves. They would rather bear those ills they have, as Shakespeare pointed out, than flee to others that they know not of. They prefer the "fleshpots of Egypt" to the ordeals of emancipation.

There is such a thing as the freedom of exhaustion. Some people are so worn down by the yoke of oppression that they give up. A few years ago in the slum areas of Atlanta, a Negro guitarist used to sing almost daily: "Been down so long that down don't bother me." This is the type of negative freedom and resignation that often engulfs the life of the oppressed.

But this is not the way out. To accept passively an unjust system   3
is to cooperate with that system; thereby the oppressed become as
evil as the oppressor. Noncooperation with evil is as much a moral
obligation as is cooperation with good. The oppressed must never
allow the conscience of the oppressor to slumber. Religion reminds
every man that he is his brother's keeper. To accept injustice or
segregation passively is to say to the oppressor that his actions are
morally right. It is a way of allowing his conscience to fall asleep.
At this moment the oppressed fails to be his brother's keeper. So
acquiescence — while often the easier way — is not the moral way. It
is the way of the coward. The Negro cannot win the respect of his
oppressor by acquiescing; he merely increases the oppressor's arrogance and contempt. Acquiescence is interpreted as proof of the
Negro's inferiority. The Negro cannot win the respect of the white
people of the south or the peoples of the world if he is willing to sell
the future of his children for his personal and immediate comfort
and safety.

A second way that oppressed people sometimes deal with oppres-   4
sion is to resort to physical violence and corroding hatred. Violence
often brings about momentary results. Nations have frequently won
their independence in battle. But in spite of temporary victories, violence never brings permanent peace. It solves no social problem; it
merely creates new and more complicated ones.

Violence as a way of achieving racial justice is both impractical   5
and immoral. It is impractical because it is a descending spiral ending
in destruction for all. The old law of an eye for an eye leaves everybody blind. It is immoral because it seeks to humiliate the opponent
rather than win his understanding; it seeks to annihilate rather than
to convert. Violence is immoral because it thrives on hatred rather
than love. It destroys community and makes brotherhood impossible.
It leaves society in monologue rather than dialogue. Violence ends by
defeating itself. It creates bitterness in the survivors and brutality in
the destroyers. A voice echoes through time saying to every potential
Peter, "Put up your sword." History is cluttered with the wreckage of
nations that failed to follow this command.

If the American Negro and other victims of oppression succumb   6
to the temptation of using violence in the struggle for freedom, future
generations will be the recipients of a desolate night of bitterness, and
our chief legacy to them will be an endless reign of meaningless chaos.
Violence is not the way.

The third way open to oppressed people in their quest for freedom   7
is the way of nonviolent resistance. Like the synthesis in Hegelian philosophy, the principle of nonviolent resistance seeks to reconcile the
truths of two opposites — the acquiescence and violence — while

avoiding the extremes and immoralities of both. The nonviolent resister agrees with the person who acquiesces that one should not be physically aggressive toward his opponent; but he balances the equation by agreeing with the person of violence that evil must be resisted. He avoids the nonresistance of the former and the violent resistance of the latter. With nonviolent resistance, no individual or group need submit to any wrong, nor need anyone resort to violence in order to right a wrong.

It seems to me that this is the method that must guide the actions 8 of the Negro in the present crisis in race relations. Through nonviolent resistance the Negro will be able to rise to the noble height of opposing the unjust system while loving the perpetrators of the system. The Negro must work passionately and unrelentingly for full stature as a citizen, but he must not use inferior methods to gain it. He must never come to terms with falsehood, malice, hate, or destruction.

Nonviolent resistance makes it possible for the Negro to remain in 9 the South and struggle for his rights. The Negro's problem will not be solved by running away. He cannot listen to the glib suggestion of those who would urge him to migrate en masse to other sections of the country. By grasping his great opportunity in the South he can make a lasting contribution to the moral strength of the nation and set a sublime example of courage for generations yet unborn.

By nonviolent resistance, the Negro can also enlist all men of 10 good will in his struggle for equality. The problem is not a purely racial one, with Negroes set against whites. In the end, it is not a struggle between people at all, but a tension between justice and injustice. Nonviolent resistance is not aimed against oppressors but against oppression. Under its banner consciences, not racial groups, are enlisted.

RESPONDING TO THE TEXT

Find the definition of *oppress* or *oppression* in the dictionary. Exactly what does King mean when he speaks of people being "oppressed" in the South in twentieth-century America? Do you think that people are still being oppressed in America today? Explain.

ENGAGING THE WRITER'S SUBJECT

1. What does King mean by the term "freedom of exhaustion" (paragraph 2)? Why is he scathing in his assessment of people who succumb to such a condition in response to oppression?

2. According to King, what is the role of religion in the battle against oppression?

3. Why does King advocate the avoidance of violence in fighting oppression, despite the short-term success violence often achieves for the victors? How do such victories affect the future?

4. According to King, how does nonviolent resistance transform a racial issue into one of conscience?

ANALYZING THE WRITER'S CRAFT

1. King's essay is easy to read and understand, and everything in it relates to his purpose. (Glossary: *Purpose*) What is that purpose? Summarize how each paragraph supports his purpose. How does the essay's organization help King achieve his purpose? (Glossary: *Organization*)

2. King says that "nonviolent resistance is not aimed against oppressors but against oppression" (paragraph 10). What does he mean by this? Why does he deflect anger and resentment away from a concrete example, the oppressors, to an abstract concept, oppression? (Glossary: *Concrete/Abstract*) How does this choice support his purpose? (Glossary: Purpose)

3. King evokes the names of Moses, Shakespeare, and Hegel in his essay. What does this tell you about his intended audience? (Glossary: *Audience*) Why does King address the audience in this way?

4. King uses division and classification to help him argue his point in this essay. What other rhetorical strategies does King use? How does each strategy, including division and classification and argument, contribute to the effectiveness of the essay?

UNDERSTANDING THE WRITER'S LANGUAGE

1. In his discussion about overcoming oppression with violence, King says that "future generations will be the recipients of a desolate night of bitterness" (paragraph 6). What image do his words evoke for you? Why do you think he chooses to use a striking metaphor here, instead of a less poetic statement? (Glossary: *Figures of Speech*)

2. King urges Negroes to avoid "falsehood, malice, hate, or destruction" (paragraph 8) in their quest to gain full stature as citizens. How does each of these terms relate to his earlier argument about avoiding violence? How does each enhance or add new meaning to his earlier argument?

3. Refer to your desk dictionary to determine the meanings of the following words as King uses them in this selection: *acquiescence* (paragraph 1), *tacitly* (1), *yoke* (2), *perpetrators* (8), *glib* (9), *sublime* (9).

WRITING SUGGESTIONS

1. Write a division and classification essay in which you follow King's model by arguing for or advocating one of the categories. Identify three methods that you can use to achieve a goal — study for a test, apply to

graduate school, or interview for a job, for example. Choose one method to advocate; then frame your essay so that the division and classification strategy helps you make your point.

2. Toward the end of his essay, King states, "By grasping his great opportunity in the South [the Negro] can make a lasting contribution to the moral strength of the nation and set a sublime example of courage for generations yet unborn" (paragraph 9). With your classmates, discuss whether the movement that King led achieved its goal of solving many of the underlying racial tensions and inequities in the United States. In terms of equality, what has happened in the United States since King's famous "I Have a Dream" speech (p. 525)? Write a paper in which you argue for or against the idea that King's "dream" is still intact. (Glossary: *Argument*)

3. In your college library and on the Internet, research the situation of African Americans in the southern United States in the 1940s and 1950s. In general, describe the living conditions there at that time. How pervasive were Jim Crow laws? How restricted were African Americans in the political arena? Why did the conditions make it so important for King to argue against both despair and violence before advocating non-violent resistance? Write an essay in which you present the conditions and use the information to provide a context for King's essay.

- To begin your research online, go to **bedfordstmartins.com /subjectsstrategies** and click on "Division and Classification" or browse the thematic directory of annotated links.

The Myth of the Latin Woman

Judith Ortiz Cofer

Author and educator Judith Ortiz Cofer was born in Hormigueros, Puerto Rico, in 1952, but her family immigrated to the United States in 1954. She grew up in New Jersey but moved south to continue her education — she received her M.A. in English from Florida Atlantic University in 1977 — and is now Franklin Professor of English and Creative Writing at the University of Georgia. Her published works include a novel, The Line of the Sun, *two collections of poetry, and several other titles that collect and combine her essays, stories, and poetry. One of these,* Silent Dancing, *a collection of essays and poetry, was awarded the Pushcart Prize for nonfiction in 1990; Cofer received an O. Henry Prize for short stories in 1994, and* An Island Like You: Stories of the Barrio *(1995) was named a Best Book of the Year by the American Library Association. Her most recent books include* The Meaning of Consuelo: A Novel *(2003) and* First Person Fiction: Call Me Maria *(2004).*

Much of Cofer's writing focuses on Hispanic issues and the culture clashes that occur between the Anglo and Hispanic communities. As she says in the following selection, which first appeared in the January 1992 issue of Glamour, *and which was later included in her book* The Latin Deli *(1993), "You can leave the island [Puerto Rico] . . . , [but] the island travels with you."*

PREPARING TO READ

In what ways has your ethnicity played a part in your life? What advantages, disadvantages, and special circumstances have you experienced because of your appearance and your cultural upbringing? Have you encountered any cultural tensions between your own heritage and what you consider to be modern American culture?

On a bus trip to London from Oxford University where I was earning some graduate credits one summer, a young man, obviously fresh from a pub, spotted me and as if struck by inspiration went down on his knees in the aisle. With both hands over his heart he broke into an Irish tenor's rendition of "Maria" from *West Side Story*. My politely amused fellow passengers gave his lovely voice the round of gentle applause it deserved. Though I was not quite as amused, I managed my version of an English smile: no show of teeth, no extreme contortions of the facial muscles — I was at this time of my life practicing reserve and cool. Oh, that British control, how I coveted it.

But "Maria" had followed me to London, reminding me of a prime fact of my life: you can leave the island, master the English language, and travel as far as you can, but if you are a Latina, especially one like me who so obviously belongs to Rita Moreno's gene pool, the island travels with you.

This is sometimes a very good thing — it may win you that extra minute of someone's attention. But with some people, the same things can make *you* an island — not a tropical paradise but an Alcatraz, a place nobody wants to visit. As a Puerto Rican girl living in the United States and wanting like most children to "belong," I resented the stereotype that my Hispanic appearance called forth from many people I met.

Growing up in a large urban center in New Jersey during the 1960s, I suffered from what I think of as "cultural schizophrenia." Our life was designed by my parents as a microcosm of their *casas* on the island. We spoke in Spanish, ate Puerto Rican food bought at the *bodega*, and practiced strict Catholicism at a church that allotted us a one-hour slot each week for mass, performed in Spanish by a Chinese priest trained as a missionary for Latin America.

As a girl I was kept under strict surveillance by my parents, since my virtue and modesty were, by their cultural equation, the same as their honor. As a teenager I was lectured constantly on how to behave as a proper *señorita*. But it was a conflicting message I received, since the Puerto Rican mothers also encouraged their daughters to look and act like women and to dress in clothes our Anglo friends and their mothers found too "mature" and flashy. The difference was, and is, cultural; yet I often felt humiliated when I appeared at an American friend's party wearing a dress more suitable to a semi-formal than to a playroom birthday celebration. At Puerto Rican festivities, neither the music nor the colors we wore could be too loud.

I remember Career Day in our high school, when teachers told us to come dressed as if for a job interview. It quickly became obvious that to the Puerto Rican girls "dressing up" meant wearing their mother's ornate jewelry and clothing, more appropriate (by mainstream standards) for the company Christmas party than as daily office attire. That morning I had agonized in front of my closet, trying to figure out what a "career girl" would wear. I knew how to dress for school (at the Catholic school I attended, we all wore uniforms), I knew how to dress for Sunday mass, and I knew what dresses to wear for parties at my relatives' homes. Though I do not recall the precise details of my Career Day outfit, it must have been a composite of these choices. But I remember a comment my friend (an Italian American) made in later years that coalesced my impressions of that day. She said that at the business school she was attending, the Puerto Rican girls always stood out for wearing "everything at once." She meant, of course, too much jewelry, too many accessories. On that day at school we were simply made the negative models by the nuns, who were themselves not credible fashion experts to any of us. But it was painfully obvious to me that to the others, in their tailored skirts and silk blouses, we must have seemed "hopeless" and "vulgar." Though I now know that most adolescents feel out of step much of the time, I also know that for the Puerto Rican girls of my generation that sense was intensified. The way our teachers and classmates looked at us that day in school was just a taste of the cultural clash that awaited us in the real world, where prospective employers and men on the street would often misinterpret our tight skirts and jingling bracelets as a "come-on."

Mixed cultural signals have perpetuated certain stereotypes — for example, that of the Hispanic woman as the "hot tamale" or sexual firebrand. It is a one-dimensional view that the media have found easy to promote. In their special vocabulary, advertisers have designated "sizzling" and "smoldering" as the adjectives of choice for describing not only the foods but also the women of Latin America. From conversations in my house I recall hearing about the harassment that Puerto Rican women endured in factories where the "boss-men" talked to them as if sexual innuendo was all they understood, and worse, often gave them the choice of submitting to their advances or being fired. 6

It is custom, however, not chromosomes, that leads us to choose scarlet over pale pink. As young girls, it was our mothers who influenced our decisions about clothes and colors — mothers who had grown up on a tropical island where the natural environment was a riot of primary colors, where showing your skin was one way to keep cool as well as to look sexy. Most important of all, on the island, women perhaps felt freer to dress and move more provocatively since, in most cases, they were protected by the traditions, mores, and laws of a Spanish/Catholic system of morality and machismo whose main rule was: *You may look at my sister, but if you touch her I will kill you.* The extended family and church structure could provide a young woman with a circle of safety in her small pueblo on the island; if a man "wronged" a girl, everyone would close in to save her family honor. 7

My mother has told me about dressing in her best party clothes on Saturday nights and going to the town's plaza to promenade with her girlfriends in front of the boys they liked. The males were thus given an opportunity to admire the women and to express their admiration in the form of *piropos:* erotically charged street poems they composed on the spot. (I have myself been subjected to a few *piropos* while visiting the island, and they can be outrageous, although custom dictates that they must never cross into obscenity.) This ritual, as I understand it, also entails a show of studied indifference on the 8 woman's part; if she is "decent," she must not acknowledge the man's impassioned words. So I do understand how things can be lost in translation. When a Puerto Rican girl dressed in her idea of what is attractive meets a man from the mainstream culture who has been trained to react to certain types of clothing as a sexual signal, a clash is likely to take place. I remember the boy who took me to my first formal dance leaning over to plant a sloppy, over-eager kiss painfully on my mouth; when I didn't respond with sufficient passion, he remarked resentfully: "I thought you Latin girls were supposed to mature early," as if I were expected to *ripen* like a fruit or vegetable, not just grow into womanhood like other girls.

It is surprising to my professional friends that even today some 9 people, including those who should know better, still put others "in their place." It happened to me most recently during a stay at a classy metropolitan hotel favored by young professional couples for weddings. Late one evening after the theater, as I walked toward my room with a colleague (a woman with whom I was coordinating an arts program), a middle-aged man in a tuxedo, with a young girl in satin and lace on his arm, stepped directly into our path. With his champagne glass extended toward me, he exclaimed "Evita!"

Our way blocked, my companion and I listened as the man half- 10 recited, half-bellowed "Don't Cry for Me, Argentina." When he finished, the young girl said: "How about a round of applause for my daddy?" We complied, hoping this would bring the silly spectacle to a close. I was becoming aware that our little group was attracting the attention of the other guests. "Daddy" must have perceived this too, and he once more barred the way as we tried to walk past him. He began to shout-sing a ditty to the tune of "La Bamba" — except the lyrics were about a girl named Maria whose exploits rhymed with her name and gonorrhea. The girl kept saying "Oh, Daddy" and looking at me with pleading eyes. She wanted me to laugh along with the others. My companion and I stood silently waiting for the man to end his offensive song. When he finished, I looked not at him but at his daughter. I advised her calmly never to ask her father what he had done in the army. Then I walked between them and to my room. My friend complimented me on my cool handling of the situation, but I confessed that I had really wanted to push the jerk into the swimming pool. This same man — probably a corporate executive, well-educated, even worldly by most standards — would not have been likely to regale an Anglo woman with a dirty song in public. He might have checked his impulse by assuming that she could be somebody's wife or mother, or at least *somebody* who might take offense. But, to him, I was just an Evita or a Maria: merely a character in his cartoon-populated universe.

Another facet of the myth of the Latin woman in the United States 11 is the menial, the domestic — Maria the housemaid or countergirl. It's true that work as domestics, as waitresses, and in factories is all that's available to women with little English and few skills. But the myth of the Hispanic menial — the funny maid, mispronouncing words and cooking up a spicy storm in a shiny California kitchen — has been perpetuated by the media in the same way that "Mammy" from *Gone with the Wind* became America's idea of the black woman for generations. Since I do not wear my diplomas around my neck for all to see, I have on occasion been sent to that "kitchen" where some think I obviously belong.

One incident has stayed with me, though I recognize it as a minor 12 offense. My first public poetry reading took place in Miami, at a restaurant where a luncheon was being held before the event. I was nervous and excited as I walked in with notebook in hand. An older woman motioned me to her table, and thinking (foolish me) that she wanted me to autograph a copy of my newly published slender volume of verse, I went over. She ordered a cup of coffee from me, assuming that I was the waitress. (Easy enough to mistake my poems for menus, I suppose.) I know it wasn't an intentional act of cruelty. Yet of all the good things that happened later, I remember that scene most clearly, because it reminded me of what I had to overcome before anyone would take me seriously. In retrospect I understand that my anger gave my reading fire. In fact, I have almost always taken any doubt in my abilities as a challenge, the result most often being the satisfaction of winning a convert, of seeing the cold, appraising eyes warm to my words, the body language change, the smile that indicates I have opened some avenue for communication. So that day as I read, I looked directly at that woman. Her lowered eyes told me she was embarrassed at her faux pas, and when I willed her to look up at me, she graciously allowed me to punish her with my full attention. We shook hands at the end of the reading and I never saw her again. She has probably forgotten the entire incident, but maybe not.

Yet I am one of the lucky ones. There are thousands of Latinas with- 13 out the privilege of an education or the entrees into society that I have. For them life is a constant struggle against the misconceptions perpetuated by the myth of the Latina. My goal is to try to replace the old stereotypes with a much more interesting set of realities. Every time I give a reading, I hope the stories I tell, the dreams and fears I examine in my work, can achieve some universal truth that will get my audience past the particulars of my skin color, my accent, or my clothes.

I once wrote a poem in which I called all Latinas "God's brown 14 daughters." This poem is really a prayer of sorts, offered upward, but also, through the human-to-human channel of art, outward. It is a prayer for communication and for respect. In it, Latin women pray "in Spanish to an Anglo God/ with a Jewish heritage," and they are "fervently hoping/ that if not omnipotent,/ at least He be bilingual."

RESPONDING TO THE TEXT

The way in which Latinas dress — and why they do so — establishes one of the primary culture clashes presented in Cofer's essay. The strict Catholic culture of Puerto Rico by and large denies young women the possibility of promiscuity, so an eye-catching outfit highlights only the beauty of the wearer without connoting a direct sexual invitation. Ironically, American culture effectively denies women the ability to wear eye-catching clothing without also sending a message to some men that the wearer expects and perhaps welcomes sexual advances. Discuss the paradox presented by the culture clash and how it relates to our society. How might American society be able to modify or separate the ties between one's appearance and the message that it sends to others?

ENGAGING THE WRITER'S SUBJECT

1. Why does Cofer say that "the island travels with you" (paragraph 1)? In what ways is that a good thing? How can it be negative?

2. How does Cofer's experience at Career Day capture the clash of American and Puerto Rican cultures with which she has struggled her entire life?

3. Advertisers have fed the stereotype of the "sizzling" Latin American woman. What gave rise to the stereotype, and how does it affect Latinas?

4. What are *piropos*? What is their place in Puerto Rican society?

5. What happens at Cofer's first public poetry reading that illustrates another stereotype that Hispanic women must confront? Despite her difficulties, why does Cofer consider herself "one of the lucky ones" (paragraph 13)?

ANALYZING THE WRITER'S CRAFT

1. How does Cofer define "cultural schizophrenia" in her essay? (Glossary: *Definition*) Why is the term so important to her overall purpose? (Glossary: *Purpose*)

2. Cofer uses personal experiences to illustrate the Latina stereotypes she identifies in her essay. (Glossary: *Examples*) Do you find her examples effective? Does she lose any credibility by not quoting or referring to Hispanic women outside of her immediate family? Explain.

3. Cofer ends her essay by discussing and quoting from one of her poems, which she calls "a prayer for communication and for respect" (paragraph 14). (Glossary: *Beginnings/Endings*) Why does she introduce poetry at the end of an otherwise prosaic essay based on personal narrative? (Glossary: *Narration*) What does the poetry communicate that the prose perhaps does not?

UNDERSTANDING THE WRITER'S LANGUAGE

1. Cofer states that " 'Maria' had followed me to London" (paragraph 1). For Cofer and for other Latinas, what does the name Maria connote?

(Glossary: *Connotation/Denotation*) How does Cofer's use of the name foreshadow the issues she presents in her essay?

2. List the adjectives Cofer uses to describe how Latinas tend to dress. What is the overall impression she gives of their style of dress? How does this impression explain the sexual stereotyping that Latinas often endure?

3. Refer to your desk dictionary to determine the meanings of the following words as Cofer uses them in this selection: *microcosm* (paragraph 3), *coalesced* (5), *innuendo* (6), *mores* (7), *menial* (11), *faux pas* (12).

WRITING SUGGESTIONS

1. Cofer's essay reveals that she categorizes herself in several ways that have nothing to do with her ethnicity. She is a poet. She is highly educated. In London, she was an expatriate. Think about the "classification" of this kind that you most aspire to represent. Do you wish to be considered a star athlete? A scholar? A person of religious faith? A premedical student with a great future as a doctor? What is it about that classification that appeals to you? What potential disadvantages does it carry, such as the implied separation from others who do not share the classification? What negative stereotypes (dumb jock, for example) might be applied to you? Do you like whatever exclusivity such a classification entails, or do you try to downplay it as much as possible so as not to set yourself apart? Explain.

2. Cofer blames the mass media for the perpetuation of Latina stereotypes. Few of us can claim that we do not hold stereotypes or assumptions that are based on preconceived notions rather than direct experience. What are some of the "myths" you have believed — and perhaps still believe — about others? How did you acquire them? Based on your experience, write an essay in which you argue for or against Cofer's contention that ethnic stereotypes are harmfully perpetuated by the media. Does the media create our values and biases, or does it merely provide us with depictions that agree with our own preconceived notions of what is true?

3. Psychologists, in trying to understand what makes people function and think the way they do, have developed new ways in which to classify people by personality typing. Research this topic at the library or on the Internet. Books like *Please Understand Me* (1978) by David Kiersey and Marilyn Bates include tests that help determine your personality type. Take one of these tests with two friends you know well. Write an essay in which you discuss the results. How well does your "type" describe you? How accurate do you think the results were for your friends? What benefits can be realized from "typing" people? What possible dangers, if any, do you see from applying this kind of typing to large numbers of people?

- To begin your research online, go to **bedfordstmartins.com /subjectsstrategies** and click on "Division and Classification" or browse the thematic directory of annotated links.

How to Detect Propaganda

Institute for Propaganda Analysis

*In 1937 a group of journalists, social scientists, and business leaders
headed by Clyde R. Miller of Columbia University established the Institute for Propaganda Analysis. The mission of the institute was to inform
the American people about the nature of propaganda and its dissemination
in a world just beginning to recognize the power and influence of mass
media. Within a few years World War II would demonstrate what a refined and deadly weapon propaganda had become. The institute was also
interested in teaching people to think critically about the information
they were receiving, to ask questions about it, to see how it was shaped
through language, and to detect the different methods of its use. To that
end the institute published books and pamphlets, none of which is still in
print with the exception of this often-reprinted selection.*

*"How to Detect Propaganda" offers both a definition of propaganda
and a division and classification of seven famous propaganda devices
used to shape the truth and our minds — often for purposes not in the
best interest of humanity.*

PREPARING TO READ

You may have heard of propaganda, but do you know what it is? Is
it good or bad? Do you think you have been the object of propaganda? If so, where and how?

If American citizens are to have clear understanding of present-day   1
conditions and what to do about them, they must be able to recognize propaganda, to analyze it, and to appraise it.

But what is propaganda?   2

As generally understood, *propaganda is expression of opinion or ac-*   3
*tion by individuals or groups deliberately designed to influence opinions or
actions of other individuals or groups with reference to predetermined ends.*
Thus propaganda differs from scientific analysis. The propagandist is
trying to "put something across," good or bad, whereas the scientist is
trying to discover truth and fact. Often the propagandist does not
want careful scrutiny and criticism; he wants to bring about a specific
action. Because the action may be socially beneficial or socially harmful to millions of people, it is necessary to focus upon the propagandist
and his activities the searchlight of scientific scrutiny. Socially desirable
propaganda will not suffer from such examination, but the opposite
type will be detected and revealed for what it is.

We are fooled by propaganda chiefly because we don't recognize it   4
when we see it. It may be fun to be fooled but, as the cigarette ads

used to say, it is more fun to know. We can more easily recognize propaganda when we see it if we are familiar with the seven common propaganda devices. These are:

1. The Name Calling Device
2. The Glittering Generalities Device
3. The Transfer Device
4. The Testimonial Device
5. The Plain Folks Device
6. The Card Stacking Device
7. The Band Wagon Device

Why are we fooled by these devices? Because they appeal to our emotions rather than to our reason. They make us believe and do something we would not believe or do if we thought about it calmly, dispassionately. In examining these devices, note that they work most effectively at those times when we are too lazy to think for ourselves; also, they tie into emotions which sway us to be "for" or "against" nations, races, religions, ideals, economic and political policies and practices, and so on through automobiles, cigarettes, radios, toothpastes, presidents, and wars. With our emotions stirred, it may be fun to be fooled by these propaganda devices, but it is more fun and infinitely more to our own interests to know how they work.

Lincoln must have had in mind citizens who could balance their emotions with intelligence when he made this remark ". . . but you can't fool all of the people all of the time."

NAME CALLING

"Name Calling" is a device to make us form a judgment without examining the evidence on which it should be based. Here the propagandist appeals to our hate and fear. He does this by giving "bad names" to those individuals, groups, nations, races, policies, practices, beliefs, and ideals which he would have us condemn and reject. For centuries the name "heretic" was bad. Thousands were oppressed, tortured, or put to death as heretics. Anybody who dissented from popular or group belief or practice was in danger of being called a heretic. In the light of today's knowledge, some heresies were bad and some were good. Many of the pioneers of modern science were called heretics; witness the cases of Copernicus, Galileo, Bruno. Today's bad names include: Fascist, demagogue, dictator, Red, financial oligarchy, Communist, muckraker, alien, outside agitator, economic royalist, Utopian, rabble-rouser, trouble-maker, Tory, Constitution-wrecker.

"Al" Smith called Roosevelt a Communist by implication when he   8
said in his Liberty League speech, "There can be only one capital,
Washington or Moscow." When "Al" Smith was running for the presidency many called him a tool of the Pope, saying in effect, "We must
choose between Washington and Rome." That implied that Mr.
Smith, if elected President, would take his orders from the Pope. Likewise Mr. Justice Hugo Black has been associated with a bad name, Ku
Klux Klan. In these cases some propagandists have tried to make us
form judgments without examining essential evidence and implications. "Al Smith is a Catholic. He must never be President." "Roosevelt
is a Red. Defeat his program." "Hugo Black is or was a Klansman. Take
him out of the Supreme Court."

Use of "bad names" without presentation of their essential mean-   9
ing, without all their pertinent implications, comprises perhaps the
most common of all propaganda devices. Those who want to *maintain
the status quo* apply bad names to those who would change it. . . . Those
who want to *change the status quo* apply bad names to those who would
maintain it. For example, the *Daily Worker* and the *American Guardian*
apply bad names to conservative Republicans and Democrats.

GLITTERING GENERALITIES

"Glittering Generalities" is a device by which the propagandist identi-   10
fies his program with virtue by use of "virtue words." Here he appeals
to our emotions of love, generosity, and brotherhood. He uses words like
truth, freedom, honor, liberty, social justice, public service, the right to
work, loyalty, progress, democracy, the American way, Constitution-
defender. These words suggest shining ideals. All persons of good will
believe in these ideals. Hence the propagandist, by identifying his individual group, nation, race, policy, practice, or belief with such ideals,
seeks to win us to his cause. As Name Calling is a device to make us
form a judgment to *reject and condemn* without examining the evidence, Glittering Generalities is a device to make us *accept and approve*
without examining the evidence.

For example, use of the phrases, "the right to work" and "social   11
justice," may be a device to make us accept programs for meeting
labor-capital problems which, if we examined them critically, we
would not accept at all.

In the Name Calling and Glittering Generalities devices, words   12
are used to stir up our emotions and to befog our thinking. In one device "bad words" are used to make us mad; in the other "good words"
are used to make us glad.

The propagandist is most effective in the use of these devices when   13
his words make us create devils to fight or gods to adore. By his use of

the "bad words," we personify as a "devil" some nation, race, group, individual, policy, practice, or ideal; we are made fighting mad to destroy it. By use of "good words," we personify as a godlike idol some nation, race, group, etc. Words which are "bad" to some are "good" to others, or may be made so. Thus, to some the New Deal is "a prophecy of social salvation" while to others it is "an omen of social disaster."

From consideration of names, "bad" and "good," we pass to institutions and symbols, also "bad" and "good." We see these in the next device. 14

TRANSFER

"Transfer" is a device by which the propagandist carries over the authority, sanction, and prestige of something we respect and revere to something he would have us accept. For example, most of us respect and revere our church and our nation. If the propagandist succeeds in getting church or nation to approve a campaign in behalf of some program, he thereby transfers its authority, sanction, and prestige to that program. Thus we may accept something which otherwise we might reject. 15

In the Transfer device, symbols are constantly used. The cross represents the Christian Church. The flag represents the nation. Cartoons like Uncle Sam represent a consensus of public opinion. Those symbols stir emotions. At their very sight, with the speed of light, is aroused the whole complex of feelings we have with respect to church or nation. A cartoonist by having Uncle Sam disapprove a budget for unemployment relief would have us feel that the whole United States disapproves relief costs. By drawing an Uncle Sam who approves the same budget, the cartoonist would have us feel that the American people approve it. Thus the Transfer device is used both for and against causes and ideas. 16

TESTIMONIAL

The "Testimonial" is a device to make us accept anything from a patent medicine or a cigarette to a program of national policy. In this device the propagandist makes use of testimonials. "When I feel tired, I smoke a Camel and get the grandest 'lift.'" "We believe the John L. Lewis plan of labor organization is splendid; C.I.O. should be supported." This device works in reverse also; counter-testimonials may be employed. Seldom are these used against commercial products like patent medicines and cigarettes, but they are constantly employed in social, economic, and political issues. "We believe that the John L. Lewis plan of labor organization is bad; C.I.O. should not be supported." 17

PLAIN FOLKS

"Plain Folks" is a device used by politicians, labor leaders, business- 18
men, and even by ministers and educators to win our confidence by
appearing to be people like ourselves — "just plain folks among the
neighbors." In election years especially do candidates show their devo-
tion to little children and the common, homey things of life. They
have front porch campaigns. For the newspaper men they raid the
kitchen cupboard, finding there some of the good wife's apple pie.
They go to country picnics; they attend service at the old frame church;
they pitch hay and go fishing; they show their belief in home and
mother. In short, they would win our votes by showing that they're
just as common as the rest of us — "just plain folks" — and, therefore,
wise and good. Businessmen often are "plain folks" with the factory
hands. Even distillers use the device. "It's our family's whiskey, neighbor; and neighbor, it's your price."

CARD STACKING

"Card Stacking" is a device in which the propagandist employs all the 19
arts of deception to win our support for himself, his group, nation, race,
policy, practice, belief, or ideal. He stacks the cards against the truth. He
uses under-emphasis and over-emphasis to dodge issues and evade facts.
He resorts to lies, censorship, and distortion. He omits facts. He offers
false testimony. He creates a smoke screen of clamor by raising a new
issue when he wants an embarrassing matter forgotten. He draws a red
herring across the trail to confuse and divert those in quest of facts he
does not want revealed. He makes the unreal appear real and the real
appear unreal. He lets half-truth masquerade as truth. By the Card
Stacking device, a mediocre candidate, through the "buildup," is made
to appear an intellectual titan; an ordinary prize fighter, a probable
world champion; a worthless patent medicine, a beneficent cure. By
means of this device propagandists would convince us that a ruthless
war of aggression is a crusade for righteousness. Card Stacking employs
sham, hypocrisy, effrontery.

THE BAND WAGON

The "Band Wagon" is a device to make us follow the crowd, to accept 20
the propagandist's program en masse. Here his theme is: "Everybody's
doing it." His techniques range from those of medicine show to dramatic spectacle. He hires a hall, fills a great stadium, marches a million
men in parade. He employs symbols, colors, music, movement, all the
dramatic arts. He appeals to the desire, common to most of us, to

"follow the crowd." Because he wants us to "follow the crowd" in masses, he directs his appeal to groups held together by common ties of nationality, religion, race, environment, sex, vocation. Thus propagandists campaigning for or against a program will appeal to us as Catholics, Protestants, or Jews; as members of the Nordic race or as Negroes; as farmers or as school teachers; as housewives or as miners. All the artifices of flattery are used to harness the fears and hatreds, prejudices, and biases, convictions and ideals common to the group; thus emotion is made to push and pull the group on to the Band Wagon. In newspaper article and in the spoken word this device is also found. "Don't throw your vote away. Vote for our candidate. He's sure to win." Nearly every candidate wins in every election — before the votes are in.

PROPAGANDA AND EMOTION

Observe that in all these devices our emotion is the stuff with which propagandists work. Without it they are helpless; with it, harnessing it to their purposes, they can make us glow with pride or burn with hatred, they can make us zealots in behalf of the program they espouse. As we said at the beginning, propaganda as generally understood is expression of opinion or action by individuals or groups with reference to predetermined ends. Without the appeal to our emotion — to our fears and to our courage, to our selfishness and unselfishness, to our loves and to our hates — propagandists would influence few opinions and few actions. 21

To say this is not to condemn emotion, an essential part of life, or to assert that all predetermined ends of propagandists are "bad." What we mean is that the intelligent citizen does not want propagandists to utilize his emotions, even to the attainment of "good" ends, without knowing what is going on. He does not want to be "used" in the attainment of ends he may later consider "bad." He does not want to be gullible. He does not want to be fooled. He does not want to be duped, even in a "good" cause. He wants to know the facts and among these is included the fact of the utilization [of] his emotions. 22

Keeping in mind the seven common propaganda devices, turn to today's newspapers and almost immediately you can spot examples of them all. At election time or during any campaign, Plain Folks and Band Wagon are common. Card Stacking is hardest to detect because it is adroitly executed or because we lack the information necessary to nail the lie. A little practice with the daily newspapers in detecting these propaganda devices soon enables us to detect them elsewhere — in radio, news-reel, books, magazines, and in expression[s] of labor unions, business groups, churches, schools, political parties. 23

RESPONDING TO THE TEXT

Think about the propaganda devices you have read about. Choose one device and list examples of its use. How effective do you think this device is? Explain.

ENGAGING THE WRITER'S SUBJECT

1. As you read the definition of propaganda given in italics (paragraph 3), what are your thoughts? Could one say that the definition provided fits our activities as writers? Why or why not? Is there some part of the definition that does not allow that conclusion? If so, what part? Explain.

2. Why is it difficult to recognize propaganda?

3. What is the most common of all propaganda devices?

4. Which of the propaganda devices do you think is most dangerous? Why?

ANALYZING THE WRITER'S CRAFT

1. What is the institute's purpose in this article? (Glossary: *Purpose*)

2. In paragraph 6, the authors include a reference to Abraham Lincoln and a partial quotation by him. How does the reference work and what does it mean?

3. Why is division and classification a useful strategy to use when writing about propaganda? How helpful is it to have the writer tell us who uses the device and where it is often encountered?

4. Some of the examples the writer uses are linked historically to the time the article was written. (Glossary: *Exemplification*) Are you hampered in your understanding of the writer's explanations by such dated examples? Is your understanding of the way each propaganda device works dependent on such references? Explain.

UNDERSTANDING THE WRITER'S LANGUAGE

1. Are there stylistic clues that let us know whether one writer or a committee of writers wrote this selection? (Glossary: *Style*) Does it matter? What tone is established in the piece, based on the writers' diction? (Glossary: *Diction; Tone*)

2. The introduction to each of the seven propaganda devices begins with the formula: "X is a device . . . ." What purpose does the repetition serve? Is the repetition helpful or annoying?

3. Refer to your desk dictionary to determine the meanings of the following words as they are used in this selection: *predetermined* (paragraph 3), *dispassionately* (5), *heretics* (7), *demagogue* (7), *oligarchy* (7), *patent medicine* (17), *beneficent* (19), *effrontery* (19), *artifices* (20), *duped* (22), *adroitly* (23).

WRITING SUGGESTIONS

1. As is readily apparent in "How to Detect Propaganda," advertisers depend on several different kinds of propaganda to win you over. Yet they use other techniques, including simple dissemination of information and misinformation, side-by-side comparisons, logical argumentation, and so on. Watch a couple of hours of television, and note the techniques used in each commercial. Then write a division and classification essay in which you present the different types of techniques and describe how advertisers use them. What techniques, other than the ones presented in this essay, are most popular?

2. Write an essay in which you compare and contrast two ads for the same product that appear in two different sources; for example, beer ads from *Vibe* and the *Advocate*, makeup ads from *Teen People* and *Vogue*, car ads from *Road and Track* and *Good Housekeeping*, or computer ads from *Wired* and *Newsweek*. (Glossary: *Comparison and Contrast*) How are the ads similar or different? What type of audience does each ad address? (Glossary: *Audience*) What propaganda techniques does each ad use, and how are those techniques keyed to the ads' audiences?

3. There have been several societies in which propaganda became frighteningly effective and was used to lead millions of people to conclusions or actions they never would have considered independently. Research a prominent society in which the leaders used propaganda as a way to "conquer the masses," as Joseph Goebbels, Adolf Hitler's minister of propaganda, once said. Nazi Germany is an excellent example. Others from the twentieth century include the Soviet Union, imperial Japan, and Italy under Mussolini. What about examples from the twenty-first century? Using your college library and the Internet to do your research, write an essay in which you present the phrases, rhetoric, and labels chosen by the leaders to shape the thinking of the "masses." What propaganda techniques did the leaders rely on? How effective were these campaigns? What questions might have caused the propaganda to fail, had enough people asked them?

• To begin your research online, go to **bedfordstmartins.com /subjectsstrategies** and click on "Division and Classification" or browse the thematic directory of annotated links.

WRITING SUGGESTIONS
FOR DIVISION AND CLASSIFICATION

1. To write a meaningful classification essay, you must analyze a body of unorganized material, arranging it for a particular purpose (Glossary: *Purpose*). For example, to identify for a buyer the most economical cars currently on the market, you might initially determine which cars can be purchased for under $20,000 and which cost between $20,000 and $30,000. Then, using a second basis of selection — fuel economy — you could determine which cars have the best gas mileage within each price range.

    Select one of the following subjects, and write a classification essay. Be sure that your purpose is clearly explained and that your bases of selection are chosen and ordered in accordance with your purpose.

    a. attitudes toward physical fitness
    b. contemporary American music
    c. reading materials
    d. reasons for going to college
    e. attitudes toward the religious or spiritual side of life
    f. choosing a hobby
    g. television comedies
    h. college professors
    i. local restaurants
    j. choosing a career
    k. college courses
    l. recreational activities
    m. ways of financing a college education
    n. parties or other social events

2. We sometimes resist classifying other people because it can seem like "pigeonholing" or stereotyping individuals unfairly. In an essay, compare and contrast two or more ways of classifying people, including at least one that you would call legitimate and one that you would call misleading. (Glossary: *Comparison and Contrast*) What conclusions can you draw about the difference between useful classifications and damaging stereotypes?

3. Both E. B. White (p. 321) and Toni Cade Bambara (p. 322) used division and classification to help explain their understanding of New York City. Bambara, however, uses other strategies, including comparison and contrast, to create a stronger image of the division between the rich, who can spend $35 on a toy clown at F.A.O. Schwarz, and the poor, who would use $35 very differently. (Glossary: *Comparison and Contrast*) She also uses narration to develop the characters of Sylvia and Miss Moore and their reactions to the prices at the toy store. (Glossary: *Narration*)

    Use division and classification to explain your school or town. What categories might you use? Would you divide your subject into different types of people the way E. B. White did? Would you classify people by their spending habits as Toni Cade Bambara did? What are the other ways in which you might explain your school or town? What other rhetorical strategies might you incorporate to strengthen your presentation? You might want to look at the Web site of your school or town to find out what categories it uses to present itself.

4. Write an essay about the types of presidents that have been elected since the invention of television. How would you organize the different presidents and elections? Would you divide the presidents by political party? By age? By their geographic origins? By their political programs — domestic, international, military, economic, and so forth? What other rhetorical strategies might you use to develop and explain your categories?

CHAPTER **9**

Definition

WHAT IS DEFINITION?

A definition explains the meaning of a word or phrase; if you have ever used a dictionary, you will be familiar with the concept of definition. Words need to be defined because their sounds and spelling hardly ever indicate exactly what they are intended to mean and because sometimes a single word can have more than one meaning. A word like *draft* can refer to a current of air, conscription, a ship's depth in the water, a bank check, the official recruiting of an athlete, or the first attempt at a piece of writing. It's amazing that this jumble of meanings can all belong to one word; but after all, words are abstract symbols and represent large and complex worlds of objects, actions, and ideas.

We can only communicate with one another properly when all of us define the words we use in the same way — and that is not always easy. What one person believes he or she is saying might be construed differently by the listener. For example, if someone told you to be *discriminatory*, you might understand the word in a manner not intended by the speaker. Let's look at how Robert Keith Miller attempts to define *discrimination* in his essay called "Discrimination Is a Virtue," which first appeared in *Newsweek* in 1980.

> We have a word in English which means "the ability to tell differences." That word is *discrimination*. But within the last twenty years, this word has been so frequently misused that an entire generation has grown up believing that "discrimination" means "racism."

People are always proclaiming that "discrimination" is something that should be done away with. Should that ever happen, it would prove to be our undoing.

Discrimination means discernment; it means the ability to perceive the truth, to use good judgment and to profit accordingly. The *Oxford English Dictionary* traces this meaning of the word back to 1648 and demonstrates that for the next 300 years, "discrimination" was a virtue, not a vice. Thus, when a character in a nineteenth-century novel makes a happy marriage, Dickens has another character remark, "It does credit to your discrimination that you should have found such a very excellent young woman."

Of course, "the ability to tell differences" assumes that differences exist, and this is unsettling for a culture obsessed with the notion of equality. The contemporary belief that discrimination is a vice stems from the compound "discriminate against." What we need to remember, however, is that some things deserve to be judged harshly: We should not leave our kingdoms to the selfish and the wicked.

Discrimination is wrong only when someone or something is discriminated against because of prejudice. But to use the word in that sense, as so many people do, is to destroy its true meaning. If you discriminate against something because of general preconceptions rather than particular insights, then you are not discriminating — bias has clouded the clarity of vision that discrimination demands.

How does Miller define *discrimination*? He mainly uses a technique called *extended definition*, a definition that requires a full discussion. This is only one of many types of definition that you could use to explain what a word or an idea means to you. The following paragraphs identify and explain several types of definition. While learning the various kinds of definition, see if you can find examples of them in Miller's article.

A *formal definition* — a definition such as that found in a dictionary — explains the meaning of a word by assigning it to a class and then differentiating it from other members of that class.

Term		**Class**	**Differentiation**
Music	is	sound	made by voices or instruments and characterized by melody, harmony, or rhythm.

Note how crucial the differentiation is here: There are many sounds — from the roar of a passing jet airplane to the fizz of soda in a glass — that must be excluded for the definition to be precise and useful. Dictionary entries often follow the class-differentiation pattern of the formal definition.

A *synonymous definition* explains a word by pairing it with another word of similar but perhaps more limited meaning.

> Music is melody.

Synonymous definition is almost never as precise as formal definition because few words share exactly the same meaning. But when the word being defined is reasonably familiar and somewhat broad, a well-chosen synonym can provide readers with a surer sense of its meaning in context.

A *negative definition* explains a word by saying what it does not mean.

> Music is not silence, and it is not noise.

Such a definition must obviously be incomplete: There are sounds that are neither silence nor noise and yet are not music — quiet conversation, for example. But specifying what something is not often helps to clarify other statements about what it is.

An *etymological definition* also seldom stands alone, but by tracing a word's origins it helps readers understand its meaning. *Etymology* itself is defined as the study of the history of a linguistic form — the history of words.

> Music is descended from the Greek word *mousikē*, meaning literally "the art of the Muse."

The Muses, according to Greek mythology, were deities and the sources of inspiration in the arts. Thus the etymology suggests why we think of music as an art and as the product of inspiration. Etymological definitions often reveal surprising sources that suggest new ways of looking at ideas or objects.

A *stipulative definition* is a definition invented by a writer to convey a special or unexpected sense of an existing and often familiar word.

> Music is a language, but a language of the intangible, a kind of soul-language.
>
> — EDWARD MACDOWELL

> Music is the arithmetic of sounds.
>
> — CLAUDE DEBUSSY

Although these two examples seem to disagree with each other, and perhaps also with your idea of what music is, note that neither is arbitrary. (That is, neither assigns to the word *music* a completely foreign meaning, as Humpty Dumpty did in *Through the Looking-Glass* when he defined *glory* as "a nice knock-down argument.") The stipulative definitions by MacDowell and Debussy help explain each composer's conception of the subject and can lead, of course, to further elaboration. Stipulative definitions almost always provide the basis for a more complex discussion. These definitions are often the subjects of an extended definition.

Sometimes a word, or the idea it stands for, requires more than a sentence of explanation. Such a longer definition — called, naturally enough, *extended definition* — may go on for a paragraph, a page, an essay, or even an entire book. It may employ any of the techniques already mentioned in this chapter, as well as the various strategies discussed throughout the text. An extended definition tends to differ greatly from a formal definition; writers use extended definition to make a specific, and often unusual, point about an idea. An extended definition of music might provide *examples*, ranging from African drumming to a Bach fugue to a Bruce Springsteen song, to develop a fuller and more vivid sense of what music is. A writer might *describe* music in detail by showing its characteristic features, or explain the *process* of composing music, or *compare and contrast* music with language (according to MacDowell's stipulative definition) or arithmetic (according to Debussy's). Each of these strategies, and others too, helps make the meaning of a writer's words and ideas clear.

Robert Keith Miller primarily used an extended definition to explain his understanding of the word *discrimination*. What other types did you find in his brief essay? Let's go through the essay again to see the various definitions that he used. To begin with, Miller used a very brief formal definition of *discrimination* [term]: "the ability [class] to tell differences [differentiation]". He then offered a negative definition (discrimination is not racism) and a synonymous definition (discrimination is discernment). Next he cited the entry in a great historical dictionary of English to support his claim, and he quoted an example to illustrate his definition. He concluded by contrasting the word *discrimination* with the compound "discriminate against." Each of these techniques helped make the case that the most precise meaning of *discrimination* is in direct opposition to its common usage today.

WHY DO WRITERS USE DEFINITION?

Since most readers have dictionaries, it might seem that writers would hardly ever have to define their terms with formal definitions. In fact, writers don't necessarily do so all the time, even when using an unusual word like *tergiversation*, which few readers have in their active vocabularies; if readers don't know it, the reasoning goes, let them look it up. But there are times when a definition is quite necessary. One of these times is when a writer uses a word so specialized or so new that it simply won't be in dictionaries; another is when a writer must use a number of unfamiliar technical terms within only a few sentences. Also, when a word has several different meanings or may mean different things to different people, writers will often state exactly the sense in which they are using the word. In each of these cases, definition serves the purpose of achieving clarity.

But writers also sometimes use definition, particularly extended definition, to explain the essential nature of the things and ideas they write about. For example, consider E. B. White's definition of *democracy*, which first appeared in the *New Yorker* on July 3, 1943.

> We received a letter from the Writers' War Board the other day asking for a statement on "The Meaning of Democracy." It presumably is our duty to comply with such a request, and it is certainly our pleasure.
>
> Surely the Board knows what democracy is. It is the line that forms on the right. It is the don't in don't shove. It is the hole in the stuffed shirt through which the sawdust slowly trickles; it is the dent in the high hat. Democracy is the recurrent suspicion that more than half of the people are right more than half of the time. It is the feeling of privacy in the voting booths, the feeling of communion in the libraries, the feeling of vitality everywhere. Democracy is a letter to the editor. Democracy is the score at the beginning of the ninth. It is an idea which hasn't been disproved yet, a song the words of which have not gone bad. It's the mustard on the hot dog and the cream in the rationed coffee. Democracy is a request from a War Board, in the middle of a morning in the middle of a war, wanting to know what democracy is.

Such writing goes beyond answering the question, "What does _____ mean exactly?" to tackle the much broader and deeper question "What is _____, and what does it represent?" In fact, every selection in this chapter is written as an extended definition.

Although exploring a term and what it represents is often the primary object of such a definition, sometimes writers go beyond giving a formal definition; they also use extended definitions to make persuasive points. Take the Miller essay, for example (p. 382). The subject of Miller's extended definition is clearly the word *discrimination*. His purpose, however, is less immediately obvious. At first it appears that he wants only to explain what the word means. But by the third sentence he is distinguishing what it does not mean, and at the end it's clear he's trying to persuade readers to use the word correctly and thus to discriminate more sharply and justly themselves. Jo Goodwin Parker in "What Is Poverty?" (p. 399) later in this chapter also uses extended definitions to make persuasive points.

AN ANNOTATED STUDENT ESSAY USING DEFINITION

Originally a native of New York City, Howard Solomon Jr. studied in France as part of the American Field Services Intercultural Program in high school, and he majored in French at the University of Vermont. Solomon's other interests include foreign affairs, languages, photography, and cycling; in his wildest dreams, he imagines becoming an international lawyer. For the following essay, Solomon began by interviewing students in his dormitory, collecting information and opinions that he eventually brought together with his own experiences to develop a definition of *best friends*.

Best Friends

Howard Solomon Jr.

Introduction: writer provides brief definition of best friend.

Best friends, even when they are not a part of our day-to-day lives, are essential to our well-being. They supply the companionship, help, security, and love that we all need. It is not easy to put into words exactly what a best friend is, because the matter is so personal. From time to time, however, we may think about our best friends — who they are, what characteristics they share, and why they are so important to us — in order to gain a better understanding of ourselves and our relationships.

Purpose: In defining best friend, writer comes to new understanding of self and relationships.

Organization: Writer uses sequence of interview questions for structure.

I recently asked several people for their opinions on the subject, beginning with the qualities they valued in their own best friends. They all agreed on three traits: reciprocity, honesty, and love. Reciprocity means that one can always rely on a best friend in times of need. A favor doesn't necessarily have to be returned; but best friends will return it anyway, because they want to. Best friends are willing to help each other for the sake of helping and not just for personal gain. One woman said that life seemed more secure because she knew her best friend was there if she ever needed help.

Three-part answer to question 1: What qualities do you value in a best friend?

1

2

Honesty in a best friendship is the   3
sharing of feelings openly and without reserve. The people I interviewed said they
could rely on their best friends as confi-
dants: They could share problems with their
best friends and ask for advice. They also
felt that, even if best friends were critical
of each other, they would never be hurtful or
spiteful.

Love is probably the most important   4
quality of a best friend relationship,
according to the people I interviewed.
They very much prized the affection and enjoyment they felt in the company of their
best friends. One man described it as a
"gut reaction," and all said it was a different feeling from being with other
friends. Private jokes, looks, and gestures create personal communication
between best friends that is at a very
high level — many times one person knows
what the other is thinking without anything
being said. The specifics differ, but almost everyone I talked to agreed that a
special feeling exists, which is best
described as love.

Answers to
question 2: Who
can be a best
friend?

I next asked who could be a best friend   5
and who could not. My sources all felt it was
impossible for parents, other relatives, and
people of the opposite sex (especially husbands or wives) to be best friends. One woman
said such people were "too inhibitive." Personally, I disagree — I have two best friends
who are women. However, I may be an exception, and most best friends may fit the
above requirements. There could be a good
reason for this, too: Most of the people I
interviewed felt that their best friends
were not demanding, while relatives and
partners of the opposite sex can be very
demanding.

Answers to question 3: How many best friends can a person have?

To the question of how many best friends one can have, some in my sample responded that it is possible to have several best friends, although very few people can do so; others said it was possible to have only a very few best friends; and still others felt they could have just one — that single friend who is most outstanding. It was interesting to see how ideas varied on this question. Although best friends may be no less special for one person than another, people do define the concept differently.

6

Answers to question 4: How long does it take to become a best friend?

Regarding how long it takes to become best friends and how long the relationship lasts, all were in agreement. "It is a long hard process which takes a lot of time," one woman explained. "It isn't something that can happen overnight," suggested another. One man said, "You usually know the person very well before you consider him your best friend. In fact you know everything about him, his bad points as well as his good points, so there is little likelihood that you can come into conflict with him." In addition, everyone thought that once a person has become a best friend, he or she remains so for the rest of one's life.

7

Writer highlights an important difference in responses from men and women.

During the course of the interviews I discovered one important and unexpected difference between men and women regarding the qualities of their best friends. The men all said that a best friend usually possessed one quality that stood out above all others — an easygoing manner or humor or sympathy, for example. One of them told me that he looked not for loyalty but for honesty, for someone who was truthful, because it was so rare to find this quality in anyone. The women I surveyed, however, all responded that they looked for a well-rounded person

8

who had many good qualities. One said that a person who had just one good quality and not several would be "too boring to associate with." Does this difference hold true beyond my sample? If so, it means that men and women have quite different definitions of their best friends.

Personal example: writer tells what he learned about best friends at the time of his father's death.

I have always wondered why my own best friends were so important to me; but it wasn't until recently that something happened to make me really understand my relationship with my best friends. My father died, and this was a crisis for me. Most of my friends gave me their condolences. But my best friends did more than that: they actually supported me. They called long distance to see how I was and what I needed, to try and help me work out my problems or simply to talk. Two of my best friends even took time from their spring break and, along with two other best friends, attended my father's memorial service; none of my other friends came. Since then, these are the only people who have continued to worry about me and talk to me about my father. I know that whenever I need someone they will be there and willing to help me. I know also that whenever they need help I will be ready to do the same for them.

Conclusion: writer gives personal definition of best friend.

Thesis

Yet, I don't value my best friends so much just for what they do for me. I simply enjoy their company more than anyone else's. We talk, joke, play sports, and do all kinds of things when we are together. I never feel ill at ease, even after we've been apart for a while. However, the most important thing for me about best friends is the knowledge that I am never alone, that there are others in the world who care about my well-being as much as I do about theirs. Surely this is a comforting feeling for everyone.

Analyzing Howard Solomon Jr.'s Essay of Definition: Questions for Discussion

1. How does Solomon define best friend in his opening paragraph?
2. According to the people Solomon surveyed, what three qualities are valued most in a best friend?
3. Which of these qualities is considered the most important? Why?
4. How do men's and women's definitions of a best friend differ? Do you agree with Solomon's informants?
5. In what ways do Solomon's interviews enhance his own definition of best friend?
6. In the final analysis, why does Solomon think people value their best friends so much?

SUGGESTIONS FOR WRITING A DEFINITION ESSAY

Determine Your Purpose

Whatever your subject, make sure you have a clear sense of your purpose. Why are you writing a definition? If it's only to explain what a word or phrase means, you'll probably run out of things to say in a few sentences, or you'll find that a good dictionary has already said them for you. An effective extended definition should attempt to explain the essential nature of a thing or an idea, whether it be *photosynthesis* or *spring fever* or *Republicanism* or *prison* or *common sense*.

Often the challenge of writing a paper using the rhetorical strategy of definition is in getting your audience to understand your particular perception of the term or idea you are trying to define and explain. Take, for example, the selection below from a student essay. For many years, the citizens of Quebec, one of Canada's ten provinces, have been debating and voting on the issue of secession from Canada. At the core of this volatile issue is the essential question of Canadian identity. As you will see from the student's introduction, the Quebecois define themselves very differently from other Canadians.

Quebecois Are Canadians

The peaceful formation of Canada as an independent nation has led to the current identity crisis in Quebec. The Quebecois perceive themselves to be different from all other Canadians because of their French ancestry and their unique history as both rulers and minorities in Canada. In an attempt to create a unified Canada the government has tried to establish a common Canadian culture through the building of a transcontinental railroad, a nationalized medical system, a national arts program, a national agenda, and the required use of both French and English in all publications and on all signs. As the twenty-first century begins, however, Canadians, especially the Quebecois, continue to grapple with the issue of what it means to be a Canadian, and unless some consensus can be reached on the definition of the Canadian identity, Quebec's attempt to secede from Canada may succeed.

This introductory paragraph establishes the need to define the terms *Canadians* and *Quebecois*. Implicit in any discussion of the meanings for these two terms is another rhetorical strategy: comparison and contrast. The writer might go on to use other strategies, such as description or exemplification, to highlight common characteristics or differences of the Canadians and Quebecois. Judging from the title, it is clear that an argument (see Chapter 11) will be made that, based on the definitions, Quebecois are Canadians.

When you decide on your topic, consider an idea or term that you would like to clarify or explain to someone. For example, Howard Solomon Jr. hit on the idea of defining what a best friend is. He recalls that "a friend of mine had become a best friend, and I was trying to figure out what had happened, what was different. So I decided to explore what was on my mind." At the beginning, you should have at least a general idea of what your subject means to you, as well as a sense of the audience you are writing your definition for and the impact you want your definition to achieve. The following advice will guide you as you plan and draft your essay.

Formulate a Thesis Statement

A strong, clear thesis statement is critical in any essay. When writing an essay using extended definition, you should formulate a thesis statement that states clearly both the word or idea that you want to define or explain and the way in which you are going to present your thoughts. Here are two examples from this chapter.

- "We have a word in English which means 'the ability to tell differences.' That word is *discrimination*. But within the last twenty years, this word has been so frequently misused that an entire generation has grown up believing that 'discrimination' means 'racism.'" Robert Keith Miller's thesis statement tells us that he will be discussing the word *discrimination* and how it is not the same as racism.

- "As the twenty-first century begins, however, Canadians, especially the Quebecois, continue to grapple with the issue of what it means to be a Canadian, and unless some consensus can be reached on the definition of the Canadian identity, Quebec's attempt to secede from Canada may succeed." Here, the writer makes it clear that the identity of both the Canadians and the Quebecois will be defined. This thesis statement also conveys a sense of the urgency of discussing these definitions.

As you begin to develop your thesis statement, ask yourself, "What is my point?" Next ask yourself, "What types of definitions will be most useful in making my point?" If you can't answer these questions yet, write some ideas down and try to determine your main point from these ideas.

Once you have settled on an idea, go back to the two questions above and write down your answers to them. Then combine the answers into a single-sentence thesis statement. Your eventual thesis statement does not have to be one sentence, but this exercise can be an effective way of focusing your point.

Consider Your Audience

What do your readers know? If you're an economics major in an undergraduate writing course, you can safely assume that you know your subject better than most of your readers do, and so you will have to explain even very basic terms and ideas. If, however, you're writing a paper for your course in econometrics, your most important reader — the one who grades your paper — won't even slow down at your references to *monetary aggregates* and *Philips Curves* — provided, of course, that you obviously know what they mean.

Choose a Technique of Definition

How you choose to develop your definition depends on your subject, your purpose, and your readers. Many inexperienced writers believe that any extended definition, no matter what the subject, should begin with a formal "dictionary" definition or should at least introduce one before the essay has proceeded very far. This is not necessarily so; you will find that most of the essays in this chapter include no such formal definition. Assume that your readers have dictionaries and know how to use them. If, however, you think your readers do require a short, formal definition at some point, don't simply quote from a dictionary. Unless you have some very good reason for doing otherwise, put the definition into your own words — words that suit your approach and the probable readers of your essay. (Certainly, in an essay about photosynthesis, nonscientists would be baffled by an opening such as this: "The dictionary defines *photosynthesis* as 'the process by which chlorophyll-containing cells in green plants convert incident light to chemical energy and synthesize organic compounds from inorganic compounds, especially carbohydrates from carbon dioxide and water, with the simultaneous release of oxygen.'") There's another advantage to using your own words: You won't have to write "The dictionary defines . . ." or "According to *Webster's* . . ."; stock phrases like these almost immediately put the reader's mind to sleep.

Certain subjects, such as liberalism and discrimination, lend themselves to different interpretations, depending on the writer's point of view. While readers may agree in general about what such subjects mean, there will be much disagreement over particulars and therefore room for you to propose and defend your own definitions.

Solomon remembers the difficulties he had getting started with his essay on best friends. "The first draft I wrote was nothing. I tried to get a start with the dictionary definition, but it didn't help — it just put into two words what really needs hundreds of words to explain, and the words it used had to be defined, too. My teacher suggested I might get going better if I talked about my topic with other people. I decided to make it semiformal, so I made up a list of a few specific questions — five questions — and went to about a dozen people I knew and asked them. Questions like, 'What qualities do your best friends have?' and 'What are some of the things they've done for you?' And I took notes on the answers. I was surprised when so many of them agreed. It isn't a scientific sampling, but the results helped me get started."

Develop Your Organizational Plan

Once you have gathered all the information that you will need for your essay of extended definition, you will want to settle on an organizational plan that suits your purpose and your materials. If you want to show that one definition of *family* is better than others, for example, you might want to lead with the definitions that you plan to discard and end with the one that you want your readers to accept.

Howard Solomon Jr. can trace several distinct stages that his paper went through before he settled on the plan of organizing his examples around the items on his interview questionnaire. "Doing this paper showed me that writing isn't all that easy. Boy, I went through so many copies — adding some things, taking out some things, reorganizing. At one point half the paper was a definition of friends, so I could contrast them with best friends. That wasn't necessary. Then the personal stuff came in late. In fact, my father died after I'd begun writing the paper, so that paragraph came in almost last of all. On the next-to-last draft everything was there, but it was put together in a sort of random way — not completely random, one idea would lead to the next and then the next — but there was a lot of circling around. My teacher pointed this out and suggested I outline what I'd written and work on the outline. So I tried it, and I saw what the problem was and what I had to do. It was just a matter of getting my examples into the right order, and finally everything clicked into place."

Use Other Rhetorical Strategies

Although definition can be used effectively as a separate rhetorical strategy, it is generally used alongside other writing strategies. Photosynthesis, for example, is a natural process, so one logical strategy for defining it would be *process analysis*; readers who know little about biology may better understand photosynthesis if you draw an *analogy* with the eating and breathing of human beings. Common sense is an abstract concept, so its meaning could certainly be *illustrated* with concrete *examples*; in addition, its special nature might emerge more sharply through *comparison and contrast* with other ways of thinking. To define a salt marsh, you might choose a typical marsh and *describe* it. To define economic inflation or a particular disease, you might discuss its *causes and effects*. Solomon builds his essay of definition around the many examples he garnered from his interviews with other students and his own personal experiences. Before you combine strategies, however, consider the purpose of your essay and the tone that you wish to adopt. Only two requirements limit your choice of rhetorical strategy: The strategy must be appropriate to your subject, and it must help you explain your subject's essential nature.

As you read the essays in this chapter, consider all of the writing strategies that the authors have used to support their definitions. How do you think these other strategies have added to or changed the style of the essay? Are there strategies that you might have added or taken out? What strategies, if any, do you think you might use to strengthen your definition essay?

Editing Tip: Precise Language

Be sure to follow the guidelines and advice for editing an essay given in Chapter 2, "Writing Essays." The guidelines highlight those sentence-level concerns — grammar, mechanics, and punctuation — that are especially important in editing any piece of writing. While editing your essay of definition, it is important that you pay attention to your diction, your choice and use of words. Good diction is precise, accurate, and appropriate. For careful writers, it is not enough merely to come close to saying what they want to say; they select words that convey exact meaning. Perhaps Mark Twain put this best when he once said, "The difference between the almost right word and the right word is really a large matter — 'tis the difference between the lightning-bug and the lightning." Inaccurate, imprecise, or inappropriate word choice not only fails to express your intended meaning but also may cause confusion and misunderstanding for your reader. You do not need a large vocabulary to use words precisely, but you do need to know the correct meanings of the words you do use. You can ensure exactness in your writing by 1) being aware of words' denotations as well as their connotative associations, and 2) using words that are specific and concrete.

1. **Select words that accurately denote and connote what you want to say.**

The *denotation* of a word is its literal meaning or dictionary definition. Most of the time you will have no trouble with denotation, but problems can occur when words are close in meaning or sound a lot alike.

accept	v., to receive
except	prep., to exclude
affect	v., to influence
effect	n., the result; v., to produce, bring into existence
anecdote	n., a short narrative
antidote	n., a medicine for countering effects of poison
coarse	adj., rough; crude
course	n., a route, a program of instruction
disinterested	adj., free of self-interest or bias
uninterested	adj., without interest

eminent	adj., outstanding, as in reputation
immanent	adj., remaining within, inherent
imminent	adj., about to happen
principal	n., a school official; in finance, a capital sum; adj., most important
principle	n., a basic law or rule of conduct
than	conj., used in comparisons
then	adv., at that time

Consult your desk dictionary if you are not sure you are using the correct word.

Words have connotative values as well as denotative meanings. *Connotations* are the associations or emotional overtones that words have acquired. For example the word *hostage* denotes a person who is given or held as security for the fulfillment of certain conditions or terms, but it connotes images of suffering, loneliness, torture, fear, deprivation, starvation, anxiety, and other private images based on our individual associations. Because many words in English are synonyms or have the same meanings — *strength, potency, force,* and *might* all denote "power" — your task as a writer in any given situation is to choose the word with the connotations that best suit your purpose.

2. Use specific and concrete words.

Words can be classified as relatively general or specific, abstract or concrete. *General words* name groups or classes of objects, qualities, or actions. *Specific words* name individual objects, qualities, or actions within a class or group. For examples, *dessert* is more specific than *food,* but more general than *pie.* And *pie* is more general than *blueberry pie.*

Abstract words refer to ideas, concepts, qualities, and conditions — *love, anger, beauty, youth, wisdom, honesty, patriotism,* and *liberty,* for example. *Concrete words,* on the other hand, name things you can see, hear, taste, touch, or smell. *Cornbread, rocking chair, sailboat, nitrogen, computer, rain, horse,* and *coffee* are all concrete words.

General and abstract words generally fail to create in the reader's mind the kind of vivid response that concrete, specific words do. Always question the words you choose. Notice how Jo Goodwin Parker uses concrete, specific diction in the opening sentence of many paragraphs in her essay "What Is Poverty?" to paint a powerful verbal picture of what poverty is:

Poverty is getting up every morning from a dirt- and illness-stained mattress.

Poverty is being tired.

Poverty is dirt.

Poverty is staying up all night on cold nights to watch the fire, knowing one spark on the newspaper covering the walls means your sleeping children die in flames.

— Jo Goodwin Parker
"What Is Poverty?," pages 399–400

Collectively, these specific and concrete words create a memorable definition of the abstraction *poverty*.

▶ *Questions for Revising and Editing: Definition*

1. Have I selected a subject in which there is some controversy or at least a difference of opinion about the definitions of key words?

2. Is the purpose of my definition clearly stated?

3. Have I presented a clear thesis statement?

4. Have I considered my audience? Do I oversimplify material for knowledgeable people or complicate material for beginners?

5. Have I used the types of definitions (*formal definition, synonymous definition, negative definition, etymological definition, stipulative definition,* and *extended definition*) that are most useful in making my point?

6. Is my essay of definition easy to follow? That is, is there a clear organizational principle (chronological or logical, for example)?

7. Have I used other rhetorical strategies — such as illustration, comparison and contrast, and cause and effect analysis — as needed and appropriate to enhance my definition?

8. Does my conclusion stem logically from my thesis statement and purpose?

9. Have I used precise language to convey my meaning? Have I used words that are specific and concrete?

STop

What Is Poverty?

Jo Goodwin Parker

All we know about Jo Goodwin Parker is that when George Henderson, a professor at the University of Oklahoma, was preparing his 1971 book America's Other Children: Public Schools Outside Suburbia, *the following essay was mailed to him from West Virginia under Parker's name. Henderson included Parker's essay in his book, and according to him, the piece was an unpublished speech given in De Land, Florida, on December 27, 1965. Perhaps Parker is, as her essay says, one of the rural poor who eke out a difficult living just beyond view of America's middle-class majority; or perhaps she is a spokesperson for them, writing not from her own experience but from long and sympathetic observation. In either case, her definition of poverty is so detailed and forceful that it conveys, even to those who have never known it, the nature of poverty.*

PREPARING TO READ

What does it mean to you to be poor? What do you see as some of the effects of poverty on people?

You ask me what is poverty? Listen to me. Here I am, dirty, smelly, and with no "proper" underwear on and with the stench of my rotting teeth near you. I will tell you. Listen to me. Listen without pity. I cannot use your pity. Listen with understanding. Put yourself in my dirty, worn out, ill-fitting shoes, and hear me.

Poverty is getting up every morning from a dirt- and illness-stained mattress. The sheets have long since been used for diapers. Poverty is living in a smell that never leaves. This is a smell of urine, sour milk, and spoiling food sometimes joined with the strong smell of long-cooked onions. Onions are cheap. If you have smelled this smell, you did not know how it came. It is the smell of the outdoor privy. It is the smell of young children who cannot walk the long dark way in the night. It is the smell of the mattresses where years of "accidents" have happened. It is the smell of the milk which has gone sour because the refrigerator long has not worked, and it costs money to get it fixed. It is the smell of rotting garbage. I could bury it, but where is the shovel? Shovels cost money.

Poverty is being tired. I have always been tired. They told me at the hospital when the last baby came that I had chronic anemia caused from poor diet, a bad case of worms, and that I needed a corrective operation. I listened politely — the poor are always polite. The poor always listen. They don't say that there is no money for iron pills, or better food, or worm medicine. The idea of an operation is frightening and costs so much that, if I had dared, I would have laughed. Who takes care of my children? Recovery from an operation takes a long time. I have three children. When I left them with "Granny" the last time I had a job, I came home to find the baby covered with fly specks, and a diaper that had not been changed since I left. When the dried diaper came off, bits of my baby's flesh came with it. My other child was playing with a sharp bit of broken glass, and my oldest was playing alone at the edge of a lake. I made twenty-two dollars a week, and a good nursery school costs twenty dollars a week for three children. I quit my job.

Poverty is dirt. You say in your clean clothes coming from your   4
clean house, "Anybody can be clean." Let me explain about housekeeping with no money. For breakfast I give my children grits with no oleo or cornbread without eggs and oleo. This does not use up many dishes. What dishes there are, I wash in cold water and with no soap. Even the cheapest soap has to be saved for the baby's diapers. Look at my hands, so cracked and red. Once I saved for two months to buy a jar of Vaseline for my hands and the baby's diaper rash. When I had saved enough, I went to buy it and the price had gone up two cents. The baby and I suffered on. I have to decide every day if I can bear to put my cracked, sore hands into the cold water and strong soap. But you ask, why not hot water? Fuel costs money. If you have a wood fire it costs money. If you burn electricity, it costs money. Hot water is a luxury. I do not have luxuries. I know you will be surprised when I tell you how young I am. I look so much older. My back has been bent over the wash tubs for so long, I cannot remember when I ever did anything else. Every night I wash every stitch my school age child has on and just hope her clothes will be dry by morning.

Poverty is staying up all night on cold nights to watch the fire,   5
knowing one spark on the newspaper covering the walls means your sleeping children die in flames. In summer poverty is watching gnats and flies devour your baby's tears when he cries. The screens are torn and you pay so little rent you know they will never be fixed. Poverty means insects in your food, in your nose, in your eyes, and crawling over you when you sleep. Poverty is hoping it never rains because diapers won't dry when it rains and soon you are using newspapers. Poverty is seeing your children forever with runny noses. Paper handkerchiefs cost money and all your rags you need for other things. Even more costly are antihistamines. Poverty is cooking without food and cleaning without soap.

Poverty is asking for help. Have you ever had to ask for help,   6
knowing your children will suffer unless you get it? Think about asking for a loan from a relative, if this is the only way you can imagine asking

for help. I will tell you how it feels. You find out where the office is that you are supposed to visit. You circle that block four or five times. Thinking of your children, you go in. Everyone is very busy. Finally, someone comes out and you tell her that you need help. That never is the person you need to see. You go see another person, and after spilling the whole shame of your poverty all over the desk between you, you find that this isn't the right office after all — you must repeat the whole process, and it never is any easier at the next place.

You have asked for help, and after all it has a cost. You are again told to wait. You are told why, but you don't really hear because of the red cloud of shame and the rising black cloud of despair.   7

Poverty is remembering. It is remembering quitting school in junior high because "nice" children had been so cruel about my clothes and my smell. The attendance officer came. My mother told him I was pregnant. I wasn't but she thought that I could get a job and help out. I had jobs off and on, but never long enough to learn anything. Mostly I remember being married. I was so young then. I am still young. For a time, we had all the things you have. There was a little house in another town, with hot water and everything. Then my husband lost his job. There was unemployment insurance for a while and what few jobs I could get. Soon, all our nice things were repossessed and we moved back here. I was pregnant then. This house didn't look so bad when we first moved in. Every week it gets worse. Nothing is ever fixed. We now had no money. There were a few odd jobs for my husband, but everything went for food then, as it does now. I don't know how we lived through three years and three babies, but we did. I'll tell you something, after the last baby I destroyed my marriage. It had been a good one, but could you keep on bringing children in this dirt? Did you ever think how much it costs for any kind of birth control? I knew my husband was leaving the day he left, but there were no good-byes between us. I hope he has been able to climb out of this mess somewhere. He never could hope with us to drag him down.   8

That's when I asked for help. When I got it, you know how much it was? It was, and is, seventy-eight dollars a month for the four of us; that is all I ever can get. Now you know why there is no soap, no needles and thread, no hot water, no aspirin, no worm medicine, no hand cream, no shampoo. None of these things forever and ever and ever. So that you can see clearly, I pay twenty dollars a month rent, and most of the rest goes for food. For grits and cornmeal, and rice and milk and beans. I try my best to use only the minimum electricity. If I use more, there is that much less for food.   9

Poverty is looking into a black future. Your children won't play with my boys. They will turn to other boys who steal to get what they want. I can already see them behind the bars of their prison instead of behind the bars of my poverty. Or they will turn to the freedom of   10 alcohol or drugs, and find themselves enslaved. And my daughter? At best, there is for her a life like mine.

But you say to me, there are schools. Yes, there are schools. My children have no extra books, no magazines, no extra pencils, or crayons, or paper and the most important of all, they do not have health. They have worms, they have infections, they have pinkeye all summer. They do not sleep well on the floor, or with me in my one bed. They do not suffer from hunger, my seventy-eight dollars keeps us alive, but they do suffer from malnutrition. Oh yes, I do remember what I was taught about health in school. It doesn't do much good. In some places there is a surplus commodities program. Not here. The county said it cost too much. There is a school lunch program. But I have two children who will already be damaged by the time they get to school. 11

But, you say to me, there are health clinics. Yes, there are health clinics and they are in the towns. I live out here eight miles from town. I can walk that far (even if it is sixteen miles both ways), but can my little children? My neighbor will take me when he goes; but he expects to get paid, *one way or another*. I bet you know my neighbor. He is that large man who spends his time at the gas station, the barbershop, and the corner store complaining about the government spending money on the immoral mothers of illegitimate children. 12

Poverty is an acid that drips on pride until all pride is worn away. Poverty is a chisel that chips on honor until honor is worn away. Some of you say that you would do *something* in my situation, and maybe you would, for the first week or the first month, but for year after year after year? 13

Even the poor can dream. A dream of a time when there is money. Money for the right kinds of food, for worm medicine, for iron pills, for toothbrushes, for hand cream, for a hammer and nails and a bit of screening, for a shovel, for a bit of paint, for some sheeting, for needles and thread. Money to pay *in money* for a trip to town. And, oh, money for hot water and money for soap. A dream of when asking for help does not eat away the last bit of pride. When the office you visit is as nice as the offices of other governmental agencies, when there are enough workers to help you quickly, when workers do not quit in defeat and despair. When you have to tell your story to only one person, and that person can send you for other help and you don't have to prove your poverty over and over and over again. 14

I have come out of my despair to tell you this. Remember I did not come from another place or another time. Others like me are all around you. Look at us with an angry heart, anger that will help you help me. Anger that will let you tell of me. The poor are always silent. Can you be silent too? 15 *answer questions*

RESPONDING TO THE TEXT

Throughout the essay, Parker describes the feelings and emotions associated with her poverty. Have you ever witnessed or observed people in Parker's situation? What was your reaction?

ENGAGING THE WRITER'S SUBJECT

1. Why didn't Parker have the operation that was recommended for her? Why did she quit her job?

2. In Parker's view, what makes asking for help such a difficult and painful experience? What compels her to do so anyway?

3. Why did Parker's husband leave her? How does she justify her attitude toward his leaving? (Glossary: *Attitude*)

4. In paragraph 12, Parker says the following about a neighbor giving her a ride to the nearest health clinic: "My neighbor will take me when he goes; but he expects to get paid, *one way or another*. I bet you know my neighbor." What is she implying in these sentences and in the rest of the paragraph?

5. What are the chances that the dreams described in paragraph 14 will come true? What do you think Parker would say?

ANALYZING THE WRITER'S CRAFT

1. What is Parker's purpose in defining poverty as she does? (Glossary: *Purpose*) Why has she cast her essay in the form of an extended definition? What effect does this have on the reader?

2. What techniques of definition does Parker use? What is missing that you would expect to find in a more general and impersonal definition of poverty? Why does Parker leave such information out?

3. How would you characterize Parker's tone and her style? (Glossary: *Style; Tone*) How do you respond to her use of the pronoun *you*? Point to specific examples of her diction and descriptions as support for your view. (Glossary: *Diction*)

4. Parker repeats words and phrases throughout this essay. Choose several examples, and explain their impact on you. (Glossary: *Coherence*)

5. In depicting poverty, Parker uses description to create vivid verbal pictures, and she illustrates the various aspects of poverty with examples drawn from her experience. (Glossary: *Description; Exemplification*) What are the most striking details she uses? How do you account for the emotional impact of the details and images she has selected? In what ways do description and exemplification enhance her definition of poverty?

UNDERSTANDING THE WRITER'S LANGUAGE

1. Although her essay is written for the most part in simple, straightforward language, Parker does make use of an occasional striking figure of

speech. (Glossary: *Figures of Speech*) Identify at least three such figures — you might begin with those in paragraph 13 (for example, "Poverty is an acid") — and explain their effect on the reader.

2. In paragraph 10, Parker states that "poverty is looking into a black future." How does she use language to characterize her children's future?

3. Refer to your desk dictionary to determine the meanings of the following words as Parker uses them in this selection: *chronic* (paragraph 3), *anemia* (3), *grits* (4), *oleo* (4), *antihistamines* (5).

WRITING SUGGESTIONS

1. Using Parker's essay as a model, write an extended definition of a topic about which you have some expertise. Choose as your subject a particular environment (suburbia, the inner city, a dormitory, a shared living area), a way of living (the child of divorce, the physically handicapped, the working student), or a topic of your own choosing. If you prefer, you can adopt a persona instead of writing from your own perspective.

2. Write a proposal or a plan of action that would make people aware of poverty or some other social problem in your community. What is the problem? What needs to be done to increase awareness? What practical steps would you propose be undertaken once the public is made aware of the situation?

3. Write an essay of your own defining poverty. In your college library and on the Internet, research and gather statistical data on the problem as it exists today in the United States or in your state or city. Another alternative is to focus exclusively on a particular family or neighborhood as a case study.

• To begin your research online, go to **bedfordstmartins.com /subjectsstrategies** and click on "Definition" or browse the thematic directory of annotated links.

In My Tribe

Ethan Watters

Ethan Watters was born in Berkeley, California, in 1964 — right between the Baby Boom and Generation X. He grew up in the small town of Chico, California, and graduated from the University of California–Davis, where he was active on the college newspaper. After interning at Harper's *magazine, Watters made his living as a free-lancer, writing articles for magazines such as* Spin, Details, Mother Jones, Esquire, *and* GQ.

In the following essay, which first appeared in the New York Times *on October 14, 2001, Watters identifies and then defines a growing social trend among single, college-educated city dwellers — urban tribes. Watters later expanded this essay into the book* Urban Tribes: Are Friends the New Family? *(2004).*

PREPARING TO READ

How would you describe the group of friends in the popular sit-coms *Seinfeld* and *Friends*? Do these characters resemble your group of friends? How so? If not, what distinguishes the group of people with whom you associate?

You may be like me: between the ages of 25 and 39, single, a 1 college-educated city dweller. If so, you may have also had the un-pleasant experience of discovering that you have been identified (by the U.S. Census Bureau, no less) as one of the fastest-growing groups in America — the "never marrieds." In less than 30 years, the number of never-marrieds has more than doubled, apparently pushing back the median age of marriage to the oldest it has been in our country's history — about 25 years for women and 27 for men.

As if the connotation of "never married" weren't negative enough, 2 the vilification of our group has been swift and shrill. These statistics prove a "titanic loss of family values," according to *The Washington Times*. An article in *Time* magazine asked whether "picky" women were "denying themselves and society the benefits of marriage" and in the process kicking off "an outbreak of *Sex and the City* promiscuity." In a study on marriage conducted at Rutgers University, researchers say the "social glue" of the family is at stake, adding ominously that "crime rates . . . are highly correlated with a large percentage of un-married young males."

Although I never planned it, I can tell you how I became a never- 3 married. Thirteen years ago, I moved to San Francisco for what I assumed was a brief transition period between college and marriage. The problem was, I wasn't just looking for an appropriate spouse. To use the language of the Rutgers researchers, I was "soul-mate searching." Like 94 percent of never-marrieds from 20 to 29, I, too, agree with the statement "When you marry, you want your spouse to be your soul mate first and foremost." This uber-romantic view is something new. In a 1965 survey, fully three out of four college women said they'd marry a man they didn't love if he fit their criteria in every other way. I discovered along with my friends that finding that soul mate wasn't easy. Girlfriends came and went, as did jobs and apartments. The constant in my life — by default, not by plan — became a loose group of friends. After a few years, that group's membership and routines began to solidify. We met weekly for dinner at a neighborhood restaurant. We traveled together, moved one another's furniture, painted one another's apartments, cheered one another on at sporting events and open-mike nights. One day I discovered that the transition period I thought I was living wasn't a transition period at all. Something real and important had grown there. I belonged to an urban tribe.

I use the word "tribe" quite literally here: this is a tight group, with unspoken roles and hierarchies, whose members think of each other as "us" and the rest of the world as "them." This bond is clearest in times of trouble. After earthquakes (or the recent terrorist strikes), my instinct to huddle with and protect my group is no different from what I'd feel for my family.

Once I identified this in my own life, I began to see tribes everywhere I looked: a house of ex-sorority women in Philadelphia, a team of ultimate-frisbee players in Boston, and groups of musicians in Austin, Texas. Cities, I've come to believe, aren't emotional wastelands where fragile individuals with arrested development mope around self-indulgently searching for true love. There are rich landscapes filled with urban tribes.

So what does it mean that we've quietly added the tribe years as a developmental stage to adulthood? Because our friends in the tribe hold us responsible for our actions, I doubt it will mean a wild swing toward promiscuity or crime. Tribal behavior does not prove a loss of "family values." It is a fresh expression of them.

It is true, though, that marriage and the tribe are at odds. As many ex-girlfriends will ruefully tell you, loyalty to the tribe can wreak havoc on romantic relationships. Not surprisingly, marriage usually signals the beginning of the end of tribal membership. From inside the group, marriage can seem like a risky gambit. When members of our tribe choose to get married, the rest of us talk about them with grave concern, as if they've joined a religion that requires them to live in a guarded compound.

But we also know that the urban tribe can't exist forever. Those of us who have entered our mid-30's find ourselves feeling vaguely as if we're living in the latter episodes of *Seinfeld* or *Friends*, as if the plot lines of our lives have begun to wear thin. 8

So, although tribe membership may delay marriage, that is where most of us are still heading. And it turns out there may be some good news when we get there. Divorce rates have leveled off. Tim Heaton, a sociologist at Brigham Young University, says he believes he knows why. In a paper to be published next year, he argues that it is because people are getting married later. 9

Could it be that we who have been biding our time in happy tribes are now actually grown up enough to understand what we need in a mate? What a fantastic twist — we "never marrieds" may end up revitalizing the very institution we've supposedly been undermining. 10

And there's another dynamic worth considering. Those of us who find it so hard to leave our tribes will not choose marriage blithely, as if it is the inevitable next step in our lives, the way middle-class high-school kids choose college. When we go to the altar, we will be sacrificing something precious. In that sacrifice, we may begin to learn to treat our marriages with the reverence they need to survive. 11

RESPONDING TO THE TEXT

What do you imagine yourself and your friends doing in the first couple years after graduating from college? Is marriage a possibility, or do you think that belonging to an urban tribe is a more likely scenario? What is your opinion of Watters's assertion that "the tribe years [are] a developmental stage of adulthood" (paragraph 6)? Explain.

ENGAGING THE WRITER'S SUBJECT

1. In what ways does a tribe resemble a family? In what ways is tribal behavior a "fresh expression" (paragraph 6) of family values?

2. According to Watters, how do tribes come into being?

3. Although Watters admits that he never planned on belonging to "one of the fastest-growing groups in America — 'the never marrieds'" (1), it happened. In retrospect, how does he explain the fact that he's remained single?

ANALYZING THE WRITER'S CRAFT

1. For Watters, what is the literal definition of *tribe*? What are the defining characteristics of his tribe?

2. What is the purpose of Watters's essay about tribes? (Glossary: *Purpose*) What are the major points about tribes that he wants to make?

3. What examples does Watters use to illustrate his definition of an urban tribe? (Glossary: *Exemplification*)

UNDERSTANDING THE WRITER'S LANGUAGE

1. Why do you suppose Watters chose the term *urban tribe* to label the group to which he belongs? How does this label effectively capture the spirit of the phenomenon he is describing? What other labels could he have used for this "tight group, with unspoken roles and hierarchies" (4)?

2. Does the term *never married*s have the negative connotations for you that it does for Watters? (Glossary: *Connotation/Denotation*) If not, at what age do you think not being married starts having negative associations?

3. Refer to your desk dictionary to determine the meanings of the following words as Watters uses them in this selection: *median* (paragraph 1), *vilification* (2), *promiscuity* (2), *correlated* (2), *uber* (3), *havoc* (7), *gambit* (7), *blithely* (11), *reverence* (11).

WRITING SUGGESTIONS

1. Watters's invokes a literal definition of the word *tribe* — "a tight group, with unspoken roles and hierarchies, whose members think of each other as 'us' and the rest of the world as 'them'" (paragraph 4) — and then goes on to define the word in his own terms, applying his own particular situation and meaning to it. Using Watters's definition of *urban tribe* as a model, write an essay in which you build your own definition of a familiar word or term, such as *family, marriage, soul mate*, or *partner*, around its literal or traditional meaning.

2. Once Watters realized that he belonged to a specific kind of group, named it an urban tribe, and then defined it, he says he saw other tribes wherever he looked. Are such tribes unique to urban areas or the age group Watters talks about, or do you see these groups elsewhere and among other ages? Do you think that you might belong to a group that fits Watters's definition of an urban tribe? If so, how is your tribe similar to or different from Watters's? How would you define your group? What would you name your group? Why? Write an essay in which you compare and contrast the group you and your peers belong to with Watters's urban tribes. (Glossary: *Comparison and Contrast*)

3. Carefully consider the following cartoon by Marisa Acocella. What statement about the institution of marriage does the cartoon make? How do you think Watters would react to this cartoon? In his essay, Watters suggests that young people today have "quietly added the tribe years as a developmental stage to adulthood" (paragraph 6) and are therefore delaying marriage until they are mature enough "to treat our marriages with the reverence they need to survive" (11). Do you agree with Watters's suggestion that urban tribes can solve America's "marriage

crisis"? Why or why not? Do you believe a "marriage crisis" exists? Why or why not? Conduct research in your college library and on the Internet to determine the status of marriage in America and write an essay in which you explore how urban tribes can help or hinder the institution. (Glossary: *Argument; Cause and Effect Analysis*)

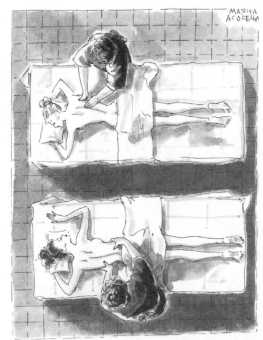

"He didn't want to end it, so I told him I wanted to get married."

- To begin your research online, go to **bedfordstmartins.com /subjectsstrategies** and click on "Definition" or browse the thematic directory of annotated links.

What's Next for Napster

Time Magazine

TimePix/Getty Images

CONNECTING IMAGE AND TEXT

On October 2, 2000, nineteen-year-old Shawn Fanning, founder of the now-infamous Napster, graced the cover of *Time* magazine. How do you "read" this photograph of the young entrepreneur? Why were Fanning and his Web site such big news at the time? What do you see in his face? In his stance? In his manner of dress? In what ways had Fanning "upended music" in 2000? What is the current status of file-sharing? Of Napster? Your observations will help guide you to the key themes and strategies in the essay that follows.

Steal This MP3 File: What Is Theft?

G. Anthony Gorry

G. Anthony Gorry is a medical educator and information technology specialist. He received his B.S. from Yale University in 1962 and pursued graduate study at the University of California–Berkeley, where he earned his M.S. in 1964, and at MIT, where he received his Ph.D. in 1967. Gorry has taught at Baylor College of Medicine and is currently a professor of management and computer science at Rice University.

In the following article, which first appeared in the Chronicle of Higher Education *on May 23, 2003, Gorry recounts an experience he had in one of his information technology courses to demonstrate how technology might be shaping the attitude of today's youth. He senses that the meaning of theft may be shifting in our ever-changing world.*

PREPARING TO READ

What for you constitutes theft? Do you recall ever stealing anything? Did you get caught? Did you have to return the item or make restitution? How did you feel about the incident at the time? How do you feel about it now?

S ometimes when my students don't see life the way I do, I recall the complaint from *Bye Bye Birdie,* "What's the matter with kids today?" Then I remember that the "kids" in my class are children of the information age. In large part, technology has made them what they are, shaping their world and what they know. For my students, the advance of technology is expected, but for me, it remains both remarkable and somewhat unsettling.

In one course I teach, the students and I explore the effects of information technology on society. Our different perspectives on technology lead to engaging and challenging discussions that reveal some of the ways in which technology is shaping the attitudes of young people. An example is our discussion of intellectual property in the information age, of crucial importance to the entertainment business.

In recent years, many users of the Internet have launched an assault on the music business. Armed with tools for "ripping" music from compact discs and setting it "free" in cyberspace, they can disseminate online countless copies of a digitally encoded song. Music companies, along with some artists, have tried to stop this perceived pillaging of intellectual property by legal and technical means. The industry has had some success with legal actions against companies that provide the infrastructure for file sharing, but enthusiasm for sharing music is growing, and new file-sharing services continue to appear.

The Recording Industry Association of America recently filed lawsuits against four college students, seeking huge damages for "an emporium of music piracy" run on campus networks. However, the industry settled those lawsuits less than a week after a federal judge in California ruled against the association in another case, affirming that two of the Internet's most popular music-swapping services are not responsible for copyright infringements by their users. (In the settlement, the students admitted no wrongdoing but agreed to pay amounts ranging from $12,000 to $17,500 in annual installments over several years and to shut down their file-sharing systems.)

With so many Internet users currently sharing music, legal maneuvers alone seem unlikely to protect the industry's way of doing business. Therefore, the music industry has turned to the technology itself, seeking to create media that cannot be copied or can be copied only in prescribed circumstances. Finding the right technology for such a defense, however, is not easy. Defensive technology must not prevent legitimate uses of the media by customers, yet it must somehow ward off attacks by those seeking to "liberate" the content to the Internet. And each announcement of a defensive technology spurs development of means to circumvent it.

In apparent frustration, some companies have introduced defective copies of their music into the file-sharing environment of the Internet, hoping to discourage widespread downloading of music. But so far, the industry's multifaceted defense has failed. Sales of CDs continue to decline. And now video ripping and sharing is emerging on the Internet, threatening to upset another industry in the same way.

Music companies might have more success if they focused on the users instead of the courts and technology. When they characterize file sharing as theft, they overlook the interplay of technology and behavior that has altered the very idea of theft, at least among young people. I got a clear demonstration of that change in a class discussion that began with the matter of a stolen book.

During the '60s, I was a graduate student at a university where student activism had raised tensions on and around the campus. In the midst of debates, demonstrations, and protests, a football player was caught leaving the campus store with a book he had not bought. Because he was well known, his misadventure made the school newspaper. What seemed to be a simple case of theft, however, took on greater significance. A number of groups with little connection to athletics rose to his defense, claiming that he had been entrapped: The university required that he have the book, the publisher charged an unfairly high price, and the bookstore put the book right in front of him, tempting him to steal it. So who could blame him?

Well, my students could. They thought it was clear that he had stolen the book. But an MP3 file played from my laptop evoked a different response. Had I stolen the song? Not really, because a student had given me the file as a gift. Well, was that file stolen property? Was it like the book stolen from the campus bookstore so many years ago? No again, because it was a copy, not the original, which presumably was with the student. But then what should we make of the typical admonition on compact-disc covers that unauthorized duplication is illegal? Surely the MP3 file was a duplication of the original. To what extent is copying stealing?

The readings for the class amply demonstrated the complexity of the legal, technical, and economic issues surrounding intellectual property in the information age and gave the students much to talk about. Some students argued that existing regulations are simply inadequate at a time when all information "wants to be free" and when liberating technology is at hand. Others pointed to differences in the economics of the music and book businesses. In the end, the students who saw theft in the removal of the book back in the '60s did not see stealing in the unauthorized copying of music. For me, that was the most memorable aspect of the class because it illustrates how technology affects what we take to be moral behavior.

The technology of copying is closely related to the idea of theft. For example, my students would not take books from a store, but they do not consider photocopying a few pages of a book to be theft. They would not copy an entire book, however, perhaps because they vaguely acknowledge intellectual-property rights but probably more because copying would be cumbersome and time-consuming. They would buy the book instead. In that case, the very awkwardness of the copying aligns their actions with moral guidelines and legal standards.

But in the case of digital music, where the material is disconnected from the physical moorings of conventional stores and copying is so easy, many of my students see matters differently. They freely copy and share music. And they copy and share software, even though such copying is often illegal. If their books were digital and thus could be copied with comparable ease, they most likely would copy and share them.

Of course, the Digital Millennium Copyright Act, along with other 13
laws, prohibits such copying. So we could just say that theft is theft,
and complain with the song, "Why can't they be like we were, perfect
in every way? . . . Oh, what's the matter with kids today?" But had we
had the same digital technology when we were young, we probably
would have engaged in the same copying and sharing of software, digital music, and video that are so common among students today. We
should not confuse lack of tools with righteousness.

The music industry would be foolish to put its faith in new protec- 14
tive schemes and devices alone. Protective technology cannot undo
the changes that previous technology has caused. Should the industry
aggressively pursue legal defenses like the suits against the four college
students? Such highly publicized actions may be legally sound and
may even slow music sharing in certain settings, but they cannot stop
the transformation of the music business. The technology of sharing is
too widespread, and my students (and their younger siblings) no longer
agree with the music companies about right and wrong. Even some of
the companies with big stakes in recorded music seem to have recognized that lawsuits and technical defenses won't work. Sony, for example, sells computers with "ripping and burning" capabilities, MP3
players, and other devices that gain much of their appeal from music
sharing. And the AOL part of AOL Time Warner is promoting its new
broadband service for faster downloads, which many people will use
to share music sold by the Warner part of the company.

The lesson from my classroom is that digital technology has unal- 15
terably changed the way a growing number of customers think about
recorded music. If the music industry is to prosper, it must change,
too — perhaps offering repositories of digital music for downloading
(like Apple's newly announced iTunes Music Store), gaining revenue
from the scope and quality of its holdings, and from a variety of new
products and relationships, as yet largely undefined. Such a transformation will be excruciating for the industry, requiring the aban-
donment of previously profitable business practices with no certain
prospect of success. So it is not surprising that the industry has responded aggressively, with strong legal actions, to the spread of file
sharing. But by that response, the industry is risking its relationship
with a vital segment of its market. Treating customers like thieves is a
certain recipe for failure.

RESPONDING TO THE TEXT

Where do you stand on file sharing? Like Gorry's students, do you freely
copy and share music or software? Do you consider all such sharing acceptable, or is there some point where it turns into theft? Explain.

ENGAGING THE WRITER'S SUBJECT

1. What is intellectual property, and how is it different from other types of property?

2. How has the music industry tried to stop "music piracy" on the Internet? What has been the success of their efforts?

3. Do you think the football player caught leaving the campus store with a book was guilty of stealing, or are you persuaded by the argument that "he had been entrapped" (paragraph 8)? Explain.

4. What does Gorry mean when he says that "the technology of copying is closely related to the idea of theft" (11)?

5. What advice do Gorry and his students have for the music industry? Is this advice realistic? Explain. What suggestions would you like to add?

ANALYZING THE WRITER'S CRAFT

1. What is Gorry's thesis, and where is it stated? (Glossary: *Thesis*)

2. Gorry's purpose is to show that there has recently been a shift in what he believes constitutes theft. (Glossary: *Purpose*) How well does he accomplish his purpose?

3. What examples does Gorry use to develop his definition of theft? (Glossary: *Exemplification*) How does he use these examples to illustrate the shift in meaning that he believes has occurred?

4. With what authority does Gorry write on the subjects of intellectual property, technology, and theft?

5. Gorry uses lyrics from the movie *Bye Bye Birdie* to introduce his essay and start his conclusion. (Glossary: *Beginnings/Endings*) Are these just gimmicky quotations or do they contribute to the substance of Gorry's essay?

6. Gorry ends paragraph 8 with the question "So who could blame him?" and then begins paragraph 9 with the response "Well, my students could," thus making a smooth transition from one paragraph to the next. (Glossary: *Transitions*) What other transitional devices does Gorry use to add coherence to his essay? (Glossary: *Coherence*)

UNDERSTANDING THE WRITER'S LANGUAGE

1. Who is Gorry's intended audience? (Glossary: *Audience*) To whom does the pronoun *we* in paragraph 13 refer? What other evidence in Gorry's diction do you find to support your conclusion about his audience? (Glossary: *Diction*)

2. How would you describe Gorry's diction — formal, objective, conversational, jargon-filled? (Glossary: *Diction; Technical Language*) Point out specific words and phrases that led you to this conclusion.

3. Refer to your desk dictionary to determine the meanings of the following words as Gorry uses them in this selection: *disseminate* (paragraph 3), *encoded* (3), *emporium* (4), *infringements* (4), *repositories* (15).

WRITING SUGGESTIONS

1. Although it is not always immediately apparent, English is constantly changing because it is a living language. New words come into the lexicon, and others become obsolete. Some words like *theft* change over time to reflect society's thinking and behavior. Another word whose definition has ignited recent debate is *marriage*. Using Gorry's essay as a model, write a paper in which you define a word whose meaning has changed over the past decade.

2. Gorry is very aware of how information technology is shaping our attitudes about the world. We're living at a time when digital technology makes it not only possible but also surprisingly easy for us to copy and share software, music, and video. Gorry does not condemn such behavior out of hand; instead, he warns that "we should not confuse lack of tools with righteousness" (paragraph 13). Write an essay in which you explore some of the ways today's technology has shaped your attitudes, especially as it "affects what we take to be moral behavior" (10). (Glossary: *Exemplification*)

3. In this age of information and technology, there is growing concern about "identity theft." Surprisingly, many Americans have not informed themselves about identity theft and how they can protect themselves against it. After conducting some research in your college library and on the Internet, write an essay in which you define identity theft and explain how such theft occurs and what can be done to reduce the chances of it happening.

- To begin your research online, go to **bedfordstmartins.com /subjectsstrategies** and click on "Definition" or browse the thematic directory of annotated links.

Ain't I a Woman?

Sojourner Truth

Sojourner Truth was born a slave named Isabella in Ulster County, New York, in 1797. After her escape from slavery in 1827, she went to New York City and underwent a profound religious transformation. She worked as a domestic servant, and as an evangelist she tried to reform prostitutes. Adopting the name Sojourner Truth in 1843, she became a traveling preacher and abolitionist, frequently appearing with Frederick Douglass. Although she never learned to write, Truth's compelling presence gripped her audience as she spoke eloquently about emancipation and women's rights. After the Civil War and until her death in 1883, she worked to provide education and employment for emancipated slaves.

At the Women's Rights Convention in Akron, Ohio, in May 1851, Truth extemporaneously delivered the following speech, as transcribed by Elizabeth Cady Stanton, to a nearly all-white audience.

PREPARING TO READ

What comes to mind when you hear the word *speech*? Have you ever attended a rally or convention and heard speeches given on behalf of a social cause or political issue? What were your impressions of the speakers and their speeches?

Well, children, where there is so much racket there must be something out of kilter. I think that 'twixt the Negroes of the South and the women of the North, all talking about rights, the white men will be in a fix pretty soon. But what's all this here talking about? 1

That man over there says that women need to be helped into carriages, and lifted over ditches, and to have the best place everywhere. Nobody ever helps me into carriages, or over mud-puddles, or gives me any best place! And ain't I a woman? Look at me! Look at my arm! I have ploughed and planted, and gathered into barns, and no man could head me! And ain't I a woman? I could work as much and eat as much as a man — when I could get it — and bear the lash as well! And ain't I a woman? I have borne thirteen children, and seen them most all sold off to slavery, and when I cried out with my mother's grief, none but Jesus heard me! And ain't I a woman? 2

Then they talk about this thing in the head; what's this they call it? [Intellect, someone whispers.] That's it, honey. What's that got to do with women's rights or negro's rights? If my cup won't hold but a pint, and yours holds a quart, wouldn't you be mean not to let me have my little half-measure full? 3

Then that little man in black there, he says women can't have as much rights as men, 'cause Christ wasn't a woman! Where did your Christ come from? Where did your Christ come from? From God and a woman! Man had nothing to do with Him. 4

If the first woman God ever made was strong enough to turn the world upside down all alone, these women together ought to be able to turn it back, and get it right side up again! And now they is asking to do it, the men better let them. 5

Obliged to you for hearing me, and now old Sojourner ain't got nothing more to say. 6

RESPONDING TO THE TEXT

What are your immediate impressions of Truth's speech? Now take a minute to read her speech again, this time aloud. What are your impressions now? Are they different, and if so, how and why? What aspects of her speech are memorable?

ENGAGING THE WRITER'S SUBJECT

1. What does Truth mean when she says, "Where there is so much racket there must be something out of kilter" (paragraph 1)? Why does Truth believe that white men are going to find themselves in a "fix" (1)?

2. What does Truth put forth as her "credentials" as a woman?

3. How does Truth counter the argument that "women can't have as much rights as men, 'cause Christ wasn't a woman" (4)?

ANALYZING THE WRITER'S CRAFT

1. What is Truth's purpose in this essay? (Glossary: *Purpose*) Why is it important for her to define what a woman is for her audience? (Glossary: *Audience*)

2. How does Truth use the comments of "that man over there" (paragraph 2) and "that little man in black" (4) to help her establish her definition of *woman*?

3. What, for you, is the effect of Truth's repetition of the question "And ain't I a woman?" four times? (Glossary: *Rhetorical Question*) What other questions does she ask? Why do you suppose Truth doesn't provide answers to the questions in paragraph 3, but does for the question in paragraph 4?

4. How would you characterize Truth's tone in this speech? (Glossary: *Tone*) What phrases in the speech suggest that tone to you?

5. Explain how Truth uses comparison and contrast to help establish her definition of *woman*, especially in paragraph 2. (Glossary: *Comparison and Contrast*)

UNDERSTANDING THE WRITER'S LANGUAGE

1. How would you describe Truth's diction in this speech? What does her diction reveal about her character and background? (Glossary: *Diction*)

2. Refer to your desk dictionary to determine the meanings of the following words as Truth uses them in this selection: *kilter* (paragraph 1), *ditches* (2), *intellect* (3), *obliged* (6).

WRITING SUGGESTIONS

1. Sojourner Truth spoke out against the injustice she saw around her. In arguing for the rights of women, she found it helpful to define *woman* in order to make her point. What social cause do you find most compelling today? Human rights? AIDS awareness? Domestic abuse? Alcoholism? Gay marriage? Racism? Select an issue about which you have strong feelings. Now carefully identify all key terms that you must define before arguing your position. Write an essay in which you use definition to make your point convincingly.

2. Sojourner Truth's speech holds out hope for the future. She envisioned a future in which women join together to take charge and "turn [the world] back, and get it right side up again" (paragraph 5). What she envisioned has, to some extent, come to pass. Write an essay in which you speculate about how Truth would react to the world as we know it. What do you think would please her? What would disappoint her? What do you think she would want to change about our society? Explain your reasoning.

3. Sojourner Truth's journey from slave to activist to speaker and, posthumously, to cultural icon was an arduous and circuitous one. In your college library and on the Internet, research Truth's life. Write an essay in which you assess her strengths and weaknesses. How was she able to overcome and transcend the deprivations and indignities of her early years? What role did religion play in her life and accomplishments? Consider what she might have done had she lived during the era of Martin Luther King Jr. Do you think her abilities and beliefs would have been effective in the age of mass media? Why or why not?

- To begin your research online, go to **bedfordstmartins.com /subjectsstrategies** and click on "Definition" or browse the thematic directory of annotated links.

A Nincompoop (FICTION)

Anton Chekhov

*One of Russia's most beloved storytellers, Anton Chekhov (1860–1904)
was born in Taganrog, in the south of Russia on the Sea of Azov. He
started writing short stories while studying medicine at the University of
Moscow. Soon after his graduation in 1884, Chekhov embarked on his
career as a writer, first as a freelance journalist and later as a playwright.
His early one-act plays, including most notably* The Bear *(1888) and*
The Wedding *(1889), met with critical acclaim. But his full-length plays
earned him lasting fame. By all accounts* Uncle Vanya *(1899),* The Sisters
(1901), and The Cherry Orchard *(1904) are among the masterworks of
modern theater. Ill health forced Chekhov to spend many of his later years
in the milder southern climate of Yalta, where he met Russian greats Mak-
sim Gorky and Leo Tolstoy. Chekhov died at the age of forty-four, shortly
after completing* The Cherry Orchard.*

In the short story "A Nincompoop," Chekhov tells the story of a gen-
tleman who teaches his children's governess a "cruel lesson" with a powerful message.*

PREPARING TO READ

When did you first become aware of class distinctions? What did it
feel like to discover that some people treated others differently
based on social class? Have people ever tried to take advantage of
you or make you feel less than adequate? Did you protest? If not,
why were you unable to express your feelings?

A few days ago I asked my children's governess, Julia Vassilyevna,   1
to come into my study.

"Sit down, Julia Vassilyevna," I said. "Let's settle our accounts. Al-   2
though you most likely need some money, you stand on ceremony
and won't ask for it yourself. Now then, we agreed on thirty rubles a
month . . ."

"Forty."   3

"No, thirty. I made a note of it. I always pay the governess thirty.   4
Now then, you've been here two months, so . . ."

"Two months and five days."   5

"Exactly two months. I made a specific note of it. That means you   6
have sixty rubles coming to you. Subtract nine Sundays . . . you know
you didn't work with Kolya on Sundays, you only took walks. And
three holidays . . ."

Julia Vassilyevna flushed a deep red and picked at the flounce of   7
her dress, but — not a word.

"Three holidays, therefore take off twelve rubles. Four days Kolya was sick and there were no lessons, as you were occupied only with Vanya. Three days you had a toothache and my wife gave you permission not to work after lunch. Twelve and seven — nineteen. Subtract . . . that leaves . . . hmm . . . forty-one rubles. Correct?" 8

Julia Vassilyevna's left eye reddened and filled with moisture. Her chin trembled; she coughed nervously and blew her nose, but — not a word. 9

"Around New Year's you broke a teacup and saucer: take off two rubles. The cup cost more, it was an heirloom, but — let it go. When didn't I take a loss! Then, due to your neglect, Kolya climbed a tree and tore his jacket: take away ten. Also due to your heedlessness the maid stole Vanya's shoes. You ought to watch everything! You get paid for it. So, that means five more rubles off. The tenth of January I gave you ten rubles . . ." 10

"You didn't," whispered Julia Vassilyevna. 11

"But I made a note of it." 12

"Well . . . all right." 13

"Take twenty-seven from forty-one — that leaves fourteen." 14

Both eyes filled with tears. Perspiration appeared on the thin, pretty little nose. Poor girl! 15

"Only once was I given any money," she said in a trembling voice, "and that was by your wife. Three rubles, nothing more." 16

"Really? You see now, and I didn't make a note of it! Take three from fourteen . . . leaves eleven. Here's your money, my dear. Three, three, three, one and one. Here it is!" 17

I handed her eleven rubles. She took them and with trembling fingers stuffed them into her pocket. 18

"*Merci*," she whispered. 19

I jumped up and started pacing the room. I was overcome with anger. 20

"For what, this — '*merci*'?" I asked. 21

"For the money." 22

"But you know I've cheated you — robbed you! I have actually stolen from you! *Why* this '*merci*'?" 23

"In my other places they didn't give me anything at all." 24

"They didn't give you anything? No wonder! I played a little joke on you, a cruel lesson, just to teach you . . . I'm going to give you the entire eighty rubles! Here they are in an envelope all ready for you . . . Is it really possible to be so spineless? Why don't you protest? Why be silent? Is it possible in this world to be without teeth and claws — to be such a nincompoop?" 25

She smiled crookedly and I read in her expression: "It is possible." 26

I asked her pardon for the cruel lesson and, to her great surprise, gave her the eighty rubles. She murmured her little "*merci*" several 27 times and went out. I looked after her and thought: "How easy it is to crush the weak in this world!"

RESPONDING TO THE TEXT

The narrator confesses to Julia that he "played a little joke on [her], a cruel lesson, just to teach [her]" (paragraph 25). What was cruel about the lesson, and what do you suppose he was intending to teach his young governess? Do young people need to be taught this cruel lesson today? Why or why not?

ENGAGING THE WRITER'S SUBJECT

1. What kind of man is the narrator? How do you feel about him at the beginning of the story? Do your feelings about him change by the end?

2. What do we know about Julia Vassilyevna? Does she change during the course of the story? If so, how do you account for the change?

3. According to the narrator, what is a *nincompoop*? Do you agree, or has *nincompoop* come to mean something else for you?

4. Why do you suppose the narrator wants to give Julia a "cruel lesson"? What does this lesson reveal about the narrator's feelings toward Julia and toward the larger class structure? Explain.

ANALYZING THE WRITER'S CRAFT

1. Chekhov's story is a classic example of the writer's dictum, "Show, don't tell." Explain how Chekhov shows us what a nincompoop is instead of telling us.

2. What does dialogue contribute to this story? (Glossary: *Dialogue*) How would the story be different if there were no dialogue?

3. Chekhov has the employer narrate his story. How would the story be different if Julia were the narrator?

4. From time to time — almost as an aside — the narrator provides a description of Julia's physical reactions to what was happening during the meeting. (Glossary: *Description*) Why is it important for the narrator to provide this information to readers?

UNDERSTANDING THE WRITER'S LANGUAGE

1. Identify six strong action verbs that Chekhov uses. (Glossary: *Verb*) What do these verbs add to his narrative? Explain.

2. Refer to your desk dictionary to determine the meanings of the following words as Chekhov uses them in this selection: *governess* (paragraph 1), *flounce* (7), *heirloom* (10), *spineless* (25).

WRITING SUGGESTIONS

1. Using Chekhov's story as a model, write a narrative in which you define *friend, jerk, survivor, procrastinator, boss, workaholic, hero, soul mate, nemesis*, or a character trait of your own choosing. (Glossary: *Narration*) Be careful to "show" your definition and not to "tell" it.

2. In the final paragraph of this story, the narrator muses to himself, "How easy it is to crush the weak in this world!" Does this story offer any insight about how to stop the exploitation of the weak by the rich and powerful? Or do we really live in a dog-eat-dog world in which everyone must have "teeth and claws"? How does one teach the weak to speak up and protest? Or should the powerful assume some responsibility to look after and protect the weak? Write an essay in which you present your views about how society should treat "the weak in this world." (Glossary: *Argument*)

3. In your college library and on the Internet research the life and work of Anton Chekhov. What was his life like? What subjects and themes did he write about? What do scholars and critics think about his writing? Write an essay in which you recount significant experiences in Chekhov's life and explain how they may have influenced his writing.

- To begin your research online, go to **bedfordstmartins.com /subjectsstrategies** and click on "Definition" or browse the thematic directory of annotated links.

WRITING SUGGESTIONS
FOR DEFINITION

1. Some of the most pressing social issues in American life today are further complicated by imprecise definitions of critical terms. Various medical cases, for example, have brought worldwide attention to the legal and medical definitions of the word *death*. Debates continue about the meanings of other controversial words, such as these:

   a. morality
   b. minority (ethnic)
   c. alcoholism
   d. cheating
   e. pornography
   f. kidnapping
   g. lying
   h. censorship
   i. remedial
   j. insanity
   k. monopoly (business)
   l. sex
   m. success
   n. happiness
   o. life
   p. equality

   Select one of these words, and write an essay in which you discuss not only the definition of the term but also the problems associated with defining it.

2. Write an essay in which you define one of the words listed below by telling not only what it is, but also what it is *not*. (For example, one could say that "poetry is that which cannot be expressed in any other way.") Remember, however, that defining by negation does not relieve you of the responsibility of defining the term in other ways as well.

   a. intelligence
   b. leadership
   c. fear
   d. patriotism
   e. wealth
   f. failure
   g. family
   h. style
   i. loyalty
   j. selflessness
   k. creativity
   l. humor

3. Karl Marx defined *capitalism* as an economic system in which the bourgeois owners of the means of production exploit the proletariat, who lack the means of production, for their own selfish gain. How would you define *capitalism*? Write an essay defining *capitalism* that includes all six types of definition: formal, synonymous, negative, etymological, stipulative, and extended.

4. *Marriage* is a word that often means different things to different people. What does *marriage* mean to you? How would you define it? Write a definition essay to explain your understanding of marriage and what it means to be married. To make your definition clearer to your reader, you might consider describing a marriage with which you are personally familiar. Perhaps it would be helpful to compare and contrast two or more different marriages. (Glossary: *Comparison and Contrast*) You could also incorporate some narration or exemplification to make your definition more powerful. (Glossary: *Exemplification; Narration*)

5. Consider the sample introduction to the essay defining Quebecois and Canadian identity (p. 391). Think about your school, town, or country's identity. How would you define its essential character? Choose a place that is important in your life, and write an essay defining its character and its significance to you.

CHAPTER 10

Cause and Effect Analysis

WHAT IS CAUSE AND EFFECT ANALYSIS?

People exhibit their natural curiosity about the world by asking questions. These questions represent a fundamental human need to find out how things work. Questioning the world around us is among the most common of human activities: "Why are babies born?" "Why do people cheat?" "What are the environmental causes of cancer?" "Why are there homeless and hungry people in America?" "What would happen if grades were abolished in colleges and universities?" "What if the stock market crashed again?" "What would happen if drunk drivers were given mandatory jail sentences?" "What would happen if the U.S. space program were expanded?" Answering questions like these means engaging in the process of *cause and effect analysis*. Whenever a question asks *why*, answering it will require discovering a *cause* or a series of causes for a particular *effect*; whenever a question asks *what if*, its answer will point out the effect or effects that can result from a particular cause. Cause and effect analysis, then, explores the relationship between events or circumstances and the outcomes that result from them.

You will have frequent opportunity to use cause and effect analysis in your college writing. For example, a history instructor might ask you to explain the causes of the Six-Day War between Israel and its neighbors. In a paper for an American literature course, you might try to determine why *Huckleberry Finn* has sparked so much controversy in a number of schools and communities. On an environmental studies exam, you might have to speculate about the long-term effects acid rain will have on the ecology of northeastern Canada and the United States. Demonstrating an understanding of cause and effect is crucial to the process of learning.

One common use of the strategy is for the writer to identify a particular causal agent or circumstance and then discuss the consequences or effects it has had or may have. In the following passage from *The Telephone* by John Brooks, it is clear from the first sentence that the author is primarily concerned with the effects that the telephone has had or may have had on modern life.

First sentence establishes purpose in the form of a question.

A series of effects with the telephone as cause.

What has the telephone done to us, or for us, in the hundred years of its existence? A few effects suggest themselves at once. It has saved lives by getting rapid word of illness, injury, or famine from remote places. By joining with the elevator to make possible the multistory residence or office building, it has made possible — for better or worse — the modern city. By bringing about a quantum leap in the speed and ease with which information moves from place to place, it has greatly accelerated the rate of scientific and technological change and growth in industry. Beyond doubt it has crippled if not killed the ancient art of letter writing. It has made living alone possible for persons with normal social impulses; by so doing, it has played a role in one of the greatest social changes of this century, the breakup of the multigenerational household. It has made the waging of war chillingly more efficient than formerly. Perhaps (though not provably) it has prevented wars that might have arisen out of international misunderstanding caused by written communication. Or perhaps — again not provably — by magnifying and extending irrational personal conflicts based on voice contact, it has caused wars. Certainly it has extended the scope of human conflicts, since it impartially disseminates the useful knowledge of scientists and the babble of bores, the affection of the affectionate and the malice of the malicious.

The bulk of Brooks's paragraph is devoted to answering the very question he poses in his opening sentence: "What has the telephone done to us, or for us, in the hundred years of its existence?" Notice that even though many of the effects Brooks discusses are verifiable or probable, he is willing to admit that he is speculating about those effects that he cannot prove.

A second common use of the strategy is to reverse the forms by first examining the effect; the writer describes an important event or problem (effect) and then examines the possible reasons (causes) for it. For example, experts might trace the causes of poverty to any or all of the following: poor education, a nonprogressive tax system, declining commitment to social services, inflation, discrimination, or even the welfare system that is designed to help those most in need.

A third use of the strategy is for the writer to explore a complex causal chain. In this selection from his book *The Politics of Energy*, Barry Commoner examines the series of malfunctions that led to the near disaster at the Three Mile Island nuclear facility in Harrisburg, Pennsylvania.

On March 28, 1979, at 3:53 A.M., a pump at the Harrisburg plant failed. Because the pump failed, the reactor's heat was not drawn off in the heat exchanger and the very hot water in the primary loop overheated. The pressure in the loop increased, opening a release valve that was supposed to counteract such an event. But the valve stuck open and the primary loop system lost so much water (which ended up as a highly radioactive pool, six feet deep, on the floor of the reactor building) that it was unable to carry off all the heat generated within the reactor core. Under these circumstances, the intense heat held within the reactor could, in theory, melt its fuel rods, and the resulting "meltdown" could then carry a hugely radioactive mass through the floor of the reactor. The reactor's emergency cooling system, which is designed to prevent this disaster, was then automatically activated, but when it was, apparently, turned off too soon, some of the fuel rods overheated. This produced a bubble of hydrogen gas at the top of the reactor. (The hydrogen is dissolved in the water in order to react with oxygen that is produced when the intense reactor radiation splits water molecules into their atomic constituents. When heated, the dissolved hydrogen bubbles out of the solution.) This bubble blocked the flow of cooling water so that despite the action of the emergency cooling system the reactor core was again in danger of melting down. Another danger was that the gas might contain enough oxygen to cause an explosion that could rupture the huge containers that surround the reactor and release a deadly cloud of radioactive material into the surrounding countryside. Working desperately, technicians were able to gradually reduce the size of the gas bubble using a special apparatus brought in from the atomic laboratory at Oak Ridge, Tennessee, and the danger of a catastrophic release of radioactive materials subsided. But the sealed-off plant was now so radioactive that no one could enter it for many months — or, according to some observers, for years — without being exposed to a lethal dose of radiation.

Tracing a causal chain, as Commoner does here, is similar to narration. The writer must organize the events sequentially to show clearly how each event leads to the next.

In a causal chain, an initial cause brings about a particular effect, which in turn becomes the immediate cause of a further effect, and so on, bringing about a series of effects that also act as new causes. The so-called domino effect is a good illustration of the idea of a causal chain; the simple tipping over of a domino (initial cause) can result in the toppling of any number of dominoes down the line (series of effects). For example, before a computer salesperson approaches an important client about a big sale, she prepares extensively for the meeting (initial cause). Her preparation causes her to impress the client (effect A), which guarantees her the big sale (effect B), which in turn results in her promotion to district sales manager (effect C). The sale she made is the most immediate and the most obvious cause of her promotion, but it is possible to trace the chain back to its more essential cause: her hard work preparing for the meeting.

While the ultimate purpose of cause and effect analysis may seem simple — to know or to understand why something happens — determining causes and effects is often a thought-provoking and complex strategy. One reason for this complexity is that some causes are less obvious than others. *Immediate causes* are readily apparent because they are closest in time to the effect; the immediate cause of a flood, for example, may be the collapse of a dam. However, *remote causes* may be just as important, even though they are not as apparent and are perhaps even hidden. The remote (and, in fact, primary) cause of the flood might have been an engineering error or the use of substandard building materials or the failure of personnel to relieve the pressure on the dam caused by unseasonably heavy rains. In many cases, it is necessary to look beyond the most immediate causes to discover the true underlying sources of an event.

A second reason for the complexity of this strategy is the difficulty of distinguishing between possible and actual causes, as well as between possible and actual effects. An upset stomach may be caused by spoiled food, but it may also be caused by overeating, by flu, by nervousness, by pregnancy, or by a combination of factors. Similarly, an increase in the cost of electricity may have multiple effects: higher profits for utility companies, fewer sales of electrical appliances, higher prices for other products that depend on electricity in their manufacture, even the development of alternative sources of energy. Making reasonable choices among the various possibilities requires thought and care.

WHY DO WRITERS USE CAUSE AND EFFECT ANALYSIS?

Writers may use cause and effect analysis for three essential purposes: to inform, to speculate, and to argue. Most commonly, they will want to inform — to help their readers understand some identifiable fact. A state wildlife biologist, for example, might wish to tell the public about the effects severe winter weather has had on the state's deer herds. Similarly, in a newsletter, a member of Congress might explain to his or her constituency the reasons changes are being made in the Social Security system. In an essay later in this chapter ("The Great Kern County Mouse War," p. 456), Kennedy P. Maize uses cause and effect analysis to inform, by exploring how disrupting the balance of nature can have disastrous effects.

Cause and effect analysis may also allow writers to speculate — to consider what might be or what might have been. To satisfy the board of trustees, for example, a university treasurer might discuss the impact an increase in tuition will have on the school's budget. A columnist for *People* magazine might speculate about the reasons for a new singer's sudden popularity. Similarly, pollsters estimate the effects that various voter groups will have on future elections, and historians evaluate how the current presidency will continue to influence American government in the coming decades.

Finally, cause and effect analysis provides an excellent basis from which to argue a given position or point of view. An editorial writer, for example, could argue that bringing a professional basketball team into the area would have many positive effects on the local economy and on the community as a whole. Educators who think that video games are a cause of delinquency and poor school performance have argued in newspapers and professional journals against the widespread acceptance of such games. Carl M. Cannon's essay "The Real Computer Virus" (p. 463) makes an absorbing and effective argument against reporters' reliance on the Internet and computer databases to find facts and quotes for their stories. This essay provides an example of how cause and effect analysis can provide the basis for an effective argument.

AN ANNOTATED STUDENT ESSAY USING CAUSE AND EFFECT ANALYSIS

Born in Brooklyn, New York, Kevin Cunningham spent most of his life in Flemington, New Jersey. While enrolled in the mechanical engineering program at the University of Vermont, Cunningham shared an apartment near the Burlington waterfront with several other students. There he became interested in the effects that private real estate development — or gentrification — would have on his neighborhood. Such development is not unique to Burlington; it is happening in the older sections of cities across the country. After gathering information for his essay by talking with people who live in the neighborhood, Cunningham found it useful to discuss both the causes and the effects of gentrification.

Gentrification

Kevin Cunningham

> I went back to Ohio, and my city
> was gone....
> — Chrissie Hynde, of the Pretenders

Thesis

My city is in Vermont, not Ohio, but soon my neighborhood will probably be gone, too. Or maybe it's I who will be gone. My street, Lakeview Terrace, lies unobtrusively in the old northwest part of Burlington and is notable, as its name suggests, for spectacular views of Lake Champlain framed by the Adirondacks. It's not that the neighborhood is going to seed — no, quite the contrary. Recently it has been Discovered, and now it is on the verge of being Gentrified. For some of us who live here, that's bad.

Description of life cycle of city neighborhoods

Cities are often assigned human characteristics, one of which is a life cycle: they have a birth, a youth, a middle age, and an old age. A neighborhood is built and settled by young, vibrant people, proud of their sturdy new homes. Together, residents and houses mature, as families grow larger and extensions get built on. Eventually, though, the neighborhood begins to show its age. Buildings sag a little, houses aren't repainted as quickly, and maintenance slips. The neighborhood may grow poorer, as the young and upwardly mobile find new jobs and move away, while the older and less successful inhabitants remain.

1

2

Decay, renewal, or redevelopment awaits aging neighborhoods.

One of three fates awaits the aging neighborhood. Decay may continue until the neighborhood becomes a slum. It may face urban renewal, with old buildings being razed, and ugly, new apartment houses taking their place. Or it may undergo redevelopment, in which government encourages the upgrading of existing housing stock by offering low-interest loans or outright grants; thus, the original character of the neighborhood may be retained or restored, allowing the city to keep part of its identity.

3

Example of Hoboken, New Jersey

An example of redevelopment at its best is Hoboken, New Jersey. In the early 1970s Hoboken was a dying city, with rundown housing and many abandoned buildings. However, low-interest loans enabled some younger residents to begin to refurbish their homes, and soon the area began to show signs of renewed vigor. Even outsiders moved in and rebuilt some of the abandoned houses. Today, whole blocks have been restored, and neighborhood life is active again. The city does well too, because property values are higher and so are property taxes. And there, at least for my neighborhood, is the rub.

4

Effects of redevelopment on Hoboken

Transition: Writer moves from example of Hoboken to his Lakeview Terrace neighborhood.

Lakeview Terrace is a demographic potpourri of students and families, young professionals and elderly retirees, homeowners and renters. It's a quiet street where kids can play safely and the neighbors know each other. Most of the houses are fairly old and look it, but already some redevelopment has begun. Recently, several old houses were bought by a real estate company, rebuilt, and sold as condominiums; the new residents drive BMWs and keep to themselves. The house where I live is owned by a Young Urban Professional couple — he's an architect — and they have renovated the place to what it must have looked like when it was new. They did a nice

5

Describes "gentrification" to date

job, too. These two kinds of development are the main forms of gentrification, and so far they have done no real harm.

Redevelopment causes property values to increase, which will cause property taxes to rise.

But the city is about to start a major property tax reappraisal. Because of the renovations, the houses on Lakeview Terrace are currently worth more than they used to be; soon there will be a big jump in property taxes. And then a lot of people will be hurt — even dispossessed from their own neighborhood.

Clem is a retired General Electric employee who has lived on Lakeview for over thirty years and who owns his home. About three years ago some condos were built on the lot next door, which didn't please Clem — he says they just don't fit in. But with higher property taxes, it may be Clem who no longer fits in. At the very least, since he's on a fixed income, he will have to make sacrifices in order to stay. Ryan works as a mailman and also owns his Lakeview Terrace home, which is across the street from the houses that were converted into condos: same cause, same effect.

Effects of gentrification on local property owners

Effects of gentrification on renters

Then there are those of us who rent. As our landlords have to pay higher property taxes, they will naturally raise rents at least as much (and maybe more, if they've spent money on renovations of their own). Some of us won't be able to afford the increase and will have to leave. "Some of us" almost certainly includes me, as well as others who have lived on Lakeview Terrace much longer than I have. In fact, the exodus has already begun, with the people who were displaced by the condo conversions.

Conclusion

Of course, many people would consider what's happening on Lakeview Terrace a genuine improvement in every way, resulting not only in better-looking houses but also in a

6

7

8

9

better class of people. I dispute that. The new people may be more affluent than those they displace, but certainly not "better," not by any standard that counts with me.

*Restatement
of thesis*

Gentrification may do wonders for a neighborhood's aesthetics, but it certainly can be hard on its soul.

Analyzing Kevin Cunningham's Essay of Cause and Effect Analysis: Questions for Discussion

1. According to Cunningham, in what way are cities like humans? What does he describe as the three possible outcomes for aging neighborhoods?

2. Cunningham presents this causal chain: Redevelopment (cause) increases property values (effect), which in turn increases property taxes upon reassessment by the city (effect), which leads to the displacement of poorer residents. What other effects of redevelopment can you think of?

3. Cunningham decries the gentrification of the neighborhood, but a neighborhood descending into disrepair is not a desirable alternative. What do you think Cunningham would like to see happen on Lakeview Terrace? How can a neighborhood fend off decay while still maintaining its "soul"?

4. Would the essay have benefited if Cunningham had proposed and speculated about a viable alternative to gentrification? Explain.

SUGGESTIONS FOR WRITING A CAUSE AND EFFECT ANALYSIS

Begin by selecting a manageable topic for your essay. In making your decision, you will need to consider both the amount of information available to you and the time you have to complete your research and writing. For a short essay due in two weeks, for example, you might concentrate on a narrowly defined topic, such as what is causing increasing numbers of students in your community to seek part-time jobs. You probably should not try to examine the reasons for the decline of American labor unions. The second topic would clearly require a significant amount of research and a more elaborate presentation; it is more suitable for a term paper. What is necessary for a successful cause and effect analysis is a clear sense of purpose as well as a careful and objective examination of the topic.

One way to approach writing a cause and effect essay would be to choose a subject (such as the Internet), to view it as a cause, and to write about the effects it has had or will have. The following sample essay introduction sets up the question of whether the effects of the Internet have been positive or negative.

```
              The Internet: Boon or Bane?
     Although the Internet has created a wonderful way to
access vast amounts of timely information, it has done
little to protect the veracity and credibility of the in-
formation itself, prompting educators and some government
officials to consider establishing a separate Internet
with more tightly controlled access. The benefits of the
Internet, however, far outweigh the adverse consequences.
The Internet can provide free access to product, news,
travel, sports, and other timely information. It also al-
lows primary and secondary sources to be easily available
to students and researchers around the world. The problem
remains, however, that the truth and reliability of the
information cannot be determined from the Internet itself.
This has raised tremendous concerns among the academic and
governmental communities, leading to discussions about
starting a more closely watched system of information. De-
spite this concern, however, the Internet has changed the
way information is distributed to the world and has had,
as a result, a tremendously positive impact on the world.
```

While the cause and effect strategy in the preceding essay could be the sole rhetorical approach, the writer has chosen to incorporate the strategy of argument (see Chapter 11). The writer not only sets out to explain the various effects of the Internet, but also to defend it against those who criticize the system for its openness. What other strategies might you add to help explain the causes and effects of the Internet? Would you, for example, compare and contrast life before the arrival of the Internet with life today?

The sample essay introduction above illustrates only one approach to writing a cause and effect essay. Another approach would be to choose an effect and to explain its causes. For example, you might decide to write about the women's soccer team at your school to explain why, after two losses, they have won five matches in a row. To do this, you could consult the coach or team members, speak to opponents, check game statistics, or watch a video of the last five matches — if you didn't happen to see them yourself. Once you have gathered and examined the relevant information, you should be ready to determine your thesis statement and to write your cause and effect essay. A possible introduction for this essay follows:

```
             Transition Game Key to Victories
        The women's soccer team has won five straight matches
against their toughest opponents. The coach, the players,
and even their opponents have ascribed their success to
the powerful transition game of the team's halfbacks.
Although each victory is won by the efforts of the whole
team, the recent victories can be attributed to the half-
backs' gaining control and possession of the ball and dom-
inating play in the quick transitions from defense to
offense and their ability to prevent their opponents from
doing the same. Clearly, in the last five matches, the
transition game has been responsible for the team's victo-
ries.
```

The purpose of the essay is to explain the success of the women's soccer team in its last five matches. Through research, the writer ascertained that the cause of the victories was the strong play of the halfbacks in controlling the transition game.

Establish Your Focus

Decide whether your essay will propose causes, talk about effects, or analyze both causes and effects. Any research you do and any questions you ask will depend on how you wish to concentrate your attention. For example, let's say that as a reporter for the school paper, you are writing a story about a fire that destroyed an apartment building in the neighborhood, killing four people. In planning your story, you might focus on the cause of the fire: Was there more than one cause? Was carelessness to blame? Was the fire of suspicious origin? You might focus on the effects of the fire: How much damage was done to the building? How many people were left homeless? What was the impact on the families of the four victims? Or you might cover both the reasons for this tragic event and its ultimate effects, setting up a sort of causal chain. Such a focus is crucial as you gather information. For example, student Kevin Cunningham decided early on that he wanted to explore what would happen (the effects) if gentrification continued on his street.

Determine Your Purpose

Once you begin to draft your essay and as you continue to refine it, make sure your purpose is clear. Do you wish your cause and effect analysis to be primarily informative, speculative, or argumentative? An informative essay allows readers to say, "I learned something from this. I didn't know that the fire was caused by faulty wiring." A speculative essay suggests to readers new possibilities: "That never occurred to me before. The apartment house could indeed be replaced by an office building." An argumentative essay convinces readers that some sort of action should be taken: "I have to agree — fire inspections should occur more regularly in our neighborhood." In his essay on gentrification, Cunningham uses cause and effect analysis to question the value of redevelopment by examining what it does to the soul of a neighborhood. Whatever your purpose, be sure to provide the information necessary to carry it through.

Formulate a Thesis Statement

All essays need a strong, clear thesis statement. When writing an essay using cause and effect, a thesis statement should clearly present either a cause and its effect(s) or an effect and its cause(s). As a third approach, your essay could focus on a complex causal chain of events. Here are a few examples from this chapter.

- "What has the telephone done to us, or for us, in the hundred years of its existence?" John Brooks's opening sentence makes it easy for the reader to know that he has chosen the telephone as his cause and that he will be exploring its effects in the essay.
- "On March 28, 1979, at 3:53 A.M., a pump at the Harrisburg plant failed." Here, Barry Commoner has chosen the failure of the pump to introduce the causal chain of events that led to the near–nuclear disaster at Three Mile Island.
- "Clearly, in the last five matches, the transition game has been responsible for the team's victories." From this sentence, the reader knows that the effect was a series of victories and that the cause was the transition game.

When you begin to formulate your thesis statement, keep these examples in mind. You can find other examples of thesis statements in the essays throughout this book. As you begin to develop your thesis statement, ask yourself, "What is my point?" Next, ask yourself, "What approach to a cause and effect essay will be most useful in making my point?" If you can't answer these questions yet, write some ideas down and try to determine your main point from these ideas.

Avoid Oversimplification and Errors of Logic

Sound and thoughtful reasoning, while present in all good writing, is central to any analysis of cause and effect. Writers of convincing cause and effect analysis must examine their material objectively and develop their essays carefully, taking into account any potential objections that readers might raise. Therefore, do not jump to conclusions or let your prejudices interfere with the logic of your interpretation or the completeness of your presentation. In gathering information for his essay, Kevin Cunningham discovered that he had to watch himself — that he had to distinguish between cause and effect and mere coincidence. "You have to know your subject, and you have to be honest. For example, my downstairs neighbors moved out last month because the rent was raised. Somebody who didn't know the situation might say, 'See? Gentrification.' But that wasn't the reason — it's that heating costs went up. This is New England, and we had a cold winter; gentrification had nothing to do with it. It's something that is just beginning to happen, and it's going to have a big effect, but we haven't actually felt many of the effects here yet."

Be sure that you do not oversimplify the cause and effect relationship you are writing about. A good working assumption is that most important matters cannot be traced to a single verifiable cause; similarly, a cause or set of causes rarely produces a single isolated effect. To be believable, your analysis of your topic must demonstrate a thorough understanding of the surrounding circumstances; there is nothing less convincing than the single-minded determination to show one particular connection. For example, someone writing about how the passage of a tough new crime bill (cause) has led to a decrease in arrests in a particular area (effect) will have little credibility unless other possible causes — socioeconomic conditions, seasonal fluctuations in crime, the size and budget of the police force, and so on — are also examined and taken into account. Of course, to achieve coherence, you will want to emphasize the important causes or the most significant effects. But be careful not to lose your reader's trust by insisting on an oversimplified "X leads to Y" relationship.

The other common problem in cause and effect analysis is lack of evidence in establishing a cause or effect. This error is known as the "after this, therefore because of this" fallacy (in Latin, *post hoc, ergo propter hoc*). In attempting to discover an explanation for a particular event or circumstance, a writer may point to something that merely preceded it in time, assuming a causal connection where none has in fact been proven. If you have dinner out one evening and the next day come down with stomach cramps, you may blame your illness on the restaurant where you ate the night before; but you do so without justification if your only proof is the fact that you ate there before-hand. More evidence would be required to establish a causal relation-ship. The *post hoc, ergo propter hoc* fallacy is often harmlessly foolish ("I failed the exam because I lost my lucky key chain"). It can, however, lead writers into serious errors of judgment and blind them to more reasonable explanations of cause and effect. And, like oversimplifica-tion, such mistakes in logic can undercut a reader's confidence. Make sure that the causal relationships you cite are, in fact, based on demon-strable evidence and not merely on a temporal connection.

Select Words That Strike a Balanced Tone

Be careful to neither overstate nor understate your position. Avoid ex-aggerations like "there can be no question" and "the evidence speaks for itself." Such diction is usually annoying and undermines your in-terpretation. Instead, allow your analysis of the facts to convince read-ers of the cause and effect relationship you wish to suggest. Do not be afraid to admit the possibility of other viewpoints. At the same time, no analytical writer convinces by understating or qualifying informa-tion with words and phrases such as *it seems that, perhaps, maybe, I think, sometimes, most often, nearly always,* or *in my opinion.* While it may be your intention to appear reasonable, overusing such qualifying words can make you sound unclear or indecisive, and it renders your analysis less convincing. Present your case forcefully, but do so honestly and sensibly.

Use Other Rhetorical Strategies

Although cause and effect analysis can be used effectively as a separate writing strategy, it is more common for essays to combine different strategies. For example, the sample essay introduction about the soc-cer team's victories could have added comparison and contrast to high-light the differences between the team's play in the two losses and in the five victories. Narration from interviews could also have been added to make the piece more colorful and more effective. The essay on the Internet could have incorporated the strategy of argument (see Chapter 11) as well as definition to defend the openness and effective-ness of the Internet. The argument could analyze exactly how the ben-efits outweigh the drawbacks, while definition could be used to focus the subject matter to better achieve the author's purpose. By combin-ing strategies, the author could have made his point more clearly and more forcefully.

You must always keep the purpose of your essay and the tone you wish to adopt in the front of your mind when combining strategies.

Without careful planning, using more than one rhetorical strategy can alter both the direction and the tone of your essay in ways that detract from, rather than contribute to, your ability to achieve your purpose.

As you read the essays in this chapter, consider all of the writing strategies that the authors have used to support their cause and effect analysis. How have these other strategies added to or changed the style of the essay? Are there strategies that you might have added or taken out? What strategies, if any, do you think you might use to strengthen your cause and effect essay? Although some essays are developed using a single rhetorical strategy, more often good writing takes advantage of several strategies to develop the writer's purpose and thesis to produce a stronger essay that is more informative, persuasive, and entertaining.

Editing Tip: Cause and Effect Signal Words

Be sure to follow the guidelines and advice for editing an essay given in Chapter 2, "Writing Essays." The guidelines highlight those sentence-level concerns of style — grammar, mechanics, and punctuation — that are especially important in editing any piece of writing. Cause and effect analysis links reasons and actions to effects. While you may think that a reason or action causes an effect, and that an effect is brought about by an action, it is necessary when writing about causes and effects to use language that accurately describes the linkage. Here is an example:

> Someone was talking very loudly on a cell phone, so I could not concentrate on my exam.

Notice that the word *so* signals the relationship between the cause, *Someone was talking very loudly on a cell phone,* and the effect, *I could not concentrate on my exam.* The sentence could be rendered as two sentences or its clauses could be joined by *and,* but the causal link would not be so clearly established.

Here is another example:

> But during a recession, demand may increase as low-wage workers rely on tips more than ever, and thus the proliferation of jars continues unabated.

> —Dalton Conley
> "Tip Jars and the New Economy," p. 451

In this example, *increase* is a causative verb that signals an action and the word *thus* signals its consequence or effect. You can ensure precision in your writing by using 1) words and phrases that high-light causal links and 2) causative verbs that describe cause-and-effect actions.

Words and Phrases That Highlight Causal Links. Certain words and phrases signal cause-and-effect relationships. They link actions to the effects that they bring about. Following are some examples:

as/as a result	hence	so/so that
because/because of	if . . . then	therefore
brought about	in order to	this is how
consequence/ consequently	influence	thus
due to	led to	what
effect/effect of/effect on	nevertheless	what followed
for/for this reason	owing to	was
	since	

Following are some examples from Dalton Conley's "Tip Jars and the New Economy."

> *So* while the benefits and origins of tipping are questionable, the social costs may be large, even as they remain hidden.

> Still better are the honoraria and grants, *since* they are promised before the work is even performed and are totally independent of the income.

> *If* workers cost more, goes the neoclassical economics argument, *then* employers will hire fewer of them.

Causative Verbs That Describe Cause-and-Effect Actions. Some verbs signal causes and effects. These verbs are known as causative verbs because they describe the action necessary to cause another action to occur. Following are some examples:

affect	dissolve	lighten
change	energize	make
convert	expand	produce
create	get	sharpen
darken	have	transform
decrease	inflate	
destroy	let	

Following are some examples in context:

> You don't need to be a shrink to see how the lessons boys learn *affect* their behavior as men.
>
> —Jon Katz
> "How Boys Become Men," p. 446

> Tipping creates what economists call a principal-agent problem. In other words, it *creates* different incentives for the worker and the owner of an establishment.
>
> —Dalton Conley
> "Tip Jars and the New Economy," p. 452

> If one pair of adult mice *produces* offspring, who in turn *produce* offspring, who in turn *produce* offspring, and so on for one year, the result will be over one million mice — unless there are predators.
>
> —Kennedy P. Maize
> "The Great Kern Country Mouse War," p. 461

▶ *Questions for Revising and Editing:*
Cause and Effect Analysis

1. Why do I want to use cause and effect: to inform, to speculate, or to argue? Does my analysis help me achieve my purpose?
2. Is my topic manageable for the essay I wish to write? Have I effectively established my focus?
3. Does my thesis statement clearly state either the cause and its effects or the effect and its causes?
4. Have I identified the nature of my cause and effect scenario? Is there a causal chain? Have I identified immediate and remote causes? Have I distinguished between possible and actual causes and effects?
5. Have I been able to avoid oversimplifying the cause and effect relationship I am writing about? Are there any errors in my logic?
6. Is my tone balanced, neither overstating nor understating my position?

(continued on next page)

(continued from previous page)

7. Is there another rhetorical strategy that I can use with cause and effect to assist me in achieving my purpose? If so, have I been able to implement it with care so that I have not altered either the direction or the tone of my essay?
8. Have I taken every opportunity to use words and phrases that signal cause and effect relationships?
9. Have I used *affect* and *effect* properly?
10. Have I avoided the phrase *the reason is because*?

Special Usage Notes for Cause and Effect

The following are two usage concerns that arise frequently when writing cause and effect essays.

1. Affect/Effect Confusion. Two words that are often confused, especially when writing cause and effect essays, are *affect* and *effect*.
Affect is a verb that means "to influence."

Staring at a computer screen for too long can affect your eyesight.

Effect is a noun that means "result."

The effect of staring at a computer screen for too long is blurry vision.

It is a good idea to check your use of these two words when you edit your essay.

2. "the reason is because". The other expression that occurs frequently in cause and effect writing is "the reason is because." It is widely regarded as redundant and should therefore be avoided. Instead use "the reason . . . is that" or "the reason why."

INCORRECT   The reason I didn't rent the apartment is because I don't have the money.

CORRECT   The reason I didn't rent the apartment is that I don't have the money.

CORRECT   The reason why I didn't rent the apartment is I don't have the money.

How Boys Become Men

Jon Katz

*Journalist and novelist Jon Katz was born in 1947. He writes with a keen
understanding of life in contemporary suburban America. Each of his
four mystery novels is a volume in the Suburban Detective Mystery series:*
The Family Stalker *(1994),* Death by Station Wagon *(1994),* The Father's Club *(1996), and* The Last Housewife *(1996). The best known
of these novels,* The Last Housewife, *won critical praise for its insights
into the pressures and conflicts experienced by young professional couples
in their efforts to achieve the American dream. It has been made into a
popular film. Katz is also the author of* Media Rants: Postpolitics in
the Digital Nation *(1997), a collection of his newspaper columns dealing primarily with the role and influence of the media in the public life of
modern America;* Virtuous Reality: How Americans Surrendered Discussion of Moral Values to Opportunists, Nitwits, and Blockheads
Like William Bennett *(1998); and* Geeks: How Two Lost Boys Rode
the Internet Out of Idaho *(2000).*

In the following essay, first published in January 1993 in Glamour,
Katz explains why many men appear insensitive.

PREPARING TO READ

How important are childhood experiences to the development of
identity? How do the rituals of the playground, the slumber party,
and the neighborhood gang help mold us as men and women? Can
you think of examples from your own experience?

Two nine-year-old boys, neighbors and friends, were walking home   1
from school. The one in the bright blue windbreaker was laughing
and swinging a heavy-looking book bag toward the head of his friend,
who kept ducking and stepping back. "What's the matter?" asked the
kid with the bag, whooshing it over his head. "You chicken?"

His friend stopped, stood still and braced himself. The bag   2
slammed into the side of his face, the thump audible all the way
across the street where I stood watching. The impact knocked him to
the ground, where he lay mildly stunned for a second. Then he struggled up, rubbing the side of his head. "See?" he said proudly. "I'm no
chicken."

No. A chicken would probably have had the sense to get out of   3
the way. This boy was already well on the road to becoming a *man*,
having learned one of the central ethics of his gender: Experience pain
rather than show fear.

Women tend to see men as a giant problem in need of solution.   4
They tell us that we're remote and uncommunicative, that we need to
demonstrate less machismo and more commitment, more humanity.
But if you don't understand something about boys, you can't understand why men are the way we are, why we find it so difficult to make
friends or to acknowledge our fears and problems.

Boys live in a world with its own Code of Conduct, a set of ruth-   5
less, unspoken, and unyielding rules:

> Don't be a goody-goody.
> Never rat. If your parents ask about bruises, shrug.
> Never admit fear. Ride the roller coaster, join the fistfight, do
> what you have to do. Asking for help is for sissies.
> Empathy is for nerds. You can help your best buddy, under cer-
> tain circumstances. Everyone else is on his own.
> Never discuss anything of substance with anybody. Grunt,
> shrug, dump on teachers, laugh at wimps, talk about comic books.
> Anything else is risky.

Boys are rewarded for throwing hard. Most other activities —   6
reading, befriending girls, or just thinking — are considered weird.
And if there's one thing boys don't want to be, it's weird.

More than anything else, boys are supposed to learn how to han-   7
dle themselves. I remember the bitter fifth-grade conflict I touched off
by elbowing aside a bigger boy named Barry and seizing the cafeteria's
last carton of chocolate milk. Teased for getting aced out by a wimp,
he had to reclaim his place in the pack. Our fistfight, at recess, ended
with my knees buckling and my lip bleeding while my friends, sympathetic but out of range, watched resignedly.

When I got home, my mother took one look at my swollen face and   8
screamed. I wouldn't tell her anything, but when my father got home I
cracked and confessed, pleading with them to do nothing. Instead, they
called Barry's parents, who restricted his television for a week.

The following morning, Barry and six of his pals stepped out from   9
behind a stand of trees. "It's the rat," said Barry.

I bled a little more. *Rat* was scrawled in crayon across my desk.   10

They were waiting for me after school for a number of afternoons   11
to follow. I tried varying my routes and avoiding bushes and hedges. It
usually didn't work.

I was as ashamed for telling as I was frightened. "You did ask for   12
it," said my best friend. Frontier Justice has nothing on Boy Justice.

In panic, I appealed to a cousin who was several years older. He   13
followed me home from school, and when Barry's gang surrounded
me, he came barreling toward us. "Stay away from my cousin," he
shouted, "or I'll kill you."

After they were gone, however, my cousin could barely stop laugh- 14
ing. "You were afraid of *them*?" he howled. "They barely came up to my
waist."

Men remember receiving little mercy as boys; maybe that's why 15
it's sometimes difficult for them to show any.

"I know lots of men who had happy childhoods, but none who 16
have happy memories of the way other boys treated them," says a
friend. "It's a macho marathon from third grade up, when you start
butting each other in the stomach."

"The thing is," adds another friend, "you learn early on to hide 17
what you feel. It's never safe to say, 'I'm scared.' My girlfriend asks me
why I don't talk more about what I'm feeling. I've gotten better at it,
but it will *never* come naturally."

You don't need to be a shrink to see how the lessons boys learn 18
affect their behavior as men. Men are being asked, more and more, to
show sensitivity, but they dread the very word. They struggle to build
their increasingly uncertain work lives but will deny they're in trouble. They want love, affection, and support but don't know how to
ask for them. They hide their weaknesses and fears from all, even
those they care for. They've learned to be wary of intervening when
they see others in trouble. They often still balk at being stigmatized as
weird.

Some men get shocked into sensitivity — when they lose their jobs, 19
their wives, or their lovers. Others learn it through a strong marriage,
or through their own children.

It may be a long while, however, before male culture evolves to 20
the point that boys can learn more from one another than how to hit
curve balls. Last month, walking my dog past the playground near my
house, I saw three boys encircling a fourth, laughing and pushing
him. He was skinny and rumpled, and he looked frightened. One boy
knelt behind him while another pushed him from the front, a trick familiar to any former boy. He fell backward.

When the others ran off, he brushed the dirt off his elbows and 21
walked toward the swings. His eyes were moist and he was struggling
for control.

"Hi," I said through the chain-link fence. "How ya doing?" 22

"Fine," he said quickly, kicking his legs out and beginning his 23
swing.

RESPONDING TO THE TEXT

Do you agree with Katz that men in general are less communicative, less
sensitive, and less sympathetic in their behavior than women? Why or why
not? Where does "Boy Justice" originate?

ENGAGING THE WRITER'S SUBJECT

1. In paragraph 12, what does Katz mean when he says, "Frontier Justice has nothing on Boy Justice"?

2. What is it that boys are supposed to learn "more than anything else" (paragraph 7)? What do you think girls are supposed to learn more than anything else?

3. How, according to Katz, do some men finally achieve sensitivity? Can you think of other softening influences on adult males?

ANALYZING THE WRITER'S CRAFT

1. This essay was originally published in *Glamour* magazine. Can you find any places where Katz addresses himself specifically to an audience of young women? Where? (Glossary: *Audience*)

2. Early in the essay, Katz refers to men as "we," but later he refers to men as "they." What is the purpose of this change?

3. Notice that in paragraphs 16 and 17, Katz quotes two friends on the nature of male development. Why is the location of these quotes crucial to the structure of the essay?

4. Katz illustrates his thesis with three anecdotes. Identify each of them. Where in the essay is each located? How do they differ? How does each enhance the author's message? (Glossary: *Narration*)

UNDERSTANDING THE WRITER'S LANGUAGE

1. In paragraph 3, Katz identifies what he describes as "one of the central ethics" of his gender. Why does he call it an ethic rather than a rule?

2. Refer to your desk dictionary to determine the meanings of the following words as Katz uses them in this selection: *remote* (paragraph 4), *machismo* (4), *empathy* (5), *resignedly* (7), *barreling* (13), *balk* (18), *stigmatized* (18).

WRITING SUGGESTIONS

1. Discuss with classmates the expectations that shape women; in your discussion you might find it helpful to share anecdotes from your own experience. (It may be helpful to review your Preparing to Read response.) Write an essay patterned on "How Boys Become Men," showing the causes and effects surrounding females growing up in American culture. You might come to the conclusion that women do not have a standard way of growing up; you could also write a cause and effect essay supporting this idea. Either way, be sure to include forceful examples.

2. The differences between men and women have always been food for controversy — and humor, as the following *New Yorker* cartoon by

Ed Fisher demonstrates. What gender stereotypes does the cartoon use in its humor? What does it say about male-female relations in general? The subject perpetually spawns a lot of discussion and debate, and a spate of recently published and widely read books have commented seriously on relationship issues. Read one of these books. (*Men Are from Mars, Women Are from Venus* by John Gray and *You Just Don't Understand* by Deborah Tannen are good examples.) Write a review presenting and evaluating the major thesis of the book you have chosen. Other than evolution, what issues make male-female relations so problematic? What can be done to bridge what the cartoon communicates is a huge "gender gap" that many of us seem to need experts, books, and teaching to understand?

"It isn't that I don't love you. It's just that I've evolved and you haven't."

3. With classmates, brainstorm a list of professions in which the character and behavior of the practitioners are sharply affected by cultural expectations (physician and professional athlete are obvious examples). Choose from this list a profession that interests you. Interview two or three people involved in the profession to discover their views about how they are expected to act, the means by which they learned to behave appropriately, and how they feel about the pressures to meet cultural expectations. Write an essay examining the causes and effects of particular professional behaviors. You may wish to support your essay with research from your college library and the Internet.

- To begin your research online, go to **bedfordstmartins.com /subjectsstrategies** and click on "Cause and Effect Analysis" or browse the thematic directory of annotated links.

SEEING/READING

Tipping Is Not a City in China

Joel Gordon

© Joel Gordon 2004

CONNECTING IMAGE AND TEXT

This photograph was taken at a Manhattan coffee shop in April 2004 and reflects an increasingly common sight at checkout counters across the country — the tip jar. People leave tips for many reasons: to ensure prompt and efficient service, out of guilt, and because servers and staff do not often make an adequate hourly wage. How do you feel about tipping? How do you "read" this photograph? When you see a tip jar do you feel obliged to drop in your loose change? What difference, if any, is there between someone waiting on you at a table and someone ringing up your order at a cash register? Is a tip warranted in both cases? What is your reaction to the message on the tip jar in this photograph? Does the message make you want to leave a tip? Why or why not? Your observations will help guide you to the key themes and strategies in the essay that follows.

Tip Jars and the New Economy
Dalton Conley

Dalton Conley is an associate professor of sociology and the director of the Center for Advanced Social Science Research at New York University. He has also taught at Yale and Princeton universities. He received his B.A. from the University of California–Berkeley and his M.A., Ph.M., and Ph.D. from Columbia University. The author of numerous articles in scholarly journals, Conley has published several books, including Being Black, Living in the Red: Race, Wealth, and Social Policy *(1999);* Honkey *(2002);* The Starting Gate: Birth Weight and Life Chances, *with Kate W. Strully and Neil G. Bennett (2003); and* The Pecking Order: Which Siblings Succeed and Why *(2004).*

In "Tip Jars and the New Economy," first published in the January 3, 2003, issue of the Chronicle of Higher Education, *Conley examines the causes for the recent proliferation of tip jars when we pay for goods or services and what significance this trend may have in an understanding of the "new economy."*

PREPARING TO READ

More and more tip jars seem to be turning up every day in familiar places — the school snack bar, where we buy our newspaper, and where we rent our videos. If tip jars are multiplying, what accounts for their increased appearance? What relationship, if any, do you think they have to the state of our economy?

I n all the hubbub about the rise and fall of the "new economy," one important trend has gone undocumented: the steady increase in the number of tip jars at restaurants, cafes, and other stores.

As far as I can tell, no official statistics are kept on the number of tip jars in consumer establishments, but over the last few years, I have noticed a staggering increase. Today you cannot order a coffee, buy a bagel, or pay for a photocopy without being asked to leave your change behind for "better service" or, alternatively, "good karma."

Their expansion to every service establishment seems to march 3
onward independent of the state of the economy. In good times the
supply of tips may be greater and thus drives their spread. But during a
recession, demand may increase as low-wage workers rely on tips more
than ever, and thus the proliferation of jars continues unabated. One
way to view the spread of tipping culture is that it represents the tri-
umph of the free market: The promise of 15 percent (or more) may spur
better service through direct economic incentives. That view rests on a
number of assumptions, however, most notably the promise of repeat
business. After all, why tip a taxi driver when you are about as likely to
get him again (and have him recognize you, the "big tipper") as to
find a pot of gold on Sixth Avenue?

In fact, the origins of the multibillion-dollar culture of tipping 4
are as vague as the reasons for its continuance. Scholars are not even
sure of the origins of the word. Some historians attribute the habit and
the word to 18th-century English coffeehouses, where collection boxes
(not unlike the tip jars of today) were often emblazoned with the words
"To Insure Promptitude" (TIP).

Other researchers date its ancestry to the Middle Ages (before capi- 5
talism), when feudal lords tossed coins to beggars on the road to insure
safe passage. And others see the origins in the Dutch word *tippen* — that
is, to tap on a table for service — or the Latin word *stips*, which translates as "gift." Although the word may be fairly recent in history, the
practice most likely long predates any of these records.

So while the benefits and origins of tipping are questionable, the 6
social costs may be large, even as they remain hidden. About 100 years
ago the German social philosopher Georg Simmel wrote a series of lectures and essays that would come to be the largest philosophical trea-
tise on money. One of his keenest observations was the way that forms
of payment affect social relations. In Simmel's view, modern society
has gone through an evolution of sorts in payment schemes. First there
was "in kind" payment. For example, a serf received some food and
shelter for tilling the soil. She wasn't much different than oxen who
were fed and stored for the night. Basic human needs were taken care
of, but the dependence of the worker on the largess of the master was,
in Simmel's view, dehumanizing.

Then came the "good old" days of craftsmen and cottage industry, 7
when workers were paid on a per-unit basis. That is, you agree on the
price for, say, a chair. The furniture maker procures the raw materials,
fashions the chair, and delivers it "on spec." If the wood is rotten, or
he makes a mistake and has to start over again, there goes his profit
margin. He bears all the risk. His wages are dependent on the quality
of the capital goods.

One step up the ladder from per-unit payment is hourly wages. 8
While many social theorists (most notably Karl Marx) saw the advent

of wage labor as something to be mourned, Simmel saw it as a further step toward worker liberation. Now the worker was privileged over the raw materials. If the wood were rotten, and the chair turned out to be no good, the worker would be paid all the same.

Even better is a salary. Now the worker is not even dependent on how much work there is to do. His salary is based on what the employer thinks is a reasonable standard of living for someone occupying that kind of position. Still better are honoraria and grants, since they are promised before the work is even performed and are totally independent of the outcome.　9

Tips, in this schema, are a big step backward. It is already bad enough that service workers are programmed to wish us a "nice day" and to plaster a perma-grin on their faces from the moment they show up to work.　10

The imposing tip jar further muddles business and sociability. If the promise of a dollar in the jar is what compels someone to be friendly, does that not cheapen smiles in general? Conversely, how can service workers and customers be on equal footing if the cashier's livelihood depends on the largess of the person ordering the mochachino? Also, studies show that aspects of the servers do affect tipping, although in a meritocratic world they should not. For instance, attractive females receive higher tips, according to at least one psychology study.　11

The presence of in-your-face money not only hurts the relationship between the customer and the service worker, it also damages the relationship between the worker and the firm. Tipping creates what economists call a principal-agent problem. In other words, it creates different incentives for the worker and the owner of an establishment. A waiter whose income largely derives from tips is more likely to give an extra scoop of ice cream to a customer. Research shows that these kinds of acts do increase tips on average, but they, of course, cut into the profit margin of the ice-cream parlor.　12

More importantly, tipping also is not good for the workers themselves. While often appearing to be tax-free revenue, tips create a high degree of income insecurity. Public-opinion research has shown that most customers would prefer that service workers were paid better wages and thereby the need for and practice of tipping could be eliminated — which leads us to the age-old debate over the minimum wage.　13

The empirical arguments against raising the minimum wage focus on the perceived loss of jobs. If workers cost more, goes the neoclassical economics argument, then employers will hire fewer of them. While the debate is far from settled, a study by economists David Card and Alan Krueger has seriously challenged that view. By comparing the changes in employment rates in neighboring areas across state　14 lines after one state raised its minimum wage and the other did not, they found no detrimental effect on labor-market opportunities resulting from wage increases. The demand for unskilled labor, it seems, may not be as elastic (that is, responsive) to price as once thought. Of course, those relationships may vary by other factors such as the state of the national and local economy, labor laws, and the local cost of living.

So — in light of research and public opinion that casts the expansion of tipping and tip jars in a negative light — why the proliferation? Again, while the lack of official statistics makes any analysis nothing more than educated conjecture, my guess is that the proliferation is at least partially the result of rising income and wealth inequality in the United States. In a recent article, the economist Paul Krugman cites a Congressional Budget Office study that found "that between 1979 and 1997, the after-tax incomes of the top 1 percent of families rose 157 percent, compared with only a 10-percent gain for families near the middle of the income distribution." The result, he writes, is that we are now at a point where the richest one-hundredth of a percent of households — a mere 13,000 households in all — enjoy "almost as much income as the 20 million poorest households."

While the rich get richer, those who serve the rich are increasingly left to appeal to the better instincts of the well off. The rich also need to have a way to release their guilt. If they tip big, then how bad can they feel for driving $40,000 SUVs and drinking their $4 coffees? (Of course, often it is the less well off who tip the most, out of insecurity.)

The cruelest irony, is that, of course, the worst-paid jobs do not even afford their workers the option to garner tips. The men and women who take the orders and bus the tables at the McDonald's and KFC restaurants of the world earn minimal (if not minimum) wages, receive no health benefits, and cannot even ask for tips. Also in this category of the untipped are maintenance and domestic workers, dishwashers, security personnel, and many other hidden service workers who work hard to ensure that we "have a nice day."

In fact, at one time, McDonald's allowed the practice, but the managers pocketed the money. When the public discovered this practice, outrage boiled over, and it was ended. So now it is only the employees in the middlebrow and high-end service establishments — ranging from Starbucks (whose employees at least get health insurance) to the funky coffee shops it competes with — who are able to paint the side of a sugar canister in bright letters asking for donations. And those of us who can afford to tip are placed in one more daily bind — do we encourage the spread of tip jars by giving? Or do we find time in our busy days to rally for better wages for the hardest working, worst paid among us?

Another double latte, please.

RESPONDING TO THE TEXT

In paragraph 15 Conley ventures a guess about the causes and effects of tipping. Why is it so difficult to say anything definitive about today's tipping culture? More specifically, why is it impossible to get any reliable statistics on the amount and nature of tipping taking place?

ENGAGING THE WRITER'S SUBJECT

1. What is the origin of the word *tip* according to Conley? Why can't we be certain of the origin of the word?

2. In paragraph 4, Conley refers to the world of tipping as a culture. Why does he see it this way?

3. According to Conley, what are some of the causes given for the increased number of tip jars today? What is his personal guess as to the cause of the increase?

4. What does Conley say is the "cruelest irony" (paragraph 17) of the tip jar economy? (Glossary: *Irony*)

ANALYZING THE WRITER'S CRAFT

1. Conley begins his article with a reference to the "new economy." What is the "new economy"? Explain.

2. Conley refers to German social philosopher Georg Simmel's observations on how "forms of payment affect social relations" (paragraph 6). How does this information support Conley's cause and effect analysis? (Glossary: *Evidence*)

3. What are the arguments for and against increasing the minimum wage? (Glossary: *Argument*) How do these arguments figure into Conley's analysis of the reasons why there are more tip jars?

4. Once he concludes with the argument against tipping, Conley recognizes that his original question persists: If tipping is so bad, why is it on the increase? (Glossary: *Argument*) What do his background arguments and his return to the original question allow him to do as an author?

5. Conley uses a brief paragraph to begin his article and an even shorter one to end it. How effective are these paragraphs? (Glossary: *Beginnings/Endings*)

UNDERSTANDING THE WRITER'S LANGUAGE

1. As a sociologist interested in connections between social relations and the economy, Conley naturally uses terms drawn from the study of economics, labor, and commerce. (Glossary: *Jargon*) For example, he uses the following terms in paragraphs 1–3 alone: *new economy, consumer establishments, recession, free market, direct economic incentives,* and *repeat business.* What other similar terms can you identify in this article? Why

are they appropriate considering his subject and audience? (Glossary: *Audience; Subject*)

2. What are the denotative and connotative dimensions of the phrase *tip jar*? (Glossary: *Connotation/Denotation*) What other terms have you heard for tip jars? How do you refer to tip jars?

3. Refer to your desk dictionary to determine the meanings of the following words as Conley uses them in this selection: *karma* (paragraph 2), *emblazoned* (4), *keenest* (6), *serf* (6), *largess* (6), *honoraria* (9), *schema* (10), *permagrin* (10), *meritocratic* (11), *garner* (17), *middlebrow* (18), *canister* (18).

WRITING SUGGESTIONS

1. Write an essay in which you analyze the effects of a hypothetical ban on tipping. Would the quality of service decline or improve? Would workers' incomes increase, stay the same, or decrease? Would more people go to restaurants and service-based establishments, or would there be no change? Explain.

2. Write an essay in which you explore your experiences with the "tipping culture." Have you ever had a job in which you received tips or had a tip jar? What did you like and dislike about it? Have you ever not left a tip? Left an overly generous tip? Why? Before you write, you might want to refer to your Connecting Image and Text response for this selection. (Glossary: *Exemplification; Narration*)

3. In paragraph 14 Conley states, "The empirical arguments against raising the minimum wage focus on the perceived loss of jobs. If workers cost more, goes the neoclassical economics argument, then employers will hire fewer of them." Do you agree? Why or why not? In your college library and on the Internet, research the issue of the minimum wage. What is the current federal minimum wage? Do you consider it a "livable wage"? Why or why not? What would be the effects of an increase? Write an essay in which you argue for or against an increase in the federal minimum wage.

• To begin your research online, go to **bedfordstmartins.com /subjectsstrategies** and click on "Cause and Effect Analysis" or browse the thematic directory of annotated links.

The Great Kern County Mouse War

Kennedy P. Maize

An environmental journalist, Kennedy P. Maize was born in Pittsburgh, Pennsylvania, in 1944. A 1966 graduate of Penn State University, Maize is a freelance writer whose articles on environmental and energy issues have appeared in Environmental Action, *the* New Republic, Analog, *and* Harper's. *In the early 1990s, Maize's interests in corporate structures and how they interact with environmental concerns led him to start his own newsletter, the* Electricity Daily. *Maize lives in Knoxville, Maryland, where he also maintains a small sheep farm.*

A letter to the editor of the local newspaper about the misguided practice of shooting vultures led Maize to research the events chronicled in the following essay. The essay, which appeared in Audubon *magazine in 1977, explores the war against the rodents of Kern County, California, in the 1920s. Maize's story serves as a lesson for today's readers about just what can happen when humans interfere with the balance of nature.*

PREPARING TO READ

What sorts of animal pests would you love to get rid of? The cockroaches overrunning your apartment, the skunks that spray your dog, the mosquitoes that make a misery of early summer, the feral cats or raccoons raiding neighborhood garbage cans? How might you go about eliminating them? How would your life be improved as a result? What other consequences might occur?

Once upon a time, some 75 years ago, the good people of Kern County, California, had an idea. They thought they were very smart. They would rid themselves of all the evil predators that killed their domestic animals, frightened their children, and made life unpleasant. 1

So in the early years of this century, the good citizens of Kern County oiled their shotguns, cleaned their traps, and brewed batches of strychnine. For 20 years they killed the evil predators — the skunk, the fox, the badger, the weasel, the snake, the owl, the hawk. Killed them all, every one they could find. The good folk of Kern County were very pleased. 2

In 1924 the good sheepmen of Kern County concocted a final solution to the "coyote problem." They hired a U.S. Biological Survey team (then part of the Department of Agriculture) to exterminate the entire coyote population. Soon there were no more coyotes in Kern County. 3

The good folk of Kern County were filled with satisfaction by what they had accomplished. They supposed they had created a pleasant paradise where their chickens would have no natural enemies, their children would never be frightened by talon or fang, and their dogs would never return stinking of skunk. Providence, they were sure, would bless their work with healthy animals, happy children, and bountiful harvests. 4

Most of the good people of Kern County were either farmers or townsmen in Taft, Tupman, McKittrick, Ford City, and other small villages. There was one city, Bakersfield, a market center with a population of under 10,000 people. Most of the good people of Kern County rarely got to Bakersfield. Despite oil derricks that dotted the landscape, Kern County in the 1920s was rural, agricultural. 5

Farming in Kern County was risky. Every year farmers planted grain in the fertile 25,000 acres of the dry bed of Buena Vista Lake. Three years out of every four the lake bed flooded in the fall, destroying the crop. But the fourth year — what a harvest for the good people of Kern County. 6

Such a year was 1926. There was kafir corn and barley in such bounty that all California took notice of Kern County's good fortune. The good merchants of Kern County rubbed their hands together as they thought about the dresses and cars and fencing and paint and other things the good farmers would buy with their grain receipts. So the good farmers reaped their grain, leaving behind 25,000 acres of stubble and scattered seed. The farmers took their grain to market and felt secure in their good fortune. 7

By October the good people of Kern County had begun to notice a minor annoyance. A farmer came to town one Saturday to buy supplies and a new shotgun, and he told the other farmers and the merchants about his little problem, "I killed nearly 500 mice in my barn last evening," he said. "You'd better sell me some poison, George." 8

Just as the storekeeper was reaching for the rat poison, his wife was telling a neighbor, "I just don't know about this cat of mine. She's getting so lazy. Seems like everywhere I look there's a mouse." 9

And there were mice. Everywhere the good people of Kern County looked, there were mice. The mice had bred in the Buena Vista Lake, unmolested by predators and well fed on residue from the harvest, until there were many millions of them. So many, in fact, that the food supply began to run out. Most were still in the dry lake bed, which looked as if it had just been cultivated, the result of mice burrowing in the ground. Mice were feeding on the grain residue, and continuing to breed. 10

A few mice, maybe a hundred thousand or so, had ventured out of the lake bed by November. The foraging vanguard increased in 11

December. They were invading barns, granaries, and houses looking for food. In some places near the lake the mice were ankle-deep. People killed them by the thousands. "The way we're slaughtering mice," one farmer said, "they'll soon be as scarce as coyotes. Now, if you'll excuse me, I have to shoot some owls I found in my silo."

If the farmer was wrong about the effect of killing thousands of mice, he can be excused his error. So far the good citizens of Kern County had fought only skirmishes in what would quickly become the Great Kern County Mouse War. But the good people of Kern County thought they had taken heroic measures and that they had won. After all, hadn't the West Side Businessmen's Club in Taft donated $50 for poisoned wheat after the county's deputy horticultural commissioner, C. H. Bowen, described the problem? Taft Mayor Clarence Williams said he would hand out the poison to the good farmers. That ought to do the trick. 12

The effort seemed to work. By Christmas of 1926 Commissioner Bowen, whom the press was calling "General" for his leadership of the war against the mice, told reporters, "By the first of the week I expect our work to be finished." *The Los Angeles Times* of December 29th reported, "Field mouse infestations at Taft and Tupman have been brought under control through the use of poisoned grain, the horticultural commissioner's office announced today." 13

But Kern County didn't understand the dimensions of its mouse problem. All the few hundred pounds of poisoned grain had accomplished was to delay hordes of mice that were marching out of the lake toward new food supplies. A cold snap at Christmas probably did as much to cause the delay as did the poisoned grain. 14

The new year of 1927 opened cold and clear, and the good people of Kern County faced the future with confidence. The mice seemed under control, and there would be prosperity ahead if they continued their eternal vigilance against the hawks, owls, coyotes, and other varmints. 15

Those good people who subscribed to the *Los Angeles Times* may have noticed a small feature article on New Year's Day. A park naturalist pointed out that the hated coyote is a very good mouser. But, of course, the article didn't mean much to the good people of Kern County. There were no coyotes in Kern County. 16

The cold snap broke on January 6th, and the mice emerged from the lake bed in a squirming, furry wave, driven by starvation. The mice had consumed every edible item in the lake bed. Scrambling up the barren, 100-foot Buena Vista Hills, the mice headed for Ford City, McKittrick, and Taft. Millions of mice were on the march toward food. U.S. Highway 399, which ran along the lake bed, became slippery with squashed mice, and cars slid into the ditches. Warning signs reading "Slow: slippery conditions" were posted. 17

Superintendent Bob Maguire of the Honolulu Oil Company put [18] men from the derricks on mouse detail. They dug trenches and spread poisoned barley. Maguire's mouse-control crew killed 50,000 mice in one day on one small piece of company property.

By January 16th, the U.S. Biological Survey was calling the affair in [19] Kern County the greatest rodent infestation in U.S. history. The only other comparable incident was a mouse migration in 1908 in Nevada. But the Biological Survey said the Nevada episode was minuscule compared with the problem in Kern County. Observers reported a "moving landscape" as mice poured over the earth in ankle-deep waves.

One January morning during the mouse invasion, a teacher at [20] Conley School near the lake, opened her desk for the day's lesson plan. A dozen mice leaped out, and she leaped out the school door, shrieking. Mice were in every wastebasket. Mice occupied the principal's office. Mice darted from classroom to classroom. Mice were everywhere.

On January 15th, a headline appeared in the *Los Angeles Times*: [21] "Army of Field Mice Kill and Eat Sheep at Taft." The article reported, "A skirmishing force of the second army of field mice reported to be invading Taft attacked, killed, and ate a sheep at the San Emidio Ranch." The unlucky ewe was kept in a small pen at the head of a canyon and was unable to escape. The article concluded dryly, "The mice have become a distinct annoyance to golfers on the Petroleum Club links on the Maricopa Road."

By January 19th, the mouse war was the *Times'* lead story on the [22] front page. The headlines said:

Pied Pipers
Lure Mice

Poison Stemming
Vast Hegira

Thousands of Rodents Prey
on Own Appetites During
Kern County Trek

"Gen." Bowen Thinks Peril
to Centers of Population
Has Been Overcome

The story was a full description of what was occurring in Kern [23] County, telling of "roads carpeted with mice" and concluding with the apt observation, "The plague has been aggravated by the fact that for many years past an unceasing warfare has been waged on the natural enemies of the invaders, such as coyotes, hawks, wildcats, and other predatory beasts and birds." The reference to the Pied Piper was a piece of a headline writer's fancy.

Folks around the country offered various ways to redress the natural balance. The northern California town of Merced offered hundreds of hungry cats to the good citizens of Kern County. But cats, it turned out, weren't much of a solution. There were just too many mice. A cat, after killing and eating a dozen or so mice, becomes sated and bored. 24

Lewis Gingery of Rushville, Missouri, told the good folks of Kern County that a couple of hundred skunks could take care of the problem. He was surprised that local skunks hadn't prevented the population increase in the first place. 25

But the good citizens of Kern County had killed all the skunks, and they still didn't understand what they had done. Mice surging up from the lake bed attracted flocks of hawks, owls, ravens, crows, vultures, and even a couple thousand seagulls which flew in from the coast. As the birds swooped down on the mice, the good people of Kern County shot-gunned them. They hung the carcasses on fenceposts to deter other feathered predators. 26

The good citizens of Kern County were losing the war against the invaders. The mice had multiplied freely over the years. The bumper crop of food in 1926 had produced a bumper crop of mice. The population spurted until the food ran out. Then tens of millions of mice found they had to migrate or starve. The mice moved inexorably. By mid-January they occupied a sector twelve by eight miles. 27

Then the war escalated. On January 19th, it was announced that the chief poison specialist and exterminator for the U.S. Biological Survey — the man who had conquered the 1908 Nevada migration — was being sent from Washington, D.C. The headline writer for the *Times* had been prescient. Stanley E. Piper was the exterminator's reassuring name. 28

Piper arrived in Kern County on Saturday, January 22nd, to examine the area and map his battle plan. On Monday he announced his intentions. Working with a full-time crew of 25 men, Piper would stage a counterattack at Buena Vista Lake. 29

Federal forces set up camp on a high spot in the middle of the dry lake, a place called Pelican Island. The crew then attempted to determine the size of the enemy forces. They dug up an acre of lake bottom and counted the mouse burrows. They counted 4,000 burrows and were stunned. They were facing an army of 100 million mice. 30

Piper quickly hauled in 40 tons of chopped alfalfa, generously laced with strychnine. Piper asked the oil companies to work harder at controlling the spread of the mice outward, and he concentrated on the lake bed. 31

By the end of February, Piper had won. But it had been a costly war. The good farmers of Kern County had lost more than a half-million 32 dollars in damaged crops, buildings, and fences. The good townsfolk had lost a similar amount in property damage and unrealized business revenues. Piper's efforts cost $5,000 for grain and supplies, paid for by the good citizens of Kern County. The great Kern County Mouse War lasted over three months, and mouse deaths amounted to unknown millions. The sweet prosperity of 1926 had turned sour.

33 If one pair of adult mice produces offspring, who in turn produce offspring, who in turn produce offspring, and so on for one year, the result will be over one million mice — unless there are predators. It is a lesson that the good people of Kern County should have learned well. It is a lesson that we all should learn well.

34 Build a better mousetrap, the old saying has it, and the world will beat a path to your door. The Great Kern County Mouse War proves that no one builds better mousetraps than nature. Let us beat a path to her door.

RESPONDING TO THE TEXT

How could the people of Kern County have dealt with the problem of local predators in other ways than systematically killing them off ?

ENGAGING THE WRITER'S SUBJECT

1. Why was it during a year of bountiful harvest that the mouse population exploded? Why were the people of Kern County initially unable to control the explosion?

2. What connection between causes and effects did the people of Kern County fail to make?

3. Why were cats not an effective solution to the mouse problem? How was the mouse war eventually won?

4. What conflicting roles did the U.S. Biological Survey play in the Mouse War?

ANALYZING THE WRITER'S CRAFT

1. What is Maize's thesis? Where in the article is it located? How does its location strengthen the impact of the essay?

2. How does Maize inject humor into his factual account? Point out some examples. Considering that the subject is a serious one, do you think that humor is appropriate? Why or why not?

3. Four times Maize cites the *Los Angeles Times* (paragraphs 13, 16, 21, 22). What are his purposes in doing so?

4. Except for the last two brief paragraphs, "The Great Kern County Mouse War" is a single extended illustration of Maize's thesis, written in the form of a historical narrative. (Glossary: *Narration*) Is one long

example sufficient to prove a point? How does he succeed or fail to succeed in turning a story into an argument? (Glossary: *Argument; Exemplification*)

UNDERSTANDING THE WRITER'S LANGUAGE

1. Maize uses the adjective "good" two dozen times to describe the people of Kern County. What is his purpose? Is he being ironic? (Glossary: *Irony*)

2. Refer to your desk dictionary to determine the meanings of the following words as Maize uses them in this selection: *strychnine* (paragraph 2), *kafir corn* (7), *residue* (10), *foraging* (11), *vanguard* (11), *horticultural* (12), *infestations* (13), *vigilance* (15), *varmints* (15), *minuscule* (19), *hegira* (22), *sated* (24), *inexorably* (27), *prescient* (28).

WRITING SUGGESTIONS

1. Many other attempts to kill "destructive" animals — not just predators, but also creatures that destroy crops or become household pests — have gone awry. Many people are familiar, for example, with the story of how the insecticide DDT was first hailed but finally banned because it was extremely harmful to many forms of life, including humans. Working with classmates and using library resources, compile a list of instances in which human efforts to eliminate a pest have precipitated a dangerous environmental imbalance. Using Maize's essay as a model, choose, research, and write the story of one of these events.

2. Some environmental crises have been precipitated not by human attempts to destroy pests, but by the introduction, either intentional or inadvertent, of a new species to a particular area. Think, for example, of the huge flocks of starlings that descend from time to time on unsuspecting midwestern towns or of the beautiful purple loosestrife that is taking over the fields of New England. What is being done to combat harmful nonnative species? Following the procedures suggested in the previous assignment, write the story of one introduced species.

3. In his book *Never Cry Wolf*, Canadian author Farley Mowat decries systematic efforts by the Canadian government to eliminate this native animal. Using your college library and the Internet, learn and write about the history of the wolf during the last fifty years on the North American continent: the reasons for attempting to eliminate wolf populations in the United States and Canada, the effects of these efforts, and the conflicts resulting from more recent efforts to reintroduce the species.

• To begin your research online, go to **bedfordstmartins.com /subjectsstrategies** and click on "Cause and Effect Analysis" or browse the thematic directory of annotated links.

The Real Computer Virus

Carl M. Cannon

Carl M. Cannon was born in San Francisco and majored in journalism at the University of Colorado. For twenty years he worked on a number of newspapers covering local and state politics, education, crime, and race relations. His reporting was instrumental in securing the freedom of a man in Georgia and a man in California who both had been wrongly convicted of murder. In 1989 Cannon's reporting on the Loma Prieta earthquake for the San Jose Mercury *won him a Pulitzer Prize. Cannon has been a staff writer for the prestigious* National Journal *since 1998, where he is now the White House correspondent. Cannon's books include* Boy Genius *(2003), a biography of George W. Bush's advisor Karl Rove, which he wrote with Lou Dubose and Jan Reid, and* The Pursuit of Happiness in Times of War *(2003), which examines the meaning and history of Jefferson's influential and quintessentially American phrase.*

In the following excerpt from "The Real Computer Virus," which first appeared in American Journalism Review *in April 2001, Cannon writes about the problems of obtaining accurate information on the Internet and correcting the misinformation frequently found and spread there.*

PREPARING TO READ

How do you go about fact-checking information from the Internet? Do you check to see who authors or sponsors the Web sites you visit? Do you use more than one or two sources for the information you need? Have you ever had reason to doubt the accuracy of information you have actually used in an assignment?

The Internet is an invaluable information-gathering tool for journalists. It also has an unmatched capacity for distributing misinformation, which all too often winds up in the mainstream media. 1

To commemorate Independence Day last year, *Boston Globe* columnist Jeff Jacoby came up with an idea that seemed pretty straightforward. Just explain to his readers what happened to the brave men who signed the Declaration of Independence. 2

This column caused big trouble for Jacoby when it was discovered that he had lifted the idea and some of its language from a ubiquitous e-mail making the rounds. It touched a particular nerve at the *Globe*, which had recently forced two well-regarded columnists to resign for making up quotes and characters. Jacoby was suspended for four months without pay, generating a fair amount of controversy, much 3 of it because he was the primary conservative voice at an identifiably liberal paper.

But there was a more fundamental issue at play than Jacoby's fail- 4 ure to attribute the information in the column: Much of what the e-mail contained was factually incorrect. To his credit, Jacoby recognized this flaw and tried, with some success, to correct it. Ann Landers, however, didn't. She got the same e-mail and simply ran it verbatim in her column.

Passing along what she described as a "perfect" Independence Day 5 column sent to her from "Ellen" in New Jersey, Ann Landers' epistle began this way:

Have you ever wondered what happened to the 56 men who signed the 6 *Declaration of Independence?*

Five signers were captured by the British as traitors and tortured before 7 *they died. Twelve had their homes ransacked and burned. Two lost their sons who served in the Revolutionary Army. . . . Nine of the 56 fought and died from wounds or hardships of the Revolutionary War. They pledged their lives, their fortunes and their sacred honor.*

Landers' column — like Ellen's e-mail — goes on from that point 8 to list names and explain the purported fates of many of the men. But this was not the "perfect" column Landers thought it was, for the simple reason that much of the information in it is simply false — as any Revolutionary War scholar would know readily.

I know because I interviewed some of them. R. J. Rockefeller, 9 director of reference services at the Maryland State Archives, reveals that none of the signers was tortured to death by the British. E. Brooke Harlowe, a political scientist at the College of St. Catherine in St. Paul, Minnesota, reports that two of the 56 were wounded in battle, rather than nine being killed. Brown University historian Gordon S. Wood points out that although the e-mail claims that for signer Thomas McKean "poverty was his reward," McKean actually ended up being governor of Pennsylvania and lived in material comfort until age 83.

And so on. What Landers was passing along was a collection of 10 myths and partial truths that had been circulating since at least 1995, and which has made its way into print in newspaper op-eds and letters-to-the-editor pages and onto the radio airwaves many times before. Mark Twain supposedly said, in a less technologically challenging time, that a lie can make it halfway 'round the world before the truth gets its boots on. The Internet gives untruth a head start it surely never needed. And what a head start: If an e-mailer sends a message to 10 people and each person who receives it passes it on to 10 more, by the ninth transmission this missive could reach a billion people.

This is the real computer virus: misinformation. Despite years of 11 warnings, this malady keeps creeping its way into the newsprint and onto the airwaves of mainstream news outlets.

One of the things that makes the Internet so appealing is that any- 12
one can pull things off of it. The other side of the coin is that anyone
can put anything on it. This poses a particular challenge for reporters
who are taught in journalism school to give more weight to the written
word (get the official records!) than to something they hearsay, word-
of-mouth at the corner barber shop. But the Web has both official documents and idle gossip, and reporters using it as a research tool — or
even a tip sheet — do not always know the difference.

"Journalists should be really skeptical of everything they read 13
online," says Sreenath Sreenivasan, a professor at the Columbia University Graduate School of Journalism. "They should be very aware of
where they are on the Web, just the way they would be if they were
on the street."

They aren't always. 14

In November 1998, the *New York Times* pulled off the Web — and 15
published — a series of riotously funny Chinese translations of actual
Hollywood hits. *The Crying Game* became "Oh No! My Girlfriend Has a
Penis!" *My Best Friend's Wedding* became "Help! My Pretend Boyfriend
Is Gay." *Batman and Robin* was "Come to My Cave and Wear this Rub-
ber Codpiece, Cute Boy."

If those seemed, in the old newsroom phrase, too good to check, it's 16
because they were. They came from an irreverent Web site called
TopFive.com, which bills itself as offering "dangerously original humor."

But even after the *Times* issued a red-faced correction, the "transla- 17
tions" kept showing up. On January 5, 1999, Peter Jennings read the
spoof of the title of the movie *Babe* ("The Happy Dumpling-To-Be Who
Talks and Solves Agricultural Problems") as if it were factual. Jennings
issued a correction 13 days later for his *World News Tonight* gaffe, but
that didn't stop things. On April 16, 1999, some of the bogus translations showed up on CNN's *Showbiz Today*. On June 10, a *Los Angeles
Times* staff writer threw one of the TopFive.com titles into his sports
column. In Hong Kong, he claimed, the title *Field of Dreams* was "Imaginary Dead Ballplayers in a Cornfield."

"What journalists need to do is learn to distinguish between the 18
crap on the Web and the good stuff," says Yale University researcher
and lecturer Fred Shapiro. "It's a crucial skill and one that some journalists need to be taught."

Even before President Clinton stirred up controversy with a slew 19
of late-term pardons and commutations, I researched and wrote a
4,000-word article on the historical and legal underpinnings of a U.S.
president's power to grant pardons, commutations, and clemency orders. One pertinent constitutional question was whether there are any
real restrictions on the presidential pardon authority.

Logging onto Lexis-Nexis, I found several relevant, in-depth law 20
review articles. Some of them cited Internet links to the original cases

being cited. In fact these were highlighted "hyperlinks," meaning that with a single click of my mouse I was able to read the controlling Supreme Court cases dating back to Reconstruction. Within seconds of clicking on those Supreme Court links, I was gazing at the actual words of Salmon P. Chase, the chief justice appointed by Abraham Lincoln. Justice Chase answered my question rather unequivocally: "To the executive alone is entrusted the power of pardon," he wrote with simple eloquence, "and it is granted without limit."

21 This is not an isolated example. I cover the White House for *National Journal* and, like many of my colleagues, I have developed an utter reliance on the Internet. I do research and interviews online, find phone numbers, check facts and spellings, and research the clips. I can read court cases online, check presidential transcripts, find the true source of quotes, and delve into history.

22 Some days this is a tool that feels like a magic wand. The riches of the Web are as vast as the journalist's imagination.

23 The point of these examples is that the Internet has rapidly become such a valuable research tool that it's hard to remember how we did our jobs without it. Need that killer Shakespeare reference to truthtelling from *As You Like It* to spice up that Clinton legacy piece? Log on and find it. Fact-checking the Bible verses slung around by the candidates during the 2000 presidential election? The Bible is not only on the Web but is searchable with a couple of keystrokes. Attorney General John Ashcroft's Senate voting record is there, too, along with his controversial interview with *Southern Partisan* magazine.

24 Yet in recent months I have found myself quietly checking the validity of almost everything I find in cyberspace and whenever possible doing it the old-fashioned way: consulting reference books in libraries, calling professors or original sources on the phone, double-checking everything. I don't trust the information on the Net very much anymore. It turns out the same technology that gives reporters access to the intellectual richness of the ages also makes misinformation ubiquitous. It shouldn't come as a surprise, but a tool this powerful must be handled with care.

25 These problems are only going to get worse unless Net users — and journalists — get a whole lot more careful. According to the Nielsen/NetRatings released on February 15, 168 million Americans logged onto the Web in the first month of the new millennium.

26 Seven years ago, *American Journalism Review* warned that an overreliance on Lexis-Nexis was leading to a "misinformation explosion." Since that time, the number of journalists using the data retrieval service has increased exponentially; at many news organizations, libraries have been phased out and reporters do their own searches. This has led, predictably, to an entire subgenre of phony quotes and statistics that won't die.

Sometimes the proliferation of errors carries serious implications. A   27
couple of years ago, Diane Sawyer concluded a *PrimeTime Live* interview
with Ellen DeGeneres the night her lesbian television character "came
out" by reciting what Sawyer called "a government statistic": gay teenagers are "three times as likely to attempt suicide" as straight teenagers.

This factoid, which Sawyer said was provided to her by DeGeneres,   28
is a crock.

Sleuthing by a diligent reporter named Delia M. Rios of Newhouse   29
News Service revealed that this figure is not a government statistic, but
rather the opinion of a single San Francisco social worker. In fact, a
high-level interagency panel made up of physicians and researchers
from the U.S. Department of Health and Human Services, the Centers
for Disease Control, the National Institute of Mental Health, and other
organizations concluded that there is no evidence that "sexual orientation and suicidality are linked in some direct or indirect manner."

Yet, the bogus stat is still routinely cited by certain gay-rights ac-   30
tivists, and thanks to Internet-assisted databases, has made its way
into the *New York Times*, the *Chicago Tribune*, the *Los Angeles Times* —
and onto prime time network television.

Joyce Hunter, onetime president of the National Lesbian and Gay   31
Health Association, insists that the available evidence suggests that both
gay and straight teens are, instead, emotionally resilient people who "go
on to develop a positive sense of self and who go on with their lives."
Other clinicians fear that this misinformation could turn into a self-
fulfilling prophecy. Peter Muehrer of the National Institutes of Health
says he worries that a public hysteria over gay-teen suicide could contribute to "suicide contagion," in which troubled gay teens come to see
suicide as a practical, almost normal, way out of their identity struggles.

Junk science on the Web — or junk history — has a way of oozing   32
into the mainstream media, often because it proves irresistible to disc
jockeys and radio talk-show hosts. The same is true of conspiracy theories and faulty understanding of the law, particularly when the in-
cendiary subject of race relations is involved.

An e-mail marked "URGENT! URGENT! URGENT!" flew like the   33
wind through the African American community for more than two
years. It warned that blacks' "right to vote" will expire in 2007. The
impetus for the e-mail was the impending expiration of the Voting
Rights Act, which has since been renewed and, in any event, no longer
has anything to do with guaranteeing anyone the right to vote.

Nonetheless, the preposterous claim was reiterated by callers to   34
African American radio talk shows. Eventually, it prompted an official
rebuttal by the Justice Department and a public disavowal by the Congressional Black Caucus. "The Web has good, useful information," observes David Bositis, senior political analyst for the Joint Center for
Political and Economic Studies. "But it also has a lot of garbage."

This particular cyberrumor was eventually traced to a naive but 35
well-intentioned college student from Chicago, who toured the South
on a promotional trip sponsored by the NAACP. The mistaken notion
that blacks' right to vote depends on the whims of Congress was given
wide circulation in a guest column in *USA Today* by Camille O. Cosby,
wife of entertainer Bill Cosby.

"Congress once again will decide whether African Americans will 36
be allowed to vote," she wrote, echoing the e-mail. "No other Americans are subjected to this oppressive nonsense."

Black leaders went to great lengths to dispel this hoax, but it ener- 37
gized black voters. The ensuing higher-than-normal black turnout in
the 1998 midterm elections helped Democrats at the polls, led to House
Speaker Newt Gingrich's demise, and may have saved Bill Clinton's job.
Could the e-mail hoax have played a role?

Other hoaxes are not so accidental. Last year, as the presidential 38
campaign began heating up, I received an e-mail from a fellow journalist alerting me to an anti–Al Gore Web site she thought contained
valuable information. It included a litany of silly statements attributed to Gore. Some of them were accurate, but several of them I recognized as being utterances of former Vice President Dan Quayle. Others
were statements never said by either Gore or Quayle.

On October 3, 1999, when liberal movie star Warren Beatty 39
spoke to Americans for Democratic Action about his political views,
he said that he wasn't the only one who worried that corporations
were a threat to democracy. Beatty said that Abraham Lincoln himself had warned that corporations are "more despotic than monarchy," adding that Lincoln also said "the money power preys upon
the nation in times of peace, and it conspires against it in times of
adversity." Beatty's populist version of Lincoln hardly squares with
his career as a corporate attorney — he represented Illinois Central
Railroad before he ran for public office — but that didn't faze modern
journalists. "That Lincoln stuff just amazed me," gushed *Newsweek*'s
Jonathan Alter on *Rivera Live*. Alter wrote that Beatty's "harshest attacks . . . were actually quotes from a speech by Abraham Lincoln."

Actually, they weren't. Lincoln's official biographer once called the 40
quote "a bold, unblushing forgery." And in a piece for History News
Service, an online site that often debunks faulty history, Lincoln scholar
Matthew Pinsker said this particular fake Lincoln citation has been
around since 1896. In his speech at the 1992 Republican National Convention, Ronald Reagan attributed phony conservative sentiments to
Honest Abe, including, "You cannot help the weak by punishing the
strong," and "You cannot help the poor by destroying the rich."

This example underscores a couple of important caveats about the 41
Web. First, bogus quotes were around a long time before the Internet.

Moreover, the Net itself is often a useful tool for those trying to correct canards.

A postscript: Three years ago, while discussing with reporters the pitfalls of the Internet, Hillary Rodham Clinton employed the line often attributed to Twain — and cited earlier in this piece — about a lie making its way halfway 'round the world before the truth could get its boots on. "Well, today," she added, "the lie can be twice around the world before the truth gets out of bed to find its boots." While fact-checking this article, I had reason to call Fred Shapiro at Yale. Perhaps because Mrs. Clinton never mentioned Twain — she attributed it to an "old saying" — my interest was piqued, and I asked Shapiro if he'd ever heard the aphorism. "I have just been intensively researching Twain quotes, and didn't come across this one," he replied. "I would assume that Twain did not say it."

Uh-oh. That sent me back into research mode. What I found is that the "Twain" quote has been around. According to a 1996 article by James Bennet of the *New York Times*, Mrs. Clinton (and Al Gore as well) used the line, with attribution to Twain. Other politicians have credited it to Twain as well. Clintonite Paul Begala, writing last year in the *Orlando Sentinel*, used it, giving Twain full credit. So did Republican stalwart Haley Barbour in a *Roll Call* op-ed. In a 1999 column in the *Chattanooga Times*, a writer named L. M. Boyd gave credit to the quote to "the sage Israel Zangwill," adding that famed CBS newsman Edward R. Murrow used it all the time.

On the Internet, the responses were even more varied. Several Web sites credited Twain while others attributed the quote to Will Rogers; Reagan-era Interior Secretary James Watt; Winston Churchill; another former British prime minister, James Callaghan; and, in one case, merely to "a French proverb."

Possibly all of these sources uttered it at one time or another. Callaghan seems to have done so on November 1, 1976, in an address to the House of Commons. But he attributed the line to the man who is probably its rightful author: a Baptist preacher from England named Charles Haddon Spurgeon, a contemporary of Twain who, according to *Benham's Book of Quotations*, wrote this line: "A lie travels 'round the world, while Truth is putting on her boots."

Amen.

RESPONDING TO THE TEXT

In paragraph 12, Cannon states, "One of the things that makes the Internet so appealing is that anyone can pull things off of it. The other side of the coin is that anyone can put anything on it." Do you agree? Why or why not?

ENGAGING THE WRITER'S SUBJECT

1. Cannon writes that one cause of journalists' errors is that they don't have much time to check their sources for accuracy. How do you respond? Do you accept that as a proper response?

2. What false understanding of the law in a cyberrumor led to a great deal of anxiety among African Americans? What seemingly unexpected effects were the result of the cyberrumor?

3. What are the causes of errors in the information found on the Internet, according to Cannon?

ANALYZING THE WRITER'S CRAFT

1. What is Cannon arguing for in this essay? (Glossary: *Argument*) What is his thesis? (Glossary: *Thesis*)

2. What evidence does Cannon cite to support the fact that misinformation on the Internet can be downright dangerous? (Glossary: *Evidence; Exemplification*)

3. Cannon begins with the story of Jeff Jacoby and the *Boston Globe*. Why is this a particularly good example for the beginning of his article? (Glossary: *Beginnings/Endings*)

4. Cannon ends with a postscript about the quotation falsely attributed to Mark Twain: "A lie can make it halfway around the world before the truth can get its boots on." Why is this an apt way of ending his essay? (Glossary: *Beginnings/Endings*)

UNDERSTANDING THE WRITER'S LANGUAGE

1. How appropriate is "The Real Computer Virus" as a title? (Glossary: *Title*) Is the comparison of misinformation to a computer virus appropriate? (Glossary: *Analogy*) Why or why not?

2. Refer to your desk dictionary to determine the meanings of the following words as Cannon uses them in this selection: *misinformation* (paragraph 1), *ubiquitous* (3), *missive* (10), *malady* (11), *gaffe* (17), *unequivocally* (20), *exponentially* (26), *impetus* (33), *despotic* (39), *populist* (39), *faze* (39), *contemporary* (45).

WRITING SUGGESTIONS

1. "According to the Nielsen/NetRatings released on February 15, 168 million Americans logged onto the Web in the first month of the new millennium" (paragraph 25). Why does Cannon cite this figure? (Glossary: *Evidence*) What does Cannon mean when he says "These problems are only going to get worse unless Net users — and journalists — get a whole lot more careful" (25). Write an essay in which you discuss possible effects of misinformation on an increasingly Web-savvy and Web-dependent public. How do incidents of incorrect reporting, such as

those Cannon discusses, affect public trust of the media? What skills will people need to better judge what they read both online and off? What measures could be implemented to ensure that information is accurate and reliable? What would the other effects of such measures be?

2. Cannon discusses how the Internet, electronic databases, and e-mail can be used to spread misinformation and disinformation. What do these two terms mean? (Glossary: *Definition*) What examples does Cannon cite as evidence of each? (Glossary: *Evidence; Exemplification*) Write an essay in which you explore the differences between misinformation and disinformation. (Glossary: *Comparison and Contrast*) In your opinion, which poses the greater threat? Why?

3. In your opinion, is the threat posed by Internet-spread disinformation dangerous enough to warrant special action? If so, why? How is this threat different from or similar to disinformation spread via television, radio, and print media? If possible, should we attempt to control Internet content? In your college library and on the Internet, research how governments have combated disinformation. Write an essay in which you explore the ethical issues such attempts would raise in a democracy and whether or not such methods should be implemented.

- To begin your research online, go to **bedfordstmartins.com /subjectsstrategies** and click on "Cause and Effect Analysis" or browse the thematic directory of annotated links.

The Lottery (*FICTION*)

Shirley Jackson

Shirley Jackson (1919–1965) was born in San Francisco, California. She received her B.A. in 1940 from Syracuse University. A novelist and writer of short stories, Jackson is considered a master of gothic horror. She was a contributor to many periodicals, including Good Housekeeping, Yale Review, *and the* New Yorker. *In 1961 she won the Edgar Allan Poe Award for the short story "Louisa, Please." Among Jackson's works are the novels* The Road through the Wall *(1948),* We Have Always Lived in a Castle *(1953), and* The Haunting of Hill House *(1959), which was adapted for the stage and several film versions; several collections of short stories; and the children's books* Life among the Savages *(1954) and* Nine Magic Wishes *(1963).*

"The Lottery," Jackson's most well-known work, was first published in the New Yorker *in 1948 and generated more mail than anything previously published by that magazine. "The Lottery" tells the story of a town that conducts a cruel, annual ritual made crueler for being repeated even though no one can remember why it is being done. According to one critic, "The Lottery" embodied Jackson's belief that "humankind is more evil than good."*

PREPARING TO READ

Think about the rituals and ceremonies in which you, your family, and friends participate. These might be religious or spiritual in nature, but they do not need to be confined to that area of your life. What is the reason for those events? Why do you participate? Do you take part simply because you have for as long as you can remember?

The morning of June 27th was clear and sunny, with the fresh warmth of a full-summer day; the flowers were blossoming profusely and the grass was richly green. The people of the village began to gather in the square, between the post office and the bank, around ten o'clock; in some towns there were so many people that the lottery took two days and had to be started on June 26th, but in this village, where there were only about three hundred people, the whole lottery took less than two hours, so it could begin at ten o'clock in the morning and still be through in time to allow the villagers to get home for noon dinner.

The children assembled first, of course. School was recently over for the summer, and the feeling of liberty sat uneasily on most of them; they tended to gather together quietly for a while before they broke into boisterous play, and their talk was still of the classroom and the teacher, of books and reprimands. Bobby Martin had already stuffed his pockets full of stones, and the other boys soon followed his example, selecting the smoothest and roundest stones; Bobby and Harry Jones and Dickie Delacroix — the villagers pronounced this name "Dellacroy" — eventually made a great pile of stones in one corner of the square and guarded it against the raids of the other boys. The girls stood aside, talking among themselves, looking over their shoulders at the boys, and the very small children rolled in the dust or clung to the hands of their older brothers or sisters.

Soon the men began to gather, surveying their own children, speaking of planting and rain, tractors and taxes. They stood together, away from the pile of stones in the corner, and their jokes were quiet and they smiled rather than laughed. The women, wearing faded house dresses and sweaters, came shortly after their menfolk. They greeted one another and exchanged bits of gossip as they went to join their husbands. Soon the women, standing by their husbands, began to call to their children, and the children came reluctantly, having to be called four or five times. Bobby Martin ducked under his mother's grasping hand and ran, laughing, back to the pile of stones. His father spoke up sharply, and Bobby came quickly and took his place between his father and his oldest brother. 3

The lottery was conducted — as were the square dances, the teenage club, the Halloween program — by Mr. Summers, who had time and energy to devote to civic activities. He was a round-faced, jovial man and he ran the coal business, and people were sorry for him, because he had no children and his wife was a scold. When he arrived in the square, carrying the black wooden box, there was a murmur of conversation among the villagers, and he waved and called, "Little late today, folks." The postmaster, Mr. Graves, followed him, carrying a three-legged stool, and the stool was put in the center of the square and Mr. Summers set the black box down on it. The villagers kept their distance, leaving a space between themselves and the stool, and when Mr. Summers said, "Some of you fellows want to give me a hand?" there was a hesitation before two men, Mr. Martin and his oldest son, Baxter, came forward to hold the box steady on the stool while Mr. Summers stirred up the papers inside it. 4

The original paraphernalia for the lottery had been lost long ago, and the black box now resting on the stool had been put into use even before Old Man Warner, the oldest man in town, was born. Mr. Summers spoke frequently to the villagers about making a new box, but no one liked to upset even as much tradition as was represented by the black box. There was a story that the present box had been made with some pieces of the box that had preceded it, the one that had been 5 constructed when the first people settled down to make a village here. Every year, after the lottery, Mr. Summers began talking again about a new box, but every year the subject was allowed to fade off without anything being done. The black box grew shabbier each year; by now it was no longer completely black but splintered badly along one side to show the original wood color, and in some places faded or stained.

Mr. Martin and his oldest son, Baxter, held the black box securely on the stool until Mr. Summers had stirred the papers thoroughly with his hand. Because so much of the ritual had been forgotten or discarded, Mr. Summers had been successful in having slips of paper substituted for the chips of wood that had been used for generations. Chips of wood, Mr. Summers had argued, had been all very well when the village was tiny, but now that the population was more than three hundred and likely to keep on growing, it was necessary to use something that would fit more easily into the black box. The night before the lottery, Mr. Summers and Mr. Graves made up the slips of paper and put them in the box, and it was then taken to the safe of Mr. Summers' coal company and locked up until Mr. Summers was ready to take it to the square next morning. The rest of the year, the box was put away, sometimes one place, sometimes another; it had spent one year in Mr. Graves's barn and another year underfoot in the post office, and sometimes it was set on a shelf in the Martin grocery and left there.

There was a great deal of fussing to be done before Mr. Summers declared the lottery open. There were the lists to make up — of heads of families, heads of households in each family, members of each household in each family. There was the proper swearing-in of Mr. Summers by the postmaster, as the official of the lottery; at one time, some people remembered, there had been a recital of some sort, performed by the official of the lottery, a perfunctory, tuneless chant that had been rattled off duly each year; some people believed that the official of the lottery used to stand just so when he said or sang it, others believed that he was supposed to walk among the people, but years and years ago this part of the ritual had been allowed to lapse. There had been, also, a ritual salute, which the official of the lottery had had to use in addressing each person who came up to draw from the box, but this also had changed with time, until now it was felt necessary only for the official to speak to each person approaching. Mr. Summers was very good at all this; in his clean white shirt and blue jeans, with one hand resting carelessly on the black box, he seemed very proper and important as he talked interminably to Mr. Graves and the Martins.

Just as Mr. Summers finally left off talking and turned to the assembled villagers, Mrs. Hutchinson came hurriedly along the path to the square, her sweater thrown over her shoulders, and slid into place in the back of the crowd. "Clean forgot what day it was," she said to Mrs. Delacroix, who stood next to her, and they both laughed softly.

"Thought my old man was out back stacking wood," Mrs. Hutchinson went on, "and then I looked out the window and the kids were gone, and then I remembered it was the twenty-seventh and came a-running." She dried her hands on her apron, and Mrs. Delacroix said, "You're in time, though. They're still talking away up there."

Mrs. Hutchinson craned her neck to see through the crowd and found her husband and children standing near the front. She tapped Mrs. Delacroix on the arm as a farewell and began to make her way through the crowd. The people separated good-humoredly to let her through; two or three people said, in voices just loud enough to be heard across the crowd, "Here comes your Missus, Hutchinson," and "Bill, she made it after all." Mrs. Hutchinson reached her husband, and Mr. Summers, who had been waiting, said cheerfully, "Thought we were going to have to get on without you, Tessie." Mrs. Hutchinson said, grinning, "Wouldn't have me leave m'dishes in the sink, now, would you, Joe?" and soft laughter ran through the crowd as the people stirred back into position after Mrs. Hutchinson's arrival. 9

"Well, now," Mr. Summers said soberly, "guess we better get started, get this over with, so's we can go back to work. Anybody ain't here?" 10

"Dunbar," several people said. "Dunbar, Dunbar." 11

Mr. Summers consulted his list. "Clyde Dunbar," he said. "That's right. He's broke his leg, hasn't he? Who's drawing for him?" 12

"Me, I guess," a woman said, and Mr. Summers turned to look at her. "Wife draws for her husband," Mr. Summers said. "Don't you have a grown boy to do it for you, Janey?" Although Mr. Summers and everyone else in the village knew the answer perfectly well, it was the business of the official of the lottery to ask such questions formally. Mr. Summers waited with an expression of polite interest while Mrs. Dunbar answered. 13

"Horace's not but sixteen yet," Mrs. Dunbar said regretfully. "Guess I gotta fill in for the old man this year." 14

"Right," Mr. Summers said. He made a note on the list he was holding. Then he asked, "Watson boy drawing this year?" 15

A tall boy in the crowd raised his hand. "Here," he said. "I'm drawing for m'mother and me." He blinked his eyes nervously and ducked his head as several voices in the crowd said things like "Good fellow, Jack," and "Glad to see your mother's got a man to do it." 16

"Well," Mr. Summers said, "guess that's everyone. Old Man Warner make it?" 17

"Here," a voice said, and Mr. Summers nodded. 18

A sudden hush fell on the crowd as Mr. Summers cleared his throat and looked at the list. "All ready?" he called. "Now, I'll read the names — heads of families first — and the men come up and take a paper out of the box. Keep the paper folded in your hand without looking at it until everyone has had a turn. Everything clear?" 19

The people had done it so many times that they only half listened [20] to the directions; most of them were quiet, wetting their lips, not looking around. Then Mr. Summers raised one hand high and said, "Adams." A man disengaged himself from the crowd and came forward. "Hi, Steve," Mr. Summers said, and Mr. Adams said, "Hi, Joe." They grinned at one another humorously and nervously. Then Mr. Adams reached into the black box and took out a folded paper. He held it firmly by one corner as he turned and went hastily back to his place in the crowd, where he stood a little apart from his family, not looking down at his hand.

"Allen," Mr. Summers said. "Anderson . . . Bentham." [21]

"Seems like there's no time at all between lotteries any more," [22] Mrs. Delacroix said to Mrs. Graves in the back row. "Seems like we got through with the last one only last week."

"Time sure goes fast," Mrs. Graves said. [23]

"Clark . . . Delacroix." [24]

"There goes my old man," Mrs. Delacroix said. She held her breath [25] while her husband went forward.

"Dunbar," Mr. Summers said, and Mrs. Dunbar went steadily to [26] the box while one of the women said, "Go on, Janey," and another said, "There she goes."

"We're next," Mrs. Graves said. She watched while Mr. Graves came [27] around from the side of the box, greeted Mr. Summers gravely, and selected a slip of paper from the box. By now, all through the crowd there were men holding the small folded papers in their large hands, turning them over and over nervously. Mrs. Dunbar and her two sons stood together, Mrs. Dunbar holding the slip of paper.

"Harburt . . . Hutchinson." [28]

"Get up there, Bill," Mrs. Hutchinson said, and the people near [29] her laughed.

"Jones." [30]

"They do say," Mr. Adams said to Old Man Warner, who stood [31] next to him, "that over in the north village they're talking of giving up the lottery."

Old Man Warner snorted. "Pack of crazy fools," he said. "Listen- [32] ing to the young folks, nothing's good enough for *them*. Next thing you know, they'll be wanting to go back to living in caves, nobody work any more, live *that* way for a while. Used to be a saying about 'Lottery in June, corn be heavy soon.' First thing you know, we'd all be eating stewed chickweed and acorns. There's *always* been a lottery," he added petulantly. "Bad enough to see young Joe Summers up there joking with everybody."

"Some places have already quit lotteries," Mrs. Adams said. [33]

"Nothing but trouble in *that*," Old Man Warner said stoutly. "Pack [34] of young fools."

"Martin." And Bobby Martin watched his father go forward. 35
"Overdyke . . . Percy."

"I wish they'd hurry," Mrs. Dunbar said to her older son. "I wish 36
they'd hurry."

"They're almost through," her son said. 37

"You get ready to run tell Dad," Mrs. Dunbar said. 38

Mr. Summers called his own name and then stepped forward pre- 39
cisely and selected a slip from the box. Then he called, "Warner."

"Seventy-seventh year I been in the lottery," Old Man Warner said 40
as he went through the crowd. "Seventy-seventh time."

"Watson." The tall boy came awkwardly through the crowd. Some- 41
one said, "Don't be nervous, Jack," and Mr. Summers said, "Take your
time, son."

"Zanini." 42

After that, there was a long pause, a breathless pause, until Mr. 43
Summers, holding his slip of paper in the air, said, "All right, fellows."
For a minute, no one moved, and then all the slips of paper were
opened. Suddenly, all the women began to speak at once, saying,
"Who is it?" "Who's got it?" "Is it the Dunbars?" "Is it the Watsons?"
Then the voices began to say, "It's Hutchinson. It's Bill," "Bill Hutchin-
son's got it."

"Go tell your father," Mrs. Dunbar said to her older son. 44

People began to look around to see the Hutchinsons. Bill Hutchin- 45
son was standing quiet, staring down at the paper in his hand. Suddenly, Tessie Hutchinson shouted to Mr. Summers, "You didn't give
him time enough to take any paper he wanted. I saw you. It wasn't fair."

"Be a good sport, Tessie," Mrs. Delacroix called, and Mrs. Graves 46
said, "All of us took the same chance."

"Shut up, Tessie," Bill Hutchinson said. 47

"Well, everyone," Mr. Summers said, "That was done pretty fast, 48
and now we've got to be hurrying a little more to get done in time."
He consulted his next list. "Bill," he said, "you draw for the Hutchinson family. You got any other households in the Hutchinsons?"

"There's Don and Eva," Mrs. Hutchinson yelled. "Make *them* take 49
their chance!"

"Daughters draw with their husbands' families, Tessie," Mr. Sum- 50
mers said gently. "You know that as well as anyone else."

"It wasn't *fair*," Tessie said. 51

"I guess not, Joe," Bill Hutchinson said regretfully. "My daughter 52
draws with her husband's family, that's only fair. And I've got no
other family except the kids."

"Then, as far as drawing for families is concerned, it's you," Mr. 53
Summers said in explanation, "and as far as drawing for households is
concerned, that's you, too. Right?"

"Right," Bill Hutchinson said.   54

"How many kids, Bill?" Mr. Summers asked formally.   55

"Three," Bill Hutchinson said. "There's Bill, Jr., and Nancy, and   56
little Dave. And Tessie and me."

"All right, then," Mr. Summers said. "Harry, you got their tickets   57
back?"

Mr. Graves nodded and held up the slips of paper. "Put them in   58
the box then," Mr. Summers directed. "Take Bill's and put it in."

"I think we ought to start over," Mrs. Hutchinson said, as quietly   59
as she could. "I tell you it wasn't *fair*. You didn't give him time enough
to choose. *Every*body saw that."

Mr. Graves had selected the five slips and put them in the box,   60
and he dropped all the papers but those onto the ground, where the
breeze caught them and lifted them off.

"Listen, everybody," Mrs. Hutchinson was saying to the people   61
around her.

"Ready, Bill?" Mr. Summers asked, and Bill Hutchinson, with one   62
quick glance around at his wife and children, nodded.

"Remember," Mr. Summers said, "take the slips and keep them   63
folded until each person has taken one. Harry, you help little Dave."
Mr. Graves took the hand of the little boy, who came willingly with him
up to the box. "Take a paper out of the box, Davy," Mr. Summers said.
Davy put his hand into the box and laughed. "Take just *one* paper," Mr.
Summers said. "Harry, you hold it for him." Mr. Graves took the child's
hand and removed the folded paper from the tight fist and held it while
little Dave stood next to him and looked up at him wonderingly.

"Nancy next," Mr. Summers said. Nancy was twelve, and her school   64
friends breathed heavily as she went forward, switching her skirt, and
took a slip daintily from the box. "Bill, Jr.," Mr. Summers said, and
Billy, his face red and his feet over-large, nearly knocked the box over
as he got a paper out. "Tessie," Mr. Summers said. She hesitated for a
minute, looking around defiantly, and then set her lips and went up
to the box. She snatched a paper out and held it behind her.

"Bill," Mr. Summers said, and Bill Hutchinson reached into the   65
box and felt around, bringing his hand out at last with the slip of
paper in it.

The crowd was quiet. A girl whispered, "I hope it's not Nancy,"   66
and the sound of the whisper reached the edges of the crowd.

"It's not the way it used to be," Old Man Warner said clearly.   67
"People ain't the way they used to be."

"All right," Mr. Summers said. "Open the papers. Harry, you open   68
little Dave's."

Mr. Graves opened the slip of paper and there was a general sigh   69
through the crowd as he held it up and everyone could see that it was
blank. Nancy and Bill, Jr., opened theirs at the same time, and both

beamed and laughed, turning around to the crowd and holding their slips of paper above their heads.

"Tessie," Mr. Summers said. There was a pause, and then Mr. Sum- 70 mers looked at Bill Hutchinson, and Bill unfolded his paper and showed it. It was blank.

"It's Tessie," Mr. Summers said, and his voice was hushed. "Show 71 us her paper, Bill."

Bill Hutchinson went over to his wife and forced the slip of paper 72 out of her hand. It had a black spot on it, the black spot Mr. Summers had made the night before with the heavy pencil in the coal-company office. Bill Hutchinson held it up, and there was a stir in the crowd.

"All right, folks," Mr. Summers said. "Let's finish quickly." 73

Although the villagers had forgotten the ritual and lost the origi- 74 nal black box, they still remembered to use stones. The pile of stones the boys had made earlier was ready; there were stones on the ground with the blowing scraps of paper that had come out of the box. Mrs. Delacroix selected a stone so large she had to pick it up with both hands and turned to Mrs. Dunbar. "Come on," she said. "Hurry up."

Mrs. Dunbar had small stones in both hands, and she said, gasp- 75 ing for breath, "I can't run at all. You'll have to go ahead and I'll catch up with you."

The children had stones already, and someone gave Davy Hutchin- 76 son a few pebbles.

Tessie Hutchinson was in the center of a cleared space by now, 77 and she held her hands out desperately as the villagers moved in on her. "It isn't fair," she said. A stone hit her on the side of the head.

Old Man Warner was saying, "Come on, come on, everyone." Steve 78 Adams was in the front of the crowd of villagers, with Mrs. Graves beside him.

"It isn't fair, it isn't right," Mrs. Hutchinson screamed, and then 79 they were upon her.

RESPONDING TO THE TEXT

Having read "The Lottery," do you now have a different view of the rituals or ceremonies in which you, your family, and friends have engaged? In your opinion, does one need to think about the rational reasons behind these events, or should their meanings be found in their enactment? Is there any danger in not thinking about one's ritualistic behavior? Explain.

ENGAGING THE WRITER'S SUBJECT

1. At what point do you begin to suspect that something terrible is going to happen? When do you figure out what it is?

2. Describe the ritual in your own words. What is the irony of this ritual? (Glossary: *Irony*) What other ironies are there in this story?

3. How are men treated differently than women in this story? Why?

4. Some critics have described what they see as the town's various classes of people. What class differences do you see and what might be Jackson's motive in drawing such distinctions?

5. The townspeople continue to live in their town knowing that yearly they will either kill another resident or be killed themselves. Why do they stay? What point about society is Jackson making?

ANALYZING THE WRITER'S CRAFT

1. What is a *scapegoat*? Is the choice of Tessie as a scapegoat random? Does she do anything or represent any views that predispose her to be stoned? Explain.

2. What is Jackson's purpose in this story? (Glossary: *Purpose*) What kinds of details does she use to create a sense of normality? To create a sense of horror? Cite examples. (Glossary: *Examples*)

3. What details does Jackson provide that make the lottery at least in part an agrarian and seasonal ritual?

4. What different attitudes toward the ritual are expressed by Old Man Warner, Tessie, Mr. Summers, and Nancy's friend? Do these attitudes remain fixed or do they change? Explain. Who do you think speaks for most of the town?

5. What is Jackson's view of humankind in your opinion? Benign? Given to occasional bouts of depravity? Deeply depraved? Cite evidence to support your assessment.

6. What effect has time had on the villagers' opinions about and the execution of the lottery? How have other villages dealt with the ritual?

UNDERSTANDING THE WRITER'S LANGUAGE

1. What significance do you see in the names of the characters in this story? What do you think their names represent or symbolize? What is the literal meaning of Delacroix? What does the name Zanini suggest?

2. What tone does Jackson establish in this story? (Glossary: *Tone*) What about her diction helps her establish that tone? (Glossary: *Diction*)

3. What is Old Man Warner's attitude toward some young people? (Glossary: *Attitude*) How is that attitude revealed?

4. Refer to your desk dictionary to determine the meanings of the following words as Jackson uses them in this selection: *paraphernalia* (paragraph 5), *perfunctory* (7), *interminably* (7), *chickweed* (32).

WRITING SUGGESTIONS

1. Write an essay in which you explain a ritual you maintain with family or friends. Discuss the reasons behind the ritual and what effects it has on you and the other participants. Perhaps it's a yearly family gathering, a polar bear club's plunge in the winter, a summer surfing reunion, a hiking date with high school chums, Thanksgiving dinner, or a regular family vacation spot.

2. Write a process analysis about a ritual in which you and your family or friends participate. It could be a religious or civic holiday observance, a yearly celebration such as a birthday or anniversary, a regular "television-watching night," or marathon end-of-the-semester study sessions. Are special foods, decorations, activities, or supplies involved? If so, what are they? How are they prepared or conducted? What paraphernalia is required for the ritual? How is it used?

3. In your college library and on the Internet, research "scapegoat rituals" such as the one in Jackson's story. What was the intention of these rituals? In what cultures were they practiced? Have any of these cultures survived into the present? A good starting point is James Fraser's *The Golden Bough*, a classic cross-cultural study of rites and rituals. Write an essay on your findings and be sure to include references to "The Lottery."

- To begin your research online, go to **bedfordstmartins.com /subjectsstrategies** and click on "Cause and Effect Analysis" or browse the thematic directory of annotated links.

WRITING SUGGESTIONS FOR CAUSE AND EFFECT ANALYSIS

1. Write an essay in which you analyze the most significant reasons why you went to college. You may wish to discuss your family background, your high school experience, people and events that influenced your decision, and your goals in college as well as in later life.

2. It is interesting to think of ourselves in terms of the influences that have caused us to be who we are. Write an essay in which you discuss two or three of what you consider the most important influences on your life. Following are some areas you may wish to consider in planning and writing your paper.

   a. a parent
   b. a book or movie
   c. a member of the clergy
   d. a teacher
   e. a friend
   f. a hero
   g. a youth organization
   h. a coach
   i. your neighborhood
   j. your ethnic background

3. Decisions often involve cause and effect relationships; that is, a person usually weighs the possible results of an action before deciding to act. Write an essay in which you consider the possible effects that would result from one decision or another in one of the following controversies.

   a. taxing cars on the basis of fuel consumption
   b. reinstituting the military draft
   c. legalizing marijuana
   d. mandatory licensing of handguns
   e. raising the mandatory fuel efficiency rating of cars
   f. cloning humans
   g. abolishing grades for college courses
   h. raising the minimum wage
   i. mandatory community service (one year) for all eighteen-year-olds
   j. banning the use of pesticides on produce
   k. requiring an ethics course in college

4. Write an essay about a recent achievement of yours or about an important achievement in your community. Explain the causes of this success. Look at all of the underlying elements involved in the accomplishment, and explain how you selected the one main cause or the causal chain that led to the achievement. To do this, you will probably want to use the rhetorical strategy of comparison and contrast. You might also use exemplification and process analysis to explain the connection between your cause and its effect.

CHAPTER 11

Argumentation

WHAT IS ARGUMENT?

The word *argument* probably brings to mind verbal disagreements we have all witnessed, if not participated in directly. Occasionally, such disputes are satisfying; you can take pleasure in knowing that you have converted someone to your point of view. More often, though, arguments like these are inconclusive and result only in anger over your opponent's stubbornness or in the frustration of realizing that you have failed to make your position understood. Such dissatisfaction is inevitable because verbal arguments usually arise spontaneously and cannot be thoughtfully planned or researched. Indeed, often it is not until later, in retrospect, that the convincing piece of evidence or the forcefully phrased assertion comes to mind.

Written arguments have much in common with verbal ones: They attempt to convince readers to agree with a particular point of view, to make a particular decision, or to pursue a particular course of action; they involve the presentation of well-chosen evidence and the artful control of language. However, writers of argument have no one around to dispute their words directly, so they must imagine their probable audience to predict the sorts of objections that may be raised. This requires that written arguments be carefully planned. The writer must settle in advance on a specific thesis or proposition rather than grope toward one, as in a verbal argument. There is a greater need for organization, for choosing the most effective types of evidence from all that is available, for determining the strategies of rhetoric, language, and style that will best suit the argument's subject, purpose, thesis, and effect on the intended audience.

Most strong arguments are constructed around an effective thesis statement. Take, for example, the following opening to the essay "The Case for Short Words" by Richard Lederer (p. 513).

Thesis statement

When you speak and write, there is no law that says you have to use big words. Short words are as good as long ones, and short, old words — like *sun* and *grass* and *home* — are best of all. A lot of small words, more than you might think, can meet your needs with a strength, grace, and charm that large words do not have.

Several examples support the thesis.

Big words can make the way dark for those who read what you write and hear what you say. Small words cast their clear light on big things — night and day, love and hate, war and peace, and life and death. Big words at times seem strange to the eye and the ear and the mind and the heart. Small words are the ones we seem to have known from the time we were born, like the hearth fire that warms the home.

Note how Lederer uses examples to support his thesis statement. When you read the whole essay, you will want to check whether Lederer's argument is well reasoned and carefully organized. You will also want to check that his argument is logical and persuasive. A strong argument will have all of these qualities.

Most people who specialize in the study of argument identify two essential categories: persuasion and logic.

Persuasive argument relies primarily on appeals to emotion, to the subconscious, even to bias and prejudice. These appeals involve diction, slanting, figurative language, analogy, rhythmic patterns of speech, and a tone that encourages a positive, active response. Examples of persuasive argument are found in the exaggerated claims of advertisers and in the speech making of politicians and social activists.

Logical argument, on the other hand, appeals primarily to the mind — to the audience's intellectual faculties, understanding, and knowledge. Such appeals depend on the reasoned movement from assertion to evidence to conclusion and on an almost mathematical system of proof and counterproof. Logical argument, unlike persuasion, does not normally impel its audience to action. Logical argument is commonly found in scientific or philosophical articles, in legal decisions, and in technical proposals.

Most arguments, however, are neither purely persuasive nor purely logical in nature. A well-written newspaper editorial that supports a controversial piece of legislation or that proposes a solution to a local problem, for example, will rest on a logical arrangement of assertions and evidence but will employ striking diction and other persuasive patterns of language to make it more effective. Thus the kinds of appeals a writer emphasizes depend on the nature of the topic, the thesis or proposition of the argument, the various kinds of support (e.g., evidence, opinions, examples, facts, statistics) offered, and a thoughtful consideration of the audience. Knowing the differences between persuasive and logical arguments is, then, essential in learning both to read and to write arguments.

Some additional types of arguments that are helpful in expanding your understanding of this strategy are described below.

Informational, or Exploratory, Argument

It is often useful to provide a comprehensive review of the various facets of an issue. This is done to inform an audience, especially one that may not understand why the issue is controversial in the first place, and to help that audience take a position. An example of this kind of argument is Jane E. Brody's "Gene-Altered Foods: A Case against Panic" (p. 574). The writer of this type of argument does not take a position but aims, instead, to render the positions taken by the various sides in accurate and clear language. Your instructors may occasionally call for this kind of argumentative writing as a way of teaching you to explore the complexity of a particular issue.

Focused Argument

This kind of argument has only one objective: to change the audience's mind about a controversial issue. Jim Scharplaz, in "Weeding Out the Skilled Farmer" (p. 579), focuses on his concern that "the main purpose of these [new] technologies [for farming] is the complete industrialization of agriculture." Being comprehensive or taking the broad view is not the objective here. If opposing viewpoints are considered, it is usually to show their inadequacies and thereby to strengthen the writer's own position. This is the kind that we usually think of as the traditional argument.

Action-Oriented Argument

This type of argument is highly persuasive and attempts to accomplish a specific task. This is the loud car salesman on your television, the over-the-top subscription solicitation in your mail, the vote-for-me-because-I-am-the-only-candidate-who-can-lower-your-taxes type of argument. The language is emotionally charged, and buzzwords designed to arouse the emotions of the audience may even be used, along with such propaganda devices as glittering generalities (broad, sweeping statements) and bandwagonism ("Everyone else is voting for me — don't be left out").

Quiet, or Subtle, Argument

Some arguments do not immediately appear to the audience to be arguments at all. They set out to be informative and objective, but when closely examined, they reveal that the author has consciously, or perhaps subconsciously, shaped and slanted the evidence in such a manner as to favor a particular position. Such shaping may be the result of choices in diction that bend the audience to the writer's perspective, or they may be the result of decisions not to include certain types of evidence while admitting others. Such arguments can, of course, be quite convincing, as there are always those who distrust obvious efforts to convince them, preferring to make their own decisions on the issues. Kennedy P. Maize's cause and effect essay, "The Great Kern County Mouse War" (p. 456), contains a powerful argument against upsetting the balance of nature.

Reconciliation Argument

Increasingly popular today is a form of argument in which the writer attempts to explore all facets of an issue to find common ground or areas of agreement. Of course, one way of viewing that common ground is to see it as a new argumentative thrust, a new assertion, about which there may yet be more debate. The object, nevertheless, is to lessen stridency and the hardening of positions and to mediate opposing views into a rational and, where appropriate, even practical outcome. Martin Luther King Jr.'s speech "I Have a Dream" (p. 525) is perhaps the greatest example of a reconciliation argument of the past century.

WHY DO WRITERS USE ARGUMENT?

True arguments are limited to assertions about which there is a legitimate and recognized difference of opinion. It is unlikely that anyone will ever need to convince a reader that falling in love is a rare and intense experience, that crime rates should be reduced, or that computers are changing the world. Not everyone would agree, however, that women experience love more intensely than men, that the death penalty reduces the incidence of crime, or that computers are changing the world for the worse; these assertions are arguable and admit differing perspectives. Similarly, a leading heart specialist might argue in a popular magazine that too many doctors are advising patients to have pacemakers implanted when they are not necessary; the editorial writer for a small-town newspaper could urge that a local agency supplying food to poor families be given a larger percentage of the town's budget; and in a lengthy and complex book, a foreign policy specialist might attempt to prove that the current administration exhibits no consistent policy in its relationship with other countries and that the State Department is in need of overhauling. No matter what forum it uses and no matter what its structure, an argument has as its chief purpose the detailed setting forth of a particular point of view and the rebuttal of any opposing views.

Classical thinkers believed that there are three key components in all rhetorical situations or attempts to communicate: the *speaker* (and for us the *writer*) who comments about a *subject* to an *audience*. For purposes of discussion we can isolate each of these three entities, but in actual rhetorical situations they are inseparable, each inextricably tied to and influencing the other two. The ancients also recognized the importance of qualities attached to each of these components that are especially significant in the case of argumentation: *ethos*, which is related to the speaker; *logos*, which is related to the subject; and *pathos*, which is related to the audience. Let's look a little closer at each of these.

Ethos (Greek for "character") has to do with the authority, the credibility, and, to a certain extent, the morals of the speaker or writer. Aristotle and Cicero, classical rhetoricians, believed that it was important for the speaker to be credible and to argue for a worthwhile cause. Putting one's argumentative skills in the service of a questionable cause was simply not acceptable. But how did one establish credibility? Sometimes it was gained through achievements outside the rhetorical arena. That is, the speaker had experience with an issue, had argued the subject before, and had been judged to be sincere and honest.

In the case of your own writing, establishing such credentials is not always possible, so you will need to be more concerned than usual with presenting your argument reasonably, sincerely, and in language untainted by excessive emotionalism. Finally, it is well worth remembering that you should always show respect for your audience in your writing.

Logos (Greek for "word"), related as it is to the subject, is the effective presentation of the argument itself. Is the thesis or claim a worthwhile one? Is it logical, consistent, and well buttressed by supporting evidence? Is the evidence itself factual, reliable, and convincing? Finally, is the argument so thoughtfully organized and so clearly presented that it has an impact on the audience and could change opinions? Indeed, this aspect of argumentation is the most difficult to accomplish but is, at the same time, the most rewarding.

Pathos (Greek for "emotion") has the most to do with the audience. The essential question is, How does the speaker or writer present an argument or a persuasive essay to maximize its appeal for a given audience? One way, of course, is through the artful and strategic use of well-crafted language. Certain buzzwords, slanted diction, or loaded language may become either rallying cries or causes of resentment in an argument.

It is worth remembering at this point that you can never be certain who your audience is; readers range along a spectrum from extremely friendly and sympathetic to extremely hostile and resistant, with a myriad of possibilities in between. The friendly audience will welcome new information and support the writer's position; the hostile audience will look for just the opposite: flaws in logic and examples of dishonest manipulation. With many arguments, there is the potential for a considerable audience of interested parties who are uncommitted. If the targeted audience is judged to be friendly, then the writer need not be as concerned with *logos* and can be less cautious and more freewheeling. If the audience is thought to be hostile, the *logos* must be the writer's immediate concern, and the language should be straightforward and objective. The greatest caution, subtlety, and critical thinking must be applied to the attempt to win over an uncommitted audience.

In general, writers of argument are interested in explaining aspects of a subject as well as in advocating a particular view. Consequently, they frequently use the other rhetorical strategies. In your efforts to argue convincingly, you may find it necessary to define, to compare and contrast, to analyze causes and effects, to classify, to describe, and to narrate. (For more information on the use of other strategies in argumentation, see the Use Other Rhetorical Strategies heading on page 501.) Nevertheless, it is the writer's attempt to convince, not explain, that is of primary importance in an argumentative essay. In this respect, it is helpful to know that there are two basic patterns of thinking and of presenting our thoughts that are followed in argumentation: *induction* and *deduction*.

Inductive reasoning moves from a set of specific examples to a general statement or principle. As long as the evidence is accurate, pertinent, complete, and sufficient to represent the assertion, the conclusion of an inductive argument can be regarded as valid; if, however, you can spot inaccuracies in the evidence or can point to contrary evidence, you have good reason to doubt the assertion as it stands. Inductive reasoning is the most common of argumentative structures.

Deductive reasoning, more formal and complex than inductive reasoning, moves from an overall premise, rule, or generalization to a more specific conclusion. Deductive logic follows the pattern of the *syllogism*, a simple three-part argument consisting of a major premise, a minor premise, and a conclusion. For example, notice how the following syllogism works.

a. All humans are mortal. *(Major premise)*
b. Catalina is a human. *(Minor premise)*
c. Catalina is mortal. *(Conclusion)*

The conclusion here is true because both premises are true and the logic of the syllogism is valid.

Obviously, a syllogism will fail to work if either of the premises is untrue.

a. All living creatures are mammals. *(Major premise)*
b. A lobster is a living creature. *(Minor premise)*
c. A lobster is a mammal. *(Conclusion)*

The problem is immediately apparent. The major premise is obviously false: There are many living creatures that are not mammals, and a lobster happens to be one of them. Consequently, the conclusion is invalid.

Syllogisms, however, can fail in other ways, even if both premises are objectively true. Such failures occur most often when the arguer jumps to a conclusion without taking obvious exceptions into account.

a. All college students read books. *(Major premise)*
b. Larry reads books. *(Minor premise)*
c. Larry is a college student. *(Conclusion)*

Both the premises in this syllogism are true, but the syllogism is still invalid because it does not take into account that other people besides college students read books. The problem is in the way the major premise has been interpreted: If the minor premise were instead "Larry is a college student," then the valid conclusion "Larry reads books" would logically follow.

It is fairly easy to see the problems in a deductive argument when its premises and conclusion are rendered in the form of a syllogism. It is often more difficult to see errors in logic when the argument is presented discursively, or within the context of a long essay. If you can reduce the argument to its syllogistic form, however, you will have much less difficulty testing its validity. Similarly, if you can isolate and examine out of context the evidence provided to support an inductive assertion, you can more readily evaluate the written inductive argument.

Consider the following excerpt from "The Draft: Why the Country Needs It," an article by James Fallows that first appeared in the *Atlantic* magazine in 1980.

> The Vietnam draft was unfair racially, economically, educationally. By every one of those measures, the volunteer Army is less representative still. Libertarians argue that military service should be a matter of choice, but the plain fact is that service in the volunteer force is too frequently dictated by economics. Army enlisted ranks E1 through E4, the privates and corporals, the cannon fodder, the ones who will fight and die, are 36 percent black now. By the Army's own projections, they will be 42 percent black in three years. When other "minorities" are taken into account, we will have, for the first time, an army whose fighting members are mainly "non-majority," or more bluntly, a black and brown army defending a mainly white nation. The military has been an avenue of opportunity of many young blacks. They may well be first-class fighting men. They do not represent the nation.
>
> Such a selective sharing of the burden has destructive spiritual effects in a nation based on the democratic creed. But its practical implications can be quite as grave. The effect of a fair, representative draft is to hold the public hostage to the consequences of its decisions, much as the children's presence in the public schools focuses parents' attention on the quality of the schools. If the citizens are willing to countenance a decision that means that someone's child may die, they may contemplate more deeply if there is the possibility that the child will be theirs. Indeed, I would like to extend this principle even further. Young men of nineteen are rightly suspicious of the congressmen and columnists who urge them to the fore. I wish there were a practical way to resurrect provisions of the amended Selective Service Act of 1940, which raised the draft age to forty-four. Such a gesture might symbolize the desire to offset the historic injustice of the Vietnam draft, as well as suggest the possibility that, when a bellicose columnist recommends dispatching the American forces to Pakistan, he might also realize that he could end up as a gunner in a tank.

Here Fallows presents an inductive argument against the volunteer army and in favor of reinstating a draft. His argument can be summarized as follows.

Assertion: The volunteer army is racially and economically unfair.
Evidence: He points to the disproportionate percentage of blacks in the army, as well as to projections indicating that, within three

years of the article's publication, more than half of the army's fighting members will be nonwhite.

Conclusion: "Such a selective sharing of the burden has destructive spiritual effects in a nation based on the democratic creed." Not until there is a fair, representative draft will the powerful majority be held accountable for any decision to go to war.

Fallows's inductive scheme here is, in fact, very effective. The evidence is convincing, and the conclusion is strong. But his argument also depends on a more complicated deductive syllogism.

a. The democratic ideal requires equal representation in the responsibilities of citizenship. *(Major premise)*
b. Military service is a responsibility of citizenship. *(Minor premise)*
c. The democratic ideal requires equal representation in military service. *(Conclusion)*

To attack Fallows's argument, it would be necessary to deny one of his premises.

Fallows also employs a number of other persuasive techniques, including an analogy: "The effect of a fair, representative draft is to hold the public hostage to the consequences of its decisions, much as the children's presence in the public schools focuses parents' attention on the quality of the schools." The use of such an analogy proves nothing, but it can force readers to reconsider their viewpoint and can make them more open-minded. The same is true of Fallows's almost entirely unserious suggestion about raising the draft age to forty-four. Like most writers, Fallows uses persuasive arguments to complement his more important logical ones.

AN ANNOTATED STUDENT ESSAY
USING ARGUMENT

Mark Jackson wrote the following essay while a student at the University of Cincinnati. Jackson's essay explores a number of arguments made in favor of a liberal arts education. In the course of the essay, Jackson rejects some of these arguments, such as the idea that a liberal arts education makes students well-rounded. He does, however, support the argument that a liberal arts education fosters critical thinking skills, and he comes to the conclusion that the ideal education would balance practical or vocational training and a grounding in the liberal arts.

The Liberal Arts:

A Practical View

Mark Jackson

Writer introduces problem: liberal arts inadequately explained.

Many students question the reasoning behind a liberal arts education. But even though they may have been forced to swallow liberal arts propaganda since junior high, students seldom receive a good explanation for why they should strive to be "well-rounded." They are told that they should value the accumulation of knowledge for its own sake, yet this argument does not convince those, like myself, who believe that knowledge must have some practical value or material benefit to be worth seeking.

First argument for liberal arts education

In "What Is an Idea?" Wayne Booth and Marshall Gregory argue convincingly that "a liberal education is an education in ideas — not merely memorizing them, but learning to move among them, balancing one against the other, negotiating relationships, accommodating new arguments, and returning for a closer look" (17). These writers propose that a liberal arts education is valuable to students because it helps to develop their analytical-thinking skills and writing skills. This is, perhaps, one of the best arguments for taking a broad range of classes in many different subjects.

Another, less convincing argument

Other, more radical arguments in favor of the liberal arts are less appealing. Lewis Thomas, a prominent scientist and physician, believes that classical Greek should form the backbone of a college student's education. This suggestion seems extreme. It is more reasonable to concentrate on the English language, since many students do not have a firm grasp of basic reading and writing skills. Freshman English and other English courses serve as a better

1

2

3

foundation for higher education than classical Greek could.

The opposition to a liberal arts curriculum grows out of the values that college-bound students learn from their parents and peers: They place an immeasurable value on success and disregard anything that is not pertinent to material achievements. Students often have trouble seeing what practical value studying a particular discipline can have for them. Teenagers who are headed for the world of nine-to-five employment tend to ignore certain studies in their haste to succeed.

Writer links personal experience to his attitude toward liberal arts.

My parents started discussing the possibility of college with me when I was in the sixth grade. They didn't think that it was important for me to go to college to become a more fulfilled human being. My mom and dad wanted me to go to college so that I might not have to live from paycheck to paycheck as they do. Their reason for wanting me to go to college has become my primary motivation for pursuing a college degree.

Personal examples used to illustrate inadequacy of some pro–liberal arts arguments.

I remember getting into an argument with my high school counselor because I didn't want to take a third year of Spanish. I was an A student in Spanish II, but I hated every minute of the class. My counselor noticed that I didn't sign up for Spanish III, so he called me into his office to hassle me. I told him that I took two years of a foreign language so that I would be accepted to college, but that I did not want to take a third year. Mr. Gallivan told me that I needed a third year of a foreign language to be a "well-rounded" student. My immediate response was "So what?!" I hated foreign languages, and no counselor was going to make me take something that I didn't want or need. I felt Spanish was a waste of time.

I frequently asked my high school coun-   7
selor why I needed to take subjects like
foreign languages and art. He never really
gave me an answer (except for the lame idea
about being "well-rounded"). Instead, Mr.
Gallivan always directed my attention to a
sign on the wall of his office which read,
"THERE'S NO REASON FOR IT. IT'S JUST OUR
POLICY!" I never found that a satisfactory
explanation.

Writer cites
authority to
explain value
of humanities
for career-minded
people.

Norman Cousins, however, does offer a   8
more reasonable explanation for the necessity of a liberal education. In his essay
"How to Make People Smaller Than They Are,"
Cousins points out how valuable the humanities are for career-minded people. He says,
"The irony of the emphasis being placed on
careers is that nothing is more valuable for
anyone who has had a professional or vocational education than to be able to deal
with abstractions or complexities, or to
feel comfortable with subtleties of thought
or language, or to think sequentially" (15).
Cousins reminds us that technical or vocational knowledge alone will not make one
successful in a chosen profession: Unique
problems and situations may arise daily in
the context of one's job, so an employee
must be able to think creatively and deal
with events that no textbook ever discussed.
The workers who get the promotions and advance to high positions are the ones who can
"think on their feet" when they are faced
with a complex problem.

Writer points to
communication
skills learned
through liberal
arts.

Cousins also suggests that the liberal   9
arts teach students communication skills
that are critical for success. A shy, intro-
verted person who was a straight A student in
college would not make a very good public
relations consultant, no matter how keen his
or her intellectual abilities. Employees who

cannot adequately articulate their ideas to a client or an employer will soon find themselves unemployed, even if they have brilliant ideas. Social integration into a particular work environment would be difficult without good communication skills and a wide range of interests and general knowledge. The broader a person's interests, the more compatible he or she will be with other workers.

Thesis   Though it is obvious that liberal arts   10
courses do have considerable practical value, a college education would not be complete without some job training. The liberal arts should be given equal billing in the college curriculum, but by no means should they become the focal point of higher education. If specialization is outlawed in our institutions of higher learning, then college students might lose their competitive edge. Maxim Gorky has written that "any kind of knowledge is useful" (22), and, of course, most knowledge is useful; but it would be insane to structure the college curriculum around an overview of all disciplines instead of allowing a student to master one subject or profession. Universities must seek to maintain an equilibrium between liberal and specialized education. A liberal arts degree without specialization or intended future specialization (such as a master's degree in a specific field) is useless unless one wants to be a professional game show contestant.

Plan of action for   Students who want to make the most of   11
college students   their college years should pursue a major course of study while choosing electives or a few minor courses of study from the liberal arts. In this way, scholars can become experts in a profession and still have a broad enough background to ensure

versatility, both within and outside the field. In a university's quest to produce "well-rounded" students, specialization must not come to be viewed as an evil practice.

12

Writer states that practical aspects of the liberal arts should be emphasized.

If educators really want to increase the number of liberal arts courses that each student takes, they must first increase the popularity of such studies. It is futile to try to get students to learn something just for the sake of knowing it. They must be given examples, such as those already mentioned, of how a liberal education will further their own interests. Instead of telling students that they need to be "well-rounded" and feeding them meaningless propaganda, counselors and professors should point out the practical value and applications of a broad education in the liberal arts. It is difficult to persuade some college students that becoming a better person is an important goal of higher education. Many students want a college education so that they can make more money and have more power. This is the perceived value of a higher education in their world.

Works Cited

Booth, Wayne, and Marshall Gregory. "What Is an Idea?" The Harper and Row Reader. 2nd ed. New York: Harper, 1988.

Cousins, Norman. "How to Make People Smaller Than They Are." The Saturday Review. Dec. 1978: 15.

Gorky, Maxim. "How I Studied." On Literature. Trans. Julius Katzer. Seattle: U of Washington P, 1973. 9–22.

Thomas, Lewis. "Debating the Unknowable." Atlantic Monthly. July 1981: 49–52.

Analyzing Mark Jackson's Essay of Argumentation: Questions for Discussion

1. Why did Jackson refuse to take Spanish III? How does his personal experience with Spanish and with his guidance counselor relate to his argument?
2. What is Jackson's thesis? Where and how does he present it?
3. Jackson employs several arguments in favor of liberal arts education. How does he classify them? What does he accomplish by including a variety of rationales regarding the validity of a "well-rounded" education?

SUGGESTIONS FOR WRITING AN ARGUMENTATION ESSAY

Writing an argument can be very rewarding. By its nature, an argument must be carefully reasoned and thoughtfully structured to have maximum effect. In other words, the *logos* of the argument must be carefully tended. Allow yourself, therefore, enough time to think about your thesis, to gather the evidence you need, and to draft, revise, edit, and proofread your essay. Sloppy thinking, confused expression, and poor organization will be immediately evident to your reader and will make for weaker arguments.

For example, you might be given an assignment in your history class to write a paper explaining what you think was the main cause of the Civil War. How would you approach this topic? First, it would help to assemble a number of possible interpretations of the causes of the Civil War and to examine them closely. Once you have determined what you consider to be the main cause, you will need to develop points that support your position. Then you will need to explain why you did not choose other possibilities, and you will have to assemble reasons that refute them. For instance, you might write an opening similar to this example.

> The Fugitive Slave Act Forced the
> North to Go to War
> While the start of the Civil War can be attributed
> to many factors — states' rights, slavery, a clash between
> antithetical economic systems, and westward expansion — the
> final straw for the North was the Fugitive Slave Act. This
> act, more than any other single element of disagreement

between the North and the South, forced the North into a
position where the only option was to fight.

Certainly, slavery and the clash over open lands in
the West contributed to the growing tensions between the
two sides, as did the economically incompatible systems
of production — plantation and manufacture — but the
Fugitive Slave Act required the North either to actively
support slavery or to run the risk of becoming a criminal
in defiance of it. The North chose not to support the
Fugitive Slave Act and was openly angered by the idea
that it should be required to do so by law. This anger
and open defiance led directly to the Civil War.

In these opening paragraphs, the author states the main argument
for the cause of the Civil War and sets up, in addition, the possible alternatives to this view. The points outlined in the introduction would
lead, one by one, to a logical argument asserting that the Fugitive
Slave Act was responsible for the onset of the Civil War and refuting
the other interpretations.

This introduction is mainly a *logical* argument. As was mentioned
before, writers often use *persuasive*, or *emotional*, arguments along with
logical ones. Persuasive arguments focus on issues that appeal to people's subconscious or emotional nature, along with their logical powers and intellectual understanding. Such arguments rely on powerful
and charged language, and they appeal to the emotions. Persuasive arguments can be especially effective but should not be used without a
strong logical backing. Indeed, this is the only way to use emotional
persuasion ethically. Emotional persuasion, when not in support of a
logical point, can be dangerous in that it can make an illogical point
sound appealing to a listener or reader.

Determine Your Thesis or Proposition

Begin by determining a topic that interests you and about which there
is some significant difference of opinion or about which you have a
number of questions. Find out what's in the news, what people are
talking about, what authors and instructors are emphasizing as important intellectual arguments. As you pursue your research, consider what
assertion you can make about the topic you chose. The more specific
this thesis or proposition, the more directed your research can become and the more focused your ultimate argument will be. While
researching your topic, however, be aware that the information may
point you in new directions. Don't hesitate at any point to modify

or even reject an initial or preliminary thesis as continued research warrants.

A thesis can be placed anywhere in an argument, but it is probably best while learning to write arguments to place the statement of your controlling idea somewhere near the beginning of your composition. Explain the importance of the thesis, and make clear to your reader that you share a common concern or interest in this issue. You may wish to state your central assertion directly in your first or second paragraph so that there is no possibility for your reader to be confused about your position. You may also wish to lead off with a particularly striking piece of evidence to capture your reader's interest.

Consider Your Audience

It is well worth remembering that in no other type of writing is the question of audience more important than in argumentation. Here again, the *ethos* and *pathos* aspects of argumentation come into play. The tone you establish, the type of diction you choose, the kinds of evidence you select to buttress your assertions, and indeed the organizational pattern you design and follow will all influence your audience's perception of your trustworthiness and believability. If you make good judgments about the nature of your audience, respect its knowledge of the subject, and correctly envision whether it is likely to be hostile, neutral, complacent, or receptive, you will be able to tailor the various aspects of your argument appropriately.

Gather Supporting Evidence

For each point of your argument, be sure to provide appropriate and sufficient supporting evidence: verifiable facts and statistics, illustrative examples and narratives, or quotations from authorities. Don't overwhelm your reader with evidence, but don't skimp either; it is important to demonstrate your command of the topic and your control of the thesis by choosing carefully from all the evidence at your disposal. If there are strong arguments on both sides of the issue, you will need to take this into account while making your choices. (See the Consider Refutations to Your Argument section on page 500.)

Choose an Organizational Pattern

Once you think that you have sufficient evidence to make your assertion convincing, consider how best to organize your argument. To some extent, your organization will depend on your method of reasoning: inductive, deductive, or a combination of the two. For example, is it necessary to establish a major premise before moving on to discuss a minor premise? Should most of your evidence precede or follow your direct statement of an assertion? Will induction work better with the particular audience you have targeted? As you present your primary points, you may find it effective to move from those that are least important to those that are most important or from those that are least familiar to those that are most familiar. A scratch outline can help, but it is often the case that a writer's most crucial revisions in an argument involve rearranging its components into a sharper, more coherent order. It is often difficult to tell what that order should be until the revision stage of the writing process.

Consider Refutations to Your Argument

As you proceed with your argument, you may wish to take into account well-known and significant opposing arguments. To ignore them would be to suggest to your readers any one of the following: You don't know about them, you know about them and are obviously and unfairly weighting the argument in your favor, or you know about them and have no reasonable answers to them. Grant the validity of the opposing argument or refute it, but respect your reader's intelligence by addressing the problems. Your readers will in turn respect you for doing so.

To avoid weakening your thesis, you must be very clear in your thinking and presentation. It must remain apparent to your readers why your argument is superior to the opposing points of view. If you feel that you cannot introduce opposing arguments because they will weaken rather than strengthen your thesis, you should probably reassess your thesis and the supporting evidence.

Avoid Faulty Reasoning

Have someone read your argument, checking sentences for errors in judgment and reasoning. Sometimes others can see easily what you can't because you are so intimately tied to your assertion. Review the following list of errors in reasoning, making sure that you have not committed any of them.

> ***Oversimplification*** — a foolishly simple solution to what is clearly a complex problem. *The reason we have a balance-of-trade deficit is that foreigners make better products than we do.*

Hasty generalization — in inductive reasoning, a generalization that is based on too little evidence or on evidence that is not representative. *It was the best movie I saw this year, and so it should get an Academy Award.*

Post hoc, ergo propter hoc ("after this, therefore because of this") — confusing chance or coincidence with causation. The fact that one event comes after another does not necessarily mean that the first event caused the second. *Every time I wear my orange Syracuse sweater to a game, we win.*

Begging the question — assuming in a premise something that needs to be proven. *Parking fines work because they keep people from parking illegally.*

False analogy — making a misleading analogy between logically connected ideas. *Of course he'll make a fine coach. He was an all-star basketball player.*

Either/or thinking — seeing only two alternatives when there may in fact be other possibilities. *Either you love your job or you hate it.*

Non sequitur ("it does not follow") — an inference or conclusion that is not clearly related to the established premises or evidence. *She is very sincere; she must know what she is talking about.*

Conclude Forcefully

In the conclusion of your essay, be sure to restate your position in different language, at least briefly. Besides persuading your reader to accept your point of view, you may also want to encourage some specific course of action. Above all, your conclusion should not introduce new information that may surprise your reader; it should seem to follow naturally, almost seamlessly, from the series of points that have been carefully established in the body of the essay. Don't overstate your case, but at the same time don't qualify your conclusion with the use of too many words or phrases like *I think, in my opinion, maybe, sometimes,* and *probably.* Rather than making you seem rational and sensible, these words can often make you sound indecisive and muddled.

Use Other Rhetorical Strategies

Although argument is one of the most powerful single rhetorical strategies, it is almost always strengthened by incorporating other strategies. In every professional selection in this chapter, you will find a number of rhetorical strategies at work.

Combining strategies is probably not something you want to think about when you first try to write an argument. Instead, let the strategies develop naturally as you organize, draft, and revise your essay. As you develop your argument essay, use the following chart as a reminder of what the eight strategies covered previously can do for you.

Strategies for Development

Exemplification	Using examples to illustrate a point or idea
Narration	Telling a story or giving an account of an event
Description	Presenting a picture in words
Process Analysis	Explaining how something is done or happens
Definition	Explaining what something is or means
Division and Classification	Dividing a subject into its parts and placing them in appropriate categories
Comparison and Contrast	Demonstrating likenesses and differences
Cause and Effect	Explaining the causes of an event or the effects of an action

As you read a draft of your essay, look for where you can use the above strategies to strengthen your argument. For example, do you need a more convincing example, a term defined, a process explained, or the likely effects of an action detailed?

Editing Tip: Sentence Variety

Be sure to follow the guidelines and advice for editing an essay given in Chapter 2, "Writing Essays." The guidelines highlight those sentence-level concerns — grammar, mechanics, and punctuation — that are especially important in editing any piece of writing. While editing your essay of argumentation, you can add interest to your writing by varying your sentence style. You should, however, seek sentence variety not as an end in itself but as a more accurate means of reflecting your thoughts and giving emphasis where emphasis is needed. Look for opportunities to achieve sentence variety by combining short, choppy sentences; varying sentence openings; and reducing compound sentences.

Combine Short, Simple Sentences to Make Your Writing More Interesting

1. Use coordinating and subordinating conjunctions to relate and connect ideas.

The coordinating conjunctions *and, but, or, nor, for, so,* and *yet* can be used to connect two or more simple sentences. A subordinating conjunction, on the other hand, introduces a subordinate clause and connects it to a main clause. Common subordinating conjunctions include:

after	before	so	when
although	even if	than	where
as	if	that	whereas
as if	in order that	though	wherever
as though	rather than	unless	whether
because	since	until	while

SHORT AND SIMPLE   Short words are as good as long ones. Short old words — like *sun* and *grass* and *home* — are best of all.

COMBINED   Short words are as good as long ones, **and** short old words — like *sun* and *grass* and *home* — are best of all.

— RICHARD LEDERER
"The Case for Short Words," p. 513

2. Use modifiers effectively.

Instead of writing a separate descriptive sentence, add an adjective modifier to convey a more graphic picture in a single sentence.

SHORT AND SIMPLE   The family that grew the soybeans by my house are farmers. And they are wonderful farmers.

COMBINED   The family that grew the soybeans by my house are *wonderful* farmers.

— JIM SCHARPLAZ
"Weeding Out the Skilled Farmer," p. 579

3. Use a semicolon or colon to link closely related ideas.

SHORT AND SIMPLE   Habitat destruction remains a serious environmental problem. In some respects it is the most serious.

COMBINED   Habitat destruction remains a serious environmental problem; in some respects it is the most serious.

— JONATHAN RAUCH
"Will Frankenfood Save the Planet?" p. 564

4. Use parallel constructions.

Parallel constructions use repeated word order or repeated grammatical form to highlight and develop a central idea. As a rhetorical device, parallelism can aid coherence and add emphasis.

SHORT AND SIMPLE   Besides, this is not about comfort. It concerns fairness.

COMBINED   Besides, this is not *about comfort* but *about fairness*.

> — ANNA QUINDLEN
> "Uncle Sam and Aunt Samantha," p. 540

Vary Your Sentence Openings

More than half of all sentences in English begin with the subject of the sentence followed by the verb and any objects. The following sentences all illustrate this basic pattern:

> Martha plays the saxophone.

> The president vetoed the tax bill before leaving Washington for the holidays.

> The upcoming lecture series will formally launch the fund-raising campaign for a new civic center.

If all the sentences in a particular passage in your essay begin this way, the effect is monotonous. With a little practice, you will discover just how flexible the English language is. Consider the different ways in which one sentence can be rewritten so as to vary its beginning and add interest.

ORIGINAL   Candidates debated the issue of military service for women and did not know that a demonstration was going on outside the auditorium.

VARIED OPENINGS   *Debating the issue of military service for women*, the candidates in the auditorium did not know that a demonstration was going on outside.

In the auditorium, the candidates debated the issue of military service for women, not knowing that a demonstration was going on outside.

As they debated the issue of military service for women, the candidates in the auditorium did not know that a demonstration was going on outside.

Another way of changing the usual subject-verb-object order of sentences is to invert — or reverse — the normal order. *Do not*, however, sacrifice proper emphasis for the sake of gaining variety.

Usual order	Inverted order
The crowd stormed out.	Out stormed the crowd.
The union will never accept that.	That the union will never accept.
They could be friendly and civil.	Friendly and civil they could be.

Do Not Overuse Compound Sentences

Like a series of short, simple sentences, too many compound sentences — two or more sentences joined by coordinating conjunctions — give the impression of haste and thoughtlessness. As you edit your paper, watch for the word *and* used as a coordinating conjunction. If you discover that you have overused *and*, try one of the following four methods to remedy the situation, giving important ideas more emphasis and making it easier for your reader to follow your thought.

1. Change a compound sentence into a simple sentence with an appositive.

COMPOUND   Richard Lederer is a linguist, and he is humorous, and he hosts a weekly radio program about language.

APPOSITIVE   Richard Lederer, *a humorous linguist*, hosts a weekly radio program about language.

2. Change a compound sentence into a simple sentence with a compound predicate.

COMPOUND   Martin Luther King Jr. chastises America for not honoring its obligations to people of color, and he dreams of a day when racism will no longer exist.

COMPOUND
PREDICATE   Martin Luther King Jr. *chastises* America for not honoring its obligations to people of color *and dreams* of a day when racism will no longer exist.

3. Change a compound sentence into a simple sentence with a phrase or phrases.

COMPOUND   Women have a number of options in the military, and the responsibilities are significant.

WITH A PHRASE   Women have a number of options in the military *with significant responsibilities.*

4. Change a compound sentence into a complex sentence.

COMPOUND   Farmers are using new technologies, and agriculture is becoming completely industrialized.

COMPLEX   *Because* farmers are using new technologies, agriculture is becoming completely industrialized.

▶   *Questions for Revising and Editing: Argumentation*

1. Is my thesis or proposition focused? Do I state my thesis well?
2. Assess the different kinds of arguments. Am I using the right technique to argue my thesis? Does my strategy fit my subject matter and audience?
3. Does my presentation include enough evidence to support my thesis? Do I acknowledge opposing points of view in a way that strengthens, rather than weakens, my argument?
4. Have I chosen an appropriate organizational pattern that makes it easy to support my thesis?
5. Have I avoided faulty reasoning within my essay? Have I had a friend read the essay to help me find problems in my logic?
6. Is my conclusion forceful and effective?
7. Have I thought about or attempted to combine rhetorical strategies to strengthen my argument? If so, is the combination of strategies effective? If not, what strategy or strategies would help my argument?
8. Have I used a variety of sentences to enliven my writing?

SEEING/READING

Rap the Vote

Ed Bailey

Ed Bailey/AP/Wide World Photos

CONNECTING IMAGE AND TEXT

In this photograph from August 20, 2002, hip-hop mogul Russell Simmons, cochairman of the Rap the Vote Advisory Board, holds a press conference in New York to announce the launch of Rap the Vote, "a voter registration, education, and empowerment campaign created to engage the hip-hop generation in political activity." How do you "read" this photograph? Do you think of hip-hop music as a form of political expression? Why or why not? What public image of hip-hop does this photograph suggest to you? Why is Simmons, a person credited by many for bringing black, hip-hop culture into the American mainstream, a good spokesperson for Rap the Vote? How successful would such a campaign be in getting you involved in the political process? Why? Your observations will help guide you to the key themes and strategies in the essay that follows.

If Hip-Hop Ruled the World
Aisha K. Finch

A 1998 graduate of Brown University, Aisha K. Finch majored in Africana Studies. Before starting work on a Ph.D. at New York University, she taught sixth- and eighth-grade students at the Brooklyn Friends School in Brooklyn, New York. Finch wrote "If Hip-Hop Ruled the World" for Essence *magazine in March 1998, during her senior year at Brown. Later Finch published the essay "Not Quite Outcasts: Hip-Hop, Black Women, Neo-Blaxploitation" (2002) in the magazine AWOL.*

In the following essay, Finch tells about her trip to Senegal, "to the Motherland in search of ancestral roots and cultural understanding." To her surprise she found the music of home — the music of America's hip-hop giants — on the streets of Dakar. This cultural disjuncture jolted her into questioning the violent and angry images of African Americans that are exported around the world through the music and lyrics of hip-hop.

PREPARING TO READ
What are your impressions of hip-hop music? Do you have a favorite hip-hop artist or group? What do you like or dislike about hip-hop? Do you find any hip-hop lyrics or videos objectionable? If so, why?

You know them well. You can pick them out anywhere. They are   1
the homeboys. The B-boys. The hip-hop kids. We see them slouched against walls, hats pulled low, hands shoved into pockets. They nod a silent greeting to a member of the crew who passes, mumble a crude appreciation for the "honeys." Searching for the elusive facade of perfect cool while gingerly holding up the walls on street corners everywhere. Atlanta. New York. Los Angeles. Even Dakar, Senegal.

I spent my first few days in Senegal trying to adjust to many   2
things: the sometimes-on-but-never-warm tap water, strangers who

greeted me as if I were family, women who created five-course meals out of fish and rice. In the midst of all this "Africanness" and cultural immersion, I was hardly prepared for a chance run-in with the former president of Death Row Records: Dr. Dre himself was blasting from the speakers of a neighborhood hangout. He was followed in turn by Warren G, Snoop Doggy Dogg, and Tupac Shakur. I had come to the Motherland in search of ancestral roots and cultural understanding, and here I was, in the French-speaking nation of Senegal, face-to-face with a spread from *Rap Pages*.

My first reaction was to smile and shake my head. I was in a foreign land with so little familiar to me, so the rhythms of black America fell on my ears like the voice of an old friend. It is no secret that hip-hop as both a musical genre and a defined lifestyle has gained recognition and popularity around the globe. Acknowledging this on a cerebral level, however, and confronting it in person are two entirely different things.

Just as in the United States, the hardcore players of hip-hop seem to have the most influence with the young people of Dakar. But what kind of message is being sent out to black people around the world when the main ambassadors of hip-hop are people like the Notorious B.I.G. and Lil' Kim? Yes, it's true that many of hip-hop's most devoted followers in Dakar don't understand standard English, much less the intricacies of black American slang. But just because they cannot dissect the individual words doesn't mean they don't grasp the message. Besides, the videos that follow closely behind leave little room for confusion as to underlying meanings.

We as African Americans seriously need to stop and think about what our music, and our popular culture in general, is saying about us. Certainly we have all heard songs whose lyrics we neither endorse nor act upon. Yet the extensive airtime allotted to songs with destructive lyrics, coupled with the visual counterpart, does take its toll. The repeated exposure to these sounds and images slowly desensitizes us to the violence, anger, and exploitative sexual images that have become staples in much of hip-hop music. Even if we don't condone these things, our initial indignation eventually subsides and then disappears altogether as we slide into the familiar seduction of pop-culture marketing at its best. I may realize that the by-now-trite image of the gun-toting gangbanger is hardly representative of black youth culture in the United States. But we would do well to remember that foreign listeners who have had little or no interaction with African Americans have no reason not to take the face on the screen or behind the album as a representative of contemporary black American morals, values, and lifestyles.

Say what you like in defense of gangsta lyrics, but there is no way to rewrite the following party scene to make it any less disturbing: A group of teenage party goers keeps right on groovin' as the sound of recorded gunshots rips through a heavy bass line. This is something I've witnessed a number of times on the home turf, and yet I had to travel four thousand miles to feel the full impact of those bullets. Maybe we've all become a little too indifferent to that sound. Or maybe those Senegalese teenagers in their baggy clothes don't quite understand that if you listen long enough, that hollow pelting can start to sound like the 3,862 black American males who were murdered in 1995 before the age of twenty-five.

The fact is, from Senegal to South Africa, from England to Japan, the export of hip-hop around the globe is more than just a pop phenomenon. So consider this: If young black America is going to be a cultural trendsetter on a global scale, why not use this to our advantage? Can you imagine what our influence could be if more groups like The Fugees or Tribe Called Quest created music and lyrics to inspire a new wave in Pan-African thinking? If hip-hop is destined to rule youth culture around the world, wouldn't you rather it be a reign that will unite and empower black people everywhere? 7

RESPONDING TO THE TEXT

Do you think Finch is correct when she warns that "we would do well to remember that foreign listeners who have had little or no interaction with African Americans have no reason not to take the face on the screen or behind the album as a representative of contemporary black American morals, values, and lifestyles" (paragraph 5)? Why or why not? Could a similar argument be made about American listeners who have had little or no interaction with African American culture? Explain.

ENGAGING THE WRITER'S SUBJECT

1. What worries Finch about the messages hardcore hip-hop players send to blacks around the world? Explain.

2. In discussing hip-hop's worldwide popularity Finch states, "Acknowledging this on a cerebral level, however, and confronting it in person are two entirely different things" (paragraph 3). What do you think Finch means? How did Finch react when confronted with American hip-hop with English lyrics playing in the French-speaking African nation of Senegal?

3. How does Finch explain our acquired insensitivity to the "violence, anger, and exploitative sexual images that have become staples in much of hip-hop music" (paragraph 5)? Do you think this insensitivity applies to forms of entertainment other than hip-hop? Explain.

4. What advice does Finch give to "young black America" (paragraph 7)? Do you agree? Why or why not?

ANALYZING THE WRITER'S CRAFT

1. In what ways is the opening paragraph a fitting beginning for this essay? (Glossary: *Beginnings/Endings*) How does it pave the way for Finch's revelation that she found the familiar in a strange place?

2. Who is Finch's audience, and what does she want them to do as a result of reading her essay? (Glossary: *Audience; Purpose*) What led you to this conclusion?

3. In paragraph 6, Finch presents the example of a disturbing party scene to counter a hypothetical defense of gangsta lyrics. (Glossary: *Exemplification*) Did you find this example persuasive? Why or why not?

4. Finch concludes her essay with three rhetorical questions. (Glossary: *Rhetorical Question*) Given their position in the essay, what effect do you think Finch intended them to have? Explain.

5. Finch's argument is structured around her experience as an African American woman surprised by the presence and popularity of American hip-hop in Senegal. (Glossary: *Narration*) In paragraph 2 she states, "In the midst of all this 'Africanness' and cultural immersion, I was hardly prepared for a chance run-in with the former president of Death Row Records: Dr. Dre himself was blasting from the speakers of a neighborhood hangout." How do Finch's narration and examples strengthen her argument? (Glossary: *Exemplification*) Explain.

UNDERSTANDING THE WRITER'S LANGUAGE

1. How would you describe Finch's tone in this essay? (Glossary: *Tone*) Is this tone appropriate given her subject and purpose? (Glossary: *Purpose; Subject*) To support your answer, cite specific words and phrases she uses.

2. Identify eight to ten strong verbs Finch uses. (Glossary: *Verb*) What do these strong verbs add to Finch's prose? Explain.

3. Refer to your desk dictionary to determine the meanings of the following words as Finch uses them in this selection: *facade* (paragraph 1), *immersion* (2), *genre* (3), *cerebral* (3), *dissect* (4), *indignation* (5), *trite* (5).

WRITING SUGGESTIONS

1. In writing about destructive hip-hop lyrics and videos, Finch states that "the repeated exposure to these sounds and images slowly desensitizes us to the violence, anger, and exploitative sexual images that have become staples in much of hip-hop music. Even if we don't condone these things, our initial indignation eventually subsides and then disappears altogether as we slide into the familiar seduction of pop-culture marketing at its best" (paragraph 5). Has American society been desensitized to the dangers of such media violence? Under the guise of seemingly innocent pop-culture marketing, have parents been duped when it comes to CDs, videos, and MTV programming? Write an essay in which you

argue for or against restrictions, such as parental warning labels, on CDs and videos with destructive lyrics or exploitative messages. Before you write, you may want to review your Preparing to Read response for this selection.

2. In paragraph 7, Finch concludes by asking the following rhetorical question: "If hip-hop is destined to rule youth culture around the world, wouldn't you rather it be a reign that will unite and empower black people everywhere?" (Glossary: *Rhetorical Question*) Do you agree that hip-hop is not a uniting or empowering force? If you disagree, write an essay explaining why hip-hop *does* "empower black people everywhere." Be sure to use examples and evidence to support your position. (Glossary: *Evidence; Exemplification*) If you agree, write an essay outlining how hip-hop can change its image. Before you write, refer to your Connecting Image and Text response for this selection.

3. In what may come as a surprise, Finch states as a matter of fact: "It is no secret that hip-hop as both a musical genre and a defined lifestyle has gained recognition and popularity around the globe" (paragraph 3). In preparation for an essay about hip-hop, research the world of hip-hop in your college library and on the Internet. You may find it helpful to consider the following questions as you begin your research. What are the origins of hip-hop music? What accounts for its widespread popularity? What exactly is a hip-hop lifestyle? How has hip-hop influenced other genres of music?

• To begin your research online, go to **bedfordstmartins.com /subjectsstrategies** and click on "Argumentation" or browse the thematic directory of annotated links.

The Case for Short Words

Richard Lederer

Born in 1938, Richard Lederer has been a lifelong student of language. He holds degrees from Haverford College, Harvard University, and the University of New Hampshire. For twenty-seven years he taught English at St. Paul's School in Concord, New Hampshire. Anyone who has read one of his more than thirty books will understand why he has been referred to as "Conan the Grammarian" and "America's wittiest verbalist." Lederer loves language and enjoys writing about its richness and usage by Americans. His books include Anguished English *(1987),* Crazy English *(1989),* Adventures of a Verbivore *(1994),* Nothing Risque, Nothing Gained *(1995), and* A Man of My Words: Reflections on the English Language *(2003). In addition to writing books, Lederer pens a weekly syndicated column called "Looking at Language" for newspapers and magazines throughout the country. He is the "Grammar Grappler" for* Writer's Digest, *the language commentator for National Public Radio, and the cohost of* A Way with Words, *a weekly radio program out of San Diego, California.*

In the following selection, a chapter from The Miracle of Language *(1990), Lederer sings the praises of short words and reminds us that well-chosen monosyllabic words can be a writer's best friends because they are functional and often pack a powerful punch. Note the clever way in which he uses short words throughout the essay itself to support his argument.*

PREPARING TO READ

Find a paragraph you like in a book that you enjoyed reading. What is it that appeals to you? What did the author do to make the writing so appealing? Do you like the vocabulary, the flow of the words, the imagery it presents, or something else?

When you speak and write, there is no law that says you have to use big words. Short words are as good as long ones, and short, old words — like *sun* and *grass* and *home* — are best of all. A lot of small words, more than you might think, can meet your needs with a strength, grace, and charm that large words do not have.

Big words can make the way dark for those who read what you write and hear what you say. Small words cast their clear light on big things — night and day, love and hate, war and peace, and life and death. Big words at times seem strange to the eye and the ear and the mind and the heart. Small words are the ones we seem to have known from the time we were born, like the hearth fire that warms the home.

Short words are bright like sparks that glow in the night, prompt   3
like the dawn that greets the day, sharp like the blade of a knife, hot
like salt tears that scald the cheek, quick like moths that flit from
flame to flame, and terse like the dart and sting of a bee.

Here is a sound rule: Use small, old words where you can. If a long   4
word says just what you want to say, do not fear to use it. But know
that our tongue is rich in crisp, brisk, swift, short words. Make them
the spine and the heart of what you speak and write. Short words are
like fast friends. They will not let you down.

The title of this chapter and the four paragraphs that you have   5
just read are wrought entirely of words of one syllable. In setting myself this task, I did not feel especially cabined, cribbed, or confined. In
fact, the structure helped me to focus on the power of the message I
was trying to put across.

One study shows that twenty words account for twenty-five percent   6
of all spoken English words, and all twenty are monosyllabic. In order of
frequency they are: *I, you, the, a, to, is, it, that, of, and, in, what, he, this,
have, do, she, not, on,* and *they.* Other studies indicate that the fifty most
common words in written English are each made of a single syllable.

For centuries our finest poets and orators have recognized and em-   7
ployed the power of small words to make a straight point between two
minds. A great many of our proverbs punch home their points with
pithy monosyllables: "Where there's a will, there's a way," "A stitch in
time saves nine," "Spare the rod and spoil the child," "A bird in the
hand is worth two in the bush."

Nobody used the short word more skillfully than William Shake-   8
speare, whose dying King Lear laments:

> And my poor fool is hang'd! No, no, no life!
> Why should a dog, a horse, a rat have life,
> And thou no breath at all? . . .
> Do you see this? Look on her; look, her lips.
> Look there, look there!

Shakespeare's contemporaries made the King James Bible a center-   9
piece of short words — "And God said, Let there be light: and there
was light. And God saw the light, that it was good." The descendants
of such mighty lines live on in the twentieth century. When asked to
explain his policy to Parliament, Winston Churchill responded with
these ringing monosyllables: "I will say: it is to wage war, by sea, land,
and air, with all our might and with all the strength that God can give
us." In his "Death of the Hired Man" Robert Frost observes that "Home
is the place where, when you have to go there,/They have to take you
in." And William H. Johnson uses ten two-letter words to explain his
secret of success: "If it is to be,/It is up to me."

You don't have to be a great author, statesman, or philosopher to 10
tap the energy and eloquence of small words. Each winter I ask my
ninth graders at St. Paul's School to write a composition composed
entirely of one-syllable words. My students greet my request with
obligatory moans and groans, but, when they return to class with their
essays, most feel that, with the pressure to produce high-sounding
polysyllables relieved, they have created some of their most powerful
and luminous prose. Here are submissions from two of my ninth
graders:

> What can you say to a boy who has left home? You can say
> that he has done wrong, but he does not care. He has left home so
> that he will not have to deal with what you say. He wants to go as
> far as he can. He will do what he wants to do.
>
> This boy does not want to be forced to go to church, to comb
> his hair, or to be on time. A good time for this boy does not lie in
> your reach, for what you have he does not want. He dreams of
> ripped jeans, shorts with no starch, and old socks.
>
> So now this boy is on a bus to a place he dreams of, a place
> with no rules. This boy now walks a strange street, his long hair
> blown back by the wind. He wears no coat or tie, just jeans and an
> old shirt. He hates your world, and he has left it.
>
> — CHARLES SHAFFER

> For a long time we cruised by the coast and at last came to a
> wide bay past the curve of a hill, at the end of which lay a small
> town. Our long boat ride at an end, we all stretched and stood up
> to watch as the boat nosed its way in.
>
> The town climbed up the hill that rose from the shore, a space
> in front of it left bare for the port. Each house was a clean white
> with sky blue or grey trim; in front of each one was a small yard,
> edged by a white stone wall strewn with green vines.
>
> As the town basked in the heat of noon, not a thing stirred in
> the streets or by the shore. The sun beat down on the sea, the land,
> and the back of our necks, so that, in spite of the breeze that made
> the vines sway, we all wished we could hide from the glare in a
> cool, white house. But, as there was no one to help dock the boat,
> we had to stand and wait.
>
> At last the head of the crew leaped from the side and strode to
> a large house on the right. He shoved the door wide, poked his
> head through the gloom, and roared with a fierce voice. Five or six
> men came out, and soon the port was loud with the clank of chains
> and creak of planks as the men caught ropes thrown by the crew,
> pulled them taut, and tied them to posts. Then they set up a rough
> plank so we could cross from the deck to the shore. We all made for
> the large house while the crew watched, glad to be rid of us.
>
> — CELIA WREN

You too can tap into the vitality and vigor of compact expression. 11
Take a suggestion from the highway department. At the boundaries of
your speech and prose place a sign that reads "Caution: Small Words
at Work."

RESPONDING TO THE TEXT

Reread a piece of writing you turned in earlier this year for any class. Analyze your choice of words, and describe your writing vocabulary. Did you
follow Lederer's admonition to use short words whenever they are appropriate, or did you tend to use longer, more important-sounding words? Is Lederer's essay likely to change the way you write papers in the future? Why or
why not?

ENGAGING THE WRITER'S SUBJECT

1. What rule does Lederer present for writing? What does he do to demonstrate the feasibility of this rule?

2. Lederer states that the twenty words that account for a quarter of all
   spoken English words are monosyllabic. So are the fifty most common
   written words. Why, then, do you think Lederer felt it was necessary to
   argue that people should use them? Who is his audience? (Glossary: *Audience*)

3. How do his students react to the assignment he gives them requiring
   short words? How do their essays turn out? What does the assignment
   teach them?

ANALYZING THE WRITER'S CRAFT

1. As you read Lederer's essay for the first time, were you surprised by his
   announcement in paragraph 5 that the preceding four paragraphs contained only single-syllable words? If not, when were you first aware of
   what he was doing? What does Lederer's strategy tell you about small
   words?

2. Lederer starts using multisyllabic words when discussing the process of
   writing with single-syllable words. Why do you think he abandons his
   single-syllable presentation? Does it diminish the strength of his argument? Explain.

3. Lederer provides two long examples of writing by his own students.
   What does he accomplish by using these examples along with ones
   from famous authors? (Glossary: *Exemplification*)

4. Lederer illustrates his argument with examples from several prominent
   authors as well as from students. (Glossary: *Exemplification*) Which of
   these examples did you find the most effective? Why? Provide an example from your own reading that you think is effective in illustrating
   Lederer's argument.

UNDERSTANDING THE WRITER'S LANGUAGE

1. Lederer uses similes to help the reader form associations and images with short words. (Glossary: *Figures of Speech*) What are some of these similes? Do you find the similes effective in the context of Lederer's argument? Explain.

2. In paragraph 9, Lederer uses such terms as *mighty* and *ringing monosyllables* to describe the passages he gives as examples. Do you think such descriptions are appropriate? Why do you think he includes them?

3. Carefully analyze the two student essays that Lederer presents. In particular, circle all the main verbs that each student uses. (Glossary: *Verb*) What, if anything, do these verbs have in common? What conclusions can you draw about verbs and strong, powerful writing?

4. Refer to your desk dictionary to determine the meanings of the following words as Lederer uses them in this selection: *cabined* (paragraph 5), *cribbed* (5), *monosyllabic* (6), *proverbs* (7), *eloquence* (10), *obligatory* (10), *vitality* (11).

WRITING SUGGESTIONS

1. People tend to avoid single-syllable words because they are afraid they will look stupid and that their writing will lack sophistication. Are there situations in which demonstrating command of a large vocabulary is desirable? If you answer yes, present one situation, and argue that the overuse of short words in that situation is potentially detrimental. If you answer no, defend your reasoning. How can the use of short words convey the necessary style and sophistication in all situations?

2. Consider the *New Yorker* cartoon by Harry Bliss on page 518. What do you think Bliss is saying, and how does he use language to make his point clear? With the exception of the word *daughter*, all the words in the caption are monosyllabic. Is language that is blunt and to the point the best or most appropriate language to use in most situations? Do you consider such language somehow more "honest" than language that "beats around the bush"? Had the teacher wished to be more tactful, what could she have said instead? How do you think Lederer would respond to this cartoon? Explain. With the cartoon and Lederer's essay in mind, write an essay in which you explore the power of short words. Be sure to use a variety of examples from your own experience and observations. (Glossary: *Exemplification*)

3. Advertising is an industry that depends on efficient, high-impact words. Choose ten advertising slogans and three jingles that you find effective. For example, "Just Do It" and "Think Different" are two prominent slogans. Analyze the ratio of short to long words in the slogans and jingles, and write an essay in which you present your findings. What is the percentage of short words? Does this percentage support or contradict Lederer's contention that short words are often best for high-impact communicating?

"Your daughter is a pain in the ass."

- To begin your research online, go to **bedfordstmartins.com /subjectsstrategies** and click on "Argumentation" or browse the thematic directory of annotated links.

The Declaration of Independence

Thomas Jefferson

President, governor, statesman, diplomat, lawyer, architect, philosopher, thinker, and writer, Thomas Jefferson is one of the most important figures in U.S. history. He was born in Albemarle County, Virginia, in 1743 and attended the College of William and Mary. After being admitted to law practice in 1767, he began a long and illustrious career of public service to the colonies and, later, the new republic.

Jefferson drafted the Declaration of Independence in 1776. Although it was revised by Benjamin Franklin and his colleagues in the Continental Congress, in its sound logic and forceful, direct style the document retains the unmistakable qualities of Jefferson's prose.

PREPARING TO READ

In your mind, what is the meaning of democracy? Where do your ideas about democracy come from?

When in the course of human events, it becomes necessary for one people to dissolve the political bonds which have connected them with another, and to assume among the Powers of the earth, the separate and equal station to which the Laws of Nature and of Nature's God entitle them, a decent respect to the opinions of mankind requires that they should declare the causes which impel them to the separation.

We hold these truths to be self-evident, that all men are created equal, that they are endowed by their Creator with certain unalienable Rights, that among these are Life, Liberty and the pursuit of Happiness. That to secure these rights, Governments are instituted among Men deriving their just powers from the consent of the governed. That whenever any Form of Government becomes destructive of these ends, it is the Right of the People to alter or to abolish it, and to institute new Government, laying its foundation on such principles and organizing its powers in such form, as to them shall seem most likely to effect their Safety and Happiness. Prudence, indeed, will dictate that Governments long established should not be changed for light and transient causes; and accordingly all experience hath shown, that mankind are more disposed to suffer, while evils are sufferable, than to right themselves by abolishing the forms to which they are accustomed. But when a long train of abuses and usurpations pursuing invariably the same Object evinces a design to reduce them under absolute Despotism, it is their right, it is their duty, to throw off such government, and to provide new Guards for their future security. Such has been the patient sufferance of these Colonies; and such is now the necessity which constrains them to alter their former Systems of Government. The history of the present King of Great Britain is a history of repeated injuries and usurpations, all having in direct object the establishment of an absolute Tyranny over these States. To prove this, let Facts be submitted to a candid world.

He has refused his Assent to Laws, the most wholesome and necessary for the public good. 3

He has forbidden his Governors to pass Laws of immediate and pressing importance, unless suspended in their operation till his Assent should be obtained; and when so suspended, he has utterly neglected to attend to them. 4

He has refused to pass other Laws for the accommodation of large districts of people, unless those people would relinquish the right of Representation in the Legislature, a right inestimable to them and formidable to tyrants only. 5

He has called together legislative bodies at places unusual, uncomfortable, and distant from the depository of their Public Records, for the sole purpose of fatiguing them into compliance with his measures. 6

He has dissolved Representative Houses repeatedly, for opposing with manly firmness his invasions on the rights of the people. 7

He has refused for a long time, after such dissolutions, to cause others to be elected; whereby the Legislative Powers, incapable of Annihilation, have returned to the People at large for their exercise; the State remaining in the mean time exposed to all the dangers of invasion from without, and convulsions within. 8

He has endeavoured to prevent the population of these States; for that purpose obstructing the Laws of Naturalization of Foreigners; refusing to pass others to encourage their migration hither, and raising the conditions of new Appropriations of Lands. 9

He has obstructed the Administration of Justice, by refusing his Assent to Laws for establishing Judiciary Powers. 10

He has made Judges dependent on his Will alone, for the tenure of their offices, and the amount and payment of their salaries. 11

He has erected a multitude of New Offices, and sent hither swarms of Officers to harass our People, and eat out their substance. 12

He has kept among us, in time of peace, Standing Armies without the Consent of our Legislature. 13

He has affected to render the Military independent of and superior to the Civil Power. 14

He has combined with others to subject us to jurisdictions foreign to our constitution, and unacknowledged by our laws; giving his Assent to their acts of pretended Legislation: 15

For quartering large bodies of armed troops among us: 16

For protecting them, by a mock Trial, from Punishment for any 17
Murders which they should commit on the Inhabitants of these
States:

For cutting off our Trade with all parts of the world: 18

For imposing Taxes on us without our Consent: 19

For depriving us in many cases, of the benefits of Trial by Jury: 20

For transporting us beyond Seas to be tried for pretended offenses: 21

For abolishing the free System of English Laws in a Neighbouring 22
Province, establishing therein an Arbitrary government, and enlarging
its boundaries so as to render it at once an example and fit instrument
for introducing the same absolute rule into these Colonies:

For taking away our Charters, abolishing our most valuable Laws, 23
and altering fundamentally the Forms of our Governments:

For suspending our own Legislatures, and declaring themselves in- 24
vested with Power to legislate for us in all cases whatsoever.

He has abdicated Government here, by declaring us out of his Pro- 25
tection and waging War against us.

He has plundered our seas, ravaged our Coasts, burnt our towns 26
and destroyed the Lives of our people.

He is at this time transporting large Armies of foreign Mercenaries 27
to compleat works of death, desolation and tyranny already begun with
circumstances of Cruelty & perfidy scarcely paralleled in the most bar-
barous ages, and totally unworthy the Head of a civilized nation.

He has constrained our fellow Citizens taken Captive on the high 28
Seas to bear Arms against their Country, to become the executioners
of their friends and Brethren, or to fall themselves by their Hands.

He has excited domestic insurrections amongst us, and has en- 29
deavoured to bring on the inhabitants of our frontiers, the merciless
Indian Savages, whose known rule of warfare is an undistinguished destruction of all ages, sexes and conditions.

In every stage of these Oppressions We Have Petitioned for Re- 30
dress in the most humble terms: Our repeated petitions have been answered only by repeated injury. A Prince, whose character is thus
marked by every act which may define a Tyrant, is unfit to be the ruler
of a free People.

Nor have We been wanting in attention to our British brethren. 31
We have warned them from time to time of attempts by their legislature to extend an unwarrantable jurisdiction over us. We have reminded them of the circumstances of our emigration and settlement
here. We have appealed to their native justice and magnanimity and
we have conjured them by the ties of our common kindred to disavow
these usurpations, which would inevitably interrupt our connections
and correspondence. They too have been deaf to the voice of justice
and of consanguinity. We must, therefore acquiesce in the necessity,

which denounces our Separation, and hold them, as we hold the rest
of mankind, Enemies in War, in Peace Friends.

We, therefore, the Representatives of the United States of America,   32
in General Congress, Assembled, appealing to the Supreme Judge of
the world for the rectitude of our intentions, do, in the Name, and by
Authority of the good People of these Colonies, solemnly publish and
declare, That these United Colonies are, and of Right ought to be Free
and Independent States; that they are Absolved from all Allegiance to
the British Crown, and that all political connection between them and
the State of Great Britain, is and ought to be totally dissolved; and that
as Free and Independent States, they have full power to levy War, conclude Peace, contract Alliances, establish Commerce, and to do all
other Acts and Things which Independent States may of right do. And
for the support of this Declaration, with a firm reliance on the protection of Divine Providence, we mutually pledge to each other our lives,
our Fortunes and our sacred Honor.

RESPONDING TO THE TEXT

Why do you think the Declaration of Independence is still such a powerful
and important document more than two hundred years after it was written?
Do any parts of it seem more memorable than others? Did any part surprise
you in this reading?

ENGAGING THE WRITER'S SUBJECT

1. Where, according to Jefferson, do rulers get their authority? What does
   Jefferson believe is the purpose of government?

2. What argument does the Declaration of Independence make for over-
   throwing any unacceptable government? What assumptions underlie
   this argument?

3. In paragraphs 3 through 29, Jefferson lists the many ways King George
   has wronged the colonists. Which of these "injuries and usurpations"
   (paragraph 2) do you feel are just cause for the colonists to declare their
   independence?

4. According to the Declaration of Independence, how did the colonists
   try to persuade the English king to rule more justly?

5. What are the specific declarations that Jefferson makes in his final paragraph?

ANALYZING THE WRITER'S CRAFT

1. The Declaration of Independence is a deductive argument; it is therefore
   possible to present it in the form of a syllogism. What is the major
   premise, the minor premise, and the conclusion of Jefferson's argument?
   (Glossary: *Syllogism*)

2. In paragraph 2, Jefferson presents certain "self-evident" truths. What are these truths, and how are they related to the intent of his argument?

3. The list of charges against the king is given as evidence in support of Jefferson's minor premise. Does he offer any evidence in support of his major premise? Why or why not? (Glossary: *Evidence*)

4. What pattern do you see to the list of grievances in paragraphs 3 through 29? Try to group them into categories. Describe the cumulative effect of this list on you as a reader.

5. Explain how Jefferson uses cause and effect thinking to justify the colonists' argument in declaring their independence. (Glossary: *Cause and Effect Analysis*)

UNDERSTANDING THE WRITER'S LANGUAGE

1. Who is Jefferson's audience, and in what tone does he address this audience? Discuss why this tone is or isn't appropriate for this document. (Glossary: *Audience*)

2. Is the language of the Declaration of Independence coolly reasonable or emotional, or does it change from one to the other? Give examples to support your answer.

3. Paraphrase the following excerpt, and comment on Jefferson's diction and syntax: "They too have been deaf to the voice of justice and of consanguinity. We must, therefore acquiesce in the necessity, which denounces our Separation, and hold them, as we hold the rest of mankind, Enemies in War, in Peace Friends" (paragraph 31). Describe the author's tone in these two sentences. (Glossary: *Diction; Tone*)

4. Refer to your desk dictionary to determine the meanings of the following words as Jefferson uses them in this selection: *effect* (paragraph 2), *prudence* (2), *transient* (2), *usurpations* (2 and 31), *evinces* (2), *despotism* (2), *candid* (2), *affected* (14), *perfidy* (27), *excited* (29), *redress* (30), *magnanimity* (31), *conjured* (31), *disavow* (31), *too* (31), *consanguinity* (31), *acquiesce* (31), *rectitude* (32), *levy* (32).

WRITING SUGGESTIONS

1. To some people, the Declaration of Independence still accurately reflects America's political philosophy and way of life; to others, it does not. What is your position on this issue? Discuss your analysis of the Declaration of Independence's contemporary relevance, and try to persuade others to your position.

2. How does a monarchy differ from American democracy? Write an essay in which you compare and contrast a particular monarchy and the presidency. How are they similar? You might also consider comparing the presidency with the British monarchy of 1776.

3. The adoption of the Declaration of Independence was, among other things, a matter of practical politics. Using your college library and the Internet, research the deliberations of the Continental Congress, and

explain how and why the final version of the Declaration of Independence evolved. For example, you might examine why the final draft differs from Jefferson's first draft.

- To begin your research online, go to **bedfordstmartins.com /subjectsstrategies** and click on "Argumentation" or browse the thematic directory of annotated links.

I Have a Dream

Martin Luther King Jr.

Civil rights leader Martin Luther King Jr. (1929–1968) was the son of a Baptist minister in Atlanta, Georgia. Ordained at the age of eighteen, King went on to earn academic degrees from Morehouse College, Crozer Theological Seminary, Boston University, and Chicago Theological Seminary. He came to prominence in 1955 in Montgomery, Alabama, when he led a successful boycott against the city's segregated bus system. The first president of the Southern Christian Leadership Conference, King became the leading spokesman for the civil rights movement during the 1950s and 1960s, espousing a consistent philosophy of nonviolent resistance to racial injustice. He also championed women's rights and protested the Vietnam War. Named Time *magazine's Man of the Year in 1963, King was awarded the Nobel Peace Prize in 1964. King was assassinated in April 1968 after speaking at a rally in Memphis, Tennessee.*

"I Have a Dream," the keynote address for the "March on Washington" in 1963, has become one of the most renowned and recognized speeches of the past century. Delivered from the steps of the Lincoln Memorial to commemorate the centennial of the Emancipation Proclamation, King's speech resonates with hope even as it condemns racial oppression.

PREPARING TO READ

Most Americans have seen film clips of King delivering the "I Have a Dream" speech. What do you know of the speech? What do you know of the events and conditions under which King presented it?

Five score years ago, a great American, in whose symbolic shadow we 1
stand, signed the Emancipation Proclamation. This momentous decree came as a great beacon light of hope to millions of Negro slaves who had been seared in the flames of withering injustice. It came as a joyous daybreak to end the long night of captivity.

But one hundred years later, we must face the tragic fact that the 2
Negro is still not free. One hundred years later, the life of the Negro is still sadly crippled by the manacles of segregation and the chains of discrimination. One hundred years later, the Negro lives on a lonely island of poverty in the midst of a vast ocean of material prosperity. One hundred years later, the Negro is still languishing in the corners of American society and finds himself an exile in his own land. So we have come here today to dramatize an appalling condition.

In a sense we have come to our nation's Capitol to cash a check. 3
When the architects of our republic wrote the magnificent words of

the Constitution and the Declaration of Independence, they were signing a promissory note to which every American was to fall heir. This note was a promise that all men would be guaranteed the unalienable rights of life, liberty, and the pursuit of happiness.

It is obvious today that America has defaulted on this promissory note insofar as her citizens of color are concerned. Instead of honoring this sacred obligation, America has given the Negro people a bad check; a check which has come back marked "insufficient funds." But we refuse to believe that the bank of justice is bankrupt. We refuse to believe that there are insufficient funds in the great vaults of opportunity of this nation. So we have come to cash this check — a check that will give us upon demand the riches of freedom and the security of justice. We have also come to this hallowed spot to remind America of the fierce urgency of *now*. This is no time to engage in the luxury of cooling off or to take the tranquilizing drug of gradualism. *Now* is the time to make real the promises of Democracy. *Now* is the time to rise from the dark and desolate valley of segregation to the sunlit path of racial justice. *Now* is the time to open the doors of opportunity to all of God's children. *Now* is the time to lift our nation from the quicksands of racial injustice to the solid rock of brotherhood.

It would be fatal for the nation to overlook the urgency of the moment and to underestimate the determination of the Negro. This sweltering summer of the Negro's legitimate discontent will not pass until there is an invigorating autumn of freedom and equality. 1963 is not an end, but a beginning. Those who hope that the Negro needed to blow off steam and will now be content will have a rude awakening if the nation returns to business as usual. There will be neither rest nor tranquility in America until the Negro is granted his citizenship rights. The whirlwinds of revolt will continue to shake the foundations of our nation until the bright day of justice emerges.

But there is something I must say to my people who stand on the warm threshold which leads into the palace of justice. In the process of gaining our rightful place we must not be guilty of wrongful deeds. Let us not seek to satisfy our thirst for freedom by drinking from the cup of bitterness and hatred. We must forever conduct our struggle on the high plane of dignity and discipline. We must not allow our creative protest to degenerate into physical violence. Again and again we must rise to the majestic heights of meeting physical force with soul force. The marvelous new militancy which has engulfed the Negro community must not lead us to a distrust of all white people, for many of our white brothers, as evidenced by their presence here today, have come to realize that their destiny is tied up with our destiny and their freedom is inextricably bound to our freedom. We cannot walk alone.

And as we walk, we must make the pledge that we shall march 7
ahead. We cannot turn back. There are those who are asking the devotees of civil rights, "When will you be satisfied?" We can never be satisfied as long as the Negro is the victim of the unspeakable horrors of police brutality. We can never be satisfied as long as our bodies, heavy with the fatigue of travel, cannot gain lodging in the motels of the highways and the hotels of the cities. We cannot be satisfied as long as the Negro's basic mobility is from a smaller ghetto to a larger one. We can never be satisfied as long as a Negro in Mississippi cannot vote and a Negro in New York believes he has nothing for which to vote. No, no, we are not satisfied, and we will not be satisfied until justice rolls down like waters and righteousness like a mighty stream.

I am not unmindful that some of you have come here out of great 8
trials and tribulations. Some of you have come fresh from narrow jail cells. Some of you have come from areas where your quest for freedom left you battered by the storms of persecution and staggered by the winds of police brutality. You have been the veterans of creative suffering. Continue to work with the faith that unearned suffering is redemptive.

Go back to Mississippi, go back to Alabama, go back to South Carolina, go back to Georgia, go back to Louisiana, go back to the slums 9
and ghettoes of our northern cities, knowing that somehow this situation can and will be changed. Let us not wallow in the valley of despair.

I say to you today, my friends, that in spite of the difficulties and 10
frustrations of the moment I still have a dream. It is a dream deeply rooted in the American dream.

I have a dream that one day this nation will rise up and live out 11
the true meaning of its creed: "We hold these truths to be self-evident; that all men are created equal."

I have a dream that one day on the red hills of Georgia the sons of 12
former slaves and the sons of former slaveowners will be able to sit down together at the table of brotherhood.

I have a dream that the state of Mississippi, a desert state swelter- 13
ing with the heat of injustice and oppression, will be transformed into an oasis of freedom and justice.

I have a dream that my four little children will one day live in a 14
nation where they will not be judged by the color of their skin but by the content of their character.

I have a dream today. 15

I have a dream that the state of Alabama, whose governor's lips 16
are presently dripping with the words of interposition and nullification, will be transformed into a situation where little black boys and black girls will be able to join hands with little white boys and white girls and walk together as sisters and brothers.

I have a dream today. 17

I have a dream that one day every valley shall be exalted, every 18
hill and mountain shall be made low, the rough places will be made
plain, and the crooked places will be made straight, and the glory of
the Lord shall be revealed, and all flesh shall see it together.

This is our hope. This is the faith with which I return to the South. 19
With this faith we will be able to hew out of the mountain of despair a
stone of hope. With this faith we will be able to transform the jangling
discords of our nation into a beautiful symphony of brotherhood. With
this faith we will be able to work together, to pray together, to struggle
together, to go to jail together, to stand up for freedom together, knowing that we will be free one day.

This will be the day when all of God's children will be able to sing 20
with new meaning.

> My country, 'tis of thee
> Sweet land of liberty,
>   Of thee I sing:
> Land where my fathers died,
> Land of the pilgrims' pride,
> From every mountainside
>   Let freedom ring.

And if America is to be a great nation this must become true. So 21
let freedom ring from the prodigious hilltops of New Hampshire. Let
freedom ring from the mighty mountains of New York. Let freedom
ring from the heightening Alleghenies of Pennsylvania!

Let freedom ring from the snowcapped Rockies of Colorado! 22

Let freedom ring from the curvaceous peaks of California! 23

But not only that; let freedom ring from Stone Mountain of Georgia! 24

Let freedom ring from Lookout Mountain of Tennessee! 25

Let freedom ring from every hill and molehill of Mississippi. From 26
every mountainside, let freedom ring.

When we let freedom ring, when we let it ring from every village 27
and every hamlet, from every state and every city, we will be able to
speed up that day when all of God's children, black men and white
men, Jews and Gentiles, Protestants and Catholics, will be able to join
hands and sing in the words of the old Negro spiritual, "Free at last!
free at last! thank God almighty, we are free at last!"

RESPONDING TO THE TEXT

King portrayed an America in 1963 in which there was still systematic oppression of African Americans. What is oppression? Have you ever felt yourself —
or have you known others — to be oppressed or part of a group that is
oppressed? Who are the oppressors? How can oppression be overcome?

ENGAGING THE WRITER'S SUBJECT

1. Why does King say that the Constitution and the Declaration of Independence act as a "promissory note" (paragraph 3) to the American people? In what way has America "defaulted" (4) on its promise?

2. What does King mean when he says that in gaining a rightful place in society "we must not be guilty of wrongful deeds" (paragraph 6)? Why is the issue so important to him?

3. When *will* King be satisfied in his quest for civil rights?

4. What, in a nutshell, is King's dream? What vision does he have for the future?

ANALYZING THE WRITER'S CRAFT

1. King delivered his address to two audiences: the huge audience that listened to him in person, and another, even larger audience. (Glossary: *Audience*) What is that larger audience? What did King do in his speech to catch its attention and to deliver his point?

2. Explain King's choice of a title. (Glossary: *Title*) Why is the title particularly appropriate given the context in which the speech was delivered? What other titles might he have used?

3. Examine the speech, and determine how King organized his presentation. (Glossary: *Organization*) What are the main sections of the speech and what is the purpose of each? How does the organization serve King's overall purpose? (Glossary: *Purpose*)

UNDERSTANDING THE WRITER'S LANGUAGE

1. King uses parallel constructions and repetition throughout his speech. Identify the phrases and words that he emphasizes. Explain what these techniques add to the persuasiveness of his argument.

2. King makes liberal use of metaphor — and metaphorical imagery — in his speech. (Glossary: *Figures of Speech*) Choose a few examples, and examine what they add to the speech. How do they help King engage his listeners' feelings of injustice and give them hope for a better future?

3. Refer to your desk dictionary to determine the meanings of the following words as King uses them in this selection: *manacles* (paragraph 2), *languishing* (2), *gradualism* (4), *inextricably* (6), *tribulations* (8), *redemptive* (8), *nullification* (16), *prodigious* (21), *curvaceous* (23).

WRITING SUGGESTIONS

1. King's language is powerful and his imagery is vivid, but the effectiveness of any speech depends partially upon its delivery. If read in monotone, King's use of repetition and parallel language would sound almost redundant rather than inspiring. Keeping presentation in mind, write a short speech that argues a point of view about which you feel strongly.

Use King's speech as a model, and incorporate imagery, repetition, and metaphor to communicate your point. Read your speech aloud to a friend to see how it flows and how effective your use of language is. Refine your presentation — both your text and how you deliver it — and then present your speech to your class.

2. King uses a variety of metaphors in his speech, but a single encompassing metaphor can be useful to establish the tone and purpose of an essay. Write a description based on a metaphor that conveys an overall impression from the beginning. Try to avoid clichés ("My dorm is a beehive," "My life is an empty glass"), but make your metaphor readily understandable. For example, you could say, "A police siren is a lullaby in my neighborhood," or "My town is a car that has gone 15,000 miles since its last oil change." Carry the metaphor through the entire description.

3. Using King's assessment of the condition of African Americans in 1963 as a foundation, research the changes that have occurred in the years following King's speech. How have laws changed? How have demographics changed? Present your information in an essay that assesses what still needs to be done to fulfill King's dream for America. Where do we still fall short of the racial equality envisioned by King? What are the prospects for the future?

- To begin your research online, go to **bedfordstmartins.com /subjectsstrategies** and click on "Argumentation" or browse the thematic directory of annotated links.

Snow *(FICTION)*

Julia Alvarez

Julia Alvarez was born in New York City in 1950, but soon after her birth, her family moved to the Dominican Republic, where she spent the first ten years of her childhood. Her return to the United States in 1960 brought her into contact with a new language and a culture steeped in the anxieties of the cold war.

Alvarez, who teaches creative writing at Middlebury College, is the author of poetry, essays, short fiction, and autobiographical novels, including How the García Girls Lost Their Accents *(1992) and* In the Time of the Butterflies *(1994). More recently, she wrote* Yo! *(1997) and* In the Name of Salome *(2000), two novels;* Something to Declare *(1998), a collection of autobiographical essays; and* The Secret Footprints *(2000), a children's story. Her newest books are* Before We Were Free *(2002) and* The Woman I Kept to Myself *(2004).*

"Snow" was published in a collection of pieces by various authors on the nuclear age. Its tone of fear and anxiety may seem strange to readers of typical college age today, but such memories are very familiar to anyone who grew up in the America of the late 1950s and early 1960s, when the threat of nuclear war prompted Americans to build backyard bomb shelters and stage community air-raid drills.

PREPARING TO READ

Whether you called it the bogeyman, the monster under the bed, or the thing in the closet, classic childhood fear takes many forms. What warnings or threats from adults really scared you when you were a child? Describe them, tell why they were so frightening, and show how you responded.

Our first year in New York we rented a small apartment with a Catholic school nearby, taught by the Sisters of Charity, hefty women in long black gowns and bonnets that made them look peculiar, like dolls in mourning. I liked them a lot, especially my grandmotherly fourth grade teacher, Sister Zoe. I had a lovely name, she said, and she had me teach the whole class how to pronounce it. *Yolan-da.* As the only immigrant in my class, I was put in a special seat in the first row by the window, apart from the other children so that Sister Zoe could tutor me without disturbing them. Slowly, she enunciated the new words I was to repeat: *laundromat, cornflakes, subway, snow.*

Soon I picked up enough English to understand holocaust was in the air. Sister Zoe explained to a wide-eyed classroom what was happening in Cuba. Russian missiles were being assembled, trained supposedly on New York City. President Kennedy, looking worried too, was on the television at home, explaining we might have to go to war against the Communists. At school, we had air-raid drills: an ominous bell would go off and we'd file into the hall, fall to the floor, cover our heads with our coats, and imagine our hair falling out, the bones in our arms going soft. At home, Mami and my sisters and I said a rosary for world peace. I heard new vocabulary: *nuclear bomb, radioactive fallout, bomb shelter*. Sister Zoe explained how it would happen. She drew a picture of a mushroom on the blackboard and dotted a flurry of chalkmarks for the dusty fallout that would kill us all.

The months grew cold, November, December. It was dark when I   3
got up in the morning, frosty when I followed my breath to school. One morning as I sat at my desk daydreaming out the window, I saw dots in the air like the ones Sister Zoe had drawn — random at first, then lots and lots. I shrieked, "Bomb! Bomb!" Sister Zoe jerked around, her full black skirt ballooning as she hurried to my side. A few girls began to cry.

But then Sister Zoe's shocked look faded. "Why, Yolanda dear,   4
that's snow!" She laughed. "Snow."

"Snow," I repeated. I looked out the window warily. All my life I   5
had heard about the white crystals that fell out of American skies in the winter. From my desk I watched the fine powder dust the sidewalk and parked cars below. Each flake was different, Sister Zoe said, like a person, irreplaceable and beautiful.

RESPONDING TO THE TEXT

In the person of Sister Zoe, Alvarez depicts a teacher who truly cares about her young students, but one whose benevolence bears sinister overtones. The reader first gets a hint of this early in the story, starting with the description of the Sisters of Charity as "dolls in mourning" (paragraph 1). In what other subtle ways does Alvarez portray Sister Zoe as a herald or personification of death?

ENGAGING THE WRITER'S SUBJECT

1. Why was Yolanda seated by the window, apart from the others in her class?

2. What does Alvarez mean by the phrase in paragraph 2, "holocaust was in the air"? Explain how the phrase "in the air" is particularly apt for the purposes of this story.

3. What is the significance of the story's final sentence? How does it relate to the central theme?

ANALYZING THE WRITER'S CRAFT

1. In literature, snow is often used as a metaphor for death because it is cold and can be a symbol for barren winter. (Glossary: *Figures of Speech*) Show how this implied metaphor serves to underscore the author's message about the threat of nuclear war. In the final paragraph, snow becomes a metaphor for something else; what does it represent at the end of the story?

2. This very short narrative touches on more than one issue important to the American culture of the early 1960s. Try to identify these issues. Which of these issues are presented directly, and which are presented indirectly? How does Alvarez pack so much content into five paragraphs?

3. In commenting on how she chose to write "Snow," Alvarez said, "Rather than becoming polemical or railing against nuclear weapons, I thought I might best 'prove' the destructiveness of nuclear weapons if I showed how a simple, poignant, and 'natural' moment becomes in this nuclear age a moment of possible holocaust for a child." How did Alvarez turn a straightforward narrative of an event into a powerful argument? Besides narration, what other rhetorical strategies does she use?

UNDERSTANDING THE WRITER'S LANGUAGE

1. Note the words *dusty* (paragraph 2) and *dust* (5). How do they relate to and differ from each other? What distinction does Alvarez make through this difference?

2. Contrast the vocabulary Yolanda was learning from Sister Zoe in paragraph 1 (*laundromat, cornflakes, subway, snow*) with the vocabulary words in paragraph 2 (*nuclear bomb, radioactive fallout, bomb shelter*). Sister Zoe must have taught her many new words; why do you think Alvarez chose these particular words for the first and second lists?

3. Refer to your desk dictionary to determine the meanings of the following words as Alvarez uses them in this selection: *enunciated* (paragraph 1), *holocaust* (2), *fallout* (2), *flurry* (2), *random* (3), *warily* (5).

WRITING SUGGESTIONS

1. Attempts are now being made to reduce the number of nuclear weapons worldwide. Should the United States continue to stockpile nuclear weapons? Why or why not? Write a paper to argue your point of view. (You may want to do some research to support your opinions.)

2. "Snow" is a very short narrative; the details have been selected carefully to support Alvarez's theme, and much that might have been said is left out. Recall a moment in your life when something happened to make you sharply aware that every person is "irreplaceable and beautiful." Briefly write the story of that moment, being sure that each detail is important. To do this, look for any details that might be distracting, and leave them out, thereby distilling your story.

3. The cold war held the United States in the grip of fear for years, especially in the late 1950s and early 1960s. In the library, look for some directives published during those years detailing how to construct and equip a backyard bomb shelter or how to behave during an air raid. You might also consider interviewing a parent, grandparent, or other person who has firsthand memories of this time period. Were these directives expressions of wisdom or of paranoia? Bring your findings together in a brief essay. You might also consider doing research in your college library as well as on the Internet and writing about the difficult task of worldwide nuclear disarmament in our post–cold war era, especially as more nations, such as India, Pakistan, and North Korea, demonstrate nuclear capabilities.

- To begin your research online, go to **bedfordstmartins.com /subjectsstrategies** and click on "Argumentation" or browse the thematic directory of annotated links.

ARGUMENT CLUSTER: WOMEN IN COMBAT

Although the draft was abolished in 1972, young men must register for the draft with the Selective Service within thirty days of their eighteenth birthday. With the wars in Afghanistan and Iraq, people are talking about reestablishing conscription. But this time there's a difference. Because of the increased presence of women in the military, people are asking if young women should be required, like their male counterparts, to register with the Selective Service and if women should be allowed to serve in combat positions. Although the debate continues, the war in Iraq made this last point somewhat moot as we learned that women had indeed been placed in harm's way — and were wounded, captured, and killed. Pictures and stories from the war zone added fuel to the debate because many of the women involved were mothers.

We have selected one photographer and four writers to give various perspectives on the debate of women in combat in hopes of provoking serious discussion and good argumentative essays about an issue that affects you and your peers. To provide context for the debate, we start with the picture of ex-POW Army Specialist Shoshana Johnson being carried on a stretcher as she prepares to fly home after receiving medical treatment from doctors at the Landstuhl Medical Center in Ramstein, Germany. In "Uncle Sam and Aunt Samantha," columnist Anna Quindlen argues that once Americans divest themselves of old-fashioned stereotypes there is only one choice — women, like men, should register for the draft. Conservative activist Linda Chavez, on the other hand, reminds us that "women are different from men, and their roles are not interchangeable," in spite of what feminists say. She asks that we consider our actions before training young women as warriors in the name of equality. Pulitzer Prize–winning journalist Anne Applebaum uses analogies from civilian life to argue that women, especially mothers, should be treated differently. She believes that "it is only when the armed forces are comfortable enough with women to treat them differently, and only when military mothers are comfortable enough to be treated differently, that we will know they have truly arrived." Finally, in "Rough Draft," Joel Beck reports on the federal discrimination lawsuit filed by five seniors at a Massachusetts high school who believe that "the way Selective Service works right now is grossly unconstitutional." He feels that now is the time to start thinking about a "different kind of draft" for our nation's young people.

PREPARING TO READ THE "WOMEN IN COMBAT" ARGUMENT CLUSTER

Equality between the sexes is the subject of many ongoing debates. Where in your own life do you still see gender inequality? With the United States fighting the war on terrorism, one of the hottest debates involving gender equity is women's role in the military. Like men, should women be required to register with the Selective Service when they turn eighteen? In combat, should women be put in roles that place them in harm's way? Should women be expected to perform the same jobs as men in time of war? Explain.

SEEING/READING

Ex-POW Army Spc.
Shoshana Johnson

Michael Probst

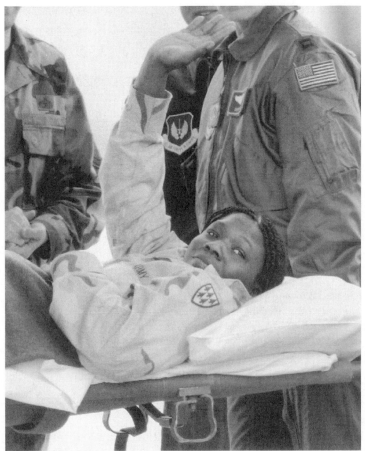

Michael Probst/AP/Wide World Photos

CONNECTING IMAGE AND TEXT

Army Spc. Shoshana Johnson waves to well-wishers as she prepares to board a plane at the U.S. air base in Ramstein, Germany, bound for Fort Bliss, Texas. A week earlier she had been a POW in Iraq. How do you "read" this photograph? What do you see in Johnson's eyes and facial expression? How did you feel when you learned that two women — Johnson and Jessica

Lynch — were among the first U.S. soldiers taken prisoner in Iraq? What were your first reactions to photographs of Johnson, Lynch, and the six other rescued POWs when they started to appear in the media in mid-April 2003? Where do you stand on the issue of women in combat? Does seeing a picture like this change your position? Explain. What about male POWs? Why do you think they receive less media attention than female POWs? Is that fair? Explain. Your observations will help guide you to the key themes and strategies in the essays that follow.

Uncle Sam and Aunt Samantha
Anna Quindlen

Born in Philadelphia in 1953, Anna Quindlen graduated from Barnard College in 1974. She became a reporter for the New York Times *and later a columnist, winning the Pulitzer Prize for her "Public and Private" column in 1992. Quindlen left the* Times *in 1994 to concentrate on writing fiction and her new column at* Newsweek *called "The Last Word." Quindlen's novels include* Object Lessons *(1991),* One True Thing *(1995),* Black and Blue *(1998), and* Blessings: A Novel *(2002). Her recent books,* How Reading Changed My Life *(1998) and* A Short Guide to a Happy Life *(2002), focus on everyday life issues, while* Loud and Clear *(2004) is a collection of essays.*

The following essay originally appeared in Quindlen's Newsweek *column in November 2001. At the time, the United States was preparing for war with the Taliban in Afghanistan. Quindlen, a mother of three, argues that women and men should both register for the draft.*

One out of every five new recruits in the United States military is female. 1

The Marines gave the Combat Action Ribbon for service in the Persian Gulf to 23 women. 2

Two female soldiers were killed in the bombing of the USS *Cole.* 3

The Selective Service registers for the draft all male citizens between the ages of 18 and 25. 4

What's wrong with this picture? 5

As Americans read and realize that the lives of most women in this country are as different from those of Afghan women as a Cunard cruise is from maximum-security lockdown, there has nonetheless been little attention paid to one persistent gender inequity in U.S. 6

public policy. An astonishing anachronism, really: While women are represented today in virtually all fields, including the armed forces, only men are required to register for the military draft that would be used in the event of a national-security crisis.

Since the nation is as close to such a crisis as it has been in more than 60 years, it's a good moment to consider how the draft wound up in this particular time warp. It's not the time warp of the Taliban, certainly, stuck in the worst part of the 13th century, forbidding women to attend school or hold jobs or even reveal their arms, forcing them into sex and marriage. Our own time warp is several decades old. The last time the draft was considered seriously was 20 years ago, when registration with the Selective Service was restored by Jimmy Carter after the Soviet invasion of, yep, Afghanistan. The president, as well as the Army chief of staff, asked at the time for the registration of women as well as men.

Amid a welter of arguments — women interfere with esprit de corps, women don't have the physical strength, women prisoners could be sexually assaulted, women soldiers would distract male soldiers from their mission — Congress shot down the notion of gender-blind registration. So did the Supreme Court, ruling that since women were forbidden to serve in combat positions and the purpose of the draft was to create a combat-ready force, it made sense not to register them.

But that was then, and this is now. Women have indeed served in combat positions, in the Balkans and the Middle East. More than 40,000 managed to serve in the Persian Gulf without destroying unit cohesion or failing because of upper-body strength. Some are even now taking out targets in Afghanistan from fighter jets, and apparently without any male soldier's falling prey to some predicted excess of chivalry or lust.

Talk about cognitive dissonance. All these military personnel, male and female alike, have come of age at a time when a significant level of parity was taken for granted. Yet they are supposed to accept that only males will be required to defend their country in a time of national emergency. This is insulting to men. And it is insulting to women. Caroline Forell, an expert on women's legal rights and a professor at the University of Oregon School of Law, puts it bluntly: "Failing to require this of women makes us lesser citizens."

Neither the left nor the right has been particularly inclined to consider this issue judiciously. Many feminists came from the antiwar movement and have let their distaste for the military in general and the draft in particular mute their response. In 1980 NOW released a resolution that buried support for the registration of women beneath opposition to the draft, despite the fact that the draft had been redesigned to eliminate the vexing inequities of Vietnam, when the sons of the working class served and the sons of the Ivy League did not. Conservatives, meanwhile, used an equal-opportunity draft as the linchpin of opposition to the Equal Rights Amendment, along with the terrifying specter of unisex bathrooms. (I have seen the urinal, and it is benign.) The legislative director of the right-wing group Concerned Women for America once defended the existing regulations by saying that most women "don't want to be included in the draft." All those young men who went to Canada during Vietnam and those who today register with fear and trembling in the face of the Trade Center devastation might be amazed to discover that lack of desire is an affirmative defense.

Parents face a series of unique new challenges in this more egalitarian world, not the least of which would be sending a daughter off to war. But parents all over this country are doing that right now, with daughters who enlisted; some have even expressed surprise that young women, in this day and age, are not required to register alongside their brothers and friends. While all involved in this debate over the years have invoked the assumed opposition of the people, even 10 years ago more than half of all Americans polled believed women should be made eligible for the draft. Besides, this is not about comfort but about fairness. My son has to register with the Selective Service this year, and if his sister does not when she turns 18, it makes a mockery not only of the standards of this household but of the standards of this nation.

It is possible in Afghanistan for women to be treated like little more than fecund pack animals precisely because gender fear and ignorance and hatred have been codified and permitted to hold sway. In this country, largely because of the concerted efforts of those allied with the women's movement over a century of struggle, much of that bigotry has been beaten back, even buried. Yet in improbable places the creaky old ways surface, the ways suggesting that we women were made of finer stuff. The finer stuff was usually porcelain, decorative and on the shelf, suitable for meals and show. Happily, the finer stuff has been transmuted into the right stuff. But with rights come responsibilities, as teachers like to tell their students. This is a responsibility that should fall equally upon all, male and female alike. If the empirical evidence is considered rationally, if the decision is divested of outmoded stereotypes, that's the only possible conclusion to be reached.

RESPONDING TO THE TEXT

Do you find Quindlen's argument for gender-blind draft registration convincing? Why or why not? What evidence does she present to dispel the "outmoded stereotypes" that dog any argument about gender equality and the military?

EXAMINING THE ISSUE CRITICALLY

1. Quindlen begins her essay with a quick list of facts and then the question, "What's wrong with this picture?" (paragraph 5) How did you answer her question? Was this an effective beginning for the issue she is writing about? (Glossary: *Beginnings/Endings*) Explain.

2. What is Quindlen's thesis? (Glossary: *Thesis*) Where does she state it? Where else might she have placed her thesis? Explain.

3. According to Quindlen, on what grounds did Congress and the Supreme Court vote down Jimmy Carter's request for gender-blind draft registration? Are these arguments still valid? Why or why not?

4. What evidence does Quindlen provide to support her claim that "neither the left nor the right has been particularly inclined to consider this issue [of a gender-blind draft] judiciously" (paragraph 11)? Do you think it is important for her to show that both liberals and conservatives are to blame for the current status of the draft registration law? Explain.

5. Toward the end of the essay, Quindlen uses a personal example to make a point about men and women and the draft. What do you think her purpose is in using her own family as an example? What does this example tell you about Quindlen herself?

Women in Combat Will Take a Toll on Our Culture

Linda Chavez

*Born in New Mexico in 1947 and raised in working-class Mexican Amer-
ican communities, Linda Chavez is a political activist and a writer. She
graduated from the University of Colorado in 1970 and pursued graduate
study at UCLA and the University of Maryland. Chavez's writings reflect
the evolution of her attitude toward ethnic diversity and multiculturalism
in the United States. She worked as a lobbyist with the National Education Association and subsequently as the assistant director of legislation
for the American Federation of Teachers (AFT) and as the editor of its
influential publication, the* American Educator. *During the Reagan administration, she served as the first female staff director of the U.S.
Commission on Civil Rights. Chavez has written widely on feminism, immigration, civil rights, and multiculturalism for* the Washington Post,
the Wall Street Journal, Commentary, National Review, *and* USA
Today. *Chavez's books include* Out of the Barrio: Toward a New Politics of Hispanic Assimilation *(1991),* Untitled on Multiculturalism
(2002), and An Unlikely Conservative: The Transformation of an Ex-
Liberal *(2002). Currently, she is president of the Center for Equal Opportunity.*

*The following essay first appeared in the online publication Town
Hall.com on April 20, 2003, as the fighting in Iraq culminated in the coalition's capture of Baghdad. In this article Chavez asks readers to consider the cultural implications of permitting women to serve in combat.*

N ow that the fighting in Iraq is all but over, it's time we ask some
hard questions about the role women soldiers played in this latest
American conflict. One woman died, and two others were taken
hostage, one of whom was severely injured, because their orders took
them close enough to danger to make the military's prohibition against
women serving in combat a mere fig leaf. Two of these women, including the female soldier who died, were also single mothers. There is no
question that these women performed bravely and honorably, but their
individual courage isn't the issue. What remains to be seen is whether it
is in our national interest — and civilization's — to send young women
and mothers into battle in the first place.

The debate over women in combat raged through much of the
1980s after the Supreme Court upheld the military's right to exclude
women from the draft largely because they were presumed unfit to
serve in combat. But with little notice or fanfare in the early 1990s,

female soldiers began performing roles that would take them ever closer to danger once fighting broke out.

At the Clinton administration's urging in 1993, Congress repealed laws that barred women from serving as members of combat aircraft and warship crews. The following year, Secretary of Defense Les Aspin repealed so-called "risk rules" that restricted women from certain jobs if they were deemed at high risk of hostile fire or capture. While the military still bars women from serving in combat per se, it no longer tries to keep them out of harm's way.

Feminists, always anxious to prove women are as tough and capable as men, applaud these changes, though I doubt many rushed down to recruiting offices in the months leading up to the war to put their principles to the test. Most young women who join the military do so to learn a skill, have a secure job with decent benefits, and serve their country. Among enlisted women, the desire to fight is minimal — only 29 percent believe women should be able to serve in combat positions, according to surveys taken by the Army in 1992. But whether some women are willing to kill — and risk being killed — to defend and serve their country isn't the point. The real issue is whether we should encourage them to do so.

No matter how much we modernists pretend otherwise, women are different from men, and their roles are not interchangeable. Females are not just smaller versions of males; they are also, on average, far less aggressive and more nurturing, qualities that suit them to be good mothers but not warriors. Not only do women do all the childbearing, but the period of their lives in which they can help perpetuate the species is far more limited than men's as well. As it so happens, females' prime childbearing years — their twenties — coincide with the age at which most male soldiers are likely to fall in combat.

Asked about the growing risk the new rules pose to soldiers who also happen to be mothers, one retired Army colonel snapped, "What about the males who get blown away? Which is worse, to lose the father of a child or the mother of a child?" It's hard to believe he didn't know the answer to that question. As tragic as the death of a father is in a young child's life, it simply can't compare to the loss of a mother.

Nor should we be concerned only with the prospect of the ultimate separation of mother and child when a female soldier dies. What about the effects of even a few months' separation of an infant or toddler from his or her soldier mom deployed halfway around the world? The military's only concern is that the soldier has a "care plan" in place so that combat readiness won't be impaired, but a generation of military dependents may be harmed by such indifference to their well-being.

In the name of equal opportunity for women in the military, we've 8
chosen to ignore nature — or worse, we're committed to altering it. We
may succeed in training succeeding generations of young women to
become warriors, but we can't begin to know the toll our hubris will
take on the individuals involved, their families, and our society.

RESPONDING TO THE TEXT

Chavez is well aware of the emotional energy surrounding the issue of allowing women to serve in combat positions. Do you think Chavez appeals
to her readers' emotions in trying to persuade them? If so, what can you
point to in her essay that led you to this conclusion?

EXAMINING THE ISSUE CRITICALLY

1. When this article was written, one woman had died and two others had
   been captured in Iraq. Since then others have died or been captured.
   How has the news of these casualties been received? Has the coverage of
   women casualties been different than that for men who have been
   killed, wounded, or captured? If so, how?

2. Although the military has rules that bar women from serving in combat
   roles, how have other rules been relaxed so that the military "no longer
   tries to keep them out of harm's way" (paragraph 3)?

3. Do you agree with Chavez's argument that "women are different from
   men, and their roles are not interchangeable" (paragraph 5)? Should
   women be denied equal opportunity in the military because they are
   nurturers, mothers, and do all the childbearing?

4. Chavez believes that "as tragic as the death of a father is in a young
   child's life, it simply can't compare to the loss of a mother" (paragraph
   6). How do you react to such a claim? Is such a comparison fair? Explain.

5. In the end, Chavez thinks that training young women to be warriors is
   not worth the unknown toll such an action will have "on the individuals involved, their families, and our society" (paragraph 8). Is it right to
   deny women equal opportunity because of some potential toll? Explain.

When Women Go to War

Anne Applebaum

Journalist, editor, and Pulitzer Prize–winning author, Anne Applebaum was born in 1964 in Washington D.C. She earned her B.A. at Yale University in 1986 and the following year was a Marshall Scholar at the London School of Economics and St. Anthony's College, Oxford. Applebaum began working as a journalist in 1988 in Poland as the Warsaw correspondent for the Economist. *While there she covered the collapse of communism in the Soviet Union and Eastern Europe. She went to London in 1992 where she worked for* Spectator *magazine and wrote a weekly column on British politics and foreign affairs for the* Daily Telegraph, *the* Sunday Telegraph, *and the* Evening Standard. *Her articles have also appeared in the* New York Times, Boston Globe, New Republic, Newsweek, Wall Street Journal, *and* Washington Post. *A specialist on Eastern European history, she authored the highly acclaimed* Between East and West: Across the Borderlands of Europe *(1994), an account of her search for cultures wiped out during the era of Stalin, and* Gulag: A History *(2003), a book for which she received the National Book Award nomination and the 2004 Pulitzer Prize for Nonfiction.*

In the following essay, first published in the Washington Post *on March 26, 2003, Applebaum joins the conversation about women in the military and speculates about what changes in official policy might be possible.*

The argument about women in combat is over. In fact, it was over three years ago, when two female sailors were among the victims of the bombing of the USS *Cole.* Women had been serving aboard U.S. combat ships only since 1994, yet these deaths — the first time any female sailor had been killed in hostile action onboard — did not lead to a reversal of policy. No special outrage accompanied the sight of "women in body bags" being brought home for burial, as many had predicted, either then or during the 1991 Persian Gulf War. Now, as we fight a new Gulf war, women constitute nearly a sixth of the armed forces. More than 90 percent of service positions, including most combat positions, are open to women. Although these facts have been noted once or twice in recent days, they have provoked no special angst. Right now, women are flying helicopters, launching missiles and dropping bombs on Iraqi cities, and American civilization has not collapsed as a result.

But if the argument about women in combat is over, the conversation about women in the military should not be — just as the conversation about women in the law, or in business, or in factories did not end when more women took those jobs. To see why, look no further than this week's front pages, some of which feature the face of Army Spc. Shoshana Johnson, a POW in Iraq and the single mother of a 2-year-old. Johnson's fate is heartbreaking, but it is not entirely unique. Johnson's child is one of tens of thousands who have been left behind while their mothers — or their mothers and their fathers — go off to war.

Is there anything wrong with that? That is, is there anything wrong with the fact that Johnson was where she was when she was, "in harm's way," as the Army puts it? Some think not. Carolyn Becraft, assistant secretary of the Navy in the Clinton administration, puts the case like this: "This is a volunteer military. Everyone who stays is there of their own free will. This is their job. These are the conditions of their employment. If they have children, they still have to be available for worldwide deployment." Official policy is no different, and no wonder. After the long struggle for acceptance, higher-ranking women in particular loathe the idea of treating mothers and fathers differently.

Dig a little deeper, though, and the angst is palpable. Very far off the record, one high-ranking Pentagon official admits to being deeply disturbed by photographs of women hugging their babies before leaving for war. "We're the United States of America. How can we ask a young woman to leave her infant?" A military women's Web site burns with acrimony. "My husband is on a ship already and we are overseas. I have no one to care for my child if we are both underway," writes one. Another has no sympathy: "As a childless single woman working hard to cover up the slack that foolish pregnant women like you give the military, I and others have every right to be mad." The awareness of a stereotype — that women get pregnant on ships in order to be sent home — leads another to describe the "shame" she felt after a planned pregnancy led to her discharge from the Navy and to write of how she longs, once again, "to serve my country with pride."

Should she be able to? In civilian life, it would be easy. Whereas many among the first generation of female lawyers, like the first generation of female fighter pilots, took two-week maternity leaves or refused to have children at all, those in the second generation — my generation — happily take off a year, or five years, or work three days a week indefinitely. This isn't because younger women have sold out, but because they, and the working world, have made a series of imperfect compromises. Women give up some seniority, and sometimes some money. In exchange, they get some time. Many, if not all, find this a fair compromise.

It is in this sense that the military now needs to catch up to the civilian world, to make that same generational shift. The American military offers its enlisted men and women enormous choices of training and education. Why shouldn't they also be offered the chance to take a few years off, and then to reenlist, with no stigma attached? The military takes dozens of factors into consideration when it deploys people. Why shouldn't single mothers be deliberately kept out of harm's way? Military traditions make some of these questions starker and harder than they would be in civilian life, but it doesn't make them illegitimate. In fact, it is only when the armed forces are comfortable enough with women to treat them differently, and only when military mothers are comfortable enough to be treated differently, that we will know they have truly arrived.

RESPONDING TO THE TEXT

In paragraph 3, Applebaum quotes "Carolyn Becraft, assistant secretary of the Navy in the Clinton administration," saying "This is a volunteer military. Everyone who stays is there of their own free will. This is their job. These are the conditions of their employment. If they have children, they still have to be available for worldwide deployment." How do you react to such a position? What changes, if any, to official policy do you think ought to be made? Explain.

EXAMINING THE ISSUE CRITICALLY

1. In her opening sentence, Applebaum concedes that "the argument about women in combat is over." Why do you think she chooses not to contest this issue?

2. According to Applebaum, what conversation about women in the military needs to take place? Why?

3. Do you think mothers should get special treatment? Why or why not? According to Applebaum, why do some military personnel, particularly higher-ranking women, "loathe the idea of treating mothers and fathers differently" (paragraph 3)?

4. In your opinion, should the military make the "generational shift" that Applebaum suggests in her final paragraph? What employment models does the civilian world offer that the military could adopt? Do you think such models would work in the military? Why or why not?

5. What is your reaction to the stereotype "that women get pregnant on ships in order to be sent home" (paragraph 4)? How does this stereotype affect the argument for equal roles for men and women in the military, in your opinion? Explain.

Rough Draft

Joel Beck

Joel Beck was born in Boston, Massachusetts, in 1976 and grew up in Foxboro. He received his B.A. in communications from Emerson College in Boston in 1998. He then took a job with WZLX radio in Boston as a promotions assistant and part-time disk jockey and on the side freelanced articles for a variety of local publications. Since 2000 he has been a full-time reporter and feature writer with Community Newspaper, a division of Boston Herald Media.

In the following essay, first published on January 27, 2003, in TownOnline.com, Beck uses a federal discrimination lawsuit filed against the U.S. government by five high school seniors from Ipswich, Massachusetts, to discuss the current system of draft registration and to explore the possibility of a draft that would involve universal service to the country.

Like most 17-year-old high school seniors, Nicole Foley has an awful lot on her plate. There are, of course, the typical activities: her schoolwork, going to swim meets, getting ready for graduation, having aspirations of one day becoming a doctor. In those ways, Foley is really no different from any of her peers at Ipswich High School. 1

It's safe to say, however, that none of Foley's classmates are involved in filing a federal discrimination lawsuit against the United States government for not allowing women to register for the military draft once they turn 18. 2

Sorry, Nicole. Looks like you're going to be all alone on that one. Trying to make women eligible for the military draft isn't exactly the kind of thing you do in high school to win friends and influence people, especially when very few 18-year-olds, male or female, have the desire to trade their Sony Playstation controllers for automatic weapons. What's next? Raising your hand at the end of class and reminding the teacher he forgot to assign homework? 3

Not quite. Foley has much bigger fish to fry. With the threat of a war with Iraq growing more likely with each passing day, talk about bringing back the draft persists (although many believe it's highly unlikely). And Foley stands by her conviction that the way Selective Service works right now is grossly unconstitutional. 4

"It seems that what people are saying (about the draft) is very outdated," Foley says. "It's like they've had this view of how our society is supposed to work and it's just ingrained in them. It's like they should be in the 1950s." 5

But Foley will also tell you that sexual discrimination is just the beginning when it comes to flaws in the draft's system. For example, history has shown that socioeconomic issues often spell doom for minorities and lower to middle class citizens when it comes to being drafted.

And somehow, the bugs in the system can seem particularly blatant when even fictional characters are left vulnerable to the draft. Like the case of "Johnny Klomberg," who received his Selective Service notification back in 1984. The only problem being, Johnny Klomberg was the invention by two California teens who used the name on a commercial mailing list for an ice cream club.

Translation: Uncle Sam will take fictional characters in his draft. But women? Forget about it.

But in times like these — with escalating conflict on the world stage and a president who seems hell bent on some sort of military action — the draft comes back into people's minds, and under scrutiny. Just ask the parents and grandparents who lived through Vietnam, and who now face the prospect of their own loved ones being forced to fight in a war in which they may have no personal interest or knowledge.

That thought certainly occurred to Danvers resident Kathy Simons when her son Evan — now a participant in Foley's lawsuit — recently received his Selective Service registration card in the mail.

"It was a terrifying moment," Kathy Simons says. "That card brought home, in a powerful way that he was old enough, eligible, and vulnerable to whatever world events might bring our way."

DINNER TALK

If all families had dinner conversations like the ones held at the Foleys', it's possible that a lot more would get accomplished in this country.

One night, during an otherwise ho-hum evening at the dinner table, Foley's stepbrother, Sam Schwartz, casually mentioned that he had filled out and mailed his Selective Service postcard, as is mandatory for all men in the U.S. when they turn 18. Naturally, Foley inquired about when she would have to do the same, and was taken aback when she was told it wasn't necessary for her to do so.

Even though women are allowed to participate in more than 90 percent of military activities, Uncle Sam still doesn't want them to register for the draft.

Enter Foley's stepfather, Boston civil rights attorney Harvey Schwartz, who recently filed the lawsuit on behalf of both Nicole and Sam and three of their friends. Schwartz readily admits that these are two of the most non-violent kids in the world, but that they each realize the enormous significance of the steps they are taking to change the law.

"Neither of the kids are particularly anxious to serve in the military," the elder Schwartz says. "Sam has said he would fight in a just war, or a war that he believed in. But I wouldn't expect either one of them to be enlisting anytime soon. 16

"On the other hand, they both pay attention to politics," he adds. "There's a lot of talk about politics at our house." 17

Foley says the reasoning behind the lawsuit is truly multi-layered. On one hand, she says it's somewhat staggering that in the year 2003 and at the height of political correctness, there remains a mindset that women should simply stay at home while the big, brave men go off and fight our wars. 18

More importantly, she says having both men and women subjected to the draft may make people think twice about whether there should even be a draft at all. That, she says, makes up the backbone of the lawsuit. 19

"I don't think there should be a draft in place and that's really what we're saying," Foley says. "I think (a draft with both men and women) would make people a little more aware that if we go in and fight a war, there's going to be consequences. People are going to have to go and fight and people are going to die. 20

"If people start thinking that it could be not only their son, but also their daughter, hopefully they would think about the consequences a little bit more." 21

AN OBSOLETE SYSTEM

In many ways, the Foley-Schwartz initiative mirrors the proposal recently brought forth by U.S. Rep. Charles Rangel, D-N.Y. 22

Rangel, in a half-serious way, has introduced a bill to Congress to bring back the draft for the first time since it was abolished in 1972. Like Foley, Rangel's motives lean toward putting a more human face on a possible draft, in the hopes of getting people to realize that there would be real people going to war, not just anonymous soldiers. 23

On the surface, Rangel's proposal may seem logical, but there are those who have their doubts about its merits. 24

"I think Charlie's point was well-made," says Rangel's colleague, Rep. John Tierney of Salem, who has spoken publicly against the United States going to war with Iraq. "But I don't think he's gotten a groundswell of support for his bill by any means. 25

"I think people are hesitant to go with a draft for a number of rea- 26
sons," Tierney says. "Logistically and financially, you don't know
whether or not you have the need for as many troops as a draft may
generate."

Given the sheer volume of troops who are already in or en route 27
to the Persian Gulf for a possible standoff with Iraq, it's difficult to
argue with Tierney's rationale. This week, the Army sent 37,000 more
troops into the Gulf, and the total is expected to reach 250,000 in the
next few weeks. That kind of manpower, coupled with the idea that
technology has advanced to the point where a war in 2003 is far different from a war like Vietnam, gives credence to the theory that a
military draft may be obsolete.

But obsolete or not, some say it could have its merits. 28

Karl Ford, a Vietnam veteran from Beverly, is on the fence when it 29
comes to reinstating the draft. But while he admits that there is really
no need for as many fighting bodies as there were in Vietnam, he
stands by the idea that the government should require people to serve
in one way or another.

"Warfare has changed a lot," Ford says. "With the way wars are 30
being fought now, yes, it is more highly technical. But even with that,
you're going to need a lot of good technical people doing this stuff.
Who's to say that the people who are volunteering and going into the
military now are the best people to do that?"

DO WE REALLY HAVE A CHOICE?

There is perhaps a touch of irony in the fact that Sam Schwartz and 31
Nicole Foley are the ones who have become anti-draft activists. Historically, they are exactly the kind of people who never get drafted in the
first place.

Realistically, a pair of smart, college-bound 18-year-old kids from 32
Ipswich stand about as much a chance of being drafted as the Red Sox
have of outbidding the Yankees for a top free agent.

But Foley realizes that there aren't many people like her in the 33
military, and that not even many politicians truly know what it's like
to have someone close to them serving in the armed forces. She's
quick to point out that of the 533 members of Congress, only one has
a child who is serving in the military. That's a number that Tierney
says strikes him as being pretty disturbing.

"You do wonder how many CEOs' kids are in (the military)," he 34
says. "I've heard a lot of people commenting on that very thought. If
your own kid was really going to go, you'd think a little harder about
this."

Amy Hasbrouck takes that one step further. As a member of the 35
Revere/Malden Committee Against War, Hasbrouck says that if the
draft was ever brought back, there would be people all over the country
marked for it well before they received their notices in the mail. And
none of them would come from Ipswich.

"Under a draft, white people and middle class people have options 36
for evading the draft," Hasbrouck says. "They do it either through de-
ferment, attending college, or through political connections their parents may have to get them out of mandatory service. So it's the poor
black people who end up serving."

While Hasbrouck commends Foley and her family for their ef- 37
forts to shed light on the issue of equality, she says allowing women
to register for the draft might only add to the already existing inequality.

"It's just going to reflect the same thing," she says. "Poor women 38
and black women are just going to be subjected to the same thing."

A DIFFERENT KIND OF DRAFT

There aren't many people in the world who will say that going to Viet- 39
nam was the best thing to ever happen to them.

Count Ford among the minority. 40

Ford was an 18-year-old, fresh-out-of-high-school kid when he de- 41
cided to enlist in the armed forces, knowing that as someone with little direction in his life, he was "prime meat" to be drafted anyway.

Ford knows full well that going to fight in combat isn't the right 42
path for everyone, but he says he definitely came back from Vietnam a
better person. Though he admits the current system for a draft needs
a lot of work, he says other young men and women might undergo the
same positive, life-changing experiences he saw from serving in the
military.

"I know of some young people who are 19 or 20 and they're really 43
floundering," Ford says. "They remind me of me. I went to 'Nam and
I'll tell you, I wouldn't trade the experience for anything. There were a
lot of negative experiences about it, but I think people do a lot of
growing up. It doesn't have to be in the military either. You could
send them to the ghetto and have them work there. A lot of people are
just too disengaged from reality. I know I was."

Realistically, Ford says he knows there is little chance of there 44
being another draft any time soon, at least not under the Bush Administration. Knowing that many Americans are already vehemently opposed to war with Iraq, he says a draft would simply throw another
monkey wrench into Bush's plans.

With that in mind, however, Congressman Tierney agrees that there 45 may be something to the idea of requiring people to serve their country in one way or another. Though not everyone would be best suited for hand-to-hand combat, he says devising a fair and equal system where people from all stretches of the country are called upon to serve may be something to think about.

"I don't think it's necessarily a bad idea," Tierney says. "Military 46 service could be just one option, depending on the slots there are to fill. But giving people the prospect of serving their country in some way, I kind of wish that option had been available when I was that age."

RESPONDING TO THE TEXT

In most discussions of the Selective Service registration and military service, gender issues tend to overshadow socioeconomic issues. What socioeconomic issues need to be considered? How, if at all, do you think these issues can be resolved?

EXAMINING THE ISSUE CRITICALLY

1. Seventeen-year-old Nicole Foley filed a lawsuit against the federal government for "not allowing women to register for the military draft once they turn 18" (paragraph 2). Does she really want to be required to register? If not, what is the purpose of her lawsuit?

2. What are the major problems with the way the Selective Service currently operates? How is it "grossly unconstitutional" (paragraph 4) as Foley claims?

3. What, if anything, is wrong with America's current all-volunteer military? Why do you suppose Rep. Charles Rangel introduced a bill to reinstate the draft system abolished in 1972? Do you think the draft is obsolete? Explain.

4. What does Beck find ironic in the fact that Nicole Foley and her stepbrother Sam Schwartz are cast in the role of "anti-draft activists"? (Glossary: *Irony*) Is it important for people like them to take a stand on this issue, or do you think they are simply grandstanding? Explain.

5. What do you think about "the idea of requiring people to serve their country in one way or another" (paragraph 45)? What advantages or disadvantages would such a "draft" have? How would a two-year commitment to serve your country affect your life? What types of jobs could you see yourself performing in such a commitment?

6. What inequalities in the draft system does Beck cite in his essay? In your opinion, would required national service solve those inequalities? Explain.

MAKING CONNECTIONS: WRITING AND DISCUSSION SUGGESTIONS FOR "WOMEN IN COMBAT"

The following questions are offered to help you start making meaningful connections among the four articles and photograph in this argument cluster. These questions can be used for class discussion, or you can choose to answer any one of them by writing an essay. If you choose the essay option, be sure to make specific references to at least two or three of the cluster articles. With several of the questions, some additional research may be required. To begin your research online, go to **bedfordstmartins.com/subjectsstrategies** and click on "Women in Combat" or browse the thematic directory of annotated links.

1. Although Quindlen, Chavez, Applebaum, and Beck address the general topic of women in combat, each approaches the issue from a different angle and cites different evidence to support his or her position. (Glossary: *Evidence*) How do you think each of the writers would use Probst's photograph of Shoshana Johnson (p. 537) to illustrate his or her points and support his or her arguments? Whose position, in your opinion, is best supported by Probst's photograph? Why? Write an essay in which you defend your conclusion. Before you write, refer to your Connecting Image and Text response for this cluster.

2. Quindlen believes that the solution to the question of draft registration is to require both men and women to register. Where do you stand on the issue of requiring both sexes to register? Using your own experience as well as evidence from the cluster readings, write an essay in which you defend your position.

3. In any discussion of women in combat, certain stereotypes about women and their social roles are bound to emerge. How have such stereotypes kept women out of combat and harm's way in the past? Have any of these stereotypes recently changed? If so, to what effect? Do you agree with Chavez's assessment that women are "far less aggressive and more nurturing [than men], qualities that suit them to be good mothers but not warriors" (paragraph 5)? In an essay consider whether or not women should be allowed to fill combat positions in time of war.

4. Applebaum believes that the "military now needs to catch up to the civilian world" (paragraph 6). She wonders why enlisted men and women shouldn't be "offered the chance to take a few years off, and then to reenlist, with no stigma attached" (6). What are the merits of her proposal? Are there any considerations that would render her plan impractical? Write an essay in which you support or oppose Applebaum's idea.

5. Beck explores "the idea of requiring people to serve their country in one way or another" (paragraph 45). Is America ready for a draft that would require universal service of all its young people? Should military service be one option under such a system, or should this public service

be kept separate from the military? What would be the advantages and disadvantages of a universal service program to the country? To the individuals serving? What obstacles would need to be overcome to ensure that this new draft was fair and equitable? Write a proposal in which you call on Congress to consider a plan for universal service, or write an essay in which you argue against such a plan.

6. One way to eliminate the debate about requiring women as well as men to register with the Selective Service would be for Congress to abolish the draft law itself. In deciding on the prudence of such an action, we should consider the following questions. Should citizens be required to perform military service, or should the military be voluntary as it is now? How can we ensure that socioeconomic factors do not define the makeup of an all-volunteer military? How do you think each of the writers in this argument cluster would respond to this question? Write an argumentative essay in which you support or oppose eliminating the draft law altogether.

7. Think of a policy in which people are treated differently based on gender, age, race, or some other distinction. The policy could be one of either your college, local government, state government, or federal government. For example, most states require that people be twenty-one to drink, eighteen to buy cigarettes, or sixteen to drive a car. Using "Uncle Sam and Aunt Samantha" as a model, write an essay in which you argue for or against your chosen policy. Try to include the policy's history in your argument to give your audience a greater understanding of the policy. (Glossary: *Audience*)

8. Using your Preparing to Read and Connecting Image and Text responses for this cluster as starting points, write an essay in which you argue for or against a certain way men and women are treated differently. Be sure to address possible objections to your point of view. For example, if you argue that women should be allowed to play professional sports alongside men, you should refute any objections that your audience might have, such as safety issues and physical differences between men and women. (Glossary: *Audience*) Be sure to provide clear and specific examples that support your position. (Glossary: *Evidence; Exemplification*)

ARGUMENT CLUSTER: GENETICALLY MODIFIED FOOD

In 1960 Dr. Seuss, in the character of Sam-I-Am, first asked children the world over, "Do you like green eggs and ham?" The knee-jerk answer to Sam's question about this strange new food was "I will not eat them anywhere. I do not eat green eggs and ham." To get some peace from Sam's constant badgering, the nameless protagonist finally agrees to try them and discovers, "I like green eggs and ham." Today discussion continues about the foods we consume, but the debate has moved beyond the pages of a children's book. The strange new foods are ones that have been genetically modified; unlike green eggs and ham, these new foods are not visibly different. Biotechnology has created a new world of agriculture that — depending upon your point of view — is either the answer to the world's food supply and environmental problems or an environmental holocaust in the making. The truth perhaps lies somewhere between these two positions.

We have selected one photographer and four writers to give various perspectives on the controversy surrounding genetically modified food in hopes of provoking serious discussion and good argumentative essays about a technology that affects the food we eat and the environment we inhabit. To provide context for the debate we start with George Olson's photograph of two workers in safety suits spraying potato seedings. In "Will Frankenfood Save the Planet?" writer Jonathan Rauch surprises most environmentalists by answering in the affirmative. His investigations led him to conclude that "biotechnology will transform agriculture, and in doing so will transform environmentalism." Biologist David Ehrenfeld believes that the so-called biotech miracles are based upon shaky science at best. In "A Techno-Pox Upon the Land," he argues that biotech corporations should come under close scrutiny as they are apt to ignore consumer fears and environmental questions in their quest for profits. Nutrition and diet expert Jane E. Brody tries to reassure readers that there's little cause for panic when it comes to genetically modified foods. In "Gene-Altered Foods: A Case Against Panic," she surveys the current and potential benefits of genetic engineering as well as the real and potential risks. Finally, in "Weeding Out the Skilled Farmer," livestock rancher Jim Scharplaz worries that biotechnology is changing the face of agriculture. With the industrialization of agriculture, America's food system is becoming controlled by a small number of powerful corporations. Scharplaz believes that this is cause for concern: "The mistake of one huge corporation could create catastrophe" for our nation's food supply.

PREPARING TO READ THE "GENETICALLY MODIFIED FOOD" ARGUMENT CLUSTER

How much do you know about the food you eat? Do you know where and how it was grown or raised? Do you look for labels that say "organic" when shopping? What have you heard or read about genetically modified foods? What questions would you like answers to before making the decision to eat genetically modified foods?

SEEING/READING

Spraying Potato Seedlings
George Olson

George Olson/Woodfin Camp & Assoc.

CONNECTING IMAGE AND TEXT

How do you "read" this photograph? What feelings does this picture of two workers — outfitted with safety suits and gas masks — spraying a field of potato seedings for agricultural pests evoke in you? Do these two figures fit your image of traditional agricultural workers? How hazardous do you think the material they are spraying is? How does the surrounding landscape strike you? In what types of situations are workers required to wear such gear? Would you be inclined to eat the food harvested from this field? Explain. Your observations will help guide you to the key themes and strategies in the essays that follow.

Will Frankenfood Save the Planet?

Jonathan Rauch

Jonathan Rauch was born in 1960 in Phoenix, Arizona. He earned his B.A. at Yale University in 1982 and then took his first job as an education reporter for the Winston-Salem Journal *in North Carolina. He later moved to Washington D.C. to work for the* National Journal, *where he continues as a contributing editor and senior writer. In addition, he is a correspondent for the* Atlantic Monthly *and a writer-in-residence at the Brookings Institution. His books include* The Outnation: A Search for the Soul of Japan *(1992),* Kindly Inquisitors: The New Attacks on Free Thought *(1993),* Demosclerosis: The Silent Killer of American Government *(1994), and* Government's End: Why Washington Stopped Working *(2000). Rauch is a frequent contributor to the* Los Angeles Times, New York Times, *and* Washington Post.

First published in the October 2003 issue of the Atlantic Monthly, *"Will Frankenfood Save the Planet?" explores the world of genetic engineering. In a surprising argument, Rauch challenges America's environmentalists to be more open to the possibilities of genetic modification, to become the "constituency for earth-friendly biotechnology."*

That genetic engineering may be the most environmentally benefi- 1
cial technology to have emerged in decades, or possibly centuries, is not immediately obvious. Certainly, at least, it is not obvious to the many U.S. and foreign environmental groups that regard biotechnology as a *bete noire*.[1] Nor is it necessarily obvious to people who grew up in cities, and who have only an inkling of what happens on a modern farm. Being agriculturally illiterate myself, I set out to look at what may be, if the planet is fortunate, the farming of the future.

It was baking hot that April day. I traveled with two Virginia state 2
soil-and-water-conservation officers and an agricultural-extension agent to an area not far from Richmond. The farmers there are national (and therefore world) leaders in the application of what is known as continuous no-till farming. In plain English, they don't plough. For thousands of years, since the dawn of the agricultural revolution, farmers have ploughed, often several times a year; and with ploughing has come runoff that pollutes rivers and blights aquatic habitat, erosion that wears away the land, and the release into the atmosphere of greenhouse

---

[1] a subject of extreme dislike [Ed.]

gases stored in the soil. Today, at last, farmers are working out methods that have begun to make ploughing obsolete.

At about one-thirty we arrived at a 200-acre patch of farmland known as the Good Luck Tract. No one seemed to know the provenance[2] of the name, but the best guess was that somebody had said something like "You intend to farm this? Good luck!" The land was rolling, rather than flat, and its slopes came together to form natural troughs for rainwater. Ordinarily this highly erodible land would be suitable for cows, not crops. Yet it was dense with wheat — wheat yielding almost twice what could normally be expected, and in soil that had grown richer in organic matter, and thus more nourishing to crops, even as the land was farmed. Perhaps most striking was the almost complete absence of any chemical or soil runoff. Even the beating administered in 1999 by Hurricane Floyd, which lashed the ground with nineteen inches of rain in less than twenty-four hours, produced no significant runoff or erosion. The land simply absorbed the sheets of water before they could course downhill.

At another site, a few miles away, I saw why. On land planted in corn whose shoots had only just broken the surface, Paul Davis, the extension agent, wedged a shovel into the ground and dislodged about eight inches of topsoil. Then he reached down and picked up a clump. Ploughed soil, having been stirred up and turned over again and again, becomes lifeless and homogeneous, but the clump that Davis held out was alive. I immediately noticed three squirming earthworms, one grub, and quantities of tiny white insects that looked very busy. As if in greeting, a worm defecated. "Plant-available food!" a delighted Davis exclaimed.

This soil, like that of the Good Luck Tract, had not been ploughed for years, allowing the underground ecosystem to return. Insects and roots and microorganisms had given the soil an elaborate architecture, which held the earth in place and made it a sponge for water. That was why erosion and runoff had been reduced to practically nil. Crops thrived because worms were doing the ploughing. Crop residue that was left on the ground, rather than ploughed under as usual, provided nourishment for the soil's biota[3] and, as it decayed, enriched the soil. The farmer saved the fuel he would have used driving back and forth with a heavy plough. That saved money, and of course it also saved energy and reduced pollution. On top of all that, crop yields were better than with conventional methods.

The conservation people in Virginia were full of excitement over no-till farming. Their job was to clean up the James and York Rivers and the rest of the Chesapeake Bay watershed. Most of the sediment

---

[2]origin [Ed.]
[3]plant and animal life [Ed.]

that clogs and clouds the rivers, and most of the fertilizer runoff that causes the algae blooms that kill fish, comes from farmland. By all but eliminating agricultural erosion and runoff — so Brian Noyes, the local conservation-district manager, told me — continuous no-till could "revolutionize" the area's water quality.

Even granting that Noyes is an enthusiast, from an environmental   7 point of view no-till farming looks like a dramatic advance. The rub — if it is a rub — is that the widespread elimination of the plough depends on genetically modified crops.

It is only a modest exaggeration to say that as goes agriculture, so   8 goes the planet. Of all the human activities that shape the environment, agriculture is the single most important, and it is well ahead of whatever comes second. Today about 38 percent of the earth's land area is cropland or pasture — a total that has crept upward over the past few decades as global population has grown. The increase has been gradual, only about 0.3 percent a year; but that still translates into an additional Greece or Nicaragua cultivated or grazed every year.

Farming does not go easy on the earth, and never has. To farm is   9 to make war upon millions of plants (weeds, so-called) and animals (pests, so-called) that in the ordinary course of things would crowd out or eat or infest whatever it is a farmer is growing. Crop monocultures, as whole fields of only wheat or corn or any other single plant are called, make poor habitat and are vulnerable to disease and disaster. Although fertilizer runs off and pollutes water, farming without fertilizer will deplete and eventually exhaust the soil. Pesticides can harm the health of human beings and kill desirable or harmless bugs along with pests. Irrigation leaves behind trace elements that can accumulate and poison the soil. And on and on.

The trade-offs are fundamental. Organic farming, for example, uses   10 no artificial fertilizer, but it does use a lot of manure, which can pollute water and contaminate food. Traditional farmers may use less herbicide, but they also do more ploughing, with all the ensuing environmental complications. Low-input agriculture uses fewer chemicals but more land. The point is not that farming is an environmental crime — it is not — but that there is no escaping the pressure it puts on the planet.

In the next half century the pressure will intensify. The United   11 Nations, in its midrange projections, estimates that the earth's human population will grow by more than 40 percent, from 6.3 billion people today to 8.9 billion in 2050. Feeding all those people, and feeding their billion or so hungry pets (a dog or a cat is one of the first things people want once they move beyond a subsistence lifestyle), and providing the increasingly protein-rich diets that an increasingly wealthy world will expect — doing all of that will require food output to at least double, and possibly triple.

But then the story will change. According to the UN's midrange   12 projections (which may, if anything, err somewhat on the high side), around 2050 the world's population will more or less level off. Even if the growth does not stop, it will slow. The crunch will be over. In fact, if in 2050 crop yields are still increasing, if most of the world is economically developed, and if population pressures are declining or even reversing — all of which seems reasonably likely — then the human species may at long last be able to feed itself, year in and year out, without putting any additional net stress on the environment. We might even be able to grow everything we need while reducing our agricultural footprint: returning cropland to wilderness, repairing damaged soils, restoring ecosystems, and so on. In other words, human agriculture might be placed on a sustainable footing forever: a breathtaking prospect.

The great problem, then, is to get through the next four or five decades with as little environmental damage as possible. That is where biotechnology comes in. 13

"Biotech" can refer to a number of things, but the relevant application here is genetic modification: the selective transfer of genes from one organism to another. Ordinary breeding can cross related varieties, but it cannot take a gene from a bacterium, for instance, and transfer it to a wheat plant. The organisms resulting from gene transfers are called "transgenic" by scientists — and "Frankenfood" by many greens.[4] 14

Gene transfer poses risks, unquestionably. So, for that matter, does traditional crossbreeding. But many people worry that transgenic organisms might prove more unpredictable. One possibility is that transgenic crops would spread from fields into forests or other wild lands and there become environmental nuisances, or worse. A further risk is that transgenic plants might cross-pollinate with neighboring wild plants, producing "superweeds" or other invasive or destructive varieties in the wild. Those risks are real enough that even most biotech enthusiasts favor some government regulation of transgenic crops. 15

What is much less widely appreciated is biotech's potential to do the environment good. Take as an example continuous no-till farming, which really works best with the help of transgenic crops. Human beings have been ploughing for so long that we tend to forget why we started doing it in the first place. The short answer: weed control. Turning over the soil between plantings smothers weeds and their seeds. If you don't plough, your land becomes a weed garden — unless you use herbicides to kill the weeds. Herbicides, however, are expensive, and can be complicated to apply. And they tend to kill the good with the bad. 16

In the mid-1990s the agricultural-products company Monsanto introduced a transgenic soybean variety called Roundup Ready. As the name implies, these soybeans tolerate Roundup, an herbicide (also 17

---

[4]environmentalists [Ed.]

made by Monsanto) that kills many kinds of weeds and then quickly breaks down into harmless ingredients. Equipped with Roundup Ready crops, farmers found that they could retire their ploughs and control weeds with just a few applications of a single, relatively benign herbicide — instead of many applications of a complex and expensive menu of chemicals. More than a third of all U.S. soybeans are now grown without ploughing, mostly owing to the introduction of Roundup Ready varieties. Ploughless cotton farming has likewise received a big boost from the advent of bioengineered varieties. No-till farming without biotech is possible, but it's more difficult and expensive, which is why no-till and biotech are advancing in tandem.

In 2001 a group of scientists announced that they had engineered a transgenic tomato plant able to thrive on salty water — water, in fact, almost half as salty as seawater, and fifty times as salty as tomatoes can ordinarily abide. One of the researchers was quoted as saying, "I've already transformed tomato, tobacco, and canola. I believe I can transform any crop with this gene" — just the sort of Frankenstein hubris that makes environmentalists shudder. But consider the environmental implications. Irrigation has for millennia been a cornerstone of agriculture, but it comes at a price. As irrigation water evaporates, it leaves behind traces of salt, which accumulate in the soil and gradually render it infertile. (As any Roman legion knows, to destroy a nation's agricultural base you salt the soil.) Every year the world loses about 25 million acres — an area equivalent to a fifth of California — to salinity; 40 percent of the world's irrigated land, and 25 percent of America's, has been hurt to some degree. For decades traditional plant breeders tried to create salt-tolerant crop plants, and for decades they failed. Salt-tolerant crops might bring millions of acres of wounded or crippled land back into production.

One of the first biotech crops to reach the market, in the mid-1990s, was a cotton plant that makes its own pesticide. Scientists incorporated into the plant a toxin-producing gene from a soil bacterium known as *Bacillus thuringiensis*. With Bt cotton, as it is called, farmers can spray much less, and the poison contained in the plant is delivered only to bugs that actually eat the crop. As any environmentalist can tell you, insecticide is not very nice stuff — especially if you breathe it, which many Third World farmers do as they walk through their fields with backpack sprayers.

Transgenic cotton reduced pesticide use by more than two million pounds in the United States from 1996 to 2000, and it has reduced pesticide sprayings in parts of China by more than half. Earlier this year the Environmental Protection Agency approved a genetically modified corn that resists a beetle larva known as rootworm. Because rootworm is American corn's most voracious enemy, this new variety has the potential to reduce animal pesticide use in America by more than 14 million pounds. It could reduce or eliminate the spraying of pesticide on 23 million acres of U.S. land.

All of that is the beginning, not the end. Bioengineers are also working, for instance, on crops that tolerate aluminum, another major contaminant of soil, especially in the tropics. Return an acre of farmland to productivity, or double yields on an already productive acre, and, other things being equal, you reduce by an acre the amount of virgin forest or savannah that will be stripped and cultivated. That may be the most important benefit of all.

Habitat destruction remains a serious environmental problem; in some respects it is the most serious. The savannahs and tropical forests of Central and South America, Asia, and Africa by and large make poor farmland, but they are the earth's storehouses of biodiversity, and the forests are the earth's lungs. Since 1972 about 200,000 square miles of Amazon rain forest have been cleared for crops and pasture; from 1966 to 1994 all but three of the Central American countries cleared more forest than they left standing. Mexico is losing more than 4,000 square miles of forest a year to peasant farms; sub-Saharan Africa is losing more than 19,000.

That is why the great challenge of the next four or five decades is not to feed an additional three billion people (and their pets) but to do so without converting much of the world's prime habitat into second- or third-rate farmland. Now, most agronomists agree that some substantial yield improvements are still to be had from advances in conventional breeding, fertilizers, herbicides, and other standbys. But it seems pretty clear that biotechnology holds more promise — probably much more. Recall that world food output will need to at least double and possibly triple over the next several decades. Even if production could be increased that much using conventional technology, which is doubtful, the required amounts of pesticide and fertilizer and other polluting chemicals would be immense. If properly developed, disseminated, and used, genetically modified crops might well be the best hope the planet has got.

Biotech companies are in business to make money. That is fitting and proper. But developing and testing new transgenic crops is expensive and commercially risky, to say nothing of politically controversial. When they decide how to invest their research-and-development money, biotech companies will naturally seek products for which farmers and consumers will pay top dollar. Roundup Ready products, for instance, are well suited to U.S. farming, with its high levels of capital spending on such things as herbicides and automated sprayers. Poor farmers in the developing world, of course, have much less buying power. Creating, say, salt-tolerant cassava suitable for growing on hardscrabble African farms might save habitat as well as lives — but commercial enterprises are not likely to fall over one another in a rush to do it.

If earth-friendly transgenics are developed, the next problem is 25 disseminating them. As a number of the farmers and experts I talked to were quick to mention, switching to an unfamiliar new technology — something like no-till — is not easy. It requires capital investment in new seed and equipment, mastery of new skills and methods, a fragile transition period as farmer and ecology readjust, and an often considerable amount of trial and error to find out what works best on any given field. Such problems are only magnified in the Third World, where the learning curve is steeper and capital cushions are thin to nonexistent. Just handing a peasant farmer a bag of newfangled seed is not enough. In many cases peasant farmers will need one-on-one attention. Many will need help to pay for the seed, too.

Finally there is the matter of using biotech in a way that actually 26 benefits the environment. Often the technological blade can cut either way, especially in the short run. A salt-tolerant or drought-resistant rice that allowed farmers to keep land in production might also induce them to plough up virgin land that previously was too salty or too dry to farm. If the effect of improved seed is to make farming more profitable, farmers may respond, at least temporarily, by bringing more land into production. If a farm becomes more productive, it may require fewer workers; and if local labor markets cannot provide jobs for them, displaced workers may move to a nearby patch of rainforest and burn it down to make way for subsistence farming. Such transition problems are solvable, but they need money and attention.

In short, realizing the great — probably unique — environmental 27 potential of biotech will require stewardship. "It's a tool," Sara Scherr, an agricultural economist with the conservation group Forest Trends, told me, "but it's absolutely not going to happen automatically."

So now ask a question: Who is the natural constituency for earth- 28 friendly biotechnology? Who cares enough to lobby governments to underwrite research — frequently unprofitable research — on transgenic crops that might restore soils or cut down on pesticides in poor countries? Who cares enough to teach Asian or African farmers, one by one, how to farm without ploughing? Who cares enough to help poor farmers afford high-tech, earth-friendly seed? Who cares enough to agitate for programs and reforms that might steer displaced peasants and profit-seeking farmers away from sensitive lands? Not politicians, for the most part. Not farmers. Not corporations. Not consumers.

At the World Resources Institute, an environmental think tank in 29 Washington, the molecular biologist Don Doering envisions transgenic crops designed specifically to solve environmental problems: crops that might fertilize the soil, crops that could clean water, crops tailored to remedy the ecological problems of specific places. "Suddenly you might find yourself with a virtually chemical-free agriculture, where your cropland itself is filtering the water, it's protecting the watershed, it's providing habitat," Doering told me. "There is still so little investment in what I call design-for-environment." The natural constituency for such investment is, of course, environmentalists.

But environmentalists are not acting as such a constituency today. They are doing the opposite. For example, Greenpeace declares on its Web site: "The introduction of genetically engineered (GE) organisms into the complex ecosystems of our environment is a dangerous global experiment with nature and evolution . . . GE organisms must not be released into the environment. They pose unacceptable risks to ecosystems, and have the potential to threaten biodiversity, wildlife, and sustainable forms of agriculture." 30

Other groups argue for what they call the Precautionary Principle, under which no transgenic crop could be used until proven benign in virtually all respects. The Sierra Club says on its Web site, 31

> In accordance with this Precautionary Principle, we call for a moratorium on the planting of all genetically engineered crops and the release of all GEOs [genetically engineered organisms] into the environment, including those now approved. Releases should be delayed until extensive, rigorous research is done which determines the long-term environmental and health impacts of each GEO and there is public debate to ascertain the need for the use of each GEO intended for release into the environment.

Under this policy the cleaner water and healthier soil that continuous no-till farming has already brought to the Chesapeake Bay watershed would be undone, and countless tons of polluted runoff and eroded topsoil would accumulate in Virginia rivers and streams while debaters debated and researchers researched. For reasons having more to do with politics than with logic, the modern environmental movement was to a large extent founded on suspicion of markets and artificial substances. Markets exploit the earth; chemicals poison it. Biotech touches both hot buttons. It is being pushed forward by greedy corporations, and it seems to be the very epitome of the unnatural. 32

Still, I hereby hazard a prediction. In ten years or less, most American environmentalists (European ones are more dogmatic) will regard genetic modification as one of their most powerful tools. In only the past ten years or so, after all, environmentalists have reversed field and embraced market mechanisms — tradable emissions permits and the like — as useful in the fight against pollution. The environmental logic of biotechnology is, if anything, even more compelling. The potential upside of genetic modification is simply too large to ignore — and therefore environmentalists will not ignore it. Biotechnology will transform agriculture, and in doing so will transform American environmentalism. 33

RESPONDING TO THE TEXT

Rauch describes himself as being "agriculturally illiterate." On a scale of one to ten, ten being extremely literate, how would you rate your own "agricultural literacy"? Have you done any farming yourself or worked on a farm? How important is it that we know how our foods are grown? After reading Rauch's essay, do you have a basic understanding of past, current, and future farming practices? What questions do you still have?

EXAMINING THE ISSUE CRITICALLY

1. In his opening sentence Rauch claims that though "genetic engineering may be the most environmentally beneficial technology to have emerged in decades, or possibly centuries," its benefit "is not immediately obvious." What does he mean by "environmentally beneficial," and what evidence does he provide? (Glossary: *Evidence*)

2. Rauch appears to have been convinced by the advocates of "continuous no-till farming" (paragraph 2). Why, according to Rauch, do traditional farmers plough? What are the negative effects of ploughing? What happens to soil when it is not ploughed? What is the "rub" of continuous no-till farming? Why do you suppose Rauch waits until after he has extolled all the benefits of no-till farming to present the "rub"?

3. Rauch claims that "farming does not go easy on the earth, and never has. To farm is to make war" (paragraph 9). Is "war" a fitting image for farming? Explain.

4. According to United Nations projections, the next four or five decades are a crucial period for the world. On what assumptions does the United Nations base its projections? Where would the United Nations like world agriculture to be by 2050? How will biotechnology help the agricultural community meet this goal? Explain.

5. In paragraphs 9–10 Rauch discusses several farming methods and their drawbacks. Why? What effect does this have on his argument?

6. It's hard to argue with the position that genetically modified crops need to be "properly developed, disseminated, and used" (paragraph 23). What are some potential risks if such practices are not followed?

7. How can genetic modification help increase future food production and decrease environmental destruction? In order for biotechnology to succeed, Rauch believes that it is essential that environmentalists become "the natural constituency for earth-friendly biotechnology" (paragraph 28). Do you think Rauch has good reason to be so optimistic that "biotechnology will transform agriculture, and in doing so will transform American environmentalism" (33)? Explain.

A Techno-Pox Upon the Land

David Ehrenfeld

David Ehrenfeld was born in 1938 in New York City. He received his B.A. in 1959 and M.D. in 1963 from Harvard University and his Ph.D. in 1966 from the University of Florida. Since 1974 he has been a professor of biology at Rutgers University. Ehrenfeld has written extensively on biology, conservation, and biotechnology in scientific journals. His books include Biological Conservation *(1970),* Conserving Life on Earth *(1972),* The Arrogance of Humanism *(1978),* Beginning Again: People and Nature in the New Millennium *(1993), and* Swimming Lessons: Keeping Afloat in the Age of Technology *(2001).*

The following essay, first published in Harper's *magazine in October 1997, was taken from the lecture "A Cruel and Transient Agriculture" that Ehrenfeld gave at Marist College in Poughkeepsie, New York, in April 1997. Here he takes biotech corporations to task for putting profits ahead of consumer and environmental concerns.*

The modern history of agriculture has two faces. The first, a happy face, is turned toward nonfarmers who live in the developed world. It speaks brightly of technological miracles, such as the "Green Revolution" and, more recently, genetic engineering, that have resulted in the increased production of food for the world's hungry. The second face is turned toward the few remaining farmers who have survived these miracles. It is downcast and silent, like a mourner at a funeral.

The Green Revolution, a fundamental change in agricultural technology, arose in the 1960s and '70s from the assumption that poverty and hunger in poor countries were the result of low agricultural productivity, that subsistence farming as it had occurred for centuries was the basis of a brutish existence. In response to this assumption, plant breeders hit on an elegant method to increase dramatically the yield of the world's most important crops, especially wheat and rice. Put simply, this plan involved redesigning the plants themselves, increasing the size of the plants' reproductive parts — the seed that we eat — and decreasing the size of the vegetative parts — the stems, roots, and leaves that we throw away. From a technical point of view, this worked. Unfortunately, that's not the end of the story. As in other seemingly simple, technical manipulations of nature, there have been undesirable and unintended consequences.

The primary problem is that Green Revolution agribusiness requires vast amounts of energy to grow and sustain these "miracle crops."

Oil must be burned to make the large quantities of nitrogen fertilizer on which these plants depend. Farmers also must invest heavily in toxic herbicides, insecticides, and fungicides; in irrigation systems; and in spraying, harvesting, and processing machinery for the weakened, seed-heavy plants. Large sums of money must be borrowed to pay for these "inputs" before the growing season starts in the hope that crop sales will allow farmers to repay the debt later in the season. When that hope is frustrated, the farmer often loses his farm and is driven into a migrant pool of cheap labor for corporate-farming operations or is forced to seek work in the landless, teeming cities.

The Green Revolution is an early instance of the co-opting of human needs by the technoeconomic system. It is not a black-and-white example: some farmers have been able to keep on farming in spite of the high inputs required; others are mixing traditional methods of farming with selected newer technologies. But the latest manifestation of corporate agriculture, genetic engineering, *is* black-and-white. Excluding military spending on fabulously expensive, dysfunctional weapons systems, there is no more dramatic case of people having their needs appropriated for the sake of profit at any cost. Like high-input agriculture, genetic engineering is often justified as a humane technology, one that feeds more people with better food. Nothing could be further from the truth. With very few exceptions, the whole point of genetic engineering is to increase the sales of chemicals and bioengineered products to dependent farmers, and to increase the dependence of farmers on their new handlers, the seed companies and the oil, chemical, and pharmaceutical companies that own them.

Social problems aside, this new agricultural biotechnology is on much shakier scientific ground than the Green Revolution ever was. Genetic engineering is based on the premise that we can take a gene from species A, where it does some desirable thing, and move it into species B, where it will continue to do that same desirable thing. Most genetic engineers know that this is not always true, but the biotech industry as a whole acts as if it were. First, genes are not like tiny machines. The expression of their output can change when they are put in a new genetic and cellular environment. Second, genes usually have multiple effects. Undesirable effects that are suppressed in species A may be expressed when the gene is moved to species B. And third, many of the most important, genetically regulated traits that agricultural researchers deal with are controlled by multiple genes, perhaps on different chromosomes, and these are very resistant to manipulation by transgenic technology.

Because of these scientific limitations, agricultural biotechnology has been largely confined to applications that are basically simpleminded despite their technical complexity. Even here we find problems.

The production of herbicide-resistant crop seeds is one example. Green Revolution crops tend to be on the wimpy side when it comes to competing with weeds — hence the heavy use of herbicides in recent decades. But many of the weeds are relatives of the crops, so the herbicides that kill the weeds can kill the crops too, given bad luck with weather and the timing of spraying. Enter the seed/chemical companies with a clever, profitable, unscrupulous idea. Why not introduce the gene for resistance to our own brand of herbicide into our own crop seeds, and then sell the patented seeds and patented herbicide as a package?

Never mind that this encourages farmers to apply recklessly large amounts of weedkiller, and that many herbicides have been associated with human sickness, including lymphoma. Nor that the genes for herbicide resistance can move naturally from the crops to the related weeds via pollen transfer, rendering the herbicide ineffective in a few years. What matters, as an agricultural biotechnologist once remarked to me, is earning enough profit to keep the company happy. 7

A related agricultural biotechnology is the transfer of bacterial or plant genes that produce a natural insecticide directly into crops such as corn and cotton. An example is Bt (*Bacillus thuringiensis*), which has been widely used as an external dust or spray to kill harmful beetles and moths. In this traditional use, Bt breaks down into harmless components in a day or two, and the surviving pests do not get a chance to evolve resistance to it. But with Bt now produced continuously inside genetically engineered crops, which are planted over hundreds of thousands of acres, the emergence of genetic resistance among the pests becomes almost a certainty. 8

Monsanto, one of the world's largest manufacturers of agricultural chemicals, has patented cottonseed containing genes for Bt. Advertised as being effective against bollworms without the use of additional insecticides, 1,800,000 acres in five southern states were planted with this transgenic seed in 1996, at a cost to farmers of not only the seed itself but an additional $32-per-acre "technology fee" paid to Monsanto. Heavy bollworm infestation occurred in spite of the special seed, forcing farmers to spray expensive insecticides anyway. Those farmers who wanted to use seeds from the surviving crop to replace the damaged crop found that Monsanto's licensing agreement, like most others in the industry, permitted them only one planting. 9

Troubles with Monsanto's genetically engineered seed have not been confined to cotton. This past May, Monsanto Canada and its licensee, Limagrain Canada Seeds, recalled 60,000 bags of "Roundup-ready" canola seeds because they mistakenly contained a gene that had not been tested by the government for human consumption. These seeds, engineered to resist Monsanto's most profitable product, the herbicide Roundup, were enough to plant more than 600,000 acres. 10

Two farmers had already planted the seeds when Monsanto discovered its mistake.

There is another shaky scientific premise of agricultural biotech- 11 nology. This concerns the transfer of animal or plant genes from the parent species into microorganisms, so that the valuable products of these genes can then be produced in large commercial batches. The assumption here is that these transgenic products, when administered back to the parent species in large doses, will simply increase whatever desirable effect they normally have. Again, this is simplistic thinking that totally ignores the great complexity of living organisms and the consequences of tampering with them.

In the United States, one of the most widely deployed instances of 12 this sort of biotechnology is the use of recombinant bovine growth hormone (rBGH), which is produced by placing slightly modified cow genes into fermentation tanks containing bacteria, then injected into lactating cows to make them yield more milk. This is done despite our nationwide milk glut and despite the fact that the use of rBGH will probably accelerate the demise of the small dairy farm, since only large farms are able to take on the extra debt for the more expensive feeds, the high-tech feed-management systems, and the added veterinary care that go along with its use.

The side effects of rBGH on cows are also serious. Recombinant 13 BGH–related problems — as stated on the package insert by its manufacturer, Monsanto — include bloat, diarrhea, diseases of the knees and feet, feeding disorders, fevers, reduced blood hemoglobin levels, cystic ovaries, uterine pathology, reduced pregnancy rates, smaller calves, and mastitis — a breast infection that can result, according to the insert, in "visibly abnormal milk." Treatment of mastitis can lead to the presence of antibiotics in milk, probably accelerating the spread of antibiotic resistance among bacteria that cause human disease. Milk from rBGH-treated cows may also contain insulin growth factor, IGF-1, which has been implicated in human breast and gastrointestinal cancers.

Another potential problem is an indirect side effect of the special 14 nutritional requirements of rBGH-treated cows. Because these cows require more protein, their food is supplemented with ground-up animals, a practice that has been associated with bovine spongiform encephalopathy, also known as "mad cow disease." The recent British epidemic of BSE appears to have been associated with an increased incidence of the disease's human analogue, Creutzfeldt-Jakob disease. There seems little reason to increase the risk of this terrible disease for the sake of a biotechnology that we don't need. If cows stay off of hormones and concentrate on eating grass, all of us will be much better off.

Meanwhile the biotechnology juggernaut rolls on, converting hu- 15 manity's collective agricultural heritage from an enduring, farmer-controlled lifestyle to an energy-dependent, corporate "process." The ultimate co-optation is the patenting of life. The Supreme Court's ruling in the case of *Diamond v. Chakrabarty* in 1980 paved the way for corporations to obtain industrial, or "utility," patents on living organisms, from bacteria to human cells. These patents operate like the patents on mechanical inventions, granting the patent holder a more sweeping and long-lasting control than had been conferred by the older forms of plant patents. The upshot of this is that farmers who save seeds from utility-patented crop plants for replanting on their own farms next year may have committed a federal crime; it also means that farmers breeding utility-patented cattle may have to pay royalties to the corporation holding the patent.

The life patents allowed by the U.S. Patent Office have been re- 16 markably broad. Agracetus, a subsidiary of Monsanto, was issued patents covering all genetically engineered cotton. The patents are currently being challenged but remain in effect until corporate appeals are exhausted. Companies such as DNA Plant Technology, Calgene, and others are taking out patents that cover many recombinant varieties of vegetable species, from garden peas to the entire genus *Brassica*, which includes broccoli, cabbage, and cauliflower. The German chemical and pharmaceutical giant Hoechst has obtained multiple patents for medical uses of a species of *Coleus*, despite the fact that this medicinal plant has been used since antiquity in Hindu and Ayurvedic medicine to treat cardiovascular, respiratory, digestive, and neurological diseases.

Somehow, in the chaos of technological change, we have lost the 17 distinction between a person and a corporation, inexplicably valuing profit at any cost over basic human needs. In doing so we have forsaken our farmers, the spiritual descendants of those early Hebrew and Greek farmers and pastoralists who first gave us our understanding of social justice, democracy, and the existence of a power greater than our own. No amount of lip service to the goal of feeding the world's hungry or to the glory of a new technology, and no amount of transient increases in the world's grain production, can hide this terrible truth.

RESPONDING TO THE TEXT

In his opening paragraph, Ehrenfeld describes the two faces of modern agriculture. One face is happy, the other is "downcast and silent." Ehrenfeld claims that the general public sees only the happy face and hears the good news of "technological miracles" in agriculture. What clues does Ehrenfeld give to explain why the public rarely sees the more somber face? Explain.

EXAMINING THE ISSUE CRITICALLY

1. What was the Green Revolution that started in the 1960s and 1970s? On what grounds does Ehrenfeld find fault with this change in agricultural practice?

2. According to Ehrenfeld, what is the real purpose of biotechnology? By the end of his essay has he convinced you that he is right? Why or why not?

3. Ehrenfeld claims that the new agricultural biotechnology is founded on shaky scientific ground. What does he think are the scientific limitations of genetic engineering?

4. What problems does Ehrenfeld find with the production of herbicide-resistant crops or crops that produce their own insecticides? What evidence does he present to support his claims? (Glossary: *Evidence*)

5. Ehrenfeld believes that recombinant bovine growth hormone (rGBH) is an example of yet one more "shaky scientific premise of agricultural biotechnology" (paragraph 11). Explain how rGBH is supposed to work — how the hormone is produced and how it is used. What are the risks associated with the use of rGBH? Do you think the claimed benefits of rGBH use outweigh the potential risks? Explain.

6. What do you think Ehrenfeld means when he says, "In the chaos of technological change, we have lost the distinction between a person and a corporation, inexplicably valuing profit at any cost over basic human needs" (paragraph 17). What is the "terrible truth" he alludes to in his closing sentence? What are the implications if we say "no" to biotechnology and instead support "traditional" agriculture? Explain.

Gene-Altered Foods:
A Case Against Panic

Jane E. Brody

Popular syndicated columnist Jane E. Brody was born in Brooklyn, New York, in 1941. She earned her B.S. from Cornell University in 1962 and her M.S. from the University of Wisconsin–Madison in 1963. After a two-year stint as a reporter for the Minneapolis Tribune, *Brody was hired by the* New York Times *to become a full-time science writer. In 1976 her popular column "Personal Health" debuted, and it has remained a mainstay of the* Times *ever since. Readers' questions, health issues in the media, and medical journal studies have provided her with topics over the years. Brody's problem with her own weight fueled her interest in food, nutrition, and diet, resulting in the publication of* Jane Brody's Nutrition Book *(1981) and the companion volume* Jane Brody's Good Food Book *(1985). When not writing, Brody lectures on health and nutrition and has starred in the PBS series* Good Health from Jane Brody's Kitchen.*

In "Gene-Altered Foods: A Case Against Panic," a "Personal Health" column from the December 5, 2000, issue of the New York Times, *Brody seeks to relieve public anxiety about the genetic modification of food.*

Ask American consumers whether they support the use of biotechnology in food and agriculture and nearly 70 percent say they do. But ask the question another way, "Do you approve of genetically engineered (or genetically modified) foods?" and two-thirds say they do not.

Yet there is no difference between them. The techniques involved and the products that result are identical. Rather, the words "genetic" and "engineer" seem to provoke alarm among millions of consumers.

The situation recalls the introduction of the M.R.I. (for magnetic resonance imaging), which was originally called an N.M.R., for nuclear magnetic resonance. The word nuclear caused such public concern, it threatened to stymie the growth of this valuable medical tool.

The idea of genetically modified foods, known as G.M. foods, is particularly frightening to those who know little about how foods are now produced and how modern genetic technology, if properly regulated, could result in significant improvements by reducing environmental hazards, improving the nutritional value of foods, enhancing agricultural productivity and fostering the survival worldwide of small farms and the rural landscape.

Without G.M. foods, Dr. Alan McHughen, a biotechnologist at the University of Saskatchewan, told a recent conference on agricultural biotechnology at Cornell, the earth will not be able to feed the ever-growing billions of people who inhabit it.

Still, there are good reasons for concern about a powerful technology that is currently imperfectly regulated and could, if inadequately tested or misapplied, bring on both nutritional and environmental havoc. To render a rational opinion on the subject and make reasoned choices in the marketplace, it is essential to understand what genetic engineering of foods and crops involves and its potential benefits and risks.

GENETICS IN AGRICULTURE

People have been genetically modifying foods and crops for tens of thousands of years. The most commonly used method has involved crossing two parents with different desirable characteristics in an effort to produce offspring that express the best of both of them. That and another approach, inducing mutations, are time-consuming and hit-or-miss and can result in good and bad characteristics.

Genetic engineering, on the other hand, involves the introduction into a plant or animal or micro-organism of a single gene or group of genes that are known quantities, genes that dictate the production of one or more desired elements, for example, the ability to resist the attack of insects, withstand herbicide treatments, or produce foods with higher levels of essential nutrients.

Since all organisms use the same genetic material (DNA), the power of the technique includes the ability to transfer genes between organisms that normally would never interbreed.

Thus, an antifreeze gene from Arctic flounder has been introduced into strawberries to extend their growing season in northern climates. But contrary to what many people think, this does not make the strawberries "fishy" any more than the use of porcine insulin turned people into pigs.

Dr. Steven Kresovich, a plant breeder at Cornell, said, "Genes should be characterized by function, not origin. It's not a flounder gene but a cold tolerance gene that was introduced into strawberries."

As Dr. McHughen points out in his new book, *Pandora's Picnic Basket: The Potential and Hazards of Genetically Modified Foods*, people share about 7,000 genes with a worm called *C. elegans*. The main difference between organisms lies in the total number of genes their cells contain, how the genes are arranged and which ones are turned on or off in different cells at different times.

CURRENT AND POTENTIAL BENEFITS

An insecticidal toxin from a bacterium called *Bacillus thuringiensis* (Bt) 13
has been genetically introduced into two major field crops, corn and
cotton, resulting in increased productivity and decreased use of pesticides, which means less environmental contamination and greater
profits for farmers. For example, by growing Bt cotton, farmers could
reduce spraying for bollworm and budworm from seven times a season to none. Bt corn also contains much lower levels of fungal toxins,
which are potentially carcinogenic.

The genetic introduction of herbicide tolerance into soybeans is 14
saving farmers about $200 million a year by reducing the number of
applications of herbicide needed to control weed growth, said Leonard
Gianessi, a pesticide analyst at the National Center for Food and Agricultural Policy, a research organization in Washington.

Genetically engineered pharmaceuticals are already widely used, 15
with more than 150 products on the market. Since 1978, genetically
modified bacteria have been producing human insulin, which is used
by 3.3 million people with diabetes.

Future food benefits are likely to accrue directly to the consumer. 16
For example, genetic engineers have developed golden rice, a yellow
rice rich in beta carotene (which the body converts to vitamin A) and
iron.

If farmers in developing countries accept this crop and if the mil- 17
lions of people who suffer from nutrient deficiencies will eat it,
golden rice could prevent widespread anemia and blindness in half a
million children a year and the deaths of one million to two million
children who succumb each year to the consequences of vitamin A
deficiency.

Future possibilities include peanuts or shrimp lacking proteins 18
that can cause life-threatening food allergies, fruits and vegetables
with longer shelf lives, foods with fewer toxicants and antinutrients,
meat and dairy products and oils with heart-healthier fats, and foods
that deliver vaccines.

REAL AND POTENTIAL RISKS

G.M. foods and crops arrived without adequate mechanisms in place 19
to regulate them. Three agencies are responsible for monitoring their
safety for consumers, farmers, and the environment: the Food and
Drug Administration, the Department of Agriculture, and the Environmental Protection Agency. But the drug agency says its law does not
allow it to require premarket testing of G.M. foods unless they contain
a new substance that is not "generally recognized as safe."

For most products, safety tests are done voluntarily by producers. 20
The recent recall of taco shells containing G.M. corn that had not
been approved for human consumption was done voluntarily by the
producer. The agency is now formulating new guidelines to test G.M.
products and to label foods as "G.M.-free" but says it lacks a legal basis
to require labeling of G.M. foods.

"In the current environment, such a label would be almost a kiss 21
of death on a product," said Dr. Michael Jacobson, director of the Center for Science in the Public Interest, a nonprofit consumer group.
"But it may be that the public is simply not going to have confidence
in transgenic ingredients if their presence is kept secret."

The introduction of possible food allergens through genetic engi- 22
neering is a major concern. If the most common sources of food
allergens — peanuts, shellfish, celery, nuts, milk, or eggs — had to pass
through an approval process today, they would never make it to market.

But consumers could be taken unaware if an otherwise safe food 23
was genetically endowed with an allergen, as almost happened with
an allergenic protein from Brazil nuts. Even if known allergenic proteins are avoided in G.M. foods, it is hard to predict allergenicity of
new proteins.

A potentially serious environmental risk involves the "escape" of 24
G.M. genes from crops into the environment, where they may harm innocent organisms or contaminate crops that are meant to be G.M.-free.

Dr. Jacobson concluded, "Now is the time, while agricultural 25
biotechnology is still young, for Congress and regulatory agencies to
create the framework that will maximize the safe use of these products, bolster public confidence in them and allow all of humankind to
benefit from their enormous potential." Two Congressional bills now
under discussion can do much to assure safer use of agricultural biotechnology, he said.

RESPONDING TO THE TEXT

Brody provides readers with a reasonably objective overview of the current
and potential benefits as well as the real and potential risks of genetically
modified foods. Do you agree with her assessment that there is no cause for
panic at present? Explain.

EXAMINING THE ISSUE CRITICALLY

1. Why do you suppose two-thirds of American consumers are alarmed by
   the words "genetically engineered" but not by the word "biotechnology"? Do these words frighten you?

2. What does Brody see as the advantages and disadvantages of genetic
   technology? Why does Brody take the time to explain what genetic

engineering involves? Does her explanation reduce any anxiety you may have had about this technology?

3. Brody is quick to qualify her praise of genetic technology with the phrase "if properly regulated" (paragraph 4). Why is proper regulation so important?

4. Michael Jacobson points to the product-labeling dilemma facing producers of genetically modified foods. He says that "in the current environment, such a label would be almost a kiss of death on a product. But it may be that the public is simply not going to have confidence in transgenic ingredients if their presence is kept secret" (paragraph 21). How can we move beyond this impasse so as to enjoy the benefits of this technology while keeping the risks in check?

Weeding Out the Skilled Farmer

Jim Scharplaz

Cattle rancher Jim Scharplaz was born in 1951 in Salina, Kansas. He holds B.S. and M.S. degrees in agricultural engineering from Kansas State University and is a licensed professional agricultural engineer. When his father was rendered unable to run the family ranch, Scharplaz gave up engineering and took on the family business. He currently lives on the ranch where he grew up. In addition to raising cattle, he has served as president of the board of the Kansas Pork Association and is on the board of the Kansas Rural Center. Scharplaz is a member of the Prairie Writers Circle, a project of The Land Institute, a natural systems agriculture research organization in Salina that is working to develop perennial grain agriculture.

In the following essay, first published in The Land Institute *on November 25, 2003, Scharplaz uses the example of his neighbor's genetically modified soybeans to raise the issue of the industrialization of agriculture and the consequences for farmers and consumers.*

Last summer, a field by my house was planted to soybeans. Walking past early in the growing season, I noticed that the field was completely free of weeds. The plant population had been reduced to the simplest possible — only soybeans grew there. These were genetically modified to resist the well-known herbicide with which the field had been treated. The herbicide had killed all other plants.

Genetically modified plants and modern herbicides are among many new technologies for farming. Some people are concerned about these technologies and their effects on human health. Others worry about the environment. I am concerned that the main purpose of these technologies is the complete industrialization of agriculture. This does not bode well for farmers, or for the rest of us.

Historically, growing soybeans, especially controlling weeds in soybeans, has been very difficult. The family that grew the soybeans by my house are wonderful farmers. They have been growing crops there for more than 50 years. Their experience, study, and inherited ability make them better able than anyone else to farm that field. Before genetically engineered soybeans, a field this weed-free would take all their skill, plus quite a bit of hand labor.

But much new technology "simplifies" farming, as the herbicide and genetically modified soybeans simplified the field next door. The knowledge required to grow the best particular plants in particular places, the valuable craft required to be a good farmer, is being lost.

579

And the farmer is increasingly dependent on an industrial food system controlled by very few, very large corporations.

A study by University of Missouri rural sociologists found that four companies own 60 percent of U.S. terminals for grain exports. Since then, agribusiness giant ADM acquired Farmland Industries' grain division, and Cenex/Harvest States joined with Cargill. The researchers report that four companies slaughter 81 percent of our beef. The top five food retailers' share of the U.S. market grew from 24 percent in 1997 to 42 percent in 2000.

The agricultural corporations co-opt the land-grant university research system so that tax dollars support research that ultimately will enhance their profits. Their legion of lawyers overwhelms the Justice Department's antitrust division, and their lobbyists essentially write the increasingly complex farm bills.

These companies spent $119 million lobbying in 1998, according to the Center for Responsive Politics. This dwarfs the $6.8 million spent by environmental groups and even the $49 million spent by military contractors that year. Individuals change jobs back and forth between corporate agribusiness and the Agriculture Department until the two are indistinguishable.

Increasing industrialization is generally assumed to go with improvements in the standard of living. But big companies mean big mistakes. Recent events show that the people who run our largest corporations are far from perfect, and some are willing to commit crimes to cover their misdeeds, both accidental and deliberate. These things have affected nearly all of us to some extent. Many folks have lost investment capital or seen their retirement funds evaporate.

As bad as these losses have been, for an agriculture increasingly controlled by fewer decision-makers, mistakes could cause far greater problems. It's not that farmers don't make mistakes. The difference is one of magnitude. One farmer's mistake has no measurable effect on our food supply. The mistake of one huge corporation could create catastrophe. Diversity in agriculture is our best guarantee of food security.

Farmers are the foundation of civilization. They are as essential to its stability as they were when agriculture began 10,000 years ago. New agricultural technologies must be judged: Is their purpose the industrialization and homogenization of farming, or the benefit of humanity?

RESPONDING TO THE TEXT

Sound agricultural practice is founded on the principle that farmers "know" the land they farm. What does it mean to you that someone "knows" the land he or she works? Explain using examples from your own experiences, observations, and reading.

EXAMINING THE ISSUE CRITICALLY

1. What does Scharplaz fear is being lost as farmers come to depend more on technology? How does the example of his neighbor illustrate his fear? Do you find his worry credible? Why or why not?

2. Scharplaz cites studies that show that America's food system is "controlled by very few, very large corporations" (paragraph 4). This situation concerns him, and it is only compounded when he sees "individuals change jobs back and forth between corporate agribusiness and the Agriculture Department until the two are indistinguishable" (7). Do you think that it is important for the Department of Agriculture to remain independent of corporate America? What could happen if the department became entangled with agribusiness?

3. What does Scharplaz mean when he states, "For an agriculture increasingly controlled by fewer decision-makers, mistakes could cause far greater problems. It's not that farmers don't make mistakes. The difference is one of magnitude" (paragraph 9)? Do you agree? Explain. In your opinion, how effective is this element of Scharplaz's argument?

4. In conclusion, Scharplaz poses a question that he believes needs to be asked of all new agricultural technologies: "Is their purpose the industrialization and homogenization of farming, or the benefit of humanity?" Do you agree that new technologies need to be questioned and challenged before they are used? Where does one draw the line when weighing the benefits to humanity against the efficiencies of industrialization? Does the industrialization of agriculture, as some claim, lead to higher standards of living? Explain.

MAKING CONNECTIONS: WRITING AND DISCUSSION SUGGESTIONS FOR "GENETICALLY MODIFIED FOOD"

The following questions are offered to help you start making meaningful connections among the four articles and photograph in this argument cluster. These questions can be used for class discussion, or you can choose to answer any one of them by writing an essay. If you choose the essay option, be sure to make specific references to at least two or three of the cluster articles. With several of the questions, some additional research may be required. To begin your research online, go to **bedfordstmartins.com/subjectsstrategies** and click on "Genetically Modified Food" or browse the thematic directory of annotated links.

1. Although Rauch, Ehrenfeld, Brody, and Scharplaz address the general topic of genetically modified food, each approaches the issue from a different angle and cites different evidence to support his or her position. (Glossary: *Evidence*) How do you think each of the writers would use Olson's photograph of workers spraying potato seedlings (p. 558) to illustrate his or her points and support his or her arguments? Whose position, in your opinion, is best supported by Olson's photograph? Why? Write an essay in which you defend your conclusion. Before you write, refer to your Connecting Image and Text response for this cluster.

2. Rauch claims that "genetic engineering may be the most environmentally beneficial technology to have emerged in decades, or possibly centuries" (paragraph 1). If that's true, why are so many environmentalists opposed to (or at best extremely cautious about) such technology? What needs to happen before environmentalists can become "the natural constituency for earth-friendly biotechnology" (28)? Write an essay in which you argue for or against environmentalists' support of genetically modified food.

3. In discussing "Roundup ready" plant varieties, Ehrenfeld states that "genes for herbicide resistance can move naturally from the crops to the related weeds via pollen transfer, rendering the herbicide ineffective in a few years" (paragraph 7). Given the possibility that desirable genes in crops could one day be expressed in undesirable weeds, should we even bother with genetic modification? Why or why not? Do the potential risks outweigh the potential benefits? Do you think scientists can solve the problem Ehrenfeld describes? Explain. Write an essay in which you argue for or against the continued development of genetically modified crops.

4. More and more people want to know what the foods they consume contain, including how much fat, carbohydrates, sodium, and cholesterol and whether the product is "organic." As Brody explains, however, the Food and Drug Administration (FDA) "lacks a legal basis to require labeling of G.M. foods" (paragraph 20). Should government require food manufacturers to label genetically modified ingredients? Do you agree with Michael Jacobson that "the public is simply not going to have confidence in transgenic ingredients if their presence is kept secret" (21)?

Explain. If "people have been genetically modifying foods and crops for tens of thousands of years" (7), is it even possible to determine what to label as genetically modified? Why or why not? Write a letter to Congress in which you argue for or against granting the FDA power to label genetically modified foods. Be mindful of your audience. (Glossary: *Audience*) Before you write, refer to your Preparing to Read response for this cluster.

5. Scharplaz reports that "the agricultural corporations co-opt the land-grant university research system so that tax dollars support research that ultimately will enhance their profits. Their legion of lawyers overwhelms the Justice Department's antitrust division, and their lobbyists essentially write the increasingly complex farm bills" (paragraph 6). Are we becoming a culture dominated by government-influencing corporations? What effect does agribusiness have on the "skilled farmer"? What could result from the close relationship between government and business? Does agribusiness hold the key to our future food needs? Do the risks outweigh the benefits of standardization in agriculture? If so, how? Write an essay in which you argue for or against what Scharplaz refers to as the "industrialization of agriculture."

6. As you were reading the essays in this argument cluster, you probably discovered that several writers drew different conclusions from the same examples. (Glossary: *Evidence; Exemplification*) To see how people can interpret the same material differently, review several of the instances — for example, genetically modified soybeans, Bt (*Bacillus thuringiensis*) crops, and "Roundup ready" plant varieties — where the same information was used to argue both for and against biotechnology. What explanations can you see for the differences in opinion? Which writers do you trust? Which do you distrust? Why? In an essay report your findings.

7. Poet and environmentalist Wendell Berry has said that "it is impossible to care more or differently for each other than we care for the land." What do you think he means? As stewards of the Earth, what responsibilities do we have toward the land? Toward each other? How can humans work in partnership with the land? Using your own experience, observations, and ideas from the readings, write an argumentative essay that answers these questions.

8. Rauch compares and contrasts organic, traditional, and low-input farming with no-till farming, which requires the use of genetically modified plants. (Glossary: *Comparison and Contrast*) In your college library and on the Internet, research one of these alternatives to no-till farming. What are its benefits and drawbacks? Which do you think is better for the environment, food production, and humans? Why? Write an essay in which you argue for increased implementation of either no-till farming or the alternative you have researched.

WRITING SUGGESTIONS FOR ARGUMENTATION

1. Think of a product that you like and want to use even though it has an annoying feature. Write a letter of complaint in which you attempt to persuade the manufacturer to improve the product. Your letter should include the following points:

   a. A statement concerning the nature of the problem
   b. Evidence supporting or explaining your complaint
   c. Suggestions for improving the product

2. Select one of the position statements that follow, and write an argumentative essay in which you defend that statement.

   a. Living in a dormitory is (*or* is not) as desirable as living off-campus.
   b. Student government shows (*or* does not show) that the democratic process is effective.
   c. America should (*or* should not) be a refuge for the oppressed.
   d. School spirit is (*or* is not) as important as it ever was.
   e. Interest in religion is (*or* is not) increasing in the United States.
   f. We have (*or* have not) brought air pollution under control in the United States.
   g. The need to develop alternative energy sources is (*or* is not) serious.
   h. America's great cities are (*or* are not) thriving.
   i. Fraternities and sororities do (*or* do not) build character.
   j. We have (*or* have not) found effective means to dispose of nuclear or chemical wastes.
   k. Fair play is (*or* is not) a thing of the past.
   l. Human life is (*or* is not) valued in a technological society.
   m. The consumer does (*or* does not) need to be protected.
   n. The family farm in America is (*or* is not) in danger of extinction.
   o. Grades do (*or* do not) encourage learning.
   p. America is (*or* is not) a violent society.
   q. Television is (*or* is not) a positive cultural force in America.
   r. America should (*or* should not) feel a commitment to the starving peoples of the world.
   s. The federal government should (*or* should not) regulate all utilities.
   t. Money is (*or* is not) the path to happiness.
   u. Animals do (*or* do not) have rights.
   v. Competition is (*or* is not) killing us.
   w. America is (*or* is not) becoming a society with deteriorating values.

3. Think of something on your campus or in your community that you would like to see changed. Write a persuasive argument that explains what is wrong and how you think it ought to be changed. Make sure you incorporate other writing strategies into your essay — for example, description, narration, or exemplification — to increase the effectiveness of your persuasive argument. (Glossary: *Description; Exemplification; Narration*)

4. Read some articles in the editorial section of today's paper, and pick one with which you agree or disagree. Write a letter to the editor that presents your point of view. Use a logical argument to support or refute the editorial's assertions. Depending on the editorial, you might choose to use different rhetorical strategies to reach your audience. (Glossary: *Audience*) You might use cause and effect, for example, to show the correct (or incorrect) connections made by the editorial. (Glossary: *Cause and Effect Analysis*)

5. Working with a partner, choose a controversial topic like the legalization of medical marijuana or any of the topics in writing suggestion 2. Each partner should argue one side of the issue. Decide who is going to write on which side of the issue, and keep in mind that there are often more than two sides to an issue. Then each of you should write an essay trying to convince your partner that your position is the most logical and correct.

CHAPTER 12

Combining Strategies

Each of the chapters of *Subjects/Strategies* emphasizes a particular rhetorical mode or writing strategy: exemplification, description, narration, process analysis, and so forth. The essays and selections within each of these chapters use the given strategy as the dominant method of development. It is important to remember, however, that the dominant strategy is rarely the only one used to develop a piece of writing. To fully explore their topics, writers find it useful and necessary to use other strategies in combination with the dominant strategy. Very seldom does an essay use one strategy exclusively. To highlight and reinforce this point, we focus on the use of multiple strategies in the Analyzing the Writer's Craft section following each professional selection.

While some essays are developed *primarily* through the use of a single mode, it is more the norm in good writing that writers take advantage of the options open to them, using multiple strategies in artful combinations to achieve memorable results. It is to this end that we have gathered the essays in this Combining Strategies chapter and ask additional questions about the author's use of multiple strategies. These essays illustrate the ways that writers use a number of strategies to support the dominant strategy. You will encounter such combinations of strategies in the reading and writing you do in other college courses. Beyond the classroom, you might write a business proposal using both description and cause and effect to make an argument for a new marketing plan. Or you might use narration, description, and exemplification to write a news story for a company newsletter or a letter to the editor of your local newspaper.

WHAT DOES IT MEAN TO COMBINE STRATEGIES?

The following essay by Sydney Harris illustrates how several strategies can be used effectively, even in a brief, concise piece of writing. Although primarily a work of definition, notice how "A Jerk" also uses exemplification and personal narrative to engage the reader and achieve Harris's purpose.

A JERK

I don't know whether history repeats itself, but biography certainly does. The other day, Michael came in and asked me what a "jerk" was — the same question Carolyn put to me a dozen years ago.

At that time, I fluffed her off with some inane answer, such as "A jerk isn't a very nice person," but both of us knew it was an unsatisfactory reply. When she went to bed, I began trying to work up a suitable definition.

It is a marvelously apt word, of course. Until it was coined, not more than 25 years ago, there was really no single word in English to describe the kind of person who is a jerk — "boob" and "simp" were too old hat, and besides they really didn't fit, for they could be lovable, and a jerk never is.

Thinking it over, I decided that a jerk is basically a person without insight. He is not necessarily a fool or a dope, because some extremely clever persons can be jerks. In fact, it has little to do with intelligence as we commonly think of it; it is, rather, a kind of subtle but persuasive aroma emanating from the inner part of the personality.

I know a college president who can be described only as a jerk. He is not an unintelligent man, nor unlearned, nor even unschooled in the social amenities. Yet he is a jerk *cum laude*, because of a fatal flaw in his nature — he is totally incapable of looking into the mirror of his soul and shuddering at what he sees there.

A jerk, then, is a man (or woman) who is utterly unable to see himself as he appears to others. He has no grace, he is tactless without meaning to be, he is a bore even to his best friends, he is an egotist without charm. All of us are egotists to some extent, but most of us — unlike the jerk — are perfectly and horribly aware of it when we make asses of ourselves. The jerk never knows.

WHY DO WRITERS COMBINE STRATEGIES?

Essays that employ thoughtful combinations of rhetorical strategies have some obvious advantages for the writer and the reader. By reading the work of professional writers, you can learn how multiple strategies can be used to your advantage — how a paragraph of narration, a vivid description, a clarifying instance of comparison and contrast, or a helpful definition can vary the interest level or terrain of an essay. More important, they answer a reader's need to know and to understand your purpose and thesis.

For example, let's suppose you wanted to write an essay on the college slang you heard used on campus. You might find it helpful to use a variety of strategies.

- *Definition* — to explain what slang is
- *Exemplification* — to give examples of slang
- *Comparison and contrast* — to differentiate slang from other types of speech, such as idioms or technical language
- *Division and classification* — to categorize different types of slang or different topics that slang terms are used for, such as courses, students, food, grades

Or let's say you wanted to write a paper on the Japanese Americans who were sent to internment camps during World War II while the United States was at war with Japan. The following strategies would be available to you.

- *Exemplification* — to illustrate several particular cases of families that were sent to internment camps
- *Narration* — to tell the stories of former camp residents, including their first reaction to their internment and their actual experiences in the camps
- *Cause and effect* — to examine the reasons why the United States government interned Japanese Americans and the long-term effects of this policy

When you rely on a single mode or approach to an essay, you may limit yourself and lose the opportunity to come at your subject from a number of different angles, all of which complete the picture and any one of which might be the most insightful or engaging and, therefore, the most memorable for the reader. This is particularly the case with essays that attempt to persuade or argue. So strong is the need, and so difficult the task, of changing readers' beliefs and thoughts that writers look for any combination of strategies that will make their arguments more convincing.

AN ANNOTATED STUDENT ESSAY USING A COMBINATION OF STRATEGIES

While a senior at the University of Vermont, English major Tara E. Ketch took a course in children's literature and was asked to write a term paper on some aspect of the literature she was studying. She knew that she would soon be looking for a teaching position and realized that any teaching job she accepted would bring her face-to-face with the difficult task of selecting appropriate reading materials. Ketch understood, as well, that she would have to confront criticism of her choices, so she decided to delve a little deeper into the subject of censorship, particularly of children's and adolescent literature. She was interested in learning more about why people want to censor certain books so that she could consider an appropriate response to their efforts. In a way, she wanted to begin to develop her own teaching philosophy with respect to text selection. Her essay naturally incorporated several rhetorical modes working in combination. As you read Ketch's essay, notice how naturally she has used the supporting strategies of definition, cause and effect, and exemplification to enhance the dominant strategy of argumentation.

Kids, You Can't Read That Book!

Tara E. Ketch

Definition of censorship and censors' activities

Censorship is the restriction or suppression of speech or writing that is thought to have a negative influence. In the case of children's and adolescent literature the censors are very often school officials, parents, or adults in the community who wish to monitor and influence what children are reading. For whatever reason, they are saying, "Kids, you can't read that book; it is not fit for your eyes." To ensure that these books do not end up in the schools, pressure groups influence school boards not to purchase them or to restrict their use if they have already been purchased. Such actions present serious questions for educators. Who will decide what materials are fit for American schoolchildren?

Cause and effect: Pressure is put on school boards, and questions are raised.

Argumentation: Who will decide on censorship issues?

The federal government has set limits on censorship and encouraged local communities to make educational decisions. In the 1968

1

2

*Exemplification:
Supreme Court
decisions*

case of <u>Emerson v. Arkansas</u>, the Supreme
Court stated, "Public education in our nation is committed to the control of state
and local authorities. Courts do not and
cannot intervene in the resolution of conflicts which arise in the daily operation of
school systems and which do not directly and
sharply implicate basic constitutional values" (Reichman 3). In 1982, the Supreme

*Cause and effect:
result of Supreme
Court decisions*

Court ruled that "local school boards may
not remove books from school library shelves
simply because they dislike the ideas contained in those books and seek by their removal to prescribe what shall be orthodox in
politics, nationalism, religion, or other
matters of opinion" (Reichman 3). These two
rulings contradict each other. The outcome
is that children's books continue to be
banned in school systems for many reasons.

*Cause and effect:
first reason why
children's and
adolescents' books
are banned*

One important reason books are banned
is family values. The censor may attack a
book because it goes against his or her personal values. For example, it may contain
"offensive" language. Most problems with
books seem to come out of the author's use
of language. This is especially true of adolescent literature. In a list of the most
frequently banned books in the 1990s, J. D.
Salinger's <u>Catcher in the Rye</u> took the number three slot because of objections to its
language. A parent found words such as <u>hell</u>,
<u>Chrissakes</u>, <u>bastard</u>, <u>damn</u>, and <u>crap</u> to be

*Exemplification:
authors' use of
language that
affronts family
values*

unacceptable (Foerstel 147). The fear was
that such language was being condoned by the
school when such a book was taught. In a debate about Katherine Paterson's <u>Bridge to
Terabithia</u>, a woman protested the use of the
words <u>snotty</u> and <u>shut up</u> along with <u>Lord</u> and
<u>damn</u>. She said, "Freedom of speech was not
intended to guarantee schools the right to
intrude on traditional family values without

3

Argumentation: Counterargument about redeeming social value is presented.

warning and regardless of the availability of non-offensive alternatives" (Reichman 38). The school board in this case decided that the book had a value that transcended the use of the few offensive words. That a book has redeeming value is the primary argument against such censorship. If we ignore all books that contain profanity, we are missing out on a lot of valuable literature.

Cause and effect: second reason why children's and adolescents' books are banned

Other people hold dear the value that children should not be exposed to anything depressing or violent. Not surprisingly, several communities have tried to get certain fairy tales banned because they are violent in nature. <u>Jack and the Beanstalk</u> and

Exemplification: violence in fairy tales

<u>Little Red Riding Hood</u> came under attack for this reason. In both cases the books were kept in the school system (Burress 283-91). The argument against their removal involved the fact that the violence was tied to fantasy. It was not in the child's everyday realm and therefore not threatening. Judy Blume's <u>Blubber</u> has been questioned for its

Exemplification: unhappy child characters

portrayal of unhappy child characters. Some parents refuse to recognize the fact that not all children have a happy and carefree existence. Judy Blume has her own ideas about childhood that she uses as an attack against such censorship. She argues, "Chil-

Argumentation: Counterargument by Judy Blume is presented.

dren have little control over their lives, and this causes both anger and unhappiness. Childhood can be a terrible time of life. No kid wants to stay a kid. . . . The fantasy of childhood is to be an adult" (West 12). <u>Bridge to Terabithia</u> has also been seen as a harsh portrayal of life because it deals

Exemplification: death of a child character

with the death of a child. Some parents want to shelter their children from the reality of death. Others find that a book such as <u>Bridge to Terabithia</u> is a natural way for

4

children to be exposed to that sensitive topic.

*Cause and effect:
third reason why
children's and
adolescents' books
are banned*

Another family value that comes into   5
play in censorship is the idea that children
should be protected from sexuality. Maurice
Sendak's <u>In the Night Kitchen</u> shows a naked
little boy, and although there is no sexual
connotation, many people were incensed by
the book. In New York, in 1990, parents
tried to have the book removed from an elementary school. In Maine, a parent wanted
the book removed because she felt it encouraged child molestation (Foerstel 201). Many
of Judy Blume's books have also come under
fire for their portrayal of sexual themes in

*Exemplification:
sexuality as topic*

adolescence. <u>Are You There, God? It's Me,
Margaret</u> has been blacklisted for its frank
discussion of menstruation and adolescent
development. <u>Forever</u> is even worse to some
because it mentions intercourse and abortion. As topics of discussion, these sub-

*Cause and effect:
explanation of
reasons for
banning books
with sexual topics*

jects are alien to many adults who grew up
in environments where sex was not talked
about; therefore, they try to perpetuate the
cycle of silence by keeping these kinds of
books from children. They may also worry
that these books will encourage sexual activity. This fear extends to textbooks that
educate children and adolescents about their
bodies and sexual reproduction. Many try to
ban gay and lesbian literature because they
feel that homosexuality is obscene and that
books about these subjects might encourage

*Exemplification:
books that discuss
gay and lesbian
themes*

homosexual behavior and lifestyles. <u>All-
American Boys</u> was donated to a California
high school, but when administrators realized
that it discussed homosexuality, the book was
seized and then "lost" (Reichman 43). Alyson
Wonderland Publications has also published
two children's books to explain the gay
lifestyle to children: Michael Willhoite's

Daddy's Roommate and Leslea Newman's Heather Has Two Mommies. These, not surprisingly, have met with a lot of opposition.

Cause and effect: fourth reason why children's and adolescents' books are banned

Often there are religious concerns as well. Religion is in many cases the foundation for people's moral beliefs. Censorship of books because of their language, violence, and sexuality happens as much in the name of religion as family values. Religion is also used as an issue in censorship for other reasons. Some people want the Bible when used as literature banned from classrooms.

Exemplification: books banned for religious reasons

Not only does teaching the Bible as literature present a problem for parents who want the Bible focused on as sacred material, but it is equally offensive to people who feel that religious documents should be kept out of the classroom (Burress 219). Sometimes religious considerations take the form of censorship of books that in any way involve the occult. The picture book Witches, Pumpkins, and Grinning Ghosts was considered inappropriate because it "interests little minds into accepting the Devil with all his evil works" (Reichman 51). Ironically, "witches" sought the banning of Hansel and Gretel because it portrayed their religion in a negative light (Reichman 50). Greek and Roman mythology has also been attacked by religious groups because it discusses gods other than the Christian one. Christians also fought to ban books on evolution that called into question their religious beliefs.

Cause and effect: fifth reason why children's and adolescents' books are banned

Yet another reason for the censorship of children's books is concern over racism and sexism. Minority groups have often made efforts to combat stereotypes and racial prejudices through censorship. The idea is that if children are exposed to sexism and racism in books, they will learn it. Mark

6

7

Exemplification: books banned for racial reasons

Twain's <u>The Adventures of Huckleberry Finn</u> is a good example of a text that has been banned because of its racist language. The use of the term <u>nigger</u> has offended many African Americans. The problem with this criticism is that the novel was not examined for its intention, which was to question the racist attitude of the South. Twain was not a racist. Nevertheless, <u>Huckleberry Finn</u> has become one of the most frequently banned books in the United States. Women have also tried to censor nursery rhymes and children's stories that reinforce negative images of women. Some have argued in opposition that to remove all books that are sexist and racist would be to remove a piece of our history that we can learn from.

Argumentation: Counterargument is presented.

Exemplification: books banned for gender bias

Argumentation: Counterargument is presented.

Central question is raised: Should we censor children's books? Answers are given.

With this brief background and a review of some of the reasons used to ban children's books, how might the question "Should we censor children's books?" be answered? On the one hand, we should realize that there are age-appropriate themes for children. For example, elementary school children should not be exposed to the ideas of rape and abortion that occur in some young adult novels. Young adults should not be exposed to extremely violent novels like Anthony Burgess's <u>A Clockwork Orange</u>, which they may not understand at such a young age. Does this mean these books should be removed from school libraries? Perhaps not. Libraries should be resources for children to broaden their horizons. If a child independently seeks out a controversial novel, the child should not be stopped from doing so. Exposure to a rich diversity of works is always advisable. A good way to decide if a book should be taught is if its message speaks to the children. What if this message is couched in profanity? If it is in a character

Argumentation: The writer provides various criteria for making decisions about what is appropriate reading for children. Discussion of these criteria generally follows the writer's sequencing of the reasons why people attempt to censor children's and adolescents' books.

8

representation, kids can understand the context without feeling compelled to emulate the behavior. If children are constantly exposed to books that throw reality in their faces in a violent way, then their attitudes will reflect it. So, it is the job of educators to present different types of materials to balance the children's exposure.

As far as sexuality goes, it's fine for   9 libraries to include children's books that focus on this subject if the objective is to educate or make transitions easier for the child. Religion, however, should not be focused on in the classroom because it causes too much conflict for different groups. This does not mean that religious works should be banned from school libraries. Children should have access to different religious materials to explore world religions and various belief systems. Lastly, if sexism and racism appear in books, those books should not automatically be banned. They can be useful tools for increasing understanding in our society.

Argumentation: Concluding statement calls for understanding and sensitivity in dealing with censorship and book selection for children and adolescents.

The efforts to censor what our children   10 are reading can turn into potentially explosive situations and cause a great deal of misunderstanding and hurt feelings within our schools and communities. If we can gain an understanding of the major reasons why people have sought to censor what our kids are reading, we will be better prepared to respond to those efforts in a sensitive and reasonable manner. More importantly, we will be able to provide the best educational opportunity for our children through a sensible approach, one that neither overly restricts the range of their reading nor allows them to read any and all books no matter how inappropriate they might be for them.

Works Cited

Burress, Lee. Battle of the Books: Literary Censorship in
    the Public Schools, 1950–1985. New York: Scarecrow,
    1989.

Foerstel, Herbert. Banned in the U.S.A.: A Reference
    Guide to Book Censorship in Schools and Public
    Libraries. London: Greenwood, 1994.

Reichman, Henry. Censorship and Selection: Issues and
    Answers to Schools. Chicago: American Library
    Association, 1993.

West, Mark. Trust Your Children: Voices against
    Censorship in Children's Literature. London: Neal-
    Schuman, 1988.

Analyzing Tara E. Ketch's Essay of
Combining Strategies: Questions for Discussion

1. What is Ketch's thesis?
2. How do the two rulings given by the U.S. Supreme Court with respect to educational decisions within communities conflict?
3. What reasons does Ketch give for why children's and adolescents' books are banned in schools?
4. How does Ketch answer the question "Should we censor children's books?" Do you agree with her?

SUGGESTIONS FOR WRITING A
COMBINING STRATEGIES ESSAY

Before you can start combining strategies in your writing, it's essential that you have a firm understanding of the purposes and workings of each strategy. Once you become familiar with how the strategies work, you should be able to recognize ways to use and combine them in your writing. Sometimes you will find yourself using a particular strategy almost intuitively. When you encounter a difficult or abstract term or concept — *liberal,* for example — you will define it almost as a matter of course. If you become perplexed because you are having trouble getting your readers to appreciate the severity of a problem, a quick review of the strategies will remind you that you could use description and exemplification. Knowledge of the individual strategies is crucial because there are no formulas or prescriptions for combining strategies. The more you write and the more aware you are of the options available to you, the more skillful you will become at thinking critically about your topic, developing your ideas, and conveying your thoughts to your readers.

Determine Your Purpose

Your purpose in writing is defined as what you are trying to achieve. The most common purposes in nonfiction writing are 1) to express your thoughts and feelings about a life experience, 2) to inform your readers by explaining something about the world around them, and 3) to persuade readers to some belief or action. Your purpose will determine the dominant strategy you use in your essay. If your major purpose is to tell a story of a river-rafting trip, you will use narration. If you wish to recreate the experience of a famous landmark for the first time, you may find description helpful. If you wish to inform your readers, you may find definition, cause and effect, process analysis, comparison and contrast, or division and classification to be best suited to your needs. If you wish to convince your readers of a certain belief or course of action, argumentation is an obvious choice.

Formulate a Thesis Statement

Regardless of the purpose you have set for yourself in writing an essay, it is essential that you commit to a thesis statement, usually a one- or two-sentence statement giving the main point of your essay.

> Party primaries are an indispensable part of the American political process.
> Antibiotics are not nearly as effective as they once were in combating infections among humans.

A question is not a thesis statement. If you find yourself writing a thesis statement that asks a question, answer the question first and then turn your answer into a thesis statement. A thesis statement can be presented anywhere in an essay, but usually it is presented at the beginning of a composition, sometimes after a few introductory sentences that set a context for it.

Determine Your Dominant Developmental Strategy

Depending on your purpose for writing, your thesis statement, and the kinds of ideas and information you have gathered in preparing to write your essay, you may use any one of the following strategies as the dominant strategy for your essay.

Strategy of Development	Purpose
Exemplification	To provide examples or cases in point
Description	To detail sensory perceptions of a person, place, or thing
Narration	To recount an event
Process analysis	To explain how to do something or how something happens
Comparison and contrast	To show similarities or differences
Definition	To provide the meaning of a term
Cause and effect analysis	To analyze why something happens and to describe the consequences of a string of events
Argumentation	To convince others through reasoning

Determine Your Supporting Strategies

The questions listed below — organized by rhetorical strategy — will help you decide which strategies will be most helpful to you in the service of the dominant strategy you have chosen for your essay and in achieving your overall purpose.

- *Exemplification.* Are there examples — facts, statistics, cases in point, personal experiences, interview quotations — that you could add to help you achieve the purpose of your essay?
- *Description.* Does a person, place, or object play a prominent role in your essay? Would the tone, pacing, or overall purpose of your essay benefit from sensory details?
- *Narration.* Are you trying to report or recount an anecdote, an experience, or an event? Does any part of your essay include the telling of a story (either something that happened to you or a person you include in your essay)?
- *Process Analysis.* Would any part of your essay be more clear if you included concrete directions about a certain process? Are there processes that readers would like to understand better? Are you evaluating any processes?

- *Comparison and contrast.* Does your essay contain two or more related subjects? Are you evaluating or analyzing two or more people, places, processes, events, or things? Do you need to establish the similarities and differences between two or more elements?

- *Division and classification.* Are you trying to explain a broad and complicated subject? Would it benefit your essay to reduce this subject to more manageable parts to focus your discussion?

- *Definition.* Who is your audience? Does your essay focus on any abstract, specialized, or new terms that need further explanation so readers understand your point? Does any important word in your essay have many meanings and need to be clarified?

- *Cause and effect analysis.* Are you examining past events or their outcomes? Is your purpose to inform, speculate, or argue about why an identifiable fact happens the way it does?

- *Argumentation.* Are you trying to explain aspects of a particular subject, and are you trying to advocate a specific opinion on this subject or issue in your essay?

Editing Tip: Wordiness

Be sure to follow the guidelines and advice for editing an essay given in Chapter 2, "Writing Essays." The guidelines highlight those sentence-level concerns of style — grammar, mechanics, and punctuation — that are especially important in editing any piece of writing. Wordiness occurs in sentences that contain words that do not contribute to the sentence's meaning. Wordiness can be eliminated by 1) using the active voice, 2) avoiding "there is" and "it is," 3) eliminating redundancies, 4) deleting empty words and phrases, and 5) simplifying inflated expressions.

1. Use the Active Rather than the Passive Voice

The active voice emphasizes the doer of an action rather than the receiver of an action. Not only is the active voice usually shorter than the passive voice, it is a much more vigorous form of expression.

PASSIVE   *The inhabitants of the town were overwhelmed* by the burgeoning mouse population.

ACTIVE   *The burgeoning mouse population overwhelmed* the inhabitants of the town.

In the *active* sentence, *The burgeoning mouse population* is made the subject of the sentence and is moved to the beginning of the sentence — a position of importance — while the verb *overwhelmed* is made an active verb.

2. Avoid "There is" and "It is"

"There is" and "It is" are expletives, words or phrases that do not contribute any meaning but are added only to fill out a sentence. They may be necessary with references to time and weather, but they should be avoided in other circumstances.

WORDY   *There were* many acts of heroism following the earthquake.

EDITED   Many acts of heroism followed the earthquake.

Notice how the edited sentence eliminates the expletive and reveals a specific subject — *acts* — and an action verb — *followed*.

3. Eliminate Redundancies

Unnecessary repetition often creeps into our writing and should be eliminated. For example, how often have you written expressions such as *I thought in my mind, point in time, large in size, completely filled,* or *academic scholar*? Edit such expressions by deleting the unnecessary words or using synonyms.

Sometimes our intent is to add emphasis, but the net effect is extra words that contribute nothing to a sentence's meaning.

REDUNDANT   A *big huge* cloud was advancing on the crowded stadium.

EDITED   A huge cloud was advancing on the crowded stadium.

REDUNDANT   After studying all night, he knew the basic and fundamental principles of his subject.

EDITED   After studying all night, he knew the principles of his subject.

4. Delete Empty Words and Phrases

There are many words and phrases that we use every day that carry no meaning and should be eliminated from our writing during the editing process. Following are examples of some words and expressions that often can be eliminated.

basically	I think/I feel/I believe
essentially	it seems to me
for all intents and purposes	kind of/sort of
generally	tend to
very, surely, truly, really	quite, extremely, severely

5. Simplify Inflated Expressions

Sometimes we use expressions we think important or authoritative people would use. However, it is best to write directly and forcefully and use clear language. Edit inflated or pompous language to its core meaning.

INFLATED   The law office hired two people *who had a complete and thorough knowledge of e-communications.*

EDITED   The law office hired two people who were e-communications experts.

▶   *Questions for Revising and Editing: Combining Strategies*

1. Do I have a purpose for my essay?
2. Is my thesis statement clear?
3. Does my dominant strategy reflect my purpose and my thesis statement?
4. Do my subordinate strategies effectively support the dominant strategy of my essay?
5. Are my subordinate strategies woven into my essay in a natural manner?
6. Have I revised and edited my essay to avoid wordiness?

The Barrio

Robert Ramírez

*Robert Ramírez was born in 1949 and was raised in Edinburg, Texas,
near the Mexican border. He graduated from the University of Texas–Pan
American and then worked in several communications-related jobs before
joining KGBT-TV in Harlingen, Texas, where he was an anchor. He then
moved to finance and worked for a time in banking and as a development
officer responsible for alumni fund-raising for his alma mater.*

*Ramírez's knowledge of the barrio allows him to paint an affection-
ate portrait of barrio life that nevertheless has a hard edge. His barrio is
colorful but not romantic, and his description raises important societal issues as it describes the vibrant community.*

PREPARING TO READ

Describe the neighborhood in which you grew up or the most
memorable neighborhood you ever encountered. Did you like it?
Why or why not? How strong was the sense of community between neighbors? How did it contrast with other neighborhoods
nearby?

The train, its metal wheels squealing as they spin along the silvery
tracks, rolls slower now. Through the gaps between the cars blinks
a streetlamp, and this pulsing light on a barrio streetcorner beats
slower, like a weary heartbeat, until the train shudders to a halt, the
light goes out, and the barrio is deep asleep.

Throughout Aztlán (the Nahuatl term meaning "land to the
north"), trains grumble along the edges of a sleeping people. From
Lower California, through the blistering Southwest, down the Rio
Grande to the muddy Gulf, the darkness and mystery of dreams en-
gulf communities fenced off by railroads, canals, and expressways.
Paradoxical communities, isolated from the rest of the town by concrete columned monuments of progress, yet stranded in the past. They
are surrounded by change. It eludes their reach, in their own backyards, and the people, unable and unwilling to see the future, or even
touch the present, perpetuate the past.

Leaning from the expressway or jolting across the tracks; one enters a different physical world permeated by a different attitude. The
physical dimensions are impressive. It is a large section of town which
extends for fifteen blocks north and south along the tracks, and then
advances eastward, thinning into nothingness beyond the city limits.
Within the invisible (yet sensible) walls of the barrio, are many, many

people living in too few houses. The homes, however, are much more numerous than on the outside.

Members of the barrio describe the entire area as their home. It is a home, but it is more than this. The barrio is a refuge from the harshness and the coldness of the Anglo world. It is a forced refuge. The leprous people are isolated from the rest of the community and contained in their section of town. The stoical pariahs of the barrio accept their fate, and from the angry seeds of rejection grow the flowers of closeness between outcasts, not the thorns of bitterness and the mad desire to flee. There is no want to escape, for the feeling of the barrio is known only to its inhabitants, and the material needs of life can also be found here.

The *tortillería* fires up its machinery three times a day, producing steaming, round, flat slices of barrio bread. In the winter, the warmth of the tortilla factory is a wool *sarape* in the chilly morning hours, but in the summer, it unbearably toasts every noontime customer.

The *panadería* sends its sweet messenger aroma down the dimly lit street, announcing the arrival of fresh, hot sugary *pan dulce*.

The small corner grocery serves the meal-to-meal needs of customers, and the owner, a part of the neighborhood, willingly gives credit to people unable to pay cash for foodstuffs.

The barbershop is a living room with hydraulic chairs, radio, and television, where old friends meet and speak of life as their salted hair falls aimlessly about them.

The pool hall is a junior level country club where 'chucos, strangers in their own land, get together to shoot pool and rap, while veterans, unaware of the cracking, popping balls on the green felt, complacently play dominoes beneath rudely hung *Playboy* foldouts.

The *cantina* is the night spot of the barrio. It is the country club and the den where the rites of puberty are enacted. Here the young become men. It is in the taverns that the young dude shows his *machismo* through the quantity of beer he can hold, the stories of *rucas* he has had, and his willingness and ability to defend his image against hardened and scarred old lions.

No, there is no frantic wish to flee. It would be absurd to leave the familiar and nervously step into the strange and cold Anglo community when the needs of the Chicano can be met in the barrio.

The barrio is closeness. From the family living unit, familial relationships stretch out to immediate neighbors, down the block, around the corner, and to all parts of the barrio. The feeling of family, a rare and treasurable sentiment, pervades and accounts for the inability of the people to leave. The barrio is this attitude manifested on the countenances of the people, on the faces of their homes, and in the gaiety of their gardens.

The color-splashed homes arrest your eyes, arouse your curiosity, 13
and make you wonder what life scenes are being played out in them.
The flimsy, brightly colored, wood-frame houses ignore no neon-
brilliant color. Houses trimmed in orange, chartreuse, lime-green, yellow, and mixtures of these and other hues beckon the beholder to
reflect on the peculiarity of each home. Passing through this land is
refreshing like Brubeck, not narcotizing like revolting rows of similar
houses, which neither offend nor please.

In the evenings, the porches and front yards are occupied with 14
men calmly talking over the noise of children playing baseball in the
unpaved extension of the living room, while the women cook supper
or gossip with female neighbors as they water their *jardines*. The gardens mutely echo the expressive verses of the colorful houses. The
denseness of multicolored plants and trees gives the house the appearance of an oasis or a tropical island hideaway, sheltered from the rest
of the world.

Fences are common in the barrio, but they are fences and not the 15
walls of the Anglo community. On the western side of town, the high
wooden fences between houses are thick, impenetrable walls, built to
keep the neighbors at bay. In the barrio, the fences may be rusty, wire
contraptions or thick green shrubs. In either case you can see through
them and feel no sense of intrusion when you cross them.

Many lower-income families of the barrio manage to maintain a 16
comfortable standard of living through the communal action of family
members who contribute their wages to the head of the family. Economic need creates interdependence and closeness. Small barefooted
boys sell papers on cool, dark Sunday mornings, deny themselves
pleasantries, and give their earnings to *mamá*. The older the child, the
greater the responsibility to help the head of the household provide for
the rest of the family.

There are those, too, who for a number of reasons have not achieved 17
a relative sense of financial security. Perhaps it results from too many
children too soon, but it is the homes of these people and their situation that numbs rather than charms. Their houses, aged and bent,
oozing children, are fissures in the horn of plenty. Their wooden homes
may have brick-pattern asbestos tile on the outer walls, but the tile is
not convincing.

Unable to pay city taxes or incapable of influencing the city to 18
live up to its duty to serve all the citizens, the poorer barrio families remain trapped in the nineteenth century and survive as best they can.
The backyards have well-worn paths to the outhouses, which sit near
the alley. Running water is considered a luxury in some parts of the barrio. Decent drainage is usually unknown, and when it rains, the water
stands for days, an incubator of health hazards and an avoidable nui-
sance. Streets, costly to pave, remain rough, rocky trails. Tires do not

last long, and the constant rattling and shaking grind away a car's life and spread dust through screen windows.

The houses and their *jardines*, the jollity of the people in an adverse world, the brightly feathered alarm clock pecking away at supper and cautiously eyeing the children playing nearby, produce a mystifying sensation at finding the noble savage alive in the twentieth century. It is easy to look at the positive qualities of life in the barrio, and look at them with a distantly envious feeling. One wishes to experience the feelings of the barrio and not the hardships. Remembering the illness, the hunger, the feeling of time running out on you, the walls, both real and imagined, reflecting on living in the past, one finds his envy becoming more elusive, until it has vanished altogether. 19

Back now beyond the tracks, the train creaks and groans, the cars jostle each other down the track, and as the light begins its pulsing, the barrio, with all its meanings, greets a new dawn with yawns and restless stretchings. 20

RESPONDING TO THE TEXT

Does Ramírez's essay leave you with a positive or negative image of the barrio? Is it a place you would like to live in, visit, or avoid? Explain your answer.

ENGAGING THE WRITER'S SUBJECT

1. Based on Ramírez's essay, what is the barrio? Why do you think that Ramírez uses the image of the train to introduce and close his essay about the barrio?

2. In paragraph 4, Ramírez states that residents consider the barrio as something more than a home. What does he mean? In what ways is it more than just a place where they live?

3. Why are the color schemes of the houses in the barrio striking? How do they contrast with houses in other areas of town? (Glossary: *Comparison and Contrast*)

4. Many of the barrio residents are able to achieve financial security. How are they able to do this? What is life like for those who cannot?

ANALYZING THE WRITER'S CRAFT

1. Explain Ramírez's use of the imagery of walls and fences to describe a sense of cultural isolation. What might this imagery symbolize?

2. Ramírez uses several metaphors throughout his essay. (Glossary: *Figures of Speech*) Identify them, and discuss how they contribute to the essay.

3. Ramírez begins his essay with a relatively positive picture of the barrio but ends on a more disheartening note. (Glossary: *Beginnings/Endings*)

Why has he organized his essay this way? What might the effect have been if he had reversed the images?

4. Did reading the essay change the connotations of the word *barrio* for you? (Glossary: *Connotation/Denotation*) If so, how?

5. Ramírez goes into detail about the many groups living in the barrio. How does his subtle use of division and classification add to his description of the barrio? (Glossary: *Classification; Division*) In what ways do the groups he identifies contribute to the unity of life in the barrio?

6. Ramírez invokes such warm images of the barrio that his statement that its inhabitants do not wish to leave seems benign. In the end, however, it has a somewhat ominous ring. How does the description of the barrio have two components, one good and one bad? What are the two sides of the barrio's embrace for the residents?

UNDERSTANDING THE WRITER'S LANGUAGE

1. Ramírez uses Spanish phrases throughout his essay. Why do you suppose he uses them? What is their effect on the reader? He also uses the words *home*, *refuge*, *family*, and *closeness*. In what ways, if any, are they essential to his purpose? (Glossary: *Purpose*)

2. Ramírez calls barrio residents "the leprous people" (paragraph 4). What does the word *leprous* connote in the context of this essay? (Glossary: *Connotation/Denotation*) Why do you think Ramírez chose to use such a strong word to communicate the segregation of the community?

3. Refer to your desk dictionary to determine the meanings of the following words as Ramírez uses them in this selection: *paradoxical* (paragraph 2), *permeated* (3), *stoical* (4), *pariahs* (4), *complacently* (9), *Chicano* (11), *countenances* (12), *fissures* (17), *adverse* (19).

WRITING SUGGESTIONS

1. Ramírez frames his essay with the image of the train rumbling past the sleeping residents. Using Ramírez's essay as a model, write a descriptive essay about where you currently live, whether it is a dorm, an apartment, or a neighborhood with an identity, such as a barrio. (Glossary: *Description*) Use a metaphorical image to frame your essay. (Glossary: *Figures of Speech*) What image is both a part of life where you live and an effective metaphor for the life you lead there?

2. Write a comparison and contrast essay in which you compare where you live now with another residence. (Glossary: *Comparison and Contrast*) Where are you the most comfortable? What about your current surroundings do you like? What do you dislike? How does it compare with your hometown, your first apartment, or another place you have lived? If and when you move on, where do you hope to go?

3. Over the past few decades, there has been a lot of attention paid to Latino communities. Latino candidates have been elected to the U.S.

Congress, there is a greater awareness of Latino issues, and the popular media have embraced many of the influences of Latino culture. There has also been some backlash, however, particularly in language issues. The English-only movement has sought to curtail the growing use of Spanish in official government functions and publications. Write an essay in which you address whether Latinos, such as those described by Ramírez, are still functional "lepers," or outsiders, in American society. Base your argument on research you do into the language issues, life in communities that have a high percentage of Latino residents, and popular media accounts of Latino issues. How much progress is real, and how much is mainly show? Do children in Latino communities today have possibilities that extend beyond their "barrio" or not? Explain.

- To begin your research online, go to **bedfordstmartins.com /subjectsstrategies** and click on "Combining Strategies" or browse the thematic directory of annotated links.

Harry Potter on Sale in Moscow
Sergei Ilnitsky

CONNECTING IMAGE AND TEXT

This photograph captures the winner of a Harry Potter look-alike contest alongside a cardboard cutout of the actor who plays Harry Potter, Daniel Radcliffe, in a Moscow bookstore in the early hours of February 7, 2004, when the Russian translation of *Harry Potter and the Order of the Phoenix* went on sale. How do you "read" this photograph? How, if at all, might the scene differ from one in an American bookstore? What Potter-related — or inspired — products do you see in this photograph? What is your reaction to them? What universal values, fears, apprehensions, and joys might account for Harry Potter's appeal among children and adults worldwide? Your observations will help guide you to the key themes and strategies in the essay that follows.

Harry Potter and the New Consumer

Andrew Blake

Andrew Blake was born in Devizes, Wiltshire, in the United Kingdom in 1955. A graduate of Cambridge University, Keele University, and Thames Polytechnic, he is currently head of Cultural Studies at King Alfred's College, Winchester, where he has been a professor since 1996. Among his publications are The Body Language: The Meaning of Modern Sport *(1996);* The Land without Music: Music, Culture, and Society in Twentieth Century Britain *(1997);* Living through Pop *(1999); and beginner's guides to the works of Salman Rushdie and J. R. R. Tolkien (2002). His latest book,* The Irresistible Rise of Harry Potter *(2002), has been translated into a number of languages, attesting to the worldwide appeal of Harry Potter.*

In "Harry Potter and the New Consumer," an excerpt from a chapter in The Irresistible Rise of Harry Potter, *Blake explains that the success of J. K. Rowling's Harry Potter books reflects a new consumerism involving adultlike children and childlike adults.*

PREPARING TO READ

If you have read any Harry Potter books, what drew you to them? Did you read them because you didn't want to be "left out" of the crowd? If you have not read any, what made them unappealing? Do you find books about fantasy, magic, or wizardry uninteresting? Did your parents or anyone else discourage you from reading Rowling's books?

Even when, wizard-cloaked and wand in hand, he is defeating monsters, Harry Potter is a contemporary boy. He therefore shops. Gazing at the latest broomsticks in the Diagon Alley shop windows, Harry desires the pleasures of retail therapy at least as much as he yearns for the lost love of parental contact. The library is important to all the stories; so is the bookshop. Flourish and Blotts, where pupils at Hogwarts buy

1

books for the coming year, has played its part in each story so far, and as with those chocolate frog collectors' cards, which have come into being since the books' success, the Potter books have had a very significant impact on the world of bookselling. Kidlit was on the rise before Harry arrived on the scene — which is why Bloomsbury set up their children's list in 1995 — but Harry has had a magical effect on the sector. Since the launch of the first novel, sales of children's fiction as a whole have increased by over 25 per cent in both Britain and the United States.

Bookselling, like publishing, is caught in the toils of globalization. 2 New technologies, economies of scale, and silly pressures on academics to produce "research outputs" mean that more titles are published every year. In the 1950s, UK publishers launched around 17,000 new titles per year; today the annual figure is in excess of 116,000. Booksellers and publishers alike concentrate on actually selling the very few titles that will make money. Best-sellers offered at a discount adorn dump-bins, steady sellers stay on the shelves, and those that don't move quickly are returned or otherwise disposed of — many are pulped within months of publication (some 300,000 books are pulped each week in the UK). The plethora of titles has consigned the traditional single-owner musty-shelved bookshop to the dump-bin of history; the book hypermarket has arisen in its place.

In BloomsburyMagazine.com and similar e-publications we see 3 the reinvention of reading in an era of literary fast-food consumerism serviced by Internet chat, celebrity singings, book prizes, and journalists' soundbites, rather than the critical opinion of academic or literary journals. Of course these innovations are also present in the Harry Potter books — though the ways in which the new consumerism is presented imply that they are not to Joanne Rowling's liking. Gilderoy Lockhart, *Chamber of Secrets*'s smarmily charismatic teacher of Defense Against the Dark Arts, is an author with a dozen titles to his name (all of which he has put on the pupils' textbook-buying list for the year), and a veteran of book signings and photo opportunities; we first meet him at a signing in Flourish and Blotts. Lockhart claims to have fought the powers of evil in a series of encounters with werewolves, hags, and vampires, but he turns out to be a lying, cowardly hypocrite whose books have ripped off other people's genuine heroism. Rita Skeeter, the celebrity journalist featured in *Goblet of Fire*, is even less positive. She digs the dirt, and invents it when it does not exist; she interviews people using magical devices that write down the answers she wants to hear, and she ignores what the interviewee actually says; she transforms into an insect in order to overhear private conversations; and she turns any considered answer into a soundbite.

Joanne Rowling may be aware of the current direction of con- 4 sumerism, and Lockhart and Skeeter (and Dudley Dursley) sound a warning about it, but that does not make Harry Potter any the less a blockbuster — and as far as book publishing was concerned a providential blockbuster — in a time of widening child-consumerism. Children's literature sales picked up in the 1990s (before Harry's arrival, we should remember) alongside sales of other children's goods. This was partly because increasing concerns over literacy and schooling's ability to deliver it were encouraging parents in most of the Western world to buy books for their children. But there is another simple reason. Children were increasingly necessary to the functioning of the market, and they were therefore addressed directly as potential consumers. In the advanced capitalist societies of the West, the adult and late-teenage markets had reached saturation point; and although population growth was slow, wealthy parents were having fewer children later in life, so the resulting offspring had more parental income available to them. Meanwhile in many parts of the developing world, the majority of the population is under twenty-one.

The teenage consumer was identified in the 1950s, and has been serviced ever since by the music and fashion industries. This is now a relatively stable market, and since capitalism prefers to expand in search of increased profits, the teenage consumer has now been joined by the preteen consumer, the target audience of the three-hour pop, Potter, and Pokémon commercials collectively known as Saturday morning television. The children's sector is a huge and expanding segment of the market for consumer goods; increasingly it is being segmented by market researchers into "children" under seven and "tweenagers" aged eight to fourteen. At the beginning of the 1990s it was estimated that Americans under twelve spent around $9 billion per year, and influenced family decisions on the spending of another $135 billion. While subsequent estimates vary widely, all are agreed that these figures have increased substantially: a recent survey estimated that the 23 million American under-fourteens spent $30 billion in 2000, while their "pester power" accounted for another $300 billion. No wonder that the market research company that carried out the latter survey concluded that

> No longer kids but still not teens, and maturing more rapidly in every way than any of their predecessors, young Americans between the ages of 8 and 14 represent an increasingly important stand-alone consumer segment. On the one hand, tweens present major marketing challenges because they are part of the most marketing-savvy and consumer-oriented generation in history and consequently are extremely aware of efforts to persuade them to buy a product or service. On the other hand, tweens offer exciting possibilities for marketers of a wide range of consumer products. Their purchasing power has grown measurably within the past decade, they are dedicated to buying the "right" brands and products for

themselves, and they have a significant influence on family purchasing decisions.[1]

Learning how to become good little consumers may begin at home in front of the television or the Internet, but it is increasingly encouraged at school. In-school marketing has mushroomed in the last quarter-century. Scholastic is among the many companies that have targeted the junior consumer through the school system. Companies such as Coca-Cola and the American Channel One, a commercial education channel, have provided educational materials "free" in return for prominent advertising opportunities. Rupert Murdoch's HarperCollins has provided free books — in return for vouchers cut from the magnate's newspapers.

6

Children are, of course, the prime target of the Harry Potter books, films, sweets, cards, and "collectable" toys. But important as shopping is for the characters in the novels, there are limits, and we can identify Rowling's very clear moral injunction about the dangers of rampant child consumption in the figure of Dudley Dursley. As well as being grossly (symbolically) overweight, Dudley is a consumer of the very worst sort, bullying his parents into buying presents such as televisions and computer games, and then hardly using them.

7

Important as tweens are, adults are more important spenders than children. They too, as well as buying for their children, buy and read the books for themselves, in very large numbers; and they too buy high-technology toys such as televisions and computer games. The boundaries between adulthood and childhood have become increasingly thin, in the West at least. The differences have been eroded by an enormous number of interacting changes. Children have become more fully physically and mentally protected, and have received the full panoply of human rights; as we've seen, they are treated as autonomous beings — as consumer citizens — at an earlier age.

8

Adults, meanwhile, have become less "grown-up." The Thatcher–Reagan revolution in values, which tried to wean people away from dependence on the welfare state (partly by closing much of it down) and encouraged "flexible" employment in which the employee took more of the risks, such as their own pension payments, attempted to create the opposite: more "grown-up" adults. Conservatives tried to reverse what they saw as the infantilization of dependence on health and pension arrangements provided by paternal state or employer. But the ideal of individual autonomy promoted as part of this change was only part of a fifty-year-long "revolution in the head"[2] in which Christianity

9

---

[1]www.MarketResearch.com — The U.S. Tweens Market

[2]A phrase elaborated in Ian MacDonald, *Revolution in the Head: The Beatles' Records and the Sixties,* 4th Estate 1994.

and other forms of social hierarchy waned in influence while some of the freedoms the church had formerly policed were legalized. Deference to authority waned. Politics became managerial rather than directional, let alone confrontational. The individual gained some sense of freedom of choice, at the massive cost of increased anxiety about employment and personal debt, at the same time as the collective sense of values held in common was in gradual decline, partly because almost all public institutions were being systematically starved of funds. Not much sense of achieved adulthood there. We were infinitely freer — to feel chained by debt to a world whose significant meanings seemed to revolve around purchase: another form of dependency, of infantilization. Welcome to the real world, as Morpheus says in *The Matrix*.

Those chains of debt form capitalism's unhelpful replacement for   10 the paternal bonds of the welfare state. Capitalism doesn't want to pay people enough money — not because it can't, but because it wants them to borrow. That way, it can plan the future for both cash and credit, and layer the repayment of debt into our life calendars as an incentive to work. Therefore it wants to teach people to become indebted, preferably as early as possible. In the late 1990s, UK students, for example, began to leave university in significant debt, as they have done in much of Europe, and the United States, for several generations. But the cost structures in Britain are different; housing for purchase or rent is particularly expensive. This means that young people in their twenties are unlikely to be able to afford housing of their own; a flatshare* culture has developed, in which groups of people, collectively renting property, form substitute families in which there are no roles differentiated by age. Many make it to thirty in this position, with more disposable income by this time but without the independence from family that has been associated with adulthood — in the West — since the industrial revolution moved the majority of people from relatively static rural communities to more mobile urban spaces.

People still do, eventually, move through extended adolescence   11 and become family adults, but in late marriages, with fewer children, and constrained by those property prices to big mortgages — so they rebind themselves into the same chains of debt that had characterized their early twenties. This discourages risk, experiment, choice. It's because of this constraining of independence that the Middle England of Privet Drive, Little Whinging, and the Dursleys, is characterized by extreme anxiety over being seen as "perfectly normal, thank you very much"[3] within the world of clipped hedges and little social contact, which characterizes suburbia.

---

*roommate. (Ed.)
[3]*Soccerer's Stone*, p. 1.

This is the world of "bowling alone," in the phrase used by Ameri-   12
can sociologist Robert Putnam. Putnam's gloomy view of the present
and future of community (in the United States, though his thoughts
apply elsewhere) goes like this. Once upon a time people went bowling
in social groups and leagues, and they did many other things in groups
as well. But since the 1960s the number of people enrolled in sociable
organizations — such as boy scouts, the Red Cross, even parent–teacher
associations — has fallen, and continues to fall. By the 1990s, he
claimed, most people were happier going bowling alone than as part of
a group. This stood for a loss of confidence in the collective, and it was
matched by the withdrawal of many Americans from the democratic
process and from any other active participation in community building,
and by a rising of mistrust of government — and arguably also by rising
rates of depression and suicide. Putnam's thoughts about the decline of
community have been echoed by others — the 2001 election in the UK,
for instance, saw the smallest turnout since the establishment of mass
democracy. Researchers reported that many young people (the least
likely age group to vote) simply refused to engage with politics or community beyond their own limited groups of friends and workmates.

All that's left is to spend — even if you are already in debt. With   13
neither political leadership nor a sense of collective identity, culture is
about consumption rather than performance. A vicar, retiring in 1999,
observed the long-term changes in his parish in Peterlee, County
Durham, since his arrival in 1964 (note the cultural difference in the
value ascribed to bowling!):

> When I came there were amateur operatics, drama groups,
> choral societies. They have all gone. Just as the youngsters, in my
> early years, were delighted to go hiking in the Cleveland hills but
> they now only want to go to the leisure center or bowling. They
> enjoy the commercial; they want to spend. Something has gone in
> the spirit.[4]

By this standard, and produced within this culture, the Harry Potter
books are of course contemporary political documents. The action takes
place against a very wide-ranging background of families, family substitutes, and family and community politics. Hogwarts and its houses
(each with its ghost); the other schools; the very different family values
of the Dursleys, the Weasleys, and the Malfoys — and the complex
racial and class politics that surround these families' relationships —
each represent aspects of the contemporary politics of the family and

---

[4]The Rev. Keith Wordhouse, quoted in Paul Vallely, "Back in Tyne," *Independent Magazine*, 24 April 1999, p. 21.

the search for community. This search is stepped up at the end of *Goblet of Fire* as the wizarding world begins to divide into opposing camps.

However, Harry's position in this quest is ambivalent. Harry arrives 14 at Hogwarts as an outsider in two complementary and contradictory respects: He is new to the wizarding world, but he is already famous and permanently marked as "the boy who lived" at Voldemort's expense. As the series progresses, Harry seems increasingly to be "bowling alone," striving for the achievement of adulthood through heroic individualism, dislocated from his actual family, his step-family, and often from his (few) school friends. This can be seen as modelling variations on typical teenagehood, with its social anxieties redoubled by the self-consciousness of puberty, and we might well expect that Harry and friends will find it easier to be close in book five and after. But for Harry all this teenage individualizing comes with the pretty constant feeling that someone in the wizarding world is trying to kill him — not his friends or community, just him — whether Voldemort, Sirius Black, or even Professor Snape. But though he wants to be part of a community (and pays his winnings to the Weasley twins so that they can all share laughter), he still wants the latest high-performance broomstick for himself, and he can still go off and practice Quidditch when there is a family or political crisis (as he and the Weasley boys do in *Goblet of Fire*, despite his "leaden stomach"[5] as he waits to hear from Sirius Black — to the disgust of Hermione). Retail therapy and sport substituting for emotional contact — no wonder so many childlike adults identify with him.

And no wonder the Harry Potter industry provides the material 15 goods for those identifiers: The generations are joined through the act of consumption. The books are constantly being repackaged, including "adult" paperback editions and also a number of expensively bound volumes suitable for the conspicuous consumer. Doubtless the videos and DVDs of the movies will be similarly packaged and repackaged. They are joined by objects seemingly more squarely aimed at children. Harry's face adorns Coca-Cola cans — even though so far the company agrees that it would be out of place for him to drink Coke in the movies. Everything that could be taken from the books and films seems to be available in Muggle-friendly form, from (cheap) chocolate frog collectors' cards or Bertie Bott's Every Flavor Beans, complete with genuinely unpleasant horseradish flavor, to (more than pocket money) soft-toy versions of Norbert the baby dragon, to (very expensive) Lego versions of Hogwarts School itself. And there are plenty of Web sites and in-store promotional posters to tell you about it all, and to encourage you to save, bully your parents, or otherwise spend,

---

[5]*Goblet of Fire*, p. 134.

spend, spend. The "free" CD-ROM released with the film soundtrack recording (which sold well enough to enter the "classical charts") contains a downloadable screensaver that is an animated advertisement for a Harry Potter computer game — something else to buy. Thus the new generations become the new consumers, and Harry Potter, having done his bit for the future of publishing, plays another significant part in the development of consumer capitalism.

Capitalism is, as the truism has it, global; certainly the much-translated Harry has repeated his Bloomsbury trick for child-consumer capitalism the world over (that free CD-ROM includes trailers with subtitles in French, German, Italian, Korean, and Thai). One of the many recent analyses of children as consumers has concluded blandly that 16

> before there is a geographic culture there is a children's culture; that children are very much alike all over the industrialized world. The result is that they very much want the same things; that they generally translate their needs into similar wants that tend to transcend culture. Therefore it appears that fairly standardized multinational marketing strategies to children around the globe are viable.[6]

Harry's impact cannot be characterized quite so simply, of course. The books are at one level "fairly standardized," but they have been *translated* into American English, for example — notoriously with the title of the first volume, which in American is *Harry Potter and the Sorcerer's Stone*. Other Americanisms include "trash" for rubbish and, stupidly, "scotch tape" for Rowling's enjoyable pun "spellotape." The translators, facing the challenge of such unusual or invented words, have perforce come up with versions of the stories that are subtly tailored to their audience's expectations, and subtly different from the Rowling originals. But however you localize the translation, Harry is very English, and goes to a very English-style school. How far can this map, which I have so far principally related to the UK at the present time, act as a template for Harry Potter's global success?

An essay by Polish research student Justyna Kita, posted on a British Council Web site, sums up what Harry means to readers worldwide. "I got *Harry Potter and the Philosopher's Stone* as a present and my first thought was 'Why not? At least I will find out why the British are so crazy about it.' I started reading out of curiosity not expecting anything extraordinary. But the book was captivating from the start."[7] 17

---

[6]Barrie Gunther and Adrian Furnham, *Children as Consumers*, Routledge 1998, p. 8.

[7]Justyna Kita, "Harry Potter — The Mystery of the Global Phenomenon," British Council Poland Web site. http://elt.britcoun.org.pl — accessed November 2001.

She goes on to praise the constant witty wordplay, but especially likes the school setting and its juxtaposition of the familiar and the magical, and the author's weaving of the dark side into the everyday events of school life.

This typical response (from someone with no direct connection with the private boarding school or the class structure that supports it) goes some way to explaining why Harry Potter has become truly globalized. But it is hard to imagine a Polish story, however well written, affecting the world in the same way. This is partly to do with the general fit of English — including literature as well as language — into the world's culture. Some people would assume that English literature can't be global in the same sense as Hollywood film. Though, certainly, the intensity of global marketing of all things Harry has increased since the deal with Warner Brothers was signed, they'd be wrong. Thanks to the cultural connections established through the British empire (including the establishment of English in the American colonies in the seventeenth century), English is a globally important language. Thanks to the nineteenth-century invention of "English Literature" — which solidified as an academic category at the height of empire — this cultural category became a model for the rest of the world. Thanks to the flourishing of British *popular* fiction in the late nineteenth century, and to the cadet relationship that developed between British fiction and Hollywood at the start of the twentieth, three fantasy characters have become the most important non-religious global cultural icons in history.

Harry Potter is the third of these — after Sherlock Holmes and James Bond, each of whom also offered magical solutions to widely shared problems. Sherlock Holmes first appeared in the English press in 1887, two years after the crimes of Jack the Ripper became public. Holmes, the gentlemanly private detective with hyperrational skills of deduction, offered a positive fictional contrast to the (largely working-class) police's failure to catch "Jack." Holmes proved so popular that he was revived after death by Sir Arthur Conan Doyle, his originating author. Many others have written Sherlock Holmes stories. He has so far been the subject of at least sixty films (including Spielberg's 1985 *Young Sherlock Holmes*, much of which was based at a public school; the film's scriptwriter was Chris Columbus, the director of the first two Harry Potter movies). There have been many television series — including a recent U.S. cartoon series, *Sherlock Holmes in the Twenty-Second Century* and a Canadian-made sequence of TV shows that launched in 2000. The innumerable books and journals have been joined by innumerable Web sites. The various Sherlock Holmes societies anticipated *Star Trek* fans in their zeal to dress as Holmes, Watson *et al.* and to take part in "murder weekends" and other adventures, which they still do.

James Bond first appeared in Ian Fleming's novel *Casino Royale* in 20
1953. When the novels began to appear in paperback, Bond was taken
up as a newspaper strip-cartoon character, in the *Daily Express*. In the
first twenty-five years of Bond's fictional existence, the novels sold
over 27 million paperbacks in the UK alone. The first Bond film, *Doctor
No*, appeared in 1962; the series shows no sign of ceasing. The magic
Bond offered in the mid-1950s was to portray a British agent who actually spied for Britain. Like Holmes, Bond was (slightly ambivalently)
killed by an author who was tired of him, at the end of *From Russia
with Love*, but as with Holmes, public pressure forced Fleming to resurrect Bond. Then, from the early 1960s, the films reinvented Bond as a
universal figure rather than a mere Brit. Following Fleming's lead (in
and after *Goldfinger*) the movies' plots moved away from Cold War
ideological confrontations and instead represented the global threat of
organized crime, invoking fears that prefigured our current collective
concern over globalization. Through his defeat of a sequence of money-
making villains intent on world domination, Bond has magically, and
repeatedly, saved us from the excesses of global capitalism. The mer-
chandising of Bond memorabilia — notably models of the various
"Bond cars" — grew alongside the films from the early 1960s, and the
videos/DVDs are constantly repackaged for new moments of consumption such as Christmas. There are several very popular computer
games in which the player becomes Bond.

And now we have Harry — a character who has already appeared 21
in books; on audio tape, film, and computer games; and who is the
subject of much World Wide Web activity. Harry Potter is a suburban
English child. So far, so far from global. But he is an orphan, doesn't
like the adults or children around him, and perceives their behavior to
him as structured oppression. So he is also a literary and psychological
universal, anticipated in fairy tales and other stories from all over the
world. But he then goes beyond the sources, and well beyond the position reflected in much literature and other entertainment for young
people — whether *Peter Pan* or *Clueless* — in which "over twenty-one"
equates to "of no interest," and being young is everything. He meets a
world in which adults aren't all oppressors or boring pedants. Some
are clearly on his side, though not themselves merely childish — Ha-
grid and Dumbledore are far more sympathetic adults than the adults
in most school stories. These few carefully selected non-parental
adults help the children to achieve a precocious collective independence, and they allow Joanne Rowling to build on the orphan scenario and address a whole raft of issues around childhood, adulthood,
and the boundaries in between — touching subtly on the perceived
crises in masculinity, changing child/parent relationships, and so on.
These too are universal issues, as important in the public discourse of
Japan as in the suburbs of the South-East of (Middle) England.

RESPONDING TO THE TEXT

In paragraph 4, Blake refers to "a time of widening child-consumerism" that began before the first Harry Potter book appeared in the late 1990s. Do you agree that children today have much more sway — or "pester power" — over parents than children a generation ago? If so, why? How does child-focused marketing today compare to when you were younger?

ENGAGING THE WRITER'S SUBJECT

1. Who are "tweenagers"? Why are they important for the new consumerism, according to Blake? How did a recent survey describe this segment of the consumer market? (Glossary: *Description*)

2. What is globalization? How does it figure into the big picture of the issues Blake discusses? (Glossary: *Definition*)

3. According to Blake, what societal factors have contributed to making the Harry Potter books popular among adults?

4. What Harry Potter product tie-ins does Blake discuss? According to Blake, how do these "branded" products help spread J. K. Rowling's books across the globe?

5. In paragraph 18, Blake states, "it is hard to imagine a Polish story, however well written, affecting the world in the same way [as Harry Potter]." Do you agree? Why or why not? What evidence does Blake cite to support his argument? (Glossary: *Argument; Evidence*)

6. Can we assume that J. K. Rowling is in favor of the relationship between education and consumerism? Why or why not? Is her position ironic? (Glossary: *Irony*)

7. Why does Blake think that English is a globally important language?

ANALYZING THE WRITER'S CRAFT

1. Blake's title, "Harry Potter and the New Consumer," is an obvious play on the titles of J. K. Rowling's books. (Glossary: *Title*) Given Blake's subject, how effective is his title? (Glossary: *Subject*) Can you think of titles that would work as well or better?

2. Blake is an academic and cultural theorist. How would you describe his style: playful, academic, reserved? (Glossary: *Style*) Why? What does Blake's style tell you about his intended audience? (Glossary: *Audience*)

3. In paragraph 10, Blake states, "Capitalism doesn't want to pay people enough money — not because it can't, but because it wants them to borrow. That way, it can plan the future for both cash and credit, and layer the repayment of debt into our life calendars as an incentive to work." How does Blake's assessment of capitalism support his analysis of Harry Potter's global popularity? (Glossary: *Evidence*)

4. Why does Blake conclude with a discussion of the tradition he sees in the movement from Sherlock Holmes to James Bond to Harry Potter as

internationally famous British literary characters? (Glossary: *Beginnings/ Endings*)

5. Blake uses exemplification to argue his point in this essay. What other strategies does Blake use? How does each strategy, including definition, cause and effect analysis, and argument, contribute to the effectiveness of this essay?

UNDERSTANDING THE WRITER'S LANGUAGE

1. A British citizen, Blake uses British English. Cite several examples of this British diction. (Glossary: *Diction*) How might an American say the same thing?

2. What is Blake's attitude toward the material he presents? (Glossary: *Attitude*) Does he like Rowling's Harry Potter books?

3. Blake's language is creative and lively. He is adept at using innovative phrases such as "dump-bin of history" (paragraph 2), "pester power" (5), and "flatshare culture" (10). Identify other interesting phrases in Blake's essay. What do they mean, and how did they affect your reading of the essay?

4. Refer to your desk dictionary to determine the meanings of the following words as Blake uses them in this selection: *globalization* (paragraph 2), *pulped* (2), *plethora* (2), *providential* (4), *rampant* (7), *pension* (9), *paternal* (9), *autonomy* (9), *infantilization* (9), *vicar* (13), *ambivalent* (14), *perforce* (16), *pedants* (21).

WRITING SUGGESTIONS

1. Blake says that "the children's sector is a huge and expanding segment of the market for consumer goods; increasingly it is being segmented by market researchers into 'children' under seven and 'tweenagers' aged eight to fourteen" (paragraph 5). Write an essay in which you compare and contrast a television or print advertisement for a children's product with one for a tweenagers' product. (Glossary: *Comparison and Contrast*) How are they similar? How are they different? How can you tell which segment is being targeted? Explain. Where were the advertisements placed? What does this placement tell you about their intended audience? (Glossary: *Audience*)

2. In paragraph 14 Blake states, "Retail therapy and sport substituting for emotional contact — no wonder so many childlike adults identify with [Harry Potter]." Do you agree with Blake's assessment? Why or why not? Are there other examples from recent pop culture that could also be applied to Blake's observation? Write an essay in which you defend or refute Blake's position on Harry Potter's success. (Glossary: *Argument*) To what, in your opinion, does Harry Potter owe his global fame? You might find it helpful to refer to your Connecting Image and Text response for this selection.

3. As Benjamin R. Barber states in his classic essay "Jihad vs. McWorld," globalization is an "onrush of [Western, often American] economic and ecological forces that demand integration and uniformity and that mesmerize the world with fast music, fast computers, and fast food." In your college library and on the Internet, research the issue of globalization. What are the threats and benefits of a globalized world? What are globalization's causes and effects? (Glossary: *Cause and Effect Analysis*) In your opinion, is globalization a uniting or dividing force? Explain. How have people in the United States and abroad reacted to globalization? (Glossary: *Exemplification*) Write an essay in which you present your findings.

• To begin your research online, go to **bedfordstmartins.com /subjectsstrategies** and click on "Combining Strategies" or browse the thematic directory of annotated links.

On Being a Cripple

Nancy Mairs

Nancy Mairs, a poet and writer, was born in Long Beach, California, in 1943. She attended Wheaton College in Massachusetts, where she earned a B.A. in English in 1964. From 1964 until 1972, Mairs took a number of teaching and writing jobs around Boston, and it was during this period that she learned she had multiple sclerosis and experienced major depression. In 1972, Mairs decided to pursue a career in writing and entered the creative writing program at the University of Arizona, where she earned an M.F.A. in poetry (1975) and then a Ph.D. in English (1984). In works like Plaintext *(1986),* Carnal Acts *(1990), and* Waist High in the World *(1997), which consist mostly of autobiographical essays, Mairs has refused to deny or cover up the specificities of her life as a woman. In fact, Mairs has often used the most intimate details of her inner life as the essential material of her art. Through her writing, Mairs has called into question what can and cannot be revealed about one's life in writing for a public audience.*

"On Being a Cripple" is an essay from her critically acclaimed Plaintext. *In this essay, she writes poignantly about living with MS and about the strategies she has developed to cope with it. But, more important, she has written of the ways in which "being a cripple" has intensified and even enhanced her artistic vision.*

PREPARING TO READ

The word *cripple* carries powerful connotations. What visual and emotional responses does it arouse in you? Do you object to the word? Why or why not?

> To escape is nothing. Not to escape is nothing.
>
> — LOUISE BOGAN

The other day I was thinking of writing an essay on being a cripple. I was thinking hard in one of the stalls of the women's room in my office building, as I was shoving my shirt into my jeans and tugging up my zipper. Preoccupied, I flushed, picked up my book bag, took my cane down from the hook, and unlatched the door. So many movements unbalanced me, and as I pulled the door open I fell over backward, landing fully clothed on the toilet seat with my legs splayed in front of me: the old beetle-on-its-back routine. Saturday afternoon, the building deserted, I was free to laugh aloud as I wriggled back to my feet, my voice bouncing off the yellowish tiles from all directions.

Had anyone been there with me, I'd have been still and faint and hot with chagrin. I decided that it was high time to write the essay.

First, the matter of semantics. I am a cripple. I choose this word to name me. I choose from among several possibilities, the most common of which are "handicapped" and "disabled." I made the choice a number of years ago, without thinking, unaware of my motives for doing so. Even now, I'm not sure what those motives are, but I recognize that they are complex and not entirely flattering. People — crippled or not — wince at the word "cripple," as they do not at "handicapped" or "disabled." Perhaps I want them to wince. I want them to see me as a tough customer, one to whom the fates/gods/viruses have not been kind, but who can face the brutal truth of her existence squarely. As a cripple, I swagger.

But, to be fair to myself, a certain amount of honesty underlies my choice. "Cripple" seems to me a clean word, straightforward and precise. It has an honorable history, having made its first appearance in the Lindisfarne Gospel in the tenth century. As a lover of words, I like the accuracy with which it describes my condition: I have lost the full use of my limbs. "Disabled," by contrast, suggests an incapacity, physical or mental. And I certainly don't like "handicapped," which implies that I have deliberately been put at a disadvantage, by whom I can't imagine (my God is not a Handicapper General), in order to equalize chances in the great race of life. These words seem to me to be moving away from my condition, to be widening the gap between word and reality. Most remote is the recently coined euphemism "differently abled," which partakes of the same semantic hopefulness that transformed countries from "undeveloped" to "underdeveloped," then to "less developed," and finally to "developing" nations. People have continued to starve in those countries during the shift. Some realities do not obey the dictates of language.

Mine is one of them. Whatever you call me, I remain crippled. But I don't care what you call me, so long as it isn't "differently abled," which strikes me as pure verbal garbage designed, by its ability to describe anyone, to describe no one. I subscribe to George Orwell's thesis that "the slovenliness of our language makes it easier for us to have foolish thoughts." And I refuse to participate in the degeneration of the language to the extent that I deny that I have lost anything in the course of this calamitous disease; I refuse to pretend that the only differences between you and me are the various ordinary ones that distinguish any one person from another. But call me "disabled" or "handicapped" if you like. I have long since grown accustomed to them; and if they are vague, at least they hint at the truth. Moreover, I use them myself. Society is no readier to accept crippledness than to accept death, war, sex, sweat, or wrinkles. I would never refer to another person as a cripple. It is the word I used to name only myself.

I haven't always been crippled, a fact for which I am soundly grateful. To be whole of limb is, I know from experience, infinitely more pleasant and useful than to be crippled; and if that knowledge leaves me open to bitterness at my loss, the physical soundness I once enjoyed (though I did not enjoy it half enough) is well worth the occasional stab of regret. Though never any good at sports, I was a normally active child and young adult. I climbed trees, played hopscotch, jumped rope, skated, swam, rode my bicycle, sailed. I despised team sports, spending some of the wretchedest afternoons of my life sweaty and humiliated, behind a field-hockey stick and under a basketball hoop. I tramped alone for miles along the bridle paths that webbed the woods behind the house I grew up in. I swayed through countless dim hours in the arms of one man or another under the scattered shot of light from mirrored balls, and gyrated through countless more as Tab Hunter and Johnny Mathis gave way to the Rolling Stones, Creedence Clearwater Revival, Cream. I walked down the aisle. I pushed baby carriages, changed tires in the rain, marched for peace.

When I was twenty-eight I started to trip and drop things. What at first seemed my natural clumsiness soon became too pronounced to shrug off. I consulted a neurologist, who told me that I had a brain tumor. A battery of tests, increasingly disagreeable, revealed no tumor. About a year and a half later I developed a blurred spot in one eye. I had, at last, the episodes "disseminated in space and time" requisite for a diagnosis: multiple sclerosis. I have never been sorry for the doctor's initial misdiagnosis, however. For almost a week, until the negative results of the tests were in, I thought that I was going to die right away. Every day for the past nearly ten years, then, has been a kind of gift. I accept all gifts.

Multiple sclerosis is a chronic degenerative disease of the central nervous system, in which the myelin that sheathes the nerves is somehow eaten away and scar tissue forms in its place, interrupting the nerves' signals. During its course, which is unpredictable and uncontrollable, one may lose vision, hearing, speech, the ability to walk, control of bladder and/or bowels, strength in any or all extremities, sensitivity to touch, vibration, and/or pain, potency, coordination of movements — the list of possibilities is lengthy and yes, horrifying. One may also lose one's sense of humor. That's the easiest to lose and the hardest to survive without.

In the past ten years, I have sustained some of these losses. Characteristic of MS are sudden attacks, called exacerbations, followed by remissions, and these I have not had. Instead, my disease has been slowly progressive. My left leg is now so weak that I walk with the aid of a brace and a cane; and for distances I use an Amigo, a variation on the electric wheelchair that looks rather like an electrified kiddie car. I no longer have much use of my left hand. Now my right side is weakening as well. I still have the blurred spot in my right eye. Overall, though, I've been lucky so far. My world has, of necessity, been circumscribed by my losses, but the terrain left me has been ample enough for me to continue many of the activities that absorb me: writing, teaching, raising children and cats and plants and snakes, reading, speaking publicly about MS and depression, even playing bridge with people patient and honorable enough to let me scatter cards every which way without sneaking a peek.

Lest I begin to sound like Pollyanna, however, let me say that I don't like having MS. I hate it. My life holds realities — harsh ones, some of them — that no right-minded human being ought to accept without grumbling. One of them is fatigue. I know of no one with MS who does not complain of bone-weariness; in a disease that presents an astonishing variety of symptoms, fatigue seems to be a common factor. I wake up in the morning feeling the way most people do at the end of a bad day, and I take it from there. As a result, I spend a lot of time *in extremis* and, impatient with limitation, I tend to ignore my fatigue until my body breaks down in some way and forces rest. Then I miss picnics, dinner parties, poetry readings, the brief visits of old friends from out of town. The offspring of a puritanical tradition of exceptional venerability, I cannot view these lapses without shame. My life often seems a series of small failures to do as I ought.

I lead, on the whole, an ordinary life, probably rather like the one I would have led had I not had MS. I am lucky that my predilections were already solitary, sedentary, and bookish — unlike the world-famous French cellist I have read about, or the young woman I talked with one long afternoon who wanted only to be a jockey. I had just begun graduate school when I found out something was wrong with me, and I have remained, interminably, a graduate student. Perhaps I would not have if I'd thought I had the stamina to return to a full-time job as a technical editor; but I've enjoyed my studies.

In addition to studying, I teach writing courses. I also teach medical students how to give neurological examinations. I pick up freelance editing jobs here and there. I have raised a foster son and sent him into the world, where he has made me two grandbabies, and I am still escorting my daughter and son through adolescence. I go to Mass every Saturday. I am a superb, if messy, cook. I am also an enthusiastic laundress, capable of sorting a hamper full of clothes into five subtly differentiated piles, but a terrible housekeeper. I can do italic writing and, in an emergency, bathe an oil-soaked cat. I play a fiendish game of Scrabble. When I have the time and the money, I like to sit on my front steps with my husband, drinking Amaretto and smoking a cigar, as we imagine our counterparts in Leningrad and make sure that the sun gets down once more behind the sharp childish scrawl of the Tucson Mountains.

This lively plenty has its bleak complement, of course, in all the things I can no longer do. I will never run again, except in dreams, and one day I may have to write that I will never walk again. I like to go camping, but I can't follow George and the children along the trails that wander out of a campsite through the desert or into the mountains. In fact, even on the level I've learned never to check the weather or try to hold a coherent conversation: I need all my attention for my wayward feet. Of late, I have begun to catch myself wondering how people can propel themselves without canes. With only one usable hand, I have to select my clothing with care not so much for style as for ease of ingress and egress, and even so, dressing can be laborious. I can no longer do fine stitchery, pick up babies, play the piano, braid my hair. I am immobilized by acute attacks of depression, which may or may not be physiologically related to MS but are certainly its logical concomitant.

These two elements, the plenty and the privation, are never pure, nor are the delight and wretchedness that accompany them. Almost every pickle that I get into as a result of my weakness and clumsiness — and I get into plenty — is funny as well as maddening and sometimes painful. I recall one May afternoon when a friend and I were going out for a drink after finishing up at school. As we were climbing into opposite sides of my car, chatting, I tripped and fell, flat and hard, onto the asphalt parking lot, my abrupt departure interrupting him in midsentence. "Where'd you go?" he called as he came around the back of the car to find me hauling myself up by the door frame. "Are you all right?" Yes, I told him, I was fine, just a bit rattly, and we drove off to find a shady patio and some beer. When I got home an hour or so later, my daughter greeted me with "What have you done to yourself?" I looked down. One elbow of my white turtleneck with the green froggies, one knee of my white trousers, one white kneesock were blood-soaked. We peeled off the clothes and inspected the damage, which was nasty enough but not alarming. That part wasn't funny: The abrasions took a long time to heal, and one got a little infected. Even so, when I think of my friend talking earnestly, suddenly, to the hot thin air while I dropped from his view as though through a trap door, I find the image as silly as something from a Marx Brothers movie.

I may find it easier than other cripples to amuse myself because I live propped by the acceptance and the assistance and, sometimes, the amusement of those around me. Grocery clerks tear my checks out of my checkbook for me, and sales clerks find chairs to put into dressing rooms when I want to try on clothes. The people I work with make sure I teach at times when I am least likely to be fatigued, in places

I can get to, with the materials I need. My students, with one anonymous exception (in an end-of-the-semester evaluation) have been unperturbed by my disability. Some even like it. One was immensely cheered by the information that I paint my own fingernails; she decided, she told me, that if I could go to such trouble over fine details, she could keep on writing essays. I suppose I became some sort of bright-fingered muse. She wrote good essays, too.

The most important struts in the framework of my existence, of course, are my husband and children. Dismayingly few marriages survive the MS test, and why should they? Most twenty-two- and nineteen-year-olds, like George and me, can vow in clear conscience, after a childhood of chickenpox and summer colds, to keep one another in sickness and in health so long as they both shall live. Not many are equipped for catastrophe: the dismay, the depression, the extra work, the boredom that a degenerative disease can insinuate into a relationship. And our society, with its emphasis on fun and its association of fun with physical performance, offers little encouragement for a whole spouse to stay with a crippled partner. Children experience similar stresses when faced with a crippled parent, and they are more helpless, since parents and children can't usually get divorced. They hate, of course, to be different from their peers, and the child whose mother is tacking down the aisle of a school auditorium packed with proud parents like a Cape Cod dinghy in a stiff breeze jolly well stands out in a crowd. Deprived of legal divorce, the child can at least deny the mother's disability, even her existence, forgetting to tell her about recitals and PTA meetings, refusing to accompany her to stores or church or the movies, never inviting friends to the house. Many do.

But I've been limping along for ten years now, and so far George and the children are still at my left elbow, holding tight. Anne and Matthew vacuum floors and dust furniture and haul trash and rake up dog droppings and button my cuffs and bake lasagne and Toll House cookies with just enough grumbling so I know that they don't have brain fever. And far from hiding me, they're forever dragging me by racks of fancy clothes or through teeming school corridors, or welcoming gaggles of friends while I'm wandering through the house in Anne's filmy pink babydoll pajamas. George generally calls before he brings someone home, but he does just as many dumb thankless chores as the children. And they all yell at me, laugh at some of my jokes, write me funny letters when we're apart — in short, treat me as an ordinary human being for whom they have some use. I think they like me. Unless they're faking. . . .

Faking. There's the rub. Tugging at the fringes of my consciousness always is the terror that people are kind to me only because I'm a cripple. My mother almost shattered me once, with that instinct mothers have — blind, I think, in this case, but unerring nonetheless — for striking blows along the fault-lines of their children's hearts, by telling me, in an attack on my selfishness, "We all have to make allowances for you, of course, because of the way you are." From the distance of a couple of years, I have to admit that I haven't any idea just what she meant, and I'm not sure that she knew either. She was awfully angry. But at the time, as the words thudded home, I felt my worst fear, suddenly realized. I could bear being called selfish: I am. But I couldn't bear the corroboration that those around me were doing in fact what I'd always suspected them of doing, professing fondness while silently putting up with me because of the way I am. A cripple. I've been a little cracked ever since.

Along with this fear that people are secretly accepting shoddy goods comes a relentless pressure to please — to prove myself worth the burdens I impose, I guess, or to build a substantial account of goodwill against which I may write drafts in times of need. Part of the pressure arises from social expectations. In our society, anyone who deviates from the norm had better find some way to compensate. Like fat people, who are expected to be jolly, cripples must bear their lot meekly and cheerfully. A grumpy cripple isn't playing by the rules. And much of the pressure is self-generated. Early on I vowed that, if I had to have MS, by God I was going to do it well. This is a class act, ladies and gentlemen. No tears, no recriminations, no fainthearted-ness. 18

One way and another, then, I wind up feeling like Tiny Tim, peer-ing over the edge of the table at the Christmas goose, waving my crutch, piping down God's blessing on us all. Only sometimes I don't want to play Tiny Tim. I'd rather be Caliban, a most scurvy monster. Fortunately, at home no one much cares whether I'm a good cripple or a bad cripple as long as I make vichyssoise with fair regularity. One eve-ning several years ago, Anne was reading at the dining-room table while I cooked dinner. As I opened a can of tomatoes, the can slipped in my left hand and juice spattered me and the counter with bloody spots. Fatigued and infuriated, I bellowed, "I'm so sick of being crippled!" Anne glanced at me over the top of her book. "There now," she said, "do you feel better?" "Yes," I said, "yes, I do." She went back to her reading. I felt better. That's about all the attention my scurviness ever gets. 19

Because I hate being crippled, I sometimes hate myself for being a cripple. Over the years I have come to expect — even accept — attacks of violent self-loathing. Luckily, in general our society no longer con-nects deformity and disease directly with evil (though a charismatic once told me that I have MS because a devil is in me) and so I'm al-lowed to move largely at will, even among small children. But I'm not sure that this revision of attitude has been particularly helpful. Physical 20 imperfection, even freed of moral disapprobation, still defies and vio-lates the ideal, especially for women, whose confinement in their bod-ies as objects of desire is far from over. Each age, of course, has its ideal, and I doubt that ours is any better or worse than any other. Today's ideal woman, who lives on the glossy pages of dozens of mag-azines, seems to be between the ages of eighteen and twenty-five; her hair has body, her teeth flash white, her breath smells minty, her un-derarms are dry; she has a career but is still a fabulous cook, especially of meals that take less than twenty minutes to prepare; she does not ordinarily appear to have a husband or children; she is trim and deeply tanned; she jogs, swims, plays tennis, rides a bicycle, sails, but does not bowl; she travels widely, even to out-of-the-way places like Finland and Samoa, always in the company of the ideal man, who possesses a nearly identical set of characteristics. There are a few exceptions. Though usually white and often blonde, she may be black, Hispanic, Asian, or Native American, so long as she is unusually sleek. She may be old, provided she is selling a laxative or is Lauren Bacall. If she is selling a detergent, she may be married and have a flock of strikingly messy children. But she is never a cripple.

Like many women I know, I have always had an uneasy relation-ship with my body. I was not a popular child, largely, I think now, because I was peculiar: intelligent, intense, moody, shy, given to unex-pected actions and inexplicable notions and emotions. But as I entered adolescence, I believed myself unpopular because I was homely: my breasts too flat, my mouth too wide, my hips too narrow, my clothing never quite right in fit or style. I was not, in fact, particularly ugly, old photographs inform me, though I was well off the ideal; but I carried this sense of self-alienation with me into adulthood, where it regener-ated in response to the depredations of MS. Even with my brace I walk with a limp so pronounced that, seeing myself on the videotape of a television program on the disabled, I couldn't believe that anything but an inchworm could make progress humping along like that. My shoulders droop and my pelvis thrusts forward as I try to balance my-self upright, throwing my frame into a bony S. As a result of contrac-tures, one shoulder is higher than the other and I carry one arm bent in front of me, the fingers curled into a claw. My left arm and leg have wasted into pipe-stems, and I try always to keep them covered. When I think about how my body must look to others, especially to men, to whom I have been trained to display myself, I feel ludicrous, even loathsome.

At my age, however, I don't spend much time thinking about my appearance. The burning egocentricity of adolescence, which assures one that all the world is looking all the time, has passed, thank God, and I'm generally too caught up in what I'm doing to step back, as I used to, and watch myself as though upon a stage. I'm also too old to believe in the accuracy of self-image. I know that I'm not a hideous crone, that in fact, when I'm rested, well dressed, and well made up, I look fine. The self-loathing I feel is neither physically nor intellectually substantial. What I hate is not me but a disease.

I am not a disease.   23

And a disease is not — at least not singlehandedly — going to deter-   24
mine who I am, though at first it seemed to be going to. Adjusting to a chronic incurable illness, I have moved through a process similar to that outlined by Elizabeth Kübler-Ross in *On Death and Dying*. The major difference — and it is far more significant than most people recognize — is that I can't be sure of the outcome, as the terminally ill cancer patient can. Research studies indicate that, with proper medical care, I may achieve a "normal" life span. And in our society, with its vision of death as the ultimate evil, worse even than decrepitude, the response to such news is, "Oh well, at least you're not going to *die*." Are there worse things than dying? I think that there may be.

I think of two women I know, both with MS, both enough older   25
than I to have served as models. One took to her bed several years ago and has been there ever since. Although she can sit in a high-backed wheelchair, because she is incontinent she refuses to go out at all, even though incontinence pants, which are readily available at any pharmacy, could protect her from embarrassment. Instead, she stays at home and insists that her husband, a small quiet man, a retired civil servant, stay there with her except for a quick weekly foray to the supermarket. The other woman, whose illness was diagnosed when she was eighteen, a nursing student engaged to a young doctor, finished her training, married her doctor, accompanied him to Germany when he was in the service, bore three sons and a daughter, now grown and gone. When she can, she travels with her husband; she plays bridge, embroiders, swims regularly; she works, like me, as a symptomatic-patient instructor of medical students in neurology. Guess which woman I hope to be.

At the beginning, I thought about having MS almost incessantly.   26
And because of the unpredictable course of the disease, my thoughts were always terrified. Each night I'd get into bed wondering whether I'd get out again the next morning, whether I'd be able to see, to speak, to hold a pen between my fingers. Knowing that the day might come when I'd be physically incapable of killing myself, I thought perhaps I ought to do so right away, while I still had the strength. Gradually I came to understand that the Nancy who might one day lie inert under a bedsheet, arms and legs paralyzed, unable to feed or bathe herself, unable to reach out for a gun, a bottle of pills, was not the Nancy I was at present, and that I could not presume to make decisions for that future Nancy, who might well not want in the least to die. Now the only provision I've made for the future Nancy is that

when the time comes — and it is likely to come in the form of pneumonia, friend to the weak and the old — I am not to be treated with machines and medications. If she is unable to communicate by then, I hope she will be satisfied with these terms.

Thinking all the time about having MS grew tiresome and intrusive, especially in the large and tragic mode in which I was accustomed to considering my plight. Months and even years went by without catastrophe (at least without one related to MS), and really I was awfully busy, what with George and children and snakes and students and poems, and I hadn't the time, let alone the inclination, to devote myself to being a disease. Too, the richer my life became, the funnier it seemed, as though there were some connection between largesse and laughter, and so my tragic stance began to waver until, even with the aid of a brace and cane, I couldn't hold it for very long at a time.

After several years I was satisfied with my adjustment. I had suffered my grief and fury and terror, I thought, but now I was at ease with my lot. Then one summer day I set out with George and the children across the desert for a vacation in California. Part way to Yuma I became aware that my right leg felt funny. "I think I've had an exacerbation," I told George. "What shall we do?" he asked. "I think we'd better get the hell to California," I said, "because I don't know whether I'll ever make it again." So we went on to San Diego and then to Orange, and up the Pacific Coast Highway to Santa Cruz, across to Yosemite, down to Sequoia and Joshua Tree, and so back over the desert to home. It was a fine two-week trip, filled with friends and fair weather, and I wouldn't have missed it for the world, though I did in fact make it back to California two years later. Nor would there have been any point in missing it, since in MS, once the symptoms have appeared, the neurological damage has been done, and there's no way to predict or prevent that damage.

The incident spoiled my self-satisfaction, however. It renewed my grief and fury and terror, and I learned that one never finishes adjusting to MS. I don't know now why I thought one would. One does not, after all, finish adjusting to life, and MS is simply a fact of my life — not my favorite fact, of course — but as ordinary as my nose and my tropical fish and my yellow Mazda station wagon. It may at any time get worse, but no amount of worry or anticipation can prepare me for a new loss. My life is a lesson in losses. I learn one at a time.

And I had best be patient in the learning, since I'll have to do it like it or not. As any rock fan knows, you can't always get what you want. Particularly when you have MS. You can't, for example, get cured. In recent years researchers and the organizations that fund research have started to pay MS some attention even though it isn't fatal; perhaps they have begun to see that life is something other than a quantitative phenomenon, that one may be very much alive for a very long time in a life that isn't worth living. The researchers have made some progress toward understanding the mechanism of the disease: It may well be an autoimmune reaction triggered by a slow-acting virus. But they are nowhere near its prevention, control, or cure. And most of us want to be cured. Some, unable to accept incurability, grasp at one treatment after another, no matter how bizarre: megavitamin therapy, gluten-free diet, injections of cobra venom, hypothermal suits, lymphocytopharesis, hyperbaric chambers. Many treatments are probably harmless enough, but none are curative.

The absence of a cure often makes MS patients bitter toward their   31
doctors. Doctors are, after all, the priests of modern society, the new shamans, whose business is to heal, and many an MS patient roves from one to another, searching for the "good" doctor who will make him well. Doctors too think of themselves as healers, and for this reason many have trouble dealing with MS patients, whose disease in its intransigence defeats their aims and mocks their skills. Too few doctors, it is true, treat their patients as whole human beings, but the reverse is also true. I have always tried to be gentle with my doctors, who often have more at stake in terms of ego than I do. I may be frustrated, maddened, depressed by the incurability of my disease, but I am not diminished by it, and they are. When I push myself up from my seat in the waiting room and stumble toward them, I incarnate the limitation of their powers. The least I can do is refuse to press on their tenderest spots.

This gentleness is part of the reason that I'm not sorry to be a crip-   32
ple. I didn't have it before. Perhaps I'd have developed it anyway — how could I know such a thing? — and I wish I had more of it, but I'm glad of what I have. It has opened and enriched my life enormously, this sense that my frailty and need must be mirrored in others, that in searching for and shaping a stable core in a life wrenched by change and loss, change and loss, I must recognize the same process, under individual conditions, in the lives around me. I do not deprecate such knowledge, however I've come by it.

All the same, if a cure were found, would I take it? In a minute. I   33
may be a cripple, but I'm only occasionally a loony and never a saint. Anyway, in my brand of theology God doesn't give bonus points for a limp. I'd take a cure; I just don't need one. A friend who also has MS startled me once by asking, "Do you ever say to yourself, 'Why me, Lord?'" "No, Michael, I don't," I told him, "because whenever I try, the only response I can think of is 'Why not?'" If I could make a cosmic deal, who would I put in my place? What in my life would I give up in exchange for sound limbs and a thrilling rush of energy? No one. Nothing. I might as well do the job myself. Now that I'm getting the hang of it.

RESPONDING TO THE TEXT

According to the old saying, every cloud has a silver lining. Mairs weighs both the positive and negative sides of dealing with a difficult illness. Why and how does adversity bring out the good in people? Consider her responses as well as your own.

ENGAGING THE WRITER'S SUBJECT

1. Why does Mairs choose to identify herself by the term *cripple*? What objections does she have to terms more generally accepted in American culture today (i.e., *disabled, handicapped*)? How do you think she would respond to the more current phrase, *physically challenged*?

2. Mairs says she had been planning to write this essay for some time. What incident finally prompted her to do it? What is noteworthy about her response to this incident?

3. In paragraph 5, review the normal activities Mairs engaged in as a child and young adult. Why do you think she chooses to list these particular activities?

ANALYZING THE WRITER'S CRAFT

1. For what purpose does Mairs introduce her essay with the quote from Louise Bogan? (Glossary: *Purpose*) How does this quote bear on her topic?

2. Although this long essay covers many years and numerous ideas, it flows seamlessly for the reader. In large measure, this unity is brought about by the use of careful transitions from paragraph to paragraph. (Glossary: *Transitions; Unity*) Find several examples of transitions that move the piece forward effectively even though the paragraphs they connect are quite different in form or content.

3. Mairs says that an MS sufferer may lose many things in life, including a sense of humor, "the easiest to lose and the hardest to survive without" (paragraph 7). What are some of the many ways she shows that she has not lost hers? Is humor appropriate in a piece of writing about such a dire topic?

4. Mairs does not recount her struggles with MS as a strict narrative in chronological order. (Glossary: *Narration*) Why do you think she chooses to structure her essay largely on the contrast between past and present? (Glossary: *Comparison and Contrast*)

5. Throughout this essay, Mairs uses brief narrative vignettes, such as her dropping a can of tomatoes or her family trip to California, to exemplify her points about living with multiple sclerosis. (Glossary: *Exemplification; Narration*) Explain how these two strategies together support Mairs's purpose.

6. Mairs's extended definition makes a point about how events in life often lead to choices and varying results — for example, her description of two different women with multiple sclerosis in paragraph 25.

(Glossary: *Definition; Description*) Point out some places where Mairs uses cause and effect to support her extended definition and her main point. (Glossary: *Cause and Effect Analysis*)

UNDERSTANDING THE WRITER'S LANGUAGE

1. What does Mairs mean when she says, at the end of paragraph 3, "Some realities do not obey the dictates of language"? By what example does she illustrate this assertion? (Glossary: *Exemplification*)

2. Why does Mairs describe herself as a "bright-fingered muse" at the end of paragraph 14? Beyond the incident she describes here, what is the significance of the phrase? In what ways do you think this phrase reflects the way Mairs views herself?

3. Refer to your desk dictionary to determine the meanings of the following words as Mairs uses them in this selection: *splayed* (paragraph 1), *chagrin* (1), *euphemism* (3), *calamitous* (4), *disseminated* (6), *requisite* (6), *degenerative* (7), *circumscribed* (8), *venerability* (9), *predilections* (10), *concomitant* (12), *muse* (14), *corroboration* (17), *recriminations* (18), *charismatic* (20), *disapprobation* (20), *depredations* (21), *decrepitude* (24), *largesse* (27), *intransigence* (31).

WRITING SUGGESTIONS

1. Mairs says, "I lead, on the whole, an ordinary life" (paragraph 10). Many of her readers could be excused for considering it quite extraordinary. What is an ordinary life? How much of what one considers ordinary depends upon one's perspective? Write an essay in which you define an ordinary life, including examples of how you follow and fail to follow your own definition. (Glossary: *Definition*)

2. Interview a student or faculty member at your college or university who would meet Mairs's definition of a "cripple." How does this person's experience of academic life compare with hers? With what particular difficulties and successes has your interviewee been faced? Write an essay illustrating the life led in an academic institution by the person you interviewed. (Glossary: *Exemplification*)

3. Many laws have been enacted at both the national and the state levels to provide equal access and opportunities for people with disabilities. Acquaint yourself with the major laws in your area, with the effects of these laws, and with the cost of implementing them. Do the research in your college library and on the Internet. How much responsibility — in terms of money, time, and adaptive technology — should a society assume for people who need special accommodations? Write an essay in which you examine the role you feel society should play in the lives of the disabled.

- To begin your research online, go to **bedfordstmartins.com /subjectsstrategies** and click on "Combining Strategies" or browse the thematic directory of annotated links.

Shooting an Elephant

George Orwell

George Orwell (1903–1950) was capable of capturing the reader's imagination as few writers have ever done. Born in Bengal, India, but raised and educated in England, he chose to work as a civil servant in the British colonies after his schooling and was sent to Burma at nineteen as an assistant superintendent of police. Disillusioned by his firsthand experiences of public life under British colonial rule, he resigned in 1929 and returned to England to begin a career in writing. He captured the exotic mystery of life in the colonies, along with its many injustices and ironies, in such works as Down and Out in Paris and London *(1933) and* The Road to Wigan Pier *(1937). His most famous books are, of course,* Animal Farm *(1945), a satire on the Russian Revolution, and* 1984 *(1949), a chilling novel set in an imagined totalitarian state of the future. Orwell maintained a lifelong interest in international social and political issues.*

"Shooting an Elephant" was published in the British magazine New Writing *in 1936. Adolf Hitler, Benito Mussolini, and Joseph Stalin were in power, building the "younger empires" that Orwell refers to in the second paragraph, and the old British Empire was soon to decline, as Orwell predicted. In this essay, Orwell tells of a time when, in a position of authority, he found himself compelled to act against his convictions.*

PREPARING TO READ

Have you ever acted against your better judgment to save face with your friends or relatives? What motivated you to take the action that you did, and what did you learn from the experience?

In Moulmein, in Lower Burma, I was hated by large numbers of people — the only time in my life that I have been important enough for this to happen to me. I was subdivisional police officer of the town, and in an aimless, petty kind of way anti-European feeling was very bitter. No one had the guts to raise a riot, but if a European woman went through the bazaars alone somebody would probably spit betel juice* over her dress. As a police officer I was an obvious target and was baited whenever it seemed safe to do so. When a nimble Burman tripped me up on the football field and the referee (another Burman) looked the other way, the crowd yelled with hideous laughter. This happened more than once. In the end the sneering yellow

---

*The juice of an Asiatic plant whose leaves are chewed to induce narcotic effects. (Ed.)

faces of young men that met me everywhere, the insults hooted after me when I was at a safe distance, got badly on my nerves. The young Buddhist priests were the worst of all. There were several thousands of them in the town and none of them seemed to have anything to do except stand on street corners and jeer at Europeans.

All this was perplexing and upsetting. For at that time I had already made up my mind that imperialism was an evil thing and the sooner I chucked up my job and got out of it the better. Theoretically — and secretly, of course — I was all for the Burmese and all against the oppressors, the British. As for the job I was doing, I hated it more bitterly than I can perhaps make clear. In a job like that you see the dirty work of Empire at close quarters. The wretched prisoners huddling in the stinking cages of the lockups, the grey, cowed faces of the long-term convicts, the scarred buttocks of the men who had been flogged with bamboos — all these oppressed me with an intolerable sense of guilt. But I could get nothing into perspective. I was young and ill-educated and I had had to think out my problems in the utter silence that is imposed on every Englishman in the East. I did not even know that the British Empire is dying, still less did I know that it is a great deal better than the younger empires that are going to supplant it. All I knew was that I was stuck between my hatred of the empire I served and my rage against the evil-spirited little beasts who tried to make my job impossible. With one part of my mind I thought of the British Raj* as an unbreakable tyranny, as something clamped down, in *saecula saeculorum*,** upon the will of prostrate peoples; with another part I thought that the greatest joy in the world would be to drive a bayonet into a Buddhist priest's guts. Feelings like these are the normal by-products of imperialism; ask any anglo-Indian official, if you can catch him off duty.

One day something happened which in a roundabout way was enlightening. It was a tiny incident in itself, but it gave me a better glimpse than I had had before of the real nature of imperialism — the real motives for which despotic governments act. Early one morning the subinspector at a police station the other end of town rang me up on the phone and said that an elephant was ravaging the bazaar. Would I please come and do something about it? I did not know what I could do, but I wanted to see what was happening and I got on to a pony and started out. I took my rifle, an old .44 Winchester and much too small to kill an elephant, but I thought the noise might be useful *in terrorem*. Various Burmans stopped me on the way and told me about the elephant's doings. It was not, of course, a wild elephant, but a tame

2

3

---

*British rule, especially in India. (Ed.)
**From time immemorial. (Ed.)

one which had gone "must."* It had been chained up, as tame elephants always are when their attack of "must" is due, but on the previous night it had broken its chain and escaped. Its mahout,** the only person who could manage it when it was in that state, had set out in pursuit, but had taken the wrong direction and was now twelve hours' journey away, and in the morning the elephant had suddenly reappeared in the town. The Burmese population had no weapons and were quite helpless against it. It had already destroyed somebody's bamboo hut, killed a cow and raided some fruit stalls and devoured the stock; also it had met the municipal rubbish van and, when the driver jumped out and took to his heels, had turned the van over and inflicted violences upon it.

The Burmese subinspector and some Indian constables were waiting for me in the quarter where the elephant had been seen. It was a very poor quarter, a labyrinth of squalid bamboo huts, thatched with palmleaf, winding all over a steep hillside. I remember that it was a cloudy, stuffy morning at the beginning of the rains. We began questioning the people as to where the elephant had gone and, as usual, failed to get any definite information. That is invariably the case in the East; a story always sounds clear enough at a distance, but the nearer you get to the scene of events the vaguer it becomes. Some of the people said that the elephant had gone in one direction, some said that he had gone in another, some professed not even to have heard of any elephant. I had almost made up my mind that the whole story was a pack of lies, when we heard yells a little distance away. There was a loud, scandalized cry of "Go away, child! Go away this instant!" and an old woman with a switch in her hand came round the corner of a hut, violently shooing away a crowd of naked children. Some more women followed, clicking their tongues and exclaiming; evidently there was something that the children ought not to have seen. I rounded the hut and saw a man's dead body sprawling in the mud. He was an Indian, a black Dravidian coolie,*** almost naked, and he could not have been dead many minutes. The people said that the elephant had come suddenly upon him round the corner of the hut, caught him with its trunk, put its foot on his back and ground him into the earth. This was the rainy season and the ground was soft, and his face had scored a trench a foot deep and a couple of yards long. He was lying on his belly with arms crucified and head sharply twisted to one side. His face was coated with mud, the eyes wide open, the teeth bared and grinning with an expression of unendurable agony. (Never

---

*That is, gone into an uncontrollable frenzy. (Ed.)
**The keeper and driver of an elephant. (Ed.)
***An unskilled laborer. (Ed.)

tell me, by the way, that the dead look peaceful. Most of the corpses I have seen looked devilish.) The friction of the great beast's foot had stripped the skin from his back as neatly as one skins a rabbit. As soon as I saw the dead man I sent an orderly to a friend's house nearby to borrow an elephant rifle. I had already sent back the pony, not wanting it to go mad with fright and throw me if it smelled the elephant.

The orderly came back in a few minutes with a rifle and five cartridges, and meanwhile some Burmans had arrived and told us that the elephant was in the paddy fields below, only a few hundred yards away. As I started forward practically the whole population of the quarter flocked out of the houses and followed me. They had seen the rifle and were all shouting excitedly that I was going to shoot the elephant. They had not shown much interest in the elephant when he was merely ravaging their homes, but it was different now that he was going to be shot. It was a bit of fun to them, as it would be to an English crowd; besides they wanted the meat. It made me vaguely uneasy. I had no intention of shooting the elephant — I had merely sent for the rifle to defend myself if necessary — and it is always unnerving to have a crowd following you. I marched down the hill, looking and feeling a fool, with the rifle over my shoulder and an ever-growing army of people jostling at my heels. At the bottom, when you got away from the huts, there was a metalled road* and beyond that a miry waste of paddy fields a thousand yards across, not yet ploughed but soggy from the first rains and dotted with coarse grass. The elephant was standing eight yards from the road, his left side towards us. He took not the slightest notice of the crowd's approach. He was tearing up bunches of grass, beating them against his knees to clean them and stuffing them into his mouth.

I had halted on the road. As soon as I saw the elephant I knew with perfect certainty that I ought not to shoot him. It is a serious matter to shoot a working elephant — it is comparable to destroying a huge and costly piece of machinery — and obviously one ought not to do it if it can possibly be avoided. And at that distance, peacefully eating, the elephant looked no more dangerous than a cow. I thought then and I think now that his attack of "must" was already passing off; in which case he would merely wander harmlessly about until the mahout came back and caught him. Moreover, I did not in the least want to shoot him. I decided that I would watch him for a little while to make sure that he did not turn savage again, and then go home.

But at that moment, I glanced round at the crowd that had followed me. It was an immense crowd, two thousand at the least and growing every minute. It blocked the road for a long distance on either

---

*A road made of broken or crushed stone. (Ed.)

side. I looked at the sea of yellow faces above the garish clothes — faces all happy and excited over this bit of fun, all certain that the elephant was going to be shot. They were watching me as they would watch a conjuror about to perform a trick. They did not like me, but with the magical rifle in my hands I was momentarily worth watching. And suddenly I realized that I should have to shoot the elephant after all. The people expected it of me and I had got to do it; I could feel their two thousand wills pressing me forward, irresistibly. And it was at this moment, as I stood there with the rifle in my hands, that I first grasped the hollowness, the futility of the white man's dominion in the East. Here was I, the white man with his gun, standing in front of the unarmed native crowd — seemingly the leading actor of the piece; but in reality I was only an absurd puppet pushed to and fro by the will of those yellow faces behind. I perceived in this moment that when the white man turns tyrant it is his own freedom that he destroys. He becomes a sort of hollow, posing dummy, the conventionalized figure of a sahib.* For it is the condition of his rule that he shall spend his life in trying to impress the "natives," and so in every crisis he has got to do what the "natives" expect of him. He wears a mask, and his face grows to fit it. I had got to shoot the elephant. I had committed myself to doing it when I sent for the rifle. A sahib has got to act like a sahib; he has got to appear resolute, to know his own mind and do definite things. To come all that way, rifle in hand, with two thousand people marching at my heels, and then to trail feebly away, having done nothing — no, that was impossible. The crowd would laugh at me. And my whole life, every white man's life in the East, was one long struggle not to be laughed at.

But I did not want to shoot the elephant. I watched him beating   8
his bunch of grass against his knees, with that preoccupied grandmotherly air that elephants have. It seemed to me that it would be murder to shoot him. At that age I was not squeamish about killing animals, but I had never shot an elephant and never wanted to. (Somehow it always seems worse to kill a *large* animal.) Besides, there was the beast's owner to be considered. Alive, the elephant was worth at least a hundred pounds; dead, he would only be worth the value of his tusks, five pounds, possibly. But I had got to act quickly. I turned to some experienced-looking Burmans who had been there when we arrived, and asked them how the elephant had been behaving. They all said the same thing: He took no notice of you if you left him alone, but he might charge if you went too close to him.

It was perfectly clear to me what I ought to do. I ought to walk up   9
to within, say, twenty-five yards of the elephant and test his behavior.

---

*A title of respect when addressing Europeans in colonial India. (Ed.)

If he charged, I could shoot; if he took no notice of me, it would be safe to leave him until the mahout came back. But also I knew that I was going to do no such thing. I was a poor shot with a rifle and the ground was soft mud into which one would sink at every step. If the elephant charged and I missed him, I should have about as much chance as a toad under a steamroller. But even then I was not thinking particularly of my own skin, only of the watchful yellow faces behind. For at that moment, with the crowd watching me, I was not afraid in the ordinary sense, as I would have been if I had been alone. A white man mustn't be frightened in front of "natives"; and so, in general, he isn't frightened. The sole thought in my mind was that if anything went wrong those two thousand Burmans would see me pursued, caught, trampled on, and reduced to a grinning corpse like that Indian up the hill. And if that happened it was quite probable that some of them would laugh. That would never do. There was only one alternative. I shoved the cartridges into the magazine and lay down on the road to get a better aim.

The crowd grew very still, and a deep, low, happy sigh, as of people who see the theater curtain go up at last, breathed from innumerable throats. They were going to have their bit of fun after all. The rifle was a beautiful German thing with cross-hair sights. I did not then know that in shooting an elephant one would shoot to cut an imaginary bar running from ear-hole to ear-hole. I ought, therefore, as the elephant was sideways on, to have aimed straight at his ear-hole; actually I aimed several inches in front of this, thinking the brain would be further forward. 10

When I pulled the trigger I did not hear the bang or feel the kick — one never does when a shot goes home — but I heard the devilish roar of glee that went up from the crowd. In that instant, in too short a time, one would have thought, even for the bullet to get there, a mysterious, terrible change had come over the elephant. He neither stirred nor fell, but every line of his body had altered. He looked suddenly stricken, shrunken, immensely old, as though the frightful impact of the bullet had paralyzed him without knocking him down. At last, after what seemed a long time — it might have been five seconds, I dare say — he sagged flabbily to his knees. His mouth slobbered. An enormous senility seemed to have settled upon him. One could have imagined him thousands of years old. I fired again into the same spot. At the second shot he did not collapse but climbed with desperate slowness to his feet and stood weakly upright, with legs sagging and head drooping. I fired a third time. That was the shot that did for him. You could see the agony of it jolt his whole body and knock the last remnant of strength from his legs. But in falling he seemed for a moment to rise, for as his hind legs collapsed beneath him he seemed to tower upward like a huge rock toppling, his trunk reaching skywards like a tree. He trumpeted, for the first and only time. And then down 11 he came, his belly towards me, with a crash that seemed to shake the ground even where I lay.

I got up. The Burmans were already racing past me across the mud. It was obvious that the elephant would never rise again, but he was not dead. He was breathing very rhythmically with long rattling gasps, his great mound of a side painfully rising and falling. His mouth was wide open. I could see far down into caverns of pale pink throat. I waited a long time for him to die, but his breathing did not weaken. Finally I fired my two remaining shots into the spot where I thought his heart must be. The thick blood welled out of him like red velvet, but still he did not die. His body did not even jerk when the shots hit him, the tortured breathing continued without a pause. He was dying, very slowly and in great agony, but in some world remote from me where not even a bullet could damage him further. I felt I had got to put an end to that dreadful noise. It seemed dreadful to see the great beast lying there, powerless to move and yet powerless to die, and not even to be able to finish him. I sent back for my small rifle and poured shot after shot into his heart and down his throat. They seemed to make no impression. The tortured gasps continued as steadily as the ticking of a clock.

In the end I could not stand it any longer and went away. I heard later that it took him half an hour to die. Burmans were bringing dahs* and baskets even before I left, and I was told they had stripped his body almost to the bones by the afternoon.

Afterwards, of course, there were endless discussions about the shooting of the elephant. The owner was furious, but he was only an Indian and could do nothing. Besides, legally I had done the right thing, for a mad elephant has to be killed, like a mad dog, if its owner fails to control it. Among the Europeans opinion was divided. The older men said I was right, the younger men said it was a damn shame to shoot an elephant for killing a coolie, because the elephant was worth more than any damn Coringhee coolie. And afterwards I was very glad that the coolie had been killed; it put me legally in the right and it gave me sufficient pretext for shooting the elephant. I often wondered whether any of the others grasped that I had done it solely to avoid looking a fool.

RESPONDING TO THE TEXT

Even though Orwell does not want to shoot the elephant, he does. How does he rationalize his behavior? On what grounds was Orwell legally in the right? What alternatives did he have? What do you think Orwell learned from this incident?

---

*Heavy knives. (Ed.)

ENGAGING THE WRITER'S SUBJECT

1. What do you suppose would have happened had Orwell not sent for an elephant rifle?

2. What is imperialism, and what discovery about imperialism does Orwell make during the course of the event he narrates?

3. What does Orwell mean when he says, "I was very glad that the coolie had been killed" (paragraph 14)?

4. What is the point of Orwell's final paragraph? How does that paragraph affect your response to the whole essay?

ANALYZING THE WRITER'S CRAFT

1. Why do you think Orwell is so meticulous in establishing the setting for his essay in paragraphs 1 and 2?

2. What do you think was Orwell's purpose in telling this story? (Glossary: *Purpose*) Cite evidence from the text that indicates to you that purpose. Does he accomplish his purpose?

3. Orwell is quick to capitalize on the ironies of the circumstances surrounding the events he narrates. (Glossary: *Irony*) Identify any circumstances you found ironic, and explain what this irony contributes to Orwell's overall purpose.

4. What part of the essay struck you most strongly? The shooting itself? Orwell's feelings? The descriptions of the Burmans and their behavior? What is it about Orwell's prose that enhances the impact of that passage for you? Explain.

5. Orwell wrote "Shooting an Elephant" some years after the event occurred. What does his account of the event gain with the passage of time? Explain.

6. "Shooting an Elephant" is, first of all, a narrative; Orwell has a story to tell. (Glossary: *Narration*) But Orwell uses other strategies in support of narration to help develop and give meaning to his story. Identify passages in which Orwell uses description, exemplification, and cause and effect analysis, and explain how each enhances the incident he narrates. (Glossary: *Cause and Effect Analysis; Description; Exemplification*)

UNDERSTANDING THE WRITER'S LANGUAGE

1. A British citizen, Orwell uses British English. Cite several examples of this British diction. (Glossary: *Diction*) How might an American say the same thing?

2. Identify several of the metaphors and similes that Orwell uses, and explain what each adds to his descriptions in this essay. (Glossary: *Figures of Speech*)

3. Orwell advocates using strong action verbs because they are vivid and eliminate unnecessary modification. (Glossary: *Verb*) For example, in

paragraph 1 he uses the verb *jeer* instead of the verb *yell* plus the adverb *derisively*. Identify other strong verbs that you found particularly striking. What do these strong verbs add to Orwell's prose style?

4. Refer to your desk dictionary to determine the meanings of the following words as Orwell uses them in this selection: *baited* (paragraph 1), *intolerable* (2), *supplant* (2), *tyranny* (2), *despotic* (3), *ravaging* (3), *labyrinth* (4), *squalid* (4), *miry* (5), *garish* (7), *squeamish* (8), *devilish* (11), *senility* (11).

WRITING SUGGESTIONS

1. Write an essay recounting a situation in which you felt compelled to act against your convictions. (Glossary: *Narration*) Before you start writing, you may find it helpful to consider one or more of the following questions and to review your Preparing to Read response for this essay. How can you justify your action? How much freedom of choice did you actually have, and what were the limits on your freedom? On what basis can you refuse to subordinate your convictions to others' or to society's?

2. Consider situations in which you have been a leader, like Orwell, or a follower. As a leader, what was your attitude toward your followers? As a follower, what did you feel toward your leader? Using Orwell's essay and your own experiences, what conclusions can you draw about leaders and followers? Write an essay in which you explore the relationship between leaders and followers.

3. Hardly a week goes by that some government official, community leader, or businessperson does not make the local or national news for some face-saving action. In your college library and on the Internet, collect and analyze several examples of public leaders caught in the act of covering for themselves. What, in your opinion, is the real story in each case? How successful was each person in his or her attempts to save face? What is your opinion of these people now that you understand what they have been up to? Explain.

• To begin your research online, go to **bedfordstmartins.com /subjectsstrategies** and click on "Combining Strategies" or browse the thematic directory of annotated links.

On Dumpster Diving

Lars Eighner

Born in Texas in 1948, Lars Eighner attended the University of Texas–Austin. After graduation, he wrote essays and fiction, and several of his articles were published in magazines like Threepenny Review, *the* Guide, *and* Inches. *A volume of short stories,* Bayou Boy and Other Stories, *was published in 1985. Eighner became homeless in 1988 when he left his job as an attendant at a mental hospital. The following piece, which appeared in the* Utne Reader, *is an abridged version of an essay that first appeared in* Threepenny Review. *The piece eventually became part of Eighner's startling account of the three years he spent as a homeless person,* Travels with Lizbeth *(1993). His publications include the novels* Pawn to Queen Four *(1995) and* Whispered in the Dark *(1996) and the nonfiction book* Gay Cosmos *(1995).*

Eighner uses a number of rhetorical strategies in "On Dumpster Diving," but pay particular attention to the importance of his delineation of the "stages that a person goes through in learning to scavenge" to the success of the essay as a whole.

PREPARING TO READ

Are you a pack rat, or do you get rid of what is not immediately useful to you? Outside of the usual kitchen garbage and empty toothpaste tubes, how do you make the decision to throw something away?

I began Dumpster diving about a year before I became homeless. 1

I prefer the term *scavenging*. I have heard people, evidently meaning 2 to be polite, use the word *foraging*, but I prefer to reserve that word for gathering nuts and berries and such, which I also do, according to the season and opportunity.

I like the frankness of the word *scavenging*. I live from the refuse of 3 others. I am a scavenger. I think it a sound and honorable niche, although if I could I would naturally prefer to live the comfortable consumer life, perhaps — and only perhaps — as a slightly less wasteful consumer owing to what I have learned as a scavenger.

Except for jeans, all my clothes come from Dumpsters. Boom 4 boxes, candles, bedding, toilet paper, medicine, books, a typewriter, a virgin male love doll, coins sometimes amounting to many dollars: all came from Dumpsters. And, yes, I eat from Dumpsters, too.

There is a predictable series of stages that a person goes through in 5 learning to scavenge. At first the new scavenger is filled with disgust and self-loathing. He is ashamed of being seen.

This stage passes with experience. The scavenger finds a pair of running shoes that fit and look and smell brand-new. He finds a pocket calculator in perfect working order. He finds pristine ice cream, still frozen, more than he can eat or keep. He begins to understand: people do throw away perfectly good stuff, a lot of perfectly good stuff.

At this stage he may become lost and never recover: All the Dumpster divers I have known come to the point of trying to acquire everything they touch. Why not take it, they reason, it is all free. This is, of course, hopeless, and most divers come to realize that they must restrict themselves to items of relatively immediate utility.

The finding of objects is becoming something of an urban art. Even respectable, employed people will sometimes find something tempting sticking out of a Dumpster or standing beside one. Quite a number of people, not all of them of the bohemian type, are willing to brag that they found this or that piece in the trash.

But eating from Dumpsters is the thing that separates the dilettanti from the professionals. Eating safely involves three principles: using the senses and common sense to evaluate the condition of the found materials; knowing the Dumpsters of a given area and checking them regularly; and seeking always to answer the question "Why was this discarded?"

Yet perfectly good food can be found in Dumpsters. Canned goods, for example, turn up fairly often in the Dumpsters I frequent. I also have few qualms about dry foods such as crackers, cookies, cereal, chips, and pasta if they are free of visible contaminants and still dry and crisp. Raw fruits and vegetables with intact skins seem perfectly safe to me, excluding, of course, the obviously rotten. Many are discarded for minor imperfections that can be pared away.

A typical discard is a half jar of peanut butter — though nonorganic peanut butter does not require refrigeration and is unlikely to spoil in any reasonable time. One of my favorite finds is yogurt — often discarded, still sealed, when the expiration date has passed — because it will keep for several days, even in warm weather.

No matter how careful I am I still get dysentery at least once a month, oftener in warm weather. I do not want to paint too romantic a picture. Dumpster diving has serious drawbacks as a way of life.

I find from the experience of scavenging two rather deep lessons. The first is to take what I can use and let the rest go. I have come to think that there is no value in the abstract. A thing I cannot use or make useful, perhaps by trading, has no value, however fine or rare it may be.

The second lesson is the transience of material being. I do not suppose that ideas are immortal, but certainly they are longer-lived than material objects.

The things I find in Dumpsters, the love letters and rag dolls of so 15
many lives, remind me of this lesson. Now I hardly pick up a thing
without envisioning the time I will cast it away. This, I think, is a
healthy state of mind. Almost everything I have now has already been
cast out at least once, proving that what I own is valueless to someone.

I find that my desire to grab for the gaudy bauble has been largely 16
sated. I think this is an attitude I share with the very wealthy — we
both know there is plenty more where whatever we have came from.
Between us are the rat-race millions who have confounded their selves
with the objects they grasp and who nightly scavenge the cable channels for they know not what.

I am sorry for them. 17

RESPONDING TO THE TEXT

In paragraph 15, Eighner writes, "I hardly pick up a thing without envisioning the time I will cast it away. This, I think, is a healthy state of mind."
React to this statement. Do you think such an attitude is healthy or de-
featist? If many people thought this way, what impact would it have on our
consumer society?

ENGAGING THE WRITER'S SUBJECT

1. What stages do beginning Dumpster divers go through before they become what Eighner terms "professionals" (paragraph 9)? What examples does Eighner use to illustrate the passage through these stages?
   (Glossary: *Exemplification*)

2. What three principles does one need to follow in order to eat safely
   from Dumpsters? What foods are best to eat from Dumpsters? What are
   the risks?

3. What two lessons has Eighner learned from his Dumpster diving experiences? Why are they significant to him?

ANALYZING THE WRITER'S CRAFT

1. Eighner's essay deals with both the immediate, physical aspects of
   Dumpster diving, such as what can be found in a typical Dumpster and
   the physical price one pays for eating out of them, and the larger, abstract issues that Dumpster diving raises, such as materialism and the
   transience of material objects. (Glossary: *Concrete/Abstract*) Why does he
   describe the concrete things before he discusses the abstract issues raised
   by their presence in Dumpsters? What does he achieve by using both
   types of elements?

2. Eighner's account of Dumpster diving focuses primarily on the odd
   appeal and interest inherent in the activity. Paragraph 12 is his one
   disclaimer, in which he states, "I do not want to paint too romantic a

picture." Why does Eighner include this disclaimer? How does it add to the effectiveness of his piece? Why do you think it is so brief and abrupt?

3. Eighner uses many rhetorical techniques in his essay, but its core is a fairly complete process analysis of how to Dumpster dive. (Glossary: *Process Analysis*) Summarize this process analysis. Why do you think Eighner did not title the essay "How to Dumpster Dive"?

4. Dumpster diving has had a profound effect on Eighner and the way he lives. How do his explanations of choices he makes, such as deciding which items to keep, enhance his presentation of the practical art of Dumpster diving?

5. Discuss how Eighner uses exemplification to bring the world of Dumpster diving to life. (Glossary: *Exemplification*) What characterizes the examples he uses?

6. Writers often use process analysis in conjunction with other strategies, especially argument, to try to improve the way a process is carried out. (Glossary: *Argument; Process Analysis*) In this essay, Eighner uses a full process analysis to lay out his views on American values and materialism. How is this an effective way to combine strategies? Think of other arguments that could be strengthened if they included elements of process analysis.

UNDERSTANDING THE WRITER'S LANGUAGE

1. Eighner says he prefers the word *scavenging* to *Dumpster diving* or *foraging*. What do those three terms mean to him? Why do you think he finds the discussion of the terms important enough to discuss at the beginning of his essay? (Glossary: *Diction*)

2. According to Eighner, "eating from Dumpsters is the thing that separates the dilettanti from the professionals" (paragraph 9). What do the words *dilettante* and *professional* connote to you? (Glossary: *Connotation/Denotation*) Why does Eighner choose to use them instead of the more straightforward *casual* and *serious*?

3. Eighner says, "The finding of objects is becoming something of an urban art" (paragraph 8). What does this sentence mean to you? Based on the essay, do you find his use of the word *art* appropriate when discussing any aspect of Dumpster diving? Why or why not?

4. Refer to your desk dictionary to determine the meanings of the following words as Eighner uses them in this selection: *foraging* (paragraph 2), *pristine* (6), *bohemian* (8), *dilettanti* (9), *transience* (14), *sated* (16).

WRITING SUGGESTIONS

1. Write a process analysis in which you relate how you acquire a consumer item of some importance or expense to you. (Glossary: *Process Analysis*) Do you compare brands, store prices, and so on? (Glossary: *Comparison and*

Contrast) What are your priorities — must the item be stylish or durable, offer good overall value, give high performance? How do you decide to spend your money? In other words, what determines which items are worth the sacrifice?

2. In paragraph 3 Eighner states that he "live[s] from the refuse of others." How do his confession and the following *New Yorker* cartoon by Peter Steiner affect you? Do you think that we have "become a throwaway society"? If so, how? How do Eighner's accounts of homelessness and Dumpster diving make you feel about your own consumerism and trash habits? Write an essay in which you examine the things you throw away in a single day. What items did you get rid of? Why? Could those items be used by someone else? Have you ever felt guilty about throwing something away? If so, what was it and why?

"We've certainly become a throwaway society."

3. Speak with someone in the department or company that handles garbage disposal on your campus or in your area. How much waste is produced in your dorm, campus, or town each day? Is there a problem with where to put all this garbage? What can you do to reduce your contributions to the garbage stream? In your college library and on the Internet, conduct research on waste on your campus or in your area. Write an essay in which you present your findings. What suggestions do you have for improving the way waste is currently handled? Discuss the future of waste disposal and what people can do to be less wasteful.

• To begin your research online, go to **bedfordstmartins.com /subjectsstrategies** and click on "Combining Strategies" or browse the thematic directory of annotated links.

WRITING SUGGESTIONS FOR COMBINING STRATEGIES

1. Select a piece you have written for this class in which you used one primary writing strategy, and rewrite it using another. For example, choose a description you wrote in response to an exercise at the end of Chapter 4, and redraft it as a process analysis. Remember that the choice of a writing strategy influences the writer's "voice" — a descriptive piece might be lyrical, while a process analysis might be straightforward. How does your voice change along with the strategy? Does your assumed audience change as well? (Glossary: *Audience*)

   If time allows, try this exercise with someone else in your class. Exchange a piece of writing with another student, and rewrite it using a different strategy. Discuss the choices you each made.

2. Select an essay you have written this semester, either for this class or another class. What was the primary writing strategy you used? Build upon this essay by integrating another strategy. For example, if you wrote an argument paper for a political science class, you might try using narrative to give some historical background to the paper. (Glossary: *Argument; Narration*) For a paper in the natural sciences, you could use subjective description to open the paper up to nonscientists. (Glossary: *Objective/ Subjective*) How does this new strategy affect the balance of your paper? Does the new strategy require you to change anything else about your paper?

3. The choice of a writing strategy reflects an author's voice — the persona he or she assumes in relation to the reader. Read back through any personal writing you've done this semester — a journal, letters to friends, e-mail. Can you identify the strategies you use outside of "formal" academic writing, as part of your natural writing voice? Write a few pages analyzing these strategies and your writing "voice," using one of the rhetorical strategies studied this term. For example, you could compare and contrast your e-mail postings to your letters home. (Glossary: *Comparison and Contrast*) Or you could do a cause and effect analysis of how being at college has changed the tone or style of your journal writing. (Glossary: *Cause and Effect Analysis*)

CHAPTER 13

Writers on Writing

Like any other craft, writing involves learning basic skills as well as more sophisticated techniques that can be refined and then passed between practitioners. Some of the most important lessons a student writer encounters may come from the experiences of other writers: suggestions, advice, cautions, corrections, encouragement. This chapter contains essays in which writers discuss their habits, difficulties, and judgments while they express both the joy of writing and the hard work it can entail. These writers deal with the full range of the writing process — from freeing the imagination in journal entries to correcting punctuation errors for the final draft — and the advice they offer is pertinent and sound. The skills and techniques presented here can help you exert more control over your writing and, in the process, become more confident of how best to achieve your goals.

Five Principles for Getting Good Ideas

Jack Rawlins

Jack Rawlins is a professor of composition and literature at California State University at Chico. He earned his B.A. at the University of California–Berkeley in 1968 and his Ph.D. from Yale University in 1972. He is the author of The Writer's Way *(2002), a text now in its fifth edition, which has a loyal following among teachers and students of composition.*

In the following excerpt from his book, Rawlins presents his five principles for getting good ideas.

PREPARING TO READ

How do you get essay ideas? Do you struggle to find good ideas? Do you follow the advice in Chapter 2 (pages 19–44) about focusing a topic and establishing a thesis? Do you wait for a lightbulb to go on in your head? Reflect on how you came upon the ideas you used in your previous essays. What lessons can you draw from your past experiences in thinking up good ideas for your writing?

Brains that get good ideas follow five principles: 1

Don't begin with a topic.
Think all the time.
To get something out, put something in.
Go from little, concrete things to big, abstract things.
Connect.

We'll talk about each in turn.

DON'T BEGIN WITH A TOPIC

Essays rarely begin with subject matter alone. Why would a per-   2
son say out of the blue, "I think I'll write about linoleum, or the national debt"? Nor are the kernels of essays always "good ideas" — they

often aren't *ideas* at all, in the sense of whole assertions. Thinking begins in lots of ways:

> With a question: "Is there any real difference between the Republicans and the Democrats anymore?" "Why is Ralph so mad at me?"
>
> With a problem: "I'm always behind in my work." "Violent crimes against women are on the increase."
>
> With a purpose: "I want to tell people about what's really going on in this class." "I want to let people know about alternatives to traditional medicine."
>
> With a thesis: "There are cheaper, healthier alternatives to regular grocery stores." "Old people are the victims of silent injustice in our culture."
>
> With a feeling: anger, frustration, surprise.
>
> With a sensation or image: a smell, a glimpse of a bird in flight, an eye-catching TV ad.

What shall we call that thing an essay begins with — the seed, the spark, the inspiration, the sense of "gotcha"? I'll call it a prompt.

THINK ALL THE TIME

If you have a sense of humor, you know that the surest way to prevent   3
yourself from being funny is to have someone (even yourself) demand that you be funny *now*. Comedians have always bemoaned the fact that people introduce them to friends by saying, "This is Milton. He's a riot. Be funny, Milton." Thinking's the same way. Being put on the spot is the surest way of preventing the creative juices from flowing.

So don't expect to discover a good prompt by sitting down for a   4
scheduled half-hour of profundity. Minds that think well think all the time. One prolific student wrote that she goes through the world "looking for *writable* things" and is thought weird by her friends because she scribbles notes to herself at parties.

Thinking all the time sounds like work, but it isn't. Your mind   5
works all the time whether you want it to or not, the same way your body moves all the time. Any yogi will tell you that it takes years of practice to learn to turn the mind *off*, even for a minute or two. And it's physiologically impossible for your brain to get tired, which is why you can study or write all day, go to bed, and find your mind still racing while your body cries for rest. So I'm really not asking your brain to do anything new; I'm just asking you to *listen* to it.

TO GET SOMETHING OUT, PUT SOMETHING IN

One popular, poisonous image for thinking is the light bulb flashing on over someone's head — the notion that ideas spring from within us, caused by nothing. To become good thinkers, we have to replace that image with another; think of ideas as billiard balls set in motion when something collides with them. Ideas are *re*actions — we have them in response to other things.

A thinker thinks as life passes through him and does what I call "talking back to the world." Many of us separate our input and output modes; we are either putting information into our brains or asking our brains to produce thoughts, but we don't do both at the same time. I call such people data sponges. But the best time to try to get things out is when things are going in. Let them bounce off you and strike sparks. People do this naturally until they've been taught to be passive; try reading a book to a three-year-old, and listen to her react to everything she hears and sees, or take her to a movie and watch her struggle not to talk back to the screen.

Are you a data sponge? To find out, answer the following questions.

Do you find yourself mentally talking back to the newspaper when you read it?

Do you write in the margins of books you read?

Are at least 25 percent of the notes you take during course reading or lectures your own thoughts, questions, doubts, and reactions?

As you meet up with life's outrages, do you find yourself complaining to imaginary audiences?

After a movie, do you feel like you're going to burst until you find someone to talk about it?

When you listen to a speaker or a teacher, do you find yourself itching to get to the question-and-answer period?

If you said yes to these questions, you're not a sponge. If you said no, you're going to have to practice your reacting skills.

GO FROM LITTLE, CONCRETE THINGS TO BIG, ABSTRACT THINGS

This principle is a logical consequence of the one before. Since ideas come best in reaction to life's incoming billiard balls, the best thinking follows a predictable course: from little, concrete bits of experience to large abstract implications. You see an ad on TV and start thinking about it, and it leads you to speculations on American consumerism, media manipulation, and the marketing of women's bodies. You overhear a snippet of conversation between a parent and child at the grocery store and start thinking about it, and it leads you to speculations on American child-rearing practices, the powerlessness of children, parental brainwashing, and antiyouth bigotry.

Here's what going from little particulars to big issues is like. I was 10 sitting doing nothing one day when my eyes fell on a box of Girl Scout cookies. The box had on it a picture of a girl and the slogan, "I'm not like anyone else." I reacted. I thought, "Gosh, that sounds lonely." And I valued the reaction enough to notice it and think about it. It led me to a big issue: How does Americans' love of individuality affect their ability to be members of a culture? And I formulated a thesis: Americans love their individuality so much that they'll cut themselves off from everything and everyone to get it. Being unlike everyone else is a curse, because it means you're separated from other human beings by your differentness. I was raised a proud individualist, and I've only recently realized that the reward for being unique is loneliness.

I went from little things to big issues when I drew essays out of one 11 writer's life. When she mentioned that she couldn't drink too heavily in high school because it would affect her shot-putting, I instantly saw the abstract issue illustrated by her experience: People who have things they love dare not practice self-destructive behavior, because they'll destroy what they love in the process. So alcoholism or drug abuse is neither a crime nor a disease nor a moral failure in the individual; it's a symptom of a social failure, the failure of our society to offer the alcoholic or drug addict a life too precious to risk destroying.

Beginning writers want to start with large abstractions, in the mis- 12 taken belief that the bigger the topic is, the more there is to say about it. It doesn't work out that way. Usually the first sentence of the essay tells whether the writer knows this or not. Essays on friendship that begin "Friendship is one of the most important things in life" are doomed, because the writer doesn't know it. Essays that begin "Mary was my best friend in high school" will thrive, because the writer does know it.

CONNECT

Those who think well make connections between things. An essay be- 13 gins when two previously unrelated bits in the brain meet and discover a connection. Usually a new stimulus hitches up with an old bit stored long ago in the memory; the incoming billiard ball hits an old one that's just lying there, and they fly off together.

It's hard to learn the connecting skill if you don't have it already. 14
Here's what it feels like inside. One day I was sitting in an English
Department faculty meeting, and we were discussing an administrative change. A colleague said, "We couldn't do that until we were sure
our people would be protected." I thought momentarily, "I wonder
how he knows who 'his people' are?" Months later I was vacationing
in a small mountain town and picked up the local newspaper. On the
front page was an article about the firing of a group of non-union construction workers. The boss had asked the union for workers, but none
were available, so he trained out-of-work mill workers. Later the union
rep showed up, announced that union workers were now available,
and insisted that the others be fired. Something clicked, and I had an
essay. My colleague's attitude and the union rep's were the same: I'll
watch out for "my people," and everyone else can watch out for himself. I wanted to talk about why people think that way and how they
learn to rise above it.

How did I make that connection? Incredible as it sounds, and un- 15
beknownst to me, I must have been checking everything that came
into my brain against the faculty-meeting remark for a possible connection. Or perhaps I had opened a file in my mind labeled "people
who think in terms of those who belong and those who don't" and
dumped anything related in there as it came along.

I just read a great essay by Arthur Miller connecting the current 16
prayer-in-school political debate with his memories of saying the
Pledge of Allegiance in elementary school. What brought the two
things together? Miller must have checked prayer in schools against
everything in his memory relating to state-mandated loyalty and
come up with recollections of third grade. That sounds exhausting,
but we all know that when something clicks in memory, we haven't
"worked" at all — in fact, the way to bring the connection that's on
the tip of the tongue to the surface is to forget about it and let the subconscious do its work unwatched.

The more unlike two things are and the less obvious the connection be- 17
tween them is, the fresher and more stimulating the connection is when you
make it. Finding a connection between mountain climbers and sky-
divers is merely okay; finding a connection between inflation rates and
the incidence of breast cancer will make the world open its eyes. This is
the Head Principle. Mr. Head was an aviation engineer who got interested in downhill skiing. Apparently no one had ever connected aircraft
technology and skiing before; Mr. Head took a few runs down the hill
and realized that he could make a better ski if he simply made it according to the principles and with the materials used in making airplane
wings. He invented the Head ski, the first metal ski, and made millions
of dollars. He then did the same thing in tennis, by inventing the
Prince racket. Apparently aircraft engineers didn't play tennis either.

The Head Principle says you can't predict what will connect with 18 what. So you can't tell yourself what information to seek. You can only take in experience and information voraciously and stir it all up together. If I had been formally researching stupid faculty remarks, I'd never have thought to read up on northern Californian construction workers. If you're writing about Charles Dickens and you read only about Charles Dickens, you're just guaranteeing you won't make any connections except those other Dickens scholars have already made. Instead, go read *Psychology Today*, read Nixon's memoirs, see a movie, watch a documentary on insect societies, or visit a mortuary. As you talk back to all of it, keep asking yourself, "What is this like? When have I thought things like this before? When was the last time I reacted like this?" When I read about the construction workers, I reacted, and I remembered that I'd had a conversation with myself like that one before sometime. Perhaps that's the key to connecting.

It's easy to block ideas from coming by practicing the exact oppo- 19 site of our idea-getting principles. Just set aside a time for idea-getting, cut yourself off from the outside world by locking yourself in a stimulus-free study room, and muse on a cosmic abstraction. If you're doing any of that, your idea-getting regimen needs overhauling.

RESPONDING TO THE TEXT

What parts of Rawlins's advice will be most helpful for you? Why? Are you already practicing one or more of his principles? Explain.

REFLECTING AND DISCUSSING

1. What does Rawlins mean by a *prompt*?

2. Rawlins advises against beginning your writing by thinking about a topic. What is wrong with thinking about a topic? How does he suggest you begin?

3. What is a "data sponge"? Are you one? How do you know? What does Rawlins suggest you do if you are a data sponge?

4. What is the point of Rawlins's story about his faculty meeting and the piece in the newspaper "about the firing of a group of non-union construction workers" (paragraph 14)?

5. What, according to Rawlins, is the "Head Principle"? What is Mr. Head an example of for Rawlins?

Shitty First Drafts

Anne Lamott

Born in San Francisco in 1954, Anne Lamott graduated from Goucher College in Baltimore and is the author of six novels, including Rosie *(1983),* Crooked Little Heart *(1997),* All the New People *(2000), and* Blue Shoes *(2002). She has also been the food reviewer for* California *magazine, a book reviewer for* Mademoiselle, *and a regular contributor to Salon.com's "Mothers Who Think" column. Her nonfiction books include* Operating Instructions: A Journal of My Son's First Year *(1993), in which she describes her adventures as a single parent, and* Tender Mercies: Some Thoughts on Faith *(1999), in which she charts her journey toward faith in God.*

In the following selection, taken from Lamott's popular book about writing, Bird by Bird *(1994), she argues for the need to let go and write those "shitty first drafts" that lead to clarity and sometimes brilliance in subsequent drafts.*

PREPARING TO READ

Many professional writers view first drafts as something they have to do before they can begin the real work of writing — revision. How do you view the writing of your first drafts? What patterns, if any, do you see in your writing behavior when working on them? Is the work liberating or restricting? Pleasant or unpleasant?

Now, practically even better news than that of short assignments is the idea of shitty first drafts. All good writers write them. This is how they end up with good second drafts and terrific third drafts. People tend to look at successful writers, writers who are getting their books published and maybe even doing well financially, and think that they sit down at their desks every morning feeling like a million dollars, feeling great about who they are and how much talent they have and what a great story they have to tell; that they take in a few deep breaths, push back their sleeves, roll their necks a few times to get all the cricks out, and dive in, typing fully formed passages as fast as a court reporter. But this is just the fantasy of the uninitiated. I know some very great writers, writers you love who write beautifully and have made a great deal of money, and not *one* of them sits down routinely feeling wildly enthusiastic and confident. Not one of them writes elegant first drafts. All right, one of them does, but we do not like her very much. We do not think that she has a rich inner life or that God likes her or can even stand her. (Although when I mentioned this to my priest friend Tom, he said you can safely assume you've created God in your own image when it turns out that God hates all the same people you do.)

Very few writers really know what they are doing until they've done it. Nor do they go about their business feeling dewy and thrilled. They do not type a few stiff warm-up sentences and then find themselves bounding along like huskies across the snow. One writer I know tells me that he sits down every morning and says to himself nicely, "It's not like you don't have a choice, because you do — you can either type or kill yourself." We all often feel like we are pulling teeth, even those writers whose prose ends up being the most natural and fluid. The right words and sentences just do not come pouring out like ticker tape most of the time. Now, Muriel Spark is said to have felt that she was taking dictation from God every morning — sitting there, one supposes, plugged into a Dictaphone, typing away, humming. But this is a very hostile and aggressive position. One might hope for bad things to rain down on a person like this.

For me and most of the other writers I know, writing is not rapturous. In fact, the only way I can get anything written at all is to write really, really shitty first drafts.

The first draft is the child's draft, where you let it all pour out and then let it romp all over the place, knowing that no one is going to see it and that you can shape it later. You just let this childlike part of you channel whatever voices and visions come through and onto the page. If one of the characters wants to say, "Well, so what, Mr. Poopy Pants?," you let her. No one is going to see it. If the kid wants to get into really sentimental, weepy, emotional territory, you let him. Just get it all down on paper, because there may be something great in those six crazy pages that you would never have gotten to by more rational, grown-up means. There may be something in the very last line of the very last paragraph on page six that you just love, that is so beautiful or wild that you now know what you're supposed to be writing about, more or less, or in what direction you might go — but there was no way to get to this without first getting through the first five and a half pages.

I used to write food reviews for *California* magazine before it folded. (My writing food reviews had nothing to do with the magazine folding, although every single review did cause a couple of canceled subscriptions. Some readers took umbrage at my comparing mounds of vegetable puree with various ex-presidents' brains.) These reviews always took two days to write. First I'd go to a restaurant several times with a few opinionated, articulate friends in tow. I'd sit there writing down everything anyone said that was at all interesting or funny. Then on the following Monday I'd sit down at my desk with my notes, and try to write the review. Even after I'd been doing this for years, panic would set in. I'd try to write a lead, but instead I'd write a couple of dreadful sentences, xx them out, try again, xx everything out, and then feel despair and worry settle on my chest like an x-ray apron. It's over, I'd think, calmly. I'm not going to be able to get the magic to work this time. I'm ruined. I'm through. I'm toast. Maybe, I'd think, I can get my old job back as a clerk-typist. But probably not. I'd get up and study my teeth in the mirror for a while. Then I'd stop, remember to breathe, make a few phone calls, hit the kitchen and chow down. Eventually I'd go back and sit down at my desk, and sigh for the next ten minutes. Finally I would pick up my one-inch picture frame, stare into it as if for the answer, and every time the answer would come: all I had to do was to write a really shitty first draft of, say, the opening paragraph. And no one was going to see it.

So I'd start writing without reining myself in. It was almost just 6 typing, just making my fingers move. And the writing would be *terrible*. I'd write a lead paragraph that was a whole page, even though the entire review could only be three pages long, and then I'd start writing up descriptions of the food, one dish at a time, bird by bird, and the critics would be sitting on my shoulders, commenting like cartoon characters. They'd be pretending to snore, or rolling their eyes at my overwrought descriptions, no matter how hard I tried to tone those descriptions down, no matter how conscious I was of what a friend said to me gently in my early days of restaurant reviewing. "Annie," she said, "it is just a piece of *chick*en. It is just a bit of *cake*."

But because by then I had been writing for so long, I would eventu- 7 ally let myself trust the process — sort of, more or less. I'd write a first draft that was maybe twice as long as it should be, with a self-indulgent and boring beginning, stupefying descriptions of the meal, lots of quotes from my black-humored friends that made them sound more like the Manson girls than food lovers, and no ending to speak of. The whole thing would be so long and incoherent and hideous that for the rest of the day I'd obsess about getting creamed by a car before I could write a decent second draft. I'd worry that people would read what I'd written and believe that the accident had really been a suicide, that I had panicked because my talent was waning and my mind was shot.

The next day, though, I'd sit down, go through it all with a col- 8 ored pen, take out everything I possibly could, find a new lead somewhere on the second page, figure out a kicky place to end it, and then write a second draft. It always turned out fine, sometimes even funny and weird and helpful. I'd go over it one more time and mail it in.

Then, a month later, when it was time for another review, the 9 whole process would start again, complete with the fears that people would find my first draft before I could rewrite it.

Almost all good writing begins with terrible first efforts. You need 10 to start somewhere. Start by getting something — anything — down on paper. A friend of mine says that the first draft is the down draft — you just get it down. The second draft is the up draft — you fix it up. You try to say what you have to say more accurately. And the third draft is the dental draft, where you check every tooth, to see if it's loose or cramped or decayed, or even, God help us, healthy.

What I've learned to do when I sit down to work on a shitty first draft is to quiet the voices in my head. First there's the vinegar-lipped Reader Lady, who says primly, "Well, *that's* not very interesting, is it?" And there's the emaciated German male who writes these Orwellian memos detailing your thought crimes. And there are your parents, agonizing over your lack of loyalty and discretion; and there's William Burroughs, dozing off or shooting up because he finds you as bold and articulate as a houseplant; and so on. And there are also the dogs: let's not forget the dogs, the dogs in their pen who will surely hurtle and snarl their way out if you ever *stop* writing, because writing is, for some of us, the latch that keeps the door of the pen closed, keeps those crazy ravenous dogs contained.

Quieting these voices is at least half the battle I fight daily. But this is better than it used to be. It used to be 87 percent. Left to its own devices, my mind spends much of its time having conversations with people who aren't there. I walk along defending myself to people, or exchanging repartee with them, or rationalizing my behavior, or seducing them with gossip, or pretending I'm on their TV talk show or whatever. I speed or run an aging yellow light or don't come to a full stop, and one nanosecond later am explaining to imaginary cops exactly why I had to do what I did, or insisting that I did not in fact do it.

I happened to mention this to a hypnotist I saw many years ago, and he looked at me very nicely. At first I thought he was feeling around on the floor for the silent alarm button, but then he gave me the following exercise, which I still use to this day.

Close your eyes and get quiet for a minute, until the chatter starts up. Then isolate one of the voices and imagine the person speaking as a mouse. Pick it up by the tail and drop it into a mason jar. Then isolate another voice, pick it up by the tail, drop it in the jar. And so on. Drop in any high-maintenance parental units, drop in any contractors, lawyers, colleagues, children, anyone who is whining in your head. Then put the lid on, and watch all these mouse people clawing at the glass, jabbering away, trying to make you feel like shit because you won't do what they want — won't give them more money, won't be more successful, won't see them more often. Then imagine that there is a volume-control button on the bottle. Turn it all the way up for a minute, and listen to the stream of angry, neglected, guilt-mongering voices. Then turn it all the way down and watch the frantic mice lunge at the glass, trying to get to you. Leave it down, and get back to your shitty first draft.

A writer friend of mine suggests opening the jar and shooting 15
them all in the head. But I think he's a little angry, and I'm sure nothing like this would ever occur to you.

RESPONDING TO THE TEXT

What do you think of Lamott's use of the word *shitty* in her title and in the
essay itself? Is it in keeping with her tone? (Glossary: *Tone*) Are you offended
by the word? Why or why not? What would be lost or gained if she used a
different word?

REFLECTING AND DISCUSSING

1. Lamott says that the perception most people have of how writers work
   is different from the reality. She refers to this in paragraph 1 as the "fantasy of the uninitiated." What does she mean?

2. In paragraph 7 Lamott refers to a time when, through experience, she
   "eventually let [herself] trust the process — sort of, more or less." She is
   referring to the writing process, of course, but why "more or less"? Do
   you think her wariness is personal, or is she speaking for all writers? Explain.

3. From what Lamott has to say, is writing a first draft more about content
   or psychology? Do you agree when it comes to your own first drafts? Explain.

4. What is Lamott's thesis, and where is it located? (Glossary: *Thesis*)

5. Lamott adds humor to her argument for "shitty first drafts." Give some
   examples. Does her humor add or detract from the points she makes?
   Explain.

6. In paragraph 5, Lamott narrates her experiences in writing a food review, during which she refers to an almost ritualistic set of behaviors.
   (Glossary: *Narration*) What is her purpose in telling her readers this story
   about her difficulties? (Glossary: *Purpose*) Is this information helpful for
   us? Explain.

Writing for an Audience

Linda Flower

Linda Flower is a professor of English at Carnegie-Mellon University, where she directed the Business Communication program for a number of years. She has been a leading researcher on the composing process, and the results of her investigations have shaped and informed her influential writing text Problem-Solving Strategies for Writing, *now in its fifth edition (1999).*

In this selection, which is taken from that text, Flower's focus is on audience — the people for whom we write. She believes that writers must establish a "common ground" between themselves and their readers that lessens their differences in knowledge, attitudes, and needs. Although we can never be certain who might read what we write, it is nevertheless important for us to have a target audience in mind. Many of the decisions that we make as writers are influenced by that real or imagined reader.

PREPARING TO READ

Imagine for a moment that you just received a speeding ticket for going sixty-five miles per hour in a thirty-mile-per-hour zone. How would you describe the episode to your best friend? To your parents? To the judge in court? Sketch out the three versions. How do you account for the differences?

The goal of the writer is to create a momentary common ground between the reader and the writer. You want the reader to share your knowledge and your attitude toward that knowledge. Even if the reader eventually disagrees, you want him or her to be able for the moment to *see things as you see them*. A good piece of writing closes the gap between you and the reader.

ANALYZE YOUR AUDIENCE

The first step in closing that gap is to gauge the distance between the two of you. Imagine, for example, that you are a student writing your parents, who have always lived in New York City, about a wilderness survival expedition you want to go on over spring break. Sometimes obvious differences such as age or background will be important, but the critical differences for writers usually fall into three areas: the reader's *knowledge* about the topic; his or her *attitude* toward it, and his or her personal or professional *needs*. Because these differences often exist, good writers do more than simply express their meaning; they pinpoint the critical differences between themselves and their reader and design their writing to reduce those differences. Let us look at these areas in more detail.

Knowledge

This is usually the easiest difference to handle. What does your reader need to know? What are the main ideas you hope to teach? Does your reader have enough background knowledge to really understand you? If not, what would he or she have to learn?

Attitudes

When we say a person has knowledge, we usually refer to his conscious awareness of explicit facts and clearly defined concepts. This kind of knowledge can be easily written down or told to someone else. However, much of what we "know" is not held in this formal, explicit way. Instead it is held as an attitude or image — as a loose cluster of associations. For instance, my image of lakes includes associations many people would have, including fishing, water skiing, stalled outboards, and lots of kids catching night crawlers with flashlights. However, the most salient or powerful parts of my image, which strongly color my whole attitude toward lakes, are thoughts of cloudy skies, long rainy days, and feeling generally cold and damp. By contrast, one of my best friends has a very different cluster of associations: to him a lake means sun, swimming, sailing, and happily sitting on the end of a dock. Needless to say, our differing images cause us to react quite differently to a proposal that we visit a lake. Likewise, one reason people often find it difficult to discuss religion and politics is that terms such as "capitalism" conjure up radically different images.

As you can see, a reader's image of a subject is often the source of attitudes and feelings that are unexpected and, at times, impervious to mere facts. A simple statement that seems quite persuasive to you, such as "Lake Wampago would be a great place to locate the new music camp," could have little impact on your reader if he or she simply doesn't visualize a lake as a "great place." In fact, many people accept uncritically any statement that fits in with their own attitudes — and reject, just as uncritically, anything that does not.

Whether your purpose is to persuade or simply to present your perspective, it helps to know the image and attitudes that your reader already holds. The more these differ from your own, the more you will have to do to make him or her *see* what you mean.

Needs

When writers discover a large gap between their own knowledge and at- 7
titudes and those of the reader, they usually try to change the reader in
some way. Needs, however, are different. When you analyze a reader's
needs, it is so that you, the writer, can adapt to him. If you ask a friend
majoring in biology how to keep your fish tank from clouding, you
don't want to hear a textbook recitation on the life processes of algae.
You expect a friend to adapt his or knowledge and tell you exactly
how to solve your problem.

The ability to adapt your knowledge to the needs of the reader 8
is often crucial to your success as a writer. This is especially true in
writing done on a job. For example, as producer of a public affairs
program for a television station, 80 percent of your time may be
taken up planning the details of new shows, contacting guests, and
scheduling the taping sessions. But when you write a program proposal to the station director, your job is to show how the program
will fit into the cost guidelines, the FCC requirements for relevance,
and the overall programming plan for the station. When you write
that report your role in the organization changes from producer to
proposal writer. Why? Because your reader needs that information in
order to make a decision. He may be *interested* in your scheduling
problems and the specific content of the shows, but he *reads* your report because of his own needs as station director of the organization.
He has to act.

In college, where the reader is also a teacher, the reader's needs are 9
a little less concrete but just as important. Most papers are assigned as
a way to teach something. So the real purpose of a paper may be for
you to make connections between two historical periods, to discover
for yourself the principle behind a laboratory experiment, or to develop and support your own interpretation of a novel. A good college
paper doesn't just rehash the facts; it demonstrates what your reader,
as a teacher, needs to know — that you are learning the thinking skills
his or her course is trying to teach.

Effective writers are not simply expressing what they know, like a 10
student madly filling up an examination bluebook. Instead they are
using their knowledge: reorganizing, maybe even rethinking their
ideas to meet the demands of an assignment or the needs of their
reader.

RESPONDING TO THE TEXT

What does Flower believe constitutes a "good college paper" (paragraph 9)?
Do you agree? Why or why not?

REFLECTING AND DISCUSSING

1. How, according to Flower, does a competent writer achieve the goal of closing the gap between himself or herself and the reader? How does a writer determine what a reader's "personal or professional needs" (paragraph 2) are?

2. What, for Flower, is the difference between knowledge and attitude? Why is it important for writers to understand this difference?

3. In paragraph 4, Flower discusses the fact that many words have both positive and negative associations. How do you think words come to have associations? (Glossary: *Connotation/Denotation*) Consider, for example, such words as *home, anger, royalty, welfare, politician,* and *strawberry shortcake.*

4. Flower wrote this selection for college students. How well did she assess your knowledge, attitude, and needs about the subjects of a writer's audience? Does Flower's use of language and examples show a sensitivity to her audience? Provide specific examples to support your view. (Glossary: *Examples*)

5. When using technical language in a paper on a subject you are familiar with, why is it important for you to know your audience? (Glossary: *Audience*) Explain. How could your classmates, friends, or parents help you?

Simplicity

William Zinsser

Born in New York City in 1922, William Zinsser was educated at Princeton University. After serving in the army in World War II, he worked at the New York Herald Tribune *as an editor, writer, and critic. During the 1970s he taught a popular course in nonfiction at Yale University, and from 1979 to 1987 he was general editor of the Book-of-the-Month Club. Zinsser has written more than a dozen books, including* The City Dwellers *(1962),* Pop Goes America *(1966),* Spring Training *(1989), and three widely used books on writing:* On Writing Well *(6th ed., 1998),* Writing with a Word Processor *(1983), and* Writing to Learn *(1988). Currently, he teaches at the New School in New York City, and his freelance writing regularly appears in leading magazines.*

The following selection is taken from On Writing Well. *This book grew out of Zinsser's many years of experience as a professional writer and teacher. In this essay, Zinsser exposes what he believes is the writer's number one problem — "clutter." He sees Americans "strangling in unnecessary words, circular constructions, pompous frills, and meaningless jargon." His solution is simple: Writers must know what they want to say and must be thinking clearly as they start to compose. Then self-discipline and hard work are necessary to achieve clear, simple prose. No matter what your experience as a writer has been, you will find Zinsser's observations sound and his advice practical.*

PREPARING TO READ

Some people view writing as "thinking on paper." They believe that by seeing something written on a page they are better able to "see what they think." Write about the relationship, for you, between writing and thinking. Are you one of those people who likes to "see" ideas on paper while trying to work things out? Or do you like to think through ideas before writing about them?

Clutter is the disease of American writing. We are a society strangling in unnecessary words, circular constructions, pompous frills, and meaningless jargon.

Who can understand the viscous language of everyday American commerce: the memo, the corporation report, the business letter, the notice from the bank explaining its latest "simplified" statement? What member of an insurance or medical plan can decipher the brochure explaining his costs and benefits? What father or mother can put together a child's toy from the instructions on the box? Our national tendency is to inflate and thereby sound important. The airline pilot who announces that he is presently anticipating experiencing considerable precipitation wouldn't think of saying it may rain. The sentence is too simple — there must be something wrong with it.

But the secret of good writing is to strip every sentence to its cleanest components. Every word that serves no function, every long word that could be a short word, every adverb that carries the same meaning that's already in the verb, every passive construction that leaves the reader unsure of who is doing what — these are the thousand and one adulterants that weaken the strength of a sentence. And they usually occur in proportion to education and rank.

During the 1960s the president of my university wrote a letter to mollify the alumni after a spell of campus unrest. "You are probably aware," he began, "that we have been experiencing very considerable potentially explosive expressions of dissatisfaction on issues only partially related." He meant the students had been hassling them about different things. I was far more upset by the president's English than by the students' potentially explosive expressions of dissatisfaction. I would have preferred the presidential approach taken by Franklin D. Roosevelt when he tried to convert into English his own government's memos, such as this blackout order of 1942:

> Such preparations shall be made as will completely obscure all Federal buildings and non-Federal buildings occupied by the Federal government during an air raid for any period of time from visibility by reason of internal or external illumination.

"Tell them," Roosevelt said, "that in buildings where they have to keep the work going to put something across the windows."

Simplify, simplify. Thoreau said it, as we are so often reminded, and no American writer more consistently practiced what he preached. Open *Walden* to any page and you will find a man saying in a plain and orderly way what is on his mind:

> I went to the woods because I wished to live deliberately, to front only the essential facts of life, and see if I could not learn what it had to teach, and not, when I came to die, discover that I had not lived.

How can the rest of us achieve such enviable freedom from clutter? The answer is to clear our heads of clutter. Clear thinking becomes clear writing; one can't exist without the other. It's impossible for a muddy thinker to write good English. You may get away with it for a paragraph or two, but soon the reader will be lost, and there's no sin so grave, for the reader will not easily be lured back.

Who is this elusive creature, the reader? The reader is someone with 8
an attention span of about 30 seconds — a person assailed by other
forces competing for attention. At one time these forces weren't so numerous: newspapers, radio, spouse, home, children. Today they also
include a "home entertainment center" (TV, VCR, tapes, CDs), pets, a
fitness program, a yard and all the gadgets that have been bought to
keep it spruce, and that most potent of competitors, sleep. The person
snoozing in a chair with a magazine or a book is a person who was
being given too much unnecessary trouble by the writer.

It won't do to say that the reader is too dumb or too lazy to keep 9
pace with the train of thought. If the reader is lost, it's usually because
the writer hasn't been careful enough. The carelessness can take any
number of forms. Perhaps a sentence is so excessively cluttered that
the reader, hacking through the verbiage, simply doesn't know what it
means. Perhaps a sentence has been so shoddily constructed that the
reader could read it in several ways. Perhaps the writer has switched
pronouns in mid-sentence, or has switched tenses, so the reader loses
track of who is talking or when the action took place. Perhaps Sentence B is not a logical sequel to Sentence A — the writer, in whose
head the connection is clear, hasn't bothered to provide the missing
link. Perhaps the writer has used an important word incorrectly by not
taking the trouble to look it up. The writer may think "sanguine" and
"sanguinary" mean the same thing, but the difference is a bloody big
one. The reader can only infer (speaking of big differences) what the
writer is trying to imply.

Faced with such obstacles, readers are at first tenacious. They blame 10
themselves — they obviously missed something, and they go back over
the mystifying sentence, or over the whole paragraph, piecing it out like
an ancient rune, making guesses and moving on. But they won't do this
for long. The writer is making them work too hard, and they will look
for one who is better at the craft.

Writers must therefore constantly ask: What am I trying to say? 11
Surprisingly often they don't know. Then they must look at what they
have written and ask: Have I said it? Is it clear to someone encounter-
ing the subject for the first time? If it's not, some fuzz has worked its
way into the machinery. The clear writer is someone clearheaded
enough to see this stuff for what it is: fuzz.

I don't mean that some people are born clearheaded and are there- 12
fore natural writers, whereas others are naturally fuzzy and will never
write well. Thinking clearly is a conscious act that writers must force
upon themselves, as if they were working on any other project that requires logic: adding up a laundry list or doing an algebra problem. Good
writing doesn't come naturally, though most people obviously think it
does. Professional writers are constantly being bearded by strangers who
say they'd like to "try a little writing sometime" — meaning when they

retire from their real profession, which is difficult, like insurance or real estate. Or they say, "I could write a book about that." I doubt it.

Writing is hard work. A clear sentence is not accident. Very few 13 sentences come out right the first time, or even the third time. Remember this in moments of despair. If you find that writing is hard, it's because it *is* hard. It's one of the hardest things people do.

RESPONDING TO THE TEXT

What assumptions does Zinsser make about readers? According to Zinsser, what responsibilities do writers have to readers? How do these responsibilities manifest themselves in Zinsser's writing?

REFLECTING AND DISCUSSING

1. What exactly is clutter? When do words qualify as clutter, and when do they not?

2. In paragraph 2, Zinsser states that "Our national tendency is to inflate and thereby sound important." What do you think he means by inflate? Provide several examples to illustrate how people use language to inflate.

3. One would hope that education would help in the battle against clutter, but, as Zinsser notes, wordiness "usually occur[s] in proportion to education and rank" (paragraph 4). Do your own experiences or observations support Zinsser's claim? Explain.

4. Zinsser believes that writers need to ask themselves two questions — "What am I trying to say?" and "Have I said it?" — constantly as they write. How would these questions help you eliminate clutter from your own writing? Give some examples from one of your essays.

5. In order "to strip every sentence to its cleanest components," we need to be sensitive to the words we use and know how they function within our sentences. For each of the "adulterants that weaken the strength of a sentence," which Zinsser identifies in paragraph 3, provide an example from your own writing.

6. Zinsser knows that sentence variety is an important feature of good writing. Locate several examples of the short sentences (seven or fewer words) he uses in this essay, and explain how each relates in length, meaning, and impact to the sentences around it.

The Maker's Eye: Revising Your Own Manuscripts

Donald M. Murray

Born in Boston, Massachusetts, in 1924, Donald M. Murray taught writing for many years at the University of New Hampshire, his alma mater. He has served as an editor at Time *magazine, and he won the Pulitzer Prize in 1954 for editorials that appeared in the* Boston Globe. *Murray's published works include novels, short stories, poetry, and sourcebooks for teachers of writing, like* A Writer Teaches Writing *(1968),* The Craft of Revision *(1991), and* Learning by Teaching *(1982), in which he explores aspects of the writing process.* Write to Learn *(6th ed., 1998), a textbook for college composition courses, is based on Murray's belief that writers learn to write by writing, by taking a piece of writing through the whole process, from invention to revision.*

In the following essay, first published in the Writer *in October 1973 and later revised, Murray discusses the importance of revision to the work of the writer. Most professional writers live by the maxim that "writing is rewriting." And to rewrite or revise effectively, we need to become better readers of our own work, open to discovering new meanings, and sensitive to our use of language. Murray draws on the experiences of many writers to make a compelling argument for careful revising and editing.*

PREPARING TO READ

Thinking back on your education to date, what did you think you had to do when teachers told you to revise a piece of your writing? How did the request to revise make you feel? Write about your earliest memories of revising some of your writing. What kinds of changes do you remember making?

When students complete a first draft, they consider the job of writing done — and their teachers too often agree. When professional writers complete a first draft, they usually feel that they are at the start of the writing process. When a draft is completed, the job of writing can begin.

That difference in attitude is the difference between amateur and professional, inexperience and experience, journeyman and craftsman. Peter F. Drucker, the prolific business writer, calls his first draft "the zero draft" — after that he can start counting. Most writers share the feeling that the first draft, and all of those which follow, are opportunities to discover what they have to say and how best they can say it.

To produce a progression of drafts, each of which says more and 3
says it more clearly, the writer has to develop a special kind of reading
skill. In school we are taught to decode what appears on the page as
finished writing. Writers, however, face a different category of possibility and responsibility when they read their own drafts. To them the
words on the page are never finished. Each can be changed and rearranged, can set off a chain reaction of confusion or clarified meaning. This is a different kind of reading which is possibly more difficult
and certainly more exciting.

Writers must learn to be their own best enemy. They must accept 4
the criticism of others and be suspicious of it; they must accept the
praise of others and be even more suspicious of it. Writers cannot depend on others. They must detach themselves from their own pages so
that they can apply both their caring and their craft to their own
work.

Such detachment is not easy. Science-fiction writer Ray Bradbury 5
supposedly puts each manuscript away for a year to the day and then
rereads it as a stranger. Not many writers have the discipline or the time
to do this. We must read when our judgment may be at its worst, when
we are close to the euphoric moment of creation.

Then the writer, counsels novelist Nancy Hale, "should be critical 6
of everything that seems to him most delightful in his style. He
should excise what he most admires, because he wouldn't thus admire
it if he weren't . . . in a sense protecting it from criticism." John Ciardi,
the poet, adds, "The last act of the writing must be to become one's
own reader. It is, I suppose, a schizophrenic process, to begin passionately and to end critically, to begin hot and to end cold; and, more
important, to be passion-hot and critic-cold at the same time."

Most people think that the principal problem is that writers are 7
too proud of what they have written. Actually, a greater problem for
most professional writers is one shared by the majority of students.
They are overly critical, think everything is dreadful, tear up page after
page, never complete a draft, see the task as hopeless.

The writer must learn to read critically but constructively, to cut 8
what is bad, to reveal what is good. Eleanor Estes, the children's book
author, explains: "The writer must survey his work critically, coolly, as
though he were a stranger to it. He must be willing to prune, expertly
and hard-heartedly. At the end of each revision, a manuscript may
look . . . worked over, torn apart, pinned together, added to, deleted
from, words changed and words changed back. Yet the book must
maintain its original freshness and spontaneity."

Most readers underestimate the amount of rewriting it usually 9
takes to produce spontaneous reading. This is a great disadvantage to
the student writer, who sees only a finished product and never watches

the craftsman who takes the necessary step back, studies the work carefully, returns to the task, steps back, returns, steps back, again and again. Anthony Burgess, one of the most prolific writers in the English-speaking world, admits, "I might revise a page twenty times." Roald Dahl, the popular children's writer, states, "By the time I'm nearing the end of a story, the first part will have been reread and altered and corrected at least 150 times. . . . Good writing is essentially rewriting. I am positive of this."

Rewriting isn't virtuous. It isn't something that ought to be done. 10 It is simply something that most writers find they have to do to discover what they have to say and how to say it. It is a condition of the writer's life.

There are, however, a few writers who do little formal rewriting, 11 primarily because they have the capacity and experience to create and review a large number of invisible drafts in their minds before they approach the page. And some writers slowly produce finished pages, performing all the tasks of revision simultaneously, page by page, rather than draft by draft. But it is still possible to see the sequence followed by most writers most of the time in rereading their own work.

Most writers scan their drafts first, reading as quickly as possible to 12 catch the larger problems of subject and form, and then move in closer and closer as they read and write, reread and rewrite.

The first thing writers look for in their drafts is *information*. They 13 know that a good piece of writing is built from specific, accurate, and interesting information. The writer must have an abundance of information from which to construct a readable piece of writing.

Next writers look for *meaning* in the information. The specifics 14 must build to a pattern of significance. Each piece of specific information must carry the reader toward meaning.

Writers reading their own drafts are aware of *audience*. They put 15 themselves in the reader's situation and make sure that they deliver information which a reader wants to know or needs to know in a manner which is easily digested. Writers try to be sure that they anticipate and answer the questions a critical reader will ask when reading the piece of writing.

Writers make sure that the *form* is appropriate to the subject and 16 the audience. Form, or genre, is the vehicle which carries meaning to the reader, but form cannot be selected until the writer has adequate information to discover its significance and an audience which needs or wants that meaning.

Once writers are sure the form is appropriate, they must then look 17 at the *structure,* the order of what they have written. Good writing is built on a solid framework of logic, argument, narrative, or motivation which runs through the entire piece of writing and holds it together. This is the time when many writers find it most effective to outline as a way of visualizing the hidden spine by which the piece of writing is supported.

The element on which writers may spend a majority of their time   18
is *development*. Each section of a piece of writing must be adequately developed. It must give readers enough information so that they are satisfied. How much information is enough? That's as difficult as asking how much garlic belongs in a salad. It must be done to taste, but most beginning writers underdevelop, underestimating the reader's hunger for information.

As writers solve development problems, they often have to con-   19
sider questions of *dimension*. There must be a pleasing and effective proportion among all the parts of the piece of writing. There is a continual process of subtracting and adding to keep the piece of writing in balance.

Finally, writers have to listen to their own voices. *Voice* is the force   20
which drives a piece of writing forward. It is an expression of the writer's authority and concern. It is what is between the words on the page, what glues the piece of writing together. A good piece of writing is always marked by a consistent, individual voice.

As writers read and reread, write and rewrite, they move closer and   21
closer to the page until they are doing line-by-line editing. Writers read their own pages with infinite care. Each sentence, each line, each clause, each phrase, each word, each mark of punctuation, each section of white space between the type has to contribute to the clarification of meaning.

Slowly the writer moves from word to word, looking through lan-   22
guage to see the subject. As a word is changed, cut, or added, as a construction is rearranged, all the words used before that moment and all those that follow that moment must be considered and reconsidered.

Writers often read aloud at this stage of the editing process, mut-   23
tering or whispering to themselves, calling on the ear's experience with language. Does this sound right — or that? Writers edit, shifting back and forth from eye to page to ear to page. I find I must do this careful editing in short runs, no more than fifteen or twenty minutes at a stretch, or I become too kind with myself. I begin to see what I hope is on the page, not what actually is on the page.

This sounds tedious if you haven't done it, but actually it is fun.   24
Making something right is immensely satisfying, for writers begin to learn what they are writing about by writing. Language leads them to meaning, and there is the joy of discovery, of understanding, of making meaning clear as the writer employs the technical skills of language.

Words have double meanings, even triple and quadruple mean-   25
ings. Each word has its own potential of connotation and denotation. And when writers rub one word against the other, they are often rewarded with a sudden insight, an unexpected clarification.

The maker's eye moves back and forth from word to phrase to sentence to paragraph to sentence to phrase to word. The maker's eye sees the need for variety and balance, for a firmer structure, for a more appropriate form. It peers into the interior of the paragraph, looking for coherence, unity, and emphasis, which make meaning clear. 26

I learned something about this process when my first bifocals were prescribed. I had ordered a larger section of the reading portion of the glass because of my work, but even so, I could not contain my eyes within this new limit of vision. And I still find myself taking off my glasses and bending my nose toward the page, for my eyes unconsciously flick back and forth across the page, back to another page, forward to still another, as I try to see each evolving line in relation to every other line. 27

When does this process end? Most writers agree with the great Russian writer Tolstoy, who said, "I scarcely ever reread my published writings, if by chance I come across a page, it always strikes me: all this must be rewritten; this is how I should have written it." 28

The maker's eye is never satisfied, for each word has the potential to ignite new meaning. This article has been twice written all the way through the writing process [. . .]. Now it is to be republished in a book. The editors made a few small suggestions, and then I read it with my maker's eye. Now it has been re-edited, re-revised, re-read, and re-re-edited, for each piece of writing to the writer is full of potential and alternatives. 29

A piece of writing is never finished. It is delivered to a deadline, torn out of the typewriter on demand, sent off with a sense of accomplishment and shame and pride and frustration. If only there were a couple more days, time for just another run at it, perhaps then . . . 30

RESPONDING TO THE TEXT

Murray notes that writers often reach a stage in their editing where they read aloud, "muttering or whispering to themselves, calling on the ear's experience with language" (paragraph 23). What do you think writers are listening for? Try reading several paragraphs of Murray's essay aloud. Explain what you learned about his writing. Have you ever read your own writing aloud? If so, what did you discover?

REFLECTING AND DISCUSSING

1. How does Murray define *information* and *meaning* (paragraphs 13–14)? Why is the distinction between the two terms important?

2. What are the essential differences between revising and editing? What types of language concerns are dealt with at each stage? Why is it important to revise before editing?

3. According to Murray, when in the writing process do writers become concerned about the individual words they are using? What do you think Murray means when he says in paragraph 24 that "language leads [writers] to meaning"?

4. The phrase "the maker's eye" appears in Murray's title and in several places throughout the essay. What do you suppose he means by this? Consider how the maker's eye could be different from the reader's eye.

5. What does Murray see as the connection between reading and writing? How does reading help the writer? What should writers be looking for in their reading? What kinds of writing techniques or strategies does Murray use in his essay? Why should we read a novel or magazine article differently than we would a draft of one of our own essays?

6. According to Murray, writers look for information, meaning, audience, form, structure, development, dimension, and voice in their drafts. What rationale or logic do you see, if any, in the way Murray has ordered these items? Are these the kinds of concerns you have when reading your drafts? Explain.

The Transformation of Silence Into Language and Action

Audre Lorde

Audre Lorde (1934–1992) was a professor of English at Hunter College in New York City. Born in New York, she studied at Hunter and at Columbia University. Her published works include several volumes of poetry, such as Undersong: Chosen Poems Old and New *(1982); essay collections like* Sister Outsider *(1984) and* Burst of Light *(1988); and an autobiography,* Zami: A New Spelling of My Name *(1982). Her book of poems* The Arithmetics of Distance *was published posthumously in 1993.*

Lorde presented the following speech at the 1977 Modern Language Association Convention. It was later reprinted in her book Sister Outsider. *In this highly personal speech she manages to make her message a universal one.*

PREPARING TO READ

Think about how important it is for you to voice your thoughts and beliefs. Do you sometimes feel frustrated by what seems your powerlessness to influence your circumstances, particularly as a young person and a student? Comment on what role your speaking out may be able to play in helping you take control of your world.

I have come to believe over and over again that what is most important to me must be spoken, made verbal and shared, even at the risk of having it bruised or misunderstood. That the speaking profits me, beyond any other effect. I am standing here as a Black lesbian poet, and the meaning of all that waits upon the fact that I am still alive, and might not have been. Less than two months ago I was told by two doctors, one female and one male, that I would have to have breast surgery, and that there was a 60 to 80 percent chance that the tumor was malignant. Between that telling and the actual surgery, there was a three-week period of the agony of an involuntary reorganization of my entire life. The surgery was completed, and the growth was benign.

But within those three weeks, I was forced to look upon myself and my living with a harsh and urgent clarity that has left me still shaken but much stronger. This is a situation faced by many women, by some of you here today. Some of what I experienced during that time has helped elucidate for me much of what I feel concerning the transformation of silence into language and action.

In becoming forcibly and essentially aware of my mortality, and   3
of what I wished and wanted for my life, however short it might be,
priorities and omissions became strongly etched in a merciless light,
and what I most regretted were my silences. Of what had I *ever* been
afraid? To question or to speak as I believed could have meant pain, or
death. But we all hurt in so many different ways, all the time, and
pain will either change or end. Death, on the other hand, is the final
silence. And that might be coming quickly, now, without regard for
whether I had ever spoken what needed to be said, or had only be-
trayed myself into small silences, while I planned someday to speak,
or waited for someone else's words. And I began to recognize a source
of power within myself that comes from the knowledge that while it is
most desirable not to be afraid, learning to put fear into a perspective
gave me great strength.

I was going to die, if not sooner then later, whether or not I had   4
ever spoken myself. My silences had not protected me. Your silence
will not protect you. But for every real word spoken, for every attempt
I had ever made to speak those truths for which I am still seeking, I
had made contact with other women while we examined the words to
fit a world in which we all believed, bridging our differences. And it
was the concern and caring of all those women which gave me
strength and enabled me to scrutinize the essentials of my living.

The women who sustained me through that period were Black   5
and white, old and young, lesbian, bisexual, and heterosexual, and we
all shared a war against the tyrannies of silence. They all gave me a
strength and concern without which I could not have survived intact.
Within those weeks of acute fear came the knowledge — within the
war we are all waging with the forces of death, subtle and otherwise,
conscious or not — I am not only a casualty, I am also a warrior.

What are the words you do not yet have? What do you need to say?   6
What are the tyrannies you swallow day by day and attempt to make
your own, until you will sicken and die of them, still in silence? Perhaps
for some of you here today, I am the face of one of your fears. Because
I am woman, because I am Black, because I am lesbian, because I am
myself — a Black woman warrior poet doing my work — come to ask
you, are you doing yours?

And of course I am afraid, because the transformation of silence into   7
language and action is an act of self-revelation, and that always seems
fraught with danger. But my daughter, when I told her of our topic
and my difficulty with it, said, "Tell them about how you're never really a whole person if you remain silent, because there's always that
one little piece inside you that wants to be spoken out, and if you
keep ignoring it, it gets madder and madder and hotter and hotter,

and if you don't speak it out one day it will just up and punch you in the mouth from the inside."

In the cause of silence, each of us draws the face of her own fear — 8 fear of contempt, of censure, or some judgment, or recognition, of challenge, of annihilation. But most of all, I think, we fear the visibility without which we cannot truly live. Within this country where racial difference creates a constant, if unspoken, distortion of vision, Black women have on one hand always been highly visible, and so, on the other hand, have been rendered invisible through the depersonalization of racism. Even within the women's movement, we have had to fight, and still do, for that very visibility which also renders us most vulnerable, our Blackness. For to survive in the mouth of this dragon we call america, we have had to learn this first and most vital lesson — that we were never meant to survive. Not as human beings. And neither were most of you here today, Black or not. And that visibility which makes us most vulnerable is that which also is the source of our greatest strength. Because the machine will try to grind you into dust anyway, whether or not we speak. We can sit in our corners mute forever while our sisters and our selves are wasted, while our children are distorted and destroyed, while our earth is poisoned; we can sit in our safe corners mute as bottles, and we will still be no less afraid.

In my house this year we are celebrating the feast of Kwanza, the 9 African-american festival of harvest which begins the day after Christmas and lasts for seven days. There are seven principles of Kwanza, one for each day. The first principle is Umoja, which means unity, the decision to strive for and maintain unity in self and community. The principle for yesterday, the second day, was Kujichagulia — self-determination — the decision to define ourselves, name ourselves, and speak for ourselves, instead of being defined and spoken for by others. Today is the third day of Kwanza, and the principle for today is Ujima — collective work and responsibility — the decision to build and maintain ourselves and our communities together and to recognize and solve our problems together.

Each of us is here now because in one way or another we share a 10 commitment to language and to the power of language, and to the reclaiming of that language which has been made to work against us. In the transformation of silence into language and action, it is vitally necessary for each one of us to establish or examine her function in that transformation and to recognize her role as vital within that transformation.

For those of us who write, it is necessary to scrutinize not only 11 the truth of what we speak, but the truth of that language by which we speak it. For others, it is to share and spread also those words that are meaningful to us. But primarily for us all, it is necessary to teach by living and speaking those truths which we believe and know beyond understanding. Because in this way alone we can survive, by taking part in a process of life that is creative and continuing, that is growth.

And it is never without fear — of visibility, of the harsh light of scrutiny and perhaps judgment, of pain, of death. But we have lived through all of those already, in silence, except death. And I remind myself all the time now that if I were to have been born mute, or had maintained an oath of silence my whole life long for safety, I would still have suffered, and I would still die. It is very good for establishing perspective.

And where the words of women are crying to be heard, we must each of us recognize our responsibility to seek those words out, to read them and share them and examine them in their pertinence to our lives. That we not hide behind the mockeries of separations that have been imposed upon us and which so often we accept as our own. For instance, "I can't possibly teach Black women's writing — their experience is so different from mine." Yet how many years have you spent teaching Plato and Shakespeare and Proust? Or another, "She's a white woman and what could she possibly have to say to me?" Or, "She's a lesbian, what would my husband say, or my chairman?" Or again, "This woman writes of her sons and I have no children." And all the other endless ways in which we rob ourselves of ourselves and each other.

We can learn to work and speak when we are afraid in the same way we have learned to work and speak when we are tired. For we have been socialized to respect fear more than our own needs for language and definition, and while we wait in silence for that final luxury of fearlessness, the weight of that silence will choke us.

The fact that we are here and that I speak these words is an attempt to break that silence and bridge some of those differences between us, for it is not difference which immobilizes us, but silence. And there are so many silences to be broken.

RESPONDING TO THE TEXT

Lorde's speech recognizes the need we all have to express ourselves and the importance of doing so. She speaks of the forces that work to maintain our silence. Have you ever felt the need to speak or write? Have you ever been intimidated into silence? What were the circumstances of your remaining silent? What were the circumstances of your speaking or writing what was on your mind? What advice can you give those who remain silent? How might they eventually experience the hearing of their own voices?

REFLECTING AND DISCUSSING

1. What did the trauma of Lorde's breast surgery make apparent to her?
2. What exactly are the silences to which Lorde refers? Why does she think it's necessary for women to break those silences?

3. Lorde refers to fear repeatedly. Is the fear of death the only thing she worries about? Explain.

4. Who is Lorde's audience? (Glossary: *Audience*) Where and how does she address those in her audience? What effect do those direct addresses have on you as a reader of the text of her speech? Are they distracting or helpful? Explain.

5. What does Lorde say about the differences between herself and the members of her audience? (Glossary: *Audience*) What do they share, and why does Lorde see it as important?

6. Why do you suppose Lorde shares with her audience what her daughter told her she should say in her speech? (Glossary: *Audience*)

7. In paragraph 9, Lorde talks about Kwanza, "the African-american festival of harvest which begins the day after Christmas and lasts for seven days" (paragraph 9). What is her point in discussing Kwanza? (Glossary: *Purpose*) Why do you think she does not capitalize the word *american*?

CHAPTER 14

Writing
Documented Essays

A documented paper is not very different from the other writing in your college writing course. You will find yourself drawing heavily on what you learned in Chapter 2 (pages 19–44). First you determine what you want to say, then you decide on a purpose, consider your audience, develop a thesis, collect your evidence, write a first draft, revise and edit, and prepare a final copy. What differentiates the documented paper from other kinds of papers is your use of outside sources and how you acknowledge them. In this chapter, you will learn how to locate and use print and Internet sources; how to evaluate these sources; how to take useful notes; how to summarize, paraphrase, and quote your sources; how to integrate your notes into your paper; how to acknowledge your sources; and how to avoid plagiarism. You will also find extensive guidelines for documenting your essay in Modern Language Association (MLA) style.

Your library research will involve working with both print and electronic sources. In both cases, however, the process is essentially the same. Your aim is to select the most appropriate sources for your research from the many that are available on your topic.

PRINT SOURCES

In most cases, you should use print sources (books, newspapers, periodicals, encyclopedias, pamphlets, brochures, and government publications) as your primary tools for research. Most print sources, unlike many Internet sources, are reviewed and refereed by experts in the field, are approved and overseen by a reputable publishing company or organization, and are examined by editors and fact checkers for accuracy and reliability. Unless you are instructed otherwise, you should always use print sources in your research.

To find print sources, search through your library's reference works, card catalog, periodical indexes, and other databases to generate a preliminary listing of books, magazine and newspaper articles, public documents and reports, and other sources that look as if they might help you explore or answer your research question. At this early stage, it is better to err on the side of listing too many sources rather than finding yourself trying later to relocate those you discarded too hastily.

Previewing Print Sources

Although you want to be thorough in your research, you will soon realize that you do not have time to read every source you collect. Rather, you must preview your sources to decide what you will read, what you will skim, and what you will simply eliminate. Here are some suggestions for previewing your print sources.

QUESTIONS FOR PREVIEWING PRINT SOURCES

1. Is the book or article directly related to the specific research question you are trying to answer?
2. Are any of the books or articles obviously outdated (for example, a source on nuclear energy published in the 1960s)?
3. Have you checked tables of contents and indexes in books to locate the material that is important and relevant to your topic?
4. If an article appears to be what you are looking for, have you read the abstract or the opening paragraphs?
5. Is it necessary to quickly read the entire article to be sure that it is relevant?

Developing a Working Bibliography

For each work that you think might be helpful, make a separate bibliography card, using a 3- by 5-inch index card. As your collection of bibliography cards grows, alphabetize the cards by the authors' last names. By using a separate card for each book or article, you can continually edit your working bibliography, dropping sources that are not helpful and adding new ones.

Make sure you record all the necessary information about each source for which you make a bibliography card. You will use the cards to compile the final bibliography, or the list of works cited, for your paper.

For books, record the following information:

- All authors; any editors or translators
- Title and subtitle
- Edition (if not the first)
- Publication data: city, publishing company, and date
- Call number

For periodical articles, record the following information:

- All authors
- Title and subtitle
- Title of journal, magazine, or newspaper
- Volume and issue numbers
- Date
- Page numbers

Using correct bibliographic form ensures that your entries are complete, reduces the chance of introducing careless errors, and saves time when you prepare your final list of works cited. You will find MLA style guidelines for your list of works cited on pages 702–708.

Evaluating Print Sources

Before beginning to take notes, you should read your sources and evaluate them for their reliability and relevance in helping you answer your research question. Examine your sources for the writers' main ideas. Pay particular attention to abstracts or introductions, tables of contents, section headings, and indexes. Also, look for information about the authors themselves — information that will help you determine their authority and perspective on the issues.

QUESTIONS FOR EVALUATING PRINT SOURCES

1. Is your source focused on your particular research question?
2. Is your source too abstract, too general, or too technical for your needs?
3. Does your source build on current thinking and existing research in the field?

4. Does your source promote a particular view, or is it meant to inform?

5. What biases, if any, does your source exhibit?

6. Is the author of your source an authority on the issue? Do other writers mention the author of your source in their work?

INTERNET SOURCES

You will find that Internet sources can be informative and valuable additions to your research; for example, you might find a just-published article from a university laboratory or a news story in your local newspaper's online archives. Generally, however, Internet resources should be used alongside print sources and not as a replacement for them. While print sources are published under the guidance of a publisher or an organization, anyone with access to a computer and a modem can put text and pictures on the Internet; there is no governing body that checks accuracy. The Internet offers a vast number of useful and carefully maintained resources, but it also contains many bogus facts and many examples of rumor, conjecture, and unreliable information. It is your responsibility to evaluate whether or not you can trust a given Internet source.

Your Internet research will almost certainly produce many more sources than you can reasonably use. By carefully previewing Web sites and other Internet sources, developing a working bibliography of potentially useful ones, and evaluating them for their reliability, you will ensure that you are making the best use of Internet sources in researching your topic.

If you do not know how to access the Internet, or if you need more instruction on conducting Internet searches, go to your campus computer center for more information, or consult one of the many books written for Internet beginners.

Previewing Internet Sources

The key to successful Internet research is being able to identify the sites that will help you the most. The following questions will help you weed out the sources that hold no promise.

QUESTIONS FOR PREVIEWING INTERNET SOURCES

1. Scan the Web site. Do the contents and links appear to be related to your research topic?

2. Can you identify the author of the site? Are the author's credentials available?

3. Has the site been updated within the last six months? This information is usually provided at the bottom of the Web page. Updating is not always necessary, especially if your topic is not a current one and information about it is deemed to be somewhat stable.

If you answer "No" to any of these questions, you should consider eliminating the source from further consideration.

Developing a Working Bibliography

Just as for print sources, you must maintain accurate records for the Internet sources you use. Here is what you need for each source:

- All authors or sponsoring agents
- Title and subtitle of document
- Title of complete work (if applicable)
- Document date (or date "last modified")
- Date you accessed the site
- Publishing data for print version (if available)
- Address of the site, URL (uniform resource locator), or network path

See pages 705–707 for the latest MLA guidelines for electronic sources.

Evaluating Internet Sources

Because the quality of sources on the Internet varies tremendously, you will need guidelines for evaluating the information you find there. Here are some techniques to help you evaluate the validity of the sites you have included in your working bibliography.

QUESTIONS FOR EVALUATING INTERNET SOURCES
- Type of Web page

    Who hosts the Web site? Often the URL (the Internet version of an address) domain name suffix can give you an indication of the type of information provided and the type of organization that hosts the site.

    Common top-level domain names include these:

    .com — business/commercial

    .edu — educational institution

    .gov — government sponsored

    .mil — military

.net — various types of networks

.org — nonprofit organization

- Authority/author

  Is it clear what individual or company is responsible for the site?

  Can you verify if the site is official, actually sanctioned by an organization or company?

  What are the author's or company's qualifications for writing on this subject?

  Is there a way to verify the legitimacy of this individual or company? Are there links to a home page or résumé?

- Purpose and audience

  What appears to be the author's or sponsor's purpose or motivation?

  Who is the intended audience?

- Objectivity

  Are advertising, opinion, and factual information clearly distinguished?

  What biases, if any, can you detect?

- Accuracy

  Is important information documented through links so that it can be verified or corroborated in other sources?

  Is the text well written and free of careless errors in spelling and grammar?

- Coverage and currency

  Is there any indication that the site is still under construction?

  For sources with print equivalents, is the Web version more or less extensive than the print version?

  How detailed is the treatment of the topic?

  Is there any indication of the currency of the information (date of last update or statement regarding frequency of updates)?

- Ease of use

  Is the design and navigation of the site user-friendly? Do all the links work, and do they take you to relevant information? Can you return to the home page easily? Are the graphics helpful, or are they simply window dressing?

You can also find sources on the Internet itself that offer useful guidelines for evaluating electronic sources. One excellent example was created by reference librarians at the Wolfgram Memorial Library of Widener University; see <www2.widener.edu/Wolfgram-Memorial -Library/webevaluation/webeval.htm>.

Internet Research: Subject Directories and Keyword Searches

Using Subject Directories to Refine Your Research Topic. The subject directories on the home pages of search engines make it easy to browse various subjects and topics, a big help if you are undecided about your exact research question or if you simply want to see if there is enough material to supplement your research work with print sources. Often the most efficient approach to Web research is to start with the subject directories provided by most search engines. Once you choose a subject area in the directory, you can select more specialized subdirectories and eventually arrive at a list of sites closely related to your topic.

Suppose you want to research bilingualism in American schools, and you are using the search engine Google (<www.google.com>). Figure 14.1 is the "Web Directory" screen where you would start your search. Your first task would be to choose, from the sixteen topics listed, the subject area most likely to contain information on bilingualism in education. Remember that just as you often need to browse through the tables of contents and indexes of numerous books on a given subject to uncover the three or four that will be most useful to you, more than one general subject area in a Web directory may seem appropriate on the surface.

Figure 14.1

The most common question students have at this stage in a Web search is, How can I tell if I'm looking in the right place? If more than one subject area sounds plausible, you will have to dig more deeply into each of their subdirectories, using logic and the process of elimination to determine which one is likely to produce the best Web site listings for your topic. In most cases, it doesn't take long — usually just one or two clicks — to figure out whether you're searching in the right subject area. If you click on a subject area and none of the topics listed in its subdirectories seems to pertain even remotely to your research topic, try a different subject area. For example, in Fig. 14.1 you might be tempted to click on "News," which has a "Current Events" link. If you do, you'll find that none of the current events topics listed seems to relate to language, education, or bilingualism, which is a strong sign that "News" is the wrong subject area for your topic. Similarly, although the "Reference" subject area contains an "Education" link, you'll find that the subdirectories listed there do not pertain to language in schools or bilingualism. The third, most logical, possibility in this case is "Society." Clicking on this subject area takes you to a screen that lists forty more subject areas, including one for "Language and Linguistics," a logical place to find sites on bilingualism in education. For "Language and Linguistics" alone, there are 3,766 Web sites listed, so chances are good that some of those sites address your subject.

When you click on "Language and Linguistics," you arrive at a screen listing categories of sites related to language study. Because you are interested in bilingualism, the "Bilingualism" option is a natural choice (see Figure 14.2). Clicking on this link takes you to a screen where you find three directory entries, including "Bilingual Education," and a listing of Web sites for bilingualism. By clicking on "Bilingual Education," you arrive at a screen (see Figure 14.3) that lists potentially valuable Web sites, including the NCBE home page (the description for this site identifies NCBE as the National Clearinghouse for Bilingual Education), the Center for Applied Linguistics, "American Shibboleth: Ebonics" posted by Cambridge Scientific Abstracts, and "Teaching Indigenous Languages" posted by Northern Arizona University. In some cases, clicking on a Web site link may bring you directly to a page containing an article on your topic. For example, clicking on "American Shibboleth: Ebonics" takes you directly to a ten-page overview and linguistic analysis of the Ebonics controversy, released online in September 2000.

Using Keyword Searches to Find Specific Information. When you type in a keyword in the "Search" box on a search engine's home page, the search engine goes looking for Web sites that match your term. One problem with keyword searches is that they can produce tens of thousands of matches, making it difficult to locate sites of immediate

Figure 14.2

Figure 14.3

value. For that reason, make your keywords as specific as you can, and make sure that you have the correct spelling. It is always a good idea to consult the help screens or advanced search instructions for the search engine you are using before initiating a keyword search. Once you start a search, you may want to narrow or broaden it depending on the number of hits, or matches, you get.

▶ *Refining Keyword Searches on the Web*

While some variation in command terms and characters exists among electronic databases and popular search engines on the Internet, the following functions are almost universally accepted. If you have a particular question about refining your keyword search, seek assistance by clicking on "Help" or "Advanced Search."

- Use quotation marks or parentheses to indicate that you are searching for words in exact sequence — e.g., "whooping cough"; (Supreme Court).
- Use AND or a plus sign (+) between words to narrow your search by specifying that all words need to appear in a document — e.g., tobacco AND cancer; Shakespeare + sonnet.
- Use NOT or a minus sign (−) between words to narrow your search by eliminating unwanted words — e.g., monopoly NOT game, cowboys−Dallas.
- Use OR to broaden your search by requiring that only one of the words need appear — e.g., buffalo OR bison.
- Use an asterisk (*) to indicate that you will accept variations of a term — e.g., "food label*."

When using a keyword search, you need to be careful about selecting the keywords that will yield the best results. If your word or words are too general, your results can be at best unwieldy and at worst not usable at all. During her initial search for her paper on cougars, an endangered cat indigenous to North America, student Dorothy Adams typed in "cougar" (see Figure 14.4). To her surprise, this produced 189,830 hits, mostly for products carrying the name or for teams with cougars as mascots. After surveying the suggested "Related Searches," Adams decided to type in "mountain lion

Figure 14.4

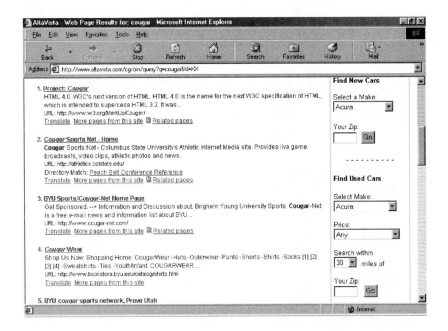

cougar." This search yielded 4,140 hits, still too many for Adams's purposes. In an effort to narrow her search even more, she tried "mountain lion cougar AND endangered" — a search that yielded a far more manageable 48 hits (see Figure 14.5). Among these hits, she located a Web page entitled "Puma, Mountain Lion, Cougar, Catamount," produced by the Natural History Museum of Los Angeles County (see Fig. 14.6). This site was a perfect starting point for Adams; it provided her with sound information about cougars and related big cats.

NOTE TAKING

As you read, take notes. You're looking for ideas, facts, opinions, statistics, examples, and evidence that you think will be useful in writing your paper. As you work through the articles, look for recurring themes, and mark the places where the writers are in agreement and where they differ in their views. Try to remember that the effectiveness of your paper is largely determined by the quality — not necessarily the quantity — of your notes. The purpose of a research paper is not to present a collection of quotes that show you've read all the material and

Figure 14.5

Figure 14.6

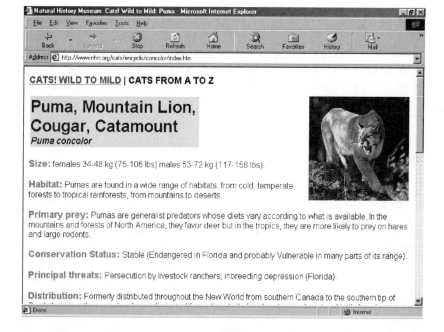

can report what others have said about your topic. Your goal is to analyze, evaluate, and synthesize the information you collect — in other
words, to enter into the discussion of the issues and thereby take ownership of your topic. You want to view the results of your research from
your own perspective and arrive at an informed opinion of your topic.

Now for some practical advice on taking notes: First, be systematic. As a rule, write one note on a card, and use cards of uniform size,
preferably 4- by 6-inch cards because they are large enough to accommodate even a long note on a single card and yet small enough to be
easily handled and carried. More important, when you get to the planning and writing stage, you will be able to sequence your notes according to the plan you have envisioned for your paper. Furthermore,
should you decide to alter your organizational plan, you can easily re-
order your cards to reflect those revisions.

Second, try not to take too many notes. One good way to help decide whether to take a note is to ask yourself, "How exactly does this
material help prove or disprove my thesis?" You might even try envisioning where in your paper you could use the information. If it does
not seem relevant to your thesis, don't bother to take a note.

Once you decide to take a note, you must decide whether to summarize, paraphrase, or quote directly. The approach that you take is
largely determined by the content of the passage and the way you envision using it in your paper. All of the examples in the following discussion are taken from articles in *Subjects/Strategies*.

Summary

When you *summarize* material from one of your sources, you capture
in condensed form the essential idea of a passage, article, or entire
chapter. Summaries are particularly useful when you are working with
lengthy, detailed arguments or long passages of narrative or descriptive background information where the details are not germane to the
overall thrust of your paper. You simply want to capture the essence of
the passage while dispensing with the details because you are confident that your readers will readily understand the point being made or
do not need to be convinced about the validity of the point. Because
you are distilling information, a summary is always shorter than the
original; often a chapter or more can be reduced to a paragraph, or
several paragraphs to a sentence or two. Remember, in writing a summary you should use your own words.

Consider the following paragraphs in which Richard Lederer compares big words with small words.

> When you speak and write, there is no law that says you have
> to use big words. Short words are as good as long ones, and short,
> old words — like *sun* and *grass* and *home* — are best of all. A lot of

small words, more than you might think, can meet your needs with a strength, grace, and charm that large words do not have.

Big words can make the way dark for those who read what you write and hear what you say. Small words cast their clear light on big things — night and day, love and hate, war and peace, and life and death. Big words at times seem strange to the eye and the ear and the mind and the heart. Small words are the ones we seem to have known from the time we were born, like the hearth fire that warms the home.

— RICHARD LEDERER,
"The Case for Short Words," page 513

A student wishing to capture the gist of Lederer's point without repeating his detailed contrast wrote the following summary.

Summary Note Card

> Short words
>
> Lederer favors short words for their clarity, familiarity, durability, and overall usefulness.
>
> Lederer, 513

Paraphrase

When you *paraphrase* a source, you restate the information in your own words instead of quoting directly. Unlike a summary, which gives a brief overview of the essential information in the original, a paraphrase seeks to maintain the same level of detail as the original to aid readers in understanding or believing the information presented. A paraphrase presents the original information in approximately the same number of words, but in the paraphraser's own wording. To put it another way, your paraphrase should closely parallel the presentation of ideas in the original but should not use the same words or sentence structure as the original. Even though you are using your own words in a paraphrase, it's important to remember that you are borrowing ideas and therefore must acknowledge the source of these ideas with a citation.

How would you paraphrase the following passage from a speech by Martin Luther King Jr.?

But one hundred years later [after the Emancipation Proclamation], we must face the tragic fact that the Negro is still not free. One hundred years later, the life of the Negro is still sadly crippled by the manacles of segregation and the chains of discrimination. One hundred years later, the Negro lives on a lonely island of poverty in the midst of a vast ocean of material prosperity. One hundred years later, the Negro is still languishing in the corners of American society and finds himself an exile in his own land.

— MARTIN LUTHER KING JR.,
"I Have a Dream," page 525

The following note card illustrates how one student paraphrased the passage from King's speech.

Paraphrase Note Card

Unfulfilled promises

On the one hundredth anniversary of the Emancipation Proclamation, African Americans find themselves still a marginalized people. African Americans do not experience the freedom that other Americans do. In a land of opportunity and plenty, racism and poverty affect the way they live their lives, separating them from mainstream society.

King, 525

In most cases, it is better to summarize or paraphrase materials — which by definition means using your own words — instead of quoting verbatim (word for word). Capturing an idea in your own words ensures that you have thought about and understood what your source is saying.

Direct Quotation

When you directly *quote* a source, you copy the words of your source exactly, putting all quoted material in quotation marks. When you make a quotation note card, carefully check for accuracy, including punctuation and capitalization. Be selective about what you choose to quote; reserve direct quotation for important ideas stated memorably, for especially clear explanations by authorities, and for arguments by proponents of a particular position in their own words.

Consider, for example, Deborah Tannen's powerful contrast between the ways boys and girls communicate:

> The girls in my study tended to talk at length about one topic, but the boys tended to jump from topic to topic. The second-grade girls exchanged stories about people they knew. The second-grade boys teased, told jokes, noticed things in the room, and talked about finding games to play. The sixth-grade girls talked about problems with a mutual friend. The sixth-grade boys talked about 55 different topics, none of which extended over more than a few turns.

> — DEBORAH TANNEN,
> "Sex, Lies, and Conversation," page 314

Quotation Note Card

Conversation differences

"The girls in my study tended to talk at length about one topic, but the boys tended to jump from topic to topic. The second-grade girls exchanged stories about people they knew. The second-grade boys teased, told jokes, noticed things in the room, and talked about finding games to play. The sixth-grade girls talked about problems with a mutual friend. The sixth-grade boys talked about 55 different topics, none of which extended over more than a few turns."

Tannen, 314

On occasion, you'll find a useful passage with some memorable wording in it. Avoid the temptation to quote the whole passage; instead you can combine summary or paraphrase with direct quotation.

Consider the following paragraph from Rosalind Wiseman's essay on schoolgirls' roles in cliques.

Information about each other is currency in Girl World. The Banker creates chaos everywhere she goes by banking information about girls in her social sphere and dispensing it at strategic intervals for her own benefit. For instance, if a girl has said something negative about another girl, the Banker will casually mention it to someone in conversation because she knows it's going to cause a conflict and strengthen her status as someone "in the know." She can get girls to trust her because when she pumps them for information it doesn't seem like gossip; instead, she does it in an innocent, I'm-trying-to-be-your-friend way.

— ROSALIND WISEMAN
"The Queen Bee and Her Court," page 342

Note how the student who took the following note was careful to put quotation marks around all words that have been borrowed directly.

Quotation and Summary Note Card

> Clique characters
>
> Perhaps the most dangerous character in the clique is the Banker, who "creates chaos everywhere she goes by banking information about girls in her social sphere and dispensing it at strategic intervals for her own benefit. For instance, if a girl has said something negative about another girl, the Banker will casually mention it to someone in conversation because she knows it's going to cause a conflict and strengthen her status as someone 'in the know.'"
>
> Wiseman, 342

Taking Notes on Internet Sources

Working from the computer screen or from a printout of it, you can take notes just as you would with print sources. You will need to decide whether to summarize, paraphrase, or quote directly the information you wish to borrow. Use the same 4- by 6-inch index card system that you use with print sources. The medium of the Internet, however, has an added advantage. An easy and accurate technique for capturing passages of text from the Internet is to copy the material into a separate computer file on your hard drive or floppy disk. You can use your mouse to highlight the portion of the text you want to save and then use the Copy and Paste features to add it to your file of research notes. You can also use the same commands to capture the bibliographic information you will need later.

INTEGRATING QUOTATIONS INTO YOUR TEXT

Whenever you want to use borrowed material, be it a summary, paraphrase, or a quotation, it's best to introduce the material with a *signal phrase* — a phrase that alerts the reader that borrowed information is to follow. A signal phrase usually consists of the author's name and a verb. Well-chosen signal phrases help you integrate quotations, paraphrases, and summaries into the flow of your paper. Besides, signal phrases let your reader know who is speaking and, in the case of summaries and paraphrases, exactly where your ideas end and someone else's begin. Never confuse your reader with a quotation that appears suddenly without introduction in your paper. Unannounced quotations leave your reader wondering how the quoted material relates to the point you are trying to make.

UNANNOUNCED QUOTATION

Despite the current focus on jazzy design and slick surfaces, "[computers'] guts have traditionally mattered quite a bit; the PC boom viewed from one angle was nothing but an endless series of announcements about bits and megahertz and RAM" (Walker, 146).

In the following revision, the writer has integrated the quotation into the text not only by means of a signal phrase, but in a number of other ways as well. By giving the name of the speaker and referring to his credentials the writer provides more context so that the reader can better understand how the writer meant for the quotation to fit into the discussion.

INTEGRATED QUOTATION

Although the current trend in electronics is jazzy design and slick surfaces, Rob Walker, *New York Times* marketing reporter, notes that "guts have traditionally mattered quite a bit; the PC boom viewed from one angle was nothing but an endless series of announcements about bits and megahertz and RAM" (146).

How well you integrate a quote, paraphrase, or summary into your paper depends partly on varying your signal phrases and, in particular, choosing a verb for the signal phrase that accurately conveys the tone and intent of the writer you are citing. If a writer is arguing, use the verb *argues* (or *asserts*, *claims*, or *contends*); if the writer is contesting a particular position or fact, use the verb *contests* (or *denies*, *disputes*, *refutes*, or *rejects*). In using verbs that are specific to the situation in your paper, you bring your readers into the intellectual debate as well as avoid the monotony of repeating such all-purpose verbs as *says* or *writes*.

You should always try to use a signal phrase that fits the situation in your essay. The following are just a few examples of how you can vary signal phrases to add interest to your paper.

Malcolm X confesses that . . .
As linguist Deborah Tannen has observed, . . .
According to blog creator Matt Haughey, . . .
Steven E. Ambrose, noted historian, emphasizes . . .
Judith Ortiz Cofer rejects the widely held belief that . . .
Iris Chang enriches our understanding of . . .

Here are other verbs that you might use when constructing signal phrases.

acknowledges	declares	points out
adds	endorses	reasons
admits	grants	reports
believes	implies	responds
compares	insists	suggests
confirms		

DOCUMENTING SOURCES

Whenever you summarize, paraphrase, or quote a person's thoughts and ideas, and when you use facts or statistics that are not commonly known or believed, you must properly acknowledge the source of your information. You must document the source of your information whenever you

- Quote a source word for word
- Refer to information and ideas from another source that you present in your own words as either a paraphrase or a summary
- Cite statistics, tables, charts, or graphs

You do not need to document

- Your own observations, experiences, and ideas
- Factual information available in a number of reference works (known as "common knowledge")
- Proverbs, sayings, and familiar quotations

A reference to the source of your borrowed information is called a *citation*. There are many systems for making citations, and your citations must consistently follow one of these systems. The documentation style recommended by the Modern Language Association (MLA) is commonly used in English and the humanities and is the style used for student papers throughout this book. Another common system is American Psychological Association (APA) style, which is used in the social sciences. In general, your instructor will tell you which system to use. For more information on documentation styles, consult the appropriate manual or handbook. For MLA style, consult the *MLA Handbook for Writers of Research Papers,* 6th ed. (New York: MLA, 2003).

There are two components of documentation in a research paper: the *in-text citation*, placed in the body of your paper, and the *list of works cited*, which provides complete publication data on your sources and is placed at the end of your paper.

In-Text Citations

Most in-text citations, also known as parenthetical citations, consist of only the author's last name and a page reference. Usually, the author's name is given in an introductory or signal phrase at the beginning of the borrowed material, and the page reference is given in parentheses at the end. If the author's name is not given at the beginning, it belongs in the parentheses along with the page reference. The parenthetical reference signals the end of the borrowed material and directs your readers to the list of works cited should they want to pursue a source. You should treat electronic sources as you would print sources; keep in mind that some electronic sources use paragraph numbers instead of page numbers.

Consider the following examples of in-text citations from a student paper that borrows information from essays in *Subjects/Strategies*.

IN-TEXT CITATIONS (MLA STYLE)

The draft is in the news again, but this time the argument has a new twist: whether <u>women</u>, along with men, should be

Citation with author's name in the signal phrase

called upon to serve their country during time of need. Columnist and cultural critic Anna Quindlen notes that "while women are represented today in virtually all fields, including the armed forces, only men are re- quired to register for the military draft that would be used in the event of a national-security crisis" (539). Although equal responsibilities for equal rights is a persuasive argument when it comes to the issue of women and the draft, many people believe that "no matter how much we

Citation with author's name in parentheses

modernists pretend otherwise, women are dif- ferent from men, and their roles are not in- terchangeable" (Chavez, 543).

LIST OF WORKS CITED (MLA STYLE)

Chavez, Linda. "Women in Combat Will Take a Toll on Our Culture." <u>Subjects/Strategies</u>. 10th ed. Eds. Paul Eschholz and Alfred Rosa. Boston: Bedford/St. Martin's, 2005. 542-44.

Quindlen, Anna. "Uncle Sam and Aunt Samantha." <u>Subjects/Strategies</u>. 10th ed. Eds. Paul Eschholz and Alfred Rosa. Boston: Bedford/St. Martin's, 2005. 538-40.

In the preceding example, page references are to the articles as they appear here in *Subjects/Strategies*. For articles and books located in the library, consult the following MLA guidelines for the list of works cited or the appropriate manual or handbook.

List of Works Cited

In this section, you will find general guidelines for creating a list of works cited, followed by sample entries designed to cover the citation situations you will encounter most often. Make sure that you follow the formats as they appear on the following pages.

General Guidelines

- Begin the list on a fresh page following the last page of text.
- Organize the list alphabetically by the author's last name. If the entry has no author name, alphabetize by the first major word of the title.

- Double-space the list.
- Begin each entry at the left margin. If the entry is longer than one line, indent the second and subsequent lines five spaces or one-half inch.
- Do not number the entries.

Books

BOOK BY ONE AUTHOR

List the author's last name first, followed by a comma and the author's first name. Underline the title, which goes next. Follow with the city of publication and a shortened version of the publisher's name — for example, *Houghton* for Houghton Mifflin, or *Cambridge UP* for Cambridge University Press. End with the year of publication.

Kitwana, Bakari. <u>Why White Kids Love Hip Hop</u>. New York: Basic, 2005.

BOOK BY TWO OR THREE AUTHORS

List the first author (following the order on the title page) in the same way as for a single-author book; list subsequent authors, first name first, in the order in which they appear on the title page.

Douglas, Susan, and Meredith Michaels. <u>The Mommy Myth: The Idealization of Motherhood and How It Has Undermined Women</u>. New York: Free, 2004.

BOOK BY FOUR OR MORE AUTHORS

List the first author in the same way as for a single-author book, followed by a comma and the abbreviation *et al.* ("and others").

Beardsley, John, et al. <u>Gee's Bend: The Women and Their Quilts</u>. Atlanta: Tinwood, 2002.

Or you may list the first author in the same way as for a single-author book, followed by a comma and then the names of all subsequent authors, first name first, in the order in which they appear on the title page. (Note, however, that if you choose this method your in-text citations must list each author's last name, matching the corresponding entry in your Works Cited page.)

Beardsley, John, William Arnett, Paul Arnett, Jane
     Livingston, and Alvia J. Wardlaw. <u>Gee's Bend: The</u>
     <u>Women and Their Quilts</u>. Atlanta: Tinwood, 2002.

TWO OR MORE SOURCES BY THE SAME AUTHOR

List two or more sources by the same author in alphabetical order by
title. List the first source by the author's name. After the first source,
in place of the author's name substitute three unspaced hyphens followed by a period.

Twitchell, James B. <u>Branded Nation: When Culture Goes</u>
     <u>Pop</u>. New York: Simon, 2004.
——. "The Branding of Higher Ed." <u>Forbes</u> 25 Nov. 2002: 50.
——. <u>Living It Up: America's Love Affair with Luxury</u>. New
     York: Columbia UP, 2002.

REVISED EDITION

Grout, Donald J., and Claude V. Palisca. <u>A History of</u>
     <u>Western Music</u>. 6th ed. New York: Norton, 2000.

EDITED BOOK

Du Bois, W. E. B. <u>The Education of Black People: Ten</u>
     <u>Critiques, 1906–1960</u>. Ed. Herbert Aptheker. New
     York: Monthly Review, 2003.

TRANSLATION

Tzu, Sun. <u>The Art of War</u>. Trans. Wu Sun Lin. San
     Francisco: Long River, 2003.

ANTHOLOGY

Eschholz, Paul, and Alfred Rosa, eds. <u>Subjects/Strategies</u>.
     10th ed. Boston: Bedford/St. Martin's, 2005.

SELECTION FROM AN ANTHOLOGY

Finch, Aisha K. "If Hip-Hop Ruled the World."
     <u>Subjects/Strategies</u>. 10th ed. Eds. Paul Eschholz and
     Alfred Rosa. Boston: Bedford/St. Martin's, 2005.
     508–12.

SECTION OR CHAPTER FROM A BOOK

Rufus, Anneli. "Bizarre as I Wanna Be." <u>Party of One: The</u>
     <u>Loner's Manifesto</u>. New York: Marlowe, 2003.

Periodicals

ARTICLE IN A JOURNAL WITH CONTINUOUS PAGINATION THROUGHOUT AN ANNUAL VOLUME

Some journals paginate issues continuously, by volume; that is, the page numbers in one issue pick up where the previous issue left off. For these journals, the year of publication, in parentheses, follows the volume number.

Lachman, Lilach. "Time, Space, and Illusion: Between
    Keats and Poussin." Comparative Literature 55
    (2002): 293-319.

ARTICLE IN A JOURNAL WITH SEPARATE PAGINATION IN EACH ISSUE

Some journals paginate by issue; each issue begins with page 1. For these journals, follow the volume number with a period and the issue number. Then give the year of publication in parentheses.

Hilmes, Michele. "Where Is PBS's Oprah?: Media Studies
    and the Fear of the Popular." Journal of
    Communication 54.1 (2004): 174-177.

ARTICLE IN A MONTHLY MAGAZINE

List author(s) the same way as for books. List the article's title in quotation marks, followed by the publication's title, which should be underlined. Abbreviate all months except May, June, and July. If an article in a magazine or newspaper is not printed on consecutive pages — for example, an article might begin on page 45, then skip to 48 — include only the first page, followed by a plus sign.

Kaiser, Charles. "Civil Marriage, Civil Rights." The
    Advocate Mar. 2004: 72.

ARTICLE IN A WEEKLY OR BIWEEKLY MAGAZINE

Bartlett, Donald L., and James B. Steele. "Why We Pay So
    Much for Drugs." Time 2 Feb. 2004: 45+.

ARTICLE IN A NEWSPAPER

If the newspaper lists an edition, add a comma after the date and specify the edition.

Wheeler, Ginger. "Weighing In on Chubby Kids: Smart
    Strategies to Curb Obesity." Chicago Tribune 9 Mar.
    2004, final ed.: C11+.

EDITORIAL (SIGNED/UNSIGNED)

Jackson, Derrick Z. "The Winner: Hypocrisy." Editorial.
Boston Globe 6 Feb. 2004, 3rd ed.: A19.
"Rescuing Education Reform." Editorial. New York Times 2
Mar. 2004, late ed.: A22.

LETTER TO THE EDITOR

Liu, Penny. Letter. New York Times 17 Jan. 2004, late
ed.: A14.

Internet Sources

Citations for Internet sources follow the same rules as citations for
print sources, but several additional pieces of information are required
to cite an Internet source: date of source's electronic publication (if
available), date you accessed the source, and the source's URL. Additionally, citations for different types of Internet sources require different types of information, so be sure to review the models that follow.
(Note: When writing a citation for an Internet source, MLA style requires that you break URLs only *after* a slash.)

ENTIRE WEB SITE (SCHOLARLY PROJECT, INFORMATION
DATABASE, OR PROFESSIONAL WEB SITE)

List the site's title first, underlined, followed by the editor, compiler,
or person responsible for maintaining or updating the site. Next include the date of the site's last update, if known; the name of the
sponsoring organization, if known; the date of your access; and the
URL, in angle brackets.

BBC: Religion & Ethics. 2004. British Broadcasting Company.
29 June 2004 <http://www.bbc.co.uk/religion/ethics/
index.shtml>.
The Victorian Web. Ed. George P. Landow. 21 Dec. 2002.
Brown U. 10 Jan. 2005 <http://www.victorianweb.org>.

SHORT WORK FROM A WEB SITE

"Designer Babies." BBC: Religion & Ethics. 2004. British
Broadcasting Company. 29 June 2004 <http://
www.bbc.co.uk/religion/ethics/issues/designer_babies/
index.shtml>.
Wojtczak, Helena. "The Women's Social & Political Union."
The Victorian Web. Ed. George P. Landow. 21 Dec.
2002. Brown U. 10 Jan. 2005 <http://
www.victorianweb.org/gender/wojtczak/wspu.html>.

PERSONAL HOME PAGE

Walker, Rob. Home page. 14 Mar. 2004. 18 Mar. 2004
    <http://robwalker.net>.

ONLINE BOOK

Whitman, Walt. <u>Leaves of Grass</u>. 1900. <u>Bartleby.com: Great
    Books Online</u>. Ed. Steven van Leeuwen. 2004. 6 Mar.
    2004 <http://www.bartleby.com/142>.

SECTION OR CHAPTER FROM AN ONLINE BOOK

Whitman, Walt. "Crossing Brooklyn Ferry." <u>Leaves of
    Grass</u>. 1900. <u>Bartleby.com: Great Books Online</u>. Ed.
    Steven van Leeuwen. 2005. 6 Feb. 2005
    <http://www.bartleby.com/142/86.html>.

ARTICLE IN AN ONLINE SCHOLARLY JOURNAL

Drury, Nevill. "How Can I Teach Peace When the Book Only
    Covers War?" <u>The Online Journal of Peace and
    Conflict Resolution</u> 5.1 (2003). 18 Mar. 2005
    <http://www.trinstitute.org/ojpcr/5_1finley.htm>.

ARTICLE IN AN ONLINE MAGAZINE

Dicarlo, Lisa. "Six Degrees of Tiger Woods." <u>Forbes</u> Mar.
    2004. 19 Apr. 2005 <http://forbes.com/business/
    2004/03/18/x_ld_0318nike.html>.

ARTICLE IN AN ONLINE NEWSPAPER

Bhatt, Sanjay. "Got Game? Foundation Promotes Chess as
    Classroom Learning Tool." <u>Seattle Times Online</u> 15 Mar.
    2004. 18 Apr. 2004 <http://seattletimes.nwsource.com/
    html/education/2001879251_chess15m.html>.

ARTICLE IN AN ONLINE REFERENCE WORK

"Chili Pepper." <u>Encyclopedia Britannica</u>. 2004.
    Encyclopedia Britannica Premium Service. 11 Dec. 2004
    <http://www.britannica.com/eb/article?eu=24458>.

ARTICLE FROM A LIBRARY SUBSCRIPTION SERVICE

Follow the guidelines for citing an article from a print periodical. Complete the citation by providing the name of the database, underlined, if known; the name of the subscription service; the name of the library, with city and state abbreviation; date of your access; and main search page URL, in angle brackets.

Strimel, Courtney B. "The Politics of Terror: Rereading
    <u>Harry Potter</u>." <u>Children's Literature in Education</u>
    Mar. 2004: 35-53. <u>Academic Search Premier</u>. EBSCO.
    Skidmore College Lib., Saratoga Springs, NY. 22 Feb.
    2005 <http://www.epnet.com>.

E-MAIL
Johnson, Gregory S. "Re: Headings and Subheadings."
    E-mail to Paul A. Eschholz. 12 Jan. 2005.

ONLINE POSTING
Cook, Hardy M. "Falstaff and Other 'Heavy' Costumes."
    Online posting. 17 Mar. 2004. Shaksper: The Global
    Electronic Shakespeare Conf. 1 Apr. 2005
    <http://www.shaksper.net/archives/2004/0700.html>.

Other Nonprint Sources

TELEVISION OR RADIO PROGRAM
"The New Americans." <u>Independent Lens</u>. Narr. Don Cheadle.
    Writ. Gita Saedi, Gordon Quinn, and Steve James.
    PBS. KLRN, San Antonio. 31 Mar. 2004.

FILM OR VIDEO RECORDING
<u>Schindler's List</u>. Dir. Steven Spielberg. Perf. Liam
    Neeson, Ralph Fiennes, and Ben Kingsley. 1993. DVD.
    Universal, 2004.

PERSONAL INTERVIEW
Kozalek, Mark. Personal interview. 22 Jan. 2005.

LECTURE
England, Paula. "Gender and Inequality: Trends and
    Causes." President's Distinguished Lecture Series.
    U. of Vermont. Memorial Lounge, Burlington.
    22 Mar. 2004.

A NOTE ON PLAGIARISM

The importance of honesty and accuracy in doing library research can't be stressed enough. Any material borrowed word for word must be placed within quotation marks and be properly cited; any idea, explanation, or argument you have paraphrased or summarized must be documented, and it must be clear where the paraphrased material begins and ends. In short, to use someone else's ideas, whether in their original form or in an altered form, without proper acknowledgment is to be guilty of plagiarism. And plagiarism is plagiarism even if it is accidental. A little attention and effort at the note-taking stage can go a long way toward eliminating the possibility of inadvertent plagiarism. Check all direct quotations against the wording of the original, and double-check your paraphrases to be sure that you have not used the writer's wording or sentence structure. It is easy to forget to put quotation marks around material taken verbatim or to use the same sentence structure and most of the same words — substituting a synonym here and there — and record it as a paraphrase. In working closely with the ideas and words of others, intellectual honesty demands that we distinguish between what we borrow — and therefore acknowledge in a citation — and what is our own.

While writing your paper, be careful whenever you incorporate one of your notes into your paper: Make sure that you put quotation marks around material taken verbatim, and double-check your text against your note card — or, better yet, against the original if you have it on hand — to make sure that your quotation is accurate. When paraphrasing or summarizing, make sure you haven't inadvertently borrowed key words or sentence structures from the original.

To learn more about how you can avoid plagiarism, go to the "Tutorial on Avoiding Plagiarism" at <bedfordstmartins.com/plagiarismtutorial>. There you will find information on the consequences of plagiarism, tutorials explaining what sources to acknowledge, how to keep good notes, how to organize your research, and how to appropriately integrate sources. Exercises are included throughout the tutorial to help you practice skills like integrating sources and recognizing acceptable paraphrases and summaries.

Using Quotation Marks for Language Borrowed Directly

Whenever you use another person's exact words or sentences, you must enclose the borrowed language in quotation marks. Without quotation marks you give your reader the impression that the wording is your own. Even if you cite the source, you are guilty of plagiarism if you fail to use quotation marks. The following example demonstrates both plagiarism and a correct citation for a direct quotation.

ORIGINAL SOURCE

Some Chinese-Americans found profit in perpetuating these stereotypes. Up through the 1930's, white and Chinese tour guides alike invented stories about a mysterious, labyrinthine world under Chinatown streets, filled with narcotics and brothels.

— Iris Chang
"Fear of SARS, Fear of Strangers," page 64

PLAGIARISM

Some Chinese-Americans found profit in perpetuating these stereotypes. Up through the 1930's, according to Iris Chang, white and Chinese tour guides alike invented stories about a mysterious, labyrinthine world under Chinatown streets, filled with narcotics and brothels (65–66).

CORRECT CITATION OF BORROWED WORDS IN
QUOTATION MARKS

According to Iris Chang, "some Chinese-Americans found profit in perpetuating these stereotypes. Up through the 1930's, white and Chinese tour guides alike invented stories about a mysterious, labyrinthine world under Chinatown streets, filled with narcotics and brothels" (65–66).

Using Your Own Words and Word Order
When Summarizing and Paraphrasing

When summarizing or paraphrasing a source you need to use your own language. Pay particular attention to word choice and word order, especially if you are paraphrasing. Remember, it is not enough simply to use a synonym here or there and think you have paraphrased the source; you *must* restate the idea from the original in your own words, using your own style and sentence structure. In the following example, notice how plagiarism can occur when care is not taken in the wording or sentence structure of a paraphrase. Notice that in the acceptable paraphrase, the student writer uses her own language and sentence structure.

ORIGINAL SOURCE

Capitalism doesn't want to pay people enough money — not because it can't, but because it wants them to borrow. That way, it can plan the future for both cash and credit, and layer the repayment of debt into our life calendars as an incentive to work. Therefore, it wants to teach people to become indebted, preferably as early as possible.

— ANDREW BLAKE
"Harry Potter and the New Consumer," page 613

UNACCEPTABLY CLOSE WORDING

According to Blake, capitalism doesn't pay us enough so that we will have to borrow more and more and, in turn, work more and more in order to repay all the debt. Capitalism, therefore, wants people to become indebted as early as possible (613).

UNACCEPTABLY CLOSE SENTENCE STRUCTURE

Blake believes that capitalism doesn't pay people enough — because it wants them to borrow. That way it can plan the future for both cash and credit, and make debt repayment a reason to continue working. Subsequently, capitalism needs people to become indebted, as soon as possible (613).

ACCEPTABLE PARAPHRASE

According to Blake, the capitalist system relies on debt. This is supported by a cycle of low wages for workers, which leads workers to borrow money and use credit to make up the difference in their income, which then leads workers to keep working so that they can pay off the debt they have accumulated (613).

▶ *Preventing Plagiarism*

Questions to Ask about Direct Quotations

- Do quotation marks clearly indicate the language that I borrowed verbatim?
- Is the language of the quotation accurate, with no missing or misquoted words or phrases?
- Do brackets or ellipsis marks clearly indicate any changes or omissions I have introduced?
- Does a signal phrase naming the author introduce each quotation? Does the verb in the signal phrase help establish a context for each quotation?
- Does a parenthetical page citation follow each quotation?

(*continued on next page*)

(continued from previous page)

Questions to Ask about Summaries and Paraphrases

- Is each summary and paraphrase written in my own words and style?
- Does each summary and paraphrase accurately represent the opinion, position, or reasoning of the original writer?
- Does each summary and paraphrase start with a signal phrase so that readers know where my borrowed material begins?
- Does each summary and paraphrase conclude with a parenthetical page citation?

Questions to Ask about Facts and Statistics

- Do I use a signal phrase or some other marker to introduce each fact or statistic that is not common knowledge so that readers know where the borrowed material begins?
- Is each fact or statistic that is not common knowledge clearly documented with a parenthetical page citation?

Finally, as you proofread your final draft, check all your citations one last time. If at any time while you are taking notes or writing your paper you have a question about plagiarism, consult your instructor for clarification and guidance before proceeding.

A DOCUMENTED STUDENT ESSAY

Krista Gonnerman's essay grew out of reading *Subjects/Strategies*. Her assignment was to write a documented essay on a current topic of debate. She knew from experience that to write a good essay, she would have to choose a topic she cared about. She also knew that she should allow herself time to gather her ideas and to focus her topic. After reading several selections in the Argument and Cause and Effect Analysis chapters and closely observing the trends of television advertising, Gonnerman found her topic. She started to see this paper as an opportunity to become more informed, to articulate her position, and to explore her observations.

Gonnerman began by brainstorming about her topic. She listed all the ideas, facts, questions, arguments, refutations, and causes and effects that came to mind as she thought about prescription drug advertisements. She then went to the library to find additional information and located several sources. Once confident that she had enough information, she made a rough outline of an organizational pattern. Keeping this pattern in mind, Gonnerman wrote a first draft. Later she went back and examined it carefully, assessing how it could be improved.

Gonnerman was writing this essay in the second half of the semester, after she had read a number of essays and had learned the importance of good paragraphing, unity, and sound organization. In revising her first draft, Gonnerman found where phrases and even whole sentences could be added to clarify her meaning. She moved some sentences, added transitions, and rewrote her concluding paragraphs to make them more forceful and persuasive. As you read Gonnerman's final draft, notice how she develops each of her paragraphs, how she uses specific information and examples to support her thesis, and how she uses the MLA in-text citation system to acknowledge her sources. Finally, notice how Gonnerman uses her opening paragraph to establish a context for her essay and how she uses her concluding paragraph to bring her essay back full circle.

Pharmaceutical Advertising

Krista Gonnerman

Turn on the television, wait for the commercial   1
breaks, and you are guaranteed to see them: direct-to-
consumer (DTC) pharmaceutical advertisements. In fact,
"Americans now see an average of nine prescription ads
per day on televison" (McLean). Allegra, an allergy medication; Celebrex, a medication for arthritis pain; Clar-
inex, another allergy medication; Detral, a pill to help
control overactive bladder; Lamisil, a drug to combat
toenail fungus; Lipitor, a medication used to lower cholesterol; Nexium, an acid reflux medication; Procrit, a
medication meant to increase red blood cell production;
Viagra, a medication for impotence; Vioxx, an anti-
inflammatory medication; Zoloft, an antidepressant — the
list of drugs currently promoted on television seems
endless and overwhelming. Flashy, celebrity endorsed,
emotionally appealing, with snappy tag lines and occasionally catchy tunes, these thirty-second sound bites
typically show healthy people enjoying life. According to
one source, the pharmaceutical industry "has tripled
drug advertising since 1996 to nearly $2.5 billion a
year. . . . Of the print and broadcast ads, 60% were for

just 20 medications" ("NJBIZ"). Industry spending is "up
28% from 1999 and 40 times the $55 million spent on mass
media ads in 1991" (McLean); in 1998 alone, the drug companies spent more than $500 million solely on television
advertising (West).

   The most significant and largely encompassing cause   2
behind this veritable explosion of pharmaceutical advertisements on television occurred in 1997 when the Federal
Drug Administration (FDA) relaxed the regulations oversee-
ing pharmaceutical advertising on television. Prior to
1997, the FDA regulations addressing prescription drug
advertisements were so strict that few manufacturers
bothered to promote their drugs in the media. Those drug
manufacturers who sought to advertise on television were
restricted to broadcasting "a drug's name without stating
its purpose. Or stating a drug's purpose without saying
its name. Or stating a drugs [sic] name and medical purpose only if the patient insert was scrolled on the
screen" (West). But in 1996 the pharmaceutical industry
filed a freedom of speech challenge and won, and in
August 1997 the FDA's Division of Drug Marketing and Communications issued the revised regulations that are still
in effect today. Currently, "drug companies can now tell
viewers . . . what their drug is used for without reciting or scrolling the entire Patient Insert; a major
statement of serious side effects and a phone number or
other route of obtaining the rest of the information" is
now all that is required of the commercial (West). No
longer hampered by restrictions, the pharmaceutical industry began in 1997 and has continued to focus its advertising budget on television: "The National Institute
for Health Care Management in Washington reports that
$1.8 billion was spent on d-t-c pharmaceutical advertis-
ing last year [1999], with $1.1 billion on TV"
(Liebeskind).

   A second, but debatable, cause may originate in pa-   3
tients becoming more proactive in their own healthcare.
Both Carol Lewis, writing in FDA Consumer, and Dr. Sidney
Wolfe, writing in the New England Journal of Medicine,
note that beginning in the mid-1980s there was an increase in the number of individuals (1) seeking more

medical information than they were being given by their
doctors and (2) making medical decisions affecting their
own healthcare. Lewis and Wolfe suggest that based on the
pharmaceutical industry's awareness of this groundswell,
the industry may have begun producing ads aimed at such
consumers. Yet beyond this anecdotal, undocumented evidence by Lewis and Wolfe, there is little to support the
suggestion that greater patient involvement led to the
dramatic increase in pharmaceutical advertisements on
television.

Other causes for the proliferation of pharmaceutical   4
advertisements have been suggested, but these ideas lack
merit. For example, it has been suggested that since many
individuals do not want to make the necessary lifestyle
changes, such as exercising and eating healthier, changes
that would result in true health benefits, the pharmaceutical industry began running commercials, in part, to encourage individuals to seek out their doctors as a first
step toward a healthier life. But the pharmaceutical industry is a for-profit industry, and its DTC commercials
look to market products for the primary purpose of enhancing pharmaceutical companies' bottom lines, not to
encourage consumers to embrace healthier lifestyles that
will lead to their — potentially — not needing medications.

In a similar vein, "The Coalition for Healthcare   5
Communication, a group of advertising agencies and medical publications dependent on drug advertising, said
that an analysis of leading published consumer surveys
provides strong evidence that [DTC] advertising of
prescription drugs is a valued source of health care
information" ("Drug Industry"). In other words, the pharmaceutical industry began running the ads as a way of
providing information-hungry patients with reliable
knowledge. But as Maryann Napoli sarcastically notes,
"Anyone trying to sell you something isn't going to give
you the most balanced picture of the product's effectiveness and risks." Or as Dr. Wolfe writes, "The education
of patients . . . is too important to be left to the
pharmaceutical industry, with its pseudo educational campaigns designed, first and foremost, to promote drugs."

The 1997 FDA regulatory revisions on media adver-   6
tisements provided the pharmaceutical industry the opportunity to inundate television with its products. But as
consumers we should not blindly accept what we see in the
industry's thirty-second sound bites. While we can use
the information conveyed in the commercials to help us
make more informed decisions about our own healthcare or
use the information in consultation with our physicians,
we must never forget that the commercials are meant to
sell products, and if those products improve our health,
it is merely a consequence of the industry's primary
intention.

Works Cited

"Drug Industry Study Finds Direct-to-Consumer Ads Help
    Customers." Health Care Strategic Management July
    2001: 10.

Liebeskind, Ken. "Targeted Ads for New Drugs a Shot in
    the Arm." Editor & Publisher Nov. 2000: 33.

Lewis, Carol. "The Impact of Direct-to-Consumer
    Advertising." FDA Consumer Mar/Apr. 2003: 9.
    Master FILE Premier. EBSCO. Rose-Hulman Inst. of
    Tech. Lib., Terre Haute, IN. 20 May 2003
    <http://epnet.com>.

McLean, Candis. "The Real Drug Pushers."
    Report/Newsmagazine 19 Mar. 2001: 38-42. MasterFILE
    Premier. EBSCO. Rose-Hulman Inst. of Tech. Lib.,
    Terre Haute, IN. 20 May 2003 <http://epnet.com>.

Napoli, Maryann. "Those Omnipresent Prescription Drug Ads:
    What to Look Out For." Healthfacts June 2001: 3.

"NJBIZ." Business News New Jersey 25 Feb. 2002: 3-5.
    MasterFILE Premier. EBSCO. Rose-Hulman Inst. of
    Tech. Lib., Terre Haute, IN. 20 May 2003
    <http://epnet.com>.

West, Diane. "DTC Ponders the Twilight Zone of TV
    Advertising." Pharmaceutical Executive May 1999:
    A4-A8. MasterFILE Premier. EBSCO. Rose-Hulman Inst.
    of Tech. Lib., Terre Haute, IN. 20 May 2003
    <http://epnet.com>.

Wolfe, Sidney M. "Direct-to-Consumer Advertising —
     Education or Emotion Promotion?" <u>New England Journal
     of Medicine</u> 346.7 (2002): 524-26. <u>MasterFILE
     Premier.</u> EBSCO. Rose-Hulman Inst. of Tech. Lib.,
     Terre Haute, IN. 20 May 2003 <http://epnet.com>.

Glossary of Rhetorical Terms

Abstract   See *Concrete/Abstract.*

Allusion   An allusion is a passing reference to a familiar person, place, or thing drawn from history, the Bible, mythology, or literature. An allusion is an economical way for a writer to capture the essence of an idea, atmosphere, emotion, or historical era, as in "The scandal was his Watergate," or "He saw himself as a modern Job," or "Everyone there held those truths to be self-evident." An allusion should be familiar to the reader; if it is not, it will add nothing to the meaning.

Analogy   Analogy is a special form of comparison in which the writer explains something unfamiliar by comparing it to something familiar: "A transmission line is simply a pipeline for electricity. In the case of a water pipeline, more water will flow through the pipe as water pressure increases. The same is true of a transmission line for electricity." See also the discussion of analogy on pages 274–75.

Analytical Reading   Reading analytically means reading actively, paying close attention to both the content and the structure of the text. Analytical reading often involves answering several basic questions about the piece of writing under consideration:

1. What does the author want to say? What is his or her main point?

2. Why does the author want to say it? What is his or her purpose?

3. What strategy or strategies does the author use?

4. Why and how does the author's writing strategy suit both the subject and the purpose?

5. What is special about the way the author uses the strategy?

6. How effective is the essay? Why?

For a detailed example of analytical reading, see pages 8–13 in Chapter 1.

Appropriateness   See *Diction.*

Argument   Argument is one of the four basic types of prose. (Narration, description, and exposition are the other three.) To argue is to attempt to convince the reader to agree with a point of view, to make a given decision, or to pursue a particular course of action. Logical argument is based on reasonable explanations and appeals to the reader's intelligence. See Chapter 11 for further discussion of argumentation. See also *Logical Fallacies; Persuasion.*

Assertion   The thesis or proposition that a writer puts forward in an argument.

Assumption   A belief or principle, stated or implied, that is taken for granted.

Attitude   A writer's attitude reflects his or her opinion of a subject. For example, a writer can think very positively or very negatively about a subject. In most cases, the writer's attitude falls somewhere between these two extremes. See also *Tone.*

Audience   An audience is the intended readership for a piece of writing. For example, the readers of a national weekly newsmagazine come from all walks of life and have diverse opinions, attitudes, and educational experiences. In contrast, the readership for an organic chemistry journal is made up of people whose interests and educational backgrounds are quite similar. The essays in this book are intended for general readers — intelligent people who may lack specific information about the subject being discussed.

Beginnings/Endings   A *beginning* is the sentence, group of sentences, or section that introduces an essay. Good beginnings usually identify the thesis or controlling idea, attempt to interest the reader, and establish a tone. Some effective ways in which writers begin essays include (1) telling an anecdote that illustrates the thesis, (2) providing a controversial statement or opinion that engages the reader's interest, (3) presenting startling statistics or facts, (4) defining a term that is central to the discussion that follows, (5) asking thought-provoking questions, (6) providing a quotation that illustrates the thesis, (7) referring to a current event that helps establish the thesis, or (8) showing the significance of the subject or stressing its importance to the reader.

An *ending* is the sentence or group of sentences that brings an essay to closure. Good endings are purposeful and well planned. Endings satisfy readers when they are the natural outgrowths of the essays themselves and convey a sense of finality or completion. Good essays do not simply stop; they conclude.

Cause and Effect Analysis   Cause and effect analysis is one of the types of exposition. (Process analysis, definition, division and classification, exemplification, and comparison and contrast are the others.) Cause and effect analysis answers the question *why?* It explains the reasons for an occurrence or the consequences of an action. See Chapter 10 for a detailed discussion of cause and effect analysis. See also *Exposition.*

Claim   The thesis or proposition put forth in an argument.

Classification   Classification, along with division, is one of the types of exposition. (Process analysis, definition, comparison and contrast, exemplification, and cause and effect analysis are the others.) When classifying, the writer arranges and sorts people, places, or things into categories according to their differing characteristics, thus making them more manageable for the writer and more understandable for the reader. See Chapter 8 for a detailed discussion of classification. See also *Division; Exposition.*

Cliché   A cliché is an expression that has become ineffective through overuse. Expressions such as *quick as a flash, dry as dust, jump* for *joy,* and *slow as molasses* are all clichés. Good writers normally avoid such trite expressions and seek instead to express themselves in fresh and forceful language.

Coherence   Coherence is a quality of good writing that results when all sentences, paragraphs, and longer divisions of an essay are naturally connected. Coherent writing is achieved through (1) a logical sequence of ideas (arranged in chronological order, spatial order, order of importance, or some other appropriate order), (2) the thoughtful repetition of key words and ideas, (3) a pace suitable for your topic and reader, and (4) the use of transitional words and expressions. Coherence should not be confused with unity. (See *Unity.*) See also *Transitions.*

Colloquial Expressions   A colloquial expression is characteristic of or appropriate to spoken language or to writing that seeks its effect. Colloquial expressions are informal, as *chem, gym, come up with, be at loose ends, won't,* and *photo* illustrate. Thus, colloquial expressions are acceptable in formal writing only if they are used purposefully.

Comparison and Contrast   Comparison and contrast is one of the types of exposition. (Process analysis, definition, division and classification, exemplification, and cause and effect analysis are the others.) In comparison and contrast, the writer points out the similarities and differences between two or more subjects in the same class or category. The function of any comparison and contrast is to clarify — to reach some conclusion about the items being compared and contrasted. See Chapter 7 for a detailed discussion of comparison and contrast. See also *Exposition.*

Conclusions   See *Beginnings/Endings.*

Concrete/Abstract   A *concrete* word names a specific object, person, place, or action that can be directly perceived by the senses: *car, bread, building, book, Abraham Lincoln, Chicago,* or *hiking.* An *abstract word,* in contrast, refers to general qualities, conditions, ideas, actions, or relationships that cannot be directly perceived by the senses: *bravery, dedication, excellence, anxiety, stress, thinking,* or *hatred.*

Although writers must use both concrete and abstract language, good writers avoid using too many abstract words. Instead, they rely on concrete words to define and illustrate abstractions. Because concrete words affect the senses, they are easily comprehended by the reader.

Connotation/Denotation   Both connotation and denotation refer to the meanings of words. *Denotation* is the dictionary meaning of a word, the literal meaning. *Connotation,* on the other hand, is the implied or suggested meaning of a word. For example, the denotation of *lamb* is "a young sheep." The connotations of lamb are numerous: *gentle, docile, weak, peaceful, blessed, sacrificial, blood, spring, frisky, pure, innocent* and so on. Good writers are sensitive to both the denotations and the connotations of words, and they use these meanings to their advantage in their writing. See also *Slanting.*

Controlling Idea   See *Thesis.*

Deduction   Deduction is the process of reasoning from a stated premise to a necessary conclusion. This form of reasoning moves from the general to the specific. See Chapter 11 for a discussion of deductive reasoning and its relation to argumentative writing. See also *Induction; Syllogism.*

Definition   Definition is one of the types of exposition. (Process analysis, division and classification, comparison and contrast, exemplification, and cause and effect analysis are the others.) Definition is a statement of the meaning of a word. A definition may be either brief or extended, part of an essay or an entire essay itself. See Chapter 9 for a detailed discussion of definition. See also *Exposition.*

Denotation   See *Connotation/Denotation.*

Description   Description is one of the four basic types of prose. (Narration, exposition, and argument are the other three.) Description tells how a person, place, or thing is perceived by the five senses. Objective description reports these sensory qualities factually, whereas subjective description gives the writer's interpretation of them. See Chapter 4 for a detailed discussion of description.

Dialogue   Dialogue is conversation that is recorded in a piece of writing. Through dialogue writers reveal important aspects of characters' personalities as well as events in the narrative.

Diction   Diction refers to a writer's choice and use of words. Good diction is precise and appropriate — the words mean exactly what the writer intends, and the words are well suited to the writer's subject, intended audience, and purpose in writing. The word-conscious writer knows that there are differences among *aged, old,* and *elderly; blue, navy,* and *azure;* and *disturbed, angry,* and *irritated.* Furthermore, this writer knows in which situation to use each word. See also *Connotation/Denotation.*

Division Like comparison and contrast, division and classification are separate yet closely related mental operations. Division involves breaking down a single large unit into smaller subunits or breaking down a large group of items into discrete categories. For example, the student body at your college or university can be divided into categories according to different criteria (by class, by home state or country, by sex, and so on).

Dominant Impression A dominant impression is the single mood, atmosphere, or quality a writer emphasizes in a piece of descriptive writing. The dominant impression is created through the careful selection of details and is, of course, influenced by the writer's subject, audience, and purpose. See also the discussion on pages 113–14 in Chapter 4.

Draft A draft is a version of a piece of writing at a particular stage in the writing process. The first version produced is usually called the *rough draft* or *first draft* and is a writer's beginning attempt to give overall shape to his or her ideas. Subsequent versions are called *revised drafts.* The copy presented for publication is the *final draft.*

Editing During the editing stage of the writing process, the writer makes his or her prose conform to the conventions of the language. This includes making final improvements in sentence structure and diction, and proofreading for wordiness and errors in grammar, usage, spelling, and punctuation. After editing, the writer is ready to prepare a final copy.

Emphasis Emphasis is the placement of important ideas and words within sentences and longer units of writing so that they have the greatest impact. In general, the end has the most impact, and the beginning nearly as much; the middle has the least. See also *Organization.*

Endings See *Beginnings/Endings.*

Essay An essay is a relatively short piece of nonfiction in which the writer attempts to make one or more closely related points. A good essay is purposeful, informative, and well organized.

Ethos A type of argumentative proof having to do with the ethics of the arguer: honesty, trustworthiness, and even morals.

Evaluation An evaluation of a piece of writing is an assessment of its effectiveness or merit. In evaluating a piece of writing, you should ask the following questions: What is the writer's purpose? Is it a worthwhile purpose? Does the writer achieve the purpose? Is the writer's information sufficient and accurate? What are the strengths of the essay? What are its weaknesses? Depending on the type of writing and the purpose, more specific questions can also be asked. For example, with an argument you could ask: Does the writer follow the principles of logical thinking? Is the writer's evidence convincing?

Evidence Evidence is the data on which a judgment or argument is based or by which proof or probability is established. Evidence usually takes the form of statistics, facts, names, examples or illustrations, and opinions of authorities.

Examples Examples illustrate a larger idea or represent something of which they are a part. An example is a basic means of developing or clarifying an idea. Furthermore, examples enable writers to show and not simply tell readers what they mean. The terms *example* and *illustration* are sometimes used interchangeably. See also the discussion of exemplification on pages 45–47 in Chapter 3.

Exemplification Exemplification is a type of exposition. (Definition, division and classification, comparison and contrast, cause and effect analysis, and process analysis are the others.) With exemplification the writer uses examples — facts, opinions, samples, and anecdotes or stories — to support a generali and to make it more vivid, understandable, and persuasive. See Chapter 3 for tailed discussion of exemplification. See also *Examples*.

Exposition Exposition is one of the four basic types of prose. (Narration, de scription, and argument are the other three.) The purpose of exposition is to clarify, explain, and inform. The methods of exposition presented in this text are process analysis, definition, division and classification, comparison and contrast, exemplification, and cause and effect analysis. For a detailed discussion of each of these methods of exposition, see the appropriate chapter.

Fact A piece of information presented as having a verifiable certainty or reality.

Fallacy See *Logical Fallacies*.

Figures of Speech Figures of speech are brief, imaginative comparisons that highlight the similarities between things that are basically dissimilar. They make writing vivid and interesting and therefore more memorable. The most common figures of speech are these:

Simile — An implicit comparison introduced by *like* or *as*: "The fighter's hands were *like* stone."

Metaphor — An implied comparison that uses one thing as the equivalent of another: "All the world's a stage."

Personification — A special kind of simile or metaphor in which human traits are assigned to an inanimate object: "The engine coughed and then stopped."

Focus Focus is the limitation that a writer gives his or her subject. The writer's task is to select a manageable topic given the constraints of time, space, and purpose. For example, within the general subject of sports, a writer could focus on government support of amateur athletes or narrow the focus further to government support of Olympic athletes.

General See *Specific/General*.

Idiom An idiom is a word or phrase that is used habitually with a particular meaning in a language. The meaning of an idiom is not always readily apparent to nonnative speakers of that language. For example, *catch cold, hold a job, make up your mind,* and *give them a hand* are all idioms in English.

Illustration See *Examples*. Also see Chapter 3.

Induction Induction is the process of reasoning to a conclusion about all members of a class through an examination of only a few members of the class. This form of reasoning moves from the particular to the general. See Chapter 11 for a discussion of inductive reasoning and its relation to argumentative writing. Also see *Deduction*.

Introductions See *Beginnings/Endings*.

Irony Irony is the use of words to suggest something different from their literal meaning. For example, when Jonathan Swift proposes in "A Modest Proposal" that Ireland's problems could be solved if the people of Ireland fattened their babies and sold them to the English landlords for food, he meant that almost any other solution would be preferable. A writer can use irony to establish a special relationship with the reader and to add an extra dimension or twist to the meaning of a word or phrase.

Jargon See *Technical Language*.

Logical Fallacies A logical fallacy is an error in reasoning that renders an argument invalid. Some of the more common logical fallacies are these:

Oversimplification — The tendency to provide simple solutions to complex problems: "The reason we have inflation today is that OPEC has unreasonably raised the price of oil."

ollow") — An inference or conclusion that does not
premises or evidence: "It was the best movie I saw
't an Academy Award."

after this, therefore because of this") — Confusing
with causation. Because one event comes after an-
ot necessarily mean that the first event caused the sec-
caught a cold at the hockey game, but I certainly didn't
ent there."

question — Assuming in a premise that which needs to be proven: "If
American autoworkers built a better product, foreign auto sales would not be
so high."

False analogy — Making a misleading analogy between logically unconnected
ideas: "He was a brilliant basketball player; therefore, there's no question in
my mind that he will be a fine coach."

Either/or thinking — The tendency to see an issue as having only two sides: "Used
car salespeople are either honest or crooked."

See also Chapter 11.

Logical Reasoning See *Deduction; Induction.*

Logos A type of argumentative proof having to do with the logical qualities of an
argument: data, evidence, and factual information.

Metaphor See *Figures of Speech.*

Narration Narration is one of the four basic types of prose. (Description, exposition, and argument are the other three.) To narrate is to tell a story, to tell
what happened. Although narration is most often used in fiction, it is also important in nonfiction, either by itself or in conjunction with other types of
prose. See Chapter 5 for a detailed discussion of narration.

Objective/Subjective *Objective* writing is factual and impersonal, whereas
subjective writing, sometimes called *impressionistic* writing, relies heavily on personal interpretation. For a discussion of objective description and subjective description, see Chapter 4.

Opinion An opinion is a belief or conclusion not substantiated by positive
knowledge or proof. An opinion reveals personal feelings or attitudes or states a
position. Opinion should not be confused with argument.

Organization In writing, organization is the thoughtful arrangement and presentation of one's points or ideas. Narration is often organized chronologically.
Exposition may be organized from simplest to most complex or from most familiar to least familiar. Argument may be organized from least important to
most important. There is no single correct pattern of organization for a given
piece of writing, but good writers are careful to discover an order of presentation
suitable for their audience and their purpose.

Paradox A paradox is a seemingly contradictory statement that may nonetheless be true. For example, "We little know what we have until we lose it" is a
paradoxical statement.

Paragraph The paragraph, the single most important unit of thought in an
essay, is a series of closely related sentences. These sentences adequately develop
the central or controlling idea of the paragraph. This central or controlling idea,
usually stated in a topic sentence, is necessarily related to the purpose of the
whole composition. A well-written paragraph has several distinguishing characteristics: a clearly stated or implied topic sentence, adequate development,
unity, coherence, and an appropriate organizational strategy.

Parallelism Parallel structure is the repetition of word order or form either
within a single sentence or in several sentences that develop the same central

idea. As a rhetorical device, parallelism can aid coherence and add emphasis. Roosevelt's statement, "I see one third of a nation ill-housed, ill-clad, ill-nourished," illustrates effective parallelism.

Pathos A type of argumentative proof having to do with audience: emotional language, connotative diction, and appeals to certain values.

Personification See *Figures of Speech.*

Persuasion Persuasion, or persuasive argument, is an attempt to convince readers to agree with a point of view, to make a given decision, or to pursue a particular course of action. Persuasion appeals heavily to the emotions, whereas logical argument does not. For the distinction between logical argument and persuasive argument, see Chapter 11.

Point of View Point of view refers to the grammatical person of the speaker in an essay. For example, a first-person point of view uses the pronoun *I* and is commonly found in autobiography and the personal essay; a third-person point of view uses the pronouns *he, she,* or *it* and is commonly found in objective writing. See Chapter 5 for a discussion of point of view in narration.

Prewriting Prewriting encompasses all the activities that take place before a writer actually starts a rough draft. During the prewriting stage of the writing process, the writer selects a subject area, focuses on a particular topic, collects information and makes notes, brainstorms for ideas, discovers connections between pieces of information, determines a thesis and purpose, rehearses portions of the writing in his or her mind or on paper, and makes a scratch outline. For some suggestions about prewriting, see Chapter 2.

Process Analysis Process analysis is a type of exposition. (Definition, division and classification, comparison and contrast, and cause and effect analysis are the others.) Process analysis answers the question *how?* and explains how something works or gives step-by-step directions for doing something. See Chapter 6 for a detailed discussion of process analysis. See also *Exposition.*

Publication The publication stage of the writing process is when the writer shares his or her writing with the intended audience. Publication can take the form of a typed or an oral presentation, a photocopy, or a commercially printed rendition. What's important is that the writer's words are read in what amounts to their final form.

Purpose Purpose is what the writer wants to accomplish in a particular piece of writing. Purposeful writing seeks to *relate* (narration), to *describe* (description), to *explain* (process analysis, definition, division and classification, comparison and contrast, and cause and effect analysis), or to *convince* (argument).

Revision During the revision stage of the writing process, the writer determines what in the draft needs to be developed or clarified so that the essay says what the writer intends it to say. Often the writer needs to revise several times before the essay is "right." Comments from peer evaluators can be invaluable in helping writers determine what sorts of changes need to be made. Such changes can include adding material, deleting material, changing the order of presentation, and substituting new material for old.

Rhetorical Question A rhetorical question is a question that is asked but requires no answer from the reader. "When will nuclear proliferation end?" is such a question. Writers use rhetorical questions to introduce topics they plan to discuss or to emphasize important points.

Rough Draft See *Draft.*

Sequence Sequence refers to the order in which a writer presents information. Writers commonly select chronological order, spatial order, order of importance, or order of complexity to arrange their points. See also *Organization.*

Simile See *Figures of Speech.*

Slang Slang is the unconventional, very informal language of particular sub-groups of a culture. Slang, such as *bummed, coke, split, hurt, dis, blow off,* and *cool,* is acceptable in formal writing only if it is used purposefully.

Slanting The use of certain words or information that results in a biased view-point.

Specific/General *General words* name groups or classes of objects, qualities, or actions. *Specific words,* in contrast, name individual objects, qualities, or actions within a class or group. To some extent, the terms *general* and *specific* are rela-tive. For example, *dessert* is a class of things. *Pie,* however, is more specific than *dessert* but more general than *pecan pie* or *chocolate cream pie.*

Good writing judiciously balances the general with the specific. Writing with too many general words is likely to be dull and lifeless. General words do not create vivid responses in the reader's mind as concrete, specific words can. However, writing that relies exclusively on specific words may lack focus and direction — the control that more general statements provide.

Strategy A strategy is a means by which a writer achieves his or her purpose. Strategy includes the many rhetorical decisions that the writer makes about or-ganization, paragraph structure, syntax, and diction. In terms of the whole essay, strategy refers to the principal rhetorical mode that the writer uses. If, for exam-ple, a writer wishes to show how to make chocolate chip cookies, the most effec-tive strategy would be process analysis. If it is the writer's purpose to show why sales of American cars have declined in recent years, the most effective strategy would be cause and effect analysis.

Style Style is the individual manner in which a writer expresses ideas. Style is cre-ated by the author's particular selection of words, construction of sentences, and arrangement of ideas.

Subject The subject of an essay is its content, what the essay is about. Depend-ing on the author's purpose and the constraints of space, a subject may range from one that is broadly conceived to one that is narrowly defined.

Subjective See *Objective/Subjective.*

Supporting Evidence See *Evidence.*

Syllogism A syllogism is an argument that utilizes deductive reasoning and consists of a major premise, a minor premise, and a conclusion. For example:

All trees that lose leaves are deciduous. (*Major premise*)

Maple trees lose their leaves. (*Minor premise*)

Therefore, maple trees are deciduous. (*Conclusion*)

See also *Deduction.*

Symbol A symbol is a person, place, or thing that represents something beyond itself. For example, the eagle is a symbol of the United States, and the bear is a symbol of Russia.

Syntax Syntax refers to the way in which words are arranged to form phrases, clauses, and sentences as well as to the grammatical relationship among the words themselves.

Technical Language Technical language, or jargon, is the special vocabulary of a trade or profession. Writers who use technical language do so with an aware-ness of their audience. If the audience is a group of peers, technical language may be used freely. If the audience is a more general one, technical language should be used sparingly and carefully so as not to sacrifice clarity. See also *Diction.*

Thesis A thesis is a statement of the main idea of an essay. Also known as the *controlling idea,* a thesis may sometimes be implied rather than stated directly.

Title A title is a word or phrase set off at the beginning of an essay to identify the subject, to capture the main idea of the essay, or to attract the reader's attention.

A title may be explicit or suggestive. A subtitle, when used, extends or restricts the meaning of the main title.

Tone Tone is the manner in which a writer relates to an audience — the "tone of voice" used to address readers. Tone may be described as friendly, serious, distant, angry, cheerful, bitter, cynical, enthusiastic, morbid, resentful, warm, playful, and so forth. A particular tone results from a writer's diction, sentence structure, purpose, and attitude toward the subject. See also *Attitude.*

Topic Sentence The topic sentence states the central idea of a paragraph and thus limits and controls the subject of the paragraph. Although the topic sentence most often appears at the beginning of the paragraph, it may appear at any other point, particularly if the writer is trying to create a special effect. Also see *Paragraph.*

Transitions Transitions are words or phrases that link sentences, paragraphs, and larger units of a composition to achieve coherence. These devices include parallelism, pronoun references, conjunctions, and the repetition of key ideas, as well as the many conventional transitional expressions, such as *moreover, on the other hand, in addition, in contrast,* and *therefore.* Also see *Coherence.*

Unity Unity is achieved in an essay when all the words, sentences, and paragraphs contribute to its thesis. The elements of a unified essay do not distract the reader. Instead, they all harmoniously support a single idea or purpose.

Verb Verbs can be classified as either strong verbs (*scream, pierce, gush, ravage,* and *amble*) or weak verbs (*be, has, get,* and *do*). Writers prefer to use strong verbs to make their writing more specific, more descriptive, and more action filled.

Voice Verbs can be classified as being in either the active or the passive voice. In the active voice, the doer of the action is the grammatical subject. In the passive voice, the receiver of the action is the subject:

Active: Glenda questioned all of the children.

Passive: All of the children were questioned by Glenda.

Writing Process The writing process consists of five major stages: prewriting, writing drafts, revision, editing, and publication. The process is not inflexible, but there is no mistaking the fact that most writers follow some version of it most of the time. Although orderly in its basic components and sequence of activities, the writing process is nonetheless continuous, creative, and unique to each individual writer. See Chapter 2 for a detailed discussion of the writing process. See also *Draft; Editing; Prewriting; Publication; Revision.*

Submitting Essays for Publication Consideration

Please let us see the essays you'd like us to consider for publication that were written using *Subjects/Strategies*. Send them with this Essay Submission Form and the Agreement Form on the back to: Subjects/ Strategies — Student Essays, Bedford/St. Martin's, 33 Irving Place, 10th Floor, New York, NY 10003.

Essay Submission Form

Student's name _____

Instructor's name _____

School _____

Department _____

Address _____

_____

_____

Course name & number _____

Below, please indicate the chapter in *Subjects/Strategies* for which you would like us to consider this essay.

❐ Exemplification   ❐ Definition

❐ Description   ❐ Cause and Effect Analysis

❐ Narration   ❐ Argumentation

❐ Process Analysis   ❐ Combining Strategies

❐ Comparison and Contrast   ❐ Writing Documented Essays

❐ Division and Classification

Agreement Form

I hereby assign to Bedford/St. Martin's ("Bedford") all of my rights, title, and interest throughout the world, including without limitation, all copyrights, in and to my essay, _____ (tentative title), and any notes and drafts pertaining to it (the sample essay and such materials being referred to as the "Essay").

I understand that Bedford in its discretion has the right but not the obligation to publish the Essay in any form(s) or format(s) that it may desire; that Bedford may edit, revise, condense, or otherwise alter the Essay as it deems appropriate in order to prepare the same for publication; and that Bedford is under no obligation to publish the Essay. I understand that Bedford has the right, but not the obligation, to use and to authorize the use of my name as author of the Essay in connection with any work that contains the Essay (or a portion of it).

I represent that the Essay is wholly original and was completely written by me, that publication of it will not infringe upon the rights of any third party, and that I have not granted any rights in it to any third party.

In the event Bedford determines to include any part of the Essay in _Subjects/Strategies_, I will receive one free copy of that work on publication and an honorarium of $100.00.

This Agreement constitutes the entire agreement between us concerning its subject matter and shall inure to the benefit of the successors, assignees, and licensees of Bedford.

Student's signature: _____

Student's name: _____Date:___ /___/___

Be sure to provide us with **_time-stable information_** _below. Please type or print clearly._

Address(es): _____

_____

_____

Phone(s): _____

E-mail(s): _____

Acknowledgments

Edward Abbey. "Aravaipa Canyon." From *Down the River* by Edward Abbey. Copyright © 1982 by Edward Abbey. Used by permission of Dutton, a division of Penguin Group (USA) Inc.

Diane Ackerman. "When the Leaves Turn Color in the Fall." From *A Natural History of the Senses* by Diane Ackerman. Copyright © 1990 by Diane Ackerman. Used by permission of Random House, Inc.

Mortimer Adler. "How to Mark a Book." From the *Saturday Review of Literature*, July 6, 1940. Reprinted by permission.

AltaVista screen shots. © 2004 Overture Services, Inc. Reprinted by permission.

Julia Alvarez. "Snow." From *How The Garcia Girls Lost Their Accents*. Copyright © 1991 by Julia Alvarez. Published by Plume, an imprint of Dutton Signet, a division of Penguin USA and originally in hardcover by Algonquin Books of Chapel Hill. Reprinted by permission of Susan Bergholz Literary Services, New York. All rights reserved.

Stephen E. Ambrose. Excerpt from *Crazy Horse and Custer* by Stephen Ambrose. Copyright © 1975 Stephen Ambrose. Used by permission of Doubleday, a division of Random House, Inc.

Anne Applebaum. "When Women Go to War." © 2003. From the *Washington Post*. Reprinted by permission.

Isaac Asimov. "Those Crazy Ideas." Ralph M. Vicinanza. Published by permission of The Estate of Isaac Asimov. C/o Ralph M. Vicinanza, Ltd.

David P. Bardeen. "Not Close Enough for Comfort." From *The New York Times*. First published in *The New York Times*, February 29, 2004. Reprinted with permission from the author.

Joel Beck. "Rough Draft." From www.towneonline.com. January 24, 2003. Reprinted by permission of the author.

Andrew Blake. "Harry Potter and the New Consumer." From *The Irresistible Rise of Harry Potter.* Copyright © 2002 by Andrew Blake. Reprinted by permission of Verso Books.

Suzanne Britt. "Neat People vs. Sloppy People." Copyright © Suzanne Britt. Reprinted by permission.

Jane E. Brody. "Gene-Altered Food: A Case Against Panic." From *The New York Times*, 2000. Copyright © 2000 The New York Times Company. Reprinted with permission.

Christopher Callahan. "Anatomy of an Urban Legend." From *American Journalism Review*, November 2001. © 2001. Reprinted by permission of the author.

Carl M. Cannon. "The Real Computer Virus." From *American Journalism Review*, April 2001. Copyright © 2001 American Journalism Review. Reprinted with permission.

Iris Chang. "Fear of SARS, Fear of Strangers." From *The New York Times*, Op-ed page, May 21, 2003. Copyright © 2003 The New York Times. Reprinted by permission.

Linda Chavez. "Women in Combat Will Take Toll on Our Culture. © 2003 Creators Syndicate, Inc. Reprinted by permission.

Anton Chekhov. "A Nincompoop." From *Anton Chekhov: Selected Stories* by Anton Chekhov, translated by Ann Dunnigan. Copyright © 1960 by Ann Dunnigan. Used by permission of Dutton Signet, a division of Penguin Group (USA) Inc.

Sandra Cisneros. "House on Mango Street." From *The House on Mango Street.* Copyright © 1984 by Sandra Cisneros. Published by Vintage Books, a division of Random House, Inc., and in hardcover by Alfred A. Knopf in 1994. Reprinted by permission of Susan Bergholz Literary Services, New York. All rights reserved.

Judith Ortiz Cofer. "The Myth of the Latin Woman." From *The Latin Deli: Prose and Poetry* by Judith Ortiz Cofer. Copyright © 1993 by Judith Ortiz Cofer. Reprinted by permission of the University of Georgia Press.

Dalton Conley. "Tip Jars and the New Economy." From *Chronicle of Higher Education*, Vol. 49, Issue 17, January 3, 2003. Reprinted by permission of the author.

Annie Dillard. "Getting Caught." From *An American Childhood* by Annie Dillard. Copyright ©1987 by Annie Dillard. Reprinted by permission of HarperCollins Publishers, Inc.

Rita Dove. "Loose Ends." From *The Poet's World*, Library of Congress. © 1995 by Rita Dove. Reprinted by permission of the author.

David Ehrenfeld. "A Techno-Pox Upon the Land." From the October 1997 issue of *Harper's Magazine*. Copyright © 1997 by Harper's Magazine. Reprinted by special permission. All rights reserved.

Lars Eighner. "On Dumpster Diving" from *Travels with Lizbeth* by Lars Eighner. ©1993 by Lars Eighner. Reprinted by permission of St. Martin's Press, LLC.

Aisha K. Finch. "If Hip-Hop Ruled the World." Reprinted with permission.

Linda Flower. "Writing for an Audience." From *Problem Solving Strategies for Writing*. Copyright © 1993. Reprinted by permisson of Thomson Learning.

Thomas L. Friedman. "My Favorite Teacher." From *The New York Times*, January 9, 2001, Letters to the Editor. Reprinted by permission of the author.

Natalie Goldberg. "Be Specific" from *Writing Down the Bones: Freeing the Writer Within* by Natalie Goldberg. ©1986 by Natalie Goldberg. Reprinted by permission of Shambhala Publications, Inc., Boston www.shambhala.com.

Google screen shots. © 2003 Google. Reprinted by permission.

G. Anthony Gorry. "Steal This MP3 File: What is Theft?" From *Chronicle of Higher Education*, Vol. 49, Issue 37, May 23, 2003, p. B20. Copyright © 2003. Reprinted by permission of G. Anthony Gorry, Friedkin Professor of Management and Professor of Computer Science, Rice University.

Matt Haughey. "Building an Online Community: Just Add Water." © 2001 by Matt Haughey. Reprinted by permission of the author.

Shirley Jackson. "The Lottery." From *The Lottery and Other Stories* by Shirley Jackson. Copyright © 1948, 1949 by Shirley Jackson. Copyright © renewed 1976, 1977 by Laurence Hyman, Barry Hyman, Mrs. Sarah Webster and Mrs. Joanne Schnurer. Reprinted by permission of Farrar, Straus, & Giroux, LLC.

Jon Katz. "How Boys Become Men." Originally published in *Glamour*, January 1993. Copyright © 1993 by Jon Katz. Reprinted by permission of International Creative Management, Inc.

Martin Luther King, Jr. Excerpt from "The Ways of Meeting Oppression" in *Stride Toward Freedom*. Copyright © 1958 Martin Luther King Jr. Copyright renewed 1986 by Coretta Scott King. "I Have a Dream" speech delivered on the steps at the Lincoln Memorial, Washington, D.C., August 28, 1963. Copyright © 1963 Martin Luther King Jr. Copyright renewed 1991 by Coretta Scott King. Reprinted by arrangement with The Heirs to the Estate of Martin Luther King Jr., c/o Writers House as agent for the proprietor.

Anne Lamott. "Shitty First Drafts." From *Bird by Bird* by Anne Lamott. Copyright © 1994 by Anne Lamott. Used by permission of Pantheon Books, a division of Random House, Inc.

Richard Lederer. "The Case for Short Words." From *The Miracle of Language* by Richard Lederer. ©1991 by Richard Lederer. Reprinted with the permission of Atria Books, an imprint of Simon & Schuster Adult Publishing Group.

Audre Lorde. "The Transformation of Silence into Language and Action." From *Sister Outsider* by Audre Lorde. Copyright © 1984 by Audre Lorde. Reprinted by permission of The Crossing Press, a division of Ten Speed Press, Berkeley, CA 94707. www.tenspeed.com.

Nancy Mairs. "On Being a Cripple." From *Plaintext* by Nancy Mairs. Copyright ©1986 The Arizona Board of Regents. Reprinted by permission of University of Arizona Press.

Kennedy P. Maize. "The Great Kern County Mouse War." From *Audubon*, vol. 79, November 1977. Reprinted by permission.

Malcolm X. "Coming to an Awareness of Language." From *The Autobiography of Malcolm X* by Malcolm X and Alex Haley. Copyright © 1964 by Alex Haley and Malcolm X. Copyright © 1965 by Alex Haley and Betty Shabazz. Used by permission of Random House, Inc.

Steve Martin. "The Death of My Father." First appeared in *The New Yorker*, June 24, 2002. Copyright © 2002 by Steve Martin. Reprinted by permission of International Creative Management, Inc.

Cherokee Paul McDonald. "A View from the Bridge." From *Sun Sentinel, Sunshine* magazine, Ft. Lauderdale, Fl. Reprinted by permission of the author.

Del Miller. "Mac or PC: There Is Simply No Comparison!" Copyright © 2003 by Del Miller. Reprinted by permission of the author.

Donald M. Murray. "The Maker's Eye: Revising Your Own Manuscripts." Originally published in *The Writer*, October 1973. Reprinted by permission of the author.

Natural History Museum, Los Angeles County. Screen shot of wild cats! © Natural History Museum of Los Angeles County Foundation. Reprinted by permission.

George Orwell. "Shooting an Elephant." From *Shooting an Elephant and Other Essays* by George Orwell. Copyright © 1950 by Sonia Brownell Orwell and renewed 1978 by Sonia Pitt-Rivers. Reprinted by permission of Harcourt, Inc. Copyright © George Orwell 1936. Reproduced by permission of A.M. Heath & Co. Ltd. On behalf of Bill Hamilton as the Literary Executor of the Estate of the Late Sonia Brownell Orwell and Martin Seeker & Warburg Ltd.

Jo Goodwin Parker. "What Is Poverty?" From *America's Other Children: Public Schools Outside Suburbia* by George Henderson. University of Oklahoma Press. Reprinted by permission of the publisher.

Anna Quindlen. "Uncle Sam and Aunt Samantha." Published in *Newsweek*, November 2001. © 2001 by Anna Quindlen. Reprinted by permission of International Creative Management, Inc.

Robert Ramirez. "The Barrio." Reprinted by permission of the author.

Jonathan Rauch. "Will Frankenfood Save the Planet?" From *Atlantic Monthly*, October 2003. © 2003 by Jonathan Rauch. Reprinted by permission of the author.

Jack P. Rawlins. "Five Principles for Getting Good Ideas." From *The Writer's Way*, Second Edition. Copyright © 1992 by Houghton Mifflin Company. Used with permission.

Paul Roberts. "How to Say Nothing in 500 Words." From *Understanding English* by Paul Roberts. Copyright © 1958 by Paul Roberts. Copyright renewed. Reprinted by permission of Pearson Education, Inc.

Jim Scharplaz. "Weeding Out the Skilled Farmer." From *The Writers Circle* at The Land Institute, published online: www.landinstitute.org. Reprinted by permission of the author.

Deborah Tannen. "How to Give Orders Like a Man." From *You Just Don't Understand* by Deborah Tannen. Copyright ©1990 by Deborah Tannen. Reprinted with permission of HarperCollins Publishers, Inc.

Judith Viorst. "The Truth about Lying." Originally appeared in *Redbook*. Copyright © 1981 by Judith Viorst. Reprinted by permission of Lescher & Lescher, Ltd. All rights reserved.

Index

Abbey, Edward ("Aravaipa Canyon"), 107, 108, 116, 124–29
Abstract words, 397–98
Ackerman, Diane ("Why Leaves Turn Color in the Fall"), 256–61
Action-oriented argument, 485–86
Active voice, 599–600
in process analysis, 219–20
Adler, Mortimer ("How to Mark a Book"), 226–32
Affect/effect, 443
"Ain't I a Woman?" (Truth), 417–19
Alvarez, Julia ("Snow"), 531
Ambiguous pronoun reference, 224
Ambrose, Stephen E. ("Crazy Horse and Custer as Young Warriors"), 306–11
American Psychological Association (APA) style, 700

Analogy, 274–75
Analyzing, 8
"Anatomy of an Urban Legend" (Callahan), 248–55
Annotating the text, 5–6
Applebaum, Anne ("When Women Go to War"), 545–47
"Aravaipa Canyon" (Abbey), 107, 108, 116, 124–29
Argument (argumentation), 21–22, 483–585. *See also* Combination of strategies
action-oriented, 485–86
annotated student essay using, 491–97
definition of, 483–86
focused, 485
informational (exploratory), 485
logical, 484–85
persuasive, 484
questions for revising and editing, 506
quiet (subtle), 486

Argument *(continued)*
  readings
    "The Case for Short Words"
      (Lederer), 513–18
    "The Declaration of
      Independence" (Jefferson),
      519–24
    "Ex-POW Army Spc.
      Shoshana Johnson"
      [photograph] (Probst),
      537–38
    "Gene-Altered Foods: A Case
      Against Panic" (Brody),
      574–78
    "Genetically Modified Food"
      argument cluster, 556–83
    "If Hip-Hop Ruled the
      World" (Finch), 508–12
    "I Have a Dream" (King),
      525–30
    "Rap the Vote" [photograph]
      (Bailey), 507–8
    "Rough Draft" (Beck), 548–53
    "Snow" (Alvarez), 531–34
    "Spraying Potato Seedlings"
      [photograph] (Olson), 558
    "A Techno-Pox Upon the
      Land" (Ehrenfeld), 568–73
    "Uncle Sam and Aunt
      Samantha" (Quindlen),
      538–41
    "Weeding Out the Skilled
      Farmer" (Scharplaz),
      579–83
    "When Women Go to War"
      (Applebaum), 545–47
    "Will Frankenfood Save the
      Planet?" (Rauch), 559–67
    "Women in Combat"
      argument cluster, 535–36,
      553–55
    "Women in Combat Will
      Take a Toll on Our
      Culture" (Chavez), 542–44
  reasons for using, 486–91
  reconciliation, 486
  suggestions for writing,
    497–506, 584–85
    audience, 499
    conclusion, 501
    determining your thesis or
      proposition, 498–99
    faulty reasoning, avoiding,
      500–501
    organizational pattern, 499
    other rhetorical strategies,
      501–2
    refutations to your
      argument, considering,
      500
    supporting evidence, 499
As, parallel constructions in
  comparisons with, 286–87
Asimov, Isaac ("Those Crazy
  Ideas"), 80–91
Assignments, understanding,
  20–21
Audience
  for argumentation, 499
  for definition, 393
  for description, 113
  knowing your, 22
  for process analysis, 221–22

Bailey, Ed ("Rap the Vote"
  [photograph]), 507–8
Bardeen, David P. ("Not Close
  Enough for Comfort"),
  193–97
"Barrio, The" (Ramírez), 602–7
Beck, Joel ("Rough Draft"), 548–53
Begging the question, 501
Beginnings, 36
"Be Specific" (Goldberg), 59–62
Biographical note, 3
Blake, Andrew ("Harry Potter and
  the New Consumer"),
  609–21

Block comparison, 273, 274
Books, citations of, 702–3
Brainstorming, 24
Britt, Suzanne ("Neat People vs. Sloppy People"), 293–97
Brody, Jane E. ("Gene-Altered Foods: A Case Against Panic"), 574–78
"Building an Online Community: Just Add Water" (Haughey), 262–69

Callahan, Christopher ("Anatomy of an Urban Legend"), 248–55
Cannon, Carl M. ("The Real Computer Virus"), 463–71
"Case for Short Words, The" (Lederer), 513–18
Cause and effect analysis, 26, 426–82. *See also* Combination of strategies
annotated student essay using, 430–34
definition of, 426–27
questions for revising and editing, 440
readings
"The Great Kern County Mouse War" (Maize), 456–62
"How Boys Become Men" (Katz), 444–48
"The Lottery" (Jackson), 472–81
"The Real Computer Virus" (Cannon), 463–71
"Tip Jars and the New Economy" (Conley), 450–55
"Tipping Is Not a City in China" [photograph] (Gordon), 449–50
reasons for using, 427–30

suggestions for writing, 434–40, 482
avoiding oversimplification and errors of logic, 438–39
balanced tone, 439
determining your purpose, 437
establishing your focus, 436
other rhetorical strategies, 439–40
thesis statement, 437
Chang, Iris ("Fear of SARS, Fear of Strangers"), 64–69
Chavez, Linda ("Women in Combat Will Take a Toll on Our Culture"), 542–44
Chekhov, Anton ("A Nincompoop"), 420–23
"Chinese Commuter in Shanghai" [photograph] (Cortes IV), 63–64
Cisneros, Sandra ("The House on Mango Street"), 151–54
Citations, 700–702
Classification, 25–26. *See* Division and classification
Cofer, Judith Ortiz ("The Myth of the Latin Woman"), 365–71
Colon, to link closely related ideas, 503
Combination of strategies, 586–649
annotated student essay using, 589–96
definition of, 587
questions for revising and editing, 601
readings
"The Barrio" (Ramírez), 602–7
"Harry Potter and the New Consumer" (Blake), 609–21
"Harry Potter on Sale in Moscow" [photograph] (Ilnitsky), 608–9

Combination of strategies,
readings *(continued)*
"On Being a Cripple" (Mairs),
622–34
"On Dumpster Diving"
(Eighner), 644–48
"Shooting an Elephant"
(Orwell), 635–43
reasons for using, 587–88
suggestions for writing an essay
using, 596–601, 649
determining your purpose,
597
dominant developmental
strategy, 597–99
thesis statement, 597
"Coming to an Awareness of
Language" (Malcolm X),
174–78
Comma splices, 171
Comparison and contrast, 26,
272–320. *See also*
Combination of strategies
analogy as a special form of,
274–75
annotated student essay using,
277–81
definition of, 272–73
questions for revising and
editing, 287
readings
"Crazy Horse and Custer as
Young Warriors"
(Ambrose), 306–11
"Mac or PC: There Is Simply
No Comparison!" (Miller),
299–305
"Macs and PCs Have Never
Been So Compatible"
[photograph] (Microsoft),
298–99
"Neat People vs. Sloppy
People" (Britt), 293–97
"Sex, Lies, and Conversation"
(Tannen), 312–18

"Two Ways of Seeing a River"
(Twain), 288–92
reasons for using, 276–77
suggestions for writing, 319–20
drawing a conclusion from
the comparison, 284–85
organizing points of
comparison, 283–84
parallel constructions, 285–87
points of comparison, 282–83
purpose, 282
subjects should be in the
same class, 281–87
thesis statement, 282
Compound sentences, 505–6
Conclusion
of argumentation, 501
from a comparison, 284–85
of division and classification,
333
Concrete words, 397–98
Conjunctions
coordinating, 503
subordinating, 503
Conley, Dalton ("Tip Jars and the
New Economy"), 450–55
Connotations, 397
Content and rhetorical
highlights, 3
Context, of narration, 158–59, 166
Controlling ideas, in
exemplification, 56–57
Coordinating conjunctions, 503
Cortes, Claro, IV ("Chinese
Commuter in Shanghai"
[photograph]), 63–64
"Crazy Horse and Custer as
Young Warriors"
(Ambrose), 306–11

Daemmrich, Bob ("Nobody
Knows I'm Gay"
[photograph]), 192
"Death of My Father, The"
(Martin), 130–36

"Declaration of Independence, The" (Jefferson), 519–24
Deductive reasoning, 488–91
Definition, 26, 37–44, 382–425. *See also* Combination of strategies
annotated student essay using, 387–91
definition of, 382–83
etymological, 384
extended, 385
formal, 383
negative, 384
questions for revising and editing, 398
readings
"Ain't I a Woman?" (Truth), 417–19
"In My Tribe" (Watters), 405–9
"A Nincompoop" (Chekhov), 420–23
"Steal This MP3 File: What Is Theft?" (Gorry), 411
"What Is Poverty?" (Parker), 399–404
"What's Next for Napster" ([photograph]) (*Time* magazine), 410–11
reasons for using, 385–86
stipulative, 384–85
suggestions for writing, 391–98, 424–25
audience, 393
choosing a technique of definition, 393–94
determining your purpose, 391–92
organizational plan, 394–95
other rhetorical strategies, 395
thesis statement, 392–93
synonymous, 384
Denotation, 396–97
Description, 105–56. *See also* Combination of strategies

annotated student essay using, 108–11
definition of, 105–6
objective, 107
questions for revising and editing, 118
readings
"Aravaipa Canyon" (Abbey), 107, 108, 116, 124–29
"The Death of My Father" (Martin), 130
"The Guts of a New Machine" (Walker), 138–50
"The House on Mango Street" (Cisneros), 151–54
"A View from the Bridge" (McDonald), 119–23
reasons for using, 107–8
suggestions for writing, 111–18, 155–56
collecting sensory details about your subject, 112–13
description in the service of an idea, 112
determining your purpose, 111
dominant impression, 113–14
figurative language, 115–17
focusing the subject of your description, 111–12
identifying audience, 113
organization, 114–15
organizing details to create a vivid picture, 114–15
selecting details with purpose in mind, 113
specific strong nouns and verbs, 115
Details
organizing, to create a vivid picture, 114–15
selection of, in narration, 159
that "show, don't tell," in narration, 167

Dialogue, in narration, 169–70
Diction, for process analysis,
    221–22
Dillard, Annie ("Getting
    Caught"), 179–85
Directional process analysis, 211
Direct quotations, 696–98
    plagiarism and, 709–11
Division and classification,
    321–81. *See also*
    Combination of strategies
annotated student essay using,
    325–28
in combination with other
    strategies, 333–34
definition and features of,
    321–24
questions for revising and
    editing, 336
readings
    "Girls on a Stoop"
        [photograph] (Felix),
        337–38
    "How to Detect Propaganda"
        (Institute for Propaganda
        Analysis), 372–79
    "The Myth of the Latin
        Woman" (Cofer), 365–71
    "The Queen Bee and Her
        Court" (Wiseman),
        338–51
    "The Truth about Lying"
        (Viorst), 352–59
    "The Ways of Meeting
        Oppression" (King),
        360–64
reasons for using, 325
suggestions for writing,
    329–36, 380–81
    conclusion, 333
    establishing appropriate
        characteristics, 331–32
    headings and subheadings
        for clarification, 334
    organization, 332–33

other rhetorical strategies,
    333–34
    purpose, 329–30
    thesis statement, 330–31
Documented essays, 681–716
    documenting sources in,
        699–707
    Internet sources for, 684–92
    note taking for, 691–98
    plagiarism and, 708–11
    print sources for, 681–84
    student essay, 711–16
Dominant impression
    in description, 113–14
    description and, 107

Editing, 36–37
Editing tips
    cause and effect signal words,
        441–43
    figurative language, 115–18
    headings and subheadings,
        334–36
    parallel constructions, 285–87
    precise language, 396–98
    pronoun references, 223–25
    run-on sentences, comma
        splices, and sentence
        fragments, 170–72
    sentence variety, 502–6
    strong topic sentences and
        unified paragraphs, 56–58
    wordiness, 599–601
Effect/affect, 443
Ehrenfeld, David ("A Techno-Pox
    Upon the Land"), 568–73
Eighner, Lars ("On Dumpster
    Diving"), 644–48
Either/or thinking, 501
Empty words and phrases, 600
Endings, 35
Ethos, 487
Etymological definition, 384
Evaluative process analysis,
    212–13

Exemplification, 45–104. *See also*
Combination of strategies
annotated student essay using,
48–52
definition of, 45–47
questions for revising and
editing, 58
readings
"Be Specific" (Goldberg),
59–62
"Chinese Commuter in
Shanghai" [photograph]
(Cortes IV), 63
"How to Give Orders Like a
Man" (Tannen), 70–79
"In Search of Our Mothers'
Gardens" (Walker), 92–102
"Those Crazy Ideas"
(Asimov), 80–91
reasons for using, 47–48
suggestions for writing, 52–58,
103–4
choosing relevant examples,
54
gathering more examples
than you can use, 53–54
representativeness of
examples, 55
sharing your work with
others, 56
strong topic sentences and
unified paragraphs, 56–58
transitions, 56
Expletives, 600
"Ex-POW Army Spc. Shoshana
Johnson" [photograph]
(Probst), 537–38
Expressive writing, 21
Extended definition, 385
Extended metaphors, 116–17

False analogy, 501
Faulty reasoning, 500–501
"Fear of SARS, Fear of Strangers"
(Chang), 64–69

Felix, Stefanie ("Girls on a Stoop"
[photograph]), 337–38
Figurative language, 115–17
Finch, Aisha K. ("If Hip-Hop
Ruled the World"),
508–12
First drafts, 31–32
"Five Principles for Getting Good
Ideas" (Rawlins), 651–56
Flower, Linda ("Writing for an
Audience"), 662–65
Focused argument, 485
Focusing the subject of your
description, 111–12
Formal definition, 383
Freewriting, 23
Fused sentences (run-on
sentences), 170–71

"Gene-Altered Foods: A Case
Against Panic" (Brody),
574–78
Generating ideas and collecting
information, 23–30
brainstorming, 24
determining your strategy,
28–29
journals, 23
organization, 30
rhetorical strategies, 24–26
thesis statements, 26–28
"Genetically Modified Food"
argument cluster, 556–83
"Getting Caught" (Dillard),
179–85
"Girls on a Stoop" [photograph]
(Felix), 337–38
Goldberg, Natalie ("Be Specific"),
59–62
Gordon, Joel
"Tipping Is Not a City in China"
[photograph], 449–50
"World Trade Center Disaster,
September 11, 2001"
[photograph], 247–48

Gorry, G. Anthony ("Steal This MP3 File: What Is Theft?"), 411

"Great Kern County Mouse War, The" (Maize), 456–62

"Guts of a New Machine, The" (Walker), 138–50

"Harry Potter and the New Consumer" (Blake), 609–21

"Harry Potter on Sale in Moscow" [photograph] (Ilnitsky), 608–9

Hasty generalization, 501

Haughey, Matt ("Building an Online Community: Just Add Water"), 262–69

Headings, 334–36

Headnote, 3

"House on Mango Street, The" (Cisneros), 151–54

"How Boys Become Men" (Katz), 444–48

"How to Detect Propaganda" (Institute for Propaganda Analysis), 372–79

"How to Give Orders Like a Man" (Tannen), 70–79

"How to Mark a Book" (Adler), 226–32

"How to Say Nothing in 500 Words" (Roberts), 233–46

Ideas
  controlling in exemplification, 56–57
  generating, 23–30
  brainstorming, 24
    determining your strategy, 28–29
    journals, 23
    organization, 30
    rhetorical strategies, 24–26
    thesis statements, 26–28

"If Hip-Hop Ruled the World" (Finch), 508–12

"I Have a Dream" (King), 525–30

Ilnitsky, Sergei ("Harry Potter on Sale in Moscow" [photograph]), 608–9

Immediate causes, 429

Implied pronoun references, 225

Impressionistic description (subjective description), 107–8

Inductive reasoning, 488

Inflated expressions, 601

Information, generating ideas and collecting, 23–30
  brainstorming, 24
  determining your strategy, 28–29
  journals, 23
  organization, 30
  rhetorical strategies, 24–26
  thesis statements, 26–28

Informational argument, 485

Informational process analysis, 211–12

Informative writing, 21

"In My Tribe" (Watters), 405–9

"In Search of Our Mothers' Gardens" (Walker), 92–102

Institute for Propaganda Analysis ("How to Detect Propaganda"), 372–79

Internet sources
  citations for, 705–7
  for documented essays, 684–92
  evaluating, 685–86
  keyword searches and, 688–91
  previewing, 684–85
  subject directories and, 687–88
  working bibliography of, 685

In-text citations, 701–2

iPodLounge.com ("Shane Holding his iPod" [photograph]), 137

It is, 600

Jackson, Shirley ("The Lottery"), 472–81

Jefferson, Thomas ("The Declaration of Independence"), 519–24

Journal prompt, 3

Journals, 23

Katz, Jon ("How Boys Become Men"), 444–48

Keyword searches, 688–91

King, Martin Luther, Jr. ("I Have a Dream"), 525–30

King, Martin Luther, Jr. ("The Ways of Meeting Oppression"), 360–64

Lamott, Anne ("Shitty First Drafts"), 657–61

Lederer, Richard ("The Case for Short Words"), 513–18

List of works cited, 701–7

Logic, errors of, in cause and effect analysis, 438–39

Logical argument, 484–85

Logos, 487–88

Long, Shannon ("Wheelchair Hell: A Look at Campus Accessibility"), 49–52

Lorde, Audre ("The Transformation of Silence Into Language and Action"), 676–80

"Lottery, The" (Jackson), 472–81

McDonald, Cherokee Paul ("A View from the Bridge"), 119–23

"Mac or PC: There Is Simply No Comparison!" (Miller), 299–305

"Macs and PCs Have Never Been So Compatible" [photograph] (Microsoft), 298–99

Mairs, Nancy ("On Being a Cripple"), 622–34

Maize, Kennedy P. ("The Great Kern County Mouse War"), 456–62

"Maker's Eye, The: Revising Your Own Manuscripts" (Murray), 670–75

Malcolm X ("Coming to an Awareness of Language"), 174–78

Martin, Steve ("The Death of My Father"), 130–36

Metaphors, 116

Microsoft ("Macs and PCs Have Never Been So Compatible" [photograph]), 298–99

Miller, Del ("Mac or PC: There Is Simply No Comparison!"), 299–305

Mixed metaphors, 117

Modern Language Association (MLA) style, 700–701

Modifiers, 503

Murray, Donald M. ("The Maker's Eye: Revising Your Own Manuscripts"), 670–75

"Myth of the Latin Woman, The" (Cofer), 365–71

Narration, 157–208. *See also* Combination of strategies

annotated student essay using, 160

definition and features of, 157–59

questions for revising and editing, 172

readings

"Coming to an Awareness of Language" (Malcolm X), 174–78

"Getting Caught" (Dillard), 179–85

Narration, readings *(continued)*
  "Nobody Knows I'm Gay"
    [photograph]
    (Daemmrich), 192
  "Not Close Enough for
    Comfort" (Bardeen), 193–97
  "Stranger Than True"
    (Winston), 186–91
  "A Worn Path" (Welty),
    198–206
  reasons for using, 159–60
  suggestions for writing,
    165–73, 207–8
  consistent verb tenses,
    168–69
  context, 166
  details that "show, don't
    tell," 167
  dialogue, 169–70
  narrative time for emphasis,
    169
  organization, 167–68
  point and purpose, 165–66
  point of view, 166–67
  selecting a topic, 165
  transitional words, 169
Narrative point, 165–66
Narrative time for emphasis, 169
"Neat People vs. Sloppy People"
  (Britt), 293–97
Negative definition, 384
"Nincompoop, A" (Chekhov),
  420–23
"Nobody Knows I'm Gay"
  [photograph]
  (Daemmrich), 192
Nonprint sources. *See also*
  Internet sources
  citations for, 707
Non sequitur, 501
"Not Close Enough for Comfort"
  (Bardeen), 193–97
Note taking, 691–98
Nouns, specific and strong, 115

Objective description, 107
Olson, George ("Spraying Potato
  Seedlings" [photograph]),
  558
"On Being a Cripple" (Mairs),
  622–34
"On Dumpster Diving" (Eighner),
  644–48
Organization, 30
  of argumentation, 499
  of definition, 394–95
  of details to create a vivid
    picture, 114–15
  of division and classification,
    332–33
  of examples, 55–56
  of narration, 159, 167–68
  of points of comparison, 283–84
Orwell, George ("Shooting an
  Elephant"), 635–43
Oversimplification, avoiding,
  438, 500
Overview, reading to get an, 5

Paragraphs, unified, 56–57
Parallel constructions, 285–87, 504
Paraphrasing, 694–95
  plagiarism and, 709–11
Parker, Jo Goodwin ("What Is
  Poverty?"), 399–404
Passive voice, 219–20, 599–600
Pathos, 488
Peer critiquing, 32–33
Periodicals, citations of, 704–5
Personification, 117
Persuasive argument, 484
Photographs and visual texts,
  13–16
Plagiarism, 708–12
Point-by-point comparison,
  273–74
Point of view
  in narration, 159
  narration and, 166–67

Points of comparison, 282–83
Post hoc, ergo propter hoc, 501
Post hoc, ergo propter hoc fallacy,
    438–39, 501
Precise language, 396–98
Prereading, 3–5
Prewriting, 20–23
Print sources. *See also* Books;
    Periodicals
for documented essays, 681
Probst, Michael ("Ex-POW Army
    Spc. Shoshana Johnson"),
    537–38
Process analysis, 209–71. *See also*
    Combination of strategies
annotated student essay using,
    213–17
definition of, 209–10
directional, 211
evaluative, 212–13
informational, 211–12
questions for revising, 225
readings
    "Anatomy of an Urban
      Legend" (Callahan), 248–55
    "Building an Online
      Community: Just Add
      Water" (Haughey), 262–69
    "How to Mark a Book"
      (Adler), 226–32
    "How to Say Nothing in 500
      Words" (Roberts), 233–46
    "Why Leaves Turn Color in
      the Fall" (Ackerman),
      256–61
    "World Trade Center
      Disaster, September 11,
      2001" [photograph]
      (Gordon), 247–48
reasons for using, 210–13
suggestions for writing,
    218–25, 270–71
    active voice and strong
      action verbs, 219–20

audience and diction,
    221–22
clear purpose, 218
knowledge of your subject,
    218
organization, 218–19
transitions, 219
testing the effectiveness of,
    222–23
Pronoun-antecedent references,
    223–25
Proofreading, 36–37
Proposition, in argumentation,
    498–99
Publication information, 3
Purpose
of cause and effect analysis, 437
of combination of strategies, 597
of comparison and contrast, 282
of definition, 391–92
of description, 111
descriptive details and, 113
determining your, 21–22
of division and classification,
    329–30
of narration, 165–66

"Queen Bee and Her Court, The"
    (Wiseman), 338–51
Quiet argument, 486
Quindlen, Anna ("Uncle Sam
    and Aunt Samantha"),
    538–41
Quotations
direct, 695–97
    plagiarism and, 708–11
integrating into your text,
    698–99
unannounced, 698

Ramírez, Robert ("The Barrio"),
    602–7
"Rap the Vote" [photograph]
    (Bailey), 507–8

Rauch, Jonathan ("Will
Frankenfood Save the
Planet?"), 559–67
Rawlins, Jack ("Five Principles for
Getting Good Ideas"),
651–56
Reading
getting the most out of your,
2–13
questions to ask while, 8
writing process and, 16–18
"Real Computer Virus, The"
(Cannon), 463–71
"Reason is because," 443
Reconciliation argument, 486
Redundancies, 600
Relevant examples, choosing, 54
Remote causes, 429
Rereading, 5
Revising, 33–36
the large elements of your
essay, 33–35
the small elements of your
essay, 35–36
Rhetorical strategies, 24–26
Roberts, Paul ("How to Say
Nothing in 500 Words"),
233–46
"Rough Draft" (Beck), 548–53
Run-on sentences (fused
sentences), 170–71

Scharplaz, Jim ("Weeding Out
the Skilled Farmer"),
579–83
Scratch outlines, 28
Semicolon, to link closely related
ideas, 503
Sensory details about your
subject, collecting, 112–13
Sentence fragments, 172
Sentence openings, varying,
504–5
Sentences, compound, 505–6
Sentence variety, 502–6

"Sex, Lies, and Conversation"
(Tannen), 312–18
"Shane Holding his iPod"
[photograph]
(iPodLounge.com), 137
Shifts, 221
"Shitty First Drafts" (Lamott),
657–61
"Shooting an Elephant" (Orwell),
635–43
Similes, 115–16
"Simplicity" (Zinsser), 666–69
"Snow" (Alvarez), 531–34
Specific and concrete words,
397–98
"Spraying Potato Seedlings"
[photograph] (Olson), 558
"Steal This MP3 File: What Is
Theft?" (Gorry), 411–16
Stipulative definition, 384–85
"Stranger Than True" (Winston),
186–91
Strong nouns, in description, 115
Strong verbs
in description, 115
in process analysis, 219–20
Subheadings, 334–36
Subject areas, 22
Subject directories, 687–89
Subjective description
(impressionistic
description), 107–8
Subordinating conjunctions, 503
Subtle argument, 486
Summarizing, 693–94
plagiarism and, 709–11
Supporting evidence, in
argumentation, 499
Synonymous definition, 384

Tannen, Deborah
"How to Give Orders Like a
Man," 70–79
"Sex, Lies, and Conversation,"
312–18

"Techno-Pox Upon the Land, A"
(Ehrenfeld), 568–73
Than, parallel constructions in
comparisons with, 286–87
There is, 600
Thesis, 26
in argumentation, 498–99
Thesis statements, 26–28
cause and effect analysis, 437
combination of strategies, 597
comparison and contrast, 282
definition, 392–93
division and classification,
330–31
"Those Crazy Ideas" (Asimov),
80–91
Time magazine ("What's Next for
Napster" [photograph]),
410–11
"Tip Jars and the New Economy"
(Conley), 450–55
"Tipping Is Not a City in China"
[photograph] (Gordon),
449–50
Title, 3
Topics, 22
for narration, 165
Topic sentences, in
exemplification, 56–58
"Transformation of Silence Into
Language and Action, The"
(Lorde), 676–80
Transitional words and phrases
in narration, 169
in process analysis, 219
Transitions, in exemplification,
56
Truth, Sojourner ("Ain't I a
Woman?"), 417–19
"Truth about Lying, The"
(Viorst), 352–59
Twain, Mark ("Two Ways of
Seeing a River"), 288–92
"Two Ways of Seeing a River"
(Twain), 288–92

Unannounced quotation, 698
"Uncle Sam and Aunt Samantha"
(Quindlen), 538–41

Vague pronoun reference, 224
Verbs, specific and strong, 115
Verb tenses, consistent
in narration, 168–69
in process analysis, 220–21
"View from the Bridge, A"
(McDonald), 119–23
Viorst, Judith ("The Truth about
Lying"), 352–59

Walker, Alice ("In Search of Our
Mothers' Gardens"),
92–102
Walker, Rob ("The Guts of a New
Machine"), 138–50
Watters, Ethan ("In My Tribe"),
405–9
"Ways of Meeting Oppression,
The" (King), 360–64
"Weeding Out the Skilled
Farmer" (Scharplaz),
579–83
Welty, Eudora ("A Worn Path"),
198–206
"What Is Poverty?" (Parker),
399–404
"What's Next for Napster"
[photograph] (*Time*
magazine), 410–11
"Wheelchair Hell: A Look at
Campus Accessibility"
(Long), 49–52
"When Women Go to War"
(Applebaum), 545–47
"Why Leaves Turn Color in
the Fall" (Ackerman),
256–61
"Will Frankenfood Save the
Planet?" (Rauch), 559–67
Winston, Barry ("Stranger Than
True"), 186–91

Wiseman, Rosalind ("The Queen Bee and Her Court"), 338–51
"Women in Combat" argument cluster
preparing to read the, 535–36
writing and discussion suggestions for, 553–55
"Women in Combat Will Take a Toll on Our Culture" (Chavez), 542–44
Wordiness, 599–601
Working bibliography
for Internet sources, 685

for print sources, 682–83
"World Trade Center Disaster, September 11, 2001" [photograph] (Gordon), 247–48
"Worn Path, A" (Welty), 198–206
"Writing for an Audience" (Flower), 662–65
Writing process, 20–37
prewriting, 20–23
reading and, 16–18

Zinsser, William ("Simplicity"), 666–69

Where can you find more help?
At bedfordstmartins.com.

We have a wide variety of Web sites designed to help students with their most common writing concerns. You'll find advice from experts, models you can rely on, and exercises that will tell you right away how you're doing. And it's all free and available any hour of the day.

Need help with grammar problems?
Exercise Central
bedfordstmartins.com/exercisecentral

Want to see what other papers for your course look like?
Model Documents Gallery
bedfordstmartins.com/modeldocs

Stuck somewhere in the research process? (Maybe at the beginning?)
The English Research Room
bedfordstmartins.com/researchroom

Wondering whether a Web site is good enough to use in your paper?
Tutorial for Evaluating Online Sources
bedfordstmartins.com/onlinesourcestutorial

Having trouble figuring out how to cite a source?
Research and Documentation Online
bedfordstmartins.com/resdoc

Confused about plagiarism?
The St. Martin's Tutorial on Avoiding Plagiarism
bedfordstmartins.com/plagiarismtutorial

Want to learn more features of your word processor?
Using Your Word Processor
bedfordstmartins.com/wordprocessor

Trying to improve the look of your paper?
Using Your Word Processor to Design Documents
bedfordstmartins.com/docdesigntutorial

Need to create slides for a presentation?
Preparing Presentation Slide Tutorial
bedfordstmartins.com/presentationslidetutorial

Interested in creating a Web site?
Web Design Tutorial
bedfordstmartins.com/webdesigntutorial